D0841292

Complete Angler's Guide to™
OREGON
John Shewey

Fishing Titles Available from Wilderness Adventures Press, Inc.™

Flyfishers Guide to™

Flyfisher's Guide to Alaska

Flyfisher's Guide to Arizona

Flyfisher's Guide to the Big Apple

Flyfisher's Guide to Chesapeake Bay

Flyfisher's Guide to Colorado

Flyfisher's Guide to the Florida Keys

Flyfisher's Guide to Freshwater Florida

Flyfisher's Guide to Idaho

Flyfisher's Guide to Montana

Flyfisher's Guide to Michigan

Flyfisher's Guide to Minnesota

Flyfisher's Guide to Missouri & Arkansas

Flyfisher's Guide to Nevada

Flyfisher's Guide to the New England Coast

Flyfisher's Guide to New Mexico

Flyfisher's Guide to New York

Flyfisher's Guide to the Northeast Coast

Flyfisher's Guide to Northern California

Flyfisher's Guide to Northern New England

Flyfisher's Guide to Oregon

Flyfisher's Guide to Pennsylvania

Flyfisher's Guide to Saltwater Florida

Flyfisher's Guide to Texas

Flyfisher's Guide to the Texas Gulf Coast

Flyfisher's Guide to Utah

Flyfisher's Guide to Virginia

Flyfisher's Guide to Washington

Flyfisher's Guide to Wisconsin & Iowa

Flyfisher's Guide to Wyoming

Flyfisher's Guide to Yellowstone National Park

On the Fly Guide to™

On the Fly Guide to the Northwest

On the Fly Guide to the Northern Rockies

Anglers Guide to™

Complete Anglers Guide to Oregon

Angler's Guide to the West Coast

Saltwater Angler's Guide to the Southeast

Saltwater Angler's Guide to Southern California

Best Fishing Waters™

California's Best Fishing Waters

Colorado's Best Fishing Waters

Idaho's Best Fishing Waters

Montana's Best Fishing Waters

Oregon's Best Fishing Waters

Washington's Best Fishing Waters

Field Guide to™

Field Guide to Fishing Knots

Fly Tying

Go-To Flies™

Flyfishing Adventures™

Montana

Complete Angler's Guide to™
OREGON
John Shewey

Complete Angler's Guide to™ Series

Wilderness
Adventures
Press, Inc.™

Belgrade, Montana

Published by Wilderness Adventures Press, Inc.™
45 Buckskin Road
Belgrade, MT 59714
866-400-2012
Website: www.wildadvpress.com
email: books@wildadvpress.com

Second Edition 2011

Printed in South Korea.

ISBN 978-1-932098-86-0 (8-09206-98860-6)

Table of Contents

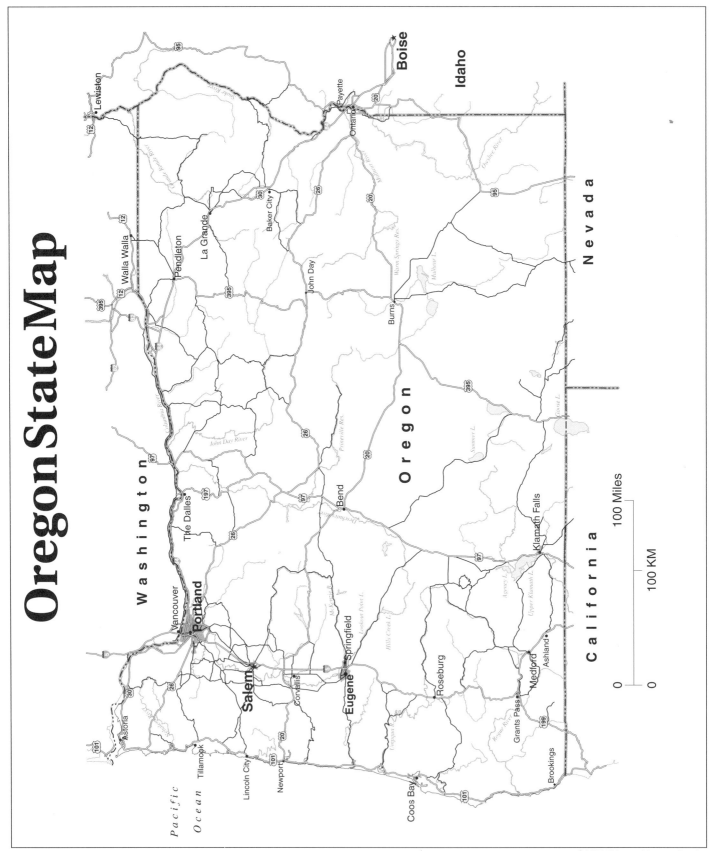

Oregon State Map

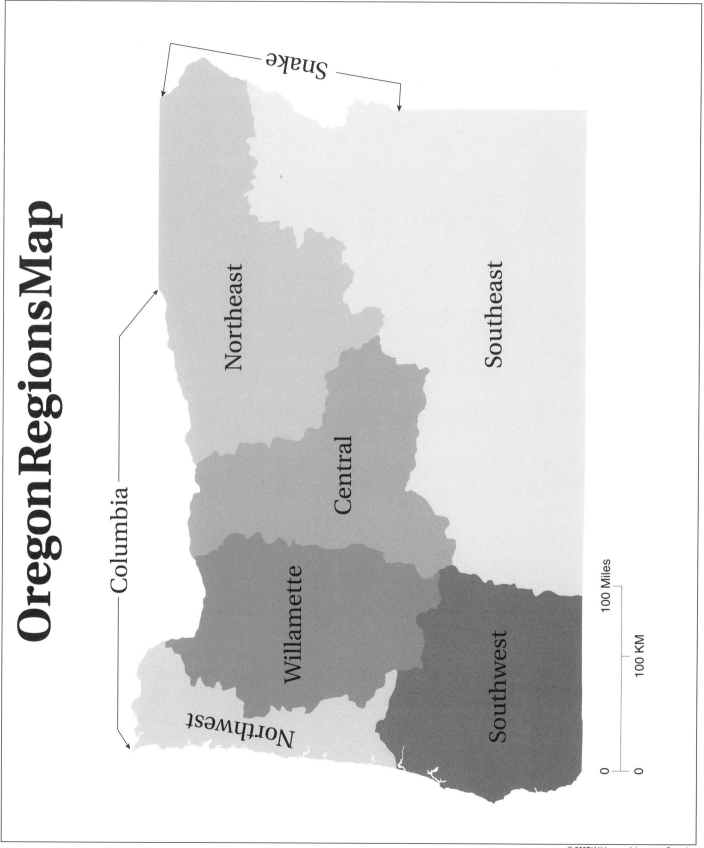

Oregon Regions Map

Snake

Northeast

Southeast

Columbia

Central

Willamette

Northwest

Southwest

100 Miles

100 KM

Introduction

I f one word could encapsulate fishing in Oregon, that word would be diversity. The state's diverse geography and numerous climate zones create a varied assemblage of unique landscapes and a wide range of options for anglers.

The Pacific Ocean creates a temperate climate for western Oregon, and provides fertile fishing grounds for numerous saltwater species, ranging from halibut, rockfish, and lingcod, to salmon and tuna. Where the ocean meets terra firma, rich intertidal waters, beaches, and bays offer seemingly boundless opportunity for surfperch, bottom fish, and shellfish. Mighty rivers and modest streams draw salmon, steelhead, and sea-run cutthroat home from ocean waters, providing myriad options for anglers seeking anadromous fishes, or even shad or striped bass in some waters. Far-reaching runs of steelhead and chinook salmon even penetrate to inland tributaries of the mighty Columbia River, creating world-class fisheries in places like the Willamette Basin, the Deschutes River, and the Grande Ronde River.

Western Oregon is more or less bisected north to south by the Coast Range which, in southern Oregon, yields to the more imposing Siskiyou Range. Immediately west of these ranges is the Pacific slope proper and in many places the mountains quite rapidly plunge to the sea. To the east of the coastal highlands are the state's most fertile valleys—the Willamette, Umpqua, and Rogue valleys—all so rich in farmlands that traditional crops are rapidly yielding to more and more acres of wine grapes. Through these valleys flow their namesake rivers as well as countless tributaries. They offer fisheries so varied that in many places anglers might easily spend a morning fishing for salmon or steelhead and then spend that evening pursuing trout or smallmouth bass or any of a host of other species.

The face of fishing changes as the foothills edging the east side of these valleys climb into the Cascade Mountain range, which is punctuated dramatically by bedazzling, snow-capped volcanic peaks. High-elevation lakes, many of them hike-in destinations, abound, and tumbling mountain creeks hold populations of wild trout. The Cascades create a rain shadow; they devour so much rain and snow from the usual west-to-east-moving weather that little remains for central and eastern Oregon. So the landscape changes rapidly and dramatically from the verdant forests and valleys of western Oregon to the parched high desert east of the mountains. Suddenly the land becomes thirsty and a handful of major rivers—the Deschutes, John Day, and Klamath—gather virtually all available drainages and create some of the state's most renowned fishing destinations.

As central and south central Oregon transition subtly into eastern Oregon, the state is bisected yet again. In the southeast—Lake County, Harney County, and Malheur County—there are vast areas with no outside drainage, making this region the northernmost edge of the much larger Great Basin, which envelopes much of Nevada. Some of Oregon's most remote trout and warmwater fisheries attract adventurous anglers to the so-called "Oregon Outback."

To the north meanwhile, the Columbia and Snake Rivers gather all the waters from the remainder of eastern Oregon. Here, in north central and northeastern Oregon, diversity is again prominently on display. The region is endowed with countless fisheries, from little known ranch-country ponds to stunning alpine lakes; from sturgeon in the Columbia River to native redband trout high in the Blue Mountains.

If the diversity of fishing opportunities in Oregon seems daunting, such is reason to rejoice, for a fine conundrum indeed is the problem of indecision on where to go because so many options present themselves. Of course a guidebook such as this leaves plenty for anglers to discover on their own. In nearly three decades of wandering, fishing gear in hand, all over this state I am continually amazed at just how little I really know. I've sampled waters from the highest lakes to the most remote beaches; from the most out-of-the-way desert waters to the busiest rivers; from dredging Mackinaw from Odell Lake to plucking tiny brook trout from small lakes in the Eagle Cap Wilderness; and from epic battles with huge steelhead to nonstop action for feisty surfperch.

Yet I often feel that I've barely scratched the surface and, if not for the help of many people—especially countless fishing friends, and personnel from the Oregon Department of Fish & Wildlife, Bureau of Land Management, and U.S. Forest Service—I could never have assembled this guide. So use this book as just that: a guide that will in some cases give you specific information from my personal store of experiences and in some cases give you enough details to start you in the right direction, leaving plenty of room for discovery. Embrace the discovery.

John Shewey
February 2007

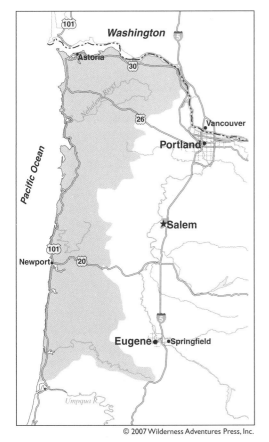

© 2007 Wilderness Adventures Press, Inc.

Northwest Zone

Oregon's north and central coast offers myriad productive salmon and steelhead streams, ranging from the big, popular rivers like the Nestucca, Siletz and Trask, to the smaller flows like the Kilchis, Necanicum and Lake Creek. Indeed it is salmon and steelhead for which the Oregon coast is most revered by anglers, and all of the rivers are busy places during the peak of the fall and winter seasons. As a general rule, chinook and coho salmon appear in the bays and lower rivers during August, with peak fishing usually from late August through early October. In a few rivers, especially in the Tillamook area, late chinook runs arrive between Thanksgiving and Christmas, hence the local term "Holiday Runs."

In most Oregon waters, fishing for coho salmon has been sharply curtailed and generally only fin-clipped fish are available for harvest. The same is true with steelhead in the Northwest Zone. In fact, before fishing any steelhead and salmon streams in this zone, a careful perusal of the current regulations is in order. In addition to salmon and steelhead, the central and north coast streams enjoy runs of unique sea-run cutthroat trout. In years past, these fish have been called "harvest trout" because they enter the rivers between late July and late October. Sea-run cutthroat trout typically range from 10 to 16 inches in length, but they can reach 24 inches. They are aggressive, exciting fish, eager to pounce on flies, spinners, and spoons.

Of course the Northwest Zone offers far more than salmon, steelhead, and sea-run cutthroat. After all, this zone runs from the western end of the Columbia River south to the Siuslaw River drainage. The entire coastal strip offers an array of lake fishing opportunities and these become increasingly prevalent and productive on the central coast, where sand-dune lakes in the Florence area range in size from 2 to 2,000 acres and offer everything from stocked trout to trophy-class largemouth bass.

Meanwhile, in the Coast Range to the east, many small forest streams offer good prospects for small, wild cutthroat trout in very pretty surroundings. The tiny mountain trout streams are not for everyone: Often they require some fairly aggressive bushwhacking. But the rewards are bejeweled little native trout and solitude. Be sure to check regulations, because many streams are closed to protect juvenile salmon and steelhead, while others are open only to catch-and-release fishing.

Naturally, the Northwest Zone offers boundless options for enjoying the bounty of the Pacific Ocean. Charter fishing fleets operate out of all the port towns and target salmon, halibut, tuna, and a wide variety of bottomfish, ranging from lingcod and cabezon to rockfish and greenling. The bays themselves boast good jetty-fishing prospects for rockfish, seaperch, surfperch, greenling, lingcod, cabezon, herring, and other species. And of course the estuary salmon fishing is nothing short of outstanding most years at places like Alsea Bay and Tillamook Bay.

The bays and harbors also offer abundant crab and shellfish with ample opportunity to harvest both, even for people without boats. Most of the port communities offer public crabbing/fishing docks and piers and in many towns you can rent crabbing gear—or even boats—from local merchants. Shellfish opportunities range from digging razor clams on broad, sandy beaches to mucking around in the mud for gapers. Myriad species of shellfish are available for harvest.

Also, the central and north coast areas feature some of the state's most productive beaches for redtail surfperch and a host of smaller surfperch species. The redtails have long ranked as one of the most popular saltwater fish available to shore-bound anglers and the Northwest Zone is certainly richly endowed with the vast, sandy beaches where these fish thrive.

One of the great attributes of the Oregon coast is that it offers year-round action. There is always something to do, whether it is fishing the beaches for surfperch during spring, crabbing the bays during summer, trolling for chinook salmon during autumn, or drifting a river for winter steelhead during January or February. Even when the rivers are blown out during winter, you can toss jigs off the jetties in pursuit of bottomfish; if the salmon runs let you down, take an offshore trip for lingcod or rockfish; if you weary of the crowded steelhead rivers, drop a small pram in a coastal dune lake and fish for trout. The mild coastal weather and the abundance of opportunity leave something for everyone here, no matter the time of year.

Northwest Zone Contacts:

Oregon Department of Fish & Wildlife
North Coast Watershed District Office
4907 Third Street
Tillamook, OR 97141
503-842-2741

ODFW Marine Resources Program (Fish Division)
2040 SE Marine Science Drive
Newport, OR 97365
541-867-4741

ODFW Newport Field Office
2040 SE Marine Science Drive
Newport, OR 97365
541-867-4741 or 541-867-0300

ODFW Mapleton Satellite Office
Mapleton Ranger District
Mapleton, OR 97453
541-991-7838

ODFW Big Creek Hatchery
Rt. 4 Box 594
Astoria, OR 97103
503-458-6512

ODFW Cedar Creek Hatchery
33465 Highway 22
Hebo, OR 97122
503-392-3485

ODFW Fall Creek Hatchery
2418 E Fall Creek Road
Alsea, OR 97324
541-487-4152

ODFW Gnat Creek Hatchery
Rt. 2 Box 2198
Clatskanie, OR 97016
503-455-2234

ODFW Klaskanine Hatchery
82635-202 Hatchery Road
Astoria, OR 97103
503-325-3653

ODFW North Nehalem River Hatchery
36751 Fish Hatchery Lane
Nehalem, OR 97131
503-368-6828

ODFW Salmon River Hatchery
575 N North Bank Road
Otis, OR 97368
541-994-8606

ODFW Trask River Hatchery
15020 Chance Road
Tillamook, OR 97141
503-842-4090

Siuslaw National Forest Supervisor's Office
4077 S.W. Research Way
P.O. Box 1148
Corvallis, Oregon 97339
541-750-7000

Hebo Ranger District
31525 Hwy 22
Hebo, OR 97122
503-392-5100

Suislaw National Forest, Waldport Office
1130 Forestry Lane
Waldport, Oregon 97394
541-563-8449

Suislaw National Forest, Florence Office
4480 Highway 101, Bldg. G
Florence, OR 97439
541-902-8526

Oregon Dunes NRA Visitor Center
855 Highway Avenue
Reedsport, OR 97467
541-271-6000

Tillamook State Forest District Office
5005 East Third Street
Tillamook, OR 97141
503-842-2545

Bureau of Land Management Salem District
1717 Fabry Rd. SE,
Salem, Oregon 97306
503-375-5646

Bureau of Land Management, Eugene District
2890 Chad Drive
Eugene, OR 97408-7336
541-683-6600

Alder Lake (Lane County)

campground

This small coastal sand-dune lake is one of three small trout lakes near Alder Dune Campground 6 miles north of Florence. The other two are Buck Lake and Dune Lake. All three lakes are liberally supplied with legal-size rainbow trout, with stockings occurring several times between January and September. In recent years, ODFW has included some of its "larger" and "trophy" size fish in the stocking effort at these lakes, and each of them is capable of over-wintering a few trout. All three are fairly popular, but you can enjoy consistent success during early spring before the summer tourists arrive on the coast. You can fish from the bank here but, at just a few acres in size, these lakes are perfect for float tubes. Alder Lake covers 3 acres and is perfect for, and popular with, kids. The USFS helps the cause by maintaining a trail around the lake and by trimming a lot of the lakeside brush at selected locations to create easy fishing access. Just south of Alder Lake, 2-acre Dune Lake offers similar opportunities and is a good place for kids. It offers a pleasant lakeside picnic spot. The east shoreline is private property, but most of the remaining shoreline is easy to access. Fishing is best in spring and early summer. Alder Dune Campground offers 39 sites and has water, but is only open from mid-May through September.

Alsea Bay (Waldport)

boat ramp, services

Alsea Bay at Waldport is best known for its fall chinook salmon fishery, which peaks from late August through late September. Most fishing is done by boat and the bay can get quite crowded during years with large salmon runs. This estuary system also supports decent opportunities for Dungeness crab, clams, surfperch, sea-run cutthroat and even a few flounder. If you have a boat, drop crab traps along the main channel from the highway bridge west. This same channel, especially near the mouth of the bay, is a good bet for both salmon and perch, with perch fishing best in the spring.

Broad, firm, user-friendly low-tide sand flats on both sides of the bay—especially down-bay from the bridge—offer good prospects for digging clams, and anglers catch a few salmon by casting into the channel from the sand bars when tide levels permit. If you can avoid the ever-present herds of seals, bank fishing for salmon is also possible from the north spit and from Yaquina John Point on the south spit.

East from the Bay Bridge, the flats adjacent to Devil's Bend and Mud Shepherd Point on the north bank can produce good clamming and the adjacent channel is a good bet for salmon trolling. Most salmon anglers fish bait, especially herring, but jigs, blades, and plugs or plug/bait combos are quite popular as well.

Some half dozen or more private marinas offer launching and docking facilities along Hwy 34 just east of Waldport, and the city operates nice public docks/launch. For information, call the Port of Alsea at 541-563-3872. Dock of the Bay Marina, in Walport near the city docks, offers moorage, rental boats and kayaks, rental crabbing gear and clamming gear, and plenty of friendly advice (541-563-2003). To reach the docks and Dock of the Bay Marina, turn east on Hwy 34 in Waldport and then turn left on Broadway.

Always bear in mind that Alsea Bay has no maintained channel or jetties to provide safe navigation to or from the ocean. During ebb tides, dangerous conditions exist at the mouth of the bay. Nelson Wayside State Park offers non-motorized boat access to Eckman Lake (see separate listing herein). Waldport has ample lodging options, but always make reservations, whether you are staying at an RV park or motel. The town attracts plenty of tourists to compete for room space with the salmon anglers. The Port of Alsea website directs you to plenty of options: www.portofalsea.com.

If you are new to crabbing and clamming, the historic Alsea Bay Bridge Interpretive Center in Waldport, operated by the Oregon Parks and Recreation Department with help from the Waldport Chamber of Commerce, offers clamming and crabbing demonstrations led by guides from the Oregon Parks and Recreation Department. A schedule is usually posted in the Interpretive Center during the visitor season. Locations and times vary with the tides.

Alsea River

boat ramp, campground

One of Oregon's top rivers for winter steelhead and also a fair bet for sea-run cutthroat and chinook salmon, the Alsea River begins at the convergence of its forks about 25 miles southwest from Corvallis. From there, the Alsea winds its way almost 60 miles down to Waldport. Though lots of private property abuts the river, access is generally quite good—better, in fact, than most coastal steelhead rivers. Anglers fish from the bank and from boats, and the river offers a number of easy-to-navigate float segments.

Winter steelhead, mostly of hatchery origin, but with a few natives as well, arrive between mid-December and early March, with January being the top month. The hatchery fish are bound mostly for the North Fork and for Fall Creek. Sea-run cutthroat enter the Alsea as early as July and are available through October. The sea-runs disperse throughout the river system but the lower end of the river, from Alsea Bay up to the town of Tidewater, is a good bet if you have a boat with a motor. The slow-moving, structure-rich water in this section is perfect habitat for sea-runs. Chinook salmon appear by late August and most of the catch comes by way of trolling or plug fishing from the bay up to Tidewater.

Steelhead anglers enjoy the best success on the upper two-thirds of the river, from the town of Alsea down to Mike Bauer Wayside, a public park with a boat ramp located about 17 miles upriver from Waldport. Bauer Wayside is a popular bank-fishing area for both steelhead and salmon.

On the upper river, no boats are allowed upstream from the launch at Mill Creek Park, located about 2 miles west of Alsea. Downstream from Mill Creek, the Alsea River boasts no less than a dozen boat launch sites as follows, beginning at Mill Creek Park:

- Mill Creek Park: Paved ramp with parking.
- Campbell Park: Paved ramp with parking.

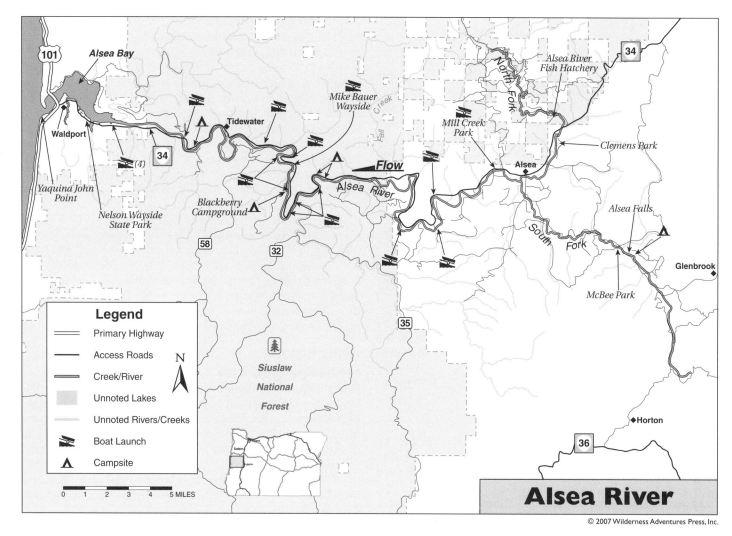

Alsea River

- Salmonberry Park: South bank on Salmonberry Road. Gravel ramp with parking.
- Missouri Bend Park: Long pole slide requiring at least 100-foot rope. Ample parking.
- Fall Creek: Private gravel launch.
- River's Edge: Paved ramp and parking.
- Stony Point: Unimproved ramp with parking along road.
- Five Rivers: Unimproved ramp off the old highway above the bridge.
- The Maples Ramp: Paved ramp with parking, also called "The Launching Ramp."
- Blackberry Park: Paved ramp with parking.
- Mike Bauer Wayside: Mostly a high-water ramp.
- Rock Crusher: Unimproved launch site on ODOT property.
- Hellion Rapids: Dirt slide with parking along road.
- Barclay Breaks: Unimproved take-out not good for low water.

Most of these sites, along with quite a few others, offer good access to the river for bank fishing. Camping is available at Blackberry Campground near Bauer Wayside and at Salmonberry Campground on the upper river. Quite a number of steelhead guides operate on the Alsea, but do-it-yourself drift boaters should bring two vehicles because shuttle service is hard to come by. All other services are available down at Waldport and in the Corvallis area.

Alsea River, North Fork

The North Fork Alsea offers a good run of hatchery winter steelhead and fishing is generally fair-to-good from January through February, despite difficult access. Private property is prevalent. Most of the fishing pressure is concentrated on the easy-to-reach section from Alsea River Fish Hatchery down to Clemens Park on State Route 34. This section of the river is only about 30 minutes from Corvallis: Head west through Philomath and just west from there, turn south on Alsea Highway. A few miles farther downstream, the North Fork joins the South Fork Alsea to form the main river.

The accessible section of river just north of the highway bridge along Fish Hatchery Road offers about 150 yards of very popular river frontage. It can get crowded. The hatchery itself, just up the road, has some access for fishing and signs there direct anglers to accessible sections of the river. Clemens Park itself offers access to about a half mile of river frontage and a good trail follows this section of the river. Confrontations with landowners are too common on this river, so anglers should respect private property and ask for permission if in doubt about access. Don't be surprised to be denied that permission. A few of the landowners allow fishing for a small fee.

Another popular fishing access site is Honey Grove Bridge, about a mile north from the town of Alsea. As you head south on the highway from Clemens Park, watch for a left-hand turn leading over the bridge. Normally the North Fork has been closed to steelhead fishing upstream from the hatchery (located north of the highway—watch for the road adjacent to the highway bridge). Check the most current regulations, however, as consideration has been given to extending the deadline.

All methods are productive on the popular North Fork and the best fishing usually lasts from late December through mid-February. However, steelhead often show up as early as mid-December and most years, fresh fish are still arriving by early March. The river fishes best at slightly elevated water levels and often clears in a day or less after a heavy rain. Less popular than the winter steelhead run, the North Fork's run of anadromous cutthroat trout can produce a few 14- to 18-inch beauties. They are never common, but a handful of enthusiasts enjoy fairly consistent success during September and October using flies or small spinners (be sure to check current regulations).

Alsea River, South Fork

A fair cutthroat trout stream, the South Fork Alsea joins the North Fork at the little community of Alsea, about 25 miles from Corvallis. From Corvallis, follow Hwy 20 west through Philomath to a left-hand turn on State Route 34, the Alsea Highway. At Alsea, turn south across the river on the road pointing to Lobster Valley and then take the left-hand turn on South Fork Alsea River Road. The river runs through an accessible mix of private and BLM lands, with fishing access available at a number of key locations along the road. The most popular general-use spot is Alsea Falls Recreation Area, a BLM site with a network of trails and a campground. Just upstream is the bridge at McBee Park, which is the angling deadline on the South Fork.

The South Fork, despite heavy timber harvest in the drainage, remains a rather attractive little trout stream. Fishing is best between early summer and mid-autumn. The South Fork is also open (up to the falls) for steelhead fishing and it kicks out a decent number of hatchery fish during January and February, though not nearly so many as the North Fork. In years past, ODFW has trucked surplus hatchery steelhead down to the lower end of the South Fork, making them available for harvest. Call ODFW in Corvallis or call the hatchery to find out if such drops are scheduled.

Barney Reservoir (Washington County)
Boat or float tube recommended

A large, secluded reservoir in the Coast Range southwest from Henry Hagg Lake, Barney Reservoir offers catch-and-release, flies/artificial lures-only fishing for cutthroat trout, a few of which get surprisingly large. Roads in the area subject to both heavy logging traffic on weekdays and to being gated. The primary route goes through Yamhill on Pike Road, which eventually becomes Turner Creek Road. The parking area is a pullout marked by large cement barriers, and launching requires dragging the boat a few yards to the lake. The reservoir is subject to closure if too many people ignore the simple rules: no fires, no off-road vehicles, no gas motors, no camping, and of course no leaving piles of garbage behind. The fishing can be fair to good from late spring into summer and again in the fall, but Barney is remote, subject to attracting people who ignore the fishing regulations, and a place lone anglers might want to avoid. In other words, take a few friends and don't leave anything valuable in the vehicle.

Battle Lake (Tillamook County)
Hike-in, float tube recommended

A diminutive lake in the Coast Range northeast of Hebo, Battle Lake offers fair to good fishing for stocked rainbow trout in a rather secluded forest setting. From Hebo to the south or Tillamook to the north, follow Highway 101 to the tiny community of Hemlock. Then head east on East Beaver Creek Road (the turn is next to Beaver Creek Artichokes) about 3 miles to a right-hand turn on Forest Road 8172 and follow this road to the second right-hand turn, about 2 miles up. Park at the gate and hike down this road about 1.25 miles to a short left-hand spur leading to the lake. The Hebo Ranger District Map from Siuslaw National Forest is helpful. Battle Lake is generally stocked once each spring with about 700 legal-size rainbow or cutthroat trout. Fishing is best from the firsts stocking through June. Though just 2 acres in size, Battle Lake is great for float tubes because the shoreline tends toward the marshy side.

Bay City Reservoir (Tillamook County)

A half-acre impoundment located east of Bay City, this tiny reservoir is stocked once each April with 500 legal-size cutthroat trout, so the best fishing occurs shortly thereafter and things slow down considerably as summer rolls around. From Bay City (south of Garibaldi along the east shore of Tillamook Bay), head north on Fifth Street to a right turn on Ocean Street. Turn left at the stop sign and go half a mile to a right-hand swing onto Patterson Creek Road and then another right on Jacoby Creek Road. After another half mile, take the left-hand fork at the Y-intersection. If the road is gated, you can walk to the lake.

Bear Creek (Clatsop County)

An attractive, swift, medium-sized stream entering the Columbia River at the tiny hamlet of Svenson, about 10 miles east of Astoria, Bear Creek offers fair prospects for winter steelhead. The wild fish must be released, but the creek gets enough fin-clipped steelhead to draw a fair number of anglers during the peak of the run from late December through early March. Svenson Market Road leads south from Hwy 30 at Svenson, more or less following the creek up to a private timber-company road, which is gated. From the gate, you must walk up the road to the creek. Downstream from the end of the road, much of the creek flows across private lands, so be sure to ask permission to fish. Be sure to check current regulations for season dates.

Bear Creek
(Salmon River drainage/Lincoln County)
closed waters

Beaver Creek (Lincoln County)
boat ramp

A small stream located 8 miles south of Newport, Beaver Creek reaches Hwy 101 and the ocean at Ona Beach State Park. The lower end of the creek, from the county road bridge 3 miles down to the mouth, is largely slack water and offers lots of good habitat for sea-run cutthroat, which run from July through October. This reach is fishable by small boat or canoe, especially if you use the tide to your advantage. Easier still is a small boat powered with a small gas or electric motor. Cast flies or lures into the abundant cover to search for the cutthroat. The stretch of Beaver Creek running through Ona Beach State Park also offers fair prospects for sea-run cutthroat trout and is easy to access in the park. Resident cutthroat occupy the diminutive upper reaches of the creek (flies/artificial lures only), where access is limited by private property. Beaver Creek also draws a small run of winter steelhead and is open for hatchery (fin-clipped) steelhead most of the year (except during April and May) as far up as the county bridge in Ona on North Beaver Creek Road. North Beaver Creek Road turns east off the highway opposite the entrance to Ona Beach State Park and the first right-hand turn from Beaver Creek Road leads down to the launch site. The next crossing upstream is at South Beaver Creek Road, but the surrounding land is private, so boaters must do up and back trips (round trip is about 3 miles). The area around the mouth of Beaver Creek, on the wide-open sand beach at Ona Beach, is an excellent place to seek redtail surfperch. Beaver Creek is currently closed to salmon fishing, but check current regulations.

Beaver Creek (Tillamook County)

A tributary to the Nestucca River, Beaver Creek offers fair-to-good fishing for sea-run cutthroat from July through October. The stream also hosts a small run of winter steelhead (open for hatchery fish December 1 through March 31 below the West Fork). Beaver Creek flows alongside the highway for several miles between the little hamlets of Hemlock and Beaver. East Beaver Creek Road follows the east fork for 10 miles, but the fishing is best in the lower few miles. Private

property abounds on the drainage so be certain to seek permission when appropriate.

Beaver Creek, North (Tillamook County)

This small tributary of Beaver Creek flows through private property on its short journey down to the town of Hemlock. North Beaver Creek has a run of anadromous cutthroat in the fall, but access is difficult.

Beneke Creek (Clatsop County)
no bait

A small, but lengthy tributary to the Nehalem, reaching the river at Jewell, Beneke Creek offers fair fishing for small, resident cutthroat trout and a very occasional sea-run cutthroat trout. Access is good along the county road that follows the creek north from Jewell. From Hwy 26 east from Elsie, turn north at the signs to Jewell (Fishhawk Falls Highway).

Beverly Beach (Lincoln County)

Beverly Beach is the northernmost extension of Moolack Beach, forming a contiguous sand beach of nearly 5 miles in length between Yaquina Head on the south and Otter Rock on the north. See Moolack Beach.

Big Creek (Clatsop County)

A fair producer of hatchery winter steelhead, and also offering fisheries for fin-clipped spring Chinook and wild fall Chinook salmon, Big Creek flows into the Columbia River near the town of Knappa, about 15 miles east of Astoria. Public access is limited to just a few places, so the stream gets rather crowded when conditions are right and the fish are running. The two most popular spots are the stretches of public water below the hatchery and at a county park near Hwy 30. Anglers also fish at the railroad trestle near the mouth of the creek. Be sure to read the regulations carefully for season dates on Big Creek, as the creek has several different closures in place. At times the creek has been open to coho salmon fishing. Upstream from the hatchery weir, Big Creek is open only for catch-and-release trout fishing from late May through August (no bait allowed for trout angling).

Big Creek Fish Hatchery, which rears steelhead, coho salmon and chinook salmon, is located about 2 miles south of the highway. Watch for the signs to Knappa and then turn south off the highway on Hillcrest Loop Road. Head south about a mile and a half to Big Creek Road and turn left to reach the hatchery. Downstream from the closed-area markers, anglers have about half a mile of public access. Big Creek County Park sits on the east bank adjacent to the highway and is also reached by Hillcrest Ridge Road. It includes 36 acres, but no facilities.

Winter steelhead fishing peaks on Big Creek during December and January, though a few fish often reach the creek by Thanksgiving. Coho and chinook salmon arrive from August through early November, but the entire creek below the hatchery is closed to fishing for the month of September.

Late August can be a good time to find fresh salmon in the creek, especially if heavy rains blanket the drainage for a few days toward the end of the month (which seems to happen every other year or so). October fishing can be fair for salmon. Upstream from the hatchery, Big Creek has a fair population of small, wild cutthroat trout. If the road is gated, you must hike or bike into the upper drainage. All trout fishing is strictly catch and release and few people fish this section of the creek.

Striped seaperch are hefty, super-strong denizens of the rocky surf zone and rock jetties all along the Oregon coast.

Big Creek (Lane County)

A slow to fair producer of winter steelhead, Big Creek is a fairly steep, short stream that reaches the Pacific about halfway between Yachats and Florence. Big Creek Road provides good access, turning east off Hwy 101 at Roosevelt Beach, a mile south of Ocean Beach and a mile north of Washburn State Park. Big Creek also receives runs of fall chinook salmon and sea-run cutthroat, but the stream is currently closed to fishing from April 1 through October 31. Only fin-clipped steelhead may be kept during the November-through-March open season.

Big Creek (Lincoln County)

campground

A small, short stream crossing under Hwy 101 north of Yachats, Big Creek produces just a few sea-run cutthroat during September and October. Most of the creek flows through public lands on the Siuslaw National Forest, but the road running east into the drainage provides only minimal access, so most anglers fish near the highway. Be sure to check current regulations for trout fishing in this zone. The beach here is a productive area for redtail surfperch. Camping is available at Tillicum Beach State Park.

Big Creek Reservoirs (Lincoln County)

A pair of similar-sized stocked-trout reservoirs on the outskirts of Newport, Big Creek Reservoirs #1 and #2 offer close-to-home fishing for anglers in the local area. They are stocked as early as February and then several more times during the spring and late summer, with reservoir #1 receiving about 11,000 legal-size rainbows annually and reservoir #2 receiving about 20,000 annually. At times ODFW adds a few of its "larger" and "trophy" plants to the mix. Trout fishing holds up into July and when the water cools in autumn, a few trout are typically still available. The reservoirs offer quite a few brown bullhead and yellow perch, as well as bluegill and a few decent-sized largemouth bass. Bank fishing is most popular, but a float tube or small boat certainly offers the advantage when targeting bass. The access road for reservoir #1 offers the best access there, while reservoir #2 has lots of bank access. Gas boat motors are not allowed (there is a primitive boat launch at the west end of reservoir #2, but there are no other facilities).

The reservoirs, covering about 20 acres each, are located immediately northeast of Newport on Big Creek Road. If you're coming from the north on Highway 101, watch for a left-hand turn on NE 32nd/NE Harney Road across the highway from Agate Beach Wayside, on the north end of town. Follow NE Harney to a left-hand turn onto Big Creek Road. From the south, follow the highway through downtown Newport to a right turn on NE 12th Street and then head east to a left-hand turn on Fogarty Street, which becomes Big Creek Road. Reservoir #2 is half a mile past reservoir #1.

Big Elk Creek (Lincoln County)

For its size, Big Elk Creek is a decent producer of fall chinook salmon and hatchery winter steelhead. The salmon fishery peaks in October and the steelheading is best in January and early February (check regulations for current open seasons). Big Elk Creek is a tributary of the Yaquina River and reaches the river at tiny Elk City, more or less due east of Toledo. The creek draws its headwaters off the west flanks of Mary's Peak. The angling deadline for salmon and steelhead is at the bridge downstream from Grant Creek, west (downstream) from Harlan.

There's some decent public access along the stretch below Grant Creek, but much of Big Elk Creek flows through private lands, even though the road follows closely alongside the stream. When in doubt, seek landowner permission. To reach the upper end of the fishery near Harlan, head west from Corvallis or east from Newport on Hwy 20. At Burnt Woods, turn south on the Harlan-Burnt Woods Road, following it down to Harlan. From there you can drive the entire length of the creek along the narrow, winding Harlan Road. To reach the lower end of the creek at Elk City, it's easier to turn south off the highway at Elk City Road about 6 miles east from Toledo (and a few miles east of Pioneer Summit).

Not surprisingly considering the extensive private land on the creek, much of the fishing pressure occurs at just a few places, including Big Elk Campground a few miles downstream from Harlan and at the park in Elk City.

Blind Slough (Clatsop County)
boat recommended, boat ramp

Blind Slough is a productive warm-water fishery along the Columbia River just north of Knappa. The slough offers good fishing for largemouth bass, bluegill, yellow perch, brown bullhead, and a host of less common species, along with an occasional salmon, jack salmon, and cutthroat trout. Jackson Road on the north bank offers public access to the slough and you can drop a float tube or similar small craft in here, but a boat is a better option if you want to make a full day adventure out of it. Launch 4 miles to the northeast at Aldrich Point and run down to the slough. Fishing for bass, perch, and panfish peaks from May through September. Kayakers paddle Blind Slough from time to time, and certainly such craft provide a convenient way to fish for bass and panfish. If you decide to fish by kayak, launch at the Knappa docks.

Bob Creek (Lane County)
closed waters

Buck Lake (Lane County)
see Alder Lake

Cannon Beach (Clatsop County)

Cannon Beach and the super-popular touristy town of the same name lies just south of Tillamook Head and about 15 miles south of Seaside. The beach here is marginally productive for surfperch and generally fishable only very early in the morning unless you want a lot of company in the form of beach strollers. Better bet is to try Arcadia Beach a few miles south, and then head back to Cannon Beach for lunch at one of the many fine restaurants.

Cape Meares Lake (Tillamook County)
boat ramp

From mid-March through early May legal rainbow and cutthroat trout are stocked in this 120-acre lake. During the winter, excess hatchery adult steelhead are sometimes released into the lake. In this situation, the steelhead are considered trout and are subject to the "no more than two fish over 20 inches" trout bag limit. Largemouth bass, bluegill, and brown bullheads are also present; however the bluegill and bullhead populations are very low and angling success is poor.

From downtown Tillamook, turn west on Third Street and then turn right on Bay Ocean Road. This road leads 5 miles to the lake, which sits along the north side of the road. Bank angling is available most of the way along the road, and a

public angling dock is located along the shore next to the road. A boat ramp is available off the main highway just past the angling dock (5 mph speed limit). A dike access road also runs along the dike on the east edge of the lake. Parking is available at the end of the road and it is a short walk back to the lake.

Carter Lake (Lane County)
boat ramp, campground

One of the sand dune lakes along the central Oregon coast, Carter Lake lies alongside the west side of Hwy 101, about 8 miles south from Florence and 2 miles south of the Siltcoos Lake turn-off. Carter is regularly and liberally stocked with rainbow trout from February through May and the fishing usually holds up through June; the lake also offers yellow perch and a few largemouth bass. The lake level varies considerably from year to year. During dry years, bank access is very good, as the receded water line leaves a sand beach around the lake's circumference. At 28 acres total, and stretching for about a mile north-to-south, Carter Lake offers enough room to spread out, yet it is small enough to cover easily if you bring a small boat. The lake has a good boat ramp on the east shore opposite the campground. Carter Lake is protected enough to avoid the wind quite often.

Cemetery Lake (Clatsop County)

Located adjacent to Ocean View Cemetery south of Warrenton, this 10-acre lake offers fair prospects for warmwater species including yellow perch, crappie, and largemouth bass. A float tube is handy here. From Hwy 101 on the Warrenton side of Youngs Bay, head south about a mile past the mall and then turn right on Route 105. After a mile, turn left on South Main Avenue and then take the next right on Cemetery Road. Access to the lake is from the cemetery. Several other nearby lakes are private, including Long, Wild Ace, and Leinenweber Lakes.

Clatskanie Slough (Columbia County)
boat recommended

A consistent producer of bass and other warm-water species, Clatskanie Slough is a productive backwater of the Columbia River near the town of Clatskanie, north of Hwy 30. Bank fishing opportunities are rather limited, but you can drop small boats off the banks along Erickson Dike Road. Fishing for bass and crappie peaks from April through September.

Clear Lake (Lane County)

Accessible only by a mile-long hike across the dunes, or by permission from one of the few homeowners along the shoreline, Clear Lake, just north of Florence and east of Highway 101, serves as a water source for the Heceta Water District. Largemouth bass and yellow perch, as well as some wild cutthroat trout, inhabit this 150-acre lake, the middle and largest lake in the north-to-south-oriented chain that includes Collard, Ackerly, and Munsel. Public use is minimal.

Cleawox Lake (Lane County)

boat ramp, boat recommended, float tube recommended, campground

Located mostly within the sprawling and popular Honeyman State Park south of Florence, Cleawox Lake is a fair producer of warmwater species—brown bullhead, yellow perch, large-mouth bass—and of stocked rainbow trout. ODFW stocks this popular lake during spring with upwards of 20,000 rainbow trout and fishing for them holds up into mid-summer. The main body of the lake spreads out over about 60 acres and a narrow arm reaches well to the north, extending almost a mile from the main lake. When the water warms during summer, use a watercraft to target trout in the deeper center area of the lake. An unimproved launch site is available for small boats and access is from a large day-use area , and Honeyman State Park includes a convenience store and rental canoes/kayaks. Information is available at http://www.oregonstateparks.org/park_134.php. Cleawox is a fair bet for late winter/early spring and late fall fishing when the ever-present summer crowds thin out.

Coffenbury Lake (Clatsop County)

boat ramp, campground

A good bet for stocked rainbow trout during the spring, 50-acre Coffenbury Lake is the largest of several lakes in Fort Stevens State Park, located on Clatsop Spit in the northwest-ernmost corner of Oregon. Coffenbury Lake is stocked liber-ally several times during the year and fishing tends to hold up well through mid-summer. Autumn stockings allow for some good fishing around the busy Labor Day weekend, and in recent years, ODFW has stocked 14- to 16-inch trout for the fall fishing. Usually ODFW adds a few surplus hatchery steel-head to the mix during winter and spring. During summer, when the water warms, fishing action turns to the lake's yellow perch, brown bullhead, and bluegill.

Coffenbury Lake stretches for about a mile from north to south and is sandwiched between low sand dunes. The lake offers handicap-accessible fishing platforms, a good boat ramp, and a good trail system. Rental canoes are available during the summer months, when the lake gets quite busy. Follow Hwy101 west from Astoria or north from Seaside and watch for the signs to Fort Stevens State Park. The park offers two other fishable lakes containing warm-water species. Cra-bapple Lake has largemouth bass and yellow perch; Creep-n-Crawl Lake has bluegill. Both get weedy by mid-summer. The state park requires an access fee and offers myriad activities in addition to fishing. For more information, visit http://www.oregonstateparks.org/park_179.php.

Collard Lake (Lane County)

Collard Lake is a 30-acre natural lake located just north of Florence, east of Highway 101. It is the uppermost lake in the Clear/Ackerly/Munsel Lakes chain and its shoreline is entire-ly private, though some of the homes are typically available for rental, which provides renters access to the lake (check

with the Florence Area Chamber of Commerce, 541-997-3128). Otherwise homeowner permission is required to fish the shoreline or launch a canoe, kayak, or other small craft (motors are not allowed). The lake has yellow perch, large-mouth bass, bluegill, and wild cutthroat trout. Collard Lake has three distinct basins connected by narrow "necks."

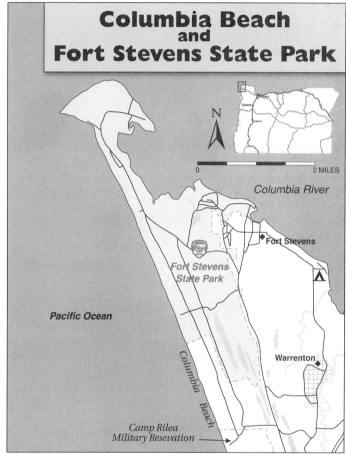

© 2007 Wilderness Adventures Press, Inc.

Columbia Beach (Clatsop County)

Picturesque Columbia Beach, site of the wreck of the ship *Peter Iredale*, forms the western edge of sprawling Fort Stevens State Park and is the state's northernmost beach. A broad expanse of sand, this beach is traditionally one of Or-egon's best bets for razor clams and recent seasons have been very productive. Columbia Beach is closed to the taking of razor clams from July 15 through September 30 and frequent-ly on all or parts of the Oregon coast, the season is closed due to elevated levels of natural toxicity in the clams. Be sure to consult current regulations and check with ODFW for toxicity closures. Columbia Beach is also a fine destination for redtail surfperch, though their numbers along this beach seem to vary considerably from year to year. The state park offers easy access to the beach by way of a network of trails and also offers ample camping space.

Cook Creek (Tillamook County)

A significant tributary to the lower Nehalem River, Cook Creek offers opportunities for hatchery winter steelhead (all wild fish must be released) and sea-run cutthroat. Salmon enter the creek at about the same time as the sea-run cutthroat, but salmon fishing is currently closed here to protect spawning fish. The creek also has a few small resident cutthroat trout, but not enough to warrant a lot of effort. Sea-run fish arrive as early as July if summer rainfall occurs; otherwise, Cook Creek's modest, but fishable run peaks from mid-September through early October. Winter steelhead arrive in modest numbers by late December, with the best prospects on the lower few miles of the creek during January and February.

Cook Creek Road provides good access to the creek, most of which runs through public lands on the Tillamook State Forest. From Hwy 101 immediately north of Wheeler, turn east at Nehalem Junction onto SR 53. After about a mile, turn south on the Miami River Road and then left onto Foss Road, leading up the Nehalem River. After a few miles, watch for the turn onto Cook Creek Road.

Crabapple Lake (Clatsop County)
see Coffenberry Lake

Creep-n-Crawl Lake (Clatsop County)
see Coffenberry Lake

Crescent Lake (Tillamook County)

A rather unproductive, shallow, 10-acre bass fishery near Hwy 101, Crescent Lake sits immediately north of Lytle Lake at the town of Manhattan Beach, about 2 miles north of Rockaway Beach.

Cullaby Lake (Clatsop County)
boat ramp

Cullaby is a 220-acre lake offering good fishing for stocked trout, brown bullhead, yellow perch, bluegill and crappie, but a solid population of largemouth bass is the big attraction here. Cullaby sits just east of Hwy 101, about 9 miles north of Seaside. One half mile south of the Sunset Beach turn-off (yellow flashing signal light), watch for an east-bound turn-off on Cullaby Lake Road, which leads down to Carnahan County Park and boat launch on the north end of the lake. At the south end, Cullaby Lake Park offers another launch site and access.

Fishing for stocked trout is best in the spring and early summer, before the water warms and the weeds begin to grow. Bank fishing is available at the parks, but a boat is handy, especially for fishing the structure-rich shorelines on the other side of the lake where bass and bluegill thrive. The lake is a popular with recreational boaters/watersports enthusiasts during summer when the action peaks for warm-water species, but speed limits are in effect for the shoreline and the coves, so anglers can enjoy good fishing even when the lake is busy.

Deadwood Creek (Lane County)

Not particularly productive during its open steelhead season, lengthy Deadwood Creek is a tributary to the far more popular Lake Creek, which in turn is a major tributary of the Siuslaw River. The creek has wild winter steelhead, which must be released, along with a few fin-clipped fish. The open section extends from the mouth up to the West Fork confluence. The season runs from January 1 to March 31 and the creek is closed to salmon angling. Trout fishing (for wild cutthroat) is allowed with flies and artificial lures from late May through September 30 from the mouth to the forks (check current regulations for exact opening date and bag limits, which are currently set at two fish per day with an 8-inch minimum length). Follow SR 36 west from Triangle Lake or northeast from Swisshome. Most of the land along the creek is private, so when in doubt, ask permission.

Depoe Bay (Lincoln County)
boat ramp, charters, services

Depoe Bay, the so-called "World's Smallest Harbor," is located in the town of the same name about halfway between Lincoln City and Newport. Several charter boat services operate out of Depoe Bay, whose narrow channel through the rocks requires no bar crossing and is thus considered one of the easier accesses to the ocean—at least during calm weather. During even moderately rough surf or heavy swell conditions, the narrow passage in and out of the harbor requires a great deal of expertise for safe negotiation. Consequently the bay's charter, commercial, and recreational boats are often stranded at home when the Coast Guard deems the passage out to be too dangerous. This occurs often during winter.

The bay is enclosed by rugged rocky shoreline, which provides ideal habitat for bottomfish and striped perch. Anglers willing to carefully navigate the rocks during periods of calm water stand a good chance at catching rockfish, greenling, cabezon, and perch, mostly on bait, but also on jigs. This is not for the frail or faint of heart; the rocks are slippery and the breaking waves can be brutal and unpredictable. Wear an emergency personal floatation device. Spring is generally best, but be sure to choose periods of minimal water movement between high and low tides. Early morning is best most days because the wind often blows later in the day. During summer, the kelp beds can grow thick enough to create problems, but they also provide cover for fish. Be very careful when fishing from the rocks, keep an eye on the ocean, and memorize the tide tables for the day.

Outside the bay, charter boats target the full range of available species, with bottomfish being the year-round draw. Charters here also book trips for halibut and salmon during their respective seasons and also for tuna during summer and early fall most years. The salmon fishery for chinook and coho is especially well known at Depoe Bay, so book your trip well in advance. With ready access to prime fishing grounds, Depoe Bay charter operators book trips as short as two hours. For contact information, go to www.depoebaychamber.org and click on "Charter Fishing".

The harbor itself often proves a fair-to-good crabbing destination because the boat docks are open to the public during daylight hours. If the fishing boats are working, you can usually buy crab bait at the little charter-boat office adjacent to the docks. If they don't have bait, you'll have to head for Harry's Bait & Tackle down in Newport. A few rockfish, greenling, and perch are taken by anglers fishing from the rocks enclosing the boat channel into the harbor immediately below the highway bridge. But beware the slippery surfaces. This channel fishes best at low light. Try white jigs of ½- to 1-ounce or drift bait below a float.

Devils Lake (Lincoln City)
boat ramp, boat recommended, campground, services
A large natural lake sprawling along the east edge of Lincoln City, Devils Lake is largely surrounded by secluded homes and neighborhoods, so bank fishing is limited to a handful of public access areas. Boat access is very good. The lake offers fair fishing for stocked rainbow trout, along with brown bullhead, bluegill, yellow perch, and largemouth bass. Devils Lake earned prominence in the 1980s when ODFW introduced fast-growing Chinese grass carp to combat rampant aquatic weed growth in the lake. Over a period of several years, more than 32,000 of the carp were introduced to the lake. The ploy worked and the protected carp attained impressive sizes.

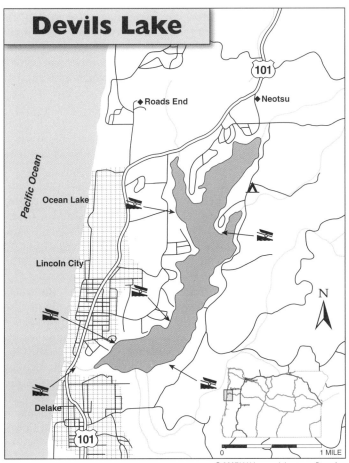

© 2007 Wilderness Adventures Press, Inc.

The lake has six different boat ramps and a state park, which is split into two halves on opposite shores. East Devils Lake State Park is located on the southeast shore and Devils Lake State Park sits on the southwest shore. East Devils Lake Road wraps around the more scenic and secluded east edge of the lake, meeting Hwy 101 just east of town to the north and near the factory-outlet mall on the south.

Drift Creek (Alsea River drainage)
One of two Drift Creeks in Lincoln County, this version reaches Alsea Bay a few miles east of Waldport and offers fishing for steelhead, salmon, and sea-run cutthroat trout. The stream's lower 25 miles, from Bohanon Falls, are open for hatchery steelhead and chinook salmon. There is no open season on coho salmon here. Most of the creek's steelhead, however, are wild and must be released. Access is quite difficult owing to extensive private property on most of the creek and steep, rugged country on the upper watershed, much of which is encompassed by the Drift Creek Wilderness Area. Thus most of the chinook salmon fishing effort is made by boat below the head of tide on the lower end of the creek. Launch at the ramp in Waldport for the short run up to the mouth of Drift Creek.

Drift Creek (Siletz River drainage)
hike-in
A fine salmon and steelhead fishery, highly regarded for its run of big, native winter steelhead, Drift Creek is a tributary to Siletz Bay south of Lincoln City. Prior to the advent of catch-and-release regulations for the creek's wild steelhead, annual harvest was as high as 1,700 fish in 1986 and catches of between 600 and 700 steelhead per year were typical. Managed for wild steelhead, with catch-and-release rules firmly in place for them, Drift Creek is less popular now than just two decades ago. The creek still receives a fair number of fin-clipped steelhead, but wild fish are far more common.

During the fall, the creek offers a fair-to-good fishery for chinook salmon and during a good year salmon anglers harvest several hundred fish from this medium-sized stream. Sea-run cutthroat trout are also fairly common in the creek after the first August freshets, and catch-and-release fishing for them generally remains good through October and even into November. The lower end of the creek, below the head of tide, is good water for cutthroat and accessible by canoe or kayak from Siletz Bay.

Access to Drift Creek is good for anglers who don't mind hiking because the roads rarely dip close to the stream. The popular lower half of the creek is accessible by walking in from Drift Creek Road (the creek is to the south of the road). The easiest and most popular access point is in the vicinity of the Drift Creek Mennonite Camp, about 12 miles upstream from the turn-off on Hwy 101. Here you can hike up or down the creek and, at low water, wading anglers can cross back and forth.

You can reach the Drift Creek road from three directions. Just south of Lincoln City, along the northeast edge of Siletz Bay, Drift Creek Road turns east from the highway adjacent to the mouth of the creek. Follow this road about 1.5 miles up to a right-hand turn, then half a mile south to a left-hand turn. This road, which winds its way through the drainage above the creek, becomes FR 19 when you reach the National Forest boundary after a mile. This road continues past the Mennonite Camp and eventually comes out on the Siletz River Highway. If you're coming from Hwy 22/18 north of Lincoln City, you can also take the Bear Creek Road from Rose Lodge. This road takes you down to Schooner Creek and a left-hand turn on CR 108, leading down to Drift Creek Road.

Dune Lake (Lane County)
see Alder Lake

Eckman Lake (Lincoln County)
boat ramp, boat recommended

Eckman Lake spans about 50 acres and sits just south of the lower Alsea River, a few miles east from Waldport. Eckman is stocked with several thousand rainbow trout during spring and also supports brown bullhead and a few largemouth bass. The boat ramp provides easy access for small craft. Follow Hwy 34 west from Alsea or east from Waldport and watch for signs (about 2.5 miles east from Hwy 101). Usually the ODFW holds a kid's fishing day at Eckman during mid May.

Ecola Creek (Clatsop County)

Ecola Creek, which reaches the Pacific at Cannon Beach, is home to wild steelhead, salmon, and cutthroat trout, and is currently open for steelhead fishing from November through March. All wild fish must be released, but the creek produces a few stray fin-clipped steelhead, mostly from mid-December through January. The creek is closed to all fishing from April 1 through October.

Elbow Lake (Douglas County)
float tube recommended, boat recommended, boat ramp

Elbow Lake lies alongside Hwy 101 north of Winchester Bay, about 7 miles north of Reedsport, and about a mile south of the boat ramp and campground at Tahkenitch Lake. You will drive alongside the 12-acre lake, which sits along the west side of the road and is signed. From the south, it is 3.5 miles from Sparrow Park Lane, which sits near the top of the grade outside of Gardiner. Elbow has a few warmwater fish (largemouth bass and yellow perch) and is stocked regularly with 12-inch-plus trout, along with some standard issue, legal-size fish. Carryovers here tend to be fat and range from 12 to 18 inches, though they are never plentiful. You can fish from the bank, but the irregular shoreline is very brushy, making access troublesome and fly-casting difficult. A float tube, raft, pram, or similar lightweight craft is perfectly suited to exploring the structure-filled shoreline margins and the cove on the lake's west side. An unimproved launch serves boaters. Despite its proximity to the highway, Elbow Lake never seems to draw crowds and fishing tends to hold up from early spring through early summer.

Erhart Lake (Lane County)
float tube recommended, campground

This small, popular trout lake sits along the east side of Hwy 101, about 8 miles south of Florence and about 1 mile south from the Siltcoos River. Covering 5 acres, Erhart is not marked by any signs, but is clearly visible from the highway, 1 mile north from the Siltcoos Campground entrance. Very limited parking for this lake is available in the highway pullouts, but the better option is to pay the fee to park at the Siltcoos Trailhead parking lot immediately to the south and also on the east side of the highway. The lake's brushy shoreline makes a float tube or similar small craft advantageous. Erhart is stocked regularly through the spring and the stocking allotment usually includes quite a few of the ODFW's 12-plus-inch "larger" trout and 16-plus-inch "trophy" trout. Fishing tends to be good from late February through June. Waxmyrtle and Lagoon Campgrounds are located west of Hwy 101. The turnoff for these campgrounds is just north of Erhart Lake.

Esmond Creek (Lane/Douglas County)

A fair-to-good producer of small, wild cutthroat—along with an occasional sea-run cutthroat—Esmond Creek is a tributary of the Siuslaw River. It reaches the Siuslaw about 20 miles east from Florence and is accessible from a county road that follows most of the creek. From Eugene, head west on Hwy 126 for about 32 miles to Austa (sight of the Wildcat Creek Covered Bridge) and then head south on the Siuslaw River Road. This road winds along the river for about 10 miles before reaching the mouth of Esmond Creek and a right-hand turn on Esmond Creek Road, which follows the creek. On the upper watershed, Esmund Lake offers good fishing for small cutthroat trout.

Esmond Lake (Lane County)
see Esmond Creek

Fishhawk Creek (Clatsop County)
no bait

Fishhawk Creek and its tributaries, Little Fishhawk and Hamilton Creeks, are small streams on the Nehalem River drainage. After gathering the tributary streams, Fishhawk Creek joins Beneke Creek near Jewell, which then flows into the Nehalem. Fishhawk Creek is best known for its elk herd and the state maintains viewing areas on the lower end of the creek. Public access beyond the viewing areas is prohibited, so fishing is limited to the upper two-thirds of the creek. Another worthwhile stop—and a good access point to the creek—is 100-foot-high Fishhawk Creek Falls, located 3 miles west of the main elk viewing area. Clatsop County's Lee Wooden-Fishhawk Falls Park spans 55 acres and has a footbridge across the creek with a trail to the falls. These streams offer fair catch-and-release fishing for small, wild coastal cutthroat trout, with the best fishing being from early June through September. Fishhawk Creek is the most accessible because it runs near SR 202, the Nehalem Highway, heading from Jewel up to Tidewater Summit. From Hwy 26, watch for the sign to

Jewell just east from Elsie (Fishhawk Falls Road). The tributary streams are difficult to access owing to extensive private lands.

Fishhawk Lake is also restricted to flies and artificial lures.

Five Rivers (Alsea River drainage)

A major tributary to the mainstem Alsea River, Five Rivers itself offers fair-to-good prospects for winter steelhead as far up the river as the angling deadline at Buck Creek. The river reaches the Alsea about halfway between Waldport to the west and the town of Alsea to the east. Both wild and hatchery steelhead enter Five Rivers, but all wild fish must be released. The steelhead fishing peaks from late December through early February, with most of the effort near the mouth of the river and at a few select spots along the road that follows Five Rivers. Fall chinook, sea-run cutthroat, and coho salmon also return to this attractive little river, though there is currently no open season for coho. Sea-run cutts, though never numerous, are usually available by September, especially after the first rains. Resident cutthroat are fairly common, but quite small. The river and all its tributaries are closed above Buck Creek, and salmon angling is limited to the lower 2.5 miles of the river below Cascade Creek.

There's a classic old covered bridge at Fisher, just south of the Buck Creek confluence. Fisher School Covered Bridge, rather garish in its bright red paint, spans Five Rivers and was built in 1919. It is the only survivor of three such covered bridges originally built on the Five Rivers drainage. Five Rivers takes its name from the fact that its flows derive from five primary tributaries: Alder Creek, Cougar Creek, Buck Creek, Crab Creek, and Cherry Creek.

Fogarty Creek (Lincoln County)

A tiny creek reaching the ocean at Fogarty Creek State Park north of Depoe Bay, Fogarty Creek offers marginal opportunities for native cutthroat and is generally not worth the effort.

Fogarty Creek Beach (Lincoln County)

A rugged and steep little beach a mile north of Boiler Bay, Fogarty Creek Beach offers fair-to-good prospects for surfperch. Fish bait and stay well back from the surf-line here because the steep beach creates some big, dangerous breakers. At low tide you can access the rocks on the beach and pick up an occasional rockfish, greenling, or striped perch. Watch for the signs for Fogarty Creek State Park. Early morning is best, especially during the first two hours of incoming water. Do not fish this beach during winter or during times of extreme tides.

Georgia Lakes (Lane County)
float tube recommended, campground

Georgia and North Georgia Lakes are situated just east of Hwy 101, south of Florence and south of the Siltcoos River. The two Georgia Lakes cover about 2 acres each. There are no signs along the highway marking the lakes and parking is available at several small highway turnouts. The lakes are stocked several times each spring with rainbow trout. The shoreline is forested but brushy, making float tubes very useful, especially for fly casters. Several campgrounds are located nearby, along with several other productive lakes. The Georgia Lakes don't appear on most maps, but the Siuslaw National Forest Map shows Erhart Lake and the Georgia Lakes are just to the north, about 7.5 miles south of Florence.

Gleneden Beach (Lincoln County)

A decent beach for redtail surfperch (at times downright productive), Gleneden Beach lies just south of Siletz Bay at the town of the same name. The beach, not visible from the highway, is generally rather quiet, even during the tourist season. Look for the signs to Gleneden Beach State Wayside.

Gnat Creek (Clatsop County)
campground

A small, swift-moving tributary to the Columbia River about 20 miles east of Astoria, Gnat Creek offers fair-to-good prospects for hatchery winter steelhead, along with fisheries for fin-clipped coho salmon and chinook salmon. The winter steelhead fishing peaks from December through late February and this small creek attracts quite a lot of angling pressure. Some years, the fin-clipped winter fish show as early as late November. Gnat Creek reaches the Columbia at Aldrich Point, northeast of Knappa and the creek is crossed by Hwy 30 near Gnat Creek Fish Hatchery. The hatchery offers 2.5 miles of accessible water, with trails leading down to the campground. Most of the fishing pressure occurs here and down to Blind Slough. Be sure to check current ODFW regulations for open seasons.

Hamilton Creek (Clatsop County)
see Fishhawk Creek

Hebo Lake (Tillamook County)

Located in the hills east of the town of Hebo, this 2-acre lake is stocked with legal-size trout several times during spring, and provides fair-to-good fishing into mid-summer. Since some of the fish over-winter, Hebo Lake offers a chance to do a little wintertime lake fishing. During the winter, you must park at the top of the gated access road and walk a short distance down to the lake. Hebo Lake offers a developed, seasonal use (summer) Forest Service campground. Additional fish are stocked in June for Free Fishing Day activities conducted by U.S. Forest Service personnel.

From Hebo take Hwy 22 a quarter-mile east, and then take a left onto Forest Service Road 14. Go 4 miles to signs that direct you to the lake a short distance off the main road. A trail surrounds the lake and barrier-free piers provide opportunity for disabled anglers. Boats are permitted on the lake, but internal combustion motors are not allowed. The lake is perfectly suited to float tubes and attracts a handful of fly anglers.

Holiday Beach (Lincoln County)

Holiday Beach offers 5 miles of wide open, gentle-gradient sand beach just south of Newport and is prime habitat for redtail surfperch, along with smaller surfperch species. Access is from South Beach State Park on the north (south from the Yaquina Bay Bridge) and from Lost Creek State Recreation Site, 6 miles south of Newport. Except for the north end near the state park, Holiday Beach is lightly used compared to other nearby surfperch beaches. It fishes best during spring and early summer on early morning incoming tides. Most anglers fish bait, but periods of calm ocean conditions allows jig anglers and even fly anglers to fish from the surf line.

Hult Pond (Lane County)

boat ramp

An old log pond alternately known as Horton Lake, Hult Reservoir, Hult Marsh, and Mill Pond, this fairly popular 40-acre impoundment on the headwater stretch of Lake Creek offers fair prospects for cutthroat trout, brown bullhead, bluegills, some largemouth bass, as well as a few wild rainbows. The reservoir sits in an attractive wooded area and is usually ac-

The Kilchis River is best known for its run of chum salmon. Photo by Todd York

cessible year-round. A boat is handy and the reservoir has an unimproved boat ramp. The BLM camping area is undeveloped but used frequently. Hult Pond is about 28 miles northwest of Eugene in the foothills of the Coast Range, and about 10 road miles northeast from Triangle Lake. From Eugene or Corvallis, follow Hwy 99 to the Cheshire turn-off (SR 36) south of Junction City. A few miles before you reach Triangle Lake, turn north on Horton Road and continue another mile from Horton to BLM Road 15-7-35 leading to the reservoir.

Humbug Creek (Nehalem River drainage)

no bait

Humbug Creek flows alongside Hwy 26 for a few miles near Camp 18 and then joins the Nehalem River south of Elsie. The creek's two forks drain opposite sides of a broad system of ridges west of Humbug Mountain and north of the highway. Both forks and the mainstem of the creek offer fair-to-good prospects for catch-and-release angling for small, native cutthroat trout. Don't expect to find lots of fish and don't expect to find any fish over about 8 inches. The highway has a few pullouts along the creek broad enough for anglers to park. Most of the drainage runs through a mix of private timber company lands and other private property, but access is decent. The East Fork flows for several miles through lands administered by Tillamook State Forest and a good forest road follows this branch of the creek. Fishing is best during the dry season, from late June through September.

Indian Creek (Siuslaw drainage)

A significant tributary to Lake Creek, which in turn is a major tributary of the Siuslaw River, Indian Creek offers a modest-to-decent run of wild winter steelhead from January through March, but they are protected from harvest. The best fishing prospects are usually from late January through late February and all wild fish must be released. A few fin-clipped fish show up and these are available for harvest. Trout fishing is open during summer below the West Fork and is only fair (no bait). Indian Creek joins Lake Creek at Indiola, 3 miles north of Swisshome on SR 36. The only public access is a 2.5-mile-long stretch of the lower creek flowing through Siuslaw National Forest lands in the vicinity of Indian Creek Campground, a primitive site about 2 miles northwest from Indiola on Indian Creek Road.

Kilchis River (Tillamook County)

boat ramp

Best known for its fishable run of chum salmon, the Kilchis River is one of the major Tillamook Bay tributary streams and also hosts runs of winter steelhead, chinook salmon, and sea-run cutthroat. The catch-and-release chum salmon season runs for two months from mid-September to mid-November. Chum salmon, which typically range from 8 to 14 pounds, used to be widespread on the Oregon coast, especially in the north, and were the subject of intense commercial harvest many decades ago on the lower Columbia. Nowadays

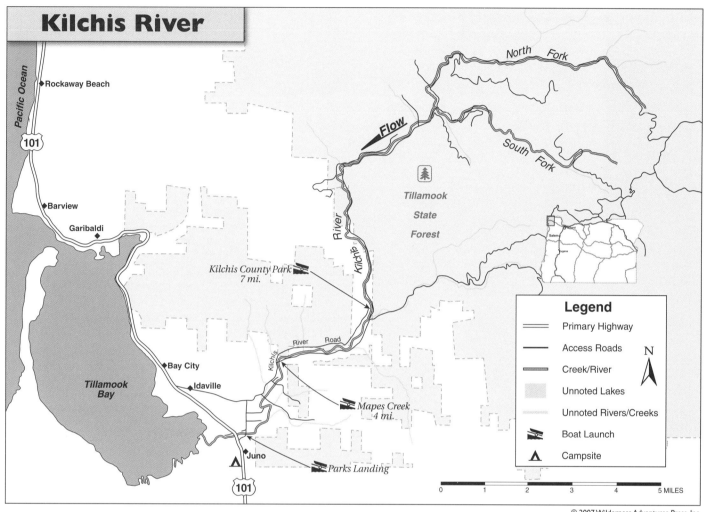

Kilchis River

Pacific Ocean
101
◆ Rockaway Beach
◆ Barview
Garibaldi ◆
Tillamook Bay
◆ Bay City
◆ Idaville
▲ Juno
101

North Fork
Flow
South Fork
Tillamook State Forest
River
Kilchis
Kilchis County Park 7 mi.
River Road
Kilchis
Mapes Creek 4 mi.
Parks Landing

Legend

═══	Primary Highway
───	Access Roads
───	Creek/River
▒▒▒	Unnoted Lakes
⋯⋯	Unnoted Rivers/Creeks
⛵	Boat Launch
▲	Campsite

N

0 1 2 3 4 5 MILES

only the Kilchis and nearby Miami Rivers offer fishing seasons on chum salmon.

Also known as "dog salmon" because of their large, sharp canine-like teeth, chum salmon are regarded as perhaps the best pound-for-pound fighter of the five species of Pacific salmon. Likely this is true for fresh-run fish, though many anglers pursue chum salmon that are well past prime condition. Beware the sharp teeth—I've seen them pierce fingers and 6mm neoprene waders.

During years when late September freshets draw chum into the Kilchis, anglers often find bright, fresh, aggressive salmon in the river. Bright is a relative term because chum salmon start to darken even before entering fresh water and soon develop their characteristic bronzy-colored slashes along the flanks. Chum salmon also endear themselves to anglers for their willingness to chase and grab lures and flies, with chartreuse colors being especially popular.

The Kilchis also enjoys good runs of winter steelhead from late December through March, with quite a few fin-clipped fish available for harvest. Fall chinook salmon ascend the river between late August and early November and a second, lesser-known run of kings arrives during December. This so-called "holiday run" of fall chinook salmon boasts some of the largest fish of the year, with 30-plus-pound fish being typical. During autumn, a modest run of sea-run cutthroat heads up the Kilchis, most of them in the 10- to 14-inch range. A sparse run of spring chinook salmon arrives during May. See current regulations for season dates and harvest allowances on salmon.

Access is problematic on the Kilchis, especially on the highly productive and coveted lower river; so much of the angling pressure is concentrated at just a few places. The uppermost access is at Kilchis County Park, about 5 miles from Hwy 101 and at the end of the road. The park has more than half a mile of good bank access and is a good bet for steelhead and chinook salmon. You can hike upstream from the park, but after a short distance, the trail begins to climb into steep canyon country with very little access to the river.

Heading downstream from the park, the road on the south bank, which crosses over the Logging Bridge, offers access at two locations along the river. The first is about a mile up the road at a gravel bar site maintained by Bay City. Another mile up the road is a small picnic area with some river access.

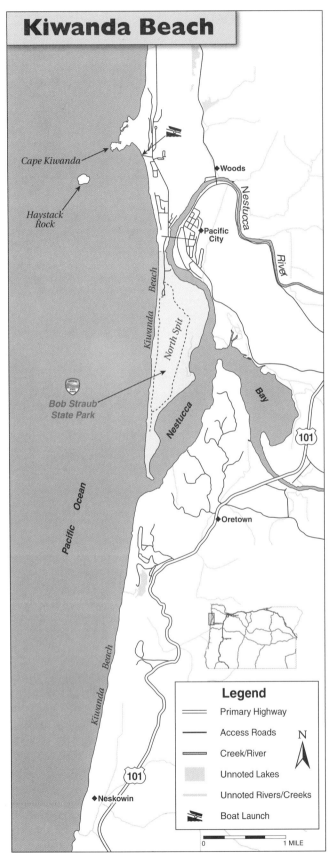

Kiwanda Beach

Cape Kiwanda

Haystack Rock

Bob Straub State Park

Kiwanda Beach

North Spit

Pacific Ocean

Kiwanda Beach

Woods

Nestucca River

Pacific City

Nestucca Bay

101

Oretown

101

Neskowin

Legend

—— Primary Highway

—— Access Roads

—— Creek/River

Unnoted Lakes

Unnoted Rivers/Creeks

Boat Launch

N

0   1 MILE

© 2007 Wilderness Adventures Press, Inc.

The Curl Road Bridge, the first bridge off to the east of Kilchis River Road, is a pay-to-fish location with a fee box for depositing the modest fee levied by the property owner. The Logger Bridge, the next bridge upstream, has a boat ramp and some bank access both above and below. Kilchis River Road ends at Kilchis County Park, which offers good access to the river. The park section is better for steelhead angling because the chum salmon that swim into the upper tend to be quite dark.

The Kilchis is easy to float in a drift boat, but boaters must take care to avoid conflict with bank anglers on this small river. Still, a drift boat allows much better access to the river. The put-ins are located at the county park and at the Logger Bridge and the take-out is at Parks Landing on Kilchis River Road, less than a quarter mile east of Hwy 101. Some anglers, using drift boats and prams with motors, launch at Parks Landing (the head of tide) and run downstream to fish for salmon. The lower river has a 5 mph speed limit.

To reach the Kilchis from Hwy 101 in Tillamook, head north from town about 3 miles to a signed right-hand turn on Alderbrook Road. You will cross the river near the Parks Landing ramp and then the road heads north to a right-hand turn on Kilchis River Road. Curl Road heads to the right after about half a mile and the Logging Bridge is on your right after another mile. From the north on Hwy 101, head south through Bay City and watch for a left-hand turn on the north extent of Alderbrook Road, leading 2 miles to Kilchis River Road.

Kiwanda Beach (Pacific City)

As a whole, Kiwanda Beach stretches for almost 10 miles from the north edge of Neskowin on the south, past the mouth of the Nestucca River and up to Cape Kiwanda near Pacific City. South of the Nestucca River, Kiwanda beach offers excellent prospects for redtail surfperch, particularly at Winema Beach (see separate listing herein).

The beach at Pacific City is famous for its dory fleet. The boats launch and land through the surf here. Likewise, adventurous and experienced sea-kayakers can have a ball fishing the rocks just offshore during calm periods during the summer. If you fit in this group, take along a spinning rod and a variety of jigs and paddle within casting range of the rocks and sea stacks. Greenling, rockfish, and striped perch abound and a few lingcod and cabezon show up as well. Also fish the sand bottoms, behind the surf zone, for perch and flounder.

One charter fishing service operates off the beach here, taking clients offshore for bottomfish, salmon, and even halibut. Haystack Fishing is supposedly the world's only licensed, beach-launched dory fishing charter (503-965-7555). They offer a variety of trips, mostly running from four to six hours in length.

Often the north end of the beach itself is too busy during the summer—lots of tourists and surfers. But if you arrive at dawn you can fish an hour or two for redtail surfperch. To get there, turn off Hwy 101 at the Pacific City exit and follow the road to a left-hand turn at the main intersection in town.

Cross the river and take an immediate right, then continue north until you see the large parking lot on the left, adjacent to the Pelican Bay Brewery, which I recommend for a post-fishing-trip meal and ale.

The south end of the beach, near the mouth of the Nestucca River, is one of the area's best beaches for redtails. The beach is part of Bob Straub State Park, which occupies the broad spit forming the barrier that encloses Nestucca Bay. Watch for the park entrance after you cross the Nestucca River in Pacific City. You can walk down from there or you can drive down the beach. The north bank of the Nestucca's mouth is easily accessible from here and provides a chance for fresh-run salmon during August and September. The river's mouth also offers surfperch and some flounder. Harbor seals frequently haul out here.

Klaskanine River (Clatsop County)

A popular and sometimes productive stream for hatchery-produced steelhead, chinook salmon, and coho salmon (no coho seasons in recent years), the Klaskanine River flows into the Youngs River about 5 miles south of Astoria. The most popular venue is the hatchery on the river's North Fork, where anglers converge in fairly substantial numbers during the autumn salmon runs and during the December-through-February winter steelhead runs. From Astoria, follow SR 202 (Nehalem Highway) up to the hatchery. Other than at the hatchery, bank access is quite limited. The North Fork is closed to salmon and steelhead angling above Olney Bridge from September 1 through October 15, and during this same period the entire South Fork is closed. Check current regulations for season parameters. The county boat launch on Youngs River Road offers some bank-fishing prospects as well as the county park about a mile below the hatchery. Boat anglers fish the mouth of the Klaskanine, launching at the county ramp: At Olney, turn south off SR 202 and cross the river on Youngs River Road.

Klickitat Lake (Lincoln County)

A small woodland lake full of stumps and logs located in the rolling hills west of Mary's Peak, Klickitat Lake offers fair-to-good fishing for small cutthroat trout. Bank fishing is easy, though you can certainly drop a float tube in (advantageous for fly fishers, but watch the stumps and logs). You can get there from three directions and all require rather lengthy, winding drives on gravel roads. The shortest route from Corvallis is to head for Philomath and then turn south on SR34 (Alsea Highway). Two miles south of Alsea Summit and the road to Mary's Peak, turn west on BLM Road 10 and follow the road about 12 miles to the lake. From Waldport, head up the Alsea and then turn north on Fall Creek Road, following it about 11 miles until it ends. Turn right to reach the lake. From Newport, head east on Hwy 20 to a right-hand turn on the Harlan Road at Burnt Woods. Drive down to Harlan and then head south about 7 miles to the lake on BLM Road 10.

Lake Creek (Lane County)
boat ramp, boat recommended

A major tributary to the Siuslaw River, Lake Creek—itself more of a river than a creek—is best known for its winter steelhead fishing. The river has both hatchery and wild winter steelhead and only fin-clipped fish may be kept. Steelhead, including a few trophy-class fish, enter Lake Creek as early as mid-December, with the peak of the run during January and February. Fresh fish continue to arrive into March. A modest run of chinook salmon provides another fishing opportunity with peak fishing from September through October.

Lake Creek flows almost entirely through private property on its swift journey from Triangle Lake down to the Siuslaw at Swisshome. State Route 36 follows the creek, providing ready access at a few popular bank-fishing holes, but be sure to seek permission before entering private property along the river. Many steelhead anglers float the stream, which tends to run clear or nearly so most of the time and which clears rapidly after a major rainstorm.

The uppermost launch site is a pole slide at Greenleaf Creek. The lower takeouts are unimproved ramps at Deadwood Landing and at Schindler Park. Don't drift below Schindler's unless you want to tangle with Class IV rapids at The Horn, located about a mile below Schindler and about 1.5 miles above the Siuslaw confluence. You can drift the lower end of the river by launching at Konnie Memorial Park and drifting down a few miles to Tide Wayside on the Siuslaw.

To reach Lake Creek, follow Hwy 126 west from Eugene or east from Florence. On the west side of the Siuslaw River at Mapleton, head north on SR 36 toward Swisshome, about 8 miles up the road. Schindler Park is about 3 miles upstream from Swisshome, Deadwood Landing about 4 miles farther. The pole slide at Greenleaf Creek is another 9 miles upstream and some additional bank-fishing access is available at a few spots on the upper stretch. The angling deadline for steelhead is the mouth of Fish Creek, 2 miles below Triangle Lake. Be sure to check current regulations for Lake Creek. At this time, the creek's tributaries are closed to all fishing

Lake Lytle (Tillamook County)

Spanning 65 acres and sitting right alongside Hwy 101 at Rockaway Beach, Lake Lytle offers fair fishing for stocked rainbow trout and sometimes for stocked cutthroat trout. The lake also is home to some good-size largemouth bass, but they are uncommon. You'll need a small boat or float tube to go after the bass, which generally occupy the brushy, weedy drop-offs and edges along the south and east shorelines. Bass anglers are allowed one fish per day and the largemouths here typically weigh 3 to 6 pounds.

Trout anglers fish by boat and from the public-access areas along the shoulder of the highway, including a public fishing pier. The boat ramp is on the north end of the lake off 12th Street. Lake Lytle gets rather weed-choked, especially along the edges, during summer so all the trout stocking occurs during spring, usually beginning around March 1. Naturally the fishing can be quite good in the days following the stockings, but generally action is rather slow here. Nonetheless, quite a few fish over-winter, so the lake kicks out a few fat 14- to 18-inch trout. It's not a bad place to spend a day fishing during a break in the winter weather.

Lily Lake (Lane County)
no bait, catch-and-release, float tube recommended

A pretty little coastal dune lake, hidden by dense scrub and supporting a rather sparse population of wild cutthroat trout, Lily Lake sits just west of Hwy 101, about 6 miles north of Florence. The lake is managed specifically for the wild cutthroat, so bait is prohibited and all fishing is catch-and-release. The trout range from 5 to 12 inches, with a rare fish reaching 15 inches, but they seem to be rather few in number. The half-mile hike begins at the Baker Beach Trailhead. About 6 miles north from Florence, turn west on Baker Beach Road.

Lobster Creek (Alsea River drainage)
no bait

A scenic tributary of Five Rivers, Lobster Creek is closed to all fishing for salmon and steelhead, but offers fair-to-good fishing for small wild cutthroat trout from the mouth up to Little Lobster Creek, above which the stream and its tributaries are closed. The trout season runs from late May through September 30. Be sure to check current regulations. From Hwy 34 (Alsea Highway), head for Five Rivers (about halfway between the towns of Alsea and Waldport). Turn south on the Five Rivers Road. After about 3.5 miles turn left, following the creek upstream to the east. Most of the land is private, so when in doubt about access, be sure to seek permission.

Loon Lake (Lane County)
float tube recommended

A pleasant little coastal dune lake offering fair fishing for stocked rainbow trout, Loon Lake sits on the west side of Hwy 101 near the entrance to Siltcoos Campground. It is not visible from the roads. The turnoff to the campground is about 10 miles north from the top of the hill north of Gardiner and across the highway from the Siltcoos Trailhead parking lot. Turn off the highway toward the campground, but after a hundred yards or so take the unmarked dirt road on your left, which heads about a quarter mile downhill to a small parking area. From there, the trail reaches the lake after about 50 yards. During spring and early summer, this is a good float tube lake.

Lost Lake (Douglas County)

A small coastal sand-dune lake, Lost Lake is lightly fished for stocked rainbow trout. Fishing is best in early and mid-spring. Covering about 5 acres and located just east of Hwy 101 south of Florence, Lost Lake is located a mile south of the south end of Carter Lake. Carter Lake is on your right as you head south on the highway, about 8 miles from Florence. Park along the highway shoulder or at the trailhead on the other side of the road.

Lost Lake (Clatsop County)

Located south of Elsie on private Longview Fiber property, Lost Lake is a fairly productive and popular 15-acre stocked-trout lake. ODFW stocks the lake with more than 8,000 fish each year, including trophy-size trout, and the fishing usually holds up throughout the spring and well into summer and even into autumn. It's a good place for a float tube or small boat, although there is no ramp. From Hwy 26, just east from Elsie, turn south on Nehalem River Road and continue 8 miles to Spruce Run County Park. Just before the park entrance, turn left on a logging road (Lost Lake Road), which leads 5 miles to the lake.

Lytle Lake (Tillamook County)
see Lake Lytle

Mercer Lake (Lane County)
boat ramp, boat recommended, campground

Mercer Lake, located just east of Hwy 101, 5 miles north of Florence, is a popular and fairly productive fishery for stocked rainbow trout and a variety of warmwater species, including largemouth bass, yellow perch, and bluegill. Bass reach at least 6 pounds and quite a few 2- and 3-pound largemouths inhabit the lake. Covering 359 acres and splintering off into myriad coves, bays, and arms, Mercer Lake offers abundant good bass cover, ranging from inlet coves and drop-offs along points, to lily pads and flooded timber.

Yellow perch are common and frequently reach 10 inches, with a few larger still. They are easy to catch on bait once you find a concentration of fish. Suspend your bait about a foot off the bottom. Trout are stocked rather liberally during spring, and fishing for them tends to be fair-to-good through May and sometimes later. During summer, the lake gets quite a bit of water-skiing traffic.

A boat is virtually required because Mercer Lake's shoreline is virtually all private property. A good county ramp is available on the south end of the lake at the end of Mercer Lake Road. Mercer Lake Resort & RV Park (800-355-3633) offers rental boats and a private dock with fishing access for guests.

Miami River (Tillamook County)

Like the Kilchis River to the south, the Miami River offers a catch-and-release season for chum salmon from mid-September through mid-November. The river also hosts runs of fall chinook, winter steelhead, and coho salmon, though there is currently no open season on coho. The fall chinook arrive from September through November, with some truly huge salmon available in December. The river's downfall is a near complete lack of easy public access. The Miami flows almost entirely across private farm and ranch lands, so most access is by permission or, in two places, by paying a modest fee.

Millport Slough (Siletz Bay)
boat recommended

A medium-size tidal slough feeding into the southeast end of

Siletz Bay, Millport Slough begins on the Siletz River across from Pike's Camp. The slough is a good bet for kayaking or canoeing for sea-run cutthroat. Years ago I would use the pullout along the highway and drop a canoe in on the bay side, then head up into the slough on the rising tide, casting streamer flies to lots of likely structure. This should still be possible. Late summer is the best time. Be sure to get out of the slough before low tide to save yourself the trouble of mucking around in the mud at the end of the trip.

Moolack Beach

Essentially the southern extension of Beverly Beach north of Newport in Lincoln County, Moolack Beach offers opportunities for surfperch, including the prized redtail surfperch. Together, Moolack and Beverly Beaches form an unbroken extension of flat, sand beach that stretches for nearly 5 miles, all adjacent to Hwy 101. Some highway shoulder parking is available near the south end of the beach, but the better option is the little parking area just off the west side of the highway (watch for the sign announcing "Moolack Beach Parking Area"), from which you must walk a ways to reach the south end of the beach where the sand begins to abut rock—often the most productive fishing area. Regardless of where you park, beware the heavy coast traffic, especially during summer. The nice wind-sheltered, shaded campground just up the road at Beverly Beach State Park is extremely popular. Reserve a spot well ahead of time (www.oregonstateparks.org).

Moolack and Beverly beaches are nothing short of crowded during the summer—not with anglers, but with tourists. Surfperch anglers should fish dusk and dawn, with the latter being the best time. Get there before sunup and fish incoming tides, especially the first hour or two of a rising tide. Stiff afternoon winds are typical here, as are strong lateral water currents. Moolack offers two creek deltas and myriad pockets and troughs that hold fish. Sand crabs, clam necks, and other traditional baits work best, though anglers casting red or pink jigs into all the likely buckets and moving quickly up or down the beach often find fish when nobody else seems to be having any luck.

Munsel Lake (Lane County)
boat ramp, boat recommended

A decent producer of warmwater fish and stocked trout, 110-acre Munsel Lake is located about 3 miles north of Florence, east of Hwy 101. Watch for the signed turn-off on Munsel Lake Road, leading about 1 mile to the lake. Munsel has an improved boat launch and a boat is a good idea here because most of the brushy shoreline lies on private lands. The lake has yellow perch and largemouth bass, as well as a few cutthroat trout and is annually stocked with nearly 10,000 rainbow trout. Such numbers intimate the lake's popularity and it sees quite a bit of pressure on spring and summer weekends. Mid-week, however, or during early spring and fall don't be surprised to find the lake deserted.

Among the stocked rainbows are quite a few of ODFW's "larger" and "trophy" fish, which are stocked at a minimum

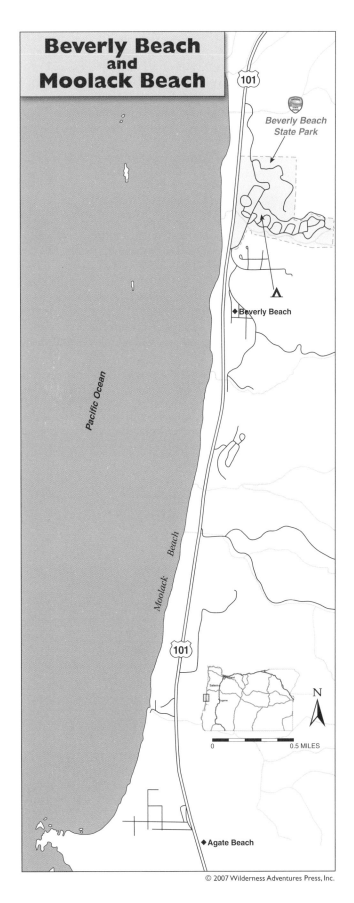

Beverly Beach
and
Moolack Beach

101

Beverly Beach
State Park

◆ Beverly Beach

Pacific Ocean

Moolack Beach

101

N

0   0.5 MILES

◆ Agate Beach

© 2007 Wilderness Adventures Press, Inc.

size of 12 and 16 inches, respectively. Hence anglers—usually trollers—can drag a 3- or 4-pound trout from Munsel. The largemouth bass are not numerous, but they typically range from 2 to 5 pounds. If you're after bass, target the flooded logs, the coves and adjacent drop-offs, and other likely cover. You'll definitely need a boat to target bass, but you can usually take a few trout and yellow perch by still fishing with bait from the banks adjacent to the boat ramp. Camping is available just to the north at Sutton Lake and at nearby Alder Dune and Baker Beach Campgrounds.

Necanicum River (Clatsop County)
boat ramp

A fairly small, but productive river for winter steelhead, the Necanicum flows alongside Hwy 26 and then Hwy 101 on its meandering path to Seaside. This river offers only minimal access, as it flows mostly through private land, so the best bet is to float the river during the January through March steelhead season. The most popular drift goes from Blotchy Creek Park down to the ODFW slide at Beerman Creek on Hwy 101. Blotchy Park, adjacent to Hwy 26 a few miles east from Hwy

101, is the site of the largest Sitka spruce tree in the United States.

The Beerman access is nothing more than a wide gravel pullout along the coast highway about 2 miles south of Seaside. Watch for the yellow ODFW sign posted on the tree. Bring a rope, as the slide here is little more than a 5-foot-wide trail through the bushes. The other option, which shortens the drift by about 2 miles, is to take out at the fee access at Johnson Construction, located off the east side of Hwy 101, where the river passes under the road.

During moderate to high flows, you can also float from Johnson's or Beerman's down to the Seaside Boat Ramp, but the tidewater section requires rowing or a small motor. During autumn, try this section (with a small motor or by kayak) for sea-run cutthroat. The Necanicum, even during winter, is just barely big enough for drift boats, but the lack of bank access makes the boat very useful. Fish mid-week or delay your launch until mid-morning to avoid clogging up the little river with too many boats (two or three boats within sight of one another is too many on this intimate river).

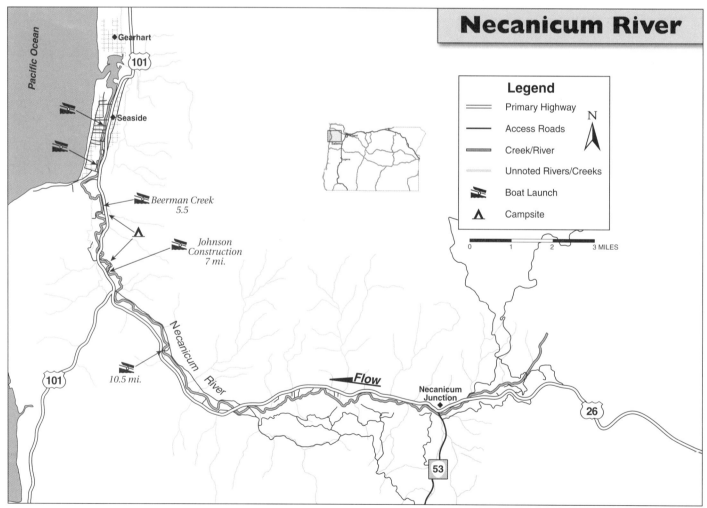

© 2007 Wilderness Adventures Press, Inc.

The Necanicum has both native and hatchery winter steelhead. The natives must be released and are most common from mid-February through March. Hatchery fish sometimes show up as early as Thanksgiving, but late December and January are better bets. Chinook salmon arrive in modest numbers during the fall. For bank anglers, access is available at Blotchy Park and just upstream along the forest roads.

Nehalem Bay (Tillamook County)
boat ramp, boat recommended

A good fishery for fall chinook salmon and also offering fair-to-good prospects for saltwater bottomfish, Nehalem Bay is located about 10 miles north of Tillamook Bay. Anglers use all methods to catch chinook salmon here, but the odds-on favorite is trolling herring. The fish show up off the mouth of the bay by mid-summer and properly equipped boats with seasoned skippers can cross the bar and fish just offshore. This bar crossing is notoriously difficult at times, so be sure to check current conditions, tide levels, and forecasts. By August the fish move into the bay and the salmon fishing remains good through October. Some fin-clipped coho salmon are also available, along with a few spring chinook, but the sprinters seem to move through quickly.

Nehalem Bay offers a broad spectrum of opportunity for saltwater species. The south jetty is a popular spot for bait and jig fishing. Commonly caught species include black rockfish, copper rockfish, greenling, and redtail surfperch. Rock breakwaters and pilings along the highway side of the bay produce pile perch, shiner perch, and a few other species. During winter and spring, anglers find fair sturgeon fishing in Nehalem Bay. Fishing by boat in the channels yields perch and a few flounder and these same channels are good crabbing locations. The bay also offers good clamming prospects for soft shells, butter clams, and a few gapers. Private docks along the bay offer access for crabbing, usually just for guests, but Brighton RV Park & Marina (503-368-5745) allows crabbing access to its docks for a modest daily fee and also rents crab rings and boats. Crab bait is for sale at their store.

Nehalem Bay State Park offers plenty of RV and camping space on the north side of the bay. Additional lodging includes Wheeler On The Bay Lodge & Marina (503-368-5858), which has private docks, rental kayaks and other amenities. All services, along with several motels, are available along Hwy 101 from Brighton and Wheeler up to Manzanita.

Nehalem River
boat ramp, boat recommended

The big, wide, slow-moving Nehalem River offers fairly productive salmon and winter steelhead fisheries, beginning with the late-summer chinook runs and ending with a chance for a few very large native steelhead during March. The Nehalem seems to put out a few 15- to 20-pound steelies every season, but this river often offers but a handful of fishable days each winter. It blows out quickly when the rainstorms hit and often remains high and un-fishable for days on end. If you're plan-

Nehalem Bay

ning a Nehalem steelhead trip, keep a back-up plan in mind and watch the weather.

Given its size, the Nehalem is best known for its plug-fishing for winter steelhead, namely on the lower end of the river below Beaver Slide. Plunking from shore is also effective. The upper river offers lots of good water for drift fishing and jig-and-bobber fishing. The best bank access is along Lower Nehalem Road above Beaver Slide, which is the put-in for the most popular drift in the river. The takeout is 6 miles downstream at Mohler Sand & Gravel. Or you can drift another 2 miles down to Roy Creek, a popular bank-fishing area.

Fall chinook salmon arrive in the Nehalem when the weather and thus the river levels are more reliable, with the run generally beginning during July. Salmon anglers on the Nehalem typically tag several thousand chinook salmon each year, but most are actually taken in the bay, making the ODFW counts for the Nehalem River a bit deceiving. Still, the tidewater stretch yields lots of fish each year and a few bright salmon are taken as far upriver as Elsie. In recent years, the Nehalem's small run of hatchery coho salmon has produced fair-to-good fishing between August and October.

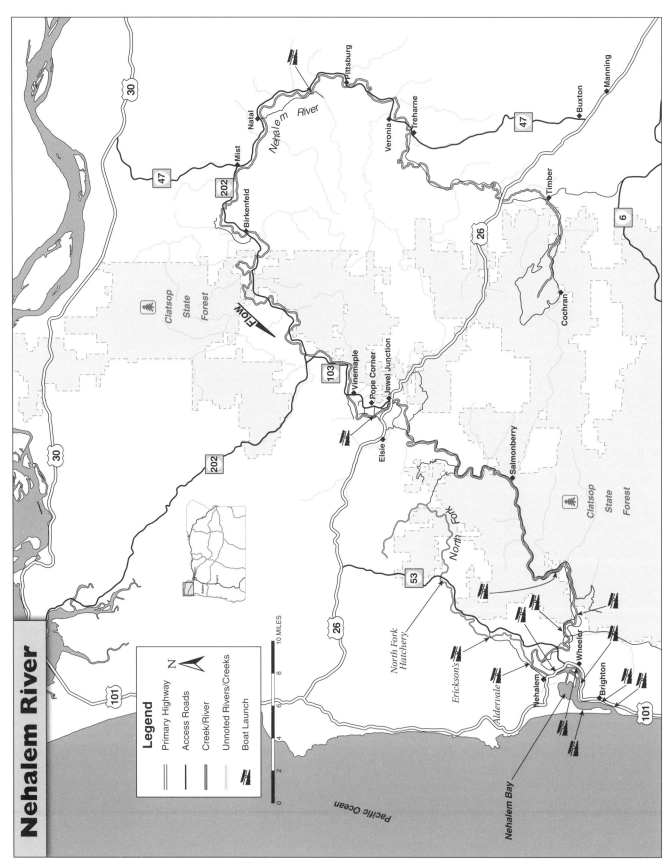

Nehalem River

The Nehalem also receives a fair run of chinook jacks, which arrive between July and October. A few fin-clipped, spring chinook salmon run the river during May and June, but the run is usually quite modest. Be sure to consult the current regulations synopsis before fishing the Nehalem.

To reach the Nehalem from the Portland area, follow Hwy 26 west toward the coast. The highway crosses the river near Jewell Junction and then a few miles farther, Lower Nehalem Road turns south (at Elsie) and picks up the river, following it most of the way.

Nehalem River, North Fork
(Clatsop/Tillamook Counties)
boat ramp

A good winter steelhead river and a fair producer of fall chinook salmon, the North Fork Nehalem is a scenic and popular river that feeds into the lowermost end of the main Nehalem River near Nehalem Bay. The most popular bank-fishing spot on the North Fork is near North Fork Hatchery (milepost 8), where lots of winter steelhead fall to bank anglers between December and March. The hatchery has a nice barrier-free fishing platform. Otherwise bank access is limited by no-trespassing signs, although several landowners have traditionally allowed anglers access to the river.

The North Fork is also a very good river for drifting anglers, but its upper drift should only be navigated by highly experienced boaters owing to some severe hazards. If you launch at the hatchery, beware of the boulders and of the three infamous and rock-filled drops known as King, Queen, and Jack Rapids, respectively. Some boaters opt for rafts with frames rather than risk beating up their drift boats here. The first take-out is a fee launch on Jim Erickson's property, about 3 miles downstream. The second drift goes from Erickson's down to the Aldervale ramp near the mouth, and presents no difficult water. It covers about 2.5 miles.

At the hatchery, anglers congregate in tight bunches during peak times, so basic gear-fishing etiquette prevails and rarely do problems occur. If you fish the hatchery waters, just expect to have lots of company. The upper drift offers good water for drift gear, jig-and-bobber fishing, and even fly angling. The lower end of the river is a good place for jigs, spoons, and other drift gear, as well as for pulling plugs.

Be sure to check current regulations for both salmon and steelhead on the North Fork. The river has a mix of wild and hatchery-produced winter steelhead. Most of the salmon are wild. From the Portland area, follow Hwy 26 west toward the coast. At Necanicum Junction, turn south on SR 53, which picks up the river and continues down to the hatchery.

Neskowin Beach Tillamook County)

Better known for its adjacent quiet resort community, Neskowin Beach also happens to be a productive destination for redtail surfperch. Fish early morning incoming tides using sand crabs or clam necks for bait. The action peaks from April through July. Neskowin is located north of Lincoln City and

north of Cascade Head. Watch for the well-marked turnoff as you follow Hwy 101 north from the Salmon River (Hwy 18 interchange) or south from Nestucca Bay.

Nestucca Bay
boat ramp, boat recommended, services

Nestucca Bay is a busy place during autumn when fall chinook depart the ocean and head for the Nestucca River. The bay's mouth is rather inaccessible because boating there is dangerous and walking in from either side of the river requires a somewhat lengthy (but easy) beach hike (or trail hike from the north). Just up from the actual mouth, however, Nestucca Bay is easy to get at by boat as it splits into the Nestucca "Arm" to the north and the Little Nestucca Arm to the southeast.

Pacific City straddles the Nestucca and provides all services, including a full-service bait and tackle store (Nestucca Sporting Goods). In addition to salmon, 1,100-acre Nestucca Bay offers perch, a few flounder, sea-run cutthroat, Dungeness crab, shrimp, and clams, not to mention some good duck hunting.

Both bank and boat anglers enjoy consistent success here and, when the salmon runs are strong, you'll be hard-pressed to find parking at the ever-popular boat ramp and access point along the Brooten Road just south of Pacific City (The Guard Rail Hole). Many boaters launch here to fish the lower bay just to the south and upstream to the north. The Pacific City Boat Ramp, just upstream, is equally popular and the adjacent "Airport Hole" puts out lots of salmon every autumn. Anglers trolling the bay, especially from Pacific City down to the Little Nestucca Arm, must heed the shallow, shifting sand shoals that predominate. Identify and stick to the main channel.

At low tide, these sand shoals and the mud flats on the Little Nestucca arm provide good clamming and shrimping opportunities. On the main channel, wait for a minus-tide and then hit the lower sand flats to collect shrimp or look for the mud bottoms for clams. The clamming (soft shells) extends up the Little Nestucca Arm to the broad mud flats, which extend for almost a mile along the east shore (behind the cattle pastures if you are looking west from Hwy 101).

The clamming flats are best accessed by boat, but you can get at them by foot on the north side. From Hwy 101, turn west on Brooten Road toward Pacific City. After about a mile, the road bends northward. Just before this point, watch on your left as the road dips close to the actual estuary, hanging just above grassy and marshy-looking tidal flats. Watch carefully and you will see a small tide channel protruding at a right angle from the road and jutting straight out toward the bay. Park on the shoulder here, climb down through the willows (there is a trail), and hike out the low dike adjacent to the tidal channel until you reach the sand at the edge of the vegetated part of the tide flat. Turn left and hike up the sand flats to reach the mud flats. This is a low-tide-only adventure, so keep an eye on the water level.

During an early morning low tide, you can fish for salmon by foot from the sand bars here; using this same access point, but doing so generally requires waders and some long-distance casting. The better shore fishing for salmon is at the Guard Rail Hole adjacent to the launch on Brooten Road just south of town. You can also fish the mouth of the river by hiking through Straub State Park. Drive through Pacific City, cross the bridge over the river and take an immediate left at the signs. Or you can drive down the beach itself from the access adjacent to the road into the state park. You can also fish from the south side of the mouth (and often have it all to yourself) by accessing from the beach adjacent to Camp Winema. Head south on Hwy 101, past the Little Nestucca and up the hill, watching for the Camp Winema sign. Turn west off the highway and follow the road until it ends at a small beach-access parking lot. Hike north, past the big rocks, until you reach the mouth of the river.

Both the Nestucca and Little Nestucca attract good numbers of sea-run cutthroat during the fall. On the Nestucca you can find them around pilings, stumps, and snags in and near Pacific City and sometimes you'll find them by casting along the edges of the sandbar on the north side of the bay where the Little Nestucca Channel meets the Big Nestucca, about half a mile down-river from the Guard Rail Hole. The Little Nestucca fishes better upstream from Hwy 101 (see listing for Nestucca River, Little).

On the Big Nestucca arm, low tides expose good clam beds along the inside of the peninsula separating the bay from the ocean. You can walk in from Straub State Park or boat down from either of the launches at Pacific City. I've seen people do this even out of small craft such as canoes—just stick close to shore and wait for the incoming tide to help with the return journey.

If you have a boat, Nestucca Bay can produce good catches of Dungeness crab. Drop traps or rings in or near the main channel on the top half of the incoming tide. The best crabbing is on the lower bay over sand bottoms, but beware of strong currents and shallow bars. While you're at it, run over to the rockpiles at Cannery Hill Point and fish for perch and an occasional greenling. The point juts into the bay from the south, separating the main bay from the Little Nestucca Arm and is accessible only by boat and fishable only at high tides. The point is also a prime spot for decoying diving ducks during fall and winter. For details on local beach fishing, see entry herein for "Kiwanda Beach."

Nestucca River
boat ramp, services

One of Oregon's most popular and most productive salmon and steelhead streams, the highly esteemed Nestucca River offers something for just about everyone. The river hosts impressive runs of winter and summer steelhead, chinook salmon, and sea-run cutthroat. It also displays a wide variety of water types along its 55-mile run from the Coast Range southeast from Tillamook to the ocean near Pacific City.

Like many Oregon coast steelhead streams, the Nestucca enjoys a generous allotment of hatchery steelhead that arrive from December through February. During late winter, the river boasts one of the region's top runs of large, native winter steelhead. Surveys conducted by Oregon Department of Fish & Wildlife indicate an estimated spawning return of 15,000 wild winter fish in 2001, preceded by an 8,000-fish return in 2000. Such returns are impressive and angler success on the Nestucca ranks among the highest on the coast. The natives are 2-, 3- and 4-salt fish and among them are a few of those elusive 20-pounders.

Each year, anglers on the Nestucca land steelhead larger than 20 pounds. Ron Byrd, owner of Nestucca Valley Sporting Goods in Hebo, recalls that in 2002 one lucky angler caught and released a 26-pound behemoth. "Most of these fish weigh a healthy 10 to 12 pounds," says Byrd, whose shop has become an institution for Nestucca River steelheaders.

Moreover, the Nestucca offers a good run of summer steelhead between late May and early October. Most of the summer fish enter the system during June, but they spread out through the river and provide good fishing until mid-summer, when low flows slow down the bite. The first freshets of late August or September stir life into the river and rejuvenate, at least to a minor extent, the summer steelhead fishing. Those same freshets draw sea-run cutthroat trout and fall chinook salmon into the river.

The salmon fishing, especially good on the lower river and in tidewater, usually peaks in September and October, but fresh fish arrive as early as August and as late as November. A modest run of fin-clipped spring chinook enters the river during May. The sea-run cutts are usually quite common and quite a few of them range from 13 to 16 inches, with a rare 20-incher in the mix.

While the Nestucca isn't the only coastal river boasting sizable runs of winter natives, it certainly ranks as the most user-friendly steelhead stream on the north coast. This medium-sized river offers plenty of access for both floaters and bank anglers. Foot access is good, especially upstream from Beaver, where you can get to the river from numerous highway pullouts and from the bridge crossings.

Highway 101 follows the river from Cloverdale north to the little town of Beaver. The highway crosses the river twice and offers several pullout areas as well. At Beaver, a good county road heads east up the river, crossing the Nestucca at each of the six bridges, which are referred to by number, starting with 1st Bridge just upstream from Beaver and progressing about 13 river miles up to 6th Bridge. From there, the road continues upstream through Blaine. In places, the road swings alongside the river, offering additional bank access. Foot access is generally difficult along the Nestucca—except on the upper river—so make sure to knock on doors for permission before crossing private property.

Bank access improves markedly upstream from the community of Blaine. The Nestucca is open to steelheading for about 12 miles upstream from Blaine and this portion is properly referred to as the "Upper River."

Comparatively small and intimate, the Upper River carries a slightly faster flow than the lower reaches and in many places twists through boulder-studded runs and pockets. My first

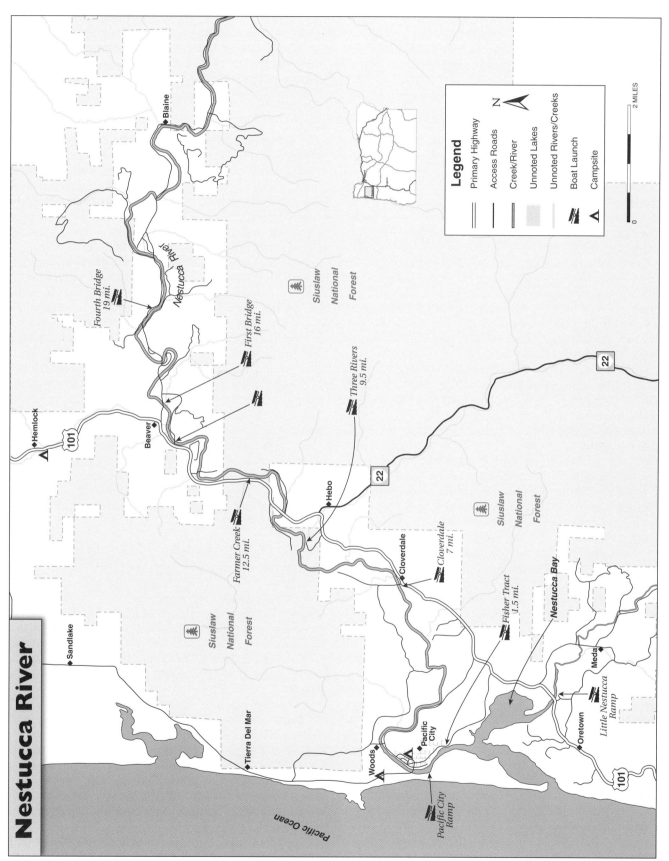

Nestucca River

Legend

Primary Highway
Access Roads
Creek/River
Unnoted Lakes
Unnoted Rivers/Creeks
Boat Launch
Campsite

N

2 MILES

0

Blaine

Fourth Bridge
19 mi.

Nestucca River

First Bridge
16 mi.

Siuslaw
National
Forest

Three Rivers
9.5 mi.

22

Hemlock

101

Beaver

Farmer Creek
12.5 mi.

Hebo

22

Siuslaw
National
Forest

Cloverdale

Cloverdale
7 mi.

Siuslaw
National
Forest

Nestucca Bay

Fisher Tract
1.5 mi.

Sandlake

Meda

Little Nestucca
Ramp

Oretown

101

Tierra Del Mar

Pacific
City

Woods

Pacific City Ramp

Pacific Ocean

© 2007 Wilderness Adventures Press, Inc.

Nestucca steelhead came from these waters many seasons ago—a lovely 9-pound hen that inhaled a Skunk wet fly and then wrapped my fly line around a rock only to eventually free herself after I pulled 30 feet of slack line off the reel and shook it out into the river.

This portion of the river upstream from Blaine is not floatable and is therefore a haven for many bank anglers who prefer to avoid the drift boat traffic common to the rest of the Nestucca. Fly anglers enjoy this upper portion of the river, as do increasing numbers of jig anglers who effectively fish the pocket water reaches along with the many productive runs and small pools. If you fish drift gear, be sure to come armed with plenty of tackle to combat the rocky bottom.

Just downstream, boaters can choose from any number of float segments, beginning with the uppermost launches at Blaine or 6th Bridge and ending as far down river as Cloverdale. Along the way are more than half a dozen launch/takeout sites, many of which require 4-wheel-drive and some of which are simple slide launches. Be forewarned, however, that upstream from Beaver, the Nestucca requires strong boating skills and local knowledge of the tricky spots, along with adequate flow to make the drift safe. First-time drifters should go with somebody who knows the water.

Inexperienced oarsmen should stick to the lower stretches, below 1st Bridge and certainly below 4th Bridge. About half way between 6th Bridge and 5th Bridge there is a tricky rapids called The Falls. The lower drifts are easy and uneventful and also access plenty of prime steelhead water. First Bridge to Farmer Creek is one of the best floats.

Plan your drift to correspond to particular water levels, saving the Upper River for those times when the river flows at 5.5 to 6 feet and moving your launches downstream as the water drops. Consistent success on the Nestucca, especially for wild steelhead, requires that you learn the entire river. Unlike the hatchery fish that often keg up at certain locales, such as Three Rivers, the wild fish spread throughout the system by mid-February. A decided advantage goes to anglers who know which holes and runs fish best at particular water levels.

The Nestucca offers steelhead water of every description and thus welcomes just about any method of pursuing these noble fish. The river has good access and can handle lots of boat traffic, leaving plenty of room for people to spread out and plenty of water for pulling plugs, side drifting, jig fishing, plunking, and fly fishing.

Pulling plugs ranks among the most popular methods for steelhead fishing on the Nestucca. Already a Northwest obsession of sorts, jigs have become markedly more popular on the Nestucca—and for good reason: They work and are especially effective in the hands of anglers who can readily identify the slots likely to hold resting steelhead. Though bait fishing is legal on the Nestucca, most local guides discourage the use of bait because of the catch-and-release regulations for wild fish. Bait is often swallowed by the fish, making proper handling and release more difficult.

Fly anglers form a vast minority on the Nestucca, but their numbers continue to increase as the river's stature as good fly

water gains a wider appreciation. The keys to successful fly angling include hitting the river when the water is running reasonably clear and low and using a line system that effectively takes the fly deep enough in the water column to tempt a steelhead to give chase.

No matter what technique you prefer, from pulling plugs to fly angling, the Nestucca offers plenty of good water conducive to all methods. Still, February and March weekends—and even weekdays during prime conditions—often draw considerable crowds to the river. Only a few years ago, the Nestucca's crowds thinned considerably as the hatchery run withered in late January. In recent seasons, however, catch-and-release fishing has taken hold as increasing numbers of sportsmen embrace a day on the water and a chance to not only catch but also release the big, muscular native fish. So the crowds are back and they continue through March.

Bank anglers can find some peace and quiet by seeking the accessible runs and pools upstream from Beaver and especially upstream from Blaine when the river drops below 4 feet. Wait for an extended high-water period to push fish into the Upper River and then head up there as soon as the water drops and the boat anglers abandon the upper drifts. Another good crowd-avoidance tactic is to make mid-day drifts, launching several hours after the early birds are underway. Likewise, on the Nestucca you can ignore the old adage that low-light conditions are best for steelhead. These February natives often go on the bite under clear skies, especially if the water carries a slight tinge of green.

Many guides work the Nestucca River for both salmon and steelhead, even sea-run cutthroat if you ask to target them. The local tackle shop and information headquarters is Nestucca River Outfitters (503-392-4269/www.nestuccariveroutfitters.com). The shop can arrange guide service and provide shuttle service.

Nestucca River, Little (Tillamook County)
boat ramp

The Little Nestucca River flows only 18 miles from its source in the Coast Range to its mouth at Nestucca Bay. The river is home to runs of chinook and coho salmon, winter steelhead, and sea-run cutthroat. Currently the river is closed to angling for coho. The fall chinook and the sea-run cutthroat arrive between late August and October and the winter steelhead, mostly natives, migrate upriver between January and early March.

Tidewater extends about a mile upstream from the Hwy 101 bridge and, other than a short stretch near the highway, the first 2 miles east of the bridge flow through private farmlands and are inaccessible from shore. This tidewater section, however, is highly productive for cutthroat and fairly good for salmon if you have a boat with a motor. The boat ramp is located near the Hwy 101 bridge. Bring a motor, because this is an up-and-back (or down-and-back if you're headed for the bay) excursion.

Upstream from the farmlands, the Little Nestucca Road follows closely along the river, providing excellent access up to the angling deadline at the hamlet of Dolph. Steelhead angling can be good all along the river above tidewater, while sea-run cutthroat angling is best from tidewater up to the county park, about a third of the way up the river. During fall, this road-accessible stretch is small water, easily waded and easily covered with a fly rod or spinning rod (barbless hooks, catch-and-release only for cutthroat). During the winter steelhead season, anglers mostly use drift gear to fish the small runs, slots, and pools that hold fish.

To reach the Little Nestucca from Hwy 101 on the west, turn east on Little Nestucca Road just north of the 101 bridge, a mile south of the turn off to Lincoln City. From the east, follow Hwy 22 south from Hebo or northerly from Grand Ronde and turn west at Dolph.

Netarts Bay (Tillamook County)
boat ramp, boat recommended, services

Offering moderately productive fishing for perch and small bottomfish, including a few flounder, Netarts Bay is primarily known as a crabbing and clamming destination. Clamming flats, for a variety of species, are literally scattered all over the bay, while the best crabbing occurs near the deeper areas, especially on the incoming and high tide during the summer and fall. You'll need a boat for crabbing and access to the good clamming areas is best by boat as well. The bay is uniformly shallow and quite safe for boaters.

Bank access is very good for clamming, as Netarts Bay/ Whiskey Creek Road runs along the entire east shoreline, while Cape Lookout State Park, which includes a nice campground, includes the south end of the bay and the entirety of Netarts Spit, which encloses the bay, separating it from the Pacific. There is no road access to the spit, but you can motor over to that side by boat at the appropriate tide levels. The little town of Netarts, on the north end of the bay near the ocean channel, offers all services along with a boat ramp. Not to worry if you don't have a boat. You can rent one at Netarts Bay RV Park & Marina (503-842-7774). The "crabbing package" includes boat/motor rental and three crab rings, and you can buy crab bait from the marina as well.

Fishing for surfperch can be good at times in the main channel near Netarts, and the beach on the ocean side of Netarts Spit is a very good beach for redtail surfperch. Fish it on an early morning incoming tide. Surfperch fishing is best from April through September. Netarts Bay kicks out a few wayward salmon during the fall.

North Lake (Tillamook County)
float tube recommended

A tiny, but attractive little wooded pond high above Hebo, North Lake is stocked early each spring with just a few hundred legal-size cutthroat trout. Much smaller and far less popular than Hebo and South Lakes, North Lake can provide decent angling for a few weeks during April and May and sometimes through June. The lake is small enough to fish from shore, but rather boggy and brushy, so a float tube is convenient. From Hebo Lake (see listing herein), continue up FR 14 another 5.75 miles.

Olalla Creek Reservoir (Lincoln County)
boat ramp, boat recommended, float tube recommended

Conveniently located near Newport and Toledo, 100-plus-acre Olalla Creek Reservoir, or just Olalla Reservoir, is stocked with rainbow trout and provides fair-to-good fishing for anglers using both bait and artificial lures or flies. The trout range from typical 9- to 12-inch keepers to some of the ODFW larger rainbows and even a few surplus hatchery steelhead. Olalla also contains largemouth bass, brown bullhead, and yellow perch. Bank fishing is rather limited, so a float tube or boat is handy (no gas motors allowed). To get there, take Hwy 20 east from Newport, past the Toledo Exit, and turn left on Ollala Road, which leads a few miles up to the reservoir.

Ona Beach (Lincoln County)

Ona Beach lies immediately south of Holiday Beach, about 8 miles south of Newport. Beaver Creek reaches the ocean here and the beach is a favorite destination for anglers seeking redtail surfperch or "pinkfins." Fishing peaks from March through June, but can be good all the way into October. Look for low tides that peak before sun-up and then fish the first two or three hours of incoming tide early in the morning. Bait anglers enjoy consistent success, but anglers armed with spinning rods and jigs or even fly rods can have good sport on this gently sloping beach. At its south end, Ona Beach is scattered with rocks and boulders where an occasional greenling or school of striped seaperch hangs out.

Perkins Lake (Lane County)

One of the myriad coastal dune lakes on the central Oregon Coast, Perkins Lake spans about 6 acres and sits alongside the west edge of Hwy 101, about 9 miles south of Florence or 6.5 miles from the top of the highway grade (Sparrow Park Road) north of Gardiner. Perkins is about 1.5 miles south of the southern end of Carter Lake. This small, brushy lake offers fair fishing for stocked rainbow trout. Parking is along the highway and there is room enough to drop a float tube or similar small craft in the water, which is advisable if you are fly angling.

Pollack Beach (Lincoln County)

Located just north of Newport, Pollack Beach is a popular tourist beach during summer, but a fair bet for redtail surfperch. Fishing is best on incoming water and at both high and low slack between April and July. Early morning is best, especially on tides of minimal water exchange. The beach usually carries quite a bit of lateral current, but also features lots of contours that create prime spots for feeding perch. Several small streams reach the ocean on the beach and these too create good fishing areas. Bait anglers do best here. Watch for the Beverly Beach State Park signs along the highway and leave your vehicle at the state parking lot. Follow the trail back under the highway to the beach. There are also a few highway shoulder pullout spots along the beach.

Recreation Pond (Columbia County)
see Trojan Pond

Road's End Beach (Lincoln City)
Located north of Lincoln City, Road's End Beach is a fair-to-good beach for redtail surfperch, especially during the spring. Often subjected to heavy lateral currents, the beach here is best fished with bait and fairly heavy sinkers. To get there, head north through Lincoln City or southwest from the Hwy 18/101 interchange. At the north edge of town, turn north (left if you are coming from the south), following the Road's End signs (Lighthouse Brewery sits near the corner at the intersection where you will head north from the highway). Before you reach the actual end of the road, watch for the public access and parking lot at Road's End State Recreation Site.

Rock Creek (Nehalem River drainage)
A long and significant tributary to the upper Nehalem River, Rock Creek heads near Hwy 26 in Clatsop County and flows easterly for 25 miles, reaching the Nehalem at Vernonia.

Rock Creek offers prospects for wild winter steelhead, but all natives must be released. A few hatchery fish stray into Rock Creek and are available for harvest. Generally angler effort is fairly light and catch rates quite low. Keasey Road follows the stream westerly from Vernonia, exclusively through private lands, so access is by permission. The upper drainage, locked away behind closed private timber roads, offers good catch-and-release fishing for small, native cutthroat trout and is open from late May through the end of August.

Salmon River (Lincoln County)
boat ramp

A popular and productive fishery for fall chinook salmon, fin-clipped coho salmon, and sea-run cutthroat, the aptly named Salmon River runs alongside Hwy 22 on its way down from the Coast Range, meeting the Pacific immediately south of Cascade Head. The mouth of the river forms a broad estuary, which itself offers good prospects for salmon and cutthroat. The salmon start to show during late August and fresh fish usually continue to arrive through October. The stream kicks

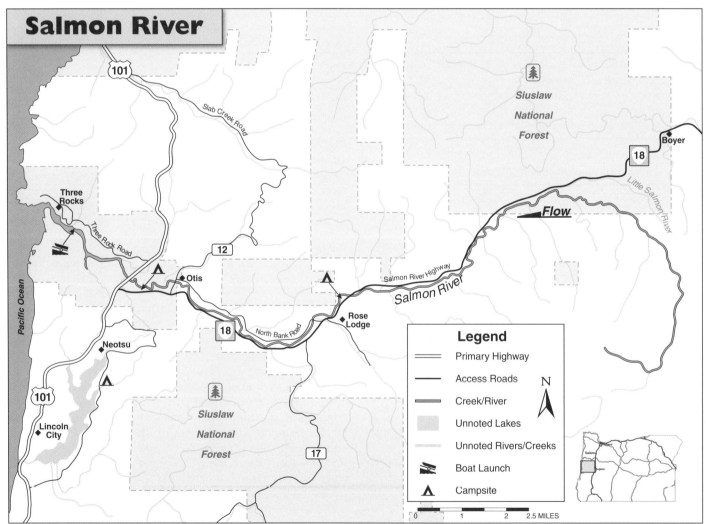

© 2007 Wilderness Adventures Press, Inc.

out a few winter steelhead and fin-clipped fish are available for harvest. Wild steelhead and wild coho salmon must be released. The salmon provide the primary fishery.

Several popular holes are located between the angling deadline below mile 12 on Hwy 22 and the bridge at Hwy 101. The popular access points are easy to find during the salmon season because each collects a lot of vehicles. An ODFW salmon hatchery, about 4 miles upriver, has access on both banks. On Hwy 22, parking is available along the shoulder and this stretch attracts lots of anglers, as does the private-land access a bit further downstream, where anglers park on the pullout and follow a trail to the river.

The Hwy 101 bridge offers lots of parking space along the highway, allowing access primarily to the north bank both above and below the bridge. A side road turns west off the highway just south of the bridge and if you can negotiate the maze of deep tidal creeks, you can walk as far as half a mile down the south bank. This tidal marsh is drained by two primary creeks, both starting small and gaining size as they snake through the flats. The mouth of the first creek, about 500 yards below the highway bridge, blocks any further foot access downstream along the river. To walk further downstream into the estuary, stick to the south rim of the grassy flats and loop around the first creek or both creeks. It's a maze, but once you learn the proper routes, you have walk-in access to the river that allows you to escape the rest of the bank angling crowds that assemble on the popular holes.

Boat access is even better on the lower river. The boat ramp is located about 2 miles downstream from the Hwy 101 bridge. From there, simply motor upriver to fish the many good holes above and below the highway. If you're after sea-run cutthroat, the lower river is best, and best fished by boat. Cast streamer flies, spinners, or small spoons along the logs, stumps, creek mouths, and cut banks. The estuary water is a good place to fish cutthroat by kayak or canoe and, at high tide, it's possible to launch such craft below the Hwy 101 bridge, but be very careful of the steep mud bank. The better option is to launch at the boat ramp on a flood tide and allow the incoming water to help move you upriver.

The boat launch is located near the end of Three Rocks Road. Follow Hwy 101 north past the Salmon River and watch for the signed left-hand turn. After about 3 miles, take the left-hand fork to the parking lot and boat ramp.

Salmon River Delta (Lincoln County)
boat ramp, boat recommended

You can't fully appreciate the beach at the mouth of the Salmon River unless you see it from high above, along the trail to Cascade Head. This tiny sand beach is enclosed and protected by Cascade Head to the north and by a tall, steep rock escarpment on the south. The only safe way to get there is to launch at the Salmon River Boat Ramp and shoot across the river to the far bank. From there you can walk down to the beach. Skilled boaters can follow the far bank downstream a little closer to the ocean to shorten the walk, but beware the treacherous currents at the delta. The beach offers good prospects for surfperch during the summer and you'll rarely see another angler. Generally this beach offers fairly calm and consistent surf during the summer, at least during tides with minimal water exchange. Anglers can successfully fish bait, jigs, and even flies here. The boat launch is located near the end of Three Rocks Road. Follow Hwy 101 north past the Salmon River and watch for the signed left-hand turn. After about 3 miles, take the left-hand fork to the parking lot and boat ramp. Beware the shallow water if you cross the river at low tide.

Tim Blount fishes the Salmon River delta for sea-run cutthroat. The lower end of the Salmon River is also a prime fishery for fall chinook and coho salmon.

Salmonberry River
(Nehalem River drainage)
catch-and-release, hike-in

A rugged, beautiful tributary to the Nehalem River, the Salmonberry is a haven for native winter steelhead. All fishing is catch-and-release unless you happen to catch a stray fin-clipped steelhead. The Salmonberry reaches the Nehalem about 15 miles upstream from Nehalem Bay, after a rather tumultuous 20-mile-long run through the Coast Range. Salmonberry-bound anglers must bring with them at least a mild sense of adventure because access to the river requires at least a short hike and for some, a rather substantial hike.

About 15 miles south of Elsie, Lower Nehalem Road crosses the mouth of the Salmonberry River. From here, you can hike up the railroad tracks to access the river, but beware the trains. The best fishing is generally found from the mouth up to the North Fork confluence. The upper river is also accessible by hiking in from the logging roads off Camp 10 Road. Consult a Tillamook County map before setting out on the maze of roads in the mountains here. The best fishing in the Salmonberry runs from late January through the end of March.

Sand Creek (Sand Lake tributary)
closed waters

Sand Lake (Tillamook County)

Sand Lake is a broad, 897-acre sand tidal plain with no major inlet. The minor inlet is a small stream called Sand Creek, which enters from the upper (north) end of the bay. On high tides, Sand Lake puts out a few chinook salmon, though not enough to stir a lot of interest from anglers, so you'll generally find the place uncrowded during the September-October peak season. Redtail and other varieties of surfperch are available near the mouth and along the beaches adjacent to both sides of the channel. Sand Lake is also a fair bet for flounder, a few sea-run cutthroat, Dungeness crabs, and a variety of clams. Thanks in a large measure to the efforts of the Trust for Public Lands and several public entities, the state was able to purchase Whalen Island and create a beautiful state park at Sand Lake. You can launch small boats at the state park and the area has become rather popular with kayakers and canoeists. Whalen Island is accessible from a bridge across a shallow channel of the bay.

Schooner Creek (Lincoln County)

Schooner Creek feeds the northeast corner of Siletz Bay and produces a few chinook salmon and a few wild winter steelhead, which must be released. Angler effort is light because the creek is not very productive. Only the lower few miles are open to angling. From its mouth up to the head of tide, Schooner Creek is prime kayak water for sea-run cutthroat that enter the creek between August and October. Launch at the public crabbing pier on the north side of the bay and head up the creek on an incoming tide.

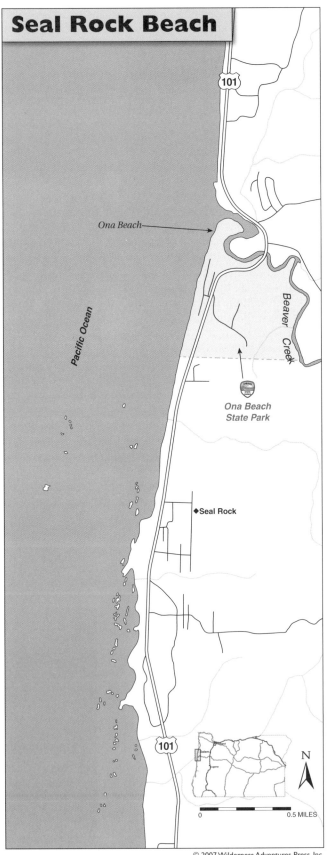

Seal Rock Beach

For anglers good at carefully negotiating the rocks, Seal Rock Beach is excellent for greenling, striped seaperch, rockfish, and other saltwater species.

Seal Rock Beach (Lincoln County)

Seal Rock Beach occupies a scenic stretch of coastline characterized by towering rock escarpments about 10 miles south of Newport. The rocks on both ends of the beach often produce good catches of striped perch and greenling along with a few black rockfish, cabezon, and lingcod. On incoming tides, fish bait for perch and greenling. At low tide, explore the rocks and probe the slots and pools with a jig. As always, be very careful when crawling around on the rocks and know your tide levels. Best fishing occurs on calm days from spring through early autumn.

During low tides, the rocky habitat of the main beach is accessible for those who can safely scamper around on the oft-slippery rocks. This central portion of the beach is sand on its upper reach, but yields to a network of ledges, boulders and escarpments that provide quite a bit of protection from the outer breakers. The pockets, pools, and channels formed by the rocks offer good prospects for greenling, along with some rockfish. You can fish them with just about any method. Try ½-ounce white jigs or fish similar lures, but bring lots of them, as you'll lose some to the rocks. Bait anglers also do well here, especially by working the deeper slots between the large rocks on an incoming tide.

At the north end of the beach, a towering escarpment reaches well out into the surf. Immediately south of this huge cliff, the beach is littered with boulders. At intermediate and high tides, greenling frequent this rock pile and at low tide you can walk out quite a ways and fish the base of the cliff and the adjacent bedrock reefs. Behind this huge escarpment, a narrow slot fills with water on incoming tides and leads directly to the outer breakers. I've heard of people catching greenling here on calm conditions, but the better water lies over the next wall of rocks to the west—very carefully climb the 10-foot-high wall and work jigs through the surge pool on the ocean side. Never try this during rough ocean conditions because sneaker waves frequent this beach.

Another huge rock marks the south end of Seal Rock Beach. At low tide you can walk out to it through the maze of small boulders that form a network of tide pools. The better fishing occurs on an incoming tide when anglers often perch atop the high rocks closer to shore and fish bait for striped seaperch and greenling. You can park along the highway shoulder to fish from these rocks on the south end of the beach. Otherwise park at the state park a mile to the north and follow the trail down to the beach. Just north of Seal Rock Beach, a nice cove forms behind a row of huge escarpments (you can see this from the trail down to Seal Rock from the state park). This is a good hole for greenling, but difficult to get to since the hillside has eroded into a cliff.

Siletz Bay (Lincoln County)
boat ramp, boat recommended, services

Sprawling Siletz Bay is a fertile estuary covering 1,400 acres formed where the Siletz River reaches saltwater. The bay lies on the west side of Hwy 101, south of Lincoln City, although tidewater extends well to the east of the highway bridge. Siletz Bay is shallow throughout and offers opportunity for pile perch, shiner perch, redtail perch, flounder, chinook salmon, and sea-run cutthroat. For the most part this is a boat fishery though some bank access is available at the mouth of Schooner Creek, along Hwy 101 south of the Siletz River bridge, along Siletz River Road east of the bridge, and on Salishan Spit on the west side of the bay.

Generally these foot access points are fishable mainly at high tides, but low tide offers the promise of good clamming throughout the bay. The Schooner Creek area is popular with clammers because of the firm bottom. Ample parking is available at a wide pullout along the highway (watch for the big rocks that mark the mouth of Schooner Creek just as you leave the south end of Lincoln City/Taft). The south end of the bay also provides good clamming. Unless you have a boat, crabbing is limited mainly to the public pier at Taft, on the north shore of the bay. This is high tide crabbing as the pier sits over shallow water, although some of the locals have perfected the art of crabbing the shallows just up from the mouth of the bay: Wearing hip boots or waders, they wade out and toss in the crab traps towards the channel, then run the rope back up to the beach. Large floats help with the retrieval process.

Boaters often enjoy good crabbing closer to the channel, generally on incoming and high tides. Likewise, you can anchor a boat near pilings and bridge abutments to cast jigs and bait for perch and flounder. Pile perch and redtail perch reach more than 2 pounds, but most of the flounder are small. Perch fishing peaks between March and August, especially for the pile perch, which wander up the Siletz channel as far as Coyote Rock, more than a mile east of the Hwy101 bridge. The bridge and its immediate vicinity rank among the best locations for pile perch and flounder, but you will need a boat to fish there. Fish the rising tide and toss in some crab rings while you're at it. You can rent boats (and crabbing equipment) at Coyote Rock RV Park & Marina (541-996-6824/www.coyote-rock.com), about a mile upstream from the bridge. Rental crab rings and bait are also available at Eleanor's Undertow Café (541-996-3800), located on the bayfront in Taft (SW 51st Street).

The Siletz River

From August through October, fall chinook and sea-run cutthroat enter the bay. Both can provide good fishing at times. Salmon anglers fare best trolling the main channel on the lower bay and still fishing around the Hwy 101 bridge and upstream in the popular salmon holes near Kernville. Cutthroat congregate near structure, so fish the logs, pilings, and other obstacles from mid-bay up to Coyote Rock. They respond best to small lures and flies fished on quick retrieves.

The beaches both north and south of the mouth of Siletz Bay are fair producers of redtail surfperch. These are good low-tide beaches that fish best on the first two hours of incoming water, especially at dawn. However, be wary of the hard-running lateral currents that form on these beaches and also watch out for the myriad huge drift logs that tend to accumulate here. Fish bait from shore rather than wading and flipping jigs.

Siletz River
boat ramp, campground

One of the best steelhead/salmon rivers on the Oregon coast, the renowned Siletz River carves a circuitous journey through the Coast Range before finally surrendering its flows to the Pacific at Siletz Bay, just south of Lincoln City. The river's best fishery is its robust run of winter steelhead, which is comprised mostly of hatchery fish, but with quite a few wild fish mixed in as well. In recent years the ODFW has switched from using Alsea river hatchery stock to producing hatchery offspring only from indigenous Siletz River broodstock. The result is fewer and fewer fin-clipped fish, especially above Moonshine Park. The winter steelhead enter the river between Thanksgiving and the end of March, with the peak being late January through March.

The Siletz also hosts a good run of summer steelhead. In fact, the Siletz and Nestucca routinely vie for the rank of third best of all the coastal summer steelhead streams; only the Rogue and North Umpqua systems—much larger and longer rivers—produce more summer fish. Most of the summer fish arrive during June, and then spread through the river system. Fishing for them holds up through most of the summer, though a hot August can and often does put a damper on the action until the fall freshets arrive. Summer fish continue to trickle into the system all summer and when the first rains come during August and September, a small but reliable push of fish moves up the river. The September and October fishing can be good.

Fall chinook salmon enter Siletz Bay as early as late July, though far more fish are available in the bay and the lower river by late August and September. The salmon run—among the ten best on the entire coast—continues well into the autumn and provides a popular troll and plug fishery in tidewater. The salmon fishing deadline is Buck Creek, on the upper end of the mainstem, though few bright salmon are taken this high in the system. The river also has a small run of spring chinook salmon available for harvest and currently the

Siletz River

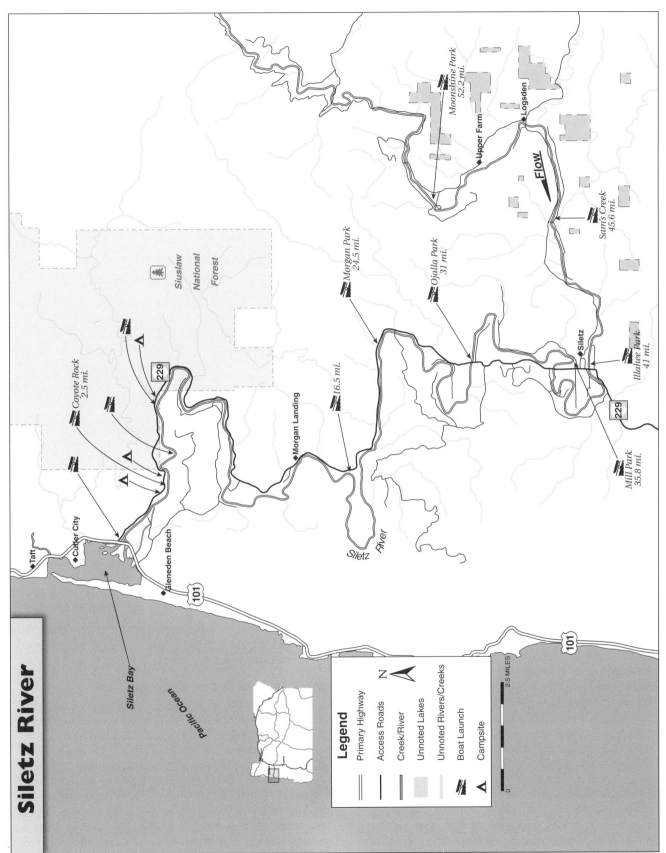

Pacific Ocean

Taft

Cutler City

Siletz Bay

Gleneden Beach

101

101

Coyote Rock
2.5 mi.

229

Siulsaw
National
Forest

Morgan Landing

16.5 mi.

Siletz   River

Morgan Park
24.5 mi.

Ojalla Park
31 mi.

Siletz

229

Mill Park
35.8 mi.

Illahee Park
41 mi.

Sam's Creek
45.6 mi.

Flow

Logsden

Upper Farm

Moonshine Park
52.2 mi.

Legend

N

‖‖‖	Primary Highway
—	Access Roads
	Creek/River
▨	Unnoted Lakes
	Unnoted Rivers/Creeks
𝕴	Boat Launch
△	Campsite

0   2.5 MILES

chinook season runs from April 1 to December 31. The river is open all year for steelhead. A fair-to-good run of sea-run cutthroat enters the river between late July and late October.

Currently only the Mainstem Siletz is open to fishing, with the deadline being below Siletz Falls, about 65 miles from the mouth. In the past, the forks provided good opportunities for summer steelhead fishing, especially during late summer and autumn. In fact the North Fork was once managed as a fly-only steelhead stream. These waters—and all Siletz tributaries—are now closed to all fishing, a situation hardly to the liking of the fly angling community. The forks of the Siletz have long been the stomping grounds of salmon and steelhead poachers and likely they are undeterred by such closures.

Because the river runs mostly through private lands, bank access to the Siletz is not very good. Moonshine Park and The Gorge, both on the upper river provide the best access. The private road above Moonshine Park is subject to closure at any time, so anglers intent on fishing The Gorge should call Georgia Pacific before making the trip (541-336-7109). These upper waters have become less popular since the inception of the Siletz broodstock program because fewer fin-clipped fish are available above Moonshine Park. Additional bank-fishing access is available just upstream from Ojalla Bridge, downstream from the town of Siletz.

Boaters definitely enjoy the advantage on the Siletz—so much so that the river gets rather busy with boat traffic during the peak of the winter steelhead runs. The floatable section spans almost 30 miles from Moonshine Park down to Morgan Park, and offers several good all-day or half-day drifts. Moonshine to Twin Bridges (Sam's Creek Launch) covers about 7 miles and is very popular and slightly technical. Before drifting it for the first time, go with someone familiar with the float. Another very popular drift covers 4 river miles from Twin Bridges to the town of Siletz (Illahee Park) and is a very good low-water option. The popular "Town Drift" covers 5 miles, sweeping around Big Bend, down to Old Mill Park. Because of the bends in the river, this 5-mile float requires only a 1-mile walk back to the put-in should you decide not to shuttle a vehicle. Five miles below Old Mill Park there is an unimproved takeout at Ojalla Bridge. The lowest drift is from Old Mill Park or Ojalla Bridge down to Morgan Park.

The uppermost drift, Moonshine to Twin Bridges, clears first after a heavy rain and is popular even at fairly high flows. If the water drops below 4.5 feet, lots of rocks get in the way, so most anglers fish this stretch at gauge levels of 5 to 7 feet. At low water, the Town Drift or the lower drifts are better. The ramp at Twin Bridges ices up from time to time during winter because it sits in the shade virtually all winter long. Also, the Old Mill-to-Morgan Park drift covers 12 miles, requiring a full day and leaving time only to fish selected spots. It's a popular float, but keep an eye on your watch.

Steelhead anglers employ a wide range of methods on the Siletz River. Drift fishing is most popular, but quite a few boaters pull plugs, especially on the lower drifts. Bait fishing is legal here, but largely discouraged owing to the difficulty in releasing wild fish unharmed after they swallow bait. Even

Greenling, rockfish, perch, and other fish inhabit the extensive jetties at Florence.

fly anglers fish winter and summer steelhead on the Siletz, especially in the Gorge upstream from Moonshine Park. Lots of guides work the river, especially during winter, and shuttle service is available through Siletz Shuttles (541-444-1111).

Siltcoos Lagoon (Lane County)

Adjacent to Lagoon Campground, just west of Hwy 101, about 7 miles south of Florence, Siltcoos Lagoon is a narrow, spruce-lined, horseshoe-shaped pond that offers stocked rainbow trout, largemouth bass, crappie, bluegill, and brown bullhead. A trail system provides access to the lagoon, but a canoe is perfect here, especially because the banks are brushy. Several times annually between February and May, ODFW stocks the lagoon with nearly 1,000 trout, mostly 8- to 10-inch "legals", but also some 12- to 14-inch fish. The trout fishing holds up throughout spring thanks to the stocking, but falls off considerably in summer.

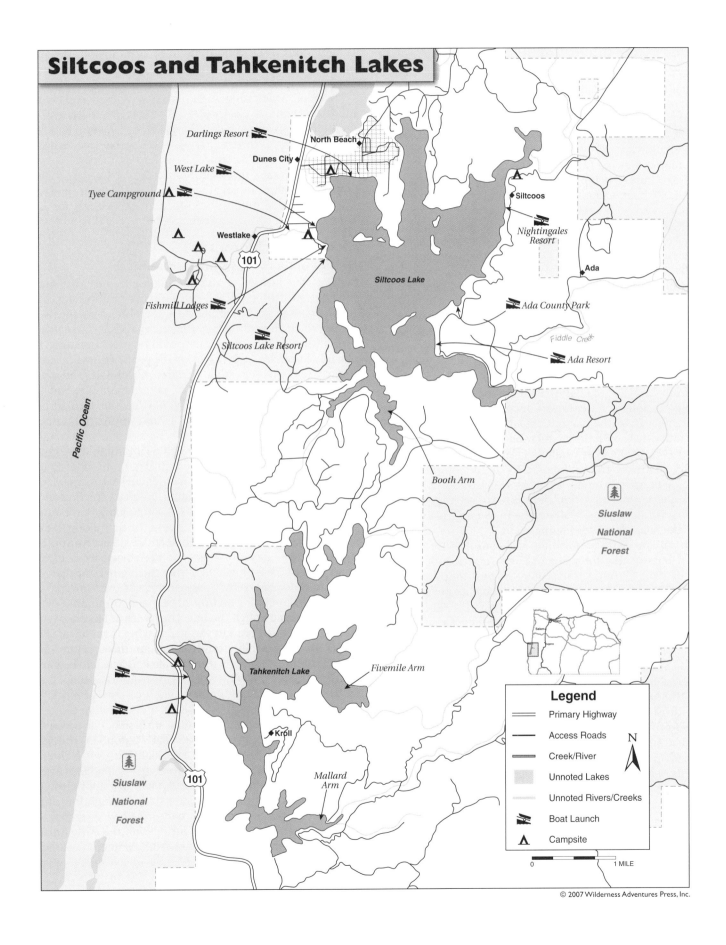

Siltcoos and Tahkenitch Lakes

Darlings Resort
North Beach
Dunes City
West Lake
Tyee Campground
Siltcoos
Nightingales Resort
Westlake
Ada
101
Siltcoos Lake
Fishmill Lodges
Ada County Park
Siltcoos Lake Resort
Fiddle Creek
Ada Resort
Pacific Ocean
Booth Arm
Siuslaw
National
Forest
Fivemile Arm
Tahkenitch Lake
Kroll
Siuslaw
National
Forest
101
Mallard
Arm

Legend

	Primary Highway
	Access Roads
	Creek/River
	Unnoted Lakes
	Unnoted Rivers/Creeks
	Boat Launch
Λ	Campsite

N

0   1 MILE

Siltcoos Lake (Lane County)
boat recommended, boat ramp, campground, services

Branching out in all directions, Siltcoos Lake covers 3,164 acres south of Florence and ranks among the state's most popular coastal fishing lakes. Siltcoos is especially well known for its propensity to produce good-sized largemouth bass, along with lots of yellow perch, brown bullhead, bluegill, crappie, stocked rainbow trout, and even a few cutthroat trout. The bass here typically weigh 1 to 4 pounds, but 5- and 6-pound fish are taken every year. Trout also grow to impressive sizes and both wild cutthroat and stocked rainbow trout reach 20 inches and commonly range from 10 to 14 inches. The lake abounds in fish food, including a localized and little-known hatch of huge mayflies called *Hexagenia* ("giant yellow mayfly"). The summer *Hexagenia* hatch occurs at dusk and, when heavy, even brings bullhead and yellow perch to the surface.

Bank-fishing access is rather limited on Siltcoos Lake owing to extensive private property on the shorelines and to lots of brush and dense tree stands. Some bank access exists around the resorts and along the west and east shorelines. The west shore is accessible by trail from Hwy 101 just to the west and from Westlake Road; the east shoreline has an access road running its length. Circuitous Canary Road gets you there—eventually—from the north: Cross the Siuslaw River at Florence and drive south on the highway 2.5 miles to a left-hand turn on Canary Road at Woahink Lake/Honeyman State Park. Canary Road delivers you to Ada Park on the southeast shore. The boat ramp here offers easy access to the productive Fiddle Creek and Booth Arms, both of which are very good bass locations. On the opposite shore, the boat ramp is located off Westlake Road near Tyee Campground.

So popular is the bass fishing at Siltcoos that the lake hosts lots of bass-fishing tournaments. Ten such events occurred here in 2003. During spring, often the best time for bass on Siltcoos, anglers use spinner baits, rubber baits, and plugs of many types. Siltcoos offers every imaginable kind of bass cover: weedbeds and lily pads, pilings and docks, submerged timber and brush, channels and steep drop-offs, shallow shoals and creek mouths. With 100 miles of shoreline, six islands and numerous coves, bays, and arms, Siltcoos offers ample room to explore and spread out.

As the weather warms during mid-summer, the bass fishing tends to slow down and the perch fishing picks up—sometimes to the point of near absurdity for anglers who still fish with bait (off the bottom to avoid bullheads). Perch fishing is a popular pastime on Siltcoos and one pragmatic way to find schools of fish is to look for congregations of boats. A 10-inch yellow perch won't raise any eyebrows and occasionally Siltcoos kicks out 2-pound perch—approaching the state record.

Trout anglers enjoy consistent success using a variety of tactics, from trolling with flasher/bait rigs, to anchoring near weed lines and still fishing with bait. Fly anglers do quite well with sinking lines and wet flies or streamer patterns. Troll the flies slowly until you find fish, then cast and retrieve. The trout fishing tends to be good more or less throughout the spring and summer, and the lake has enough carryover fish to assure decent prospects even from autumn through winter.

Siltcoos Lake enjoys the services of several lodges/marinas. Darling's Resort (541-997-2841/www.darlingsresort.com) offers moorage, a deli/store, RV park, tavern, and rental boats. Westlake Resort (541-997-3722/www.westlakeresort.com) includes rental cottages, boat rentals, tackle shop, store, and moorage facilities. Fish Mill Lodges & RV Park includes cottages, cabins, motel, docks, and rental boats (541-997-2511/ http://fishmill.tripod.com/homepage.html) for a full listing visit www.dunescity.com.

Siuslaw Bay (Florence)
boat ramp, boat recommended, services

Siuslaw Bay, located at the coastal community of Florence, offers good fishing for fall-run chinook salmon and is also highly reputed for its clamming and crabbing prospects. The bay also attracts traditionally robust runs of sea-run cutthroat. The cutthroat and salmon arrive at about the same time, from late July through October. During the peak of the salmon runs, the bay tends to get rather crowded with boats. The sea-run cutthroat, including fish up to 2 pounds, often spend quite a bit of time hanging around the bay feeding. Cast for them around current seams, flooded logs and stumps, pilings, creek mouths, and cut banks.

The bay offers extensive low-tide clamming flats, ranging from firm, sandy mud to a few places more akin to quick mud, so be careful. The catch includes cockles, soft shells, and gapers, and all are quite abundant. A few of the flats are accessible by foot, but a boat allows you to explore the numerous flats surrounding the islands and the flats along the bay's south bank, across from Florence and just east from the bay bridge. Siuslaw Bay also offers good prospects for Dungeness crabs, mostly west (down bay) from the highway bridge.

Fishing for saltwater species ranges from slow to good, with much depending on time of year and the amount of fresh water running through the bay. The jetties at Florence tend to get pounded fairly hard by the sea, making them unsafe much of the time, especially from late autumn through late spring. During summer, they are usually safe and accessible, with the south jetty almost always offering the calmest water.

The jetties here can produce good catches of black rockfish, blue rockfish, striped seaperch, and greenling, along with a few lingcod, cabezon, and redtail surfperch. Pile perch show up around the pilings and a few reach 2 pounds. Though no longer common, Siuslaw Bay still kicks out a few flounder, almost always as an incidental catch for anglers targeting other species. For bottomfish and perch, fish bait during the day and try jigs at dusk and after dark. Though few anglers target them, the Siuslaw even harbors a few sturgeon. Shad move through the bay rapidly during May and early June and are targeted primarily upstream from Mapleton, along the first few miles of Hwy 36.

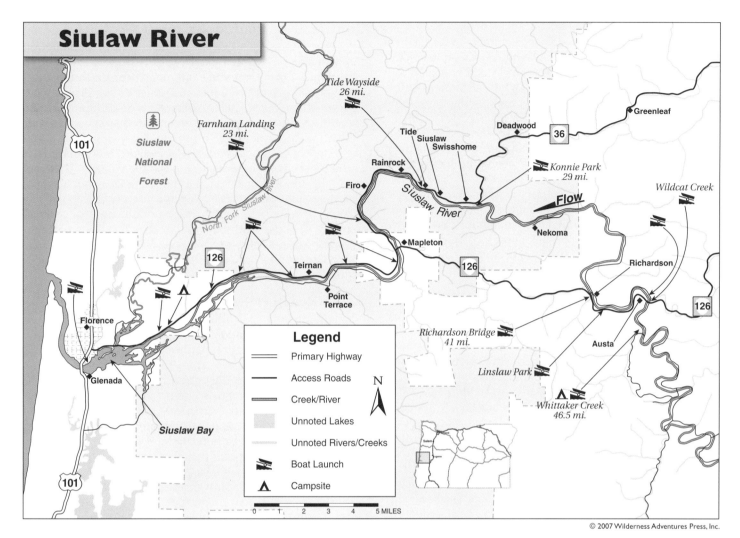

Siulaw River

Legend
- Primary Highway
- Access Roads
- Creek/River
- Unnoted Lakes
- Unnoted Rivers/Creeks
- Boat Launch
- Campsite

© 2007 Wilderness Adventures Press, Inc.

Siuslaw River (Lane County)
boat ramp

The Siuslaw River, which flows westerly through Lane County, reaching the Pacific at Florence, offers fair-to-good fishing for fall chinook salmon and sea-run cutthroat, with reasonable prospects for winter steelhead and shad. The salmon show up in August, with peak fishing during September and early October. Anglers trolling and fishing plugs on the lower river enjoy the most consistent success on salmon. Likewise, the river traditionally enjoys a rather robust run of sea-run cutthroat and the fish are most accessible to anglers with boats.

From Florence up to Mapleton, the river is wide, slow moving, and affected by the tides. Throughout this tidewater section, cutthroat anglers will find an abundance of perfect habitat for these cover-loving sea-going trout. A shallow-running pram is ideally suited to fishing here; as such craft allow easy access to the countless waterlogged stumps, logs, and pilings that attract cutthroat. Also fish the small channels between tidal islands on the lower river. The salmon, conversely, tend to stick to the main channel. Be sure to check the tide schedule because the river speeds up considerably on the ebb.

The lower Siuslaw is accessible from any number of boat launches, with the ramp at Mapleton being convenient for cutthroat anglers. There's an ODFW ramp a few miles downstream at Tieran and another gravel ramp at Cushman Store a few miles east of Florence. Additional launch/moorage sites include Sisulaw Marina & RV Park, Coast Marina RV Park, and C&D Dock. This same stretch of river can be productive for shad during the May/June run, but the better action generally occurs along a short stretch of river just above the head of tide from Mapleton to Farnham Park, along State Route 36. Access is fairly good along this stretch, which offers several large pools where shad congregate. Farnham Landing offers a pole-slide launch, which allows boaters to drift down to Mapleton.

Winter steelhead arrive in the river by late December and the runs continue into March. A mix of both wild and hatchery fish, the steelhead move quickly through tidewater, so most angling effort occurs from Mapleton upstream. The stretch from Mapleton to the mouth of Lake Creek, the river's major tributary, is especially popular and quite productive, but the steelhead fishery continues all the way up to the headwaters (for fin-clipped fish only). Currently the steelhead season runs from December through March, but check current regulations.

Upstream from Mapleton, the Siuslaw offers quite a few different options for both bank anglers and boat anglers. The uppermost launch is at the BLM Whitaker Creek Recreation Site, which also offers good bank access and is usually very busy during the peak of the run. ODFW acclimates smolts here, so many of the fish, and the anglers pursuing them, return to the accessible stretch of river from Whitaker down to Wildcat Creek. Wildcat Creek is located at the Hwy 126 bridge, just 2 miles downstream from Whitaker; and downstream from the creek, at the old Wildcat Covered Bridge, is a pole slide (Austa Landing).

The next ramp below Austa is 3 miles downstream at Linslaw Park, which offers a good improved ramp and 2 miles below Linslaw there is a pole slide at Richardson Bridge. With four launch/takeout sites located along this short stretch of river, Siuslaw boaters have plenty of access and bank anglers will find good steelhead water at each of these places. From Richardson Bridge, the run down to Swisshome covers 12 miles to the takeout at Konnie Park. This is a lengthy, but popular float that covers tons of great steelhead water. You can shorten the trip by using the unimproved primitive launch 3 miles below Richardson Bridge: Cross to the north side of the river and drive westerly down Stagecoach Road to Milepost 3.

Downstream from Konnie, ramps are located at Tide Wayside, at the aforementioned Farnham Landing (pole slide) and at Mapleton. A little used primitive launch site lies about halfway between Tide and Farnham. Mapleton offers docks, fuel, a store, and a restaurant. Currently most Siuslaw River tributaries are closed to fishing for steelhead and salmon, but several offer good fishing for small, wild cutthroat trout. Notable exceptions to the salmon/steelhead closures include Lake Creek, Sweet Creek, and the North Fork Siuslaw, which joins the main river at Florence (see separate listings herein).

Trout prospects are best on the tributaries during the summer months. Fishing is restricted to flies and artificial lures. Check current regulations for closures and catch-and-release rules. You can also try Knowles Creek, Whitaker Creek, and Esmond Creek. Access can be difficult on these creeks owing to a patchwork mix of private and public lands.

Siuslaw River, North Fork (Lane County)

A marginally productive river for hatchery winter steelhead, the North Fork Siuslaw reaches the main river at Florence. The lower half of the river is also currently open to fishing for chinook salmon. A county road follows the river, but access is very limited due to mostly private lands. Much of the steelhead fishing occurs at a few spots along the road and at a campground located on the upper river. Best salmon fishing prospects occur down in tidewater near the Hwy126 bridge.

Skookum Lake (Tillamook County)
closed waters

Slick Rock Creek (Lincoln County)
closed waters

Smith Lake (Tillamook County)

A 35-acre coastal lake located 2 miles north of Garibaldi on the west side of Hwy 101, Smith Lake is stocked each spring with about 3,000 legal-size rainbow and/or cutthroat trout (stocking occurs at the Camp Magruder dock). Private land surrounds most of this lake, so bank access is limited to the shoreline nearest the highway, accessible via a short trail. Adequate parking is available on the highway shoulder. ODFW suggests "children and older anglers would find much easier and safer access at other lakes around the county." There are no public docks or boat launches on Smith Lake, but it is possible to maneuver a small craft into the water, though you may need some help getting in and out of the water. Small numbers of largemouth bass are present, but few are caught by bank anglers, and occasionally ODFW stocks the lake with a few surplus hatchery steelhead. An RV park is located nearby.

South Beach (Newport)

Located immediately south of Yaquina Bay, South Beach is a popular tourist destination but also a fairly productive beach for redtail surfperch. Access is from South Beach State Park south of the bay bridge or from the south jetty of Yaquina Bay. South Beach forms the northernmost extent of the larger Holiday Beach, which runs south for about 5 miles and provides increasingly better surfperch prospects as you head south (see Ona Beach). At its northern terminus, South Beach abuts the south jetty of Yaquina Bay and the slot formed on the beach side of the jetty holds perch and flounder, along with an occasional salmon. Pick an early morning low tide and, from the adjacent sandbar, fish the first hour or two of incoming water by drifting bait through the slot or still fishing with a heavy weight. Try mud-shrimp, sand crabs, or clam necks.

South Lake (Tillamook County)
campground, float tube recommended

A fairly popular and pleasant 5-acre lake situated high above the town of Hebo in the Coast Range, South Lake is stocked several times each spring with legal-size cutthroats, about 6,000 of them in total for 2010. The lake is about 7 miles beyond Hebo Lake on FR 14 (see Hebo Lake herein). A short, signed spur road leads to the lake. Only electric motors are allowed on South Lake and because of the brushy, sometimes boggy shoreline, you'll want a small pram, float tube, pontoon boat, canoe, or raft. The best fishing is during spring and early summer, but South Lake can yield a few trout even during mid-winter when the weather cooperates. From May through September, fly angling can be quite productive on South Lake. Both wet flies and dry flies produce, and the lake offers decent hatches of both caddisflies and *Callibaetis* mayflies. Beware the soggy roads during winter and spring. The small, no-fee campground is unimproved.

Spring Lake (Tillamook County)

Located along the east side of Hwy 101 about 1.5 miles south of Rockaway Beach, Spring Lake covers 13 acres and offers slow to fair fishing for stocked rainbow and cutthroat trout. From time to time, ODFW dumps a few excess hatchery steelhead into the lake during spring, along with about 3,000 hatchery legals dumped in the lake between March and May. Spring Lake is surrounded by private property, leaving the highway right-of-way along the lake's west shoreline as the only public access. Parking along the highway is limited to a few wide spots, and extreme caution should be used given the heavy traffic. There are no public docks or boat launches that access this lake, but creative types could and occasionally do drop rafts and other small craft into the water. Some largemouth bass are present, but seldom caught by bank anglers.

Sunset Lake (Clatsop County)

boat ramp, boat recommended

A narrow, 2-mile-long coastal lake with stocked trout and a variety of warmwater fish, Sunset Lake sits about half a mile west of Hwy 101 a few miles south of Warrenton. Access is from the Sunset Beach Road, which crosses the lake and provides the only public bank-fishing access. From the south, the turnoff, marked by a flashing yellow signal light, is about 9 miles north of Seaside. The boat ramp here, at Sunset Lake Park, is unimproved but very serviceable and boaters enjoy a distinct advantage on the lake. Small prams, canoes, and other such craft are best as the narrow lake has a 10 mph speed limit. Sunset Lake is stocked several times each year and usually receives a modest planting of ODFW's trophy-size rainbows along with several thousand legal-size fish. Brown bullhead, yellow perch, bluegill, crappie, and largemouth bass round out the fishery.

Sutton Lake (Lane County)

boat ramp, campground, boat recommended

One of a handful of good mixed-bag lakes north of Florence, Sutton Lake offers largemouth bass, yellow perch, a few cutthroat trout, and stocked rainbow trout. The lake's 107 surface acres include two main pools connected by a narrow, short channel. Most of the shoreline is private, except for the west edge along the highway and day-use area. Sutton Campground is located on the west side of the highway. Sutton is generally only lightly fished except on weekends during early summer. The lake has a lot of good structure that attracts bass, including lily pads and downed timber, along with several small bays on the north pool and quite a few docks and pilings. The best fishing for trout is during the spring, while bass and perch fishing can be good just about any time from April through September.

Sweet Creek (Lane County)

Open to fishing for fin-clipped winter steelhead, sea-run and resident cutthroat trout, and chinook salmon (check season dates), Sweet Creek is a scenic tributary to the lower Siuslaw River, entering the river from the south 4 miles downstream from Mapleton. To reach the creek, take Hwy 126 to Mapleton and turn south on the east side of the Siuslaw (across the bridge from Mapleton). The county road follows the river's south bank to Point Terrace and Sweet Creek and from there, follow Sweet Creek Road heading south. The only public access is in the vicinity of Sweet Creek Falls and fishing is very slow most of the time, although quite a few small, wild cutthroat are available for catch-and-release fishing during the summer. A trail system takes you down to the creek and leads up to the falls. The trailhead is about 10 miles total from Hwy 126 and is marked by a small sign. There is a small paved parking lot. You can drive up the road another 1.7 miles to visit the falls, but the trail below is better for getting to the creek. Salmon anglers catch chinook near the mouth of the creek on the Siuslaw River and the creek itself is good for several dozen tagged fish each season. Only the tidewater section is open to salmon fishing.

Tahkenitch Lake (Douglas County)

boat ramp, boat recommended, campground

One of the more popular bass fisheries on the Oregon coast, Tahkenitch Lake is located about 15 miles south of Florence and a few miles north of Winchester Bay and covers 1,523 acres. The lake holds bass up to at least 10 pounds, but typical fish weigh 1 to 4 pounds. They enjoy excellent habitat in the form of abundant flooded snags, logs, stumps, brush, and other haunts. The lake is stocked regularly with rainbow trout and also hosts sizable populations of yellow perch and bluegill, along with a few wild cutthroat trout and a few warmouth (a sunfish that looks something like a cross between a crappie and a bluegill).

Though Tahkenitch Lake borders partly on a tract of 10,000 acres of largely undisturbed forest, most of the shoreline is in private hands and the remainder (the west side) is mostly too brushy for easy shoreline access. So you'll want a boat for fishing this lake, whose fingers and bays sprawl out in all directions. Indeed, the word Tahkenitch means "lake of many fingers." The best bass fishing often occurs in the Fivemile and Mallard Arms. Fivemile Arm stretches about 4 miles to the east and Mallard Arm branches off from the south end of

Tahkenitch Lake yellow perch.

the lake. Boat ramps are located just off Hwy 101 (watch for the signs to Tahkenitch Landing). There are two large campgrounds adjacent to the lake. (see map with Siltcoos Lake)

Tenmile Creek (Lane County)

A small coastal steelhead stream south of Yachats in Lane County, Tenmile Creek usually produces a few dozen finclipped winter fish each season. Wild fish are prevalent, but there is no open season for them and they must be immediately released. Currently the creek is open from November 1 through March 31 and closed the balance of the year to protect juvenile salmon and steelhead. Tenmile Creek Road follows the creek east from Hwy 101 across from Stonefield Beach. The creek flows through a lot of private property.

Thissel Pond (Lincoln County)

A nice little stocked trout pond on Fall Creek on the Alsea River drainage, Thissel provides fair-to-good fishing during the spring and early summer. From Philomath, head south on the Alsea Highway (SR 34) until you reach Fall Creek Road, about 15 miles west from the town of Alsea. The pond is alongside the road about 2.5 miles from the highway and about 1.5 miles downstream from the hatchery.

Three Rivers (Nestucca River drainage)

campground

A very popular and fairly productive tributary to the Nestucca River, Three Rivers is best known for its winter steelhead fishery. The stream also hosts runs of hatchery summer steelhead, chinook salmon and sea-run cutthroat trout. Access is very limited and the river has just a few popular and oft-busy fishing holes. The most popular spot is at the mouth of the river at Hebo and the other popular access is upstream 2 miles, at the fishing area downstream from Cedar Creek Hatchery. The lower river remains closed to all fishing from July 1 to September 30 to protect returning brood-stock chinook and coho salmon. Access on the upper river is by landowner permission except at the forest service campground. Winter steelheading—the most popular activity on Three Rivers—peaks during January and February.

Threemile Lake (Douglas County)

hike-in, float tube recommended

Brushy shorelines, a short hike, and often-slow fishing make this coastal sand dune lake rather lightly fished for its yellow perch and cutthroat trout. The lake lies just west of Hwy 101 and just north of Winchester Bay. The trail to the lake covers a bit more than half a mile and begins toward the west end of Sparrow Park Road. Sparrow Park Road is the last road leading west from Hwy 101 before the highway dips down the hill above Winchester Bay an into the town of Gardiner. From the north, the turnoff is about 5 miles south of Tahkenitch Lake. From the south, it is 2 miles north of Gardiner. Sparrow Park is rather rugged on its lower end. Watch carefully for the trailhead at the 3.3-mile mark. A longer trail heads south to the

lake from the trailhead near Tahkenitch Campground, just north of Elbow Lake. The beach in this area is open to motorized vehicles and a few anglers use ORVs to haul small boats or float tubes into the lake. When you reach the beach at the end of the road, head north 1 mile and then cut inland to the lake. A good reference is the Oregon Dunes National Recreation Area map from Siuslaw National Forest.

Tillamook Bay

boat ramp, services, charters

One of the Northwest's best all-around saltwater fisheries, Tillamook Bay offers a wide range of angling opportunities. Gathering the flows of several significant, salmon-rich tributaries—the Miami, Kilchis, Wilson, Trask, and Tillamook Rivers—this sprawling bay complex ranks among the best salmon-fishing destinations in the state. At the same time, Tillamook Bay is rich in saltwater fish, crabs, shellfish, and sturgeon.

Salmon fishing begins in April and May when modest but very fishable numbers of spring chinook run through the bay. As with the far more numerous fall chinook, most anglers fish springers by trolling with herring or other bait, or by fishing plug/bait or blade/bait combinations. The fall chinook fishery is legendary, highly productive, and very popular. These fish range from 15 to 50 pounds or more, and 25- to 35-pound salmon are common. Most of the salmon-fishing action occurs along the main channel from Barview near the jetties, southward through the east edge of the bay all the way to the mouth of the Trask and Tillamook Rivers. Included in this section are some justifiably famous salmon-fishing grounds, such as the ever-popular Ghost Hole, located about 2 miles north of Bay City.

Sturgeon fishing can be productive at times, mostly from mid-winter through mid-spring when lots of fish enter the bay. As with the salmon, most sturgeon fishing occurs in the main channel and in the old channel to the west. Falling tides concentrate the fish in the deeper water, making them more accessible to anglers who still fish with a variety of baits. While you're at it, toss crab rings into the bay, which produces decent catches of legal-size Dungeness crabs. The crabbing tends to pick up as the tide moves in and is usually best from mid-tide to peak high.

In addition to opportunities for crabbing, Tillamook Bay also offers very good clamming for soft shells, gapers, cockles, and butter clams. Ideal clam habitat exists throughout the bay complex. During extreme low tides, falling water reveals extensive mud and mud-sand flats. Bayocean Road, which runs along the bay's southwest side, offers excellent access to tidal flats. On the bay's west edge, Bayocean Peninsula juts to the north to enclose Tillamook Bay and offers access to vast clamming flats. The service road on the peninsula is gated near Cape Meares Lake, so access is by foot or bicycle. On the northeast extent of the peninsula, the so-called "Crab Pot" is a relatively protected and popular boat-access crabbing hotspot. During minus tides, it also offers excellent clamming opportunities.

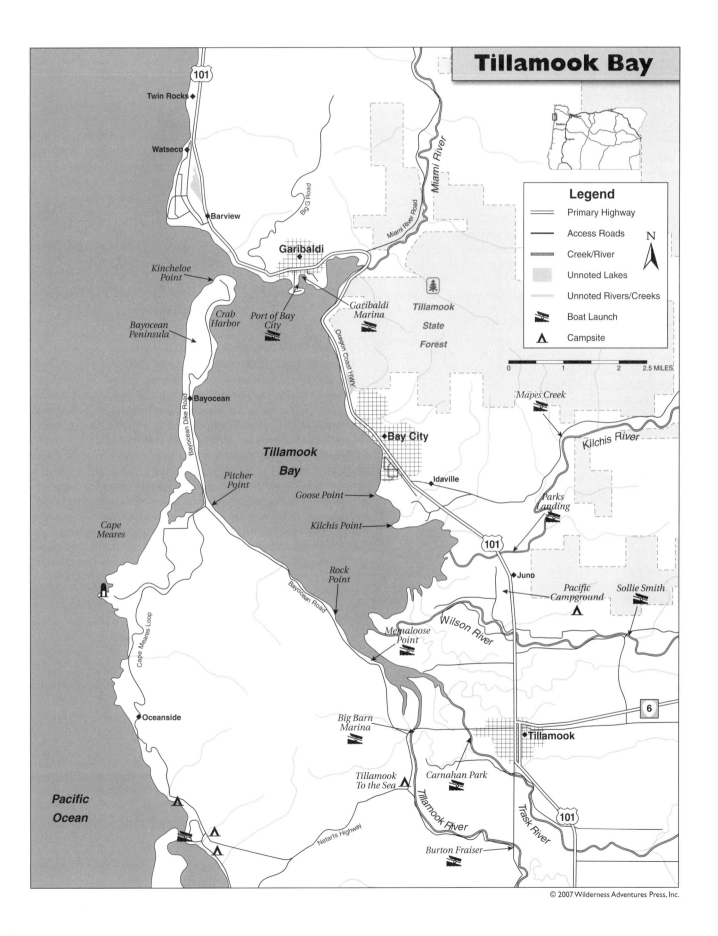

Tillamook Bay

Legend

Primary Highway

Access Roads

Creek/River

Unnoted Lakes

Unnoted Rivers/Creeks

Boat Launch

Campsite

N

0   1   2   2.5 MILES

Twin Rocks ◆

Watseco ◆

Barview ◆

Big G Road

101

Miami River

Miami River Road

Garibaldi ◆

Kincheloe Point

Crab Harbor

Port of Bay City

Garibaldi Marina

Tillamook State Forest

Bayocean Peninsula

Oregon Coast HWY

Bayocean Dike Road

Bayocean ◆

Tillamook Bay

Mapes Creek

Kilchis River

Bay City ◆

Idaville ◆

Pitcher Point

Goose Point

Parks Landing

Cape Meares

Kilchis Point

101

Rock Point

Bayocean Road

Juno ◆

Pacific Campground

Sollie Smith

Cape Meares Loop

Wilson River

Memaloose Point

Oceanside ◆

6

Big Barn Marina

Tillamook ◆

Tillamook To the Sea

Carnahan Park

Pacific Ocean

Netarts Highway

Tillamook River

Trask River

101

Burton Fraiser

© 2007 Wilderness Adventures Press, Inc.

The jetties at Tillamook Bay provide a wide array of saltwater species and fishing can be quite good, especially for rockfish and greenling. The most accessible jetty structure is found along the breakwater at Barview, more or less right along the highway. The north jetty can get nasty during periods of unsettled weather or rough seas, so use extreme caution. The south jetty is generally safer, though it absorbs some huge breakers from time to time. As always, jetty anglers should be alert and very careful. The south jetty is accessible only by boat, foot, or bicycle.

Most anglers fish the jetties with bait or with jigs, but fly fishing also enjoys modest popularity. Both fly and jig anglers often fish at night by way of lantern light, as is the custom to the south at Yaquina Bay. The light starts a food chain that ultimately leads to rockfish and other predators moving in close to feed. During daylight hours, bait fishing is more productive; though fishing a jig deep and close to the rocks can prove effective also.

Black rockfish, blue rockfish, copper rockfish, and a few other members of the *Sebastes* genus show up in the catch, with blacks being the most common. They generally range from less than a pound up to about 3 pounds. Greenling abound along the jetties, and cabezon and lingcod are fairly common. Striped seaperch occur along both jetties and redtail perch sometimes enter the bay as well. Redtails are also available on the beach west of Bayocean Peninsula, south from the south jetty. The jetties also produce an occasional salmon.

Higher in the bay, try fishing around the pilings and other wood structure for pile perch, which can be found as far south as the Sheep Corral pilings in the main channel west of Idaville. Flounder are still taken in Tillamook Bay, but they are not nearly so numerous as they were a few decades ago.

Tillamook Bay also offers offshore charter trips originating at the little port town of Garibaldi. The fleet targets chinook and coho salmon, halibut, and bottomfish. Fishing offshore for lingcod and large rockfish can be very good. Information on booking trips is available from the Garibaldi Chamber of Commerce (503-322-0301). For just about anything having to do with Tillamook Area fishing—bay or rivers—the Guide Shop ranks amongst the best possible sources of information. This full-service tackle shop resides in Tillamook (503-842-3474/www.guideshop.com).

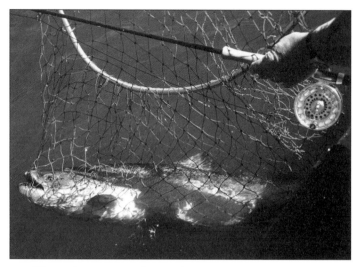

Tillamook Bay is one of Oregon's best chinook salmon fisheries.

Tillamook River
boat ramp, boat recommended

Generally the least productive and least fished of the major Tillamook Bay tributaries, the Tillamook River runs mostly through private dairy farms and other private properties, reaching the bay's south side just west of town. The primary fisheries are for fall chinook salmon and sturgeon, and most anglers fish the mouth and lower end of the river by boat, launching at the fee ramp at Memaloose Point. To get there, head west towards Bayocean from downtown Tillamook (3rd Street). During the salmon season, you can usually find a few sea-run cutthroat wandering the lower Tillamook River and a few anglers target winter steelhead during January and February. Be sure to check current regulations. Bank fishing on the Tillamook is largely limited to the public-access fishery (including handicap-access pier) adjacent to the Trask River confluence at Tillamook Tidewater Park.

Town Lake (Tillamook County)
boat ramp, boat recommended, float tube recommended

Protected from the wind by a big sand dune, Town Lake north of Pacific City can be a pleasant place to spend a day fishing for stocked rainbow and cutthroat trout. The small lake sits just off the east side of the road (behind the dune) about a mile north of the tiny town of Woods. Follow the main road (Brooten Road) through Pacific City and north, turning left to cross the Nestucca River. Head through Woods and after about a mile watch for the 9-acre lake on your right. Respect the private property abutting much of the lakeshore (public bank access extends from the power transformers to the boat ramp); parking is limited. All methods produce here and a float tube or small, carry-able boat comes in handy. The lake also offers a few largemouth bass (catch-and-release recommended) and from time to time during spring, ODFW dumps surplus hatchery steelhead into the lake.

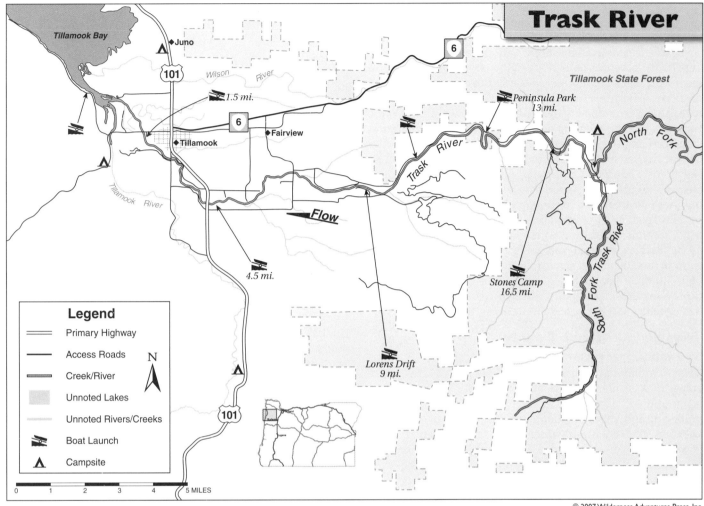

Trask River

Tillamook Bay

Juno

Wilson River

Tillamook State Forest

Peninsula Park
13 mi.

Fairview

Tillamook

Trask River

North Fork

Flow

4.5 mi.

Stones Camp
16.5 mi.

South Fork Trask River

Legend

══	Primary Highway
—	Access Roads
═	Creek/River
▨	Unnoted Lakes
	Unnoted Rivers/Creeks
✈	Boat Launch
▲	Campsite

N

Lorens Drift
9 mi.

0 1 2 3 4 5 MILES

© 2007 Wilderness Adventures Press, Inc.

Trask River (Tillamook County)

boat ramp, campground

Perhaps the best winter steelhead river on the north coast, the Trask River is highly regarded for its run of natives, some of which surpass the 20-pound mark. Most years, the steelhead run lasts from Christmas through early April. The best chance for trophy-class fish usually occurs during February and March. Though no longer stocked, the Trask hosts substantial numbers of stray hatchery steelhead from other nearby rivers, including some summer-run fish. The Trask also hosts a good run of fall chinook salmon and a small run of spring chinook salmon. Be sure to check current regulations for salmon fishing on this scenic river.

The lower end of the Trask—no doubt the best salmon and steelhead water—flows through a lot of private land and while bank access is available in several popular places, boaters enjoy the advantage. The lowermost drift, and a very popular and easy run, is from the ODFW ramp near the hatchery (Loren's) down to Hwy 101 and the takeout at Hwy 101.

There are three boat access sites upstream from Loren's. The highest drift goes from the pole-slide at Stone Camp

down to the upper takeout at Peninsula Park. Drifting below Peninsula requires boaters to negotiate some nasty water—bad enough that you can easily loose a boat; so most anglers and floaters avoid it altogether. The middle drift starts at Cedar Creek (unimproved) and goes down to Loren's. This is a short float, but allows lots of fishing time on prime water during the short days of winter. To lengthen the trip, head all the way down to the lower takeout near Hwy 101, but mind your watch. The lower takeout is located just east from the highway on Long Prairie Road, while Loren's is located about 5.5 miles upriver on Chance Road.

Drifting from the pole-slide put-in at Stone Camp down to Peninsula requires strong boating skills. Before doing it on your own, float with someone who knows the water. The lower river is generally uneventful. The Stone Camp slide (unmarked last time I was there) is located off a gravel spur road leading down just past Milepost 10 on Trask River Road. The run down to Peninsula covers about 2.5 miles.

Just about every prominent place of interest to anglers on the Trask has at least two names. Loren's Drift is also called "The Pig Farm" and sometimes "Hannekrat," though the latter spot is actually located just upstream. Peninsula Park is often called simply "The Park," and the lower gravel ramp at the park is sometimes called "Last Chance." And the list goes on.

Bank access is available at the various launch sites, including The Park, Loren's, and Stone Camp, along with a variety of pay-to-fish sites and permission-only sites located on private property. When in doubt, ask for permission to access the river. The upriver angling deadline for salmon is Trask County Park; located at the confluence of the North and South Forks. Steelhead angling is allowed in the forks from the December 1 through March 31. Bark Shanty Creek is the deadline on the North Fork; Edwards Creek is the deadline on the South Fork and only adipose fin-clipped steelhead may be kept. All tributary streams are closed to angling.

The Trask River tends to clear rather quickly and takes a while to blow out during winter storms. It fishes just fine at moderately high water levels and anglers employ the full spectrum of steelhead and salmon fishing methods, from pulling plugs and bait fishing to jig-and-float fishing and fly angling. Quite a few steelhead guides work the river, so if you're new to this water a guided trip can cut down on the learning curve.

Triangle Lake (Lane County)
boat ramp, boat recommended, campground

A very popular, 293-acre multi-use natural lake west of Eugene, Triangle Lake offers a productive fishery for a mix of warmwater and coldwater species, including bass, bluegill, brown bullhead, and yellow perch, along with cutthroat trout and kokanee. The lake is also very popular with pleasure boaters, jet skiers, and water skiers during summer. In fact, prior to the construction of Fern Ridge Lake, Triangle Lake was the favorite local water-sports destination for the Eugene area.

Triangle Lake is surrounded by homes, so shoreline access is somewhat limited. Fishing by boat is better because the boat allows you to work the abundant shoreline structure. The largemouth bass range from a pound or so up to about 5 pounds. They are fairly common, but small fish predominate. Bluegill abound and constitute a very popular fishery. Because of the summer boat traffic, fish the lake early and late in the day, or wait until after Labor Day, when the crowds thin out.

Easiest access to Triangle Lake is from old Hwy 99 northwest from Eugene and just south of Junction City. Take SR 36 through Cheshire, heading west. From Cheshire, the drive covers about 21 winding, scenic miles. You can also get there by heading north through Elmira to a left-hand turn on Warthen Road, which leads up to Hwy 36. From the west (Florence), follow Hwy 126 east to a left-hand turn on SR 36 at Swisshome.

Trojan Pond (Columbia County)

Also known as Recreation Pond, Trojan Pond—as the name might suggest—sits adjacent to the mothballed Trojan Nuclear Reactor along Hwy 30 across the Columbia from Kalama, Washington. The pond supports bluegill, brown bullhead, and other warmwater species, but is mostly fished for stocked legal-size rainbow trout. The pond covers about 15 acres and sits along the north side of the highway.

Vernonia Lake (Columbia County)

A pleasant and productive 40-acre retired millpond in the town of Vernonia, this lake offers consistently fair-to-good action for bluegill, crappie, yellow perch, largemouth bass, and stocked rainbow trout. The pond is very popular with locals and is a great place for kids. Bank fishing is easy, with a trail circling the lake, and a small boat ramp allows for small watercraft (only electric motors allowed). The pond is full of structure that attracts bass and panfish. There are restrooms and wheelchair-accessible fishing docks and a primitive camping area has fire pits and drinking water. The pond is open all year, with the best fishing from March through June. A kid's fishing day is held here during the summer.

Waconda Beach (Lane County)
campground

A fair-to-good beach for redtail surfperch, Waconda stretches for several miles just south of Waldport. This is a low-gradient, wide, windswept sand expanse well suited to bait casting during the early morning hours, especially on the first two hours of the incoming tide. Prime season is from April through June, and you can often have much of the beach all to yourself. Good access and camping is available at Beachside State Recreation Site 3 miles south of Waldport.

Walluski River (Clatsop County)

A short, little-known river entering the lower Youngs River, just upstream from Youngs Bay at Astoria, the Walluski is currently closed to fishing for its sparse runs of steelhead and salmon. The river attracts a few sea-run cutthroat during fall, but hardly enough to warrant the effort and most of the river flows through private lands.

Westport Slough (Clatsop County)
boat recommended, boat ramp

Westport Slough is a long backwater from the Columbia River offering good fishing for a variety of warmwater species, including largemouth bass and bluegill. Westport is located about 10 miles west of Clatskanie on Hwy 30, just past the Clatsop County Line. Bank access is available from a few road approaches and bridges, or you can launch a boat at the Westport Ramp and head into the slough from there. To find the ramp at Westport, turn north off Hwy 30 at the west end of town on the road to Westport Ferry Landing. Go past King Salmon Inn and turn right to reach the ramp. The slough is ideal for kayakers, which can launch at Westport or at Beaver Boat Ramp in Clatskanie. Don't use the Beaver ramp with a large boat because the route to Westport Slough goes through (or portages over) a couple of large culverts. After launching at Beaver, kayakers must first negotiate about 3 miles on the Clatskanie River. You'll pass Beaver Slough first (on the right as you approach Anunde Island) and then veer into the left-hand channel (Beeston Slough). Watch for the big, black tidegates as you come around Anunde. These mark the portage into Westport Slough. Park a rig at Westport for the end of the trip, which covers about 12 miles.

Wilson River

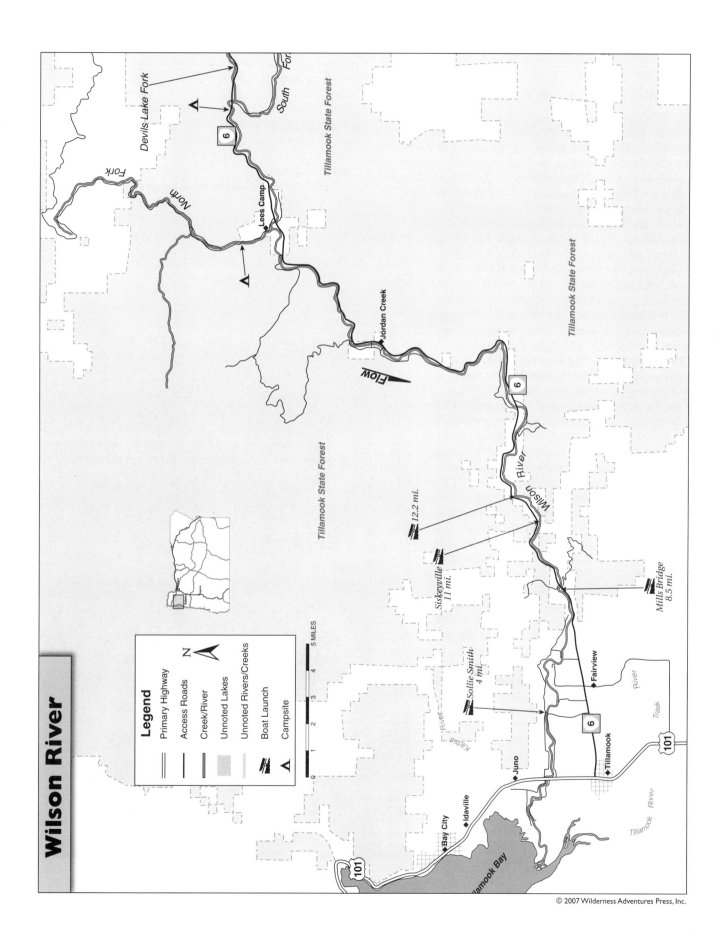

Legend

Primary Highway	
Access Roads	
Creek/River	
Unnoted Lakes	
Unnoted Rivers/Creeks	
Boat Launch	
Campsite	

N

0 1 2 3 4 5 MILES

Whittaker Creek (Lane County)
closed waters

Wilson River (Tillamook County)
boat ramp

A popular, heavily fished tributary to Tillamook Bay, the Wilson River offers good prospects for winter and summer steelhead, chinook salmon, and sea-run cutthroat. Of the Tillamook-area rivers, the Wilson is the most accessible. Highway 6 offers good bank access to the Wilson and the county has several parks scattered along the river.

Winter steelhead head up the Wilson from December through March, with the later fish being mostly wild and including a few trophy-class fish. Most years you can count on finding winter steelhead in the Wilson by Christmas, often sooner. During May, spring chinook salmon run the river and, in most years, provide a fair fishery through early June. On the heels of the springers come hatchery summer-run steelhead that range from 4 to 10-plus pounds. The summer fishing is best during June and July, but steelhead are in the river every month of the year. The lower 12 miles of the river are the most popular of all of the river's fisheries, but the summer fish (of hatchery origin) get as far upriver as Jones Creek. Fall chinook, along with a few cutthroat and coho salmon, arrive between August and November and then it's back to winter steelhead.

Be sure to read the regulations carefully for the Wilson River. Currently, fin-clipped coho salmon may be taken only below the Hwy 101 bridge. The salmon fishery downstream of the highway (for coho and chinook) is fairly popular. Put in at Sollie Smith just east from the highway, fish downriver and then motor back up to the ramp. To reach Sollie Smith, the lowermost access to the Wilson, head east from the highway on either side of the Wilson River (Wilson River Loop Road on the south side or Latimer Road on the north side).

The lower Wilson is a very popular drift boat fishery owing to the uncomplicated water and to the abundance of productive pools and runs accessible only by boat on the lower half of the river. The most popular drift, especially for salmon, runs from Mills Bridge down to Sollie Smith, covering about 5 river miles. For steelhead, many anglers prefer to launch 2.5 miles upstream at the ODFW slide at Siskeyville, about a quarter mile west from Alice's Restaurant. Another launch/takeout, 2 miles upstream from Sollie Smith, is a pay-to-launch site on the south bank at the end of Donaldson Road, but it isn't as heavily used now as it was before the big floods altered the river's flows there in 1996/97.

Two remaining launch sites, upstream from Siskeyville, present some problems and are seldom used. A very primitive slide is available near the bridge at about mile 13, but only skilled boaters should use this launch because the run immediately plunges through fast, narrow, boulder-studded water that leaves little room for mistakes at the oars. Another upriver launch is located about a mile east of Alice's Restaurant, but this site is tricky to use at most water levels, so it is largely avoided.

Bank anglers can find a wide range of river access options. Look for pullouts along the highway with easy access to the

The Wilson River offers both summer and winter steelhead.

river. The landowners in the area follow one of three tactics: They post their property against trespassing, they charge a fee for access, or they leave their property un-posted and un-fenced and allow anglers to access the river. When in doubt, always ask, but generally access along the highway is fairly easy to decipher. Downstream from Mills Bridge, bank access is difficult, though the well-known and productive Josi's Hole lies on this stretch and is accessible for a small fee. Upstream from Mills Bridge good, easy bank access continues up to about river mile 26 or so.

As you head upstream, the Wilson is increasingly precari-ous to access owing to its steep, brushy canyon. Nonetheless, those willing to park along the highway and hike down to the river can find some lightly fished water for both winter and summer steelhead. The South Fork Wilson River confluence, located near Elk Creek Campground, is the upstream deadline for fishing and all tributaries to the Wilson, except the Little North Fork, are closed to fishing.

The Wilson lies within easy reach of Portland. Follow Hwy 26 west from the city heading toward Seaside and the Oregon coast. When you reach the intersection with Hwy 6, turn left toward Tillamook. After reaching the Coast Range summit, you will follow above the river all the way to Tillamook (high above the river for the first half of the drive).

Winema Beach (Tillamook County)

Winema Beach is actually the name of a small community at the northern extent of Kiwanda Beach, located north of Neskowin. The community's name is frequently applied to the adjacent and very attractive secluded beach. An excel-lent beach for redtail surfperch, "Winema Beach" begins on the south side of the Nestucca River mouth and runs south to the beach parking area. A very readable beach with dis-tinct pockets and rips, this strip is a local favorite hotspot for surfperch and fishes best on the first half of an incoming tide. Spring and summer are best and the beach generally has enough mole crabs ("sand crabs"), that surfperch anglers can easily dig enough for their own bait along the surf line. Just be careful about the severe drop-off that forms on the beach, es-pecially between fall and spring, generally just a few yards off-shore from the big rock monolith about halfway up the beach. Because of the topography here, it's wise to scout the beach at low tide. Access is near the top of the hill a few miles south of where Hwy 101 crosses the Little Nestucca River (watch for the sign).

Woahink Lake (Lane County)

boat ramp, boat recommended, campground

This productive 726-acre sand dune lake lies a few miles south of Florence, stretching along the east side of Hwy 101. The well-marked access is through Honeyman State Park, which includes enough shoreline to provide some bank-fishing op-portunity. Nonetheless, a boat is highly advantageous in pursuing the lake's stocked rainbow trout and warm-water species, including yellow perch and largemouth bass. The lake

also has a few cutthroat trout and an occasional steelhead or salmon shows up, having negotiated Woahink Creek after swimming up the Siltcoos River and through Siltcoos Lake.

Woahink Lake is the deepest of all the Oregon coast sand dune dammed lakes. The deepest spot is 74 feet and the lake offers far less fertile, shallow shoal area than the other dune lakes. Thus largemouth bass don't thrive here, though the lake has some surprisingly large fish. Yellow perch grow to at least 12 inches and carryover trout can reach 18 inches, though the trout fishery is generally not as productive as that in Siltcoos Lake just to the south.

Honeyman State Park has two boat ramps on Woahink Lake, whose shoreline is 85 percent privately owned. Woahink attracts a lot of water skiers during summer, but fishing is better during April and May before the water-sports season really gets started. Bogs along the lakeshore support fragile and endangered populations of California Pitcher Plants, or Cobra Lilies (*Darlingtonia*). The Woahink Unit of Honeyman State Park is a day-use area (except for the group-camp area). The campground is located at Cleawox Lake on the other side of the highway and is open all year.

Yachats River (Lincoln County)

Flowing almost entirely through private property, the pretty little Yachats River offers modest but sometimes fishable runs of winter steelhead, along with a few fall chinook salmon and a few cutthroat trout. Yachats River Road follows the river upstream and provides access to a few small sections of na-tional forest lands; otherwise you must track down landown-ers for permission to fish. Most steelhead anglers fish just up from the mouth of the river during January and February. The mouth itself runs over a beach of mixed sand and rock and provides fair prospects for surfperch using bait-casting rigs.

Yaquina Bay (Newport)

boat ramp, services, charters

One of Oregon's most popular saltwater fishing destinations, Yaquina Bay at Newport offers a wide selection of activities, ranging from crabbing and clamming to fishing for a vast array of saltwater species, including perch, rockfish, cabezon, lingcod, flatfish, herring, and salmon. At the same time, the bay supports a sizeable fleet of charter vessels operating alongside the numerous commercial fishing boats.

Yaquina Bay's north and south jetties are highly reputed for producing good catches of black rockfish, blue rockfish, greenling, cabezon, striped sea perch, and a few lingcod. Black rockfish abound, although the average size and numbers have decreased over the past two decades. Blue rockfish, which sometimes reach 5 or 6 pounds in the bay, usually occupy the outermost reaches of the jetties, making them difficult to target unless the seas are calm. The same goes for the lingcod and cabezon, although juveniles of both species occupy suit-able habitat throughout the lower bay.

Most anglers fish the jetties with jigs, especially feather jigs and rubber "curly-tail" jigs, usually ranging from ¼ to ¾ ounces. Bait anglers also enjoy consistent success drifting multiple hooks under a large float. Virtually any bait works, including marine worms, clam necks, mussels, shrimp, and small baitfish. Keep your offering fairly close to the rocks, casting up current and allowing the bait to drift back down.

Even fly anglers do well off the Yaquina Bay jetties. Like jig anglers, fly fisher's mostly pursue rockfish and greenling after dark, when the fish are far more willing to chase a meal near the surface. Take along one or more lanterns and set them on the rocks a few feet above the water line. The light attracts bait, which in turn attracts rockfish and other species. Many different flies work, ranging from weighted streamers and woolly buggers to large bonefish and permit patterns. Use a fast-sinking line or a floating line coupled with a long leader and weighted fly.

Regardless of your angling method, bring along plenty of tackle when you fish the jetties. The fish live among the rocks and you'll lose plenty of lures. Also, beware of the slippery rocks—especially as the tide recedes. Be very careful negotiating these jetties and be wary of large breakers and sneaker waves, especially on the outer halves of the jetties and anywhere along the north jetty.

The south jetty is accessible by car for most of its length and includes a series of "finger-jetties" protruding at right angles into the bay. This productive jetty habitat extends inland almost to the foot of Yaquina Bay Bridge. The north jetty requires a short walk, which is well worth your time as it is not so heavily fished as the south jetty. However, rough ocean conditions frequently create dangerous breakers crashing against both sides of the north jetty, so exercise caution. Both jetties tend to fish best at incoming water and at high slack tide.

On the ocean side of both jetties, the transition zone between sand beach and rock jetty provides good habitat for perch and flounder, along with salmon and a few greenling. From the south jetty, you can easily fish the beach side of the rocks opposite the bay, especially when ocean conditions are calm. The same situation presents itself on the beach side of the north jetty, but the waves tend to be more rugged. Also keep an eye peeled for low tides that expose the productive clam beds immediately west of both ends of the bay bridge.

Back on the south side of the bay, just inside the bridge, South Beach Marina is enclosed by two rock jetties, both of which can provide good action for rockfish and sometimes greenling and perch. To reach the marina and the south jetty watch for the signs for the first exit off Hwy 101 south of the bridge. Adjacent to the long jetty enclosing the south marina is a lengthy public pier, which is very popular for crabbing and fishing. At its terminus, the pier stands high above the water, so make sure your crab rings have 75-foot ropes. Anglers fishing with bait sometimes do well from the pier, with striped perch and flounder being fairly common.

On the north side of the bay, just west of the bridge, Newport's bay front attracts a seemingly endless parade of tourists. Increasingly the bay front is home to slightly upscale res-

taurants, gift shops, and art galleries. Mo's, the decades-old chowder house, is as busy as ever and you'll stand in line for a seat during summer. Despite the hustle and bustle, the bay front offers public access for fishing and crabbing. Most of the time, the latter is the better and more productive bet. The access points are scattered along the south side of the street at Port Dock #1 (next to Undersea Gardens), Abby Street Pier, and Baystreet Pier (both at the west end of the street).

Any of these public access points, on both sides of the bay, provide ideal sites for jigging herring. They abound in the bay between late winter and spring and are especially active after dark on the rising and high-slack tides. The herring commonly range from 6 to 12 inches in length.

Harry's Bait & Tackle, a long-time fixture on the bay front, sits on the north side of the street, west from Mo's. Harry's offers tackle, bait, crab bait, rental crabbing equipment, and lots of free advice eagerly given for the asking (541-265-2407). Much of the street-side parking along the bay front is of the two-hour variety, but some all-day spots are scattered about, particularly at the west end of the strip where the street turns up the hill towards the bridge.

Just west of the main bay front area, Yaquina Bay's north shore is enclosed by a sea wall that shelters the numerous docks, which are generally off-limits to non-boat owners. If you have a small boat, fish jigs or bait right along the sea wall, especially at the upper and lower ends where large rock piles provide ideal habitat for a range of species. If the current is moving, suspend several baited hooks under a float and drift them right along the wall. The sea wall extends inland to the ever-popular and sprawling Embarcadaro Hotel. Several charter fleets operate off the docks near the Embarcadaro.

For boaters, these middle reaches of the bay provide good prospects for both Dungeness and red rock crab. Incoming and high tides are best. If you don't own crab rings or traps, you can rent them from Harry's Bait & Tackle. This middle section of Yaquina Bay, from the bridge east to King's Slough on the south and Sawyer's Landing on the north, also provides lots of boat-fishing opportunity.

Striped perch, common from The Embarcadaro to the mouth of the bay, tend to congregate near rock structure and pile perch, which become more common as you head up the bay, prefer wood structure in the form of old pilings, sea-walls, and the like. Both species prefer bait, but they'll certainly take small jigs. Boaters can also fish the rock structures on both sides of the bay. If you're fishing by foot, you are limited to the two rock jetties that enclose South Beach Marina along with a handful of other rock structures scattered about the bay. Black rockfish and greenling are fairly common and the middle bay also kicks out quite a few copper rockfish and a few other Sebastes species.

A little further up the bay, on the north side just east of the Embarcadaro, is the "Natural Gas Pier," identifiable by the big green gas storage tank. A public, wheelchair accessible pier here offers both crabbing and fishing access, but only at high

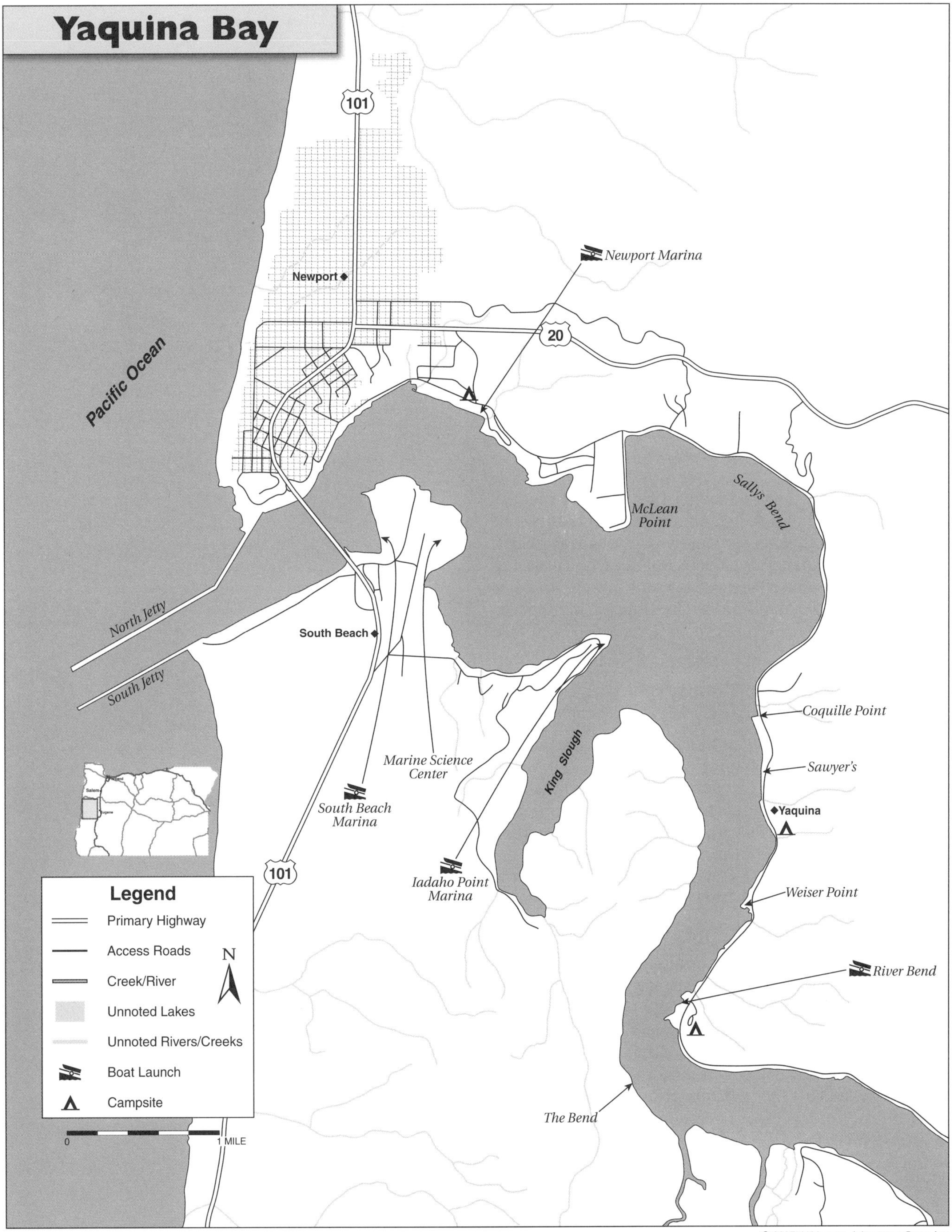
Yaquina Bay
101
Newport Marina
Newport
20
Pacific Ocean
Sallys Bend
McLean Point
North Jetty
South Beach
South Jetty
Coquille Point
King Slough
Marine Science Center
Sawyer's
South Beach Marina
Yaquina
101
Iadaho Point Marina
Weiser Point
Legend
Primary Highway
Access Roads
Creek/River
Unnoted Lakes
Unnoted Rivers/Creeks
Boat Launch
Campsite
N
River Bend
The Bend
0
1 MILE

tide. At low tide, the extensive flats here are usually good for clamming and for collecting mud-shrimp. Bay Road follows along the flats before reaching Sawyer's near "Coquille Point," where you can rent small boats year-round for fishing and crabbing in the bay. The rock structure nearby is a good high-tide bet for pile perch.

From Sawyer's, Bay Road follows the north shore all the way up to the town of Toledo, providing bank access in several places. The upper bay is popular with sturgeon and perch anglers (pile perch) and also offers extensive flats for digging soft-shell clams. This entire reach of the Bay ("The Narrows"), from Sawyer's up to Toledo, provides fair-to-good fishing for fall chinook salmon between late August and late October. On the south side of the bay, boaters troll for salmon in King's Slough. Immediately west of King's Slough, extensive flats behind the Marine Science Center are popular with clam and shrimp diggers. If you have a boat, fish and crab the edge of these flats, along the bay channel, as the tide rises. Perch and flounder feed here, as do sturgeon (spring) and salmon (fall). If you are on foot, you can access the flats here from the Marine Science Center or from Idaho Point: From Hwy 101 south of the bay bridge.

Charters operating out of Yaquina Bay offer a variety of trips for bottomfish, salmon, halibut, and albacore tuna. The halibut and salmon seasons are strictly controlled, so keep a sharp eye on season dates. Book your halibut trip as soon as the dates are announced in the spring. Tuna follow the warm ocean currents, which sometimes reach within 50 miles of Oregon's coast during the summer. Usually tuna trips will take you out 30 to 100 miles, so these trips last at least 12 hours.

Yaquina River (Lincoln County)
boat ramp, boat recommended

Mostly fished in tidewater for fall chinook salmon, the Yaquina River drains into Yaquina Bay at Newport and the river's lower end forms a long arm extending up the bay to the east. The salmon fishing is done mostly by boat from September through November. The bay itself yields far more salmon than the river. The uppermost boat launch is in Elk City and the next is downriver on the way to Toledo at Cannon Quary Park. Additional launch sites are available in Toledo and Newport.

Youngs River (Clatsop County)

Offering some opportunity for salmon and steelhead fishing, the Youngs River is a tributary to Youngs Bay near Astoria. The river offers slow to fair summer and fall catch-and-release fishing for wild cutthroat trout. The lower river, below the first highway bridge, is open to salmon and steelhead fishing at certain times of the year (check current regulations). The upper river is accessible by a network of private logging roads that spur off the Youngs River Loop Road. The loop road accesses Youngs River Falls.

Southwest Zone

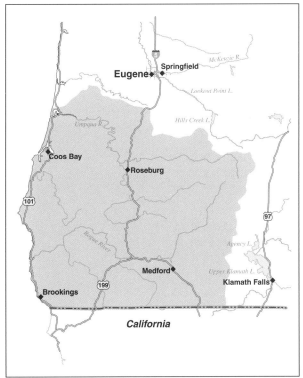

© 2007 Wilderness Adventures Press, Inc.

Oregon's diverse Southwest Zone boasts two of the state's—and the world's—most famous steelhead and salmon rivers. Both the Rogue and the Umpqua Rivers have earned their lofty reputations through decades of providing some of the finest salmon and steelhead fishing in North America and they continue to do so today thanks in a large measure to their own astonishing productivity and to some foresight in fisheries management. These two river systems remain the major draw for anglers in southwestern Oregon, but this corner of the state has far more to offer.

The south coast enjoys comparative obscurity in many ways because it sits a long ways from Oregon's major population centers. This relative isolation means that anglers can enjoy some degree of peace and quiet on the region's salmon and steelhead streams even during the peak runs. Certainly crowds can assemble on prime waters at prime times of the respective seasons, but anglers are equally likely to find runs, pools, and even long stretches of river devoid of competition, especially on the lesser-known flows. Few out-of-the-area anglers have ever cast a line on productive waters like the West Fork Millicoma or Winchuck Rivers, just to name two of the myriad productive waters that are home to fine runs of fall chinook salmon and winter steelhead.

The coastal bounty of southern Oregon is hardly limited to the rivers and creeks draining west from the Siskiyou and Coast Range Mountains. Southern Oregon's port cities—including Brookings, Bandon, Charleston, and others—host sizable charter-fishing fleets for good reason: These rich Pacific waters offer excellent prospects for a wide range of off-shore recreational fishing opportunities. Meanwhile, the beaches, bays, and headlands provide important and productive fisheries for saltwater denizens like rockfish and surfperch, along with seasonal fisheries for salmon and sturgeon.

Of course the Southwest Zone boasts its inland fisheries as well, including the aforementioned Rogue and Umpqua River systems. The latter offers an astonishing array of top-flight fisheries: steelhead, salmon, shad, smallmouth bass, and more. The interior counties also present a diverse array of both coldwater and warmwater fisheries. Some of the state's best prospects for bass and panfish are found in southwestern Oregon and trout fisheries range from well-known waters to remote, lightly fished mountain lakes and streams.

The headquarter communities in southwestern Oregon are as diverse in personality as are the region's waters in fisheries. Key places include Ashland, Medford, Grants Pass, and Roseburg; all situated along the I-5 corridor, which provides ready access to the area, along with the aforementioned coastal towns. But the small, oft-remote hamlets frequently offer better testimony to southwest Oregon's history and flavor. This is a part of Oregon where fishing excursions should include a little extra time to see the sights.

Southwest Zone Contacts:

ODFW Southwest Regional Office
4192 N Umpqua Hwy
Roseburg, OR 97407
541-440-3353

ODFW Rogue Watershed District Office
1495 E. Gregory Road
Central Point, OR 97502
541-826-8774

ODFW, Gold Beach Field Office
29907 Airport Way
Gold Beach, OR 97444
541-247-7605

ODFW Charleston Field Office
63538 Boat Basin Drive
Charleston, OR 97420
541-888-5515

ODFW Brookings Field Office
16217 W. Hoffeldt, Times Square West Complex
Harbor, OR 97415
541-412-7364

Rogue-Siskiyou National Forests
333 West 8th St.
Medford OR 97503-0209
541-858-2200

Rogue River National Forests
Siskiyou Mountains Ranger District, Applegate Office
6941 Upper Applegate Road
Jacksonville, OR 97530
541-899-3800

Rogue River National Forest
Siskiyou Mountains Ranger District, Ashland Office
645 Washington Street
Ashland, OR 97520
541-552-2900

Rogue River National Forest
High Cascades Ranger District, Butte Falls Office
800 Laurel Street
Butte Falls, OR 97522
541-865-2700

Rogue River National Forest
High Cascades Ranger District, Prospect Office
47201 Highway 62
Prospect, OR 97536
541-560-3400

Siskiyou National Forest
Chetco Ranger District
539 Chetco Avenue
Brookings, OR 97415
541-412-6000

Siskiyou National Forest
Wild Rivers Ranger District
200 NE Greenfield Road
Grants Pass OR 97528
541-471-6500

Siskiyou National Forest
Gold Beach Ranger District
29279 Ellensburg Avenue
Gold Beach OR 97444
541-247-3600

Siskiyou National Forest
Wild Rivers Ranger District, Cave Junction Office
26568 Redwood Hwy.
Cave Junction OR 97523
541-592-4000

Siskiyou National Forest
Powers Ranger District
42861 Highway 242
Powers OR 97466
541-439-6200

Siuslaw National Forest
Mapleton Ranger District
4480 Hwy. 101, Bldg. G
Florence, OR 97439
541-902-8526

Oregon Dunes NRA Visitor Center
855 Highway Avenue
Reedsport, Oregon 97467
541-271-3611

Umpqua National Forest
2900 NW Stewart Parkway
Roseburg, OR 97470
541-672-6601

Umpqua National Forest
Cottage Grove Ranger District
78405 Cedar Park Road
Cottage Grove, OR 97424
541-767-5000

Diamond Lake Ranger District
2020 Toketee Reservoir Road
Idleyld Park, OR 97447
541-498-2531

North Umpqua Ranger District
18782 N. Umpqua Hwy.
Glide, OR 97443
541-496-3532

Tiller Ranger Station
27812 Tiller-Trail Hwy.
Tiller, OR 97484
541-825-3201

Bureau of Land Management
Coos Bay District Office
Umpqua Resource Area
Myrtlewood Resource Area
1300 Airport Lane
North Bend, OR 97459
541-756-0100

Bureau of Land Management
Medford District Office – Butte Falls, Ashland, Grants
Pass and Glendale Resource Area
3040 Biddle Road
Medford, OR 97504
541-618-2200

Bureau of Land Management
Roseburg District Office
South River and Swiftwater Resource Areas
777 NW Garden Valley Blvd.
Roseburg, OR 97470
541-440-4930

Oregon International Port of Coos Bay
125 Central Avenue, Suite 300
Coos Bay, OR 97420
541-267-7678

Charleston Marina
63534 Kingfisher Drive
Charleston, OR 97420
541-888-2548

Coos Bay Visitor Center
50 Central Ave.
Coos Bay, OR 97420
541-269-0215

Bay Area Chamber of Commerce
145 Central Ave.
Coos Bay, OR 97420
541-266-0868

Bandon Chamber of Commerce
P.O. Box 1515
Bandon, OR 97411
541-347-9616

Port of Bandon
P.O. Box 206
Bandon, OR 97411
541-347-3206

Reedsport-Winchester Bay Chamber of Commerce
Highway 101 and Oregon 38
Reedsport, OR 97467
541-271-3495

Port of Umpqua
P.O.Box 388
Reedsport, OR 97467
541-271-2232

Port of Brookings-Harbor
16408 Lower Harbor Road
Harbor, OR 97415
541-469-2218

Oregon Coast Visitors Association
137 NE First Street
Newport, OR 97365
541-574-2679

Agate Reservoir (Jackson County)
boat ramp

Located a few miles northeast of Medford and east of the Jackson County Sports Park, 216-acre Agate Reservoir is a fair fishery for a variety of warmwater species including bass, bluegill, and crappie, along with stocked rainbow trout. From I-5, take the SR 62 Exit (Exit 30) and head east and then north to a right-hand turn onto Hwy 140. When you reach the golf club (Stoneridge), turn right onto East Antelope Road and follow the signs down to Agate Lake County Park.

The reservoir also has plenty of yellow perch and brown bullhead, and is stocked during spring, usually in both April and May, with several thousand legal-sized rainbow trout. The reservoir features a lot of riprap structure, which attracts bass and other fish. The steeper shoreline areas adjacent to the dam are good places for bank fishing and, in general, bank fishing is productive with bait or with jigs. A pram, pontoon, or float tube is useful here (no gas motors allowed). If you have a boat or tube, try fishing the brushy shallows on the back end of the reservoir.

Agate Reservoir is open year round and makes a decent, close-to-town place for a little afternoon fishing between November and March. The trout fishing is best during April and May, while fishing for the more abundant warmwater species peaks from May through June and again in the fall. The county park has an improved boat ramp and picnic area.

All Sports Park Pond (Grants Pass)
See Reinhart Park Pond

Alta Lake
see Sky Lakes Wilderness

Applegate Lake (Jackson County)
boat recommended, boat ramp, campground

A varied and productive reservoir near the California border southwest of Medford, Applegate Lake (or Applegate Reservoir) offers good prospects for smallmouth bass, crappie, largemouth bass, stocked rainbow trout, and sometimes stocked chinook salmon. Rarely do the fish here reach trophy size, but respectable bass and crappie are fairly common, while some carryover trout, along with the salmon, reach 16 to 18 inches.

The reservoir draws quite a bit of fishing pressure, along with quite a few campers and hikers. Luckily the fishing can be excellent during May before the crowds begin to assemble for the summer, and during the fall when the crowds disperse. Even during summer, however, the fishing remains consistent. Shoreline access is plentiful and lots of people still fish with bait from the bank. A boat is useful, especially for serious bass and crappie anglers.

The water level is drawn down regularly throughout the spring and summer but, at full pool, the lake spans about 1,000 acres and spreads out into various arms where lots of flooded structure provides ideal habitat for crappie and bass. By late summer, Applegate Lake shrinks to somewhere between 300 and 700 acres. Once the reservoir levels drop, look for smallmouth and crappie holding along rocky drop offs and points, often fairly deep. A fishfinder helps find them and jigs are especially productive.

From I-5, take Exit 33 at Central Point (just north of Medford) and head southwest, following the signs to Jacksonville. Continue south through Jacksonville and down to Ruch. From Ruch, head south on Applegate Road until you reach the reservoir. The road wrapping around the reservoir's western shoreline accesses three campgrounds and two day-use areas. Hart-Tish Campground, the most popular recreation site on the reservoir, offers about ten camp sites, drinking water, flush toilets, a boat ramp (not useable at low water), nice views of the Red Buttes area, and a manicured lawn sloping down to the water. Carberry and Watkins Campgrounds are more primitive, offering 24 tent sites between them. They are located on the far southwest corner of the reservoir (Carberry Arm), where, at high water, myriad flooded trees and stumps provide good bass and crappie habitat.

A second boat ramp is located along the west shoreline, half a mile before you reach Watkins Campground. Also, anglers fishing the lake during fall or winter can use the low-water boat launch (gravel) across the dam at French Gulch. Here a gravel road heads down to the waterline. There are two trailer-size camping sites near the launch road.

The reservoir offers two hike-in/boat-in campgrounds, Tipsu-Tyee and Hart Point, each with five tent spots and both on the Squaw Arm on the west side of the lake. The Squaw Arm is a favorite area for bass, crappie, and trout fishing. To get there by trail, turn left when you reach the dam and follow CR 959 about 3 miles to a right-hand turn on FR 100, leading to the Squaw Arm Parking Area. Hart Point is a short walk down the trail and Tipsu-Tyee lies about 1.5 miles by trail from the parking area. You can access the east-side trail from the south by driving around the west edge of the lake, crossing the Carberry Arm and then turning left toward the Seattle Bar Picnic Area. Continue past the picnic area and follow FR 1041 until it ends at the trail.

Applegate River (Jackson/Josephine Counties)

The Applegate River is an important tributary to the Rogue River. It runs primarily through agrarian lands south of Grants Pass and Gold Hill. The river offers good runs of both hatchery and wild winter steelhead and also gets a few autumn half-pounders in its lower stretch. The hatchery-produced steelhead arrive as early as December, but the season opens January 1 and the run peaks during January and February. The run of wild steelhead peaks during February and March. Only fin-clipped fish may be kept, and that includes both rainbow and cutthroat trout.

Because the river abounds with hatchery steelhead, ODFW frequently must resist pressure from local anglers to extend the fishing season beyond the March 31 closure. However, biologists fear that extending the season would create too

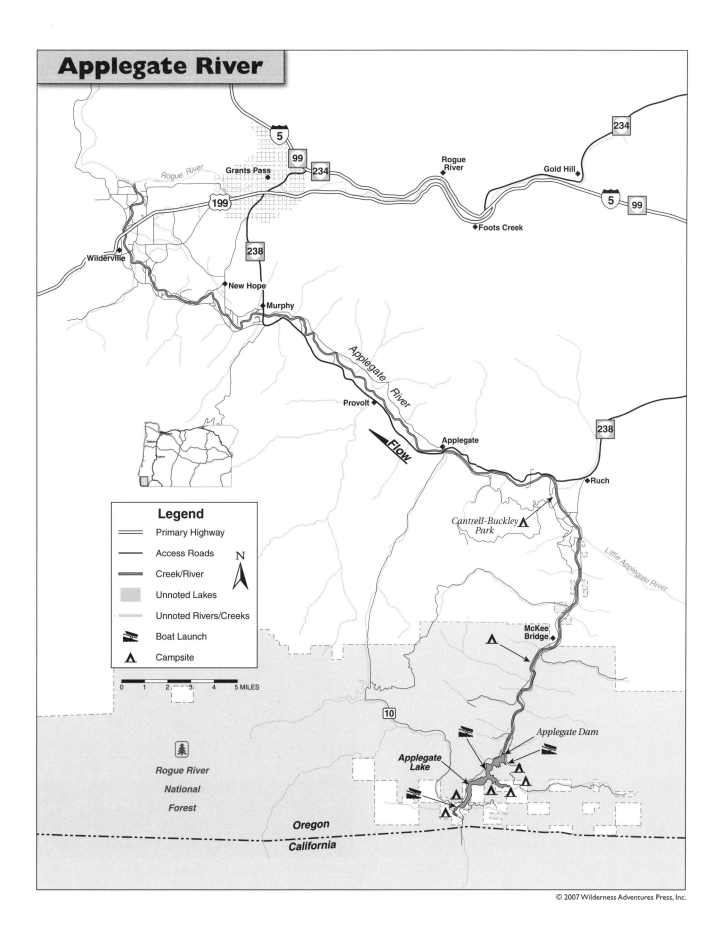

Applegate River

Legend

Primary Highway

Access Roads

Creek/River

Unnoted Lakes

Unnoted Rivers/Creeks

Boat Launch

Campsite

N

0 1 2 3 4 5 MILES

Rogue River

Grants Pass

Wilderville

New Hope

Murphy

Provolt

Applegate River

Flow

Applegate

Rogue River

Gold Hill

Foots Creek

Ruch

Cantrell-Buckley Park

Little Applegate River

McKee Bridge

Rogue River

National

Forest

Applegate Lake

Applegate Dam

Oregon

California

much opportunity for less-than-scrupulous anglers to pursue wild steelhead while the fish are on or near their spawning grounds. Often during April the river gets low and clear enough that spotting such fish is easy. In any event, be sure to consult current regulations before fishing the Applegate.

Applegate Dam is the upstream extent of the steelhead fishery, although most of the angling pressure occurs below the confluence of the Little Applegate River near the community of Ruch. Applegate Road (SR 238) follows the river from Murphy to Ruch. You can reach the Applegate from Grants Pass to the north or from Medford (and Jacksonville) to the northeast. If you're coming from the south, watch for signs to Jacksonville.

Road access to the Applegate is quite good. South of Grants Pass, Fish Hatchery Road (north bank) and South Side Road follow the river west (downstream) from Murphy, where SR 238 crosses the river. West of Grants Pass, Hwy 199 crosses the Applegate about 2 miles above the mouth, providing access to several well-known steelhead pools, including Old Bridge Hole, Slate Creek Pool, and the Tavern Hole.

Upstream from Murphy, there are several popular walk-in access points and several popular pools requiring landowner permission for access. Highway 238 follows the south bank from Murphy to the town of Applegate and then crosses over to follow the river's north bank. North Applegate Road follows the north bank between Murphy and Applegate. About a mile below the mouth of the Little Applegate, Cantrall-Buckley Park is a popular access point and offers several productive pools. The park covers 88 acres and includes 1.75 miles of riverfront. The park has a large, first-come, first-served campground with 30 campsites (no hookups).

Most Applegate steelhead anglers fish with drift gear or bait (fishing for steelhead with bait is currently legal here) and the local area also has quite a few dedicated fly-rod enthusiasts who enjoy consistently good success on the river.

Ashland Creek (Jackson County)
hike-in

A tributary to the Rogue River—and of one of the few such tributaries open to fishing—Ashland Creek is best known because it provides a serene backdrop as it flows through Lithia Park in the town of Ashland. The creek offers fair trout fishing, mostly upstream from the city and is fairly popular with some local anglers. The best fishing for small natives is above Reeder Reservoir, a city water-supply facility in the hills south of Ashland. At the top of the reservoir, Ashland Creek splits into its East and West Forks.

Access is by foot, beginning at the reservoir or off FR 2060, which runs along the ridge above the East Fork, circles around the drainage to the south and then wraps back to the north to Ashland. From the road, you must hike the steep slopes down to the creek, or hike downstream from the road crossings. FR 2060 crosses the upper end of both forks. This route, popular with mountain bikers, is called Lithia Loop, but the road is technically Ashland Loop Road.

From I-5, take Exit 14 and head west into town. Turn right on Siskiyou Boulevard, which becomes Lithia Way. Follow the signs to Lithia Park and from there, head for the south end of the park and take Granite Street along Ashland Creek for about a mile to a fork where Glenview Drive goes to the left. Follow Glenview half a mile to Ashland Loop Road, which becomes FR 2060 after crossing onto the National Forest. The entire loop road is sometimes closed during the summer fire season. Best fishing is between early May and late June and during the autumn. Currently bait is allowed.

Babyfoot Lake (Josephine County)
hike-in

This popular, and easy-to-reach 4-acre lake sits near the edge of the Kalmiopsis Wilderness Area and offers fair fishing for stocked brook trout. The hike covers 1 mile and the lake sits at 4,000 feet. Follow Hwy 199 south of Selma and then turn right (west) on Eight Dollar Mountain Road, which starts as CR 5240 and then becomes FR 4201. Follow the signs to Spur Road 4201-140. Babyfoot Lake's shoreline was severely charred during the infamous Biscuit Fire of 2003.

Black rockfish abound along jetties and rocky headlands on the southern Oregon coast.

Bastendorff Beach (Coos County)

Bastendorff is a good clamming beach and a fair-to-good location for redtail surfperch. Rarely is the beach crowded. Access is from Bastendorff Beach Park located about a quarter mile off the Cape Arago Highway, 2 miles west of Charleston. The county park here has 81 campsites.

Beal Lake

see Sky Lakes Wilderness Area

Beale Lake (Coos County)

hike-in, float tube recommended

Covering 130 acres in the Oregon Dunes National Recreation Area, Beale Lake provides good prospects for naturally reproducing largemouth bass, bluegill, and yellow perch. Access is by hiking in from the trail on Hauser Station Road, just off Hwy 101, 5.5 miles north of North Bend. You can also get there via dune buggy or similar off-road vehicle.

Bear Creek (Douglas County)

see Lake Creek

Beaver Slough (Coos County)

see Coquille River

Ben Irving Reservoir (Douglas County)

boat ramp

Spanning 250 acres at full pool, Ben Irving Reservoir is a large and popular multiple-use recreation destination located southwest of Roseburg and Winston. From I-5, take the Winston Exit (119) and head west through Winston, following SR 42 to the tiny community of Tenmile. At Tenmile, head south and watch for the signs to Ben Irving County Park.

Ben Irving is a good fishery for largemouth bass and stocked rainbow trout. ODFW begins stocking Ben Irving early in the spring and then adds fish regularly throughout the spring. The fishing holds up until hot summer weather sets in to the area. Bass fishing can be very good, especially along the channel and shoreline of the reservoir's westernmost corner, away from the usual water-skiing/water-sports activities in the main part of the lake. The bass run small—usually less than 2 pounds—but they are plentiful. Bluegill and yellow perch also abound and both are typically of modest size.

Big Butte Creek (Jackson County)

no bait

A lengthy tributary to the Rogue River, Big Butte Creek provides fair fishing for wild trout. It reaches the Rogue near Casey State Park, downstream from Lost Creek Reservoir. Access to the creek is limited by lots of private property so in many places, fishing requires landowner permission. There is some access at a few road crossings and sidings and on several parcels of BLM land between Butte Falls and the Rogue River. Currently the creek is open to trout fishing only upstream from Cobleigh Road Bridge. Cobleigh Road heads north from the Butte Falls Highway a few miles west of Butte Falls. Another access to the lower creek is near the town of Butte Falls, off Falls Road near the recycling center: Follow the road past the sewage pond and head down the next dirt road to a day-use area and overlook.

Just west of Butte Falls, the creeks splits into two forks with the North Fork offering better public access upstream from town. The North Fork has wild cutthroat, rainbow, and brook trout, with brookies being more common in the headwaters. There is no limit on the size or number of brook trout taken from the creek. To access the headwaters, you should first obtain a copy of the Butte Falls/Ashland Ranger Districts Map, available from the Rogue River/Siskiyou National Forest office in Medford. Then head east from Butte Falls and turn north on the Butte Falls-Prospect Road (CR 992). The road crosses the creek at the 1-mile mark and then runs parallel to it, at a distance, for 6 miles. Several primitive roads lead east, reaching the creek on BLM land.

East from Butte Falls, the Willow Lake Road (CR 821) follows the South Fork of Big Butte Creek for 3 miles but beyond that, the creek flows almost entirely across private ranch lands.

Bluebill Lake (Coos County)

hike-in, campground

A nice little walk-in pond just north of Coos Bay, Bluebill Lake offers fair-to-good fishing for planted rainbow trout during the spring. The lake usually gets very low by mid-summer, so the best fishing begins just after the pond is stocked in late March or early April (check ODFW's online stocking schedules). You can fish from the bank or by float tube, and a maintained trail leads around the lake's perimeter. Just north of Coos Bay, as you cross Haynes Inlet, turn west on the North Spit Road ("Transpacific Highway") and then watch for a right-hand turn leading to Horsfall Beach. You'll find the parking area and trailhead, along with Bluebill Campground, about a mile before you get to the beach.

Blue Canyon Lake

see Sky Lakes Wilderness Area

Blue Lake (South Blue Lake)

see Sky Lakes Wilderness Area

Boardman State Park (Curry County)

campground

More correctly called the Boardman State Scenic Corridor, this huge state park stretches for 12 miles along the coast north of Brookings. This scenic stretch of the coastline is characterized by rugged, steep headlands and basalt outcroppings interrupted by small sand beaches. This park was named in honor of Samuel H. Boardman, the first Oregon Parks superintendent. He and others of his generation felt this shining green emerald coastline should be saved for the public. Included in the park are stately 300-year old Sitka spruce trees, the amazing Arch Rock and Natural Bridges, and 27 miles of Oregon Coast Trail weaving through lush forests of giant trees.

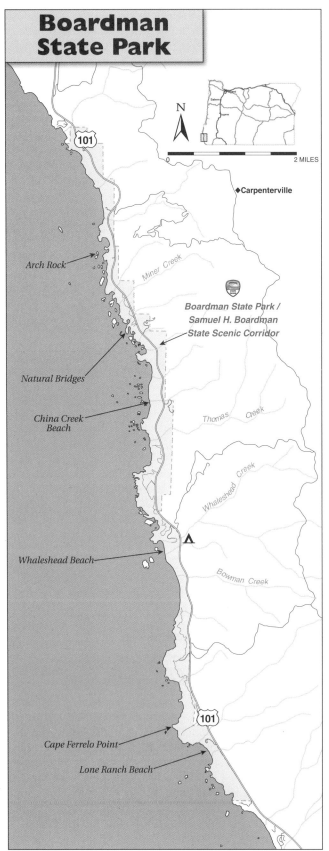

Boardman State Park

N

2 MILES

◆Carpenterville

Arch Rock

Miner Creek

Boardman State Park / Samuel H. Boardman State Scenic Corridor

Natural Bridges

China Creek Beach

Thomas Creek

Whaleshead Creek

Whaleshead Beach

Bowman Creek

101

Cape Ferrelo Point

Lone Ranch Beach

© 2007 Wilderness Adventures Press, Inc.

Boardman Park offers lots of opportunity for saltwater angling. The sand beaches—Whaleshead Beach especially—are best for surfperch and several of them are quite remote, requiring would-be anglers to hike the trail system and sometimes clamber down steep embankments. The rocky coves and rocky beaches offer opportunities for greenling, striped seaperch, and rockfish. A few places—Lone Rock Beach, for example—are very good locations for digging steamer clams.

Lone Rock Beach is fairly popular, but clam diggers are in the minority, as are surfperch anglers, who enjoy consistent success here on early-morning incoming tides. A nice path heads down from the parking area along Hwy 101, about 5 miles north of Brookings. Another smaller and less-visited beach is located just to the north, below the Cape Ferrelo Viewpoint.

Whaleshead Beach is the largest sand beach at Boardman State Park. It offers excellent prospects for redtail surfperch. Try the rocky section to the north for greenling and seaperch. The usual route down to the beach is from the steep trail at Whaleshead Beach Viewpoint along Hwy 101. The easier route, however, is from Whaleshead Beach Road, half a mile further north across from Whaleshead Resort. The next beach to the north is China Creek Beach, another good surfperch location and easily accessible from the highway by way of a trail that is just difficult enough to discourage the usual summer throng of beach enthusiasts. The trailhead is at Thomas Creek Bridge south from the beach.

North from China Creek, the beaches become much smaller and far more difficult to access. At least two of them are low-tide-only beaches. Rocky promontories and headlands in this area are used as fishing platforms by some anglers seeking striped seaperch, greenling, and rockfish. Be extremely careful, however, if you choose to fish these places as they are inherently and frequently dangerous owing to breaking waves and slippery rocks. For additional access details, contact the state park headquarters (800-551-6949).

Bolan Lake (Josephine County)
campground

Located about 30 miles southeast of Cave Junction, pretty little 12-acre Bolan Lake is a round, deep blue natural lake surrounded by dense stands of conifers. The lake is regularly stocked with brook trout and sometimes with rainbow trout, which range from 9 to 14 inches. The fishing holds up pretty well during the warm summers, although many visitors use the lake as a summer weekend swimming hole. All methods produce here and the lake is well-suited to a float tube or raft. Take Hwy 199 south to O'Brien and then head east on CR 5560/55. At the 6-mile mark, the road becomes FR 48. Continue 7 miles and turn onto FR 4812, which leads 4 miles to the lake. The lake offers a small campground and is accessible by mid-May.

Bradley Lake (Curry County)

boat ramp, boat or float tube recommended

A nice little stocked-trout lake south of Bandon, Bradley Lake is a consistent producer, especially during spring and early summer. Sand dunes protect the lake from the full force of coastal winds, making Bradley a good place to hunker down in a boat or float tube when the wind gets bad on other nearby lakes. The boat ramp is a rather rugged but serviceable affair and you'll want a boat or float tube here. The lake sits on the south end of Beach Loop Drive, 3 miles south of Bandon.

Briggs Creek (Josephine County)

closed waters

Brookings-Harbor (Curry County)

see Chetco Bay

Brush Creek (Curry County)

Brush Creek is a small stream running through Humbug Mountain State Park, a few miles south of Port Orford. The creek supports a small run of wild winter steelhead along with a few hatchery fish. The open season, for hatchery steelhead only, runs from November 1 through March 31, although few steelhead make their way into the creek before Christmas most years. The stream is closed to all angling between April 1 and October 31. The state park includes a campground and access to the lower end of the creek is good within the state park. All tributaries are closed to angling.

Buckeye Lake (Douglas County)

see Cliff Lake

Bullards Beach (Coos County)

campground

A popular tourist attraction located across the Coquille River from Bandon on the south coast, Bullards Beach is a fair-to-good surfperch location and also kicks out an occasional striped bass. This beach offers plenty of elbowroom, especially if you fish during the early morning hours; the closer to dawn, the better. Incoming tides are best here, with the first two hours of the rising water being ideal, especially when the ebb tide reaches peak low about an hour before sunrise.

Immediately to the north, Bullards Beach transitions seamlessly into the 5-mile-long Whiskey Run Beach and this entire stretch of coastline, from the mouth of the Coquille at Bullard's Beach State Park north to Whiskey Run County Park, offers excellent surf-fishing opportunities. The state park offers a very large campground and 185 sites with full hookups, a horse camp with 7 miles of trail, and plenty of beach access.

From Hwy 101 north of Bandon, turn west at the wide spot called Bullards. The signed road leads to the state park. The road to Whiskey Run Beach is 7 miles north from the turnoff to Bullards Beach.

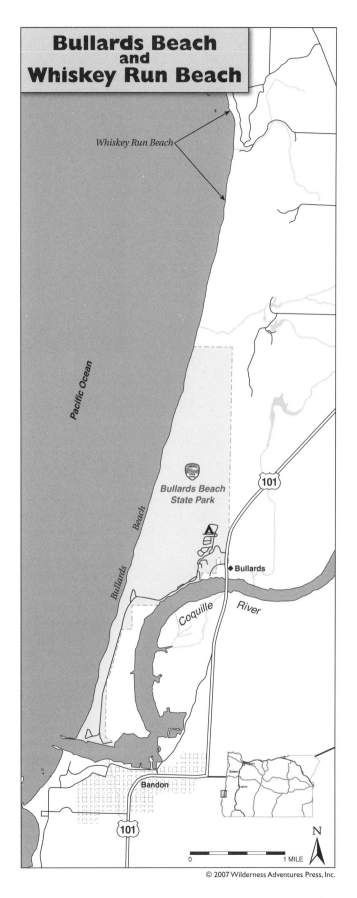

Bullards Beach and Whiskey Run Beach

© 2007 Wilderness Adventures Press, Inc.

Bullpup Lake (Douglas County)

This quiet little mountain lake, situated in the Calapooya Mountains between the Middle Fork Willamette drainage to the north and the North Umpqua drainage to the south, offers fair to good fishing for stocked brook trout, which can reach a foot long. A float tube is very useful, especially for fly fishers, owing to the brushy, tree-lined shoreline. You will want the Umpqua National Forest map to hike to Bullpup, which is accessible by mid-summer (the lake appears, but is not named, in the Oregon Atlas & Gazetteer by DeLorme Mapping, so the national forest map is needed). The Steamboat Creek Road, Forest Road 38, gets you to the area (follow Oregon Highway 138 past Steamboat Inn on the North Umpqua and before you cross the bridge over the river, turn left on FR 38), but be sure to consult the map to get to the trailhead (there are several approaches).

Sand beaches along the southern Oregon coast provide excellent fishing for redtail surfperch.

Burma Pond (Josephine County)

campground

Located about 8 miles east of the historic community of Wolf Creek (north of Grants Pass and south of Roseburg), Burma Pond is a fairly popular, wooded 4.5-acre pond regularly stocked during the spring with legal-size rainbows. The pond also has smallmouth bass and is sometimes stocked with surplus steelhead. A good trail encircles the lake, but the easiest bank fishing is from the dam. Because of the brushy shorelines, a float tube or raft is handy here (motors are prohibited). The site features a series of designated campsites and a vault toilet.

From Roseburg, exit the freeway at Exit 78 (Speaker Road) and head east on Speaker Road for about 4 miles to the end of the pavement and then about 3 more miles to a right-hand turn on BLM Road 33-5-15.2. Follow this road about half a mile until it ends at the parking area. From Grants Pass, exit the freeway at Exit 76 and turn left under the freeway and then right into Wolf Creek. Follow the frontage road to a right-hand turn on Speaker Road and head east 4 miles to the end of the pavement and then another 3 miles to a right-hand turn on BLM Road 33-5-15.2 leading to the pond. This road is steep and 4-wheel-drive vehicles are recommended.

Butterfield Lake (Coos County)

A large coastal lake in Coos County, Butterfield Lake lies entirely on private property with no public access.

Bybee Creek (upper Rogue drainage)

see Rogue River, Forks

Calamut Lake (Douglas County)

hike-in

A pretty and productive trout lake usually stocked with rainbows or brookies located high in the Cascades in the northeast corner of Douglas County, Calamut Lake is capable of producing plump fish to 15 inches, though the typical catch is about 9 inches. Calamut Lake spans about 18 acres and its much smaller neighbor, Lake Linda, is also stocked, most recently with rainbow trout. Lake Linda lies at the trailhead, 1.5 miles south of Calamut. Lake Charline sits alongside the trail half a mile south of Calamut and is not stocked. To reach the trailhead, follow Hwy 138 about 75 miles east from Roseburg to a left-hand turn on Windigo Pass Road (FR 60). After 6.5 miles, turn left on the Kelsay Valley-Calamut Loop Road and continue 2 miles to a right-hand turn on FR 6000-740. The trail is at the end of the road. These lakes are infamous for their mosquito production. Calamut sits at almost 5,900 feet and is usually accessible by mid-June.

Calapooya Creek (Douglas County)

no bait

A surprisingly decent wild trout stream making a circuitous journey through private lands in Douglas County, Calapooya Creek reaches the Mainstem Umpqua River at the hamlet of Umpqua. Interstate-5 crosses the creek just north of Sutherlin and during summer offers a tantalizing glimpse of a creek bestowed with good cutthroat trout habitat. The best trout populations occur upstream (east) from I-5, where CR 19 (take Exit 136 at Sutherlin and head straight through town eastbound) follows the creek into the foothills. Once you leave the valley, the creek flows through private timberlands and the road is usually gated upstream from the old railway signal station called Hawthorne. Access is entirely by landowner permission, but such permission is worth seeking, especially for locals. Currently the trout season here is open from late May through September 15, but check the current synopsis for details on tributary streams to the Mainstem Umpqua River.

Canton Creek (North Umpqua drainage)
closed waters

Cape Blanco State Park (Curry County)
see Elk River

Carberry Creek (Jackson County)
campground

Carberry Creek feeds into the southwest arm of Applegate Reservoir and provides generally slow-to-fair fishing for small, wild cutthroat and a few rainbows. Current regulations allow for a 2-per-day trout bag limit with a minimum size of 8 inches. Carberry produces a few keeper-sized fish, especially if you get away from the road as much as possible. Best fishing is during early summer and autumn. FR 10 follows most of the creek upstream from the reservoir.

Carey Lake
see Sky Lakes Wilderness Area

Castle Creek (Rogue River drainage)
see Rogue River, Forks

Catching Slough (Coos County)
see Coos River

Chetco Bay (Curry County)
boat ramp, campground, services, charters

The narrow bay where the Chetco meets the Pacific boasts one of the calmest, easiest bar crossings on the Oregon coast. Served by the Port of Brookings-Harbor, Chetco Bay houses both commercial and recreational ocean fishing vessels. Charter boats here enjoy consistently good success on both salmon and bottomfish. Sometimes tuna come close enough to shore to allow long-distance runs to the blue water in pursuit of them. The port facilities include everything you need if you have your own seaworthy craft. Call the port offices for a list of charter operators, local tackle shops, and for information about launching and docking private craft (541-469-2218).

A public pier is available for crabbing and fishing. Anglers sometimes get in on good fishing for striped seaperch from the pier, along with a mix of other species. Generally, however, fishing from the jetty is the better bet. Striped seaperch, black rockfish, blue rockfish, greenling, and a few lingcod are taken regularly from the jetties. Brookings enjoys a mild winter climate and during dry spells (when the bay water is clear), fishing can be very good between January and April. During spring, redtail surfperch join the list of species caught here.

Crabbing can be good on incoming and high slack tides from the public pier and also very good just outside the harbor if you're equipped with a seaworthy boat and the proper crabbing gear. Also, the beach immediately south of the south jetty produces good surfperch catches from time to time, usually during early morning incoming tides from March through June.

A large RV park (Beachfront RV Park, 541-469-5867) offers full and partial hook-up sites, camping sites and other amenities and is located immediately adjacent to the beach. During summer, when the beaches here fill with tourists, be sure to fish the surf at first light. The Brookings-Harbor area offers a wide array of options for dining and lodging, but if you're headed to the south coast during the busy summer tourist season, be sure to reserve motel rooms well ahead of time.

Chetco River (Curry County)
boat ramp

Amongst Oregon's most productive coastal salmon streams, the 52-mile-long Chetco River reaches the Pacific at Brookings-Harbor, just north of the California border. The Chetco boasts a sizeable run of fall chinook salmon, which enter the system between August and November. The salmon run usually peaks in September, sometimes October. The river's lower reaches have long been popular with fly anglers, who generally anchor prams in the river and fish sinking lines. The pram fishery can get crowded enough that ill behavior occurs from time to time.

Gear anglers generally fare better than fly anglers and the Chetco enjoys a widespread reputation for producing some of the state's largest salmon. A 40-pound chinook is hardly worthy of mention on this river and each year anglers take a few fish weighing between 50 and 60 pounds. Later, from December through March (the season closes March 31), native winter steelhead arrive in good numbers and some of these fish will push the 20-pound mark. Current south-coast regulations allow anglers to harvest one wild steelhead per day and five per season. The Chetco also receives a conservative stocking hatchery winter steelhead, totaling about 50,000 smolts annually.

With it's headwaters protected in the Kalmiopsis Wilderness, the Chetco drainage, while certainly degraded to some degree, is in better shape than the nearby Sixes, Elk and Pistol rivers. In fact, it ranks among the cleanest and most pristine coastal rivers in the state. Consequently the Chetco is generally slower to flood out and faster to drop back into shape following heavy winter rains. It can drop a foot in a day. Bank and boat angling are equally popular here and the river offers some productive and well-known access spots where plenty of salmon and steelhead are landed from shore.

The most popular stretch for salmon is the lower river (some 8 river miles). Popular bank-fishing spots include

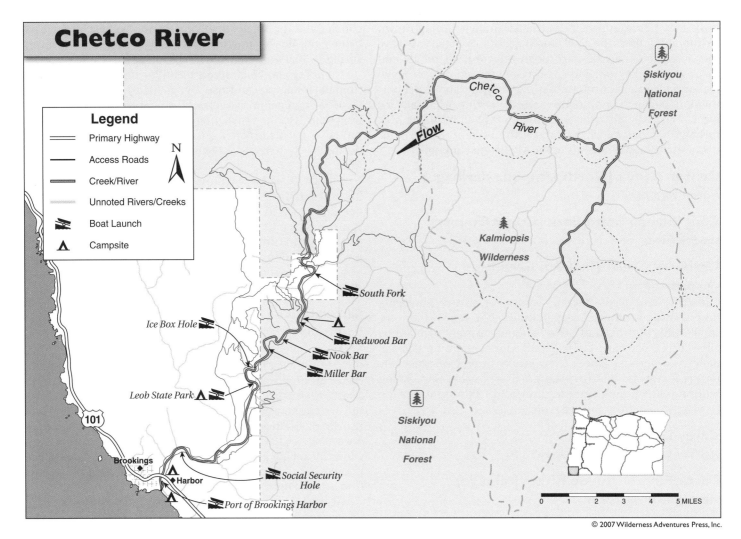

Chetco River

Legend

— Primary Highway
— Access Roads
— Creek/River
— Unnoted Rivers/Creeks
🛥 Boat Launch
Λ Campsite

N

Siskiyou National Forest

Chetco River

Flow

Kalmiopsis Wilderness

South Fork

Ice Box Hole

Redwood Bar

Nook Bar

Miller Bar

Leob State Park

Siskiyou National Forest

101

Brookings

Harbor

Social Security Hole

Port of Brookings Harbor

0 1 2 3 4 5 MILES

© 2007 Wilderness Adventures Press, Inc.

Loeb State Park (8 miles upriver), Social Security Bar (about a quarter mile west of Riverside Market on North Bank Road), and Ice Box. All three spots are signed and easy to find. Expect lots of company at Ice Box, Social Security Bar, and Loeb during the steelhead season and even more during the salmon season. The lower river (basically the river downstream from the high bridge a mile above Loeb Park) offers additional informal access points if you look carefully, but private property dominates, so always ask permission to fish when in doubt.

Boaters often launch at Loeb State Park (8 miles upriver on North Bank Road) or at the cobblestone bar below the high bridge just upstream from the park, and take out at Social Security Bar. The state park includes a campground and ample bank access (not to mention a very good steelhead run). On the South Bank Chetco Road, about a mile east of the highway, an RV Park (popular with traveling salmon anglers) allows easy access to the river. (At River's Edge RV Park, 541-469-3356). Anglers, especially those seeking winter steelhead, can enjoy first-class accommodations and meals well upriver at Chetco River Inn (between Low Water Crossing and South Fork) (www.chetcoriverinn.com, 541-251-0087).

Some steelhead anglers prefer to float the somewhat more challenging upper drifts on the Chetco. The uppermost launch is at about river mile 18 at Low Water Crossing (look for a road dipping off to the left of the main road, Forest Road 1376, with a sign for the Chetco Gorge Trail); next, a couple miles downstream, is a launch site called South Fork, located at the mouth of the South Fork of the Checto. A popular takeout for these upper launch sites is the broad coble bar ("Redwood Bar") at Little Redwood Campground (about 7 miles upstream from Second Bridge, the high bridge upstream from Loeb Park, and 14 miles above Highway 101). Little Redwood also makes a nice launch site for the drift down to Loeb or the takeout below Second Bridge. Two additional launches are located below Little Redwood, but above Second Bridge/Ice Box, these being Nook Bar and then Miller Bar. Note that all the launches on the Chetco are basically unimproved cobblestone bar sites, and the upper launches (Low Water Crossing and South Fork) often require four-wheel-drive. Forest Road 1376, upstream from Loeb Park and across Second Bridge, provides fair access to the river as it runs through the Siskiyou National Forest and through private lands. The river itself is public, but in many places private ownership of bank-side property limits access and in many other places, steep hillsides make reaching the river difficult or perilous or impossible.

Low Water Crossing marks the uppermost limit for boat access, but some 6 miles upstream, "steel bridge" crosses the river and a very rugged road turning left past the far side of the bridge leads a short distance downriver, but really offers little in the way of access to steelhead water. Some anglers also hike down from the south side of the steel bridge, a route that leads to better steelhead water than trying the north bank, across the bridge.

Midway between steel bridge and Low Water Crossing is Chetco Gorge, a very scenic stretch of river accessible only by hiking. The trick, during winter steelhead season, is reaching the trail, which runs along the far bank from Low Water Crossing, thus requiring anglers to first wade the river (at a broad tailout a few hundred yards upstream from the old bridge pilings), and then hike several miles upstream. Obviously this is impossible unless the river is running rather low. Reputedly there are one or two bushwacking routes off the forest road and into the gorge, but I don't know where they are and likely wouldn't pinpoint them if I did! Without knowing these routes, trying to drop into the gorge from the road could be extremely dangerous.

Searun cutthroat provide a third fishery on the Chetco and fishing for them can be very good at times, mostly on the lower river from the North Fork down to Highway 101. Cutthroat enter the river as early as late July in the event of a lucky summer rain storm. Otherwise, look for them after the first freshet, with the run continuing into late October.

Clear Lake (Coos County)
closed waters

Clear Lake, a 300-acre lake adjacent to Hwy 101 south of Reedsport, serves as the city water reservoir and is closed to public access.

Clear Lake (Douglas County)
closed waters

Clearwater River (Douglas County)
see Lake Creek

Cliff Lake (Douglas County)
hike-in

One of a pair of small, productive, lightly fished hike-in brook trout lakes on the upper South Umpqua watershed. The other is Buckeye Lake, just to the northwest of Cliff. Both lakes sit about 1.5 miles southwest of much larger and more popular Fish Lake in the 33,000-acre Rogue-Umpqua Divide Wilderness Area.

The lakes are fishable from the shore, although fly anglers will find a float tube to be a very useful accessory. Brook trout in these lakes range from 6 to 15 inches. In years past, both lakes have produced an occasional 3-pound brookie, but these are few and far between. Most of the fish average about 10 inches.

Both lakes sit at about 4,300 feet. To reach the trailhead, take the Tiller-Trail Highway from I-5 at Canyonville east to Tiller and then head east on the South Umpqua Road (FR 28). Follow FR 28 to a right-hand turn on FR 2823 and then a right-hand turn on FR 2830. Follow FR 2830 for 3 miles to a left-hand turn on Spur Road 600 and follow this road until it ends at the trailhead. From here, the hike to the lakes covers about 2 miles. Both lakes have some nice camping spots. You can fish these lakes in conjunction with Fish Lake, just 2 miles distant by trail.

Cliff Lake
see Sky Lakes Wilderness Area

Cooper Creek Reservoir (Douglas County)
boat ramp, boat recommended

A heavily fished warmwater and trout reservoir near Sutherlin, Cooper Creek Reservoir is locally renowned for its big bluegill and largemouth, along with rather abundant crappie. Each spring the reservoir is stocked with lots of legal-size rainbow trout (more than 10,000 annually) and the trout fishing usually holds up until about mid-May. The warmwater species enjoy plenty of ideal habitat in the arms and coves of the reservoir, especially along the lengthy south shoreline. A trail follows the banks, but access is easier by boat because of the reservoir's steep banks.

Cooper Creek Reservoir is equally popular with water skiers and pleasure boaters, hence the regulation discouraging fishing and swimming at the boat ramps, but you can

A bluegill from Cooper Creek Reservoir near Sutherlin.

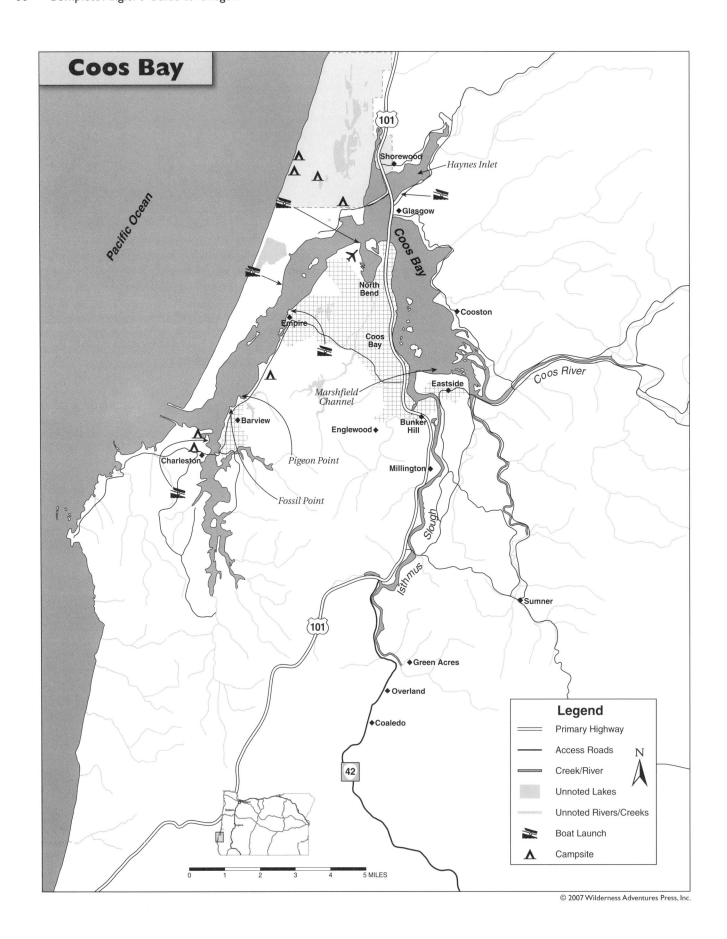

Coos Bay

Pacific Ocean

101

Shorewood

Haynes Inlet

Glasgow

Coos Bay

North Bend

Cooston

Empire

Coos Bay

Eastside

Coos River

Marshfield Channel

Barview

Englewood

Bunker Hill

Pigeon Point

Millington

Fossil Point

Charleston

Isthmus Slough

Sumner

101

Green Acres

Overland

42

Coaledo

Legend

Primary Highway

Access Roads

N

Creek/River

Unnoted Lakes

Unnoted Rivers/Creeks

Boat Launch

Campsite

0 1 2 3 4 5 MILES

© 2007 Wilderness Adventures Press, Inc.

escape the boating crowd by fishing the arms, including the Cooper Creek inlet on the far southeast corner. The city of Sutherlin holds hydroplane boat races here on Labor Day Weekend—a good time to avoid the reservoir.

Although never abundant, largemouth reach at least 7 pounds in Cooper Creek Reservoir and bluegill typically range from 5 to 8 inches in length, with a few bruisers reaching 10 inches. Crappie range from 6 to 12 inches and can provide fast and furious action when you locate a school holding off a point, along the face of the dam or around submerged structure in the coves. In recent years, ODFW has added several hundred of its trophy-size rainbow trout to the reservoir each spring, along with a liberal allotment of legal-size trout. Free fishing events are held here each June (contact ODFW for dates and specifics).

The reservoir is restricted to day-use only and has two nice picnic areas. Largely timbered slopes surround the impoundment, but the forest products company that owns most of the timber has scheduled quite a bit of clear-cutting on the drainage. Still, Cooper Creek Reservoir is an attractive and productive fishery most of the year. During the heat of summer, the trout fishing tapers off substantially, but you can usually find good warmwater action by boat. When the summer algae bloom occurs, probe the depths for crappie by casting jigs along the steep drop-offs on the south end of the reservoir.

Both of the picnic areas have a good boat ramp, along with drinking water and flush toilets. From I-5, take the Sutherlin Exit (Exit 136) and head east through town on Central Avenue. Turn right on Southside Road and follow the signs to the reservoir.

Coos Bay (Coos County)
boat ramp, services, charters

A large and long-industrialized bay on the south-central coast, Coos Bay has historically served as one of Oregon's most important ports. The bay's vast reaches offer a wide array of fisheries, the most popular of which is the fall run of chinook and coho salmon. Sturgeon, striped bass, saltwater fishes, and crabs are also significant.

Geographically speaking, the fishing begins at the bay's mouth, where rock jetties provide ideal and productive habitat for black rockfish, blue rockfish, greenling, lingcod, striped seaperch, cabezon, and a variety of other species. Additional submerged "reefs" are located inside the mouth of the bay and they, along with myriad pilings and docks, provide good fish-holding structure primarily accessible by boat. Charleston Marina is the launch point for fishing excursions into the lower bay. To reach the popular and productive south jetty, park in Bastendorff Beach County Park and walk out the jetty. Also, the community of Charleston has a nice public fishing and crabbing pier.

The north jetty is more difficult to access and requires a rather long walk from the end of the road at the Trans Pacific Parkway: From the north end of the Bay Bridge (north of Coos Bay and North Bend) turn west, crossing over the mouth of Haynes Inlet and then follow the road southwest, past the large industrial pond. You can also boat over to that side of the bay from the Empire public ramp off the west end of Newmark Avenue.

Naturally, fishing and crabbing in Coos Bay is best for those who have a boat, but don't let that fact deter you. The public piers and other access points can produce excellent catches of crabs, various species of surfperch, rockfish, and even striped bass and salmon. There are several public ramps available for those who do have a boat, which opens up countless opportunities for fishing, crabbing, and even clamming. The relatively new Eastside Ramp provides excellent and immediate access to the ever-popular fall salmon fisheries at Isthmus Slough and Marshfield Channel, both located on the east side of the community of Coos Bay.

For clamming and crabbing, boaters can take advantage of the vast sand and mud flats surrounding the bay. Make sure you know and understand the tidal movements within the bay or you risk stranding a boat on the flats. Popular clamming spots in the lower bay include the so-called Clam Island flats immediately adjacent to the edge of the north spit, and easily accessible from the ramps at Charleston and Empire. On the city side of the lower bay, clammers often congregate on the flats at Pigeon Point and Fossil Point, both located about a mile up bay from Charleston.

In addition to productive fisheries for salmon, bottomfish, perch, clams, and crabs, Coos Bay is also home to a modest run of shad and a marginal, but fishable population of striped bass. The bass can show up anywhere, though the Coos River itself has long been a popular venue. In recent years, anglers have discovered fair prospects for stripers along the beaches adjacent to the jetties at Coos Bay. Also, the lower bay attracts huge influxes of baitfish—mostly herring, smelt, and sardines—and anglers jig them from the piers and docks at Charleston and by boat outside the marina complex.

Coos River (Coos County)
boat recommended, boat ramp

The Coos River proper begins at the confluence of the South Fork Coos and Millicoma Rivers, after which the river runs for just a few miles, emptying into the southeast corner of Coos Bay. The river is best known for its striped bass and sturgeon fishing, but also supports a decent shad run during May and June and fair prospects for winter steelhead, fall chinook salmon, coho salmon, and sea-run cutthroat. Access is almost entirely by boat because the banks are private.

Striped bass are hardly numerous these days, but they still provide a viable fishery in the Coos (and nearby waters). Most anglers fish large plugs or baits. Be sure to check current regulations on stripers. Sturgeon anglers do fairly well here and increasing numbers of both chinook and coho salmon have improved the salmon fishing in recent years. The salmon runs begin during August and winter steelhead head upstream between December and March. The Coos floods out quickly and often, so always check water conditions before heading for the river.

The easiest access to the Coos is from the launch at Isthmus Slough (East Side Ramp) on the south side of the bay at the terminal end of Isthmus Slough. To get there, head east across the bridge over Isthmus Slough and then turn left, fol-

Coquille River

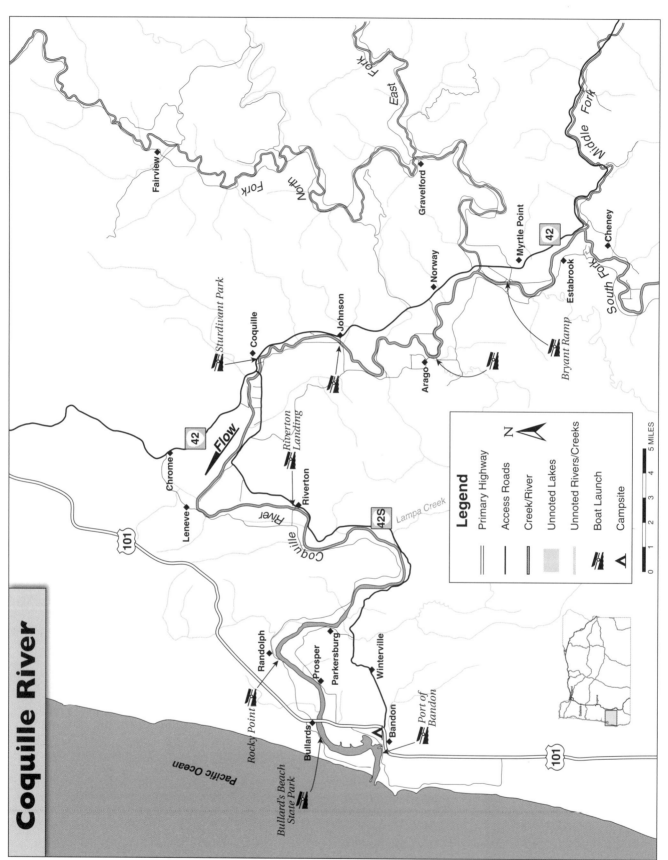

Pacific Ocean

Bullard's Beach State Park

Rocky Point

Randolph

Prosper

Bullards

Parkersburg

Winterville

Bandon

Port of Bandon

101

Leneve

Chrome

101

Flow

42

Sturdivant Park

Coquille

Riverton Landing

Riverton

Coquille River

42S

Lampa Creek

Johnson

Arago

Norway

Bryant Ramp

Estabrook

Myrtle Point

42

Cheney

South Fork

Middle Fork

East Fork

North Fork

Fairview

Graveford

Legend

N

	Primary Highway
	Access Roads
	Creek/River
	Unnoted Lakes
	Unnoted Rivers/Creeks
	Boat Launch
	Campsite

0   1   2   3   4   5 MILES

© 2007 Wilderness Adventures Press, Inc.

lowing the highway north. When the highway heads sharply to the right (east), turn left and follow the signs down to the ramp. Or you can launch upriver on the South Fork Coos (Myrtle Tree County Ramp) or on the Millicoma at Doris Place County Ramp. This is a motorboat fishery—leave the drift boat at home.

Bank-fishing access is available along the highway on the south bank near Catching Slough. Follow the highway past The Gravel Pit and continue north and then east until the road dips down close to the Coos at Catching Slough. Ample parking is available along the road shoulder. Once the road crosses to the north side of the river, it continues to provide ready bank access, but the channel—where the salmon are generally found—runs closer to the south bank. Boaters enjoy the distinct advantage and their abundance testifies to the timing of the runs: Few boats mean few salmon in the river - lots of boats, lots of salmon.

Coos River, South Fork (Coos County)
boat ramp, boat recommended

The South Fork Coos is a fair-to-good salmon and steelhead stream and also supports a good run of shad, a fair run of sea-run cutthroat and a few striped bass. The downfall is lack of public access, so most anglers fish by boat between the county-owned Myrtle Tree Boat Launch and Coos Bay. Fishing for chinook and coho salmon peaks between mid-September and mid-October, while steelhead—mostly of hatchery origin—arrive between late December and March, with the best fishing in January when water levels cooperate.

The Myrtle Tree Launch, one of the busiest ramps in Coos County during the fall salmon runs, is located just upstream from Daniel's Creek on the south bank. From Bunker Hill, on the southern outskirts of Coos Bay, head east and pick up South Coos River Road. Most of the fishing pressure is concentrated from the bay up to Coos River Fish Hatchery, located about 4 miles upstream from Myrtle Tree Launch.

Coquille River (Coos County)
boat recommended, boat ramp

If asked to name Oregon's third largest river system, few people would guess the Coquille River in southern Oregon, yet this productive, multi-pronged river drains an area covering 1,059 square miles. The Coquille River proper—the Mainstem—is actually shorter than its upriver forks, which converge near the town of Myrtle Point. From the confluence of the North and South Forks, the Coquille River winds its way north to the town of Coquille and then slowly makes its way westward, meeting the Pacific at Bandon.

The Coquille is best known for its runs of winter steelhead and fall chinook salmon, both of which provide good fishing, especially for anglers with boats. Public access for bank anglers is very limited, but if you're willing to seek landowner permission, you might gain access to some productive stretches of the Coquille. In any event, most anglers fish the river by boat, trolling or anchoring and casting for salmon and winter steelhead. Currently the Coquille is open to fishing for

fin-clipped coho salmon up to Lampa Creek at river-mile 11.5 south of Riverside. The coho season, which can be quite productive, runs from August 1 through December 31 (be sure to check current regulations).

Chinook salmon show up in the Coquille by August and sometimes as early as late July. The peak season is September through mid-November. During the salmon runs, fishing for sea-run cutthroat can be fair-to-good on the Coquille. Winter steelhead, both wild and hatchery, arrive by mid-December, but the peak of the run is in January and February. Salmon anglers fish as far downriver as the bay itself, which is also a fair bet for crabbing and for marine fish, including striped seaperch, pile perch, black rockfish, and small sole.

Anglers even find fair-to-good prospects for striped bass that prowl the Coquille, including some trophy-class fish. Cast bait or large plugs for them in the sloughs (Hatchet, Iowa, and Beaver Slough), around Johnson Island, and in the channels and edges just about anywhere from Rocky Point to Arago. During dawn and dusk, watch for stripers herding baitfish along the outer edges of the mud and sand flats on the lower river. The Coquille is also home to sturgeon, along with a decent shad run that hits the river during May and June.

The lower end of the Coquille River near Bandon and Hwy 101 provides excellent opportunities for fall chinook salmon and a variety of other fish.

After the autumn and winter rains begin, you can drift the Coquille's upper section between Myrtle Point and the city of Coquille. The drift gets easier as the river gets a little higher during the winter steelhead season. During dry years, the sluggish waters of autumn make for a slow trip. Four good boat ramps are located along this 15-odd-mile stretch of river: Bryant Ramp is located on the South Fork below Myrtle Point; the next ramp is at Arago; Coquille has two county ramps, the most popular being at Sturdivant Park, which is located just off Hwy 42 South on the west end of town.

Most anglers prefer to fish the Coquille by motorized craft, including both outboards and inboards. Motorboats use these same ramps between Myrtle Point and Coquille, along with the ramps on the lower half of the river: Riverton Landing, Rocky Point Ramp, Bullard's Beach State Park, and the Port of Bandon. Rocky Point landing sits along North River Road and the Riverton Landing is just south of Riverton on Hwy 42 South between Bandon and Coquille.

At Bandon, crabbers and anglers enjoy fairly consistent success from the public pier and from the jetties. The Bandon Jetties seem to have solid populations of black rockfish, along with an array of other species, including some greenling and seaperch. The south jetty is the most accessible, being situated at the end of Jetty Road off First Street in Bandon. To reach the north jetty, head for Bullard's Beach State Park and then the Coquille River Lighthouse. The jetties at Bandon take a pounding during periods of rough ocean conditions, so know your tide stages and be especially careful during winter and spring. Bullard's Beach itself is a good bet for redtail surfperch.

Coquille River, East Fork (Coos County)

The East Fork Coquille River is mostly known as a decent winter steelhead producer, but also kicks out a few fall chinook salmon and some sea-run cutthroat. The upper reaches are home to small, native cutthroat (check current regulations). Land ownership is a virtual checkerboard, so access can be difficult in places. From Frona Park, upstream to the ODFW markers at the lower end of Brewster Gorge, the steelhead are mostly wild and available only for catch-and-release fishing. At Frona Park itself, anglers often enjoy good success on hatchery winter steelhead. The runs here peak between early December and about mid-February. From Hwy 42 north of Myrtle Point, the Myrtle Point-Sitkum Road follows the North Fork about 5 miles up to Gravelford and from there the road continues up the East Fork.

Coquille River, Middle Fork (Douglas/Coos Counties)

A trout stream—with modest runs of wild winter steelhead and chinook salmon—the Middle Fork Coquille runs mostly alongside SR 42, the highway crossing the Coast Range between Roseburg and Myrtle Point/Coquille. From I-5, take Exit 119 and head west through Winston and then Tenmile. The highway picks up the river near Camas and then follows it all the way to the confluence with the South Fork Coquille. The highway crosses the river at least 15 times. The river has

a fair population of wild cutthroat trout, which seem to be about evenly—if sparsely—distributed along its entire length. Access is from pullouts and side roads along the highway. The river gets low and warm during summer, so the best trout fishing is during May and June. Upstream from Myrtle Creek (the creek, not the town well to the east), the Middle Fork is closed between mid-September and the end of November to protect spawning salmon. Winter steelhead arrive between late December and late February, with the best fishing on the lower end of the river. The lower river winds through agricultural lands, making access difficult; be sure to seek permission before crossing private property.

Coquille River, North Fork (Coos County)

Like the other forks of the Coquille River, the North Fork has limited bank access owing to ample private property. Nonetheless, the North Fork is a fair-to-good bet for both resident and sea-run cutthroat, winter steelhead, and fall chinook salmon. The steelhead run, which peaks from early January through February, comprises the North Fork's most popular fishery, though in some years the chinook fishing can be very

South Fork Coquille River

productive. However, during other years the river yields just a few dozen salmon during the late October-through-November run.

Currently the salmon-fishing deadline is at the East Fork Coquille confluence at Gravelford, leaving about 8 miles of river available for anglers to pursue chinook here. The most popular access point is at Laverne Falls, where a county park encompasses about a mile of good water. Heed the 200-foot-long closure extending both above and below the falls.

From the town of Coquille, head south about 3 miles to a left-hand turn heading east on Lee Valley Road, and reaching the north fork. Stay left at the Norway-Lee Valley Road and head north along the river to Rock Prairie County Park, one of the public access points. Just to the north, Coquille-Fairview Road heads upstream along the river, reaching Laverne County Park and continuing north and east into the headwaters, which are inhabited by a fair population of small, wild cutthroat trout. Sea-run cutts arrive as early as the first late-summer rains, but fishing for them improves during late September, especially if you can get access to some of the productive private-land sections between Gravelford and Fairview.

Coquille River, South Fork (Coos County)
boat ramp, boat recommended, campground
One of Coos County's best winter steelhead streams, and a fair bet for fall chinook salmon, The South Fork Coquille is a pretty and reasonably accessible river that flows into the North Fork north of Myrtle Point. The South Fork's 50-odd-mile run begins amidst steep forest ridges just north of the Rogue River drainage in the southeast corner of Coos County.

The South Fork enjoys solid runs of hatchery-produced winter steelhead, along with a fair number of natives. Peak season is mid-January through early March. A lengthy section of the river (about 12 miles) from the national forest boundary south to Coquille River Falls, is closed to all fishing. The national forest boundary is about 4 miles south of Powers and the stretch of river between town and the national forest kicks out quite a few native winter steelhead for catch-and-release anglers. Acclimation sites at Beaver Creek and Woodward Creek draw hatchery adult steelhead in substantial numbers, making these areas popular with anglers.

Access to the river is generally fair once you learn the area, with popular bank-fishing areas for plunking and drift fishing located at the mouth of Beaver Creek, at Myrtle Grove State Park and at Powers Memorial State Park. Additional bank access is available along stretches where the river fronts the highway (Powers Road). Watch for pullouts used by bank anglers, especially between milepost 4 and 5.

Boats come in handy and many anglers either float the river or motor up a short section of the lower river. Boat launches are located along Powers South Road at Orchard Park, 2 miles south of the town of Powers; at Baker Creek, 3 miles downstream from Powers; and at Beaver Creek, about 3 miles downstream from Baker Creek. Only the Beaver Creek ramp is paved.

Fall chinook salmon enter the river by September, but the legal salmon-fishing season begins during October, with the peak fishing varying from year to year. Generally mid-October through mid-November is best. The salmon fishing deadline is the Gaylord Bridge on the lower river, about 10 miles north of Powers (no bank access at Gaylord Bridge).

The upper section of the South Fork—a rugged and scenic little mountain river—is currently open to fishing for wild trout, with a no-bait restriction in effect from late May through August. Check current regulations, however, before embarking on a fishing trip here. This part of the river offers good fishing for small cutthroat trout and USFS campgrounds are scattered throughout the reach from Coquille River Falls up to the headwaters at Eden Valley. Forest Road 33 follows the river south from Powers to the falls and then FR 3348 heads east up the river above the falls.

Copeland Creek (Rogue River drainage)
see Rogue River, Forks

Cow Creek (Douglas County)
no bait
Cow Creek cuts a wide, sweeping arc through southern Douglas County, heading in the Cascade foothills southeast of Myrtle Creek and soon reaching Galesville Reservoir. Below the reservoir, Cow Creek continues on a westerly course, catching up with I-5 at Azalea and then running near the freeway for about 8 miles. Then the creek makes a broad, circuitous loop to the north and then back to the east to finally meet the South Umpqua River near Riddle, located along I-5 about 15 miles north from Azalea.

Though access is severely limited by private property, Cow Creek—a significant tributary to the South Umpqua River—offers fair prospects for winter steelhead, smallmouth bass, and small, native cutthroat trout. The steelhead fishery occurs primarily on the lower end of the stream and only hatchery fish may be taken. In general, you'll need to gain access by talking to the landowners. Hatchery steelhead are available from late December through late February. Smallmouth bass occur at least as far upstream as Union Creek and as you drive up the creek, access improves from the road and from several BLM parcels of land located on the creek. The bass fishing is generally spotty and the bass rarely attain much size except on the lower few miles of the creek.

Trout fishing can be quite good on certain sections of Cow Creek. Bait is prohibited during the late-May-through-September-15 trout season (check current regulations). Best trout action (for small, wild cutthroat) occurs in the Middle Creek-to-Reuben stretch and in the headwater reaches above Galesville Reservoir. On both sections, you'll find a mix of public and private land, but access is generally good.

Crater Creek (Rogue River drainage)
see Rogue River, Forks

Crissey Field Beach (Curry County)
Crissey Field is the first beach accessible after you cross the California border coming into Oregon. This beach extends up to and includes the mouth of the Winchuck River—an

excellent clamming spot. Crissy Field is a good—sometimes very good—beach for redtail surfperch, especially during the spring. Check the tide lines for dead sand crabs. When sand crabs are abundant here, so too are surfperch. Access is from Crissey Field State Recreation Area and from Winchuck Wayside, both alongside Hwy 101 south of Brookings.

Denman Wildlife Area Ponds (Jackson County)

A popular location for fishing, waterfowl hunting, and bird watching, Ken Denman Wildlife Area encompasses 1,920 acres along the Rogue River a few miles north of Medford. The area has more than a dozen small ponds teaming with panfish and bass and a few of the ponds are also stocked with legal-size rainbow trout during the spring.

The largest and most popular fishery is Whetstone Pond, located adjacent to the wildlife area headquarters building. In recent years, ODFW has worked to create a special Youth Angling Enhancement Program here, which includes stocking the pond with extra trout in time for spring break. Adults are asked to voluntarily leave Whetstone Pond to the kids during this time period. Like the other ponds, Whetstone also has fair-to-good fishing for largemouth bass and panfish.

To reach Denman Wildlife Area, take Exit 33 from I-5 at Central Point (immediately north of Medford) and head east on Pine Street. Turn left on Table Rock Road and then left on East Gregory Road (watch for the wildlife area signs).

Diamond Lake (Douglas County)
boat ramp, boat recommended, campground, services

For decades Diamond Lake has ranked among Oregon's most revered and productive stillwater fisheries for big trout. The attraction has always been two-fold: excellent fishing for rainbows up to 6 or more pounds and spectacular mountain scenery. In the 1990s, Diamond Lake's fishery suffered the devastating blow of being illegally infested with tui chub. Likely someone transported live chub to the lake for use as bait—in violation of state law—and within a few years in the 1990s, the chub population exploded and the millions of chub ate everything in sight, leaving insufficient forage for Diamond Lake to support its usual dense population of large trout.

This episode was a repeat of a chub infestation in the 1940s, which had similar consequences. Diamond Lake is naturally a fishless lake. The Oregon Department of Fish and Wildlife introduced fish in 1910, which began the economic returns

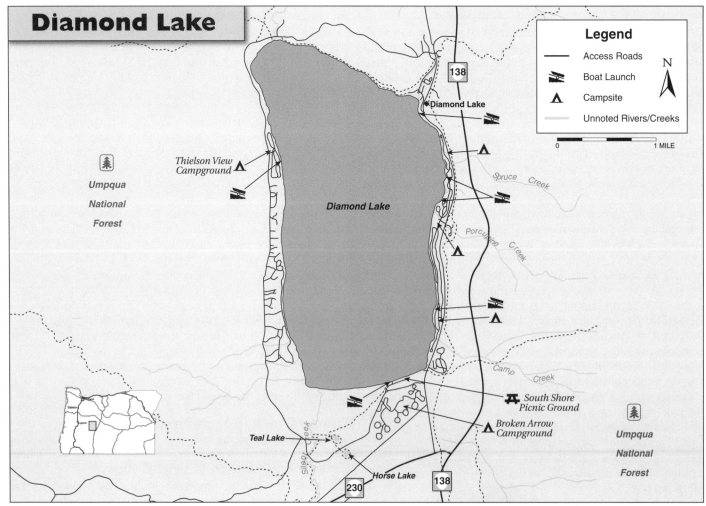

from the lake. But rainbow trout fisheries began to decline in the 1940s when tui chub multiplied. So, in 1954, Diamond Lake was poisoned with Rotenone, killing every living thing in the lake. Because there were few pre-surveys and post-monitoring, it is unknown how devastating this treatment was to the rest of the ecosystem. Nonetheless the re-introduced rainbow trout fared well. For some years afterwards, Diamond Lake enjoyed a boom in recreation dollars and fishing permits, even exceeding 100,000 anglers per year.

With tui chub once again infesting the lake, ODFW decided to stock the lake with Klamath Lake-strain redband trout (sometimes called Williamson River rainbows). These highly piscivorous trout feed heavily on chub in their native range in the Klamath Basin to the south of Diamond Lake. Likewise they

Though it has suffered severely from infestation by tui chub, likely because they were used illegally as live bait, Diamond Lake is poised to return to its former status as one of the region's top fisheries for rainbow trout.

fed heavily on Diamond Lake's tui chub, creating a fair-to-good fishery at the lake until the chub problem was addressed a few years later. ODFW also stocks the lake annually with rainbows from the Desert Springs Hatchery.

Still, the chub infestation showed few signs of slowing down, so the lake was once again chemically treated, and recent seasons have witnessed a return to excellent trout fishing in this popular mountain lake. The lake is now heavily stocked with rainbow trout in a variety of age classes; in 2009 alone, ODFW dumped almost 350,000 fish in Diamond Lake.

Diamond Lake sits at 5,100 feet near the summit of the Cascade Range, between the headwater drainages of the Rogue and North Umpqua River systems. Highway 138 leads east from Roseburg and west from Hwy 97 in central Oregon, passing by Diamond Lake's east shoreline. From Medford, follow the Crater Lake Highway (SR 62) northeast and swing left when you reach SR 230. The lake, which spans about 2,800 acres, is open during the general trout season from late April through October, but some years it doesn't thaw until May. A 10-mph speed limit for boats eliminates any worry over disruption of the lake by water skiers or jet skiers.

All methods produce on Diamond Lake. Still fishing with bait (by boat) has long been a popular method on the lake, but as the chub population exploded, bait fishing became less effective—the chub tend to get at the bait before the trout ever have a chance. Top areas for bait fishing include the so-called Velveeta Hole near the northeast shoreline, the Shrimp Hole on the southwest end and the deep pool near the middle of the lake.

Trollers enjoy consistent success throughout the lake and in recent years, since the ODFW began stocking large rainbows and especially Klamath-strain redband trout into Diamond Lake, trolling with large lures, including Rapalas and similar plugs, has become one of the best ways to hook the lake's largest fish. The Klamath-strain trout reach more than 15 pounds in Diamond Lake and, in each of the past few seasons, anglers have taken quite a few 8- to 12-pound trout.

Fly anglers do well casting nymph and streamer patterns around the drop-offs and along the shallow shoal areas. Traditionally fly anglers converge near the inlets and over the weed beds on the south end of the lake. Small flies tend to attract chub, so until the chub problem is solved, stick to larger patterns, including—of course—chub patterns up to 5 inches long. Hatches of midges and *Callibaetis* mayflies allow for frequent dry-fly action, though the dry-fly fishing now hardly compares to that of the pre-chub days.

The fishing tends to hold up throughout the season except for when the water turns over during mid-summer. Many anglers try to plan their Diamond Lake outing for ice-out, when large trout gather near the feeder streams. During October, when the lake is far less crowded, try the shallow margins of the lake trolling flies or hardware.

Diamond Lake has three Forest Service campgrounds with boat ramps and a total of more than 400 campsites. You can reserve sites by calling the National Recreation Reservation System (877-444-6777) or reserve online at www.reserveusa.com. Advance reservations are available for 174 of the campsites; the remaining 226 sites are first-come, first-served.

Diamond Lake Resort (541-793-3333/www.diamondlake.net) offers myriad services and amenities: tackle shop, general store, café, dining room, pizza parlor, bar, marina, rental boats, charter fishing service, moorage rental, 42 guest cabins, large motel, gas station and more. Diamond Lake RV Park (541-793-3318/www.diamondlakervpark.com) has 160 spaces.

Dutch Herman Pond (Josephine County)

This 2-acre pond east of Wolf Creek offers planted legal-size rainbow trout along with bluegill, bullhead, and a few bass. The pond is stocked during spring, usually in April before the general trout season opens, and fishing for the trout holds up into June. From Roseburg, exit the freeway at Exit 78 (Speaker Road) and head east on Speaker Road for about 4 miles to the end of the pavement and then about 3 more miles to a right-hand turn on BLM Road 33-5-15.2. Follow this road about half a mile until it ends at the parking area. From Grants Pass, exit the freeway at Exit 76 and then turn left under the freeway and then right into Wolf Creek. Follow the frontage road to a right-hand turn on Speaker Road and head east 4 miles to the end of the pavement and then about 4 more miles. Go past the turn-off to Burma Pond (BLM Road 33-5-15.2) and stay right at the next intersection.

Eel Creek (Coos County)

Eel Creek is a tributary of Tenmile Creek and drains Eel Lake, a good stocked-trout lake just south of Winchester and Reedsport. The creek is stocked with winter steelhead smolt and provides a limited fishery for the returning adults between January and late March or early April (the season ends April 30). Access is good and Eel Creek Campground sits near the creek.

Eel Lake (Coos County)

campground, boat ramp, boat recommended, float tube recommended

Located just north of the popular Tenmile Lakes and a few miles south of Winchester Bay, Eel Lake is a consistently good trout fishery and fair warmwater fishery offering largemouth bass and crappie. The lake is regularly stocked with rainbow trout throughout the spring and also has a modest population of wild cutthroat trout. Largemouth bass reach 5 pounds here and average 1 to 2 pounds. They enjoy perfect habitat rich in wood structure, but they never seem to be numerous.

The rainbows, planted at legal size, provide the primary fishery for most anglers at Eel Lake, although a few bass specialists fish the lake regularly. Some of the rainbows carry over in this deep, 350-acre lake and reach 14 to 16 inches. Cutthroat average about 9 inches and a few residualized juvenile salmon are taken by trout anglers. During early spring, Eel Lake kicks out a few fin-clipped steelhead that range from 4 to more than 10 pounds. These fish come from Tenmile Creek and are usually caught near the Eel Lake outlet (Elk Creek) on the south end of the lake.

Eel Lake is difficult to fish from shore, although the public dock is a favorite spot for bank anglers and provides fairly consistent action for trout. The lake's shoreline is steep, brush, and lined with trees, so a boat is the way to go here. Shaped like a big "V," Eel Lake offers two long, narrow arms and both feature lots of shoreline structure and plenty of room to spread out. The launch is at Tugman State Park, which encompasses the lake's entire west arm and features a large campground with more than 100 sites. Watch for the signs along Hwy 101 about 8 miles south of Reedsport.

Elk River (Curry County)

boat recommended, campground

A small, productive salmon and steelhead stream on the south coast, Elk River reaches the ocean just north of Port Orford. The river has a good run of wild winter steelhead that range from 7 to 20 pounds. The 20-pounders are few and far between, but fish to 14 pounds are taken regularly from January through March. The run usually peaks from mid-February through March.

The Elk also offers a very good fishery for fall chinook salmon that enter the river as soon as autumn rains swell the river enough so that it breaches the sand bar that blocks access from the Pacific. Often anglers take more than 1,000 salmon per season from this small river. Most of the kings are of hatchery origin and are produced at the Elk River Hatchery, a few miles below Bald Mountain Creek, which is the angling deadline. During the fall salmon season and into the steelhead season, don't be surprised if you hook a half-pounder steelhead because these 14- to 20-plus inch summer-run fish stray from the Rogue River.

Bank access is limited to just a handful of places on the Elk, including the ever-popular stretch below the hatchery, the access at the Hwy 101 bridge, Ironhead Launch (about half a mile above the bridge), the Culvert Hole about 2 miles below the hatchery, and a few other spots. Many anglers float the Elk rather than rely on the limited bank access. The put-in is at the hatchery and the drift down to the steep, primitive launch at Ironhead. A mid-drift launch is available at the Elk River RV Park (541-332-2255). For anglers unfamiliar with the fishery here, a guide is a big help. Call Todd Hannah, 800-428-8585. One of southern Oregon's most highly reputed guides, Hannah also works on the Rogue, Sixes, and Umpqua Rivers.

At the mouth of the Elk River, the beach is a good bet for redtail surfperch between April and July. It also provides a rare opportunity to fish for chinook salmon in the surf. Staging for their autumn run up the Elk River, the salmon cruise the outer break, with best fishing from October through early November. From Hwy 101 a few miles north from Port Orford, watch for the signs to Camp Blanco State Park. From the state park, you must walk down the beach to find the mouth of the Elk. Or walk north from Paradise Point State Recreation Area, located just west of Port Orford.

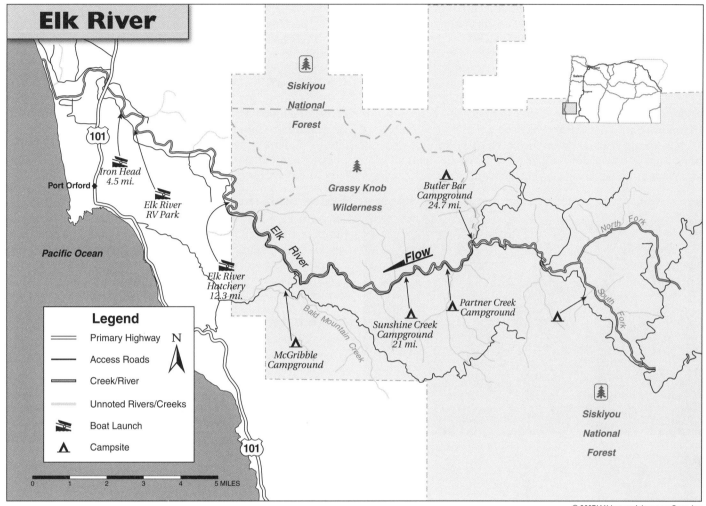

Elk River

Legend

—— Primary Highway

—— Access Roads

—— Creek/River

········· Unnoted Rivers/Creeks

Boat Launch

Campsite

N

0 1 2 3 4 5 MILES

© 2007 Wilderness Adventures Press, Inc.

Emigrant Lake (Jackson County)

boat ramp, campground

An extremely popular, oft-crowded and highly productive reservoir near Ashland, 800-acre Emigrant Lake offers a wide array of gamefish, including stocked trout, smallmouth and largemouth bass, crappie, brown bullhead, channel catfish, and bluegill. All the reservoir's species enjoy popularity with anglers, though in recent years the smallmouth bass and crappie have proven rather numerous. An 8-inch minimum length on crappie is aimed at producing more large fish in the reservoir.

Emigrant Lake is heavily supplied with hatchery rainbows and with land-locked chinook salmon (considered part of the trout catch limit); at times ODFW adds a few surplus hatchery steelhead to the mix. Brown bullhead reach decent size here and can certainly provide plenty of action when things are slow for other species.

Smallmouth thrive along rock structures and typically range from 8 to 12 inches, with a few reaching 3 pounds. Largemouth bass live in the flooded brush on the reservoir's

arms and can reach at least 6 pounds. As the reservoir is drawn down during summer, fish for largemouth bass in the channels and along the numerous points. Emigrant Lake is popular with anglers of all bents. Some people enjoy a relaxing day still fishing with bait from the dam; others hunt bass by boat in the small bays and coves. Even fly anglers, fishing by float tube or pontoon boat, enjoy consistent success.

The reservoir is also very popular with water sports enthusiasts and pleasure boaters, so during the summer, you'll want to fish early and late in the day. Fall and winter fishing can be very good at Emigrant Lake and you'll often find the place comparatively deserted. The reservoir lies just a few miles south of Ashland, just east of (and visible from) I-5. Take Exit 14 and head south, following the signs.

Empire Lakes (Coos County)

Well stocked with rainbow trout, including trophy-size fish, Upper, Middle, and Lower Empire Lakes are large urban ponds located between the towns of Coos Bay and Empire. Newmark Avenue, a main east-west route through town, offers access.

Trophy-size rainbows are generally stocked in the Upper and Lower Lakes and all three lakes also have largemouth bass, yellow perch, bluegill, and bullhead catfish.

The ponds, part of John Topits Park, offer myriad interconnecting trails that provide good access for bank fishing. A small boat, canoe, or float tube comes in handy here and indeed some of the local anglers employ float tubes to get at the productive areas hard to reach from shore. Only electric motors are allowed on boats, which can be launched at Middle Empire Lake or from the beach down from the swimming area at Lower Empire Lake. The lakes are open all year and fishing can be decent during the winter and early spring.

The three Empire Lakes are pleasant and productive fisheries located in the heart of Coos Bay/North Bend.

The various access points to Topits Park include the main entrances on Ackerman Street (Lower Empire) and Hull Street (Middle/Upper Empire), both of which turn north off Newmark Street. Southwest Oregon Community College, which maintains a trail system connected to the park open to the public, is situated on the east side of Middle Empire Lake, providing easy access (also off Newmark Street). On the north side of the lakes, you can gain access via Lakeshore Drive, where parking is available adjacent to Upper Empire Lake and where a side street (Crocker Street) dead-ends and offers parking and access to Lower Empire.

Euchre Creek (Curry County)

A small, attractive coastal stream boasting a fair run of wild winter steelhead, Euchre Creek flows into the Pacific about 10 miles north of Gold Beach. Currently this part of the coast, including Euchre Creek, is open to keeping wild steelhead (one per day/five per year), but check current regulations. Euchre Creek Road follows the creek upstream for several miles.

Expo Ponds (Jackson County)

This series of five small ponds offers fair fishing for stocked rainbow trout and warmwater species ; sometimes ODFW stocks some surplus steelhead. They are located at the Jackson County Expo Center in Central Point. From I-5, take Exit 33 heading east and follow the signs to the expo center, which is located near the freeway.

Finch Lake (Sky Lakes Wilderness)

A remote hike-in lake in the Sky Lakes Wilderness, Finch Lake is no longer stocked with brook trout and the most recent surveys indicate few if any trout remaining in the lake.

Fish Creek (Douglas County)
see Lake Creek

Fish Lake (Douglas County)
hike-in

A very pretty, fairly productive hike-in brook trout and rainbow trout lake, Fish Lake sits at about 3,400 feet on the western edge of the Rogue-Umpqua Divide Wilderness Area. The short 1.2-mile hike makes this a fairly popular summer destination and many anglers pack in a float tube or other small watercraft. The trout usually range from 8 to 12 inches, with a few reaching 18 inches, though these are uncommon.

Forest Primary Route 28 takes you to the area from either the North Umpqua Highway near Eagle Rock Campground to the north, or from Tiller on the South Umpqua River to the west. From Tiller, head up along the South Umpqua until you reach a right-hand turn on FR 2823. Follow FR 2823 to a right turn on FR 2830 and a left turn on FR 2840. Once on FR 2840 continue *past* the Fish Lake Trailhead (unless you prefer a much longer hike) and continue up to the Beaver Swamp Trailhead on Spur Road 400. Total distance from Tiller is about 32 miles. Facilities at the trailhead include parking, a picnic table, fireplace, two vault toilets, information board, and trail signs, but no water.

Fish Lake (Jackson County)
campground, boat ramp

A very popular 483-acre irrigation-storage reservoir high in the Cascades east of Medford, Fish Lake offers consistently good fishing for stocked rainbow trout that reach several pounds, along with some wild brook trout. Most anglers fish bait or troll. The lake sits at 4,642 feet, so the productive spring season starts late in here, usually by late April, and fishing tends to hold up throughout the summer and well into autumn. Some anglers ice fish the lake during January and February and Fish Lake Resort is open Wednesdays through Sundays during the winter. You'll need a Sno-park Permit during winter.

Fish Lake Resort, opened during the 1930s, offers a large RV park, campground, store, café, rental boats and canoes, moorage rental, coin-operated showers and laundry, some rustic cabins, and plenty of free fishing advice. You can reserve boats, campsites and cabins by calling ahead (541-949-8500).

At full pool the lake reaches a maximum depth of 31 feet and averages 18 feet deep. Originally a spring-fed natural lake surrounded by extinct volcanoes and lava flows, Fish Lake was modified and expanded with the addition of a dam to raise the water level to create additional storage capacity. The lake's level drops regularly during the summer. At times over the years, illegally introduced chub have invaded the lake, but thus far ODFW has kept them in check.

Several campgrounds are located at and near Fish Lake, including Fish Lake Campground and Doe Point Campground adjacent to the lodge, along with North Fork Campground, located 2 miles west of the lake on FR 37. Fish Lake Trail provides good walk-in access to much of the lake's shoreline, and popular, easy-to-reach bank-fishing areas are located near the campgrounds and resort and at the dam.

Fish Lake is located alongside Hwy 140, about 33 miles east of Medford and 38 miles west of Klamath Falls. From Medford, follow Crater Lake Highway (SR 62) north from Exit 30 off I-5. A few miles from the freeway turn right onto Hwy 140. Watch for the signs to Fish Lake.

Floras Lake (Curry County)

campground, boat ramp, boat or float tube recommended

Covering about 250 acres, Floras Lake near Port Orford is a fair fishery for stocked rainbow trout. The fish rarely exceed 13 inches and most anglers fish bait. A few fly anglers enjoy some success fishing by float tube or pontoon boat. A few wild cutthroat show up and the lake also has largemouth bass, though they are rather uncommon. Chinook and coho salmon, along with winter steelhead, migrate through the lake in modest numbers and a few are taken in the lake each year (there is currently no open season for Coho). Shoreline fishing is limited to the boat ramp area and a short bank section on the lake's northwest end, so a boat or other craft comes in handy. The boat ramp and public access is at Boice Cope Park. From Hwy 101 just south of Langlois, head west on Floras Lake Road.

Garrison Lake (Curry County)

boat ramp, boat or float tube recommended

A popular 53-acre lake on the western edge of Port Orford, Garrison Lake is a fair-to-good fishery for stocked rainbow trout and sometimes a few cutthroat. A few decent-size large-

mouth bass have inhabited the lake in the past, but an illegal bar breach drained the lake in April of 2002, shortly after ODFW had stocked about 5,000 trout. The large bass are gone and the trout stocking is done on a more conservative basis now, with several hundred fish being stocked periodically throughout the spring. Best fishing is by boat or float tube, but bank access is available at the city park and around the 12th Street Boat Ramp. To reach the park, head west on 18th Street to Pinehurst Drive. Garrison Lake usually offers quite a few carryover rainbows that average about 14 inches and a few 16-inchers show up as well.

Galesville Reservoir (Douglas County)

boat ramp, boat recommended

Little known outside the local area—but popular with Douglas County anglers—630-acre Galesville Reservoir is the county's largest reservoir and one of the best for largemouth bass. This large, clear-water reservoir is literally filled with woody debris, providing perfect bass habitat. The cover is so dense in places that the reservoir can be a tackle eater, but bass as large as 8 pounds make the effort well worthwhile. Best fishing is by boat, but plenty of anglers fish from shore.

Galesville Reservoir also offers bluegill, including a few large specimens, along with crappie and lots of stocked trout. The trout fishing peaks during April and May, when the fish are stocked. In recent years, ODFW has added quite a few surplus recycled winter steelhead to the stocking mix, providing anglers a chance at a surprise in the form of an 8- to 10-pound fish. The lake has also been stocked with trout-sized salmon, which are counted as part of your trout limit. All bass between 12 and 15 inches must be released and anglers may keep only one bass larger than 15 inches per day. Catch-and-release fishing for the bass is a good idea regardless of their size because of the mercury contamination warnings in effect for Galesville's fish.

The reservoir is open year-round, but for day-use only (7:00am to dark). Chief Miwaleta County Park offers a picnic area and boat ramp. You can also launch small boats from the shore on the Cow Creek Arm (electric motors only above the main reservoir), accessed by the county road that follows the north shoreline. To get to Galesville Reservoir, take I-5 to Exit 88 at Azalea and head east on Upper Cow Creek Road. The nearest campground is about 10 miles east on Cow Creek (Devils Flat Campground).

Game Lake (Curry County)

Game Lake is too shallow to support fish, although it is literally swarming with orange-bellied newts. The trail here, however, leads into some very scenic areas of the Kalmiopsis Wilderness Area and eventually down to Collier Bar on the Illinois River.

Glenn Creek (Coos County)

A very scenic cutthroat trout stream and tributary to the East Fork of the Millicoma River east of Coos Bay, Glenn Creek is also the site of two stunning waterfalls. Golden and Silver Falls are well worth the 24-mile drive from Hwy 101. The small parking and picnic area are located along the banks of Glenn and Silver Creeks and are shaded by large maple, alder, and Oregon myrtle trees. Hiking trails wind through scenic canyons to each of the waterfalls. The dramatic falls plunge over sheer rock cliffs to moss-covered boulders 100 feet below. Hike to the top of Golden Falls to get an eagle's-eye view of the cascading waterfall and giant old-growth firs and cedars. The creek has a good population of small, wild cutthroat, with the best fishing available to those who hike up the creek.

Grass Lake
see Sky Lakes Wilderness Area

Grave Creek (Rogue River drainage)
closed waters

Hall Lake (Coos County)
float tube recommended, campground
Located about 10 miles south of Reedsport, Hall Lake is an interestingly little cutthroat trout and largemouth bass pond recently acquired by Oregon Dunes National Recreation Area. Locals use it as a swimming hole during the summer because of the sandy beach on one side. As of this writing, a day-use area is under construction, which will include a picnic area and a network of trails, one of which will lead to nearby Shuttpelz Lake, located just to the north. Hall Lake has decent shoreline fishing possibilities, but a raft or float tube would allow you to fish the flooded snags near the center of the lake. To get there from Hwy 101, turn west on Wildwood Drive, which is located opposite the south end of Tugman State park and Eel Lake. Tugman State Park has a campground and another is located just to the south at Eel Creek.

Harris Beach (Curry County)
Productive for both surfperch and bottomfish, Harris Beach sits just north of Brookings and offers a large state park with ample room for camping. The beautiful beach here features sandy expanses semi-protected by near-shore sea stacks along with rocky stretches and cliff faces home to greenling, rockfish, and striped seaperch. Best fishing is during low-light hours and this beach can be productive at just about any tide level. Choose an early morning or evening incoming tide to fish the sand for surfperch and the occasional sole, both of which will take baits and jigs. Or fish bait along the deeper edges of the sea stacks for seaperch and greenling. Although you're likely to loose quite a few jigs to the rocks, try casting jigs over the rocky areas for black rockfish.

Hemlock Lake (Douglas County)
campground, float tube recommended
Stocked with rainbow trout and sometimes with kokanee salmon, Hemlock Lake is a fairly popular, but quiet 28-acre mountain reservoir nestled in the forest about 33 miles east-by-southeast of Glide. From Glide, turn south on Little River Road (32 miles from Roseburg) and then follow the signs to Hemlock Lake (FR 27). Or from the north, turn south across the North Umpqua River at Apple Creek Campground and follow FR4720 to a right-hand turn on FR2715 to a left-hand turn on FR 27. The lake has a boat ramp (no motors) and is ideally suited to small prams, canoes, and pontoon boats. An Umpqua National Forest Campground here offers 13 sites.

Hemlock Lake (Sky Lakes Wilderness)
A remote hike-in lake in the Sky Lakes Wilderness, Hemlock Lake is no longer stocked with brook trout and the most recent surveys indicate few if any trout remaining in the lake.

Herbert's Pond (Douglas County)
A large, popular pond located on the Tiller-Trail Highway just east of Canyonville and I-5, Herbert's Pond is regularly stocked with legal-size rainbow trout and provides fair fishing throughout the spring. When available, ODFW also stocks the pond with excess hatchery winter steelhead from the South Umpqua River. These fish usually range from 8 to 15 pounds. The pond is also home to largemouth bass, crappie, and bullhead. The crappie range from 6 to 9 inches and the bass are mostly of modest size. Many anglers fish from the bank, but any type of small watercraft can be launched from the shore (no motors allowed). Canyonville is located on I-5, 25 miles south of Roseburg.

Holst Lake (Sky Lakes Wilderness)
A remote hike-in lake in the Sky Lakes Wilderness, Holst Lake is no longer stocked with brook trout and the most recent surveys indicate few if any trout remaining in the lake.

Hoover Ponds (Jackson County)
Primarily used by dirt bike and off-road vehicle enthusiasts, Hoover Ponds is a collection of half a dozen small impoundments in Hoover Ponds County Park north of Medford. The ponds contain largemouth bass, bluegill, brown bullhead, and crappie, and fishing can be fair, but get there early in the morning on a weekday to avoid the dust and noise stirred up by the ORV crowd. From Medford, take Hwy 62 (Crater Lake Avenue) heading north and then turn right onto Hwy 140 and head east about 2 miles to the parking area.

Horseshoe Lake
see Sky Lakes Wilderness Area

Horsfall Beach (Coos County)
A good surfperch beach and also known to produce an occasional striped bass, Horsfall Beach lies north of the North Spit at Coos Bay. On Hwy 101 north of North Bend, head across Haynes Inlet and turn west towards North Spit. Then turn right at the signs to Horsfall Beach. Three campgrounds are available along the road. Between April and July, try fishing the beach at dawn for surfperch and then head for Horsfall Lake to fish for largemouth bass.

Horsfall Lake (Coos County)

hike-in, campground

More or less a sleeper, Horsfall Lake can be a very good fishery for largemouth bass up to several pounds. This sprawling, shallow dune lake sits just north of Coos Bay in the Oregon Dune National Recreational Area. Access is by foot or off-road vehicle. You can carry in a small raft, float tube, or pontoon boat, but the lake is pretty easy to wade, so a few of the regulars here just carry a pair of waders in to the lake and wade around casting to likely areas. Some years the water gets very low, but the bass seem to survive the late summer just fine and then bounce back in numbers when two or three consecutive high-water years occur.

Horsfall is lightly fished and provides ample room for anglers to spread out. The bass here, most of which weigh less than 1.5 pounds, are fairly abundant during good years and you might well catch several dozen of them during a day. The fishing peaks from mid-spring through mid-summer, but can be good even during winter with jigs fished slowly around structure. When the water warms during late springs, try top-water baits and plugs or cast popping bugs with a fly rod.

South of the lake is a campground and picnic area. You can ride or hike in beginning near the picnic area, but it's actually a shorter hike/ride from the trailhead area at Bluebill Lake just to the west. A few anglers use off-road vehicles to carry in small car-topper-type boats and small prams. From Hwy 101, as you cross Haynes Inlet of Coos Bay, turn west on the road out to the north spit and then turn right on the road to Horsfall Beach.

Howard Prairie Lake (Jackson County)

boat ramp, campground, services

Extremely popular with anglers and boaters from southern Oregon, Howard Prairie Lake (actually a reservoir), sits at about 4,500 feet in a scenic setting in the Cascades east from Ashland. The lake offers good prospects for rainbow trout and is heavily stocked by ODFW. The trout commonly reach 17 inches and many 3- to 5-pounders are taken every year. Howard Prairie likewise offers good fishing for both largemouth and smallmouth bass, including some large fish, and the reservoir is full of modest-sized brown bullhead.

Trout anglers enjoy consistent success both trolling and still fishing with bait, and bank access is very good. Trout anglers catch bass with regularity and the reservoir has increasingly attracted a contingent of serious bass anglers who fish by boat, targeting the lake's structural elements, especially in the coves, creek channels, and around the islands. Covering 1,996 acres at full pool, Howard Prairie is about 6 miles long and offers ample room to spread out, so even on crowded weekends you can find a place to have to yourself. On summer weekends, get on the lake early if you intend to troll for trout because water skiers and pleasure boaters can be rather abundant. In recent years, the odds-on favorite for trolling has been the Tazmanian Devil, usually in subdued colors.

Howard Prairie Resort maintains an informative webpage that allows anglers to get the latest news and fishing reports from the lake (www.howardprairieresort.com). The resort (541-482-1979) offers a wide range of services, including a popular restaurant, marina, rental boats, concessions, camping, and ready-to-use rental RVs set up in a nice campground. Five additional campgrounds feature a total of some 167 tent/car sites and 185 trailer sites. Boat launches are located at the

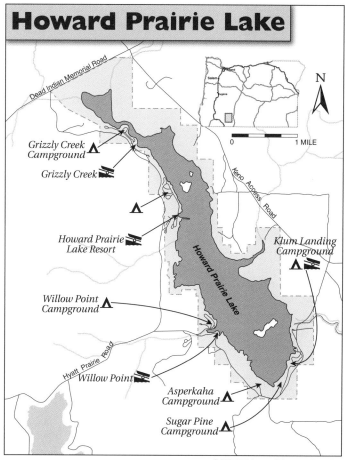

© 2007 Wilderness Adventures Press, Inc.

resort on the west shore, at Klum Landing and Willow Point on the south end of the lake and at Grizzly on the reservoir's northern arm. A recently installed wheelchair-accessible path and fishing platform is quite popular. The facilities at the lake are generally open from the beginning of fishing season in late April through the end of October when the reservoir closes to angling.

From I-5 at Ashland, take Exit 14 and then head east about 1 mile on SR 66 to a left turn on Dead Indian Memorial Road (watch for the signs to the airport and "Mountain Lakes"). Follow the road about 17 miles to the well-signed entrance to reservoir on Hyatt Prairie Road. A network of roads surrounds the reservoir.

Hubbard Creek (Curry County)
closed waters

Hunter Creek (Curry County)
This attractive little stream south of Gold Beach offers fair prospects for winter steelhead, with wild fish—including an occasional very large steelhead—arriving between February and the end of the season on March 31. Currently the creek is open for fall chinook salmon and during a good year, it will yield perhaps 50 chinooks during the October and November runs. Check current regulations before venturing to Hunter Creek and be sure to seek permission before crossing private property. Access is generally good on the road running alongside the creek. Hwy 101 crosses the creek 2 miles south of Gold Beach. Hunter Creek's delta is a fair place to try for sea-run cutthroat during September, but in recent years the entire drainage has been closed to trout angling. The adjacent beach offers decent prospects for surfperch.

Hyatt Lake, Little
see Little Hyatt Lake

Hyatt Reservoir (Jackson County)
boat ramp, campground, services
Located in the southeast corner of Jackson County, about 15 miles from Ashland, Hyatt Reservoir (often called Hyatt Lake) is a very popular, pretty and productive fishery for stocked rainbow trout. Nestled amidst high-country stands of timber, the lake also has some bass and quite a few small brown bullhead. Rainbows carry over successfully here and a number of them reach 16 or more inches. Each year anglers take a few 3- to 7-pound trout from Hyatt.

Every once in a while, 430-acre Hyatt Lake suffers water quality problems brought about by a combination of low summer reservoir levels, warm water, and algae blooms. So the late summer fishing can be rather slow at times and partial trout die-offs have occurred here in the past. Still, under favorable conditions—which are the norm— Hyatt's trout grow more quickly and average a larger size than those in nearby Howard Prairie Reservoir. The reservoir is open during the general trout season and fishing can be excellent from April through mid-June. Most years, autumn is good and the lake also produces some large trout during October.

Many anglers still fish with bait from the banks and from boats. The reservoir offers plenty of good bank fishing opportunity. Trolling is also popular and effective, especially during the early morning hours. Fly anglers fishing from float tubes and pontoon boats have become a common sight at Hyatt Lake. Boat rentals are available at Hyatt Lake Resort (541-482-3331/www.hyattlakeresorts.com) and the lake has two campgrounds. Hyatt Lake Campground on the south shore is the larger of the two, while Wildcat Campground on the east bank is a semi-primitive site.

Boat launches are located at both campgrounds and at Hyatt Lake Resort, which sits on the lake's southwest corner. Campers

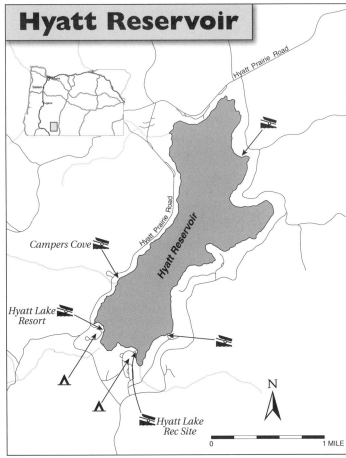

© 2007 Wilderness Adventures Press, Inc.

Cove Resort, a quaint little lodge offering camping, a popular restaurant, and other amenities, also sits along the lake's southwest shoreline (541-482-1201/www.hyattlakeresorts.com).

From I-5 at Ashland, take Exit 14 and follow Hwy 66 heading east toward Klamath Falls. After 17 miles turn north at the well-signed Hyatt Lake Road, which leads 3 miles north to the reservoir. East Hyatt Lake Road follows the east shoreline and Hyatt-Howard Prairie Road follows the west shore.

Illinois River (Curry/Josephine Counties)
boat ramp, campground, no bait, catch-and-release
One of Oregon's most ruggedly wild rivers, the 60-mile-long Illinois gathers its headwaters from extreme northern California, then runs northerly, soon plunging through a tremendous wilderness section revered by whitewater enthusiasts. Before reaching the Rogue at Agness, the Illinois River plunges through 150 rapids, including eleven Class IV rapids and one Class V plunge. The wilderness section of the river is for experienced whitewater experts only, but above and below the Kalmiopsis Wilderness, the more readily accessible parts of the river offer fair-to-good catch-and-release fishing for wild trout and fair prospects for winter-run steelhead.

Also, the Illinois usually attracts quite a few half-pounder summer-run steelhead and fishing for these 13- to 20-inch

Illinois River

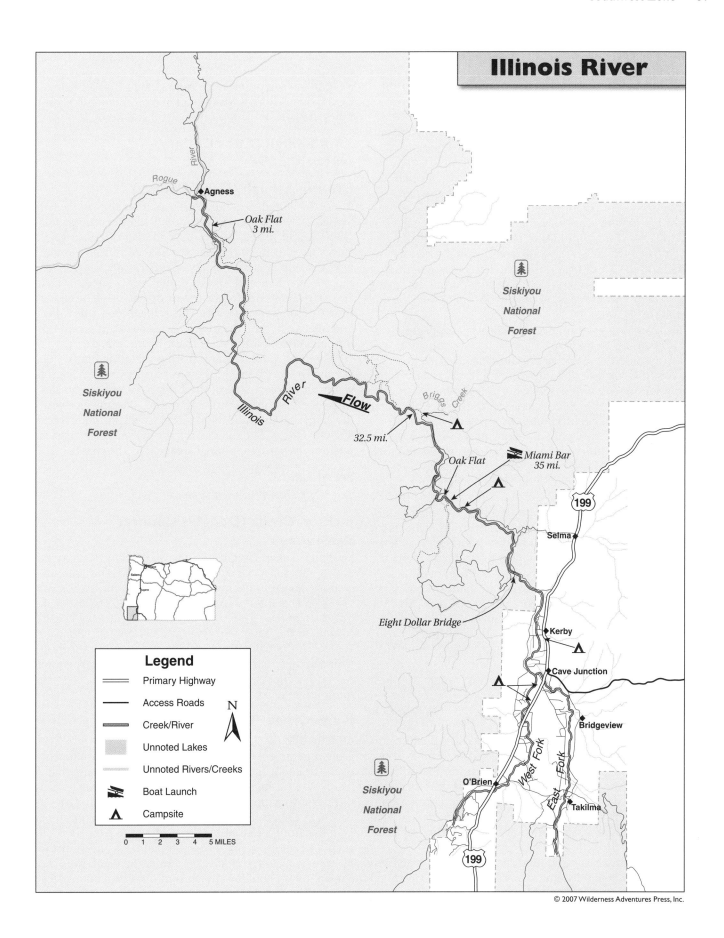

Rogue River

◆ Agness

Oak Flat
3 mi.

Siskiyou National Forest

Illinois River

Flow

32.5 mi.

Briggs Creek

Oak Flat

Miami Bar
35 mi.

Siskiyou National Forest

199

Selma ◆

Eight Dollar Bridge

Kerby ◆

Cave Junction ◆

Bridgeview ◆

Siskiyou National Forest

West Fork

East Fork

O'Brien ◆

Takilma ◆

199

Legend

═══	Primary Highway
───	Access Roads
═══	Creek/River
▓▓▓	Unnoted Lakes
┄┄┄	Unnoted Rivers/Creeks
⛴	Boat Launch
⛺	Campsite

N

0 1 2 3 4 5 MILES

steelhead can be very good at times between September and December, with October being the prime month. The lower end of the river is best for the half pounders, but these fish make it as far upstream as Cave Junction.

Unlike other southern Oregon steelhead waters, the Illinois is currently open only for catch-and-release angling and bait is not allowed. These regulations make the Illinois a haven of sorts for fly anglers and gear anglers who wish to escape the crowded waters and who don't mind releasing their catch.

Unfortunately the Illinois and its steelhead/salmon fisheries have been severely impacted by decades of intense commercial use of the watershed, hence the strict regulations here. Still, the river continues to put out some of the largest wild winter steelhead on the south coast, with the best fishing generally on the lower river during the latter stages of the run in March. The river is closed to all angling during the spring (April through most of May) to protect out-migrating juvenile steelhead and salmon.

The river is open to catch-and-release trout and steelhead angling up to Pomeroy Dam near Cave Junction, well upstream from the wilderness boundary. For all practical purposes, the rugged wilderness stretch of the river is inaccessible for angling unless you wish to include some catch-and-release trout or steelhead angling during a whitewater excursion during March. Limited by private land in places and by the rugged landscape in other places, bank access is fair between Cave Junction and Briggs Creek, where the road ends.

In the uppermost section of the river, popular bank access spots include the bridge just west of Kerby, along with Little Falls (walk-in) and Eight Dollar Bridge off Eight Dollar Mountain Road northwest of Kerby. Downstream from Eight Dollar Bridge, a rugged primitive road follows (more-or-less) along the east bank and below that, Illinois River Road follows the river for about 15 miles down to Briggs Creek. In many places, the banks are too steep to negotiate, but there are a number of good access points, including Snail Back Creek, Six Mile Creek, Swinging Bridge, Anderson Ranch, McGuires Gulch, Old Cabin Road, Miami Beach, Oak Flat, and Briggs Creek. Most of the access points are indicated by little more than wide pullouts along the road; and the last mile or so of the road, from Oak Flat to Briggs Creek, is very rough and best suited to 4-wheel-drive vehicles.

Downstream from the wilderness area, the Illinois River is largely a hike-in river, although the lowermost end is accessible by car and the river is floatable. The usual float on this stretch is from a gravel-bar launch at Oak Flat, 3 miles above the mouth near Agness. Do not confuse this Oak Flat with the Oak Flat above the wilderness area. This short drift takes you through prime steelhead water when river conditions are favorable. The river can get very low during summer, so wait for fall rains before floating the lower drift during the half-pounder season.

There is a small campground located at Oak Flats and access is from CR 450 leading south from Agness. Upstream from Oak Flat, access is by trail and increasing numbers of steelhead anglers seem to enjoy walking upriver to fish lightly pressured pools and runs. To reach the upper section of the river, follow Hwy 199 south from Grants Pass. At Selma, turn right to reach Illinois River Road or continue south a few more miles to Eight Dollar Mountain Road and Kerby.

Iowa Slough (Coos County)
see Coquille River

Isthmus Slough (Coos County)
A lengthy slough feeding Coos Bay from the south, Isthmus Slough is widely known for its fall salmon fishing for both chinook and fin-clipped coho, and also offers striped bass, sturgeon, and myriad other species. With a few exceptions, Isthmus Slough is mostly a boat fishery. Most anglers use the ramp near the mouth of the slough, off D Street in Eastside. To reach the ramp, follow the bridge across Isthmus Slough from Coos Bay and turn left. This is the route to the Coos River and Allegany. When the main road heads right (east), turn left instead and follow the signs to the boat ramp.

The most popular bank-fishing site on Isthmus Slough is at "The Gravel Pit," a large gravel parking area adjacent to the water on the east side of the bridge coming from Coos Bay. Cross the bridge and turn left toward Allegany and you'll see the large parking and bank-access area on your left. Bank anglers fare well here during the fall salmon season and boaters often fish the slough adjacent to The Gravel Pit.

Ivern Lake
see Sky Lakes Wilderness Area

Jackson Creek (Douglas County)
closed waters

Jackson Creek is a major tributary to the South Umpqua River and a sanctuary for spawning steelhead and salmon. The creek is closed to fishing year-round, but the area is worth a visit if you are interested in seeing the world's tallest or second tallest sugar pine. The tree is located along Jackson Creek Road (watch for the signs) and towers at 265 feet tall, with a girth of 7.5 feet at the base. The tree is about 24 miles north of Trail. Unfortunately, several years ago moronic vandals girdled the tree with a chainsaw and because of that act, the 400-year-old monolith may be in danger of dying.

Jenny Creek (Jackson County)
no bait, hike-in

Truly a gem of a fishery, Jenny Creek is a little-known, relatively isolated and rugged wild redband stream that flows south from Howard Prairie Reservoir, eventually crossing the California border and emptying into Iron Gate Reservoir near Copco. The lower half of the creek—running about 14 miles from SR 66 at Pinehurst down to Iron Gate—forges such a powerful spring presence that it has been discovered by expert white-water kayakers. Here the creek runs through a deep, rocky, boulder-strewn semi-arid canyon and features several falls and gorges.

Jenny Creek offers fair fishing for wild redband trout that range from 5 to 18 inches. Big fish are rare, but quite a few reach 12 inches, especially in the creek's most inaccessible reaches and where water quality is highest. Water quality would not be problematic, expect that the Talent Irrigation District diverts as much as half of the creek's flow. During summer, Jenny Creek can get precariously low, so catch-and-release-minded anglers should consider leaving the trout un-molested during July and August. The best fishing is between May and June and then again in October.

Access is mostly by foot, at least if you want to fish the best sections of the creek, but be advised that Jenny Creek flows through a mix of public and private property. Copco Road follows above the canyon, but mostly off to the east quite a ways, and various back roads lead toward the creek. Copco Road turns south off Hwy 66 just east of Pinehurst. This road is usually gated about halfway to the border, so you must access the lower end of the river from Iron Gate Reservoir, as there is no way to drive all the way through to the border. Road access has been in a state of flux in this area since the inception of the Cascade-Siskiyou National Monument; so consult the BLM in Medford before venturing into these rugged environs. There is a nice day-use area on the Jenny Creek arm of Iron Gate Reservoir in California, but of course you will need a California angling license to fish the creek's lower few miles.

Johnson Mill Pond (Coos County)

A large, retired millpond along the Coquille River between the towns of Coquille and Myrtle Point, Johnson Pond is a fishery developed jointly by the Port of Bandon and the U.S. Forest Service. The pond is stocked regularly with legal-size rainbow trout and at times with trophy-size rainbows. In recent years, the pond has quietly received plantings of trophy-size trout during October. Johnson Mill Pond also supports populations of largemouth bass and bluegill, along with brown bullhead that often reach a respectable 12 to 14 inches. The odd salmon or steelhead smolt counts as part of your trout limit—they occasionally get trapped in the pond after flood events on the Coquille.

Periodically the pond succumbs to dense weed growth, prompting clean-up projects and it has lots of structure in the form of sunken logs. Bank fishing is easy and a good trail circles the lake, but a raft or float tube is the ideal way to fish the pond. Best action occurs between April and June, but the autumn fishing can be decent also.

From Coos Bay, follow Hwy 101 south out of town and then follow the signs for Coquille and SR 42. The pond is about 3 miles south of Coquille. From I-5, take the Winston Exit (Exit 119) and follow Hwy 42 heading west along the Middle Fork Coquille. Continue north through Myrtle Point about 7 miles to the pond.

Laird Lake (Curry County)

campground

A small, forested pond near the South Fork Elk River, Laird Lake has been stocked with rainbow trout from time to time.

The 28-mile drive from Port Orford gets rugged, but the campground at Laird Lake (four spaces) is lightly used during summer. Before making the journey, check with ODFW about current stocking status for Laird Lake. From Hwy 101 north of Port Orford, head east into the highlands on Elk River Road.

Lake Creek (Douglas County)

campground

Lake Creek is the outlet stream from Diamond Lake and flows north about 10 miles to Lemolo Lake, crossing under Hwy 138 along the way. The creek supports small brook trout and brown trout, along with a few rainbows and cut-bows. Access is primarily by hiking and much of the creek flows through brushy under-story in a shallow, forested canyon. Most of the creek offers only small fish, but a few big browns run a short distance up the creek from Lemolo Lake during October. Hike up from the reservoir or walk in from the Lemolo Lake Road just south of the reservoir.

The creek's most inaccessible section begins about half a mile downstream from Diamond Lake and offers an occasional 12- to 16-inch rainbow that has escaped the lake. These are quite rare, but the rugged hike and fairly common small, wild trout make for a pleasant trek for those who don't mind some rough-and-tumble brush busting in places.

Several other small creeks in this area offer good prospects for small, wild trout, especially for anglers willing to hike along the stream banks, often through some rather dense brush. These creeks fish best between mid-summer and mid- to late September. Consult the national forest map and check out Fish Creek, Bear Creek, and the Clearwater River.

Lake In The Woods (Douglas County)

campground

A small, popular man-made lake in the forested highlands above the town of Glide (east of Roseburg), Lake In The Woods is a pretty and productive fishery for stocked rainbow trout that reach 16 inches. The fish typically range from 9 to 12 inches and all methods are productive. Both bank and boat fishing are popular, but only non-motorized boats are allowed. The lake sits at 3,200 feet and is usually accessible by late April and sometimes earlier. The 11-site campground has drinking water. From Glide, turn south on Little River Road and head into the forest for 20 miles where the pavement ends and the road becomes FR 27. Continue 7 more miles to the campground.

Lake Marie (Coos County)

campground, float tube recommended

A very pretty lake, surrounded by trees and with a scenic little beach on one end, Lake Marie resides in Umpqua Lighthouse State Park, 4 miles south of Reedsport. The lake offers fair-to-good fishing for stocked rainbow trout and a few wild cut-throat. Best fishing is during spring and fall and a float tube is handy here, especially if you are fly fishing. A mile-long trail circles the lake, but the shoreline is mostly shrouded in dense brush and trees. The beach area is popular with swimmers during the summer months.

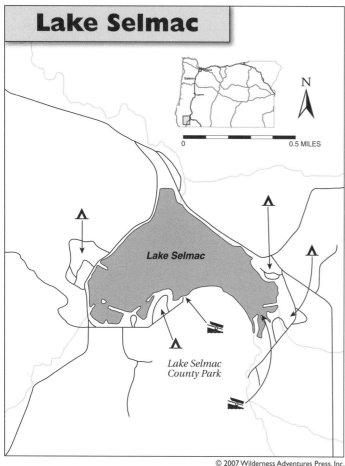

© 2007 Wilderness Adventures Press, Inc.

Lake Selmac (Josephine County)
campground, boat ramp, boat recommended

An attractive and very popular multi-purpose lake south of Grants Pass, 160-acre Lake Selmac sits nestled amidst steep, timbered hills and offers good fishing for stocked rainbow trout, crappie, brown bullhead, and other species. Largemouth bass, however, provide the lake's most prestigious and famous fishery. Selmac is managed to produce trophy-size bass and it does so with regularity, including three state record fish during a ten-year span from 1981 to1991.

These three bass weighed 10 pounds-13 ounces, 10 pounds-15 ounces, and 11 pounds-7.4 ounces, respectively. Not coincidentally, all three fish were taken during the spring—the best time to find Selmac's trophy-class bass in shallow water. Spring is spawning time for largemouth bass, so they abound in the structure-filled shallows. At the same time they enjoy easy shallow-water feeding opportunity provided by the lake's abundant prey fish. Selmac's serious bass-fishing experts—and there are quite a few of them—fish by boat, targeting big bass around the flooded stump fields, the steep drop-offs and other ideal habitat that abound here.

Shoreline access for bank angling is excellent and includes several levees that make excellent fishing platforms. Bank anglers, however, account for a small percentage of the lake's big bass. Anglers specifically targeting the bass should bring a boat and work the coves and drop-offs. Current regulations allow anglers to keep only one bass per day, regardless of size, so until you're ready to quit for the day, be sure to release all bass.

To reach Lake Selmac, take Hwy 199 south through Grants Pass. From the town of Selma, head south about half a mile on Hwy 199, then turn left on Lake Shore Drive, continuing 2.3 miles to the lake. In addition to ample campground space, the lake boasts the services of Lake Selmac Resort (541-597-2277/ www.lakeselmac.com), which offers camping, RV spaces, boat rentals, a general store and more. Lake Selmac hosts an annual ODFW Kid's Fishing Derby during early June.

Lemolo Lake (Douglas County)
boat ramp, boat recommended, campground

A very pretty 435-acre reservoir located on the upper North Umpqua watershed, Lemolo Lake is most widely known for its capacity to produce large brown trout. The browns, though often rather elusive, typically range from 2 to 8 pounds, sometimes larger, and are generally taken by anglers fishing Rapalas and other large plugs.

The best brown trout action occurs during spring and fall and the regulars often find these fish in the creek arms, especially the Lake Creek and North Umpqua arms. During the spring, fish close to shore. As summer warms the water, the browns move deeper. Late in the season, the fish again roam the shallows and relatively few people realize that good brown trout fishing occurs right at the end of the season during the last few days of October. Usually the reservoir is drawn down substantially by then, making the fishing more difficult, but the fish still seem to prefer the coves where the streams enter the reservoir. If a heavy rain silts the water, wait for the lake to clear and then fish the arms as the browns move back in.

Lemolo also offers a fair kokanee fishery, and has quite a few wild brook trout and rainbow trout, neither of which grows large. The lake has become rather popular with fly anglers, who fish by float tube, pontoon craft, and boat, targeting the brown trout both spring and fall. Large streamer patterns are best.

Lemolo Lake Resort (541-643-0750/www.lemololakeresort.com) sits right on the lakeshore and offers rental boats, lodging, a restaurant, store, and other services. From Roseburg, head east up the North Umpqua Highway (Hwy 138) towards Diamond Lake. About 73 miles from Roseburg, watch for the prominent signs to Lemolo Lake and turn left onto FR 2610 (Birds Point Road). From the highway, you'll travel about 5 miles to the lake.

Libby Pond (Curry County)

A popular 10-acre lake inland from Gold Beach, Libby Pond is regularly stocked with hatchery rainbow trout, including some of ODFW's 2-plus-pound fish. Bank access is excellent, although a raft, canoe, or float tube is handy. Just south of the Hwy 101 bridge over the Rogue River, head east on Jerry's Flat

Road (CR 595), leading about 7 miles up to the pond. The pond also has a fair population of mostly small brown bullhead.

Little Butte Creek (Jackson County)
no bait, catch-and-release

The outlet from Fish Lake, which sits in the highlands of southeastern Jackson County, North Fork Little Butte Creek offers good prospects for small, wild rainbows, cutthroat and brook trout. The stream is managed for catch-and-release fishing, except that there is no limit on non-native brook trout. Brookies are fairly common high in the drainage, where most of the public access is available. The South Fork offers a similar scenario with more public access in the Rogue River National Forest. These creeks are open from late May through October, but the best fishing begins after run-off, usually by late June.

The North and South Forks converge just south of Hwy 140 about 15 miles northeast of Medford. From the forks, Hwy 140 follows along the North Fork, while South Fork Butte Creek Road follows the creek's southern branch. The turnoff for South Fork Butte Creek Road is on Hwy 140 about 5 miles east from the Brownsboro Junction. From there, some access to the South Fork is available near the road on BLM lands, but both forks are better accessed on the National Forest lands to the east. (Little Butte Creek is closed to all fishing below the forks).

South Fork Road continues into the national forest as FR 3730, leading up to Latgawa Campground. From the campground, you can hike up the creek or follow FR 3730 up the hill to the north and watch for the first spur road on your right, which leads along the creek for about a mile. This is the South Fork's steepest section and access is only available by foot for the next 4 miles, which flow through a steep-sided forest canyon. The meandering uppermost and diminutive reach of the South Fork is easier to reach from Fish Lake and Hwy 140 to the north. Likewise, Hwy 140 at Fish Lake provides ready access to the North Fork.

Follow Hwy 140 heading east from the Crater Lake Highway at Medford (Exit 30 from I-5). Just before you reach Fish Lake, turn south on FR 37, leading south to North Fork Campground and Big Elk Guard Station. This road crosses the North Fork of Butte Creek half a mile below Fish Lake and from there you can hike up or down the stream. Alternately you can turn south of the highway 5 miles west of Fish Lake on FR 2815 and access the creek from the bridge. To reach the South Fork from Fish Lake, continue south on FR 37, which crosses the creek about a mile past Big Elk Guard Station. Or, just past the guard station, turn left on FR 3705, which leads southeast to another creek crossing and a trailhead. The trail follows the South Fork in both directions, but better access and better fishing is downstream.

Little Hyatt Lake (Jackson County)

This small reservoir sits south of much larger and more productive Hyatt Reservoir, east from Ashland. Little Hyatt Lake has a mix of warmwater species, including largemouth bass and brown bullhead, and is stocked with rainbow trout. Best fishing is in the spring. With open meadows and scattered shoreline pine trees, Little Hyatt provides easy bank fishing, although at less than 10 acres in size, it is perfectly suited to a float tube or raft. There is no formal campground, but tent campers sometimes use the meadows back from the lakeshore.

To get there from Hyatt Reservoir, head south on Hyatt Prairie Road and on the southwest corner of the reservoir, head south on Little Hyatt Lake Road. Alternately take Hwy 66 south and east from Ashland, wrapping around Emigrant Lake and heading up to Greenspring Summit, where Little Hyatt Lake Road heads north.

Little River (Douglas County)
no bait

A very pretty trout stream in its own right, Little River joins the beautiful North Umpqua at the town of Glide, east of Roseburg. At the confluence, Little River rushes headlong into the North Umpqua at a 90-degree angle, hence the name of the place: Colliding Rivers. Colliding Rivers is hardly dramatic during the low flows of summer when trout fishing peaks, but visit the place during swollen winter flows and you'll fully appreciate the name. Little River is currently open to trout angling from late May to mid-September and fishing for wild cutthroat, and a few rainbows, is generally fair. The river is easily accessed by FR 27 (Little River Road), which follows the stream to its headwaters. A nice little county park (day use) sits about 9 miles up the creek and four campgrounds are situated along the river in the Umpqua National Forest.

Lobster Creek (Curry County)
closed waters

Lone Ranch Beach
see Boardman State Park

Loon Lake (Douglas County)
boat ramp, campground, boat recommended, services

Loon Lake is a popular, deep, and scenic 260-acre lake south of the Mainstem Umpqua River about halfway between Elkton and Reedsport. The signed turnoff from Hwy 138 is 4 miles west from Scottsburg. Loon Lake was created by a major landslide about 1,400 years ago when the mountain to the west crumbled in a massive landslide. House-sized boulders dammed the creek causing the lake to form. Boulders are still visible at the entrance to Loon Lake and by the boat ramp. The lake averages less than half a mile wide and stretches for about 2 miles in length.

Popular with swimmers, water skiers, jet skiers, and pleasure boaters, Loon Lake is stocked regularly with rainbow trout and also has quite a few wild cutthroat trout. Be sure to check current regulations regarding the cutthroat. In addition to the trout, Loon Lake supports fair populations of largemouth bass (including some big ones) along with crappie, bluegill, and brown bullhead. The bass generally range from 10 to 16 inches, but a few fish to 6 pounds are available. Best fishing is during May, June, and after Labor Day weekend. If you fish the lake during the busy summer weekends, be sure to get on the water early in the morning.

The BLM's Loon Lake Recreation Site offers camping, a boat ramp, and a sandy beach with a swimming area, which gets crowded on warm summer weekends. East Shore Campground, a mile past the recreation site, has six campsites and a fishing dock. Loon Lake Resort (www.loonlakerv.com/541-559-2244) offers camping, lodging, rental boats, a café and store, and fuel.

Lost Creek Reservoir (Rogue River)
boat ramp, boat recommended, campground

A large impoundment on the upper Rogue River northeast from Medford, Lost Creek Reservoir is heavily stocked with rainbow trout and provides good fishing for well-established smallmouth bass. The trout typically range from 9 to 15 inches and a few wild cutthroat and brown trout show up in the catch as well. ODFW sometimes adds some trophy-size planters to the mix and the legal-size fish can over-winter to reach 18 or 19 inches. Best trout fishing is often in the Rogue River arm upstream (east) from the highway bridge—also a good bet for bass.

Smallmouth are fairly abundant, but they grow slowly and typically range from 8 to 14 inches in length. Once a good producer of decent-sized largemouth bass, 3,426-acre Lost Creek Reservoir still kicks out a few largemouth, but smallies predominate. The reservoir also holds bluegill, green sunfish, black crappie, and brown bullheads. The bass congregate around structure, including the rock dam and the many rocky shoreline areas. Best fishing is by boat because bank-fishing access is generally limited to the area around Stewart State Park and at the dispersed camping areas and recreation areas along the shoreline. The state park occupies most of the south shore and includes nice trails that follow the shoreline. The park also has a nice boat launch facility, campground, and other amenities.

The Lost Creek arm, which branches off from the north side of the reservoir, is a good bet for all species. Trollers do best for trout here, while bass anglers can work along the highly varied shoreline, casting to structure. One rugged back road provides minimal bank access to the Lost Creek arm; so again, a boat is the best way to fish here. Along the north shore, between the Lost Creek arm and the highway bridge, a series of coves provide good bass habitat and these are accessible only by boat or by hiking. To follow the shoreline by foot here, turn back toward the west at the north end of the highway bridge. Drive to the end of the road and walk from there.

Lost Creek Reservoir is a year-round fishery. The trout fishing peaks between April and July, but can be good any time. Fishing for smallmouth bass is best from May through October. From Medford, take Exit 30 off I-5 and head north on SR 62. Continue through Shady Cove and Trail, crossing the Rogue River above Casey State Park and then reaching the south shore of the reservoir.

Maidu Lake (Douglas County)
hike-in

Twenty-acre Maidu Lake is the source of the North Umpqua River and offers outstanding scenery along with good fishing for brook trout ranging from 6 to 16 inches. You can get there via an 8-mile hike from the west or a much shorter route beginning at the northwest corner of Miller Lake. Should you choose the longer route from the west, take Hwy 138 from Roseburg and head east toward the crest of the Cascade Range. About 4 miles east from Clearwater Falls and a mile east from the turnoff to Lemolo Lake, turn left on FR 60, the Windigo Pass Road (about 75 miles from Roseburg). Go about 4.5 miles to FR 6000-958, the Kelsay Valley Road. The trailhead for the North Umpqua Trail is at the east end of the road approximately 1.5 miles. The lake is almost 9 miles up the trail. For directions to Miller Lake, see Southeast Zone herein. From Digit Point Campground on Miller Lake, the trail heads northwest and reaches Maidu Lake after just 3 miles.

Matson Creek (Coos County)
hike-in

A rough-and-tumble tributary to the East Fork Millicoma River east of Coos Bay, Matson Creek offers fair-to-good fishing for small, wild cutthroat and an occasional sea-run cutthroat on the creek's lowermost end.

McKee Lake
see Sky Lakes Wilderness Area

McVay Wayside (Curry County)

This popular wayside just south of Brookings offers easy access to a section of beach that holds good prospects for both surfperch and clamming. A picnic area sits adjacent to the parking area. At high tides, the surf here can rise enough to leave little available beach, so lower tide levels are best for surfperch, and of course for clams. The ideal tide/time combination is the first two hours of an incoming tide at dawn on a summer morning (between fall and late spring, the surf here can get very rough).

Medco Pond (Jackson County)

A large millpond, covering more than 50 acres, Medco Pond is a popular trout and warmwater fishery located east of Shady Cove and south of Prospect. The pond is regularly stocked with legal-size rainbows. Bass, though not especially numerous, range from 1 to 3 pounds, with a few larger fish available and bluegill usually run about 4 to 7 inches in length. ODFW holds annual free fishing day events here during early June and the event usually includes a kid's fishing derby along with instructional events. Take Hwy 62 from Medford to Prospect and then head south about 10 miles on the Butte Falls-Prospect Road.

Middle Lake
see Sky Lakes Wilderness Area

Miller Lake (Rogue River National Forest)
hike-in, float tube recommended

A nice little hike-in lake in the southeast corner of Josephine County, Miller Lake lies about 8 miles north-by-northwest of Applegate Reservoir. The lake is stocked periodically by air, and the brook and rainbow trout typically range from 6 to 12 inches. Except for summer weekends, this lake is rather lightly fished and is perfectly suited to a float tube. It's an ideal location for a late September or early October outing. The hike covers about half a mile. From I-5 at Medford, take Exit 33 and follow the signs to Jacksonville. At Jacksonville continue south on SR 238 to the town of Ruch and then head south, upstream along the Applegate River. Continue around the west shoreline of Applegate Reservoir and when you reach Carberry Creek and Carberry Creek Campground, turn right on FR 10 (Carberry Creek Road). Follow FR 10 to a left-hand turn on FR 1020 and then another left-hand turn on Spur Road 1020-400. The trailhead is at the end of this road.

Millicoma Interpretive Center Pond (Coos County)

As part of the ODFW's new Youth Angling Enhancement Program, rainbow trout are stocked annually in the miniscule pond at the Millicoma Interpretive Center near Allegany. The pond, about 20 feet across, is reserved for kids-fishing only, generally during visits by youth groups from area schools. State law allows juveniles under the age of 14 to fish for free and a juvenile license is required for kids from 14 to 17 years of age. The center, located 25 miles east of Coos Bay, is staffed by volunteer host Ed Obrien, who keeps a few loaner rods on hand. The pond is stocked two or three times each spring.

The facility here is an educational "hands-on" fish hatchery where each year, hundreds of Oregon schoolchildren learn about salmon lifecycles and stream habitat, and clip the fins of hatchery fish. The facility also serves as an acclimation site for hatchery fish on the West Fork Millicoma River and as a native steelhead brood stock development site. To arrange a visit for a school or other youth group, call Obrien at 541-267-2557.

Turn north at the Allegany Store and follow the West Fork of the Millicoma River. About 6 miles from Allegany take the right fork in the road and follow the signs past the Girl Scout camp to Millicoma Interpretive Center.

Millicoma River (Coos County)
boat ramp, campground

The Millicoma River is a stream of varying personalities. It joins with the South Fork Coos to form the Coos River. Like the Coos, the Millicoma offers a good May-June fishery for shad that range from 2 to 5 pounds. The river also has a fair run of fall chinook salmon and a good run of winter steelhead, mostly of hatchery origin. The main branch of the river, influenced by tidewater, runs less than 10 meandering miles from the "town" of Allegany down to the confluence with the Coos.

This is the stretch that offers the best shad and salmon fishing and even puts out an occasional striped bass.

Many anglers fish the Millicoma by boat, motoring up from Doris Place Boat Ramp or Rooke-Higgins Park Ramp, both located along the mainstem. Camping is available in primitive sites at Rooke-Higgins. As you approach Allegany (there is no ramp at Allegany), the Millicoma narrows: Make sure you know the tide levels and times, and beware the typical load of flotsam carried by the river on falling tides.

At Allegany, the river splits into its East and West Forks. Both forks offer fair-to-good fishing for winter steelhead between late December and mid-March. On the East Fork Millicoma, bank access is available at Coos County's Nesika Park, where anglers congregate to fish several popular and productive holes and runs. Theoretically you can float a short segment of the East Fork, starting at a rugged cobble put-in about a mile above the park and taking out at the swimming hole below the park (only at winter flows). However, few

West Fork Millicoma River

people bother floating this section because of the abundant bank access and because of the difficulty in lifting a boat out of the water at the end of the short drift. East Fork Millicoma Road follows the river up from Allegany.

ODFW's Millicoma Interpretive Center is located on the West Fork, about 9 miles upstream from Allegany and much of the steelhead fishing effort is concentrated in this area, with several popular pools accessible from the center. Bank access is good for several miles upstream from the center, but you'll need a sense of adventure. West Millicoma Road crosses the river at Stonehouse Bridge, a popular public access point. At moderate flows, you can drift the lower end of the West Fork (starting at a rugged slide at the bridge), but you must first secure permission from landowner Howard Slater before using the takeout located on his property (the second house up the road from Allegany). Slater doesn't like guides using his takeout (he's had problems with them in the past), but private boaters are welcome—just knock on his door and introduce yourself first. At low water, boulders and bedrock make the drift hazardous, and be courteous of the many private land-owners along the river.

The West Fork is generally the more productive of the two forks of the Millicoma. Chinook salmon arrive as early as late August and you can be sure they are running by the boat traffic on the Millicoma mainstem. Steelhead arrive from December through March. Both forks of the Millicoma offer good fishing for resident cutthroat trout, with fish numbers increasing as you get higher into the headwater areas. The upper reaches of the West Fork flow through the 92,000-acre Elliott State Forest, one of the few large tracts of publicly owned forest in the area. Hence trout fishing access to the West Fork is quite good and the fishing peaks from June through September.

The Millicoma is easy to reach from Coos Bay. From the south end of the city (the Bay Park district) turn east on the Coos River Highway, crossing the Coos River a few miles east of town. The highway follows the Millicoma up to Allegany, where the river's East and West Forks converge. County roads lead up both forks. If you're coming from the north, you can turn east off Hwy 101 on East Bay Drive, on the north end of the bay bridge at Russell Point. After winding its way around the east edge of the bay, this road meets the Coos River Highway.

Minnehaha Creek (Rogue River drainage)
see Rogue River, Forks

Modoc Pond (Jackson County)
Modoc Pond is a 50-acre private pond near Table Rock north of Medford. There is no public access.

Muir Creek (Rogue River drainage)
see Rogue River, Forks

Mussel Creek (Curry County)
closed waters

Myers Creek (Curry County)
closed waters

Myrtle Creek (Curry County)
closed waters

National Creek (Rogue River drainage)
see Rogue River, Forks

New River (Curry County)
boat recommended

Intriguing because it runs more-or-less parallel to the beach for about 12 miles, New River is the outlet from Floras Lake, north of Port Orford. The river, which runs very slowly, offers a small run of fall chinook salmon. There are salmon in the system just about any time during autumn, but mid-October through November is usually the best time frame. Fishing for them can be spotty much of the time, but if you time it right, the river can produce chrome-bright beauties. During most years, anglers (mostly locals) take about 150 fall chinook from the New River.

The river also hosts modest runs of coho salmon during fall and of winter steelhead from late December through March, peaking toward the end of that time frame. Sea-run cutthroat provide another option and fishing for these 10- to 18-inch trout can be good at times, especially from late September through early October. Look for them around structure.

New River is best accessed by boat, although there is some good bank access available for those willing to walk the trails at the BLM access area. Gas-powered motors are prohibited, but you can easily negotiate the river with a small pram or even a canoe or pontoon boat. Just beware the heavy afternoon winds on this part of the coast. The winds can get so fierce that in recent years the south coast has become a destination for ocean wind surfing. Launch at the BLM site and run up the river. To protect snowy plovers and other wildlife, the boat launch is usually closed until September 15 and is then closed again after March 15. The access road leaves little room to turn around with a trailer, so car-top boats and other such small craft are best. You might want to throw a few crab rings or pots in the river's lowermost end, but be wary of tidal currents.

The BLM property at New River is known as Storm Ranch. The turnoff is about halfway between Bandon and Langlois, on Croft Lake Road (9 miles south of Bandon). The river derives its name from the fact that it is indeed quite new, having been born during the Great Flood of 1890, when the mouth of Floras Creek moved north. Where the creek had once flowed into the Pacific, the floodwaters scoured out a new channel that was dubbed New River. The river's mouth is dynamic, changing locations when influenced by flood events and shifting sand dunes. Currently the mouth of New River is just north of Four-Mile Creek, about 3 miles north of the entrance to Storm Ranch.

The beach adjacent to New River is a lightly fished and productive area for redtail surfperch, but access is limited by the seasonal closure on boating the river (March 15 to September 15). Watch for calm ocean conditions during early March or late September, run across the river, hike over the dunes to the beach and you stand a good chance of finding fish, especially during an early morning incoming tide.

Pear Lake
see Sky Lakes Wilderness Area

Pistol River (Curry County)

The rugged little Pistol River reaches the Pacific Ocean about 10 miles south of Gold Beach. The Pistol is home to fair runs of fall chinook salmon, native winter steelhead, and sea-run cutthroat. As with most of Curry County's small streams, the Pistol's runs are late arrivals. Most of the native steelhead arrive from late February through early April, although there are fish in the river as early as December.

The salmon and sea-run cutthroat cannot ascend the river until flows increase from fall rains (the river's mouth is usually more or less bound by a sand bar during the summer). Thus the best fishing occurs once the bar is breached, usually in October. You can find fresh salmon and cutthroat well into November, at least during years with strong returns. Don't be too surprised to hook a half-pounder size steelhead while fishing the river for sea-runs—these 13- to 18-inch steelhead sometimes stray down from the Rogue.

Access is difficult on the Pistol because most of the banks are on private property owned by timber companies. Still, you can ferret out the bank access spots (one popular hole is just below the bridge on Hwy 101) by driving up the river on North Bank Pistol River Road. Once the road ends, however, access is by walking and driving logging roads if they are open. The river has a recent history of disagreements over access between landowners (or at least one landowner) and anglers, so check with ODFW before venturing up the river and certainly before attempting to float the Pistol.

Once you figure out a few access points, the Pistol can be a good bet when other area rivers (the Chetco, Elk, and Sixes) are drawing sizable crowds. Because of its small size and the limited access, the Pistol won't stand much pressure because there isn't a lot of room to spread out.

Pit Lake (Douglas County)

A 10-acre quarry pond near Lemolo Lake on the North Umpqua River drainage, Pit Lake is stocked with brook trout that grow to about 12 inches. The pond covers about 10 acres and reaches a depth of 14 feet. Take Hwy 138 from Roseburg about 74 miles east to Lemolo Lake Junction and turn north on Fr 2610. Then turn right on FR 2610-100 and then follow the half-mile trail (Trail #1446) to the lake.

Platt I Reservoir (Douglas County)
boat ramp

A good fishery for largemouth bass, stocked rainbow trout, brown bullhead, and panfish, Platt I Reservoir sits a few miles east of Sutherlin. The reservoir gets crowded at times, but fishing tends to hold up from late March through July until the water level begins to drop. Bass reach about 7 pounds here and each year anglers catch a fair number of 3- to 5-pound largemouths, though typical fish range from 1 to 3 pounds. They thrive in the reservoir's fertile, shallow margins, which are dense with wood and brush structure.

Bass and other fish in Plat I Reservoir tend to contain elevated levels of mercury, so catch-and-release fishing is a good idea, especially for larger fish. Also, while the reservoir is open all year, bass fishing is strictly catch and release during the winter, from Nov. 1 through the month of February. Platt I Reservoir is also one of the few places in Oregon where bird-watchers can expect to see purple martins just about any time during spring or summer. The birds use nesting boxes and gourds mounted to dead snags at the reservoir. From I-5, take the Sutherlin Exit and head east through town on Nonpereil Road, watching for the signs to Plat I.

Port Orford (Curry County)

The quaint little town of Port Orford, on Hwy 101 about 30 miles south of Bandon, has a single rock jetty/breakwater that at times offers good fishing for small black rockfish, greenling, and striped seaperch. Park at the lot adjacent to the port dock and walk out the jetty. Try jigs or bait, but bring lots of tackle because if you're not loosing gear, you're not fishing in the rocks and kelp where the fish live. This is a good spot for winter fishing because the adjacent headland protects the jetty from the full force of the incoming waves.

Powers Pond (Coos County)
campground

The centerpiece of a popular county park on the Coquille River, 23-acre Powers Pond is liberally stocked with rainbows, especially during the spring and provides fair-to-good fishing through June. ODFW usually adds several hundred of its trophy-size planters to the stocking allotment for Powers Pond. The pond sits on the north edge of the town of Powers, south from Myrtle Point on Powers Highway. Warmwater fish—largemouth bass, bluegill, and brown bullhead—also inhabit the pond and the large park includes a picnic area and RV sites. The pond serves as the site for the annual Powers Fishing Derby and Free Fishing Day events, held in early June.

Red Blanket Creek (Jackson County)

Red Blanket Creek is a tributary to the Middle Fork of the Rogue River near Prospect. The creek originates high in the Cascades along the southwestern edge of Crater Lake National Park and then flows for about 15 miles through a scenic canyon. The creek offers fair fishing for small wild trout and its more remote reaches are lightly fished. Red Blanket Road follows the creek east from Prospect.

Reinhart Park Ponds

Formerly known as All Sports Park Pond, Reinhart Park Ponds are part of the very nice 57-acre Reinhart Volunteer Park adjacent to the Rogue River, less than 2 miles west of downtown

Grants Pass. The ponds are regularly stocked with rainbow trout (sometimes with excess 4- to 5-pound steelhead from a nearby Rogue River hatchery facility), with the best fishing from April through June. If you're arriving from I-5, take Exit 58 and follow the main road (NE 6th Street) through downtown to a right-hand turn on Bridge Street. Follow Bridge Street to a left-hand turn on Lincoln Street, which leads south to the park. You can also get there via foot bridge from Tussing Park, on the south bank of the Rogue behind the fairgrounds. This park features numerous amenities, including a number of picnic shelters.

Rock Creek (North Umpqua drainage)
closed waters

Rogue River
One of the most significant, lengthy and complex rivers systems in the state, southern Oregon's Rogue River also ranks amongst the world's most famous steelhead and salmon rivers. Its high repute as a steelhead fly-angling fishery is well deserved and the Rogue was among the first rivers where steelhead fly angling became a popular form of fishing. Likewise legendary is the Rogue's propensity for yielding some of the largest chinook salmon on the west coast.

The Rogue hosts runs of both spring and fall chinook salmon, with the "springers" being especially regarded as table fare and the autumn fish being renowned for their size. The Rogue's spring chinook run the river rather quickly and even high in the river system, plenty of chrome-bright fish are available during the heart of the season in May and June. Most anglers fish them with plugs or plug/bait combos. The fall chinook show up at Gold Beach—the Rogue's mouth on the south coast—beginning in August and fresh fish continue to arrive well into the fall.

The Rogue's steelhead fishery takes several forms. Most famous of the runs is that of the "half-pounders." The half-pounder steelhead are defined by a unique life history. These fish start out life like any other steelhead, living in the river as a trout until they reach smolting size. Then—like any other steelhead—their natal urge to migrate leads them to the Pacific Ocean, where they feast on the sea's bounty. But here the familiar story takes a twist. Unlike typical steelhead, half-pounders abandon their ocean-going lifestyle after just a few months. They return to their home river the same year they left her. Most half-pounders migrate out during May and return to the Rogue the following October.

Because they have spent but a few months at sea, half-pounders only grow a few inches and the typical fish ranges from 12 to 16 inches. So they are small, trout-size steelhead, but they tend towards abundance and often travel and congregate in packs numbering dozens of fish. In doing so, they form a substantial and popular fishery on the Rogue. Mixed among them are adult steelhead, including quite a few 18- to 22-inch fish that were half-pounders the previous year before returning to the ocean for a second time. Also among them

are a fair number of more typical adult steelhead that have spent one to three contiguous years at sea. These are the Rogue's largest summer-run steelhead, ranging from 5 to 15 pounds. Like the half-pounders, they ascend the river during the fall, with the peak season running from late September through November.

A second run of steelhead enters the river between December and March. These winter-run fish are prized quarry among the local anglers and the runs are typically quite robust, comprised of both hatchery and wild fish. Some of the wild fish push the 20-pound mark, but 8- to 14-pound fish are more typical. Locals enjoy a tremendous advantage on winter steelhead because they can hit the river when flows are perfect.

The Rogue offers several distinct segments. The river's upper forks converge near the pretty little town of Prospect before reaching Lost Creek Reservoir. Immediately below the reservoir lies a mile-long stretch of productive trout water deemed "The Holy Water." Next comes the "Upper Rogue,"

Ken Stanley with an Upper Rogue River steelhead.

home to one of Oregon's best autumn fisheries for 14- to 24-inch summer-run steelhead and to some fine salmon-fishing opportunities. The Upper Rogue extends from the angling deadline below Cole M. Rivers Fish Hatchery past the old Gold Ray Dam site north of Central Point and down to the old Savage Rapids Dam site east from Grants Pass. Both Gold Ray and Savage Rapids dams, as of 2010, have been removed, creating a freeflowing Rogue River all the way up to William L. Jess Dam, which impounds Lost Creek Reservoir, 157 miles from the Pacific Ocean.

Next comes the Middle Rogue, which extends from the old Savage Rapids Dam site, through Grants Pass and down to the end of the road access at Grave Creek. Below Grave Creek is the Lower Rogue, whose upper half is a unique, roadless Wild & Scenic section popular with whitewater enthusiasts. The Lower Rogue continues down to the river's terminus at Gold Beach. Each section is further described below. The term Wild & Scenic Rogue refers to the upper half of the Lower Rogue.

The Rogue River is famous for its prodigious runs of "half-pounder" steelhead—fish that return from sea after just a few months and typically span just 12 to 18 inches in length.

Holy Water

Below the dam at Lost Creek Reservoir, upstream from Shady Cove, the Rogue forms a mile-long tailwater lovingly referred to by the regional fly-fishing community as "The Holy Water." This short section of the river is home to Rogue's largest trout and to the Rogue's highest population density of trout. They thrive in a fertile, slow-moving reach with abundant insect activity, including excellent hatches of salmonflies, caddis, and various mayflies.

Of the latter, blue-winged olives hatch throughout the year, even—at times—during the middle of winter. During spring and summer, fairly predictable hatches of pale morning duns and mahogany duns bring trout to the top and summer evenings are usually abuzz with swarming caddis activity. The prime hatch season culminates during mid- to late autumn with the appearance of October caddis, the inch-long, orange-colored caddisflies that often drive trout into evening feeding frenzies. Chironomids hatch year-round and at times spawn winter dry-fly opportunities.

During times of elevated flows and during the non-hatch periods on the Holy Water, most anglers switch to fishing weighted nymphs and streamers. Streamer patterns account for some of the river's largest brown and rainbow trout. Both species reach more than 5 pounds here and typical fish range from 12 to 19 inches. Because flows vary and because the timing of the major hatches varies annually, it's a good idea to get up-to-date info on the Holy Water before venturing there. Various websites provide such details or simply call one of the local fly shops.

The Holy Water below the dam features a nice county park along the bank. Follow SR 62 northeast from Medford (or southwest from Diamond Lake), heading for Shady Cove. Before the highway crosses the Rogue east from Shady Cove, watch for the signs to Cole M. River's Fish Hatchery. Drive to the hatchery diversion dam and turn right, crossing the river at the holding ponds. Head toward the hatchery and turn left to reach the parking areas.

Rogue River, Upper

(Cole M. Rivers Hatchery to old Savage Rapids Dam site)

The Upper Rogue is a very popular and very good section of river, with an excellent autumn fishery for small adult summer-run steelhead. These fish typically range from 14 to 24 inches. Traditionally, from Rogue Elk County Park (a few miles below the fish hatchery) down to the top of Gold Ray Reservoir, the river is closed to fishing with bait from November 1 through December 31. The result of this regulation has been to create a very popular late-fall fly angling fishery for steelhead. Gear anglers are also very successful during the no-bait period. The bait ban now extends down to the old Gold Ray Dam site. However, keep an eye peeled for regulation changes dictated by the removal of the dams on the upper Rogue. And likewise because of dam removals, anglers wanting to float the river should consult ODFW about the newly free-flowing sections of the river and about any alterations the dam removal caused in other reaches of the river.

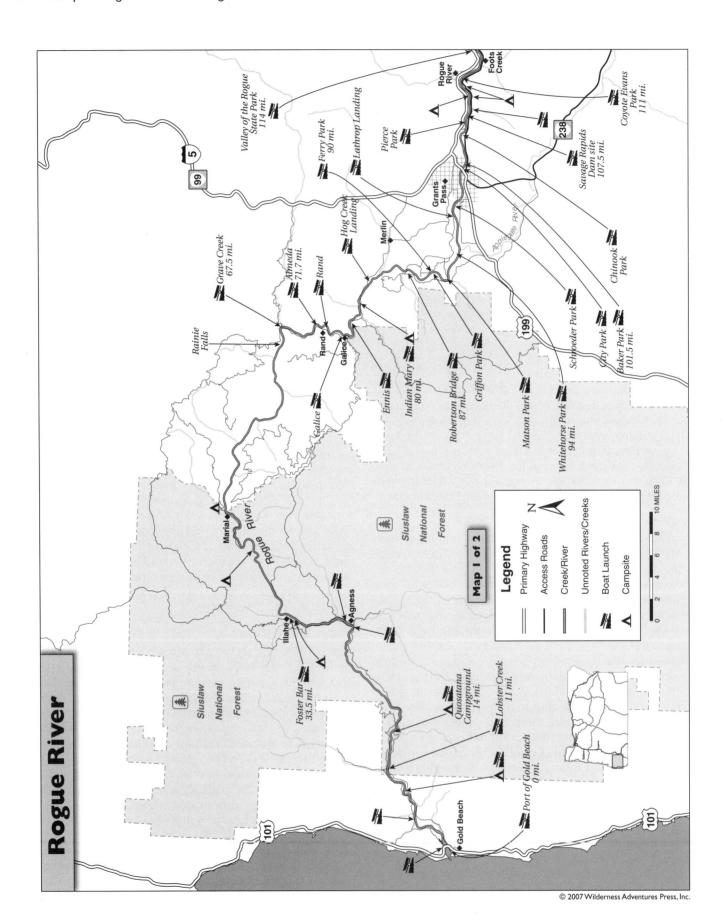

Rogue River

Valley of the Rogue State Park 114 mi.

Ferry Park 90 mi.

Lathrop Landing

Pierce Park

Rogue River

Foots Creek

Coyote Evans Park 111 mi.

238

Savage Rapids Dam site 107.5 mi.

Grants Pass

Applegate River

Merlin

Hog Creek Landing

Grave Creek 67.5 mi.

Almeda 71.7 mi.

Rand

Chinook Park

199

Schroeder Park

City Park

Baker Park 101.5 mi.

Rainie Falls

Rand

Galice

Galice

Ennis

Indian Mary 80 mi.

Robertson Bridge 87 mi.

Griffon Park

Matson Park

Whitehorse Park 94 mi.

Siuslaw National Forest

Legend

N

Primary Highway
Access Roads
Creek/River
Unnoted Rivers/Creeks
Boat Launch
Campsite

0 2 4 6 8 10 MILES

Map 1 of 2

Marial

Rogue River

Siuslaw National Forest

Agness

Illahe

Foster Bar 33.5 mi.

Quosatana Campground 14 mi.

Lobster Creek 11 mi.

Port of Gold Beach 0 mi.

Gold Beach

101

101

© 2007 Wilderness Adventures Press, Inc.

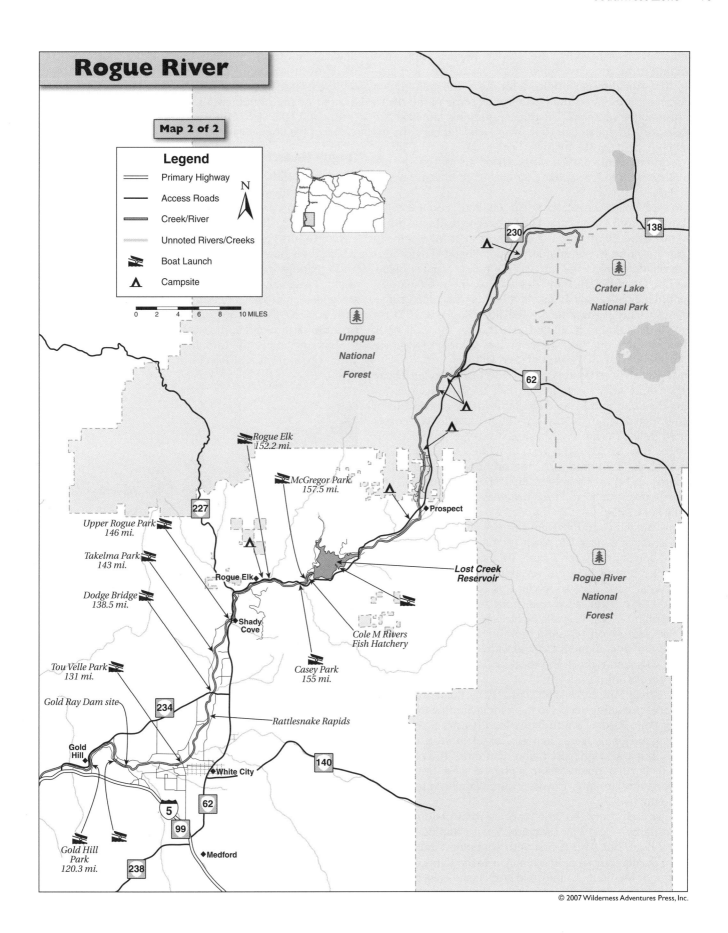

Rogue River

Map 2 of 2

Legend

≡≡≡ Primary Highway
— Access Roads
═══ Creek/River
⋯⋯ Unnoted Rivers/Creeks
🛥 Boat Launch
⛺ Campsite

N

0   2   4   6   8   10 MILES

138

230

Crater Lake National Park

Umpqua National Forest

62

🛥 *Rogue Elk 152.2 mi.*

🛥 *McGregor Park 157.5 mi.*

◆ Prospect

227

Upper Rogue Park 146 mi. 🛥

Takelma Park 143 mi. 🛥

◆ Rogue Elk

Dodge Bridge 138.5 mi. 🛥

Lost Creek Reservoir

Rogue River National Forest

◆ Shady Cove

Cole M Rivers Fish Hatchery

Casey Park 155 mi. 🛥

Tou Velle Park 131 mi. 🛥

234

Gold Ray Dam site

Rattlesnake Rapids

◆ Gold Hill

◆ White City

140

5

62

99

🛥 🛥

Gold Hill Park 120.3 mi.

◆ Medford

238

Relatively user-friendly, the Upper Rogue, while not abounding in bank access, offers some easy, short float segments that run through prime water. Also, the well-known public-access areas are situated alongside some of the river's most productive stretches. The three uppermost launches are at McGregor Park located at Cole River Fish Hatchery, the informal launch site at the highway bridge about a mile downstream, and the ramp at Casey Park. Using the McGregor Park ramp allows you to fish about 1.5 miles of good water above Casey Park.

The next boat access is at Rogue Elk Park, about 3 miles downstream from Casey Park. The McGregor-to-Rogue Elk or Casey-to-Rogue Elk drift is a good, short drift for steelhead and can be done in short order. Upper Rogue (Edgewater) Park in Shady Cove is the next access point, 5 miles below Rogue Elk. Downstream from Shady Cove, the river features two popular boat ramps at Takelma Park and Dodge Bridge, respectively. These ramps are located along Rogue River Drive on the west bank: From Shady Cove, stay on the west bank and head south along River Drive or, just before crossing the river, turn north off SR 234 east of Gold Hill.

Only experienced boaters should drift below Dodge Bridge and then only after learning the river and its hazards, including the voluminous rapids at Rattlesnake. The drift from Dodge Bridge down to the last takeout at Touvelle Park covers about 10 miles. Do not float beyond Touvelle. To reach Touvelle Park, take SR 62 to the town of White City (a few miles south of Eagle Point) and turn west on Antelope Road. Then turn north (right) on Table Rock Road. From I-5 to the south (Medford), take Exit 33 and then head east to a left-hand turn on Table Rock Road.

Below the old Gold Ray Dam site, the Upper Rogue flows mostly along and near I-5 down to the old Savage Rapids Dam site, located between Grants Pass on the west and the little community of Rogue River along I-5 to the east. The most popular bank-access area for this stretch is at Valley of the Rogue State Park, accessible from the interstate. Other good shoreline access is available at Gold Nugget Recreation Area: Take Exit 40 off I-5 and cross the river into Gold Hill. Then head upstream on SR 234 and watch for the signs. Gold Hill Park—located right in the town of Gold Hill—is another popular access point.

Downstream from Gold Hill, North River Road follows the north bank, providing access to the river at Sardine Creek and at Rocky Point Bridge. South Bank Road (Upper River Road) provides good bank access as well: Take Exit 40 (Gold Hill) from I-5, but turn right just before you cross the river into Gold Hill. Further downstream, along I-5 west from Valley of the Rogue State Park, Coyote Evans Wayside offers good access to the river.

The stretch between the two decommissioned and removed dams—Gold Ray Dam and Savage Rapids—can be fished by boat, but float it first with someone familiar with the drift, particularly since the removal of the dams changed the nature of the float. An informal launch site is located just downstream from Gold Ray Dam on the south bank. To get there, from I-5, take Exit 40 and turn right just before crossing the bridge into Gold Hill. Another informal launch site is located at the aforementioned Gold Nugget Rec Site north from Gold Hill. Gold Hill Park has a paved ramp, as do both Valley of the Rogue State Park and Coyote Evans Park.

Rogue River, Middle
(Savage Rapids Dam site to Grave Creek)

The Middle Rogue offers a tremendous and highly varied mix of water types and a great deal of both bank and boat access. The old Savage Rapids Dam site, located near I-5 a few miles east of Grants Pass, marks the beginning of the Middle Rogue, which then runs through Grants Pass before swinging north and creating some of the state's best steelhead and salmon water. From Robertson Bridge southwest of Merlin, through the spectacular Hellgate Canyon and down to the end of the road at Grave Creek, the Middle Rogue ranks among the most beautiful waterways in the state.

Bank access to the Middle Rogue is good once you learn your way around and ferret out the many access spots that

The Middle Rogue River near Hellsgate Canyon.

don't appear on river maps. Some of the public access points are obvious and come in the form of county and state parks. The accompanying map shows these. Floating anglers can navigate the Middle Rogue via drift boat, raft, or pontoon boat, but know the water before you launch because the river has myriad tricky spots, most notably the aptly named Hellsgate Canyon.

The Middle Rogue is great water for intercepting the river's run of half-pounder and adult steelhead. The river has a mix of wild and hatchery summer-run steelhead, with the latter being in the majority. Most of the Rogue's summer steelhead—which reach the middle section of the river between September and November—are of half-pounder life history. The adults, typically 18 to 24 inches in length, are simply half-pounders that made a second journey to the Pacific.

Many highly productive steelhead pools and runs are accessible from the roads along the Middle Rogue. Numerous access points are informal and little known except by local anglers, but the various public parks offer lots of very good water. These include Hog Creek Landing, Hellsgate Park, Indian Mary Park, Ennis Park, Rand, Almeda Park and Grave Creek. All of the aforementioned access sites, along with numerous informal sites, are located downstream from Robertson Bridge. Many other access points are located in and around Grants Pass, upstream from Robertson Bridge.

The Middle Rogue also offers very good prospects for spring chinook salmon between late April and early June. Most salmon anglers pursue the Rogue's salmon by boat, usually fishing plugs and plug/bait combinations. Many outstanding fishing guides work the Middle Rogue for both salmon and steelhead and anglers unfamiliar with the river would be well served to hire a guide. This section also is the home of one of the great old lodges on the river, Morrison's Rogue River Lodge (800-826-1963/www.morrisonslodge.com), as well as Galice Resort (541-476-3818/www.galice.com).

The two primary access points for the Middle Rogue are the towns of Merlin and Grants Pass. If you're heading south on I-5, Merlin is off Exit 66. Head west from the freeway, following the signs toward Merlin. Just west of town, the road splits, with Merlin-Galice Road taking a northerly approach, reaching the river near Hog Creek. The road then crosses the river and follows the south bank to Galice and then all the way down to the next bridge (and the end of road access) at Grave Creek. Once it crosses over to the south bank, Merlin-Galice Road takes you to the popular access points, including Indian Mary Park, Rand, and Almeda Park.

To reach Robertson Bridge from Merlin, take the signed left-hand fork just west of town on Robertson Bridge Road. Cross the river and turn left to reach the popular Griffin Park or turn left before crossing the river to reach Ferry Park on the east bank. Boat launch sites on the Middle Rogue are as follows, starting on the upstream end east from Grants Pass: Pierce Park, Chinook Park, Baker Park (Grants Pass), City Park (Grants Pass), Schroeder Park, Lathrop Landing, Whitehorse Park, Maston Park, Griffin Park, Ferry Park, Robertson Bridge,

Hog Creek Landing, Indian Mary Park, Ennis Park, Galice, Rand, Almeda Park, Argo, and Grave Creek.

Because of the treacherous rapids at Hellsgate Canyon, most boaters take out at Hog Creek, making the Robertson Bridge-to-Hog Creek drift quite popular during the salmon and steelhead seasons. Downstream from Hellsgate Canyon, boaters often launch at Indian Mary or Galice for the drift down to Almeda or Grave Creek. For a fine view of Hellsgate Canyon, stop at the overlook along Merlin-Galice Road.

Rogue River, Wild & Scenic
(Grave Creek to Foster Bar)

In general more popular with whitewater enthusiasts and splash-and-gigglers than with anglers, the roadless section of the Rogue from Grave Creek to Foster Bar is a unique stretch of wilderness water featuring breathtaking scenery and rugged whitewater. Most of the rafting traffic subsides by the time the steelhead arrive in the fall, so adventurous anglers can make a float-and-camp trip through the Wild & Scenic section and combine a great float with good steelheading prospects.

Once you launch at Grave Creek, you are committed to running the entire 33-mile stretch down to Foster Bar. This scenic corridor boasts numerous Class II, III, and IV rapids, not to mention Class V Rainie Falls. From May 15 through October 15, floaters must secure a BLM permit to float the Wild & Scenic Rogue. All information about the river is available from the BLM, whose website is the best place to begin your trip planning (www.or.blm.gov/rogueriver/).

The Wild & Scenic Rogue enjoys the services of several historic, rustic, river-side lodges accessible by trail or by boat. Those lodges on the upper section of the drift are usually open through mid-November, while the jet-boat- and car-accessible lodges near Foster Bar remain open all year. All the lodges require advance reservations. They are as follows, with river miles below the put-in at Grave Creek:

- Black Bar Lodge, RM 13 (541-479-6507/www.blackbarlodge.net)
- Marial Lodge, RM 24.3 (541-474-2057)
- Paradise Bar Lodge, RM 28.3 (800-525-2162/www.paradise-lodge.com);
- Half Moon Bar Lodge, RM 28.4 (888-291-8268/www.halfmoonbarlodge.com)
- Clay Hill Lodge, RM 33.2 (503-859-3772/www.clayhilllodge.com)
- Illahe Lodge, RM 39 (541-247-6111)
- Santa Anita Lodge, RM 39 (541-247-6884/www.santa-anitalodge.net)

The Wild & Scenic section of the Rogue River also offers good trail access and quite a few steelhead anglers hike down from Grave Creek to fish some of the productive pools and runs otherwise accessible only by boat. The trail on the north bank continues all the way down to Foster Bar. The west trailhead (Foster Bar) has camping, toilets, and overnight parking. Drinking water is available May through September at Illahe Campground, 1 mile downriver.

Grave Creek (east trailhead) has toilets and a small parking area along the road above the trailhead. Overnight parking and camping are not allowed at Grave Creek boat ramp area. Drinking water and camping are available about 4 miles upriver from Grave Creek, at Almeda Campground, which is open year round with drinking water available April through November.

Marial Road provides vehicle access to the middle portion of the Rogue River Trail, where Tucker Flat Campground offers six campsites. To reach Marial Road, take I-5 to Exit 80 at Cow Creek and head west, through Glendale, on Cow Creek Road. Turn left at West Fork (CR 32-8-1.1) and take the circuitous Mule Creek-Murial Road down to the river and trailhead. The Rogue River trail leads to many productive bars along the river, but climbs high above the water in many places. A trail map is available from the BLM.

Fly fishing the Middle Rogue

Technically speaking, the Rogue's federally designated Wild & Scenic section stretches for 84 miles, from the mouth of the Applegate River all the way down to Lobster Creek, well below Agness. For practical purposes, however, the truly wild section—the roadless stretch—goes from Grave Creek to Foster Bar.

Rogue River, Lower
(Foster Bar to Gold Beach)

Stretching for almost 40 miles from Foster Bar down to Gold Beach, the Rogue River's lowermost end ranks amongst the state's best fisheries for chinook salmon and steelhead. Many anglers rate the Lower Rogue as the best winter steelhead water on the entire river system. Indeed, the runs here are usually robust and include fish headed for the Applegate and Illinois Rivers, along with the Rogue and its lesser tributaries. All of the fish must negotiate the Lower Rogue and they generally do so rather quickly. Spring and fall chinook salmon abound on the Lower River and are usually mint bright. The lower river offers some good bank-accessible plunking holes and even some productive bars for steelhead fly fishing, but many anglers fish by boat.

The Lower Rogue is a river of a different nature than the rest of the Rogue and is markedly different from the Wild & Scenic section immediately above. The lower river is characterized by a broad, low-gradient flow where depths typically range from 2 to 8 feet and where most of the fish are found in less than 6 feet of water. The shallow riffles are especially good for steelhead, while the pools and deeper runs produce lots of salmon. Anglers employ a full spectrum of salmon and steelhead techniques, with pulling plugs, side drifting, bait fishing, and fly angling all enjoying equal playing time on the river.

Bank access varies quite a bit on the Lower Rogue and is good from tidewater up to Quosatana Campground, a stretch of about 13 miles. From Quosatana up to the little community of Agness (32 river miles from Gold Beach), bank access is almost nonexistent because the river runs through the precipitous Copper Canyon, where sheer 400-foot rock walls rise up from the river. In the canyon, fishing by boat is the rule and many anglers run upriver by jet-sled from the ramp at Quosatana Campground or from points as far down as the docks at Gold Beach. This scenic section of the Rogue offers lots of productive water. At Agness, the Illinois River feeds into the Rogue, creating one of the Rogue's most popular steelhead pools. Even when winter rains make the Rogue run off color, the Illinois creates a clear-water seam running a mile or more downstream.

Upstream from Agness, the river is characterized by somewhat faster water. Drift boat anglers often launch at Foster Bar for the float down to Agness. Bank anglers congregate around Foster Bar and Illahe, and also at Agness. The Rogue River Trail continues along the north bank from Foster Bar and Illahe, providing good walk-in access.

Below Quosatana Campground, angling effort is probably about equally divided between bank anglers and boat anglers. Quosatana forms a very popular bank-fishing access area, rivaled on this lower end of the river by the popularity and productivity of several other well-known holes, riffles, and bars. These include the Ferry Hole, site of the old Bagnell Ferry, along with the mouth of Lobster Creek and the Lobster Creek Campground and Bridge area. The road on the north bank leads upstream from Lobster Creek and ends at Dunkleburger Bar, where lots of steelhead congregate. A trail continues along the north bank from the end of the road. Canfield, Kimball, and Hawkins Riffles derive their names from early settlers in the area, while Boiler Riffle was named for an old ship's boiler once visible at low water.

Two roads lead along the Lower Rogue upstream from Gold Beach. The road to Agness is on the south bank (Jerry's Flat Road) and heads east just south of the bay bridge in Gold Beach. At Lobster Creek, a left-hand turn crosses over the river to Lobster Creek Campground and then continues about 4 miles along the north bank to the Dunkleburger Bar area. The bar opposite the mouth of Lobster Creek (downstream from the bridge) generally fishes best from the south bank.

The campgrounds along the Lower Rogue are usually rather busy during the prime fishing season, especially during the fall when both summer-run steelhead and fall chinook salmon are in the river. Quosatana is the largest campground with 43 sites. Lobster Creek and Foster Bar Campgrounds offer eight sites each and Illahe Campground, a mile downstream from Foster Bar, has 14 sites. Additional lodging options are available both at Agness and in Gold Beach.

Rogue River, Forks

Above Lost Creek Reservoir, the Rogue River's headwater forks flow through some of the prettiest country in the southern Cascade Range. The main river (North Fork) originates near the northwest corner of Crater Lake National Park and then flows south, with SR 230 providing ready access and following the river all the way to the town of Prospect. Trout fishing along the highway ranges from slow to quite good if you seek out-of-the-way pools that are difficult to reach. In general, the more physically demanding the access, the better the fishing for wild trout and this pattern also holds true for the Rogue's many tributary streams, including the highly scenic creeks that feed the uppermost reaches of the river. Stocked rainbow trout are available throughout most of the North Fork and they predominate in the easy-access places.

Among the North Fork's beautiful tributaries are the photogenic Muir Creek, National Creek, Copeland Creek, Mill Creek, Crater Creek, and Bybee Creek. Each of these streams offers fair fishing for small, wild trout—including some brook trout on which there is no limit on the size or number taken. The forest here has a staggering number of logging roads that form a maze of access points. Fortunately for National Creek and Copeland Creek, these roads remain at a respectable distance for the most part.

The upper stretch of the Rogue itself is easy to reach from pull-outs along the highway, several side roads, and a good trail system. Hamaker Campground, about 11 miles west from the SR230/138 intersection, offers good access to the river and the trail, along with several side roads leading to the Rogue and to several small streams in the area. Watch for the signs along the highway and then turn east (right if you are heading uphill from Prospect) to reach the campground, the river and the trail system. Before you get to the campground, a left-hand turn (FR 6530) leads north, following above the east bank of the Rogue before eventually looping back to the south to follow above National Creek.

Upper Rogue River

You'll need a map to orient yourself, but FR 6530 provides the best access to National Creek, though you'll be walking from the road and its spurs down to the creek. This road crosses back over the Rogue just upstream from the mouth of Crater Creek, another lightly-fished trout stream draining the west edge of Crater Lake National Park. Crater Creek is quite tiny by late summer and holds only a sparse trout population, but you'll likely not see another angler. The larger feeder creeks offer better fishing, and except for easy access near the highway and forest roads, fishing these streams requires a substantial physical effort to negotiate the low, but steep ravines and the blow-down-filled forestlands. Nonetheless, a mile or more of fishing along these quiet, timbered creeks is an adventure undertaken by very few anglers. They fish best with dry flies, especially from July through September.

To get to Muir Creek, whose lower end runs in part through a flower-filled bog-like forest meadow, turn west instead of east at the signs for Hamaker Campground or park at the Sno-Park about a mile farther south on the highway. You can also reach Muir Creek from the trailhead and spur road 1 mile south of the Sno-Park. By the time it reaches the highway and the confluence with the North Fork, Muir Creek is actually larger than the Rogue.

Continuing south along the highway, access to the Rogue remains good all the way down to the tiny town of Union Creek. In many places you can park on spur roads and bushwhack to the river and surprisingly few anglers go to such lengths, perhaps because of the oft-steep banks and because in many stretches the river lies out of sight from the highway.

To reach the tributary streams near Union Creek, follow the highway north from town and watch for the forest roads leading east and providing good walk-in access to Copeland Creek, Bybee Creek, and Castle Creek. Union Creek itself is the most popular trout stream in the area. It flows alongside the Crater Lake Highway (at a distance) and offers fair-to-good fishing, mostly for hatchery fish. The seldom-fished upper stretches of Union Creek flow through a canyon so steep as to make access available only to the adventurous, physically capable, mountain-goat-type anglers.

Good access to the Rogue continues all the way south to Prospect and the area offers several worthwhile landmarks: Rogue Gorge where the entire river is stuffed into an impossibly narrow basalt gorge and a majestic stand of old-growth ponderosa pines. There are several campgrounds in the area and the trail system, along with myriad forest roads, provides access to many lightly fished stretches of the river.

To reach the upper Rogue River from I-5, take the Crater Lake Highway exit (Exit 30) at Medford and follow SR 62 north through Shady Cove and past Lost Creek Reservoir. The fishing is best after the runoff subsides during late May and June. The Rogue and its tributary streams generally hold up well throughout the summer and into fall, especially in the out-of-the-way places where wild fish predominate. Most of these waters have wild rainbows and brook trout, and some also offer cutthroat and brown trout. A ranger district map is very helpful in figuring out all the access points.

South of Prospect, the Middle Fork Rogue and South Fork Rogue converge and then travel another few miles down to the Rogue River arm of Lost Creek Reservoir. Both forks offer fair fishing for small wild trout. From Prospect, turn east and follow CR 992, which crosses both forks. Easiest access, however, is from FR 37, which turns left off the county road about 3 miles east of Prospect. It crosses the Middle Fork and then heads south to eventually cross the South Fork at South Fork Campground. East from the road crossing, the Middle Fork descends from a steep gorge where access is difficult (but certainly possible for the adventurous angler). The South Fork is more accessible from several spur roads and from a trail that heads both directions from South Fork Campground.

Rough-and-Ready Creek
closed waters

Round Lake
see Sky Lakes Wilderness Area

Saunders Creek (Coos County)
see Tenmile Creek

A fine salmon and winter steelhead stream, the Sixes River is ideal for drift boats.

Saunders Lake (Coos County)
boat ramp, boat recommended, float tube recommended

A 52-acre lake located alongside Hwy 101, 7 miles north of North Bend, Saunders Lake offers good fishing during April and May for stocked rainbow trout and throughout the year for bluegill, yellow perch, and largemouth bass. You'll want a boat, float tube, canoe, or pontoon boat on Saunders Lake because shoreline access is very limited by private lakeshore property (including a few houses available for short-term rentals). A boat allows you to fish the shorelines, where structure abounds and attracts the bass and bluegill. Work your way up into the coves and arms to find both of these species. The boat ramp is an improved, paved ramp at the day-use/picnic area.

Selmac Lake (Josephine County)
see Lake Selmac

Shuttpelz Lake (Coos County)
no bait, catch-and-release, float tube recommended

A secluded little dunes lake south of Reedsport, Shuttpelz Lake is equally if not more interesting than its neighbor, Hall Lake. Shuttpelz is surrounded by dense timber on three sides and offers fair catch-and-release fishing for native cutthroat trout, some of which reach 14 inches or more. They typically range from 6 to 12 inches and the lake is lightly fished. A small waterfall prevents fish from migrating upstream from Hall Lake to Shuttpelz, creating a unique fishery offering an isolated population of native coastal cutthroat—hence the catch-and-release, no bait regulations. The western shore offers bank access, although it is rather steep, while the remainder of the shoreline is cloaked in trees and thick brush. A float tube is perfect here. The hike from Hall Lake covers about half a mile. From Hwy 101, about 10 miles south of Reedsport, turn west on Wildwood Drive (opposite the entrance to the campground at Eel Lake).

Sixes River (Curry County)
boat ramp, campground

One of the best salmon and steelhead streams on the south coast, the Sixes River is a popular destination during late fall when chinook salmon arrive and during late winter when native steelhead ascend this small river. Like the other small rivers on this part of the coast, the mouth of the Sixes tends to get more-or-less closed off to fish passage during the summer when low flows prevent adequate passage over the building sand dunes. Thus the river's salmon wait until the river levels rise during October and November. Steelhead show up as early as December, but the late-February-through-March fishing is better. The Sixes produces both salmon and steelhead to trophy size.

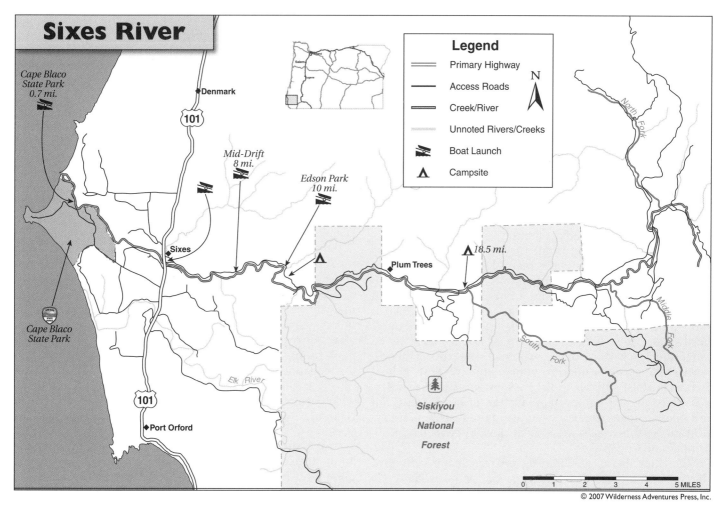

In addition, the Sixes has a fair run of sea-run cutthroat and also usually gets a few stray half-pounder steelhead from the Rogue River. Many of these half-pounders are of hatchery origin (fin-clipped) and can be kept. Current regulations also allow anglers to harvest one wild winter steelhead per day and five per year. The cutthroat trout usually start trickling into the river alongside the chinook salmon as soon as the bar is breached by rising water in mid- to late autumn. Most years—especially if the bar breaches while the water is still quite low—chinook salmon stack up in the lower tidewater pools, accessible from Cape Blanco State Park. Fishing can be very good when this happens, but word spreads quickly and the pools get crowded. The drift from Hwy 101 down to the state park is an easy and pleasant float and a good one for both salmon and cutthroat.

Bank access is fairly limited by private land, but you can get to the water at a few places between the Grange Hole at Hwy 101 and the public access at the confluence with the South Fork (where the campground is located). The confluence is the angling deadline and the river is closed above that point. Drift boat anglers usually launch at Edson Park, 4 miles east of Hwy 101 on Sixes River Road and then take out at the highway bridge (4 miles) or downstream at Cape Blanco State

Park (both sites offer unimproved gravel-bar take-outs). There are two additional launch points, one called Mid-Drift about halfway between Edson and the highway and the other a steep earthen/mud slide, un-named but fairly popular, about a mile above Edson County Park. For this one you'll need a 4-wheel-drive and ropes.

Be sure to check the most recent regulations for open seasons on the Sixes. Currently the river has different season frameworks for each species, including a trout season from late May through October. The trout season allows anglers a chance to keep two cutthroat, and some resident fish are available (mostly in the upper section of the open portion of the river) during the summer.

Skookum Lake (Douglas County)
hike-in

A good producer of 6- to 10-inch brook trout, with an occasional 15-incher, Skookum Lake is located above Devils Creek, high on the North Umpqua River drainage. As a crow flies, this 10-acre lake is about halfway between Tokatee Reservoir to the northwest and Hwy 230 to the southeast. You can there from either side. From Hwy 230, turn north on FR 3703 (Three Lakes Road) about 2 miles west from Diamond Lake. Continue for 8 miles and turn right on FR 3703-200, the Skookum Lake Road. The trailhead is at the end of the road (about 3 miles). From Hwy 138, turn south on the Fish Creek Road (FR 37) just east from the entrance to Tokatee Ranger Station and follow the signs to the trailhead. The hike covers less than a mile.

Sky Lakes Wilderness Area (Klamath County)
hike-in

Situated along the crest of the Cascade Mountains south of Crater Lake National Park, the 113,590-acre Sky Lakes Wilderness Area averages about 6 miles wide and runs north to south for 27 miles. Elevations range from 3,800 feet at the bottom of the Middle Fork Rogue River Canyon to 9,495 feet at Mt. McLoughlin. The wilderness has about 200 lakes and ponds, but only a handful of these support stocked and/ or naturally reproducing trout. The most popular areas are the Seven Lakes Basin and the Island-Horseshoe Lakes area. These basins draw quite a lot of summer visitors.

The lakes here are primarily, if not entirely, stocked with brook trout by air and several of them—like fishless high lakes throughout the west—have a long history of official and unofficial stocking efforts. Several previously fishable lakes are no longer stocked because they lie within remote parts of the wilderness managed for minimal human impact. These include Hemlock, Holst, and Finch Lakes. A few lakes in the wilderness have limited natural reproduction of brook trout, but not enough spawning occurs to maintain fishable numbers of trout, so these lakes are also stocked. They include Cliff, Middle, and Grass Lakes.

Generally the lakes within the wilderness are fairly productive and the more remote lakes can be quite good. Fly fishing is always productive, but anglers can also do quite well with small spinners and spoons. Most of the lakes are fishable from shore, but a float tube is a handy accessory, especially for fly angling. Regularly stocked lakes include Alta, Beal, Blue Canyon, Carey, Cliff, Horseshoe, Grass, Ivern, Middle, McKee, Pear, Round, and South Blue. (See also Southeast Zone for information about lakes on the eastern side of the Cascades within the Sky Lakes Wilderness).

Smith River (Coos County)
boat ramp, boat recommended, campground

Joining the Mainstem Umpqua River near Reedsport to form Winchester Bay, the Smith River is best known as one of Oregon's best destinations for striped bass. The river also hosts a decent run of winter steelhead, shad, chinook salmon, coho salmon and a few sea-run cutthroat. Currently there is no open season for coho on the Smith, but angling for steelhead and chinook can be quite good at times. From August through October, salmon are taken in tidewater by trolling and above tidewater by anglers pulling plugs and bank fishing. The best fishing is from the mouth of the North Fork down to the mouth. Steelhead—lots of wild fish and a few hatchery fish—arrive between late December and early March.

The Smith River hosts a sizeable population of striped bass, including a few trophy-class fish roaming the lower river

among the "schoolies," younger bass in the 2- to 8-pound range. The bass can be taken on bait, plugs, spoons, and even streamer flies. Bank anglers catch a few of them, but fishing for stripers in the Smith River is mostly a boat show. Bait is only allowed in the tidewater section of the lower river (where most of the bass occur). Most serious anglers pursue stripers between May and July, but the autumn fishing can be equally productive, especially during low-light periods and even after dark. During summer, look for them near the mouth of the river. A guide is extremely helpful for striper fishing here: call Dean Finnerty, (541-942-2535/www.5riversguideservice.com) or Todd Hannah, (800-428-8585/www.theoregonangler.com). Current regulations require that all stripers less than 30 inches be released unharmed and anglers are allowed to retain two keeper-sized bass in any 24-hour period.

Shad enter the lower Smith River as early as late April and the run peaks between mid-May and mid-June. Few shad run above tidewater, so the fishery is concentrated below Spencer Creek. Bank access is decent along the lower river, though many anglers fish shad by boat, either motoring up from the Bolan Island ramp or using any of the several launch sites along the river, including Noal Ranch Ramp (the most popular bank-fishing spot), Riverside Park (Schoolhouse Launch), or the fee-launch at Smith River Marina/RV Park (541-271-5370). All these sites are located along Lower Smith River Road, which heads north from Hwy 101 at Bolan Island. Noel Ranch is about 8 miles upriver and Schoolhouse another 2 miles upstream.

Good runs of sea-run cutthroat trout used to enter the Smith River as early as July and their numbers seemed to vary quite a bit from year to year. The run is severely depressed now, though they are still encountered, even well above tidewater, especially after the September and October freshets. To target them for catch-and-release action, look for structure—stumps, pilings, current seams, logs, and cut banks—and cast small spoons and spinners or streamer flies (all barbless). At the mouth of the river, these same kinds of structure sometimes attract pile perch and other saltwater fish. Depending on tide movement and river flows, the lower end of the Smith can create some heavy currents, so be wary if you are boating near the pilings or other obstacles.

The upper reaches of the Smith, upstream from the head of tide at Spencer Creek, and including the North Fork, offer many miles of good winter steelhead water. The North Fork is better than the West Fork for steelhead, and the West Fork is the better early summer catch-and-release trout stream. Peak steelhead catches occur during January and February and the forks are no longer stocked with hatchery fish so virtually all the steelhead are wild and must be released (check current regulations). The upper sections of both forks host fair populations of wild cutthroat trout ranging from 6 to 12 inches in length. Currently fishing for wild trout is catch-and-release only and no bait is allowed above tidewater areas on the Smith, the North Fork Smith, and all tributaries. Read the regulations carefully before venturing out on the Smith.

During winter, when the steelhead are running, the upper section of the Smith is usually floatable from Smith River

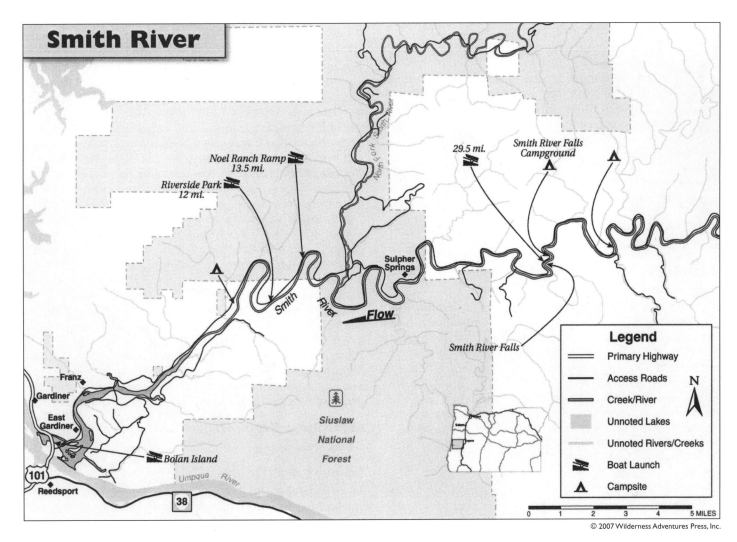

Smith River

Legend

═══	Primary Highway
───	Access Roads
───	Creek/River
▓	Unnoted Lakes
	Unnoted Rivers/Creeks
≋	Boat Launch
⛺	Campsite

© 2007 Wilderness Adventures Press, Inc.

Falls down to the pole slide at Dailey Ranch. The North Fork, though not often floated, is boat-able, but only for experienced rowers. The launch is at milepost 6 on the access road along the North Fork (FR 23) and the take-out is on the Mainstem, about a mile below the North Fork's mouth, at a steep gravel bar called Stimmermans (about river mile 12). Be especially wary of the heavy whitewater just downstream from the launch. Bank access is available from the bridge crossings along the road. The North Fork is brushy and difficult to access, but lightly fished.

Smith River Falls Campground (BLM) is about midway along the length of the stream and has eight tent/trailer sites, vault toilets, but no water. Numerous other campgrounds are present along Hwy 101 north and south of Reedsport, Oregon.

Smith River, North Fork (Josephine County)
hike-in, no bait
The Smith River of northern California fame—renowned for its runs of salmon and winter steelhead—actually has part of its modest beginnings in the mountains of southwest Oregon. Here the river is a small, steep, forested creek with a fair population of small, wild trout. It flows through rugged canyon country in the Siskiyou Range. The North Fork Smith forms the southwest border of the Kalmiopsis Wilderness Area. Access is from a network of forest roads, these in turn being accessible from the Winchuck and Chetco Rivers. You'll need a good map to travel this country.

Snag Lake (Coos County)
hike-in, float tube recommended
A 30-acre lake on the Oregon Dunes National Recreation Area, Snag Lake offers secluded fishing for naturally reproducing largemouth bass and yellow perch. Access is by hiking or off-road vehicle and this shallow, sand dune lake is a good place for a float tube, though bank-fishing access is good. The hike (or ride) begins at the end of Hauser Station Road, which heads west from Hwy 101, 5.5 miles north from North Bend. Snag Lake has been known to produce a few bass in the 3- to 5-pound range. They have lots of good cover in the form of the many dead shore-pine snags standing in the lake. The shoreline also is lined intermittently with small shore-pines, which provide shelter for primitive camping. Best fishing is between March and June.

Soda Springs Reservoir (Douglas County)

A small, narrow impoundment on the upper North Umpqua drainage, Soda Springs Reservoir is lightly fished for rainbow and brown trout. Fishing is generally slow because the reservoir doesn't have much shallow-water habitat, but an occasional 16- to 20-inch brown trout comes from these waters. The reservoir is located almost adjacent to Hwy 138 about 30 miles west from Diamond Lake and about 2 miles east from Boulder Flat Campground on the North Umpqua River.

South Blue Lake
see Sky Lakes Wilderness Area

South Umpqua River
see Umpqua River, South

Spalding Pond (Josephine County)
campground

A popular little 3-acre millpond stocked with rainbow trout, Spalding Pond sits at 3,000 feet in the forested hills southwest of Grants Pass and offers excellent handicap-access facilities, including three fishing platforms and a surfaced trail. The forest service campground, sitting near the old mill site, is primitive. To get there, head south from Grants Pass on Hwy 199 for about 18 miles to a right-hand turn on FR 25. Follow FR 25 about 7.5 miles to a left turn on FR 2524 (Spalding Mill Road) and continue 4.5 miles to the lake and campground.

Spirit Lake (Coos County)
see Horsfall Lake

Squaw Lake (Coos County)
campground

This small lake is stocked each spring with legal-size rainbows and offers fair-to-good fishing, with best action in May and June. Squaw Lake has a small, primitive campground (seven sites) and is located 22.5 miles south of Powers. From Powers, head south on the county road along the river. At the forest boundary, the road becomes Forest Primary Route 33 and heads down to Coquille Falls. Turn left on FR 3348 and then right on Spur Road 080, leading to the lake and campground. A float tube is handy here.

Though populations are depressed, sea-run cutthroat trout still run many south coast streams.

Squaw Lakes (Jackson County)
hike-in, campground

The Squaw Lakes are two scenic, natural mountain lakes near the California border south of Medford and just east from Applegate Reservoir. Lower Squaw Lake, covering 51 acres, offers rainbow and cutthroat trout, yellow perch, white crappie, brown bullhead, largemouth bass, and a few smallmouth bass. Upper Squaw Lake provides a good fishery for 8- to 12-inch native coastal cutthroat trout. A .25-mile hiking trail connects Upper and Lower Squaw Lake. The upper lake spans 20 acres.

These lakes are very popular during the summer months, but fishing tends to be good most of the time. To escape the crowds and fish these waters at their best, wait until late September when the water begins to cool. A float tube or raft comes in handy and the 300-yard hike is no detriment to carrying watercraft in to the lakes. Motors are not permitted and during the summer months, camping is by reservation only at the semi-primitive campground at Lower Squaw Lake.

Camping reservations must be made through the National Recreation reservation Service by calling 1-877-444-6777 or by reserving online at www.reserveusa.com. To reach Squaw Lakes from Jacksonville, head south on Hwy 238 for 7 miles. At the community of Ruch, turn left on Upper Applegate Road and continue south 14 miles to Applegate Dam. Cross the dam and continue heading east about 9 miles to the lakes.

Steamboat Creek (North Umpqua drainage)
closed waters

Stump Lake (Douglas County)

As its name suggests, Stump Lake is a stump-filled reservoir adjacent to Hwy 138 on the upper North Umpqua River watershed northwest of Diamond Lake. The reservoir spans about 12 acres and offers fair fishing for wild brook trout from 6 to 12 inches. You can fish by raft or float tube, but bank fishing is most popular.

Tannen Lakes (Josephine County)
hike-in, float tube recommended

Located due south of Oregon Caves Monument and just north of the California border, the two small Tannen Lakes offer fair-to-good fishing for small brook trout, with a rare fish reaching 13 inches. They are fairly popular owing to the scenic, easy hike on the Tannen Lakes Trail. The pleasant hike takes you through heavily wooded highlands. While in the area, check out the view from the road on the south side of Tannen Mountain. A float tube is handy on these lakes, especially on shallow, brushy East Tannen Lake and especially if you are fly angling. Fishing generally holds up from June through October. From Cave Junction, head south on Hwy 199 toward O'Brien and then head west on CR 5828, which becomes FR 48 and leads to FR 4812. Follow FR 4812 westerly to FR 041, leading to the trailhead.

Tenmile Creek (Coos County)

The outlet from Tenmile Lake, this slow-moving stream is best known for its winter steelhead fishery featuring both hatchery and wild fish that arrive from December through the end of the season on March 31. Lesser known are the creek's runs of both chinook salmon and sea-run cutthroat trout. The salmon fishery here has been closed in recent years, but keep an eye on the regulations for potential re-opening. The salmon arrive between September and early November.

Tenmile Creek offers a fair fishery for cutthroat, though they are best fished by floating the river in a small pram or similar easy-to-carry craft and then motoring back up. The sea-runs can appear any time between July and October, with September being the peak month. Steelhead anglers often congregate at five popular pools located at Spinreel Campground, which sits right on the creek along Hwy 101 just south of the entrance to Tenmile Lakes. ODFW plants steelhead smolts at the mouth of Saunders Creek, so the fish tend to stack up in the Spinreel area.

Even sustained rain has minimal impact on the clarity of Tenmile Creek. When the stream does color up, it clears quickly, making Tenmile a good back-up plan when the larger steelhead waters in the area remain high and dirty.

Tenmile Lakes (Coos County)
boat ramp, boat recommended, campground, services

Among Oregon's most popular multi-use waters, the two Tenmile Lakes south of Reedsport offer a wide array of angling opportunities. The best action—and the most renowned—is for largemouth bass, but Tenmile and North Tenmile Lakes also have good populations of bluegill, brown bullhead, and crappie. The bass reach double-digit weights and are numerous enough that bass clubs hold tournaments here. Most of the fish range from 1 to 3 pounds, with a fair number up to 5 pounds. Knowledgeable bass anglers—fishing by boat—often enjoy 15- to 50-plus-fish days, with the peak action running from April through July.

The bass, along with the crappie and bluegill, enjoy ideal habitat in the form of myriad narrow arms and coves rich in

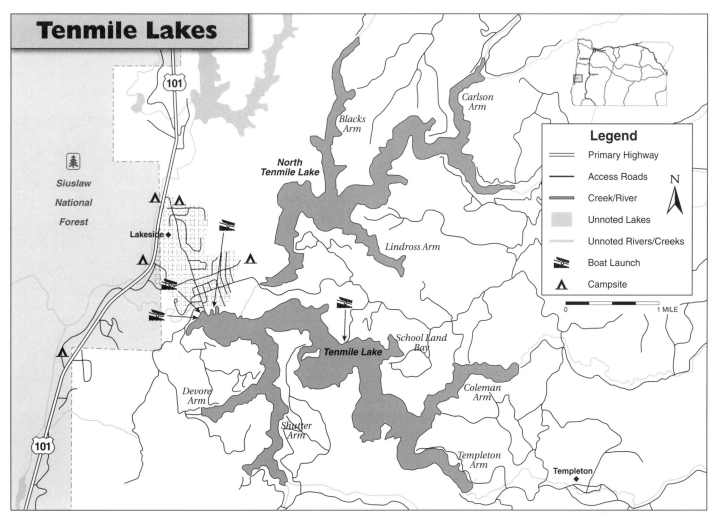

© 2007 Wilderness Adventures Press, Inc.

snags, logs, stumps, brush, weed beds, extensive lily pads, and other cover. For that matter, the numerous docks (most of them private) always seem to hold bass and crappie when the fish are holding shallow. All told these two lakes boast a combined 2,723 surface acres and 187 miles of shoreline. Even though they attract lots of anglers, lots of pleasure boaters, and lots of water sports enthusiasts, the Tenmile Lakes offer plenty of room to spread out. The narrow arms offer ample opportunity for solitude and plenty of very good fishing.

In addition to the warmwater action, Tenmile Lakes are stocked with hatchery rainbow trout and have indigenous populations of cutthroat trout, along with a few winter steelhead, coho salmon and chinook salmon that historically migrate through the lakes and into the feeder streams. Many decades of intense timber harvest in the nearby hills had the predictable result of degrading the spawning habitat, so the wild anadromous fish are not too numerous now. Trout, however, can reach several pounds in these shallow, fertile lakes and few people pursue them with regularity.

Bank access is very limited on Tenmile Lake and essentially non-existent on North Tenmile. In addition to boat ramps at 6th Street and at 8th Street in the community of Lakeside, Tenmile Lake County Park offers a large boat ramp and fishing access, along with picnic area and restrooms. The park is at the south end of 11th Street and Park Avenue, along the lake's western corner. The area also offers several privately owned campgrounds, lodges and motels, and two full-service marinas that rent boats. Tenmile Marina is in Lakeside (541-759-3137/www.tenmilemarina.com) and La Playa Marina is located further to the west along the lake's north shore (541-759-4775).

Access to the north lake is by boat only, with the ramp being located at the southwest corner at Lakeside at North Lake Resort & Marina (541-759-3515/www.northlakeresort.com). The marina offers all services, including a tackle shop. To reach Tenmile Lakes, follow Hwy 101 north from Coos Bay or south from Reedsport. The entrance is well signed.

Toketee Reservoir (Douglas County)
boat ramp, boat recommended, campground

Little known outside the area, 97-acre Toketee Reservoir is a fairly productive brown trout fishery located high on the North Umpqua River, about 20 miles from Diamond Lake. Toketee produces brown trout from 10 to 20 inches, with the big fish being few and far between. Most of the fish are less than 16 inches, but each year anglers take fish in the 3- to 4-pound range, with lures and flies being most effective, especially at the reservoir's upper end. Boat and float tube anglers enjoy the advantage here and best fishing is in the fall, although anglers can find good-to-fair action just about any time from mid-spring through summer. There is an unimproved ramp and camping area on the upper end of the reservoir. A few wild brook and rainbow trout also inhabit the reservoir. Take Hwy 138 east from Roseburg or west from Hwy 97. Watch for the signs at FR 34, 2 miles west from the turnoff to Watson Falls.

Twin Lakes (Douglas County)
hike-in

These pleasant, forested mountain lakes offer fair-to-good fishing for small brook trout from mid-June through October. The better of the two, Big Twin (or East Twin) covers 14 acres and Little Twin, or West Twin, spans 6 acres. A small camping area and a shelter are located on East Twin, and West Twin has a three-sided log shelter with picnic tables. The hike covers an easy half-mile. To reach the Twin Lakes, follow Hwy 138 about 50 miles from Roseburg, past Glide, to a right-hand turn on FR 4770 (about 3 miles east from Dry Creek Store). Follow the road about 10 miles to the trailhead.

Umpqua River, Mainstem (Douglas County)
boat ramp, boat recommended, campground

Winding through oak-clad foothills and rolling farmlands, Oregon's Mainstem Umpqua abounds with smallmouth bass and annually hosts one of the region's best runs of shad. Neither shad nor smallmouth bass are native to the drainage—nor to the state—but they create the two most prolific fisheries on the Mainstem, which begins at the convergence of the North Umpqua and South Umpqua Rivers near Roseburg.

Since their introduction to the system in the 1960s, smallmouth bass have established themselves not only throughout the Mainstem, but also well into the South Fork and into the lower North Umpqua. So prolific are the bass that 100-fish days occur regularly on the Mainstem's best reaches.

Mainstem Umpqua River

By mid-summer, when the river drops into ideal shape, the Umpqua reveals her prime, slow-moving, structure-filled bass haunts. Exposed bedrock, carved by the river into ridges, reefs, and hollows, provides perfect cover for the abundant bass. Forage abounds in the form of smaller fish, insects, and crayfish. An Oregon Department of Fish & Wildlife (ODFW) study found that the bass prefer crayfish and myriad insects over other prey despite persistent concerns in the angling community that the bass might pose a major predatory threat on migrating juvenile salmon and steelhead.

The Umpqua's prime smallmouth period stretches from July through September—a time when the Umpqua Valley enjoys hot summer weather, making a day on the river a decidedly pleasant and refreshing undertaking. Most of the river's bass are small fish, less than 10 inches in length. ODFW says that only 15 percent of the bass population is composed of fish more than 10 inches long. Among that 15 percent, however, are fish that weigh 3 to 5 pounds.

Tim Blount lands a smallmouth bass on the Mainstem Umpqua River above Elkton.

The river's best stretches are so densely populated with fish that anglers commonly hook many dozens of smallies during a daylong drift. In fact, on sunny, hot summer days, schools of small bass often drift along with you, enjoying the shadow cast by your boat or float tube. The larger bass tend to shun the schools of small fish. Look for them in the deeper, more inaccessible hideouts.

The shad run begins in May and lasts through early July. The best fishing occurs between Memorial Day and mid-June, especially during years when spring runoff is light and ends quickly. Low water during June means fast and furious shad fishing for anglers who know the good shad pools, such as those at Sawyer Rapids and Yellow Creek, among many others.

In addition to the shad and smallmouth bass, anglers pick up quite a few salmon in the Mainstem Umpqua. Fishing for spring chinook salmon peaks from mid-April through early June and fall chinook are available during September, but constitute a less-productive fishery than that afforded by the highly regarded springers. Coho salmon, winter steelhead, and summer steelhead also run through the mainstem, though they provide far more productive fisheries in the forks.

The river's winter steelhead provide a fair fishery between January and March, with February generally being the best month. These are a mix of both wild and hatchery fish ranging from 6 to 20-plus pounds. The best steelhead fishing is from the forks down to Scott Creek.

Most salmon anglers fish by boat, either motoring up from the launch just west of Scottsburg or drifting the popular stretches as far downstream as Scottsburg. These same segments are good bets for pulling plugs for winter steelhead. During the winter steelhead season, try the upper drifts west of Sutherlin: Umpqua Landing to James Wood Park or James Wood to Osprey or Yellow Creek. Yellow Creek to Elkton makes for a very long day during the short days of winter, so take out or launch at Kellogg Bridge or The Slide. Below Elkton, good steelhead (and shad and smallmouth) drifts go from Elkton RV Park (fee launch) down to Sawyer Rapids (also a fee launch). The Sawyer Rapids launch is also known as the Henderer Road Launch.

The Slide is located on the southwest bank, across the bridge and upstream from Elkton. The short, lazy drift down to Elkton takes half a day (or more if you fish every nook and cranny along the way) while the 8-mile drift from Elkton to the Sawyer Rapids Launch (across the river and downstream from Elkton) takes a full day during summer when the water flows low and slow.

The upper drifts, from the forks, past Umpqua, and down to Yellow Creek are great for bass, fair for shad, and decent for winter steelhead, but not too productive for salmon. A few fast-water areas, such Sawyer Rapids downstream from the town of Elkton, require strong boating skills, but for the most part this is easy water, most of it negotiable by pontoon boats, although drift boats are more popular. Shuttles can be arranged through the tackle shop at Arlene's Restaurant in Elkton (541-584-2555).

Salmon anglers frequent the area around Scottsburg, where slow, flat water allows for easy jet-boat access. Some anglers fish with standard motorboats, but beware the submerged ledges that can provide a severe beating to your props. Motorboats are better off staying below Scottsburg.

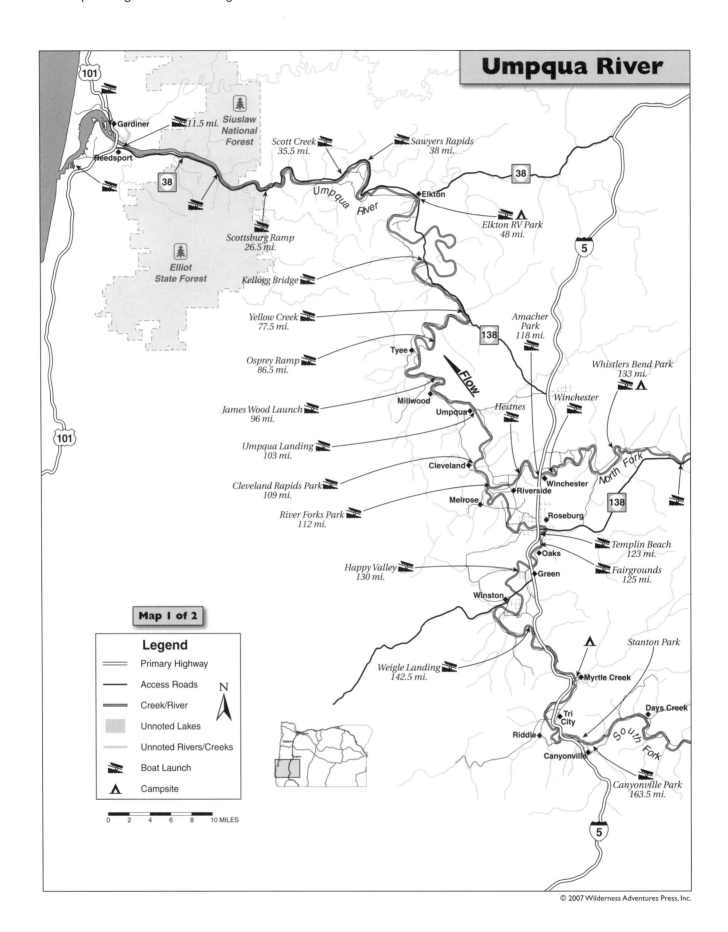

Umpqua River

101

Gardiner

11.5 mi.

Siuslaw
National
Forest

Reedsport

38

Scott Creek
35.5 mi.

Sawyers Rapids
38 mi.

Umpqua River

Elkton

38

5

Elkton RV Park
48 mi.

Scottsburg Ramp
26.5 mi.

Elliot
State Forest

Kellogg Bridge

Yellow Creek
77.5 mi.

Amacher
Park
118 mi.

Osprey Ramp
86.5 mi.

Tyee

Flow

Whistlers Bend Park
133 mi.

138

Winchester

James Wood Launch
96 mi.

Millwood

Umpqua

Hestnes

Umpqua Landing
103 mi.

Cleveland

North Fork

Cleveland Rapids Park
109 mi.

Winchester

138

Melrose

Riverside

River Forks Park
112 mi.

Roseburg

Templin Beach
123 mi.

Oaks

Happy Valley
130 mi.

Green

Fairgrounds
125 mi.

Winston

101

Map 1 of 2

Legend

— Primary Highway

— Access Roads

— Creek/River

Unnoted Lakes

Unnoted Rivers/Creeks

Boat Launch

▲ Campsite

N

Stanton Park

Weigle Landing
142.5 mi.

Myrtle Creek

Tri
City

Days Creek

Riddle

South Fork

Salem

Canyonville

Canyonville Park
163.5 mi.

0   2   4   6   8   10 MILES

5

© 2007 Wilderness Adventures Press, Inc.

Umpqua River

Map 2 of 2

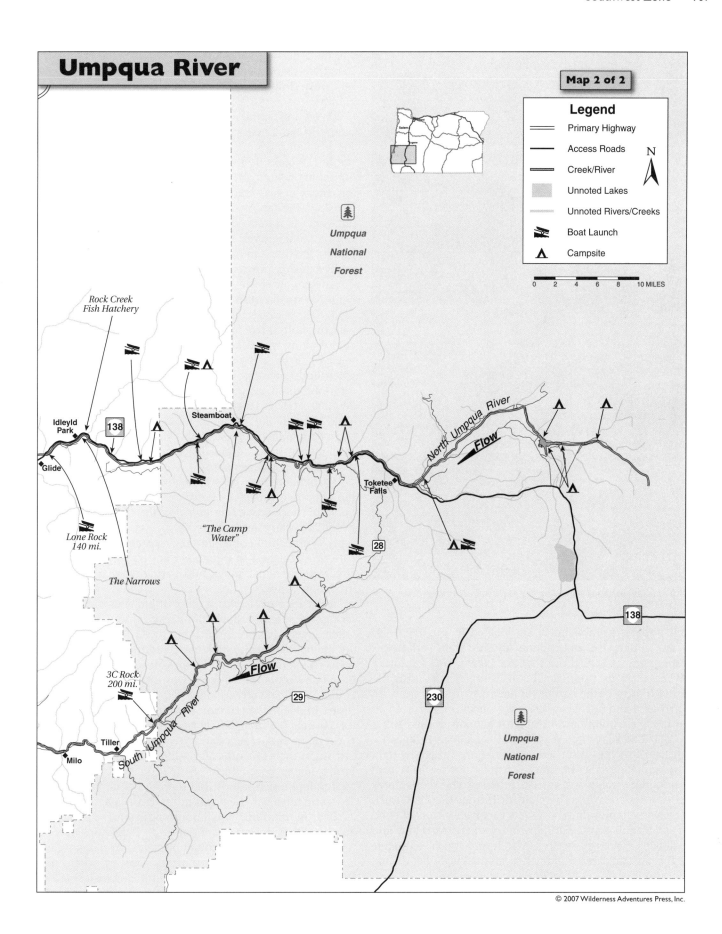

Legend

Primary Highway

Access Roads

Creek/River

Unnoted Lakes

Unnoted Rivers/Creeks

Boat Launch

Campsite

N

0 2 4 6 8 10 MILES

Umpqua

National

Forest

Rock Creek
Fish Hatchery

Idleyld
Park

138

Glide

Lone Rock
140 mi.

Steamboat

"The Camp
Water"

The Narrows

3C Rock
200 mi.

Tiller

Milo

South Umpqua River

Flow

29

North Umpqua River

Flow

Toketee
Falls

28

230

Flow

138

Umpqua

National

Forest

Bill Stanley unhooks a shad on the Mainstem Umpqua River.

spinners, herring and bait/plug or bait/blade combinations. Longtime favorites include Blue Fox Spinners and Kwikfish, but every Umpqua salmon angler has a favorite lure, bait, or combo.

If you don't mind a little exploratory legwork, you can find plenty of bank access on the Mainstem Umpqua, including the popular sites at Yellow Creek and Sawyer Rapids. State Route 138 picks up the Umpqua northwest from the town of Sutherlin (located on Interstate-5, 10 miles north of Roseburg) and more or less follows the river all the way to the Oregon Coast at Reedsport. Along the way, the highway provides bank access at many places. Yellow Creek is located upstream from Elkton; Sawyer Rapids is downstream. Both places rank among the river's most productive shad areas, so you can generally expect a crowd when the shad are running.

Anglers interested in a unique guided expedition for Umpqua smallmouth would be well advised to check out the Big K Ranch, which has private access to miles of water otherwise difficult to reach. The Big K offers lodging in 20 separate cabins along with fine meals and guided fishing on a lengthy reach of the river. Big K guides and guests adhere to the lodge's catch-and-release policy, which results in more large smallmouth than on any other stretch of the river. Contact Big K at 800-390-2445 and visit their website at www.big-k.com. Also, Todd Hannah, the Umpqua's most revered fishing guide, runs trips throughout the year on the Mainstem, focusing on shad, smallmouth bass, striped bass, and salmon (800-428-8585/www.theoregonangler.com).

For smallmouth bass, straightforward tactics prevail on the Umpqua, especially between July and September when bass are most active and enjoying the river's 70-plus-degree water. You can't go wrong with an assortment of jigs in an array of sizes and colors. Rubber worms, especially curly-tail varieties, attached to a jig-head are equally effective, as are small spoons, small plugs, and a wide range of different flies, including poppers.

Don't be surprised if a pack of smallies attacks your offering—or at least follows along as if curious but not hungry. Often several bass rush in trying to get there first. The takes are vicious. The Umpqua's clear summer flows allow you to watch most of the action. Often you can choose a lure or fly based on simply watching the way the fish respond to various colors, sizes, and styles. However, the river's larger fish often reside in deeper water, typically hiding alongside submerged (or partially submerged) ledges and reefs. Look for shaded cover in the slow reaches and for current seams created where fast water meets or runs alongside ledge rock. When holding in the deeper flows, these 14- to 18-inch bass are difficult to spot, being much less visible than the abundant small bass. Thus you must fish the water rather than cast to sighted fish.

Bear in mind that smallmouth bass tend to eat just about anything that doesn't eat them first. Rarely are they super-finicky about particular colors or styles. You'll get plenty of action with a basic selection of jigs, flies, or other lures. On the Umpqua, plenty of action sometimes translates to one of those 100-bass outings under perfect sunny skies.

Several popular salmon holes are located in this area and there are launch sites at Umpqua Wayside State Park below Scottsburg and at Scottsburg Park near town. This section of the river is the most popular salmon-fishing reach during the first month or so of the spring chinook run. Anglers show up here in March and by mid-April it's not uncommon to see two dozen boats anchored and fishing for Salmon in the Scottsburg/Wells Creek area upstream from the highway bridge.

You can fish the water above Scottsburg Bridge by drift boat by launching at Scotts Creek (1.5 miles downstream from Sawyer Rapids) and taking out at Scottsburg. The Scotts Creek Ramp is at milepost 23. The short drift from the fee-launch below Sawyer Rapids down to Scotts Creek offers lots of good water as well and is also a prime drift for shad during May and June. During the early season (March and April), springers move through this area rapidly. Fish all the inside bends and look for water from 4 to 8 feet deep. Anglers use plugs, spoons,

The river's shad are equally susceptible to jigs. One of the long-time favorite shad rigs on this river is a chartreuse curly-tail rubber worm on a ⅛- or ¼-ounce jig. If the chartreuse doesn't work—or stops producing—switch to fluorescent red, white, or purple. Fly anglers do very well fishing for shad on the Mainstem Umpqua. Typical shad darts in a range of colors will suffice. Carry them in both weighted and un-weighted versions and carry both floating and high-density sinking-tip fly lines. Over the past decade or so, many fishing guides based in southern Oregon have started guiding anglers for Umpqua shad. If you've never fished the river, consider a guided trip to help you learn the water and the best techniques.

To reach the Mainstem Umpqua at the town of Elkton, take Exit 150 or Exit 162 from I-5 and head westerly to Drain. From Drain follow the signs west to Elkton. At Elkton, SR 138 heads south, crossing the river twice and then following it for a few miles up past Yellow Creek. When the highway heads away from the river, turn right at the signs to Tyee. Tyee Road follows the river south and then east all the way to another bridge at Umpqua Landing. Nearby Henry Estates Winery is well worth the stop. Downstream from Elkton, SR 38 follows the Umpqua all the way to Winchester Bay. Arlene's, the restaurant and store in Elkton, is the hub of fishing activity on the Mainstem Umpqua and the folks there can give you good directions and excellent fishing advice.

In summary, the Mainstem Umpqua boat ramps are as follows, starting upstream and heading down the river:
- River Forks County Park sits at the top of the mainstem where the North and South Umpqua River meet
- A few miles below is Cleveland Rapids Park and boat ramp, located off Cleveland Park Road via Garden Valley Road from Roseburg or from Winchester
- Another 7 miles downstream is Umpqua Landing (from Sutherlin, take Fort McKay Road heading west)
- James Wood Launch, located along Tyee Road, about 7 miles west of Tyee Store
- Osprey Ramp, 15 miles north of Umpqua on Tyee Road
- Yellow Creek, a few miles downstream from Osprey
- Kellogg Bridge, where Hwy 138 crosses the river south of Elkton
- The Slide, across the bridge at Elkton and upstream
- Elkton RV Park
- Sawyer Rapids Ramp (cross the bridge at Elkton and head downriver for 10 miles on Henderer Road; sometimes called Henderer Road Launch)
- Scott Creek Ramp (12 miles west of Elkton on Hwy 38)
- Scottsburg Ramp (1 mile west of Scottsburg)
- Umpqua River, Mouth—see Winchester Bay

Umpqua River, North (Douglas County)
campground, boat ramp

The North Umpqua River offers two distinct halves: From the confluence with the South Umpqua River west of Roseburg, up past the tiny town of Idelyld Park, the North Umpqua is a good steelhead fishery and a fair-to-good salmon fishery. This lower end of the North Umpqua stretches for almost 40 miles and is especially kind to anglers fishing by drift boat.

Above Idelyld Park, Rock Creek—site of an ODFW fish hatchery—marks the beginning of the North Umpqua's legendary 31-mile-long fly-only section. This stretch of the river is famous for its run of summer steelhead, which attracts fly anglers from all over the world. Far fewer anglers pursue the wild trout in this section of river and changing regulations not withstanding, dry-fly action for trout can be very good on these waters. Likewise, the so-called "fly water" offers a good, but little-known run of native winter steelhead.

North Umpqua River

The fly-only water on the North Umpqua is open to anglers using both traditional fly-fishing equipment and also to anglers using spinning or casting rods. In all cases, however, only artificial flies are allowed, so those using spinning or casting gear are allowed to use a plastic bubble in order to cast the flies. Be sure to consult the most current regulations for the fly water because the rules are in a constant state of flux.

Summer steelhead arrive in the North Umpqua by June, with the bulk of the run reaching the river between early July and early October. Winter steelhead fishing picks up below Winchester Dam as early as late December. From Winchester Dam to Glide, winter fishing can be good during January, while February and March are prime months on the fly water. The North Umpqua likewise has strong runs of spring chinook and coho salmon. Winchester Dam, located just east of I-5 and just north of Roseburg, has a fish-passage facility that includes several large windows through which you can watch salmon and steelhead passing through on their journeys.

Fly-only Zone, Soda Springs Dam to Rock Creek

The 31 miles of fly-only water on the North Umpqua River ranks among the most famous and revered steelhead waters in the world. Steelhead fly fishing fanatics flock to this vibrantly beautiful river. They come to test their skills not only against the North Umpqua's remarkable fish, but also against this unique and demanding river. The North Umpqua's rich history features a litany of famous anglers past and present, among them Clarence Gordon who founded the North Umpqua Lodge, which catered to fly anglers during the middle of the 20th century.

This lodge is located across the river from the mouth of Steamboat Creek. Gordon and his angling contemporaries named most of the pools on that reach of the North Umpqua. The Boat Pool was so-named because its calm waters allowed a rowboat to ferry visitors back and forth from the road on the north bank. The Kitchen—always a coveted run—was visible from the lodge's dining hall.

Another prominent figure in North Umpqua lore, Ward Cummings guided for Gordon. Together, the two men accounted for several well-known and beautiful North Umpqua steelhead flies. The Cummings Special and the Black Gordon remain popular flies on the river, at least with anglers with an appreciation for the North Umpqua's storied past.

The North Umpqua River is famous for its lengthy fly-only stretch where anglers pursue summer- and winter-run steelhead. This summer fish took a classic style "Dee" fly.

Eventually, Gordon moved his operation to the north bank where it evolved into Steamboat Inn under the ownership of Frank and Jeanne Moore, who purchased the lodge in 1957. Moore, Gordon, Cummings, and several others formed a group called the Steamboater's Club. The Steamboater's remain to this day the watchdog of the North Umpqua. It was this group that in the 1950s, convinced the game commission of the need to create a fly-only zone on the river. The fly-only regulations have survived in the form of a 31-mile-long sanctuary set aside for fly angling.

The river's most famous pools are collectively known as "The Camp Water" and are strung along a mile-long S-curve near the mouth of Steamboat Creek. The Camp Water includes such renowned pools as Sawtooth, The Station, The Boat Pool, The Kitchen, Upper & Lower Gordon, and The Mott Pools. Many anglers on their first visit to the North Umpqua fish only the Camp Water, despite 30 additional miles of water and hundreds of productive pools and runs. The river upstream from the Camp Water is locally known as the "Upper River."

Summer steelhead arrive in the fly water by early summer. During good years mid- to late July offers fair fishing. Fish numbers continue to climb through August and September—usually the peak time on the river. Strong runs total 10,000 or more fish. Like most steelhead rivers, the North Umpqua draws a crowd when reports circulate of a voluminous summer run.

As the number of summer fish climbs, the water level drops. By late August, the river reaches its lowest flows of the year. Hot weather often brings a lull in the action, but lucky be the angler who encounters one of those rare August freshets, which usually awaken the steelhead for a time. Low water continues through September and usually well into October. The arrival of the autumn's first big rains spells an end to the

Joe Howell swings a fly for winter steelhead on the North Umpqua River.

cleated boots and a wading staff is a good idea. If you're new to this water, you can expect some of the most challenging wading of your career. Much of the river features submerged bedrock reefs of all sizes and shapes. They make for difficult footing, although many pools allow for minimal wading. During late summer, many anglers opt for shorts or pants rather than waders, but the cleated boots remain an essential item.

Anglers will find that 7- to 10-weight rods are ideally suited to this large river, where steelhead range from 5 to more than 20 pounds. Both single-hand and Spey-casting rods have their place on the river. Many different flies are both popular and productive on the North Umpqua, including the classic wet flies like the Purple Peril and Skunk, along with dry flies like the Muddler and Bomber. Spey-style steelhead flies are also popular.

The North Umpqua's fly water is easily accessible from Hwy 138, which follows virtually the entire river upstream from the lower fly-only deadline. Exit I-5 at Roseburg and watch for the signs for Diamond Lake and Hwy 138. Campgrounds are conveniently strung along the river all the way through the fly water.

Rock Creek to South Umpqua Confluence

Below the fly-only zone, the North Umpqua River continues its high-gradient run down through the foothills of the Cascade Range. Bank access is fair from the Rock Creek area down to Glide and this section includes several well-known and productive pools, including The Narrows, upstream from Idelyld Park, where the river funnels rapidly through a narrow cleft in the bedrock, and the Tavern Pool, a bit further downstream. The motel in Idelyld Park sits right above a good section of steelhead water accessible to motel guests. This section of the river is very popular with steelhead and coho salmon anglers. The coho fishery peaks during October and November.

Downstream from Glide, bank access is more limited and drift boats have a distinct advantage. The uppermost drift starts above Glide at Lone Rock Launch and runs about 4 river miles down to the county ramp in Glide. The Glide to Whistler Bend drift, covering about 10 miles, is the most popular drift on the lower river and allows anglers to fish lots of excellent steelhead water. You can drift from Whistler's Bend down to a pole-slide takeout in the small reservoir formed by Winchester Dam, but comparatively few people make this run because of the distance and inconvenience.

Whistler Bend Park also offers about a mile of access along the south bank and, as the name suggests, the park sits on a broad, sweeping bend in the river. Virtually the entire length of river through the park is good steelhead and salmon water.

low water. Despite increased flows, fishing often holds up into November.

The North Umpqua's winter steelhead run peaks from February through early April. The river's winter steelhead average larger than do their summer-run cousins, with 12- to 15-pound fish being common. During a good year, the winter run exceeds 6,000 fish, all of them natives. About half of the winter fish spawn in Steamboat/Canton Creeks and as many as 20 percent spawn upstream from the famed "Camp Water" near the confluence with Steamboat Creek. By April, one begins to see steelhead holding on shallow gravel bars in pairs and small groups. These fish are spawners and etiquette dictates that they should be left to their business, undisturbed by anglers.

Throughout the winter season, the North Umpqua runs higher than during the summer and fall, but breaks in the rainy weather cause the water to drop into fishable shape while heavy storms swell the river to unruly proportions, sometimes for days on end. Local anglers have the advantage, for they can head for the river when she drops into shape. Traveling anglers might plan a week for the North Umpqua, arrive with high hopes and then find the river swollen over its banks for the entire time. Under certain conditions, the river can jump 6 or 8 feet overnight and, during wetter-than-average winters, it might offer a scant handful of fishable days.

As with winter steelheading anywhere, timing is everything.

In most respects the North Umpqua is a physically demanding river. In many places, you must scramble down a steep highway embankment to get to the water. Then there's the wading. The North Umpqua's slippery bottom demands

Watch for the signs to Whistler's Bend about 5 miles west of Glide. The park covers 175 acres and has 25 camp sites (no hookups). Two miles west of Glide, a north turn off the highway leads across the river to North Bank Road, which follows above the river heading west and provides a handful of bank access spots.

Below Winchester Dam, the river is open to powerboats, though you don't see too many of them unless the river is full of spring chinook or winter steelhead. Jet sleds can launch at River Forks County Park and run the river as far as Amacher Park. Amacher, situated just west of I-5, is one of the most popular access points on the lower river and sits along a productive stretch of water for steelhead and salmon. River Forks Park, located at the confluence of the North and South Umpqua Rivers, also offers access to some productive bank fishing areas. Drifting from Amacher down to River Forks takes you through lots of good water. Halfway between these two parks is another launch called Hestnes Landing, located about 4 miles from the Winchester Exit on Del Rio Road.

You can launch at any of the ramps below Winchester Dam (Amacher, Hestnes, or River Forks) and drift past the North Umpqua/South Umpqua confluence and down the top end of the mainstem. This is good water for salmon, winter steelhead, and bass. If you launch at Amacher or Hestness, try the run down to Cleveland Rapids Ramp on Cleveland Rapids Road (exit the freeway at Winchester and head west on Del Rio Road and then Garden Valley Road).

The large and rather lavish River Forks Park is located on the northwest outskirts of Roseburg, about 6 miles from town. From I-5, take Exit 125 and head west and then northwest on Garden Valley Boulevard and watch for the signs. To reach Amacher Park, take Exit 129 from I-5 (also exit the freeway here to visit the fish-viewing windows on the north side of Winchester Dam).

Umpqua River, South (Douglas County)
boat ramp, campground

The South Umpqua River is primarily known for its very good smallmouth bass fishery and for its good winter steelhead runs. The steelhead, mostly of hatchery origin, arrive between early December and late March, with peak fishing being in January and February. The fish typically range from 7 to 12 pounds. Anglers fish the steelhead runs both by drifting and by bank fishing, especially from the angling deadline at Jackson Creek Bridge down to Myrtle Creek.

Jackson Creek Bridge is located in the Cascade Range, east from Tiller. From I-5, take Exit 98 at Canyonville and head east on the Tiller-Trail Road. When you reach Tiller, turn left on South Umpqua

River Road and continue another 5 miles up to the bridge and the 3C Rocks Picnic Area (the launch is at the picnic area). Quite a few bank anglers fish here during the peak of the runs and there are quite a few good pools and runs accessible from the highway downstream. Also, I-5 runs alongside the South Umpqua for about 15 miles, from Round Prairie—south of Roseburg—south to Seven Feathers Casino. Access is available from several side roads and steelhead fishing can be fair to good along the freeway when the water drops into ideal condition during the winter.

On the upper river, a popular drift segment starts at the unimproved launch site at 3C Rocks (near Jackson Creek Bridge) and ends at the Milo Boat Ramp (also unimproved). This

Mike Shewey lands a brook trout from a high lake in the Umpqua drainage.

drift covers about 11 miles. You can also launch at Milo or 2 miles further downstream at the Lavadoure Creek launch and float down to Days Creek or all the way to Canyonville Park. Days Creek to Canyonville is a good drift for the short days of winter but you can also continue another 2 miles down to the unimproved launch at Stanton Park near I-5 (access the park from Stanton Park Road), north of Canyonville. Canyonville Park is a mile east of Canyonville. Drifting this section of the river (Milo to Canyonville) allows you to fish a lot of water not accessible from the banks.

You can float the I-5 segment by launching at Canyonville Park and taking out about 5 miles downstream at Cow Creek Bar (4 miles northwest of Canyonville off the Gasley Road Exit). Or launch at Stanton Park or Cow Creek Bar and float down to Myrtle Creek or all the way to ODFW's Weigle Landing ramp, located 4 miles southeast of Winston on Hwy 99. Myrtle Creek Access is 1 mile north of Myrtle Creek on the east bank on Hwy 99. From Milo to Winston, only three of the ramps are improved: Milo, Canyonville Park, and Weigle. Be sure to scout the unimproved sites before using them.

In the Roseburg Area, boaters can choose from several good drift segments for winter steelhead angling and for spring smallmouth action. During summer and fall, the South Umpqua is simply too low and slow to drift, although you can do point-to-point paddle trips using canoes or kayaks. The Roseburg-area launch sites are as follows: Happy Valley County Park (take Exit 120 and follow Carnes Road to Happy Valley Road and then turn right on Poteet Avenue); Fairgrounds Boat Ramp at Umpqua Park (Exit 123 from I-5); Templin Beach Launch in southeast Roseburg off Templin Avenue; River Forks Park (5 miles northwest of Roseburg on Garden Valley Road). River Forks Park sits at the confluence of the North and South Umpqua Rivers.

The South Fork offers excellent smallmouth bass fishing from Canyonville to the river's mouth at River Forks Park near Roseburg. Fishing can be quite good within the city limits of Roseburg, where access is available at Stewart Park and a few other places. During the summer, when the water is low, a canoe or kayak is perfect here. You'll do plenty of paddling, but good fishing is the reward.

Union Creek (upper Rogue drainage)
see Rogue River, Forks

Vulcan Lakes (Kalmiopsis Wilderness)
hike-in

Though fishless, these beautiful hike-in wilderness lakes are worth a visit just for the scenery and, during the summer, for the amazing display of cobra lilies (Darlingtonia), which grow along the shoreline of Little Vulcan Lake.

Whaleshead Beach
see Boardman State Park

Whetstone Pond
see Denman Wildlife Area Ponds

Whiskey Run Beach (Coos County)
see Bullards Beach

Williams Creek (Josephine County)
closed waters

Williams River (Douglas/Coos County)
A small, but lengthy tributary to the South Fork Coquille, Williams River reputedly offers only mediocre fishing for resident trout and it flows almost entirely across privately owned lands in a little-known canyon west of Roseburg. Access is difficult if roads are gated, so consult the BLM office in Roseburg before venturing out to explore the area (541-440-4930). The stream is closed to salmon and steelhead angling.

Willow Lake (Jackson County)
boat ramp, campground

Willow Lake, sometimes called Willow Creek Lake or Willow Creek Reservoir, is a popular and fairly productive fishery for largemouth bass, rainbow trout, and crappie. The lake sits at about 3,000 feet and spans about 300 acres at full pool. The bass here reach about 4 pounds, but the vast majority are from 10 to 14 inches. They are reasonably abundant in the coves, along the points, and just about anywhere with good structure. Most serious bass anglers launch boats to fish the arms on the reservoir's south side. Bank anglers do well on both crappie and trout by fishing from the dam. To get there, head first for the town of Eagle Point (Exit 30 in Medford). Drive north on Hwy 62 and continue through Eagle Point about 4.5 miles to Butte Falls Junction. Turn right and follow the road 15 miles to Butte Falls and then head southeasterly on the Willow Lake Road (CR 321), which ends at the lake.

Winchester Bay (Umpqua/Smith Rivers)
boat ramp, boat recommended, services, charters

Winchester Bay is a fertile estuary where the Umpqua and Smith Rivers meet and then reach the Pacific. The bay is highly reputed as a top-flight fishery for sturgeon, salmon, and striped bass, along with saltwater denizens, such as rockfish and perch. A fleet of charter boats operates out of the harbor at Winchester Bay, targeting salmon and halibut during the respective seasons, along with a variety of bottomfish.

The stripers, including a few trophy-class fish, roam the entire bay and most anglers fish for them between late spring and mid-autumn. During the summer, they often hunt baitfish along the edges of the islands and along tidal cuts and current seams. Night fishing is especially productive for those equipped do so, but be sure you know your way around. The lower ends of Steamboat Island and Bolan Island are good places to look for bass on the falling tides, but beware that the convenient Gardener Boat Ramp is essentially a high-tide ramp. Stripers frequent the structure-filled areas around the mouth of the Smith and are found as far down the bay as the jetties and even out along the adjacent beaches.

Fishing for chinook salmon is a popular pursuit on Winchester Bay, mostly during August and September. Anglers use plug/bait combos, blade/bait combos, jigs, and bait, especially herring, anchovy, and strips of shad. Trollers can work the channels between the jaws and the big bend, and also the channels on both sides of Steamboat Island. The mouth of the Smith River and the channel running under the highway bridge on the Reedsport side of the Umpqua are also favorite spots. Many salmon anglers fish the bay proper, from the big bend below Gardener down to the jetties and even outside when conditions allow. Fin-clipped coho salmon enter the bay during summer and anglers catch quite a few of them in the same areas popular for chinook.

Sturgeon fishing is especially good in Winchester Bay—a fact anyone can appreciate upon witnessing the countless dozens of sturgeon inexplicably breaching on the Umpqua side of Bolan and Steamboat Island during a falling tide. The fish range from juvenile-size to well beyond the legal limit (currently 42 to 60 inches), and keeper-size sturgeon are fairly common.

Winchester Bay enjoys the unique and rather historic services of several of the state's most highly reputed guides, including a few who've made a living on these waters for several decades. Among the best is Todd Hanah (800-428-8585/www.theoregonangler.com), who guides everything from salmon and steelhead to stripers, smallmouth bass, and sturgeon. Others include Bob Cobb (541-271-3850/www.cobbreelfish.com) and Jerry Jarmain (800-635-5583). During the salmon season, the bay gets plenty busy with boats, so if you're new to the region, hiring a guide is a wise move. Winchester Bay's guides pursue all the system's gamefish, so be specific about what you're after.

Winchuck River (Curry County)

The scenic little Winchuck River reaches the Pacific Ocean just north of the California border. This diminutive river offers generally slow-to-fair prospects for both chinook salmon and wild winter steelhead. Both fish are late arrivers, with the fall chinook showing up after the autumn rains begin. Fishing for them peaks from late October through mid-November. Likewise, the river's steelhead run peaks during March, although there are always a few fish in the system during January and February.

Winchester Bay

Access to the Winchuck is generally limited by private property, especially on the lower river. In places, Winchuck Road swings alongside the river, and leads to the angling deadline at Wheeler Creek, where access is good. The short stretch from Wheeler Creek down to the Siskiyou National Forest boundary is generally the most popular reach because access is unfettered by private property. Anglers are not allowed to fish from boats on the Winchuck, though in decades past, the little river supported a pram fishery for fall chinook salmon. Even with the boat-angling closure, salmon anglers often tag as many as 160 chinook from the Winchuck each autumn

Upstream from the salmon/steelhead deadline at Wheeler Creek, the highly scenic Winchuck offers fair fishing for small, native cutthroat trout. They rarely exceed 10 inches in length, but they can be a lot of fun on dry flies during summer and early autumn. Be sure to check current regulations before going after the river's trout.

Winchuck Wayside
see Crissey Field Beach

Wolf Lake (Douglas County)
hike-in

Tucked away in the northern tip of the Rogue-Umpqua Divide Wilderness Area, Wolf Lake is a productive and attractive brook trout fishery. The lake is usually accessible by mid-June and fishing holds up through the summer and well into fall for brookies from 6 to 12 inches and occasionally larger. From I-5 to the west, take Exit 98 at Canyonville and head east along the South Umpqua River on the road to Tiller. At Tiller, turn left on FR 28 (South Umpqua River Road) and continue east past South Umpqua Falls and past Camp Comfort Campground. About 10 miles beyond Camp Comfort, turn right on FR 950, leading southeast to the trailhead. The hike covers about half a mile. Alternately, take Hwy 138 up the North Umpqua from Roseburg or west over the Cascades from Hwy 97 in central Oregon. Just west from Boulder Flat Campground and just east from Eagle Rock Campground, turn south on Copeland Creek Road (FR 28) and follow it south about 12 miles to a left turn on FR 950.

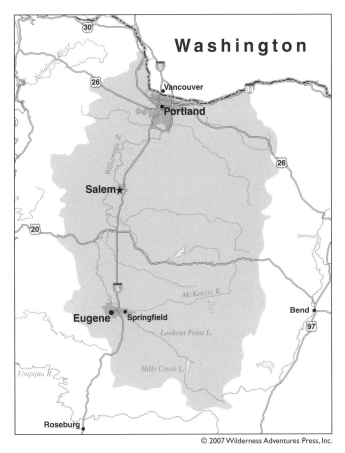

© 2007 Wilderness Adventures Press, Inc.

WillametteZone

Perhaps improbably, western Oregon's Willamette River watershed provides a remarkable array of diverse and productive options for anglers, despite simultaneously holding the state's highest population density. Indeed, 65 percent of the state's population lives in and around the fertile Willamette Valley, whose namesake river draws its headwaters from the Cascade Range southeast of Eugene, meanders its way south to north through the valley, and finally surrenders to the Columbia River near Portland. Along the way, the Willamette River not only provides some fine fishing itself, but also collects the waters from its numerous productive tributaries, including the South Santiam, North Santiam, and Molalla Rivers, not to mention the McKenzie River, famous for its rainbow trout, and the Clackamas River, renowned for its runs of salmon and steelhead.

Above the Willamette Valley, the Cascade Range offers a staggering number of small, trout-laden mountain lakes tucked away from the hustle and bustle of Oregon's largest cities. Many of these lakes are hike-in fisheries, lying within the confines of several large wilderness areas, including the Three Sisters Wilderness Area and the Mt. Jefferson Wilderness Area. The high lakes managed by ODFW's Willamette District include a mix of stocked lakes and those containing naturally reproducing populations of trout. All but a handful of the high lakes had no indigenous fish until stocking efforts began as long ago as the early 20th Century. Anglers wishing to ferret out the secrets of the high lakes would be wise to collect the best maps available, including the Ranger District maps available from the U.S. Forest Service.

Trout anglers enjoy myriad other options in the Willamette Zone. Many streams are managed for wild trout and in these places, catch-and-release, artificials-only fishing is the rule. But catch-and-keep anglers can enjoy oft-fast-paced action on the upper McKenzie River and on a variety of other streams draining the Cascade foothills. And for those who prefer a quiet day on an easy-to-reach trout pond, the Willamette Valley offers quite a lot of them, continually supplied with fish by ODFW.

Warmwater enthusiasts enjoy myriad options throughout the Willamette Zone. Henry Hagg Lake, for example, ranks among the state's better smallmouth bass destinations and the region includes many other lesser-known waters, home to teeming populations of bass, bluegill, crappie, brown bullhead, and other warmwater fishes.

And perhaps to save the best for last, the Willamette River along with the Sandy River, east of Portland, serve as literal highways for salmon and steelhead. The Willamette itself continues to be one of the state's most productive spring chinook salmon fisheries and several of its tributaries offer equally good salmon prospects, along with fine runs of hatchery-produced summer steelhead and wild winter steelhead.

The Willamette Valley offers something to satisfy every conceivable kind of angler. Some of the region's fisheries attract lots of attention, while others await only the most adventurous, exploratory anglers. Interstate 5 essentially divides the region, providing rapid north-south transit, and a host of primary and secondary highways branch off in all directions.

Willamette Zone Contacts:

North Willamette Watershed District Office
17330 SE Evelyn Street
Clackamas, OR 97015
503-673-6000

South Willamette Watershed District Office
7118 NE Vanderberg Avenue
Corvallis, OR 97330-9446
541-757-4186

Springfield Field Office
3150 E Main Street
Springfield, OR 97478-5800
541-726-3515

Mt. Hood National Forest Headquarters
16400 Champion Way
Sandy, Oregon 97055
503-668-1700

Barlow Ranger District, Dufur Ranger Station
780 NE Court Street
Dufur, Oregon 97021
541-467-2291

Clackamas River Ranger District, Estacada Ranger Station
595 NW Industrial Way
Estacada, OR 97023
(503) 630-6861

Hood River Ranger District, Hood River Ranger Station
6780 Highway 35
Parkdale, Oregon 97041
541-352-6002

Zigzag Ranger District, Zigzag Ranger Station
70220 E. Highway 26
Zigzag, Oregon 97049
503-622-3191

Willamette National Forest Supervisor's Office
Federal Building, 211 East 7th Avenue,
Eugene, OR 97440
541-225-6300

Detroit Ranger District
HC73, Box 320
Mill City, OR 97360
503-854-3366

Sweet Home Ranger District
3225 Highway 20
Sweet Home, OR 97386
541-367-5168

McKenzie River Ranger District
57600 McKenzie Hwy
McKenzie Bridge, OR 97413
541-822-3381

Middle Fork Ranger District
46375 Highway 58
Westfir, OR 97492
541-782-2283

Bureau of Land Management, Salem District
1717 Fabry Rd. SE,
Salem, Oregon 97306
503-375-5646

Bureau of Land Management, Eugene District
2890 Chad Drive
Eugene, OR 97408-7336
541-683-6600

Abernethy Lakes (Lane County)
hike-in

Upper and Lower Abernethy Lakes, located just west of Odell Lake and just south of Hwy 58, offer lots of small, naturally reproducing brook trout. Upper Abernethy covers about 4 acres and reaches a depth of 16 feet. Once stocked with a variety of different trout, Upper Abernathy is now a brook trout fishery with brookies ranging from 5 to 12 inches (few of them reach the upper end of that range). Only small brookies occupy 2-acre Lower Abernethy. The hike to the lakes covers about 1 mile. Opposite the Gold Lake turnoff, turn south off Hwy 58 onto FR 5899 and after a mile turn right onto Spur Road 505, which follows the old railroad grade and leads to the trailhead.

Abiqua Creek (Marion County)
no bait; catch & release

A nice little trout stream during summer and fall, Abiqua Creek flows entirely through private property near the town of Silverton, east from Salem. The stream offers fair-to-good catch-and-release fishing for mostly small wild cutthroat, though upstream from Abiqua Falls (river mile 19), anglers may keep two trout over 8 inches in length; throughout, the creek is fly- and artificial lures only. The best water lies east of Hwy 213, just north of Silverton (and 25 miles south of Oregon City), where the only access is at the three bridge crossings along Abiqua Creek Road. Watch for the turn-off after you cross the river on the highway. Otherwise, you'll have to knock on doors for permission, which is a good idea anyway if you intend to wade up or down the river. Save this one for late summer or fall when the water is low—then just walk up or down the river and fish the small pockets and pools. The river opens in late May to protect scarce juvenile wild winter steelhead and salmon.

Adair Pond (Benton County)

Adair Pond sits adjacent to the ODFW office at Adair Village, north of Corvallis on Hwy 99W. The lake offers fair-to-good fishing for warmwater species, including bluegill, largemouth bass, brown bullhead, and channel catfish. The pond is known for its ability to produce the occasional trophy-size bass.

Aerial Lake (Three Sisters Wilderness)
hike-in

Three-acre Aerial Lake sits among a cluster of small, high lakes in the Three Sisters Wilderness a few miles west from Elk Lake and Century Drive. Aerial offers fair action for pan-size rainbows, brook trout, and cutthroat trout. The mix of species depends on what has been stocked recently in the lake, which is planted with several hundred fish every other year. This is a pretty area and several of the lakes, including Aerial, don't see a lot of angling pressure.

The route from the Elk Lake Trailhead covers a total of 4.25 miles, if you can navigate the last mile cross country. Start out on the Sunset Lake Trail and head 1.3 miles to the Pacific Crest Trail. Follow the PCT another 1.3 miles and turn north on the Sunset Lake Trail. After passing a large pond on the left (consult the Three Sisters Wilderness Area map), cut northwest to the south shore of Sunset Lake and from there begin a due-west compass course. Aerial lies 1 mile away and you'll cross another trail en route. If you prefer to stay on the trails for the 5-mile-plus route, both the Island Meadow/Sunset Lake Trail and the Horse Lake Trail get you to Aerial (as well as the Fisher Lakes and Herb, Platt, Marten, and Mile Lakes). From the trail junction at Horse Lake, head left and then take the second right after a quarter mile (the Horse Mt. Trail). From the Sunset Trail, head half a mile past Sunset Lake and watch for a left turn at the next junction and then a right-turn shortly thereafter. Aerial sits just off the trail, behind Herb Lake (be sure to take a good topo map).

Aerial sits at an elevation of 5,550 feet and is usually accessible by late June. These are good early-season lakes despite the horrific mosquitoes. Adventurous anglers skilled in cross-country travel might want to head up to the Horse Lakes area as soon as the Century Drive loop is open as far as Elk Lake (sometime in June most years). You'll need map and compass skills if persistent snowfields blot out long sections of trail, but the fishing can be excellent and you'll have it to yourself.

Agency Creek (Yamhill County)
catch-and-release, no bait

Agency Creek, a tributary to the South Yamhill River, flows south through the Grand Ronde Indian Reservation and offers fair fishing for small, native cutthroat trout. The creek picks up nearby Yoncalla Creek (sometimes called Yoncalla River) and Wind River upon reaching the extensive private lands on its lower 7 miles. Access to the 2-mile stretch on BLM-administered lands is good, but below that stretch you will need permission. County Road 858A follows the creek: Take Hwy 22/18 west to Grand Ronde and turn right at the signs to Grand Ronde Agency. Continue north and then northwest along the creek.

Airport Pond (Lane County)
closed waters

Alameda Lake (Lane County)

Three-acre Alameda Lake sits at 5,500 feet near Emigrant Pass in the extreme southeast corner of Lane County, just west of Summit Lake. ODFW stocks Alameda with cutthroat trout and about a dozen other nearby lakes make this a nice area to explore. You can drive to Alameda on rough forest roads. To get there from the west side of the Cascades, take Hwy 58 through Oakridge. Two miles east of town, turn south on the Kitson Springs Road (FR21) towards Hills Creek Reservoir. Stay right and follow FR21 south along the west side of the reservoir. Remain on FR21 for about 32 miles until you reach a left turn on FR2154. Follow 2154 about 5 miles to a left turn on FR2160 and then watch for a short spur on the right after about a mile (half a mile north from Spur Road 393). From the east side, head for the west shore of Crescent Lake, then follow the rugged route west over Emigrant Pass. After crossing the summit take a left turn (south) on FR2160 and then watch for the first left-hand spur at Alameda Lake. The Emigrant Pass region offers lots of nice informal camping spots and forest service campgrounds are located nearby at Summit Lake (see Central Zone) and Timpanogas Lake.

Alforja Lake (Mt. Jefferson Wilderness)
hike-in

Brook trout have reproduced successfully in this small lake located just south of the Duffy Lake Trail in the Mt. Jefferson Wilderness Area. Alforja spans 4 acres, but reaches a depth of only 5 feet. Most of the fish are small and the last time I was there, in the mid-90s, the lake appeared fishless, perhaps a winterkill victim. Alforja lies near the Cincha Lakes (see listing herein).

Alice Lake (Mt. Jefferson Wilderness)
hike-in

Spanning only 1 acre, Alice Lake offers fair-to-slow fishing for brook trout and is located along the Duffy Lake Trail, 5.5 miles from the trailhead (located off the Big Meadows Road). Hike past Duffy Lake, up the hill and past Mowich Lake and past the Dixie Lakes Trail junction. Alice is on your left a short distance past the junction. The lake seems to over-winter quite well and produces a few 14-inch fish, but most are pan-size. There are three campsites here and the lake is accessible by mid- to late June. Unfortunately the 2003 B&B Complex fire scorched most of the timber along the lakeshore.

Alton Baker Canal/Pond (Lane County)

Sprawling Alton Baker Park in Eugene offers a pond and canal that are heavily stocked with rainbow trout by ODFW; the pond—very kid-friendly—also has warmwater fish, such as bluegill and brown bullhead. Each year ODFW holds one of its kid's fishing events here (check with ODFW for dates and details). This beautiful park stretches for 5 miles east to west, bounded on the south by the Willamette River, with Autzen Stadium complex—home of the University of Oregon Duck football team—to the north. The canal begins east of Interstate 5 and runs through most of the park, interrupted midway through by the pond. Access is excellent via a series of walking/running paths and parking areas. After being stocked, trout rend to disperse through the canal, with many making their way to the pond, but also swimming east past the interstate. The adjacent Willamette River (see entry herein) offers a few cutthroat and rainbows (fishing can be good during hatches of March brown mayflies in spring and on summer evenings), along with summer steelhead between June and mid-autumn. For a terrific map, visit www.eugene-or.gov/.

Amazon Creek (Lane County)

A lengthy tributary of the Long Tom River northwest of Eugene, Amazon Creek runs entirely through private property from its headwaters in Eugene down to its mouth. A few cutthroat inhabit the creek where appropriate habitat exists, but you'll need to knock on doors for permission.

Amos Lake (Lane County)
hike-in, cross-country

Amos Lake and its neighbor, Andy Lake, sit at 6,000 feet just northwest from Indigo Lake in the southernmost corner of the Willamette National Forest. Amos is shallow and covers 8 acres. Amos is stocked every other year, most recently with cutthroat trout. Most range from 8 to 12 inches. See Andy Lake herein for hiking directions.

Amstutz Lake (Three Sisters Wilderness)
hike-in, cross-country

A tiny but deep cutthroat lake high in the Three Sisters Wilderness, Amstutz is seldom fished owing to its remote location. The lake sits at 6,100 feet elevation about 3 miles southeast from popular Linton Lake. It is generally stocked every other year or so with 200 to 300 cutthroat trout and they over-winter well in the lake's depths, which reach 20 feet. Amstutz sits one-half mile west by northwest from Eileen Lake and 600 feet higher. This is spectacular country, fairly easy to navigate and offering sensational views of the nearby Three Sisters just a few miles to the east. See Eileen Lake.

Andy Lake (Lane County)
hike-in, cross-country

Andy Lake is deeper than its sister lake, Amos, and often fares better during the winter. Consequently some of its trout, stocked every few years, survive to reach 14 inches or more. In recent years, ODFW has stocked the lake with cutthroat trout. Andy Lake requires a fairly short cross-country hike. It covers about 5 acres and sits a mile northeast of Indigo Lake. Amos and Andy sit adjacent to one another and Andy is the southernmost of the pair (a third lake, with no fish, lies a quarter mile west and down slope). From Indigo's north shore, head northeast, skirting the lower slope of the ridgeline north of Sawtooth Mountain. Follow a strict compass course, as the lake is easy to miss. Wait until July to try this one since snow lingers well into summer.

Ann Lake
see Lake Ann

Anvil Lake (Mt. Hood National Forest)
hike-in

Anvil Lake, lightly stocked with cutthroat trout and also lightly fished, is a very pretty, fairly productive high-elevation, hike-in lake northwest from Timothy Lake in the Mount Hood National Forest. Forest Road 5820 leads to the short trail to the lake, but be sure to consult the national forest map before heading out. Take plenty of insect repellent: the boggy meadows and shallow lake margins provide mosquito habitat.

Averill Lake (Olallie Scenic Area)
hike-in

Liberally stocked with brook trout every other year, 13-acre Averill Lake offers consistent action for fish reaching about

13 inches. The lake sits on the western edge of the Olallie Lake Scenic Area. Fly anglers should consider a float tube here—the lake has shallow shoal areas on both ends and a deep pool in the middle. Spin fishers and bait anglers have no problems fishing from shore, and rocky shallows around much of the lake make for easy wading—the water can be surprisingly warm from mid-summer through early autumn. The shortest route arrives via the Breitenbush Road (FR46) at Detroit. Follow FR46 all the way to the Mt. Hood National Forest border and turn right on FR 4220, which heads east toward Breitenbush Lake. After half a mile turn left on Spur Road 380 and follow it to the trailhead (#719) a few hundred yards north of the overhead power lines. The hike covers an easy 1.5 miles.

Brook trout abound in the high lakes of the Cascade Range.

Ayers Pond (Eugene)

One of the suburban warmwater fisheries in Eugene, 33-acre Ayers Pond sits at the intersection of Ayers Road and North Delta Highway. The pond offers white crappie, bluegill, and largemouth bass, including an occasional big one. A float tube is handy here, but bank fishing is also productive.

Balch Creek and Tributaries (Multnomah County)
closed waters

Bays Lake (Mt. Jefferson Wilderness)
hike-in
A scenic lake in beautiful Jefferson Park, 12-acre Bays Lake provides a commanding view of magnificent Mt. Jefferson and a wealth of small, planted brook trout. A few fish reach 13 inches or more, but most run 6 to 10 inches. Jefferson Park, which features five fishable lakes, ranks among the most popular destinations in the Mt. Jefferson Wilderness Area and generally attracts quite a few visitors each weekend between late June and Labor Day weekend.

Because the area is so popular—for good reason I might add, considering the awesome view of the mountain and the lovely sub-alpine meadows—campers must use existing sites, of which there are many and pitch tents well back from the lake shores. Bays Lake offers five marked campsites; if all are occupied, camp at least 250 feet away from the lakeshore, using no-trace methods. A permanent fire ban is in effect here and throughout Jefferson Park. You can expect company, but you can also look forward to good brook trout action on a lake with myriad small bays and coves lined with rocks and small cliffs. Shoreline fishing is easy, though a float tube saves you the trouble of scrambling about on the bank.

All methods produce, and Bay's Lake offers the usual high-lakes hatch of speckled-wing dun mayflies (*Callibaetis*) that provide good dry-fly opportunity. Also carry a few patterns to imitate flying ants, alderflies (a black Elkhair Caddis works for this), midges, and caddisflies. For subsurface work, which prevails often, try a No. 8 olive Woolly Bugger trailed by a No. 14 beadhead Zugbug or Prince Nymph. Spin fishers should try tiny spoons and spinners.

Myriad trails lead up to Jefferson Park and Bays Lake. Consult the Mt. Jefferson Wilderness Area map available from the Forest Service (you can find these at many outdoor stores) or the Mt. Jefferson Wilderness map published by Geo-Graphics. If you want the shortest route into Bays Lake, head east from Salem (Hwy 22) or west from Bend. The highway squeezes across an old, narrow bridge about halfway between Marion Forks and Idanha. This is the Whitewater Creek Bridge. Immediately west of the bridge is a signed east turn onto Whitewater Road (FR 2243). Follow this road all the way to the end where you will find the White Water Trail (#3429), which reaches Bays Lake in just 5.5 miles. The trail gains about 1,000 feet in elevation the first 2 miles, but the balance is easy going.

Bear Creek (Clackamas County)

A tributary to the Pudding River, Bear Creek offers opportunity for harvest of trout (five fin-clipped trout per day) upstream from Shorty's Pond within Ivor Davies Park in Molalla. Bait is allowed. In past years, ODFW has stocked legal-size trout in both the creek and the pond. See Shorty's Pond herein for details.

Bear Lake (Hood River County)

hike-in

Located in the Mark O. Hatfield Wilderness Area east from Cascade Locks and just south of the Columbia Gorge, 2-acre Bear Lake offers consistent action on small stocked brookies ranging from 4 to 12 inches. To reach the trailhead, head south from Hood River on SR 35 or on SR 281. Then follow the signs toward the town of Dee and Punchbowl Falls. Take the road to Punchbowl Falls and Rainy Lake Campground (FR 2820). This road winds its way through the forest almost 10 miles to the trailhead for Mt. Defiance (on the right-hand side of the road, about 2 miles past the intersection with FR 2821). Rainy Lake Campground is a mile further up the road. The trail begins as a short spur leading to the Mt. Defiance Trail (#413). At the main trail, turn right and follow this trail to the next left-hand turn on Bear Lake Trail (#413A). The total distance is just over 1 mile. Bear Lake sits at 3,930 feet and is usually accessible by mid-May.

Bear Lake (Mt. Jefferson Wilderness)

hike-in, cross-country, float tube recommended

Tucked away in the northern part of the Mt. Jefferson Wilderness Area, Bear Lake offers good fishing for brook trout, which reach 14 inches. Most are smaller, but you'll have the place to yourself assuming you have the cross-country navigation skills to reach the lake. There are two fairly easy routes: The first covers 4.2 miles and climbs the trail to the top of Bear Point, gaining a total of almost 3,000 feet along the way. From there you just drop down to the lake. You'll do some steep climbing both up and down Bear Point, but it's easy if you're in decent shape. The trailhead is 5 miles up FR 4685, the South Fork Breitenbush Road. Follow Trail #3375 east for 2 miles to a left turn on the Bear Point Trail. The other reasonably short route, requiring a lot less climbing, is to approach Bear Point from the Firecamp Lakes: Head east by southeast from Sheep Lake (see listing herein) straight to Bear Point (or stay just north of the summit) and drop over the ridge to Bear Lake. This route covers less than 3.5 miles. Be sure to consult the topo map. A float tube comes in handy here and if you're fly angling be sure to bring a sinking or sink-tip line to fish the drop-offs of this deep lake. The lake offers three or four nice camp spots.

Benson Lake (Multnomah County)

Located in Benson State Park in the Columbia Gorge east of Portland and Troutdale, Benson Lake offers fair-to-good prospects for stocked rainbow trout along with a variety of warmwater fish, including largemouth bass, crappie, sunfish, and brown bullhead. The lake is easy to access from the state park, with bank access on most of the shoreline, though few people fish on the freeway (north) side of the lake. A well-worn path follows the south shore adjacent to the railroad tracks. You can launch float tubes, pontoons, kayaks, and canoes off the bank. The lake is stocked with trout from spring and through mid-autumn and has been open year-round in recent years. ODFW holds free-fishing day events here during early June (contact ODFW for dates). Benson State Park does not have a campground, but the day-use facilities, despite their proximity to the busy interstate, are nicely secluded in the woods and quite pleasant, especially on a summer day. From October through March, few people venture to 30-acre Benson Lake and as late as May—even on weekends—you can often share the entire lake with just a few other anglers. There is no westbound exit for Benson Park. Eastbound traffic uses Exit 31; westbound traffic must go 2 miles farther west, exit the freeway, turn around and head back east.

The second and larger lake at Benson Park (on the right as you drive into the park) is called Hartman Pond (formerly Wahkeena Pond) and is used as a salmon smolt-rearing pond by ODFW. It also supports lots of warmwater species, including crappies, bluegill, yellow perch, largemouth bass, and smallmouth bass, and is stocked regularly with rainbow trout. A fishing dock and boat launch is situated on the east end of the pond, next to the road into Benson Park. Bank access is fair and most bank anglers fish along the south shoreline adjacent to the tracks. A small boat or personal watercraft is useful and advantageous here.

Benson Lake

Benson Lake (Mt. Washington Wilderness)
hike-in

This popular, heavily fished lake in the Mt. Washington Wilderness holds up well throughout the season owing to generous annual stocking of rainbow and cutthroat trout (sometimes brookies are stocked instead of cutthroat). The fish range from 6 to 18 inches, with 10- to 12-inch fish common. Benson lays a mile-and-a-half west of Scott Lake, off the Old McKenzie Highway on the eastern edge of Linn County. The trail gains only 400 feet between Scott and Benson Lakes and departs from the end of the road on the west side of Scott Lake, which offers ample camping space. From Scott Lake Campground, Benson Lake is an easy day trip. Shoreline fishing abounds, but a float tube comes in handy. Benson spans 20 acres and reaches depths of 55 feet. If you want to escape the people at Benson, check out nearby Elf and Glaze Lakes, a few hundred yards to the southwest (see separate listings herein).

Berley Lakes (Mt. Jefferson Wilderness)
hike-in

Stocked every few years, Upper and Lower Berley Lakes offer good fishing for brook trout (Upper Berley) and cutthroat trout (Lower Berley) that average pan-size. A few fat 14-inchers show up from time to time in these deep 6-acre lakes. For my money, these are among the prettiest of all the lakes within the Mt. Jefferson Wilderness Area, offering commanding views of nearby Three Fingered Jack. Fly anglers should consider hauling in a float tube owing to tight casting quarters along the shorelines of the lakes; spin fishers will have no problem reaching the best water. They are located near the southern edge of the Mt. Jefferson Wilderness Area and both offer some nice campsites. To get there, take the Pacific Crest Trail or the old Santiam Lodge Trail (#3496) (both heading at the top of Santiam Summit) north to the Santiam Lake Trail (#3491). Follow the trail signed for Eight Lakes Basin and then head north 2 miles to a short side trail leading over to Lower Berley—watch for a stream crossing and then a rock cairn marking the faint trail. Upper Berley lies just to the northwest, about 300 yards beyond the end of Lower Berley. Getting to the Berley Lakes, you will hike through a lot of ghost forest burned in the 2003 B&B Complex fire, and while the dead snags may lack scenic appeal, much of the route is ripe with wildflowers and huckleberry bushes, which bear fruit in late summer. Luckily the lakes themselves were missed by the fire and remain surrounded by lush conifers.

Beth Lake (Bull of the Woods Wilderness)
hike-in, cross-country

A fairly productive brook trout lake and seldom fished, Beth Lake spans about 4 acres and sits on the Dickey Creek drainage on the north side of the Bull of the Woods Wilderness Area. This small wilderness area sits in the high Cascades on the Collawash River watershed. Its southern boundary skirts popular Elk Lake near Detroit and its northern boundary lies south of Fan Creek and Kingfisher Campgrounds on the Collawash. To reach the northern trailheads from the Portland area, head southeast, up the Clackamas River to Ripplebrook and then head south on FR 46 and at River Ford Campground, turn right on FR 63. Follow FR 63 about 6 miles south to a right-hand turn on FR 6340. From here you will want the Clackamas Ranger District Map, available from Mt. Hood National Forest. Off the end of FR 6340, a very rugged (4-wheel-drive only) spur loops around the east flank of North Dickey Peak. From the end of this spur, you can hike southwest to North Dickey Peak, and then drop down to the lake. Don't try it unless you have competent cross-country navigating skills. As of this writing the aforementioned spur road (#340) is not gated. Should that change, then you must take a more circuitous 2.5-mile hike starting at the Pansy Lake Trailhead: At the junction of FR 6340 and 6341, bear right on 6341 and follow it 4 miles down to Pansy Creek. Watch for the hiker sign before you cross the creek. Take Trail 551 to a left turn on 549. Climb uphill for about a mile to Trail 550 and make your cross-country route from there, beginning at the old burn site along the top of the ridge and losing about 500 feet of elevation to find the lake. Don't over-shoot the lake or you enter some very steep canyon country.

Betty Lake (Waldo Lake area)
hike-in, float tube recommended

A fairly popular, easy-to-reach 40-acre lake adjacent to sprawling Waldo Lake, Betty Lake is heavily stocked with rainbows and the fish tend to over-winter quite successfully. Consequently Betty Lake continues to produce quite a few 12- to 16-inch fish, though typical pan-size rainbows predominate. Follow Hwy 58 east from Oakridge to the Waldo Lake Road. Turn left and head about 5 miles to the trailhead. The hike covers an easy half-mile, making it ideal for anglers carrying float tubes. Perched at about 5,500 feet, Betty Lake is rarely accessible before mid-June. Lower Betty Lake sits about a quarter mile south of larger Betty Lake and almost adjacent to the Waldo Lake Road 3 miles north of Hwy 58. Lower Betty is stocked liberally with rainbows that can reach impressive sizes, though they average pan-size.

Big Cliff Reservoir (North Santiam drainage)
boat recommended; boat ramp

Big Cliff Reservoir lies immediately downstream of Detroit Dam on the North Santiam River east of Salem. Three miles long and only 100 yards wide, this 50-foot-deep reservoir has a well-earned reputation for producing large rainbows. Trollers, working slowly up and down the reservoir, catch most of the big rainbows, which reach at least 6 pounds. Small fish are moderately common. Big Cliff's water level fluctuates frequently and often dramatically. At full pool, this re-regulating reservoir spans about 140 acres. The rough boat launch lies at the upstream end, below Detroit Dam—watch for the access road on your right as you head towards the upper (east) end of the reservoir. Shore fishing is available near the boat ramp and also at the mouth of Sardine Creek, half a mile upstream of the dam. Campgrounds (always popular on summer weekends) are located upstream at Detroit Reservoir and all services are available in Detroit and downstream in Mill City.

Big Lake (Willamette National Forest)
campground, boat ramp

Only 4 miles south of Santiam Summit, Big Lake sprawls over a scenic 225 acres, making it one of the largest natural lakes in the Willamette National Forest. The lake is stocked with rainbow, cutthroat, and brook trout along with kokanee salmon. All four species can reach 16 or more inches, but pan-size fish prevail. Big Lake is popular with anglers and has also emerged as a favorite hangout for water skiers and boaters.

The lake offers a large campground featuring drinking water, vaulted toilets, 49 spaces (trailer spaces have a 35-foot length limit) and a good boat ramp. Eleven tent-only sites are located at the west-end of the campground (Big Lake West), near the trailhead for the Patjens Lakes (see listing herein). These walk-in sites come at a slightly higher price, aimed at discouraging the heavy use that has damaged the riparian area along the lakeshore. The day-use area also carries a nominal fee. Big Lake sits at 4,644 feet and is usually ice-free by late May.

Ice-out is the best time to avoid the summertime onslaught of boaters, swimmers, jet skiers, and water skiers, who converge on Big Lake during the pleasant summer months. If you're fishing from shore and wish to escape the crowds, try the lake's northeast corner where a small bay provides some shelter from the typical afternoon winds. Or walk the Patjens Lake Trail around to the south shore. Better yet, wait until early October—if good weather holds, the lake is largely devoid of people during mid-autumn and the fishing can be quite good. Ice fishing has become increasingly popular here in recent years.

All methods produce at Big Lake and kokanee specialists, trolling with Ford Fenders, Kokanee Killerssmall spoons and similar rigs, do quite well during early summer and fall. They seem to catch plenty of trout while trolling for kokanee. Many anglers still fish with bait from shore while others cast and retrieve spoons, spinners, and wet flies.

To reach Big Lake, head for the Santiam Summit (Hwy 20/22/126) and turn south on the road to Hoodoo Ski Area. Drive past the ski area entrance and head 4 miles down FR 2690 to the lake.

Big Slide Lake/Upper Big Slide Lake (Bull of the Woods Wilderness)
hike-in

Highly scenic, but only fairly productive most of the time (although you never know until you try, and the scenery alone is worth the hike), Big Slide Lake sits at the base of aptly named Big Slide Mountain in the Bull of the Woods Wilderness Area some 70 miles southeast from Portland. This small wilderness area sits in the high Cascades on the Collawash River watershed. Its southern boundary skirts popular Elk Lake near

Detroit and its northern boundary lies south of Fan Creek and Kingfisher Campgrounds on the Collawash. To reach the northern trailheads from the Portland area, head southeast up the Clackamas River to Ripplebrook and then head south on FR 46 and at River Ford Campground, turn left on FR 63. Follow FR 63 about 6 miles south to a right-hand turn on FR 6340. Follow 6340 until it ends at Trail 550, which heads south about 3 miles to Bull of the Woods Lookout, from which you can see Big Slide Lake about half a mile and 1,000 vertical feet to the north. Follow Trail 555/553 down to the lake (the total round-trip distance is about 10 miles). Big Slide sits at 4,300 feet and is rarely accessible before mid-June. Upper Big Slide Lake is also stocked with brook trout, and sits just up the slope beyond the end of Big Slide—few people venture to the upper lake.

This area of the wilderness boasts several other fair brook trout lakes, including Lenore, West, and Lower Welcome Lakes. Lenore spans 5 acres and is easy to fish from the shore, even offering lots of casting room for fly anglers. The last section of the trail into Lenore sits on a steep, guarded north slope and often remains snow blocked until July, though you can navigate around it. Six-acre Lower Welcome Lake, sitting at 4,200 feet, is rather brushy, but manageable from shore and a big boulder in the lake makes a nice casting platform. Diminutive West Lake sits about half a mile northwest of Lower Welcome and is fairly easy to reach by bushwhacking since the old trail connecting the two is no longer maintained and badly choked with brush and shrubs. The easiest route is to drop down to West Lake from Trail 556 west from Lower Welcome Lake.

Billy's Lake (Three Sisters Wilderness)
hike-in

A small lake in the Taylor Burn area, near the Jack Pine Way Trail in the Three Sisters Wilderness Area, Billy's is stocked regularly with cutthroat trout. Trail #3587 begins at a trailhead about a mile west of Taylor Lake on the road to Taylor Burn. From there, head north about a mile and a quarter—Billy Lake is on the left. Be sure to consult the topo map for this one, as it does not appear by name on any of the forest service maps.

Bingham Lake (Mt. Jefferson Wilderness)
hike-in, cross-country

One of the more remote lakes in the Mt. Jefferson Wilderness Area, Bingham's wild cutthroat range from 4 to 12 inches, sometimes a little larger. Small fish predominate and you'll have them to yourself. The route to this 4-acre lake requires nearly 1 mile of cross-country work. Years ago I found it by compass bushwhacking using Papoose Pond as a starting point. Consult the topo map—you'll find Bingham Lake about 5 miles east of Marion Forks. Other than the satisfaction of finding this remote lake, the small trout hardly seemed worth the blood and sweat, but it's a pretty little place and you'll find total solitude here.

Bingo Lake (Waldo Lake Wilderness)
hike-in

A 4-acre lake just half a mile west from the southern end of Waldo Lake, Bingo Lake offers fair fishing for planted brook trout. You can reach Bingo Lake from the south or west from several trails, or boat across from Shadow Bay on Waldo's southeast shore and hike over to Bingo. Bingo Lake is a worthwhile stop if you're hiking cross-country up to Bongo Lake (see listing herein) but generally not worth the trouble for its own sake. Consult the Waldo Lake Wilderness Map and Willamette National Forest Map for specific trail routes.

Birthday Lake (Waldo Lake Area)
hike-in

Located a few miles south of Waldo Lake and north of Hwy 58, 3-acre Birthday Lake offers fair-to-good fishing for small brook trout stocked every other year. The lake is deep enough to over-winter its fish, so a few reach 12 inches and every once in a while the lake kicks out a 15-incher. Most range from 6 to 9 inches. Birthday Lake sits just south of the Island Lakes in the Island Lakes Basin and the shortest route arrives from the west via the Fuji Mountain Trail (#3674), which heads at the end of FR 5883. After a quarter mile, turn right, and then continue east to the intersection with the South Waldo Trail (#3586). Turn left (north) and then take the next right (east), which is the eastern extension of the Fuji Mountain Trail. Continue about 600 yards to Birthday Lake (on your right). You'll pass Verde Lake along the way (see listing herein). FR 5883 heads north from Hwy 58, about 15 miles east from Oakridge. The area is rarely accessible before mid- to late June.

Black Creek (Lane County)

A tributary to Salmon Creek near Oakridge, Black Creek is a scenic trout stream with opportunities for harvest. The fishing is usually good between mid-summer and mid-autumn. Black Creek Road follows most of the creek and the Lilian Falls Trail follows the headwaters within the Waldo Lake Wilderness Area. Along the way, you can see some truly gargantuan Douglas firs and cedar trees at the Joe Goddard Old Growth Grove and you can enjoy beautiful Lilian Falls for the price of an easy 1-mile hike from the end of the road. In Oakridge, turn north on Crestview Street and then take a right on 1st Street, which becomes Salmon Creek Road (FR 24). Follow FR 24 to a right turn on Black Creek Road (FR 2421), which provides easy access to the stream.

Blair Lake (Lane County)
campground, small boat recommended, float tube recommended

Blair Lake is a beautiful and popular brook trout fishery located about 17 miles north-east of Oakridge in the Willamette National Forest. The wild brook trout typically range from 8 to 11 inches, but bigger fish show up often and the fishing is usually quite consistent throughout the season. The lake is surrounded by an array of habitats, ranging from lush mountain meadows to verdant evergreen forest to dry, rocky outcroppings. Wildflowers abound and the area has become a favorite destination for wildflower enthusiasts, not to mention anglers, bikers, hikers, and equestrians.

Motors are not allowed on the lake, but anglers should bring a float tube, canoe, or small boat. The shoreline is lined with brush and heavy timber so you'll enjoy a distinct advantage if you can get out on the water. Fly anglers do well here all summer as hatches of midges, mayflies, caddis, and flying ants provide ample surface action. Wet flies always do well, as do small spoons and spinners. Blair Lake spans 35 acres and reaches a depth of 21 feet. At 4,800 feet elevation, the lake is rarely accessible until late May. A small campground offers eight tent sites and requires a nominal fee paid at the parking area. The campground often fills quickly on weekends. Drinking water is available at the lake.

To reach Blair Lake, first follow Hwy 58 to the town of Oakridge. From the highway, turn north at the sign to downtown and then follow Salmon Creek Road (FR24) for 9 miles to FR 1934, the Blair Lake turnoff. Turn left on FR 1934 and head 8 miles uphill to a right-hand turn on Spur Road 733, following the road 1.3 miles to the parking area. Forest Road 1934 and Spur Road 733 are steep and usually a bit rough, so trailers and RV's are not recommended.

Blondie Lake (Three Sisters Wilderness)
hike-in, float tube recommended

Blondie Lake is a good little 5-acre rainbow and cutthroat lake located on the west edge of the Three Sisters Wilderness Area.

Tim Blount enjoys a pleasant day on lake in the Mt. Jefferson Wilderness.

From Blue River, take Hwy 126 east for 3.5 miles and turn right on FR 19 (Aufderheide National Scenic Byway). Continue on for 25 miles to FR 1958, half a mile before you reach Box Canyon Campground. Follow FR1958 east about 3 miles to a right turn on Spur Road 380. The trailhead for trail #3307 is on the south side of FR1958 just before the spur road. Follow the trail south for about a mile and a quarter and then turn left (east) when you reach the junction with the McBee Trail (#3523). Blondie Lake will be on the north side of the trail about a mile past the trail junction.

Blowout Creek (Linn County)
campground

Blowout Creek runs into the so-called "Blowout Arm" of Detroit Reservoir and offers fair fishing for small, wild trout; mostly rainbows, but also a few cutthroat and some fish that appear to be hybrids between the two species. The creek offers about 3 miles of good water, all paralleled by Blowout Creek Road (FR 10). Head east past the town of Detroit and, at the upper end of the reservoir, watch for a south turn on Blowout Creek Road. The road crosses over the North Santiam River at the head of Detroit Reservoir and then follows the south shoreline of the reservoir for 7 miles to the Blowout Creek Arm. As you head south above the reservoir, use the pullouts along the road to access the creek. Hover, Cove Creek, and Southside Campgrounds are located back down along the south shore of Detroit Reservoir, but be forewarned that they fill up quickly on summer weekends.

Blue Lake (Diamond Peak Wilderness)
hike-in, float tube recommended

This beautiful lake ranks among the most popular destinations in the Diamond Peak Wilderness and serves as an easy day trip for anglers and hikers alike. The lake offers naturally reproducing brook trout in good numbers though they rarely attain much size. Every once in a while a lucky angler hooks into a 14- to 16-inch fish. The lake covers about 20 acres and reaches a depth of 30 feet. The short hike is conducive to carrying in a float tube or other small craft.

To get there, follow Hwy 58 about 2 miles east of Oakridge and turn south onto Kitson Springs Road. Follow FR 21 about 30 miles to its junction with FR 2149, just past Indigo Springs Campground. Turn left and head 7 miles to the trailhead (Trail #3645, which continues on to Happy Lake). There are lots of nice campsites at Blue Lake, but be sure to camp at least 200 feet back from the lakeshore. This is a popular base camp for climbing 8,744-foot Diamond Peak immediately to the east.

Blue Lake (Mt. Jefferson Wilderness)
hike-in, float tube recommended

Blue Lake is a scenic, deep 10-acre brook trout fishery located in Eight Lakes Basin in the Mt. Jefferson Wilderness Area. The fish range from 8 to 12 inches and fishing is usually fair to slow. The shoreline is brushy in places and surrounded by trees, so fly anglers might want a float tube here. Campsites abound, but be sure to set up at least 200 feet back from the lake. The three routes to Blue Lake vary only by a few tenths of a mile, so take your pick from the Marion Lake Trailhead, the Pine Ridge Trailhead, or the Duffy Lake Trailhead, all accessed via Hwy 22 (North Santiam Highway) east from Salem and west from Sisters. All three routes cover between 6 and 7 miles. Plan on staying a few days to sample the myriad fishable lakes in the immediate area (see Jorn, Teto, Chiquito, Bowerman, Jenny, Melis, Marion, Red Butte, Mowich, and Grenet Lakes herein).

Blue Lake (Bull Run River)
closed waters

Blue Lake (Multnomah County)
boat ramp, boat recommended

A 60-acre lake near Troutdale, Blue Lake offers largemouth bass, crappie, bluegill, and other warmwater fish, along with stocked rainbow trout. Blue Lake County Park, large and very popular during summer, offers access to the park, including shoreline access for fishing. Nonetheless, a boat is handy here because the rest of the lakeshore lies on inaccessible private lands. Head east from Portland on I-84 and then follow the Blue Lake signs from the Exit 16.

Blue River (Lane County)

This pretty little tributary to the McKenzie River offers fair-to-good action for stocked rainbow trout and is a nice place to spend a hot summer day. The river flows for about 8 easy-access miles before reaching Blue River Reservoir. Follow Hwy 126 about 40 miles east from Springfield to the little town of Blue River. A few miles east of town turn north on Blue River Road (FR 15), which follows the east bank of Blue River Reservoir and then heads northwest along the river itself. Heavily used Mona and Lookout Campgrounds sit at the head of Blue River Reservoir.

Blue River Reservoir (Lane County)
boat recommended, campground

Located just off Hwy 126 near the McKenzie River, 1,200-acre Blue River Reservoir offers fair fishing for stocked rainbow trout with most of the action occurring during spring and early summer. Some shoreline fishing is available at various places on both sides, but the boat fishing is better, unless you arrive during a drawdown. Boat ramps are located at the upper end (Lookout Creek) and also at the Saddle Dam, a mile north of the highway off FR 15. To reach the campgrounds and boat ramps, head east past the town of Blue River and watch for the signed left-hand turn on FR 15. Mona Campground occupies the upper end of the reservoir: Follow FR 15 past Lookout Creek and then turn left over the bridge and head down the "Right Bank Access Road." FR 15 continues north along Blue River, which offers fair-to-good catch-and-keep fishing for stocked rainbow trout.

Bluegill Lake (Salem)

Bluegill Lake is the smaller of the two ponds located in Salem's Cascade Gateway Park, right next to I-5 and the Salem Airfield. This 7-acre lake offers sunfish, crappie, bullheads, and large-mouth bass. Shore fishing is okay, especially if you use bait, but serious bass anglers should launch a canoe or float tube. To get there, from I-5, take the Hwy 22/Mission Street Exit and head west toward town—you will see the pond adjacent to the south side of Mission Street just after you exit the freeway. Take the left turn at the next stoplight onto Turner Road. The entrance to the park is about a quarter mile south, on the left. The park includes picnic areas, restrooms and garbage cans, though this latter amenity seems lost on some of the anglers who show up here.

Bond Butte Pond (Linn County)

This fairly popular 35-acre pond sits close to I-5 about 18 miles north of Eugene and offers mixed-bag fishing for blue-gill, largemouth bass, channel catfish, and crappie. From Exit 209, head west on Diamond Hill Road for about a mile and then turn right (north) on Rowland Road. After about 1.5 miles turn right again, following Belts Road back over the freeway and to a left-hand turn into the pond's ODFW access area. Bank fishing is good along the rugged jeep trail on the west side of the pond and small boats or float tubes can be launched at the access area. The pond tends to get very weedy by late summer, so fish it from April through June and during mid-autumn.

Bongo Lake (Waldo Lake Wilderness)
hike-in, cross-country

This lightly fished lake in the Waldo Lake Wilderness offers naturally reproducing brook trout and usually plenty of soli-tude. Bongo covers about 8 acres and reaches a depth of 14 feet. Its brookies range from 6 to 13 inches and they feed in part on a ready supply of *Callibaetis* mayflies, Chironomids, and other insects that make this a good fly fishing lake, though all methods produce. You'll need cross-country navi-gational skills to find Bongo Lake, which occupies a broad, forested bench a little more than half a mile west by north-west of Bingo Lake, west from the southwest corner of Waldo Lake. Bingo Lake requires a 5- to 6-mile hike via either of two trails, so visitors to Bongo Lake need a strong sense of adven-ture. Consult the Waldo Lake Wilderness and Recreation Area Map available from the Willamette and Deschutes National Forests. At 5,000 feet elevation, Bongo is usually snowbound until June.

Boot Lake (Three Sisters Wilderness)
hike-in, cross-country

Boot Lake is a deep, 5-acre lake located just east of the Pacific Crest Trail east of Mink Lake in the Three Sisters Wilderness Area. Reaching it requires an easy 300-yard cross-country trek due east from Cliff Lake (see listing herein). Boot Lake is well worth your time if you are in the area and especially if you have a float tube, though this latter item is not needed to fish the lake effectively. In addition to the usual pan-size fish, Boot Lake sometimes holds a handful of fat 12- to 16-inch trout.

The shortest route (nearly 7 miles) is from the Six Lakes Trail, whose trailhead is located on Century Drive a mile south of Elk Lake. The trail is popular with horse packers, so you may have to watch your step—literally—during the summer months. When you reach the Pacific Crest Trail, continue ahead on the Six Lakes Trail until you again cross the PCT. From that junction head south another half mile to Cliff Lake or take a compass bearing on Boot Lake and head directly there from the trail junction.

Boulder Creek (Willamette National Forest)
catch-and-release, no bait

A tributary to the North Santiam River just above Detroit Res-ervoir, Boulder Creek offers fair action for small wild trout. Access is difficult. Consult the Detroit Ranger District Map, available from the ranger district office near Detroit.

Bounty Lake (Three Sisters Wilderness)
hike-in

Bounty Lake—more a deep pond than a lake, and very pretty— lies just west of the Deschutes County line and just west of the popular and scenic Sisters Mirror Lake. Bounty spans 3 acres and reaches a depth of 15 feet. Brook trout used to be the fare here, but cutthroat have been stocked in recent years. Several tiny lakes occupy the area; so consult the map to figure out which is which. These lakes are fishable from shore, but a float tube comes in handy. Fly anglers at Bounty will es-pecially benefit from a float tube owing to the steep, uneven shores and the abundant deadfalls in the water.

Bowerman Lake (Mt. Jefferson Wilderness)
hike-in

Nestled among spire-shaped fir trees, scenic Bowerman Lake offers fair-to-good fishing for stocked cutthroat trout (pre-viously brook trout have been stocked here). Located in the heavily used Eight Lakes Basin in the Mt. Jefferson Wilder-ness Area, Bowerman spans 5 acres and reaches a depth of 10 feet. The shoreline is rather brushy, but not too bad, although a float tube comes in handy throughout the area. The easiest hike to the basin is from the Pine Ridge Trail. At Milepost 70 on Hwy 22, turn east on Twin Meadows Road (look for the Camp Pioneer sign) and follow the road 5 miles uphill to the trailhead. Follow Pine Ridge Trail (#3443) east 4 miles to a right turn on the Blue Lake Trail (#3422) and after 3 miles turn left on the Bowerman Lake Trail (#3492). The Duffy Lake Trail route is about the same length but gains a lot more elevation. Use the existing campsites or be sure to camp at least 250 feet away from all the lakeshore.

Breitenbush Lake (Warm Springs Reservation)
campground

Located in the Ollalie Lakes area along the crest of the Cascade Range east from Detroit, Breitenbush Lake is the source of the North Fork Breitenbush River. This 65-acre lake offers fair fishing for small brook trout and rainbow trout, with the season generally beginning around mid- to late June. Easiest access is from Hwy 22 at Detroit: Turn east on Breitenbush Road (FR 46) and follow this road about 7 miles past Breitenbush Campground. When you climb a steep ridge and pass under the big powerlines, turn right on FR 4220, which leads about 7 rugged miles up to the lake. A Warm Springs fishing permit is not needed here.

Breitenbush River (Marion County)
campgrounds

The Breitenbush is a swift mountain river and a major feeder stream to Detroit Reservoir, entering the reservoir at the town of Detroit on Hwy 22 east from Salem. Heavily stocked with hatchery rainbow trout, the Breitenbush holds up well during the summer. The river's beauty and good fishing for keepable trout makes it a popular destination for anglers and families, especially between June and the Labor Day weekend.

Paved FR 46 follows the lower river for almost 20 miles. The upper 5 miles hangs above the South Fork, which offers mostly wild rainbows and cutthroat (8-inch minimum length). Along the way are four campgrounds (Willamette National Forest), all of which tend to fill up on popular summer weekends. Lots of primitive sites are available on and near the river.

The Breitenbush flows cold and clear all summer. Most of the trout (hatchery and wild) range from 6 to 12 inches and all methods produce here. Adventurous anglers can hike along the river to reach out-of-the-way pools, runs, and riffles or head up FR 4685 to explore the South Fork. FR 4685 departs FR46 upstream from privately owned Breitenbush Hot Springs. The Breitenbush arm of Detroit Lake is accessible by boat from the main reservoir.

All supplies and services are available in the little town of Detroit and many other productive waters in the area are open to keeping trout. (see French Creek, Detroit Reservoir, Upper North Santiam River, Big Cliff Reservoir, Tumble Lake, Leone Lake, Elk Lake, Dunlap Lake).

Brice Creek (Lane County)
campground

Pretty little Brice Creek offers fair fishing for small native cutthroat that reach 12 inches and average about 6 inches. During the general season, bait is allowed and a five-fish limit applies. Catch-and-release with artificial lures or flies applies for the balance of the year. A nice trail runs alongside much of the creek, providing ready access to this swift, steep, beautiful mountain stream that gouges out a rocky path through old-growth forest southeast of Cottage Grove. Brice Creek's upper section falls at a rate of about 215 feet per river mile, making it popular with veteran kayakers during the high-water period of spring.

The trout fishing is best during late summer and autumn, when the water is low enough to allow anglers to negotiate the banks. The stream offers numerous small waterfalls and plunge pools and a few nice summer swimming holes. Large dry flies always seem to work nicely, as do small spinners and spoons. The lower section of the creek offers a handful of 12-inch natives, but 4- to 9-inch trout predominate throughout.

Brice Creek attracts hikers, berry pickers, birdwatchers, and various other outdoor enthusiasts, but angling pressure seems to be fairly modest. Two campgrounds are located within a few miles of each other and you can access the trail from either of these or from the upper and lower trailheads. To get there, take Exit 174 off I-5 at Cottage Grove and head east on Row River Road. Follow the road around Dorena Reservoir and continue east to a right-hand turn on Brice Creek Road. The lower trailhead is a mile up the road and the upper trailhead is 8 miles up the road.

Bridal Veil Creek (Multnomah County)
catch-and-release, no bait

Famous for its beautiful waterfall that plunges off the cliffs of the Columbia Gorge, Bridal Veil Creek offers fair catch-and-release action for wild cutthroat trout above the falls. At the tiny community of Bridal Veil (Exit 28 from I-84) a gravel road follows the creek upstream for a short distance.

The Waldo Lake Wilderness offers many fishable lakes.

Brittany Lake (Waldo Lake Wilderness)
hike-in, cross-country, float tube recommended

Brittany Lake, denuded of timber by a large forest fire in 1996, offers fair-to-good fishing for stocked rainbow trout. The fish over-winter well and some reach 14 inches or more. Brittany covers 4 acres and reaches a depth of nearly 30 feet. All methods produce here, with flies and small spinners being especially good. I recommend a float tube for Brittany and for its neighbor, Mickey Lake.

To reach Brittany Lake, first head for Rigdon Lakes or Lake Kiwa, which lie just north of Waldo Lake. From the northeast corner of Lower Rigdon (the northernmost of the two Rigdon Lakes) head northeast for a quarter mile to find Brittany. From the northeast corner of Lake Kiwa, head southeast about a quarter mile to reach Brittany. Several small ponds dot the landscape here as well, but none covers more than an acre. Immediately northwest from Brittany is Mickey Lake, which spans 5 acres and offers stocked cutthroat trout, a few of which reach 16 or more inches. Stocked every other year, both lakes are lightly fished owing to the lack of formal trails reaching them, even though the nearby Rigdon Lakes are rather heavily fished. For directions to the area, see Rigdon Lakes herein and consult a map of the Waldo Lake Wilderness Area.

Bruno Lakes (Linn County)

Upper and Lower Bruno Lakes are little more than swampy ponds, but they are deep enough to over-winter small, naturally reproducing brook trout. I've not been to these lakes in many years, so I cannot report on their current status. Check them out if you don't mind a little brush busting and a mosquito-ridden bog or two. They lie just off the right-hand side as you head up Bruno Mountain Road off of Hwy 22 east from Detroit and Idanha. About 6 miles east of Idanha, look for FR 2422 heading across the North Santiam River on the south side of the highway (about a mile east from Whispering Falls Campground). Cross the bridge and head to the right. Then take a left-hand turn onto Spur Road 805. Head uphill for about a mile-and-a-half and keep a sharp eye off to the right-hand (downhill) side of the road. The ranger district map is a big help here.

Buck Lake (Clackamas County)
hike-in

A very pretty, fairly productive and generally lightly fished 10-acre rainbow brook trout lake, Buck Lake sits just a few miles west of ever-popular Timothy Lake high in the Cascades south of Mt. Hood. Follow Hwy 26 to the turn-off for Timothy Lake (Skyline Road). Follow the south shore of Timothy Lake and cross the Clackamas River at the lake's outlet dam. Then follow FR 5820 until you reach a right-hand turn on Spur 210, leading a short distance to the half-mile trail up to the lake.

Bug Lake (Lane County)

Bug Lake is a 3-acre mountain lake located on the southeastern edge of Lane County in the Willamette National Forest. The lake is stocked every other year with a few hundred rainbow trout and is lightly fished owing to its isolation and the long drive over rough forest roads. From Hwy 58, head 2 miles east of Oakridge and turn south at Kitson Springs Road (FR 21). Follow FR 21 around the west side of Hills Creek Reservoir and continue up the Middle Willamette River. One mile past Sacandaga Campground, turn south (right) on FR 2143 and head up about 12 miles to a three-way intersection. Follow the middle spur (FR 2144), which loops around 2 more miles to the lake, sitting off to the right-hand (east) side of the road. Be sure to bring along the Middle Fork ranger district map.

Bull Run River (Clackamas County)

A tributary to the Sandy River and the source of the Portland area's water supply, the Bull Run River is open only on its lowermost mile, or thereabouts, and the rest of the drainage is closed to public recreation use. The river's lower end, just above the Sandy River confluence near Dodge Park, produces a few salmon and steelhead. Only fin-clipped steelhead, chinook salmon and coho salmon may be kept and all wild fish must be released unharmed.

Burley Lakes
see Berley Lakes

Burnt Lake (Mt. Hood National Forest)
hike-in

A very pretty and popular hike-in lake in the Mt. Hood National Forest, Burnt Lake offers fair-to-good fishing for 8- to 10-inch cutthroat trout (it used to be stocked with brook trout), with a few larger fish. It makes a nice, easy-to-reach alternative to some of the oft-crowded mountain lakes closer to the highway. Burnt Lake covers 8 acres and sits at about 4,100 feet. The easy 3-mile hike runs along a creek bottom most of the way and finally switches back to climb up to the lake. Follow Hwy 26 to ZigZag and then head north on FR 18 (Lolo Pass Road). After about 5 miles, watch for the campground signs and turn off toward Riley and Lost Creek Campgrounds. Follow FR 1825 past Lost Creek Campground and take the right-hand turn when the road forks. The trail begins at the end of this road.

Nearby 7-acre Cast Lake offers similar prospects for brook trout and always seems to have a precious few fat 14-inchers available, though they can be difficult to catch. This is a great float tube lake and the hiking in this area offers lots of scenic beauty. From Burnt Lake you can follow the trail west 1.5 miles to Cast Lake. Or you can reach Cast Lake by taking Trail 773 from Riley Campground. Both lakes are easy to fish in a day's time during July and if the weather cooperates in early October you'll have them to yourself.

Burnt Top Lake (Three Sisters Wilderness)
hike-in, cross-country

A scenic and productive off-trail lake in the Three Sisters Wilderness Area, Burnt Top spans about 20 acres and reaches a depth of 28 feet. ODFW stocks the lake every other year, usually with cutthroat and/or rainbow trout, which reach at least 16 inches here; sometimes the mix includes brook trout rather than cutts. The fish typically range from 6 to 12 inches and they respond to all methods. Shoreline fishing is easy on Burnt Top (sometimes called "Top Lake"), but a float tube is a nice luxury. Spend a few days in this area to fish Burnt Top, Nash, Bounty, Denude, and Lancelot Lakes.

The easiest route to Burnt Top Lake is reached from the east via the Mirror Lake Trail (#20): Follow Century Drive from Bend past Sparks Lake and past Devils Lake. Watch for the trailhead on the right-hand side of the road, 2 miles past Devils Lake. Follow this trail 3 miles to a trail junction near Sisters Mirror Lake. Take a left and head southwest past Sisters Mirror Lake to the next trail junction. Then head cross-country up to Denude Lake, a quarter-mile to the northwest. From Denude, follow a fairly rugged but pleasant cross-country trek due west 1 mile. Just hold your elevation as you head west until you see the lake off to the right.

Alternately you can follow the Nash Lake Trail (#3527) (north of Sisters Mirror Lake) about 1.75 miles westerly before heading off cross-country to the south. The major reference point is the nearby butte called Burnt Top, which rises gently above the surrounding wilderness. The lake sits on a narrow bench just below the butte's northeast flank. When you head south off the trail, you will descend to the creek bottom and then climb steeply up to the bench below Burnt Top's slopes.

Butte Creek (Clackamas/Marion Counties)
catch-and-release, no bait

A lengthy tributary to the Pudding River, Butte Creek—in its upper reaches—flows parallel to Abiqua Creek, but one ridge farther north. Access is spotty as the creek has lots of private property until you get well above Scotts Mills. The upper-most reaches of the stream have a good population of wild cutthroat and rainbow trout, with a few reaching 10 inches. Upstream from Butte Creek Falls, at about river mile 25.5, the stream has a two-fish limit (minimum size 8 inches).

Calapooia River (Linn County)

Located in a largely rural region of the central Willamette Valley, the Calapooia River runs almost entirely through private farmlands in its lower half and through a mix of private and public timber lands in its canyon-bound upper half. Access to the lower half is difficult, but the upper reaches, upstream from the tiny town of Dollar, offer fair catch-and-release fishing for wild cutthroat and rainbow trout. The road runs alongside the creek, offering easy access.

Adventurous types might try a summertime canoe trip below Brownsville for cutthroat and warmwater species. Reputedly one can run the river all the way from Brownsville to Albany, but that's a stretch covering a staggering 33 miles. The better bet—especially for bass and crappie—would be to launch at the mouth of the river in Albany and fish upstream.

The upper reaches of the Calapooia, fished mostly by local anglers, offer easy access, but the fish are usually small, ranging from 6 to 10 inches. The fishing peaks from late June through October. Remnant populations of steelhead and spring chinook salmon exist here, but runs are severely depressed and have been for many years. The river is closed to fishing for both species.

Access to the area is easy: South of Albany and north of Eugene, take the Brownsville Exit from I-5 and head east through Brownsville. Or, from downtown Sweet Home, just head south 4 miles on SR 228 (Holley Road). From the tiny town of Holley, SR 228 roughly follows the river down to Brownsville, but access on this section is mostly non-existent. The better trout fishing is upstream. Head east on Upper Calapooia Road, which deteriorates upstream from Dollar, where the best fishing awaits. Crawfordsville Covered Bridge, erected in 1932, lies adjacent to the highway bridge at Crawfordsville, downstream from Holley. The bridge came perilously close to utter destruction during the big floods of 1996/97.

Campers Lake (Three Sisters Wilderness)
hike-in, float tube recommended

This shallow, 12-acre lake sits just east of the Old McKenzie Highway about a mile northeast from Scott Lake. Not particularly popular, Campers Lake receives about 1,000 cutthroat every few years. They reach 15 inches or so, but smaller fish prevail. To get there, park at the trailhead for Hand Lake (see listing herein) and hike east about 300 yards.

Canby Pond (Canby)

Located at Canby City Park in Canby, this small pond is stocked each spring with legal-size rainbow trout and also offers bluegill, crappie, and an occasional largemouth bass. The pond is open to fishing only by youths (under age 17) and anglers with ODFW Disabled Angler permits.

Canyon Creek (South Santiam tributary)
closed waters

Cardiac Lake (Waldo Lake Wilderness)
hike-in, cross-country, float tube recommended

A productive, isolated 3.5-acre brook and cutthroat trout fishery, Cardiac Lake sits off trail about 1 mile west of Waldo Lake. Lightly fished, the lake is 15 feet deep and offers some good-size fish to complement the typical pan-size specimens. Cardiac sits at 5,550 feet elevation, perched on the rim above Black Creek Canyon, and lies immediately east of Last Lake (see listing herein). You will need strong cross-country skills to navigate this terrain.

Use the Koch Mountain Trail (#3576) to access Cardiac Lake and nearby Fig, Photo, and Last Lakes, all of which require a bushwhacking cross-country course of upwards of 1 mile. In this case, bushwhacking serves as a precise description because some of this region grows dense stands of rhododendron. From Oakridge, head northeast on the Salmon Creek Road (FR 24) until you reach the junction where 24 becomes FR 2420 to the right (gated) and FR 2421 to the left (the main branch). This is the Black Creek Road. Follow it half a mile to a left-hand turn onto FR 2422 and follow this road all the way to its end at the trailhead. From there, the shortest route to Cardiac Lake follows a southerly compass course from the trailhead—consult you topo map first, but beware that Cardiac Lake and its neighbors are not labeled on the maps. The area is dotted with small ponds, all of which are smaller than the fishable lakes. Beware the incessant clouds of mosquitoes throughout the summer. The lake is rarely accessible before mid-summer.

Carmen Reservoir (Linn County)
campground

A diversion reservoir on the upper McKenzie River, Carmen offers good fishing for stocked rainbow trout as well as small, wild brook trout and a few native cutthroat that drift down from the gorge-bound river above. The reservoir, which spans about 40 acres, offers good shoreline fishing and is open year round. Many anglers concentrate on the area where the river flows in and bait always seems most productive there.

The deepest water (up to 25 feet) lies along the dam and the adjacent pool on the reservoir's west side and often produces the largest fish. The east half of Carmen is dominated by shallows that seem to attract a lot of brook trout. Rainbows here reach 18 inches and brookies reach at least 14 inches, but these are the uncommon extremes. Most of the 'bows range from 9 to 12 inches and the brookies typically range from 6 to 8 inches. Boats are easily launched from the shoreline.

Carmen Reservoir

Carmen is a pleasant place for a day-trip and quite family friendly. A campground nearby is secluded in the timber and a trail leads up from the reservoir, following the river and providing some stunning views of the gorge and the nearby waterfalls. The trail is probably not a good place for children owing to the steep drop-off into the narrow river gorge.

Carmen Reservoir lies just south of Clear Lake on Hwy 126, about 5 miles south of the Hwy 20/126 junction and 8 miles south from Santiam Junction. Watch for the sign on the west side of the road. The reservoir is usually accessible by May and fishing holds up into mid-autumn. Owing to its source—the cold, gin-clear waters of the upper McKenzie—Carmen rarely suffers algae blooms.

Cast Lake (Mt. Hood National Forest)
see Burnt Lake

Cedar Creek (Marion County)
catch-and-release

Cedar Creek joins the Little North Fork of the North Santiam River a few miles upstream from Elkhorn. This rugged and scenic little mountain creek offers fair-to-good catch-and-release fishing for small, wild cutthroat and rainbow trout. The lower 3 miles of the creek are fairly heavily fished and easily accessible from the gravel road that runs alongside. The upper end of Cedar Creek is brushier and less popular. To get there, follow Hwy 22 east about 24 miles from Salem. One mile past Mehama, turn left (north) on North Fork Road. Follow this road all the way up to a right-hand fork on FR 2207. Just past Shady Cove Campground, you'll pick up the creek on the left. To reach the upper section, continue up FR 2207 to a right turn on Spur Road 225. Park wherever you can and bushwhack over to the creek to the west.

Cedar Lake (Willamette National Forest)

Tiny Cedar Lake, high on the ridge north of Opal Lake, contains no fish.

Chehalem Creek (Yamhill County)
catch-and-release, no bait

Home to a few wild cutthroat, Chehalem Creek runs entirely through private lands, right through the heart of some of Oregon's best Pinot Noir country. The creek reaches the Willamette River at Newberg.

Chiquito Lake (Mt. Jefferson Wilderness)
hike-in

Chiquito Lake sits on the east edge of the Eight Lakes Basin, northeast from Jorn Lake. Chiquito, which spans about 7 acres, offers wild brook trout that reach 13 inches or so, but which usually range from 5 to 9 inches. The five designated campsites at Chiquito often offer a little more seclusion than those at Jorn, Blue, and Bowerman Lakes. Shoreline fishing is easy at Chiquito, but a float tube certainly helps reach the deep water. A rockslide borders one end of the lake while fir trees surround the remaining shoreline.

The easiest hike to the basin is achieved from the Pine Ridge Trail. At Milepost 70 on Hwy 22, turn east on Twin Meadows Road (look for the Camp Pioneer sign) and follow the road 5 miles uphill to the trailhead. Follow Pine Ridge Trail (#3443) east 4 miles to a right turn on the Blue Lake Trail (#3422) and after 3 miles turn left on the Bowerman Lake Trail (#3492). From Bowerman's north shore, follow the outlet streambed about a quarter mile north and downhill to Chiquito. The Duffy Lake Trail route is about the same length as the Pine Ridge/Blue Lake Trail route but gains a lot more elevation.

Cincha Lakes (Mt. Jefferson Wilderness)
hike-in, cross-country, float tube recommended

Two lightly fished lakes just off the Duffy Lake Trail, the Cincha and Little Cincha, usually fish quite well, though they are both tiny and are thus stocked with just a few hundred brookies or cutthroat every few years. Little Cincha, just an acre in size, is substantially deeper than 2-acre Cincha and is capable of growing 14-inch trout, though rarely. Both lakes are surrounded by dense timber, making fly casting a little precarious, but Little Cincha offers enough shoreline margin to allow you to dart a back cast through spaces in the trees and to roll cast quite easily. Cincha, while certainly fishable from shore, is tailor-made for a float tube.

To find the Cincha Lakes, follow the Duffy Lake Trail east for 1.7 miles to its intersection with the Turpentine Trail (#3490), which heads north. From the trail junction, continue a quarter mile east along the Duffy Lake Trail (count your steps) and then bushwhack about 50 yards south to Cincha Lake. The lakes are close to the trail, but obscured by dense timber. Study the terrain closely and you can sometimes make out the faint bushwhacker's trails heading to the lake. A pleasant, wooded campsite sits between Cincha and Little Cincha. Little Cincha lies immediately west of Cincha.

Clackamas River
boat ramp, campground

Often one of the busiest rivers in western Oregon, the Clackamas also ranks among the most productive steelhead and salmon rivers in the Willamette drainage. The Clackamas draws its headwaters from high in the Cascade Range southeast from Portland and east from Salem. Along its lengthy northwesterly journey, the river gathers numerous major tributaries—the Collawash, the Oak Grove, and South Forks Eagle Creek—before eventually reaching the Willamette River near Gladstone, on the southeast side of the Portland metro area.

The best fishery here, arguably, is the run of winter steelhead in the Clackamas, but the river also offers very good prospects for hatchery summer steelhead, spring chinook salmon and fin-clipped coho salmon. The winter-run steelhead are of both hatchery and wild origins and they enter the river from early December through March. Hatchery summer steelhead show up between April and September, so the Clackamas has steelhead every month of the year. The upper

Clackamas River steelhead

watershed harbors small, wild trout in relative abundance.

Just below the town of Estacada, River Mill Dam (one of three impoundments in the Estacada area) divides the so-called Lower Clackamas from the Upper Clackamas. The Clackamas Highway, SR 224, more or less follows the river for about 40 miles between the town of Clackamas and Ripplebrook Guard Station, located where the Oak Grove Fork of the Clackamas reaches the main river. From there, Mt. Hood National Forest Route 46 follows the river south and east to its headwaters and then loops back to the west, down the Breitenbush River to the town of Detroit on Hwy 22.

The Lower Clackamas is the realm of the river's highly productive salmon and steelhead runs. A boat is almost a necessity on the lower river owing to extensive and inaccessible private land along both banks. The uppermost launch site on the Lower Clackamas is at ever-popular McIver State Park, 4 miles downstream from Estacada on the south bank, off Springwater Road. McIver Park offers good access for bank fishing and is thus very popular. It also has a large campground (call 1-800-452-5687 for reservations) and showers. Though the Clackamas offers some fairly technical water, its is easily navigable in drift boats. As with any river, prospective boaters should first float the Clackamas with someone familiar with the routes.

Downstream from McIver, the Clackamas boasts five additional boat ramp sites: Feldheimer Ramp (gravel), Barton County Park, Carver Ramp, Riverside Park, and Clackamette Park respectively. The Milo-to-Barton float covers 8 miles and is extremely popular. You can avoid the whitewater at McIver Park (sometimes called Milo Park and officially named Milo McIver Park) by using the lower ramp near the lowermost picnic area. Feldheimer Ramp is situated about half way through this stretch. Barton Park to Carver covers 5.5 miles and is equally popular. Both of these drifts take you through a seemingly endless supply of good steelhead water, ranging from deep pools perfect for pulling plugs to wide, shallow tailouts and riffles ideal for spin-casting and fly fishing.

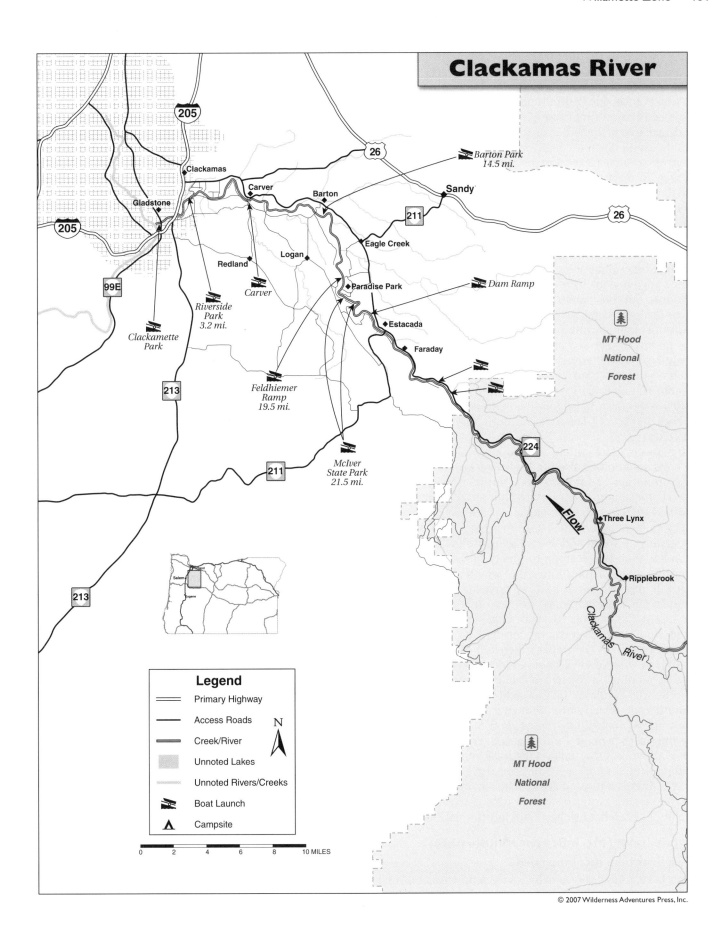

Clackamas River

Barton Park
14.5 mi.

Riverside
Park
3.2 mi.

Clackamette
Park

Carver

Feldhiemer
Ramp
19.5 mi.

McIver
State Park
21.5 mi.

Dam Ramp

MT Hood
National
Forest

Clackamette
Park

Flow

Three Lynx

Ripplebrook

Clackamas River

MT Hood
National
Forest

Legend
—— Primary Highway
—— Access Roads
—— Creek/River
▨ Unnoted Lakes
〰 Unnoted Rivers/Creeks
⛴ Boat Launch
⛺ Campsite

0   2   4   6   8   10 MILES

N

© 2007 Wilderness Adventures Press, Inc.

The lower drift on the Clackamas—popular with salmon and steelhead anglers—runs 8 miles from Carver down to Clackamette Park at the Clackamas/Willamette confluence. The ramp at Riverside Park cuts about 3 miles off the drift.

To reach Barton Park from I-205 near Gladstone, take Exit 12 and head east to the SR 224 turn-off heading south. The park is about 7 miles down the highway (watch for the signs). The boat ramp at Carver is located just upstream from the bridge at Carver. To reach Clackamette Park, take Exit 9 (McLaughlin Blvd.) from I-205 and head north. The takeout at Riverside Park is useful if you want to avoid the extremely busy ramp at Clackamette and the salmon-fishing hoglines that span the river during the run of spring chinook. Take Exit 12 heading east from I-205 and turn right on Evelyn Street, which leads to the ODFW Clackamas office.

Bank anglers don't have a lot to choose from on the Lower Clackamas, but those areas that do offer public bank fishing tend to be located on productive stretches. ODFW owns a section of shoreline running from the mouth of Clear Creek down to the bridge at Carver. The mouth of Eagle Creek (Bonnie Lure State Park) is equally popular and productive, located on the east bank about halfway between Carver and Estacada. The boat launch areas—McIver Park, Barton Park, and Riverside—also have good bank access and Cross Park and High Rocks in Gladstone are both very popular bank access sites.

The Lower "Clack" offers a rare opportunity to catch and keep coho salmon because the Eagle Creek Hatchery releases huge numbers of smolts. During autumn, the run of fin-clipped coho salmon often ranges from 40,000 to 80,000 fish and draws huge numbers of anglers to the river. The super-popular hole between the Hwy 99 bridge and the trestle gets horribly crowded and always seems to include a rather substantial snag-fest, leading to plenty of discussion about closing this spot to fishing during the salmon runs. The silvers, which will hit a wide array of lures, typically range from 6 to 9 pounds. On the Clackamas, the season is currently open from August 1 to October 31, while Eagle Creek itself is open through Nov. 31 (check current synopsis).

For trout anglers the upper watershed of the Clackamas, including its South and Oak Grove forks, offers lots of opportunity. Depending on where you fish, the upper river and the forks offer wild cutthroat, rainbow and brook trout. Except for the South Fork, which flows through a steep, deep, roadless canyon, access to the upper river is good. State Route 224 runs along the river upstream from Estacada. From the Collawash River confluence, FR 46 follows the river into the mountains, providing access to 25 miles of productive water. The best fishing is found at those places where the road swings away from the stream, requiring you to hike down to the water. These upper stretches fish best from July through September.

Clagget Lake (Mt. Jefferson Wilderness)
hike-in, float tube recommended
Clagget Lake, one of the so-called "Firecamp Lakes," is a fair brook and cutthroat trout fishery covering about 6 acres. It lies on the northwestern edge of the Mt. Jefferson Wilderness Area alongside Sheep Lake and Crown Lake. At 5,000 feet, these lakes are rarely accessible before June. To reach the Firecamp Lakes, turn east at Detroit onto Breitenbush Road and continue about 11 miles up to a right turn onto FR 4685 (South Fork Breitenbush Road), 2 miles past Cleator Bend Campground. Follow FR 4685 up the South Fork and then up a steep ridge to a right turn onto Spur Road 330. The trailhead is at the end of the spur. Crown Lake is a mile in; Clagget and Sheep Lakes are a quarter mile to the southeast. Six-acre Clagget offers eight designated campsites.

Clare Lake (Mt. Washington Wilderness)
hike-in, float tube recommended
Clare Lake sits along the popular Patjens Lake Trail south of Big Lake near the Santiam Summit. It's a 5-acre lake just west from the Patjens Lakes that is sometimes planted with brook trout or rainbow. The fish generally don't get big, but if you're headed to the Patjens Lakes (see listing herein), Clare is worth a look. See Patjens lakes for directions to the area. The lake does not appear by name on any of the maps but sits right along the western extent of the loop trail about 2 miles from the trailhead (map coordinates: T14S R7-1/2E 16S).

Clear Creek (Sandy River drainage)
hike-in, no bait, catch-and-release
A fast-flowing creek that carves out a steep forested canyon north of ZigZag, Clear Creek supports fair numbers of small, wild trout that don't see much angling pressure. The stream's upper half lies inside the Bull Run Watershed Management Area and is off-limits to public use. The lower end of the creek is fishable for about 4 miles just northeast from ZigZag. The best water is in the canyon and requires a rather troublesome hike up the creek. From ZigZag, turn north on the Lolo Pass Road (FR 18) and go 3 miles to a left-hand turn that dead ends after a mile. Hike upstream from there. The best fishing is from July through September.

Clear Fork (Clackamas County)
campgrounds, no bait, catch-and-release
A tumultuous tributary to the upper stretch of the Sandy River, Clear Fork offers fair catch-and-release fishing during summer for small, native trout. Clear Fork joins the Sandy near the Lolo Pass Road (FR 18) northeast from ZigZag. Forest Road 1828 crosses the creek near its mouth and you can hike down into the steep canyon from the LoLo Pass Road itself, which parallels the Clear Fork. Fishing is best from July through September.

Clear Lake (Linn County)
boat recommended, campground
A deep, vibrantly transparent 148-acre lake sitting near voluminous lava flows in the high Cascades, Clear Lake is the source of the famous McKenzie River. The lake supports a fair population of small, wild brook trout, with an occasional brookie reaching 15 inches (no limit on the number of brook-

ies taken), and is also heavily stocked with rainbow trout. The lake has very little viable shoreline access, so fishing is almost entirely by boat. Clear Lake is rather popular with scuba divers because of the crystal-clear waters that reveal an ancient flooded forest. Many of the old trees remain standing as if frozen in time. The forest was flooded when a lava flow blocked the river and formed the lake. On a still day with good lighting, you can peer down into the lake's depths from a boat. No motors are allowed on the lake. The boat launch is at the campground and Clear Lake Resort offers rental rowboats.

Cleary Pond (Lane County)

Located on the Fern Ridge Wildlife Management Area west of Eugene, 4-acre Cleary Pond offers slow-to-fair fishing for largemouth bass. Take 11th Street heading west out of Eugene. Outside of town, 11th Street becomes Hwy 126. Turn left on Neilson Road and follow it to the parking area for the pond.

Cleo Lake (Mt. Jefferson Wilderness)
hike-in

A little 5-acre gem hidden off the beaten path in the Mt. Jefferson Wilderness, Cleo is stocked with rainbow or cutthroat trout that can reach 16 to 18 inches if they survive three straight years without winterkill. Most of the fish range from 8 to 12 inches and they rarely seem numerous. To reach Cleo Lake, take the Pine Ridge Trail near Camp Pioneer. To find this trailhead, follow Hwy 22 about 5 miles south from Marion Forks to Forest Service Road 2261, marked "Camp Pioneer." Turn east off the highway and ascend 2261 until it ends.

Follow the Pine Ridge Trail for about half a mile until you cross a rocky creek bed. Shortly thereafter, look for a faint trail heading off to your right (this trail does not appear on most maps). Follow this trail past the first lake you come to (Scout Lake). The next similar-sized lake you find is Cleo. There is a nice camp spot on the far side of the lake, under the trees, and you can fish Cleo effectively from shore. Just a quarter mile over the hill to the southwest is Turpentine Lake and you can regain the Pine Ridge Trail by heading northeast from Cleo.

Cliff Lake (Three Sisters Wilderness)
hike-in

Cliff Lake is a popular and productive 40-acre lake in the Three Sisters Wilderness Area. It is heavily stocked with rainbows and brook trout so the fishing holds up well throughout the season, which usually begins by mid-June if not earlier. The fish over-winter successfully and Cliff Lake kicks out an occasional 16-inch rainbow. The lake lies along the east side of the Pacific Crest Trail (PCT), a mile east of Mink Lake. Many visitors arrive here via the PCT, but the shortest route (nearly 7 miles) is from the Six Lakes Trail, whose trailhead is located on Century Drive a mile south of Elk Lake. The trail is popular with horse-packers, so you may have to watch your step—literally—during the summer months. Autumn is the best time to visit this area because the entire Mink Lake Basin is devoid of people. Be prepared for cold weather by late September and arrive armed against mosquitoes during summer. Cliff Lake

offers some nice campsites and serves well as a base camp for exploring the other lakes in the area.

Coal Creek (Lane County)

A nice little tributary to the Middle Fork Willamette River above Hills Creek Reservoir in Lane County, Coal Creek offers fair-to-good fishing for small wild trout. Two miles past Oakridge, turn south on Kitson Springs Road (FR21) and follow the road around the west side of Hills Creek Reservoir. Just past Campers Creek Campground, turn south on Staley Creek Road and then take an immediate right onto FR 2133, which follows the stream for about 6 miles.

Collawash River (Clackamas River drainage)

A gem of a mountain trout stream, the Collawash offers good fishing for small, wild rainbows and cutthroat trout. Much of the river is available only to anglers willing to hike, so crowds are easy to avoid here. The river fishes best from July through September and is a great respite from the hot late-summer weather in western Oregon. The Collawash has two main forks, widely separated by the roadless Bull of the Woods Wilderness Area. The East Fork and the Hot Springs Fork converge at the Fan Creek Campgrounds and then the main branch flows about 4 miles north to join the Clackamas at River Ford Campground.

The Hot Springs Forks, named for Bagby Hot Springs on the upper (south) end of the river, is the more readily accessible of the two forks, and thus the more crowded. Forest Road 70 follows closely along the Hot Springs Fork for 7 miles. Upstream from the road, however, access is by trail only. The popular trail into Bagby Hotsprings continues up the river (a creek at this point). If you make this hike into the upper watershed, try fishing the lower end of Whetstone Creek as well.

You can also reach the East Fork Collowash from the north via the Clackamas River Road. When you get to Little Fan Creek Campground, continue left on FR 63, which follows the East Fork for about 2.5 miles before swinging off to the east. The road again approaches the river about 7 miles upstream, leaving a lengthy and productive section of easy-to-reach hike-in water that is very lightly fished. Park along the road or at either of the two or three short spur roads on the west side of the road, and bushwhack your way down to the river. The main road eventually leads down to the river and from there you can hike upstream along yet another lengthy section of walk-in-only water.

You can also get to the East Fork from Hwy 22 at Detroit. Head east on Breitenbush Road about 5 miles to a left-hand turn on the Humbug Creek Road (FR 4696). Stay on 4696 until you reach a high summit and a major 3-way intersection at the Mt. Hood National Forest Boundary. Turn left on FR 6370, which heads downhill, crosses the headwaters of the Collawash and then turns north to parallel the upper river from a distance. This road, which heads to the Round Lake parking area, washed out a few years ago about 2 miles past Round Lake. Until and unless the road is repaired, you must backtrack and then turn east and then north to take FR 6355 to continue downstream (north) above the Collawash.

Columbia Slough (Portland)
boat ramp, boat recommended

Columbia Slough is a narrow waterway running all the way across the northern section of Portland, from the mouth of the Willamette on the west, to the Columbia River well upstream from the I-205 bridge. This course takes the slough through Portland's industrial area and consequently this warmwater fishery has suffered substantial pollution over the years. Elevated PCB levels, for which ODFW has issued a warning, affect the fish. Don't eat them. In addition to toxic fish (and water), the slough suffers myriad other water quality problems, including high PH levels, low dissolved-oxygen levels, high algae levels, high coli form bacteria levels and elevated water temperatures. Nonetheless, Columbia Slough offers some very good fishing for warmwater species, and is best accessed by canoe or similar craft. Species include bullhead, yellow perch, smallmouth bass, largemouth bass, bluegill, crappie, and various non-game species. Fishing is best as the water begins to warm during spring, especially from April through June, and again during early to mid-autumn. The mouth of the slough is accessible from the Willamette River at Kelley Point Park and a network of additional canoe/kayak launch points have been established to aid increasing numbers of paddlers. Estimated straight-through, point-to-point paddle times are as follows:

- Slough headwaters to 16550 NE Airport Way: 1 hour
- 16550 NE Airport Way to 143rd Street levee: 1 hour
- 143rd Street levee to 11198 NE Simpson: 1 hour
- 11198 NE Simpson to Whitaker Slough mouth: 1.5 hours
- Whitaker Slough mouth to1880 NE Elrod levee: 1 hour
- 1880 NE Elrod levee to N. 9363 Columbia Blvd.: 2.5 hours
- 9363 N. Columbia Blvd. to North Slough mouth: 1 hour
- North Slough mouth to Kelley Point Park: 1 hour
- Slough headwaters to Kelley Point Park: 9+ hours

Colt Lake (Three Sisters Wilderness)
hike-in

Colt Lake sits north of Sunset Lake and southeast from Horse Lake in the Three Sisters Wilderness. In the past it has produced small, naturally reproducing brook trout. Check it out if you're in the area, but don't expect any sizeable fish. See Horse Lake or Sunset Lake for directions to the area.

Commonwealth Lake (Washington County)

More or less an urban fishery, Beaverton's Commonwealth Lake is an attractive, 16-acre stocked-trout lake in the Cedar Hills area. ODFW keeps the lake well stocked with legal-size

Off-trail travel can lead to terrific lakes in the Diamond Peak Wilderness.

rainbows during the spring, and warmwater species are also available. The park attracts lots of waterfowl, including a sizable population of resident geese and ducks. Park rules prohibit feeding the waterfowl. To get there, take Hwy 26 east to the Cedar Hills Blvd. exit. Turn right and take a right on Southwest Foothills Drive and follow it to a right-hand turn on Huntington Avenue, leading to the park.

Copepod Lake (Three Sisters Wilderness)
hike-in

Planted with rainbows and/or cutthroat, and also offering a few wild brook trout, Copepod Lake sits just west of the Pacific Crest Trail, northeast of Mink Lake in the Three Sisters Wilderness Area. The lake is deep (18 feet) and over-winters well. The typical trout range from 6 to 12 inches, but the 16-inchers are in there. This is good float tube country and myriad other small lakes in the immediate area make the trek with the tube well worthwhile. The shortest route arrives from the east via the Six Lakes Trail and covers about 6 miles. The trailhead is a mile south of Elk Lake on Century Drive east of Bend. Be sure to consult a topo map as the area is riddled with trails.

Corner Lake (Three Sisters Wilderness)
hike-in

This 50-acre brook trout lake sits north of Mink Lake in the Three Sisters Wilderness Area. Its wild trout range from 4 to 14 inches, but the majority are 6 to 8 inches. They are small but usually eager, and all methods produce. Trails arrive from all sides (see Mink Lake) and most anglers camp amidst the many lakes here and sample any number of them.

Corrigan Lake (Diamond Peak Wilderness)
hike-in

Beautiful, 5-acre Corrigan Lake is a popular camping area for climbers headed for 8,744-foot Diamond Peak just 2 miles to the east. Bring your camera for the view of the summit from Corrigan's west shore. Over the years, ODFW has stocked this lake with brook trout, rainbows, and most recently cutthroat trout. Most are pan-size, but the occasional 14-incher makes things exciting and the scenery is hard to beat, especially during late June and again during the fall.

To get there, follow Hwy 58 about 2 miles east of Oakridge and turn south onto Kitson Springs Road. Follow FR 21 about 30 miles to its junction with FR 2149, just past Indigo Springs Campground. Turn left on FR 2149 and head uphill about 7 miles to the Corrigan Lake Trailhead. Follow the trail for 1.5 miles and watch for a well-trodden but unmarked trail leading off to the right and down to the lake. At 6,000 feet elevation, Corrigan is rarely accessible before late June.

Cottage Grove Ponds (Lane County)

Cottage Grove Ponds, at South Lane Regional Park, offer about 15 acres of decent warmwater fishing. During the spring, ODFW also stocks legal-size rainbows. The ponds are located just off Row River Road at the truck scales. A good trail leads to the ponds, which feature bluegill, brown bullhead, and largemouth bass.

Cottage Grove Lake (Lane County)
boat ramp; campground

Located on the Coast Fork Willamette 6 miles south of Cottage Grove, this 1,200-acre reservoir enjoys a reputation for producing some of the region's biggest largemouth bass. Special regulations require catch-and-release of all bass more than 15 inches long. The reservoir abounds with ideal largemouth habitat and is fishable by boat and from shore. The reed stands in the upper end (south end) provide good fishing by boat and the shoreline offers good structure in the form of submerged outcroppings, drop-offs, rip-rap, timber, and channels.

The fishing picks up as the water warms during April and May. During summer, water skiers use the lake, but fishing holds steady until September, when the reservoir is drawn down. Once the drawn-down reservoir stabilizes, anglers continue to do fairly well until cold weather arrives. The reservoir offers three boat ramps, one at the dam on the north end, another on the southeast side at Wilson Creek Park, and another nearby at Shortridge Park. After drawdown, only the ramp near the dam is serviceable.

Cottage Grove Reservoir also offers fair fishing for white crappie and a few bluegill and brown bullhead. During spring, ODFW stocks about 18,000 legal rainbow trout. Trout fishing use (and angler use in general) has declined here in recent years, perhaps because of the posted warnings of mercury contamination.

To find the reservoir, take I-5 to the London Road Exit just south of Cottage Grove (Exit 172) and head south to the dam.

London Road follows the west shore and the Reservoir Road follows the east shore.

Cottonwood Meadows Lake (Clackamas County)
see Hideaway Lake

Cougar Lake (Linn County)
hike-in, cross-country

A deep, 2-acre brook trout lake, Cougar ranks among the most remote of the non-wilderness lakes in the Willamette National Forest. Its wild brookies, which range from 6 to 12 inches, don't see many anglers. Cougar Lake lies about 7 miles due west of Santiam Junction, but reaching the lake requires a circuitous drive through miles of logging roads. Be sure to carry a ranger district map. The route begins with FR 2047, which connects Hwy 20 on the south with Parish Lake Road and Hwy 22 on the north. From 2047 (either direction of the road is open all the way through), look for FR 2049 turning off to the east. From either direction, FR 2049 reaches Cougar Creek and doubles back sharply on itself after crossing the creek. Cougar Creek does not flow from the lake of the same name. Instead, reaching Cougar Lake requires a half-mile bushwhacking walk originating from Spur 630 or 635. Consult the map and find the lake by compass course. Snow banks can hang in here until mid-June.

Cougar Reservoir (Lane County)
campground; boat ramp

Stretching for 6 miles along the South Fork McKenzie River, Cougar Reservoir offers fair fishing for stocked rainbow trout. Most anglers use bait while still fishing or troll with lures and flashers, concentrating on the shoreline margins. During summer, keep close watch for water skiers, swimmers, and other users. The reservoir's upper end is a fairly popular off-season destination with anglers from Eugene/Springfield and surrounds.

At full pool the reservoir covers 1,280 acres and reaches depths of nearly 400 feet. The best fishing is found by boat around the edges, especially in the East Fork Arm and in the Walker Creek Arm, both located on the east side of the reservoir. When the reservoir is at full pool, bank anglers will find ready access near the campgrounds at the upper end where the South Fork McKenzie flows in, and at several places along the road, which circles the entire reservoir (gravel on the east bank). At low water, most of the reservoir is impossible to reach owing to the extremely steep shoreline. Only the upper end is fishable then and the boat ramps are unusable.

Boat ramps are located at Echo Campground on the East Fork Arm (turn left at the dam) and at Slide Creek Campground on the upper (south) end. Four campgrounds occupy the reservoir's shoreline and another (French Pete) sits just upstream along the river. There are no utilities available for RVs, but Slide Creek, Delta, and French Pete Campgrounds offer slots large enough to accommodate motor coaches and trailers. About an hour east of Eugene, Cougar Reservoir lies just southeast from the tiny community of Blue River on the McKenzie River. Follow Hwy 126 about 4 miles past Blue River and watch for the signed right-hand turn leading a few miles to the reservoir.

Coyote Creek (Lane County)

Most of Coyote Creek flows across private lands west of Eugene, but the lower end meanders through the Fern Ridge Wildlife Area and provides fair prospects for warmwater fish, especially if you fish by canoe. Follow West 11th Street heading west through Eugene. When you leave town, this becomes Hwy 126. Continue west toward Fern Ridge and turn left on Central Road. Take the next left turn on Cantrell Road, which leads back east toward the canoe launch site on Coyote Creek. Be sure to check with Fern Ridge Headquarters for closed seasons.

Coyote Lake (Mt. Jefferson Wilderness)
hike-in

Coyote Lake is a 1-acre pond located just off the Pacific Crest Trail above popular Hunt's Cove. Traditionally this 12-foot-deep lake has been stocked with brook trout. The lake sits at 5,900 feet off to the west side of the well-worn trail, nearly opposite Shale Lake, which sits on the east side of the trail. Be sure to consult a topo map to find these two small lakes. If you use the Pamelia trailhead, you'll need a limited entry permit, so opt instead for the Woodpecker Ridge Trail: From Hwy 22, turn east on Woodpecker Road (milepost 61). The road ends at the trailhead. Follow this trail east about 1.6 miles to the PCT and turn south. Follow the PCT south about 5 miles to Shale and Coyote Lakes.

Craig Lake (Mt. Jefferson Wilderness)
hike-in, cross-country

Craig Lake lies perched on a bench just below the top of Craig Butte in the southern end of the Mt. Jefferson Wilderness Area. This scenic, secluded lake offers fair-to-good fishing for brook trout while offering a commanding view of nearby Three-Fingered Jack. To find Craig, take the old Santiam Lodge Trail north from the trailhead at the top of Santiam Pass (or take the Pacific Crest Trail nearby). At the first trail junction stay left and head westerly, watching for an old, un-marked trail that used to lead to Maxwell Butte. Take this trail past Lost Creek (dry by late summer) and then pick your way up the butte to Craig Lake. The total distance is about 3.5 miles. The lake covers 5 acres and reaches a depth of 14 feet. A float tube is handy here though not necessary. At 5,280 feet, the lake is usually accessible by mid-June.

Creswell Ponds (Lane County)

The four Creswell Ponds, totaling 20 acres of shallow bass and bluegill water, sit immediately east of Interstate-5 at the Creswell exit, 8 miles south of Eugene. These ponds tend to get quite weedy by mid- to late summer, so the best fishing is from April through June.

Crescent Lake (Linn County)
hike-in, cross-country

This scenic, shallow 7-acre lake is hard to find and lightly fished. Its naturally reproducing brook trout reach 12 inches, though most are 6 to 10 inches in length. Crescent sits just north of Crescent Mountain about 8 miles west of Santiam Junction. Be sure to consult the ranger district map before trying to find this one (Detroit or Sweet Home R.D.). From Hwy 20 (west of Santiam Junction) or Hwy 22 (north of the junction), turn onto Lava Lake Road (FR 2067) and from there watch for a west turn (left if you are arriving from Hwy 20) on Spur Road 525. Follow 525 almost a mile to a left turn on 530. Follow 530 just about to its end where it reaches Crescent Creek (about 2 miles). The lake is a mile up the creek. Navigate the route by map and compass.

Mike Shewey float tubes Daly Lake.

Crown Lake (Mt. Jefferson Wilderness)

hike-in

At 12 acres, Crown Lake is the largest of the "Firecamp Lakes" located in the northern end of the Mt. Jefferson Wilderness Area. Though only 6 feet deep, Crown is stocked annually with brook trout and is fairly popular with hikers, campers, and anglers. The lake offers ten designated campsites and requires just a 1-mile hike. To reach the Firecamp Lakes, turn east at Detroit onto Breitenbush Road and continue about 11 miles up to a right turn onto FR 4685 (South Fork Breitenbush Road), 2 miles past Cleator Bend Campground. Follow FR 4685 up the South Fork and then up a steep ridge to a right turn onto Spur Road 330. The trailhead is at the end of the spur.

Cunningham Lake/Cunningham Slough (Sauvie Island)

boat recommended, boat ramp

Columbia Lake and Slough are interconnected waterways on the north end of Sauvie Island. They offer fair fishing for brown bullhead, yellow perch, bass, and other panfish. Access is by boat (or kayak), running up the slough. The nearest launch site is at the Scappose Bay ramp, off Hwy 30 south of St. Helens, and run north and across the bay to the mouth of the slough. Fishing peaks during the summer months.

Daly Lake (Linn County)

hike-in

A deep and pleasant 11-acre lake southwest from Marion Forks and west from Hwy 22, Daly Lake supports naturally reproducing populations of both cutthroat and brook trout. Neither species gets large in Daly. The cutthroat typically range from 4 to 7 inches, with the brookies a bit larger. A few brookies reach 11 inches. The fish are fairly numerous. Daly is located across the road from Parish Lake, along the east side of Spur Road 450 (a right turn off FR 2266 just before you reach the Parish Lake trailhead). See Parish Lake for directions. An easy trail leads to and then circles the lake. Shoreline access is good, but a float tube, raft, or small boat helps. Daly is usually accessible by early or mid-May.

Davis Lake (Mt. Jefferson Wilderness)

hike-in

Located in the Mt. Jefferson Wilderness near Temple Lake, 4-acre Davis Lake offers planted brook trout during years when the fish survive the winter. The easiest route to Davis is to first find Temple Lake (see directions thereunder) and then head east a few hundred yards on a faint trail. Davis isn't worth the effort on its own behalf but it's worth checking out if you happen to be at Temple.

Deer Camp Lake (Waldo Lake area)

hike-in

Sitting at about 6,000 feet just west of the Waldo Lake Wilderness, Deer Camp Lake is generally stocked every other year or so with a few hundred cutthroat trout along with a few rainbows from time to time. They can reach 14 inches in this 5-acre lake, which reaches a maximum depth of 25 feet. The lake is unnamed on most maps, but sits just south of the High Divide Trail north of Fuji Mountain. To reach the trailhead, follow Hwy 58 east from Oakridge or west from Willamette Pass. Between mileposts 50 and 51, just east from the train trestle, turn north onto Eagle Creek Road (FR 5883) and follow the road about 8 miles to a left turn on Spur Road 381. From the end of the road, follow an informal trail a short distance to its intersection with the High Divide Trail and turn east (right). Deer Camp Lake sits about 2 miles east, just south of the trail, just before you reach the edge of the wilderness area.

Deer Creek (Yamhill County)

catch-and-release, no bait

A small but lengthy tributary to the South Yamhill, Deer Creek offers fair catch-and-release fishing for small, native cutthroat trout. Though followed closely by roads, Deer Creek flows mostly through private property. When in doubt about access, knock on the nearest door. Public access is available 7 miles north of Sheridan at Deer Creek County Park, site of the largest remnant wet prairie in the lower Willamette Valley. The prairie, home to many indigenous plant species, covers about 25 acres. Highway 18 crosses the creek a few miles east of Sheridan, but the good trout water lies well upstream along the Gopher Valley Road. Turn north off SR 18 across from the Dairy Queen, half a mile east from the Sheridan exit.

Delta Ponds (Eugene)

Eugene's Delta Ponds, located along Delta Highway north of Valley River Center, are consistent producers of bluegill, crappie, bass, and bullhead. The ponds boast almost 200 total surface acres and are surrounded by scrub timber and heavy brush. Bank fishing is good for anglers using spinning gear (the crappie respond well to jigs), but local fly anglers often haul float tubes to the ponds and enjoy good fishing between late spring and early autumn.

Denude Lake (Three Sisters Wilderness)

hike-in

One of a group of small lakes that includes oft-photographed Sisters Mirror Lake, 9-acre Denude Lake is usually rather slow for small brook trout. The fish range from 6 to 10 inches, with an occasional larger fish. The area is worth a visit for the scenery, but not necessarily for the fishing alone. The shortest route is from the trailhead at Devils Lake on Cascade Lakes Highway west from Bend. These lakes are accessible from July through October (beware October snow storms).

Detroit Lake (North Santiam River)

boat ramps, campgrounds, services

Covering 3,500 acres at full pool, Detroit Lake is a popular and highly productive reservoir on the North Santiam River an hour east from Salem along Hwy 22. Heavily stocked with catchable rainbow trout, the lake is open year-round and fishing can be good any time. The peak season runs from late

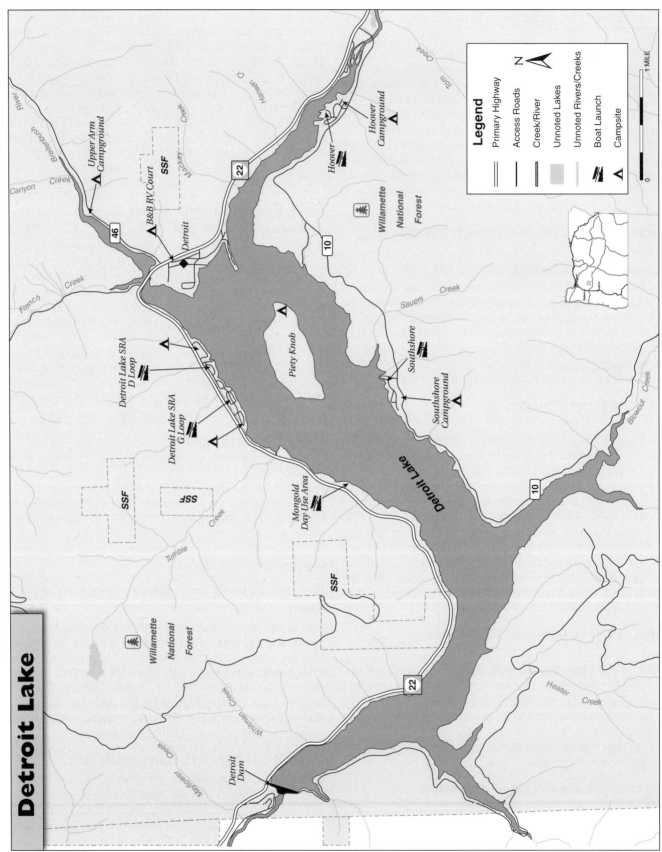

Detroit Lake

spring through summer when the reservoir is full, a time when water skiers, jet boaters and pleasure boaters abound. Trolling, both for trout and kokanee, is popular here but during the summer, trollers should be on the water early in the morning to avoid the splash-and-giggle crowd and to avoid the common afternoon winds.

Bank anglers find lots of good access points when the reservoir is full. The highway follows the lake's north shore from the dam up to Breitenbush Arm near the town of Detroit. Immediately upstream from the Detroit Dam, steep banks make access difficult, though there are a couple well-used trails. From Mongold Day Use area up to the Breitenbush Arm however, access from the highway is easy. Popular bank-fishing areas along this stretch include Mongold, Tumble Creek, Detroit Lake State Park, and the French Creek Arm (turn left just before crossing the bridge into the town of Detroit). Upstream from town, the highway again swings close to the reservoir near the popular camping area at Santiam Flats.

The south bank, likewise, offers good shoreline fishing when the reservoir is full. You can drive across Detroit Dam to reach the Kinney Creek Arm and you can cross the upper end of the lake at Blowout Bridge to reach the abundant shoreline access near Hover Campground and along the Blowout Creek Arm. During the off-season (mid-September through April), when the reservoir is drawn down, steep banks equate to more difficult and precarious shoreline access. You can scramble down the steep banks in several places to reach the water (Kinney Creek Arm, for example), but the north shore near Tumble Creek and Detroit Lake State Park offers the easiest fishing because the bank slopes gently here.

Boat anglers can fish the productive Kinney Creek and Blowout Creek Arms along with the shallows between the town of Detroit and the east shore of Piety Island. If you target kokanee or the lake's 2- to 5-pound landlocked chinook salmon, seek the deeper water near the channels from the south side of Piety Island west through the main body.

Detroit's stocked rainbows typically range from 10 to 13 inches, but the lake yields quite a few carryover fish from 14 to 16 inches in length. Most anglers still fish with bait, but all methods work. Boaters can choose from several launch sites. Mongold, located along the highway, is the most popular. Unless you arrive early in the morning, expect lines waiting to launch on summer weekends. The next public launch is just upstream at Detroit Lake State Park. There are three U.S. Forest Service-operated launch sites on the south shore (cross the upper end of the reservoir at Blowout Bridge). Improved ramps are located at Hoover and Cove Creek Campgrounds

Anglers fishing from Detroit Dam often enjoy fast action for hatchery rainbows.

and an unimproved launch sits at South Shore Campground.

The little town of Detroit offers all services, including two private marinas offering all boater services including rental boats. Reserve rental boats well ahead of time during the busy summer weekends. Call Kane's Hideaway Marina (503-854-3362/www.kanesmarina.com) or Detroit Lake Marina (503-854-3423/www.detroitlakemarina.com). Fishing tackle is available at the small stores, with the most extensive selection at Lake Center Hardware. Several restaurants offer breakfast, lunch, and dinner. During May, the town holds its annual Detroit Lake Fishing Derby and on July 4, people flock to the reservoir to watch the over-water fireworks show.

Cumulatively, campgrounds around Detroit Lake offer ample space, but they fill up rapidly and completely on summer weekends. Along the north shore where the highway runs, Detroit Lake State Park (west of town) and Santiam Flats (at the head of the lake east of town) offer the only two choices, but the south side of the reservoir offers three campgrounds (accessible by crossing the North Santiam River just above the reservoir at Blowout Bridge). Other options include the campgrounds on the Breitenbush River, which enters Detroit Lake near the town of Detroit, and any number of informal campsites located on USFS land along the roads that follow most of the reservoir's tributary streams (French Creek, Breitenbush River, Blowout Creek, and Kinney Creek).

The aforementioned tributary streams offer fair-to-good fishing as well, and are listed individually herein. A number of mountain lakes, both hike-in and drive-in, are located within easy reach of the Detroit area. See listings for Elk Lake, Leone Lake, Tumble Lake, and Opal Lake.

To reach Detroit Lake, follow Hwy 22 east from I-5 at Salem or from Central Oregon, follow Hwy 20 west from Sisters, over the Santiam Summit and down past Marion Forks and Idanha.

Dexter Reservoir (Lane County)
campground, boat ramps, campground

Covering about 1,000 acres, Dexter Reservoir is an easily accessible re-regulating reservoir on the Middle Fork of the Willamette River southeast of Eugene. Highway 58 runs along Dexter's south bank. Thanks to liberal stocking by ODFW, Dexter ranks among the area's top winter trout fishing destinations, though it is heavily infested with pike minnows. The reservoir produces lots of carryover rainbows that range from 13 to 16 inches, sometimes larger. ODFW annually dumps about 50,000 legal-size trout in Dexter, a third of them after Labor Day to support the winter fishery. Off-season fishing peaks from October through February.

During winter, bait anglers congregate at the "Causeway," which is a built-up roadway running north and south right across the reservoir to connect Hwy 58 to the community of Lowell on the north bank. The parking areas offer easy access and roadside fishing for those who prefer not to scramble

Dewey Weddington lands a trout from a wilderness lake.

around on the rocks below. The north shore is also popular with bank anglers. Boat ramps are available off Hwy 58 at Dexter State Recreation Site and on the north side at Lowell State Recreation Site.

Dexter Reservoir also offers largemouth and smallmouth bass, but most are taken incidentally to trout fishing. To get there, follow I-5 south from Eugene to the Hwy 58 Exit (Exit 188) and head east on 58, past Pleasant Hill, to the reservoir. The Causeway to Lowell turns left off the highway about half way along the reservoir.

Dinger Lake (Clackamas County)
hike-in, cross-country

A shallow, swampy lake offering fair fishing for small stocked cutthroat trout, Dinger Lake is situated about 3 miles northwest from ever-popular Timothy Lake, south from Mt. Hood. Dinger is marshy and much of the shoreline is difficult to fish. A float tube would be a bonus here and would no doubt be well worth the effort of carrying such gear the short distance to the lake. Dinger Lake is susceptible to winterkill, so keep a back-up plan in mind, but when favorable conditions persist for 2 or 3 years, some of the fish reach 13 to 14 inches. Fly anglers can enjoy good dry-fly action here during daily hatches of *Callibaetis* mayflies. There are several approaches to Dinger Lake. To avoid the marsh on the northeast shore, most people walk in from the south. Follow Hwy 26 to the turnoff for Timothy Lake (Skyline Road). Follow the south shore of Timothy Lake and cross the Clackamas River at the lake's outlet dam. Then follow FR 5820 for 3 miles to a small spur road taking off to the right (Spur 160). From the end of this road, walk northwesterly less than half a mile to the lake.

Divide Lake (Diamond Peak Wilderness)
hike-in

A superbly scenic, emerald-colored alpine pond and a fairly popular wilderness camping spot, Divide Lake sits right at the foot of Mt. Yoran in the Diamond Peak Wilderness south of Hwy 58. The lake is stocked with cutthroat every few years. The more immediate attraction for most visitors is the stunning scenery dominated by Mt. Yoran, a huge spire-like rock monolith towering above a lush sub-alpine forest of mountain hemlock and white fir. From the west, the Mt. Yoran Trail leads 4 miles to the lake. To get there, follow Hwy 58 about 2 miles east of Oakridge and turn south onto Kitson Springs Road. Stay left at the junction with FR 21 and head east along Hills Creek on FR 23 about 15 miles until you reach the Vivian Lake Trailhead near Hemlock Butte (Trail #3662). Follow #3662 half a mile to Notch Lake and then continue east on Trail #3683 to Divide Lake and Mt. Yoran. Other trails arrive from the east and south. Consult the maps.

Dixie Lake, North (Mt. Jefferson Wilderness)
hike-in

North Dixie Lake, located east of Duffy Lake in the Mt. Jefferson Wilderness, offers fair-to-good fishing for stocked trout. Its five designated campsites often offer a respite from the weekend crowds that file into Duffy and Mowich lakes, though the lake is less scenic since the 2003 B&B Complex fire scorched most of the surrounding timber. Three-acre North Dixie requires a 5-mile hike from the Duffy Lake Trailhead. Follow the Duffy Lake Trail to its intersection with the Santiam Lake Trail (the third trail junction) and turn right. Then turn east again (left) on the Dixie Lakes Trail (#3494). North Dixie lays .75 of a mile up the trail, on your left. You'll pass South Dixie first, which is too shallow to support fish.

Dixie Lake, South (Mt. Jefferson Wilderness)
hike-in

South Dixie Lake is too shallow to support fish and is not stocked, but its neighbor, North Dixie, is stocked with brook trout or cutthroat trout. See listing above.

Don Lake
hike-in, float tube recommended

Don Lake, covering about 2.5 acres, sits half a mile as the crow flies uphill from Riggs Lake, northwest from Parish Lake in the Willamette National Forest near Marion Forks. The trail into Riggs Lake continues up the hill, through stately old Douglas firs, to Don Lake, starting adjacent to the Riggs Lake inlet stream—but not following it. The hike covers about a mile and can be difficult to follow—watch for ribbon blazes. This deep, 2-acre lake has small brook trout, few of them larger than 10 inches. Fly anglers will find the steep, brushy shoreline troublesome at best, though a careful descent to the water at the lake's far corner (follow the faint trail all the way to the far end of the lake) leads to some back-casting room. Spin casters find easier prospects and a float tube is handy here, but not really worth the effort to haul in, given the tiny trout. From Hwy 22 head southeast past Marion Forks or west from Santiam Junction. Near milepost 74, turn west on Parish Lake Road (FR 2266). Follow Parish Lake Road past the Parish Lake Trailhead and about another 1.5 miles to the Riggs Lake Trailhead, which is signed. Park along the shoulder of the road on your left.

Donaca Lake (Middle Santiam Wilderness)
hike-in

Diminutive Donaca Lake sits on the eastern edge of the Middle Santiam Wilderness Area and offers fair fishing for small, wild cutthroat trout. Scenic and more than 40 feet deep, Donaca is a good place for a float tube. The hike to Donaca used to cover only about 1 mile, but a bridge washed out on a logging road crossing Pyramid Creek, adding 2 more miles. It's a lengthy drive over forest roads to get there—consult the Detroit Ranger District and Willamette National Forest maps.

Dorena Reservoir (Lane County)
boat recommended, boat ramp, campground

Boasting one of the area's best growth rates amongst its bass, trout, and crappie, 1,800-acre Dorena Reservoir sits just east

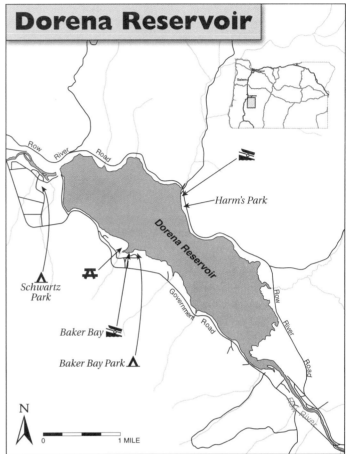

© 2007 Wilderness Adventures Press, Inc.

of Cottage Grove and offers consistently productive fishing for its myriad species. Like nearby Cottage Grove Lake, Dorena Reservoir is managed for large-size bass and anglers must release all bass more than 15 inches in length. Two-pound largemouth are fairly common and over the years Dorena has produced a handful of 10-plus-pound fish.

The bass enjoy perfect habitat in the form of submerged stumps and channels, reed stands, weed beds, and drop-offs. They commonly reach 3 pounds and grow substantially larger. The shallower and more structure-rich upper end, where the Row River flows in, offers the best bass fishing and it is essentially a boat fishing show for the bass. Dorena also offers bluegill, crappie, bullheads, and stocked rainbow trout along with the rare wild cutthroat. ODFW stocks the reservoir with about 28,000 legal-size rainbows each spring and the holdovers tend to over-winter well here, reaching lengths up to 16 inches. A mercury contamination warning is in effect for Dorena. Dorena also offers a popular and productive fishery for catfish, and the tailwater below the dam produces large trout along with a handful of steelhead and chinook salmon.

Also popular with water-sports enthusiasts, Dorena holds full pool through the summer most years and drawdown begins during early or mid-September. At full pool, use either of the ramps (one on the north side and one on the south shore), but after drawdown, only the Baker Bay ramp on the south shore is serviceable. Bank anglers congregate around the dam, mostly for trout and some crappie action. Additional bank-fishing opportunities include the Harm's Park area on the north shore and Baker Bay on the south bank.

To get there, follow I-5 to Exit 174 at Cottage Grove and turn left at the first stoplight, heading east on Row River Road. The dam is about 6 miles to the east. Row River Road continues around the north shore from its junction with Shoreline Drive, which follows the south bank. Schwartz Park (camping) sits just below the dam and two additional campgrounds are located at Baker Bay on the south shore and Harms Park on the north shore. Rental boats are available at Baker Bay during the summer.

Duffy Lake (Mt. Jefferson Wilderness)
hike-in

A scenic and popular 31-acre lake in the Mt. Jefferson Wilderness Area, Duffy offers consistent action for brook and cutthroat trout (rainbows have also been stocked in some years). The fish range from 8 to 12 inches with an occasional fish to 16 or 18 inches. Duffy Lake sits adjacent to the trail leading into Eight Lakes Basin and requires an easy 3.5-mile hike that gains a modest 800 feet en route.

The Duffy Lake Trailhead lies east of Hwy 22 immediately south of the North Santiam River Bridge near milepost 76. After crossing the river, watch for a left-hand turn to Big Meadows. A little more than half a mile in, the road forks. The left-hand fork leads down to Big Meadows while the right-hand fork leads to the Duffy Lake Trailhead. Big Meadows offers a horse camp and horse trail that parallels the foot trail most of the way to Duffy Lake. (Horse packers frequent the Duffy Lake area).

All methods produce on Duffy Lake, with fly fishing and spin fishing being most popular and highly productive. The lake offers a decent hatch of Callibaetis (speckled-wing dun) Mayflies from June through September. On still days, the hatch provides good mid-day dry-fly opportunities. Otherwise try basic sub-surface flies (woolly bugger, Prince Nymph, Zugbug, etc.), Rooster Tails, or small spoons. Even though bank fishing is easy here, many anglers carry in a float tube or other small watercraft. The Duffy Lake Trail heads up the upper reach of the North Santiam River, which though diminutive in the wilderness, offers good fishing for small brookies and a few cutthroat. Invariably the trout reside in the deeper pools and runs. In places the river is close to the trail and in others anglers are better off following the riverbed to get at the best water. Try dry flies or small spinners and spoons.

Duffy Lake offers ample camping space with 12 established sites. Campers must use these established sites and use the existing fire rings or must camp at least 250 feet from the lakeshore. Beautiful and productive Mowich Lake lies just 15 minutes up the trail past Duffy and you can easily set up camp at Mowich for a few days while you fish Duffy to the south and Eight Lakes Basin immediately to the northeast. Duffy

Peak (5,835 feet) towers above the lake and is a relatively easy, though brushy climb for a fine view of the surrounding wilderness.

Duffy Lake, Little (Mt. Jefferson Wilderness)
hike-in, cross-country

This diminutive brook trout lake sits a quarter mile southeast from Duffy Lake and just northeast of the connector trail (#3491) that heads from Duffy down to Santiam Lake. Consult your map. A float tube comes in handy and the brook trout rarely exceed 10 inches, although the occasional fat 14-incher makes Little Duffy worth the time if you're in the neighborhood.

Dumbell Lake (Three Sisters Wilderness)
hike-in

Located in ever popular Mink Lake Basin in the heart of the Three Sisters Wilderness Area, Dumbbell Lake is typically not very productive for small brook trout, though it has its moments when good hatches of Callibaetis mayflies occur. See Mink Lake for directions to the area. Dumbbell, which covers about 6 acres, sits at the north edge of the basin, right along the Pacific Crest Trail. A side trail leading west to nearby Nightshade, Sandy, and Krag Lakes delivers you to somewhat inferior, but much quieter campsites, provided you can survive the mosquitoes. The two Nightshade Lakes offer slow-to-fair fishing for small brook trout; Krag and Sandy Lakes are not stocked.

Dunlap Lake (Willamette National Forest)
float tube recommended, small boat recommended

A small, fairly popular lake not too far from the town of Detroit, Dunlap offers fair-to-good fishing for pan-size brook trout and rainbows. A float tube or small boat is handy on this 7-acre lake situated just east of Elk Lake, high above the Breitenbush River. To get there, follow Breitenbush Road (FR 46) east from Detroit for 5 miles and turn left on Humbug Road (FR 4696). After a mile take another left onto Elk Lake Road. The first 3 miles are easy going but full of big, deep potholes. The next 2 miles are steep, badly wash-boarded, rocky and rugged and the final quarter mile, while flat, is full of big, sharp rocks and nasty potholes. Take your time getting there. At the top of the ridge, the road branches in several directions—stay left, following the sign to Elk Lake and after a quarter mile watch for a short left-hand spur accessing Dunlap Lake. The road is usually open all the way to the lake by around the third week in June.

Eagle Creek (Clackamas County)

This very popular and productive Clackamas River tributary offers both fin-clipped coho salmon and a good run of winter steelhead. With fairly robust coho returns to the Eagle Creek Hatchery in recent years, the creek's salmon fishery now garners as much attention from anglers as the long-popular steelhead fishing. In the Clackamas River, the silver salmon are usually available from late August through at least late October, with Eagle Creek's fishery picking up around late September. Chinook salmon arrive in more modest numbers during spring, and winter steelhead are in the creek from December through at least late March. Even a few stray summer steelhead show up.

Eagle Creek enters the Clackamas River about 6 miles north of Estacada and is crossed by SR 224. Public access is fairly limited on Eagle Creek; the salmon/steelhead fishery extends from the mouth up to Eagle Creek Hatchery. To reach the primary access points, including the hatchery, Eagle Fern County Park, and Lower Ladder, take SR 224 to an east turn on Wildcat Mountain Road. Then turn onto Eagle Fern Road and then onto George Road, which leads to the hatchery. Bonnie Lure State Park, at the mouth of Eagle Creek, is another very popular access point—turn off the highway at Burnett Road and turn left on Doty Road.

Eagle Creek clears quite rapidly after a heavy rain, making it a very popular post-storm fishery for winter-run steelhead, almost all of which are of hatchery origin. Wild fish (intact adipose fins) must be released, including wild salmon. Eagle Creek is a bank-access-only fishery and is not floatable.

Eastern Brook Lake (Waldo Lake Wilderness)
hike-in

As its name suggests, this 11-acre wilderness lake used to be stocked regularly with brook trout. In recent years, however, ODFW has stocked the lake with rainbows and cutthroat, most of which range from 8 to 12 inches with a few larger fish. Eastern Brook is an easy .75-mile hike from the campground at Taylor Burn: Follow the Wahanna Trail south .25 mile to a right-hand fork leading .5 of a mile to Eastern Brook Lake. It's an easy half-day or day trip from the campground. To reach Taylor Burn from Hwy 58 to the south, turn north on the Waldo Lake Road (FR 5897) 3 miles east of Salt Creek Falls. Follow Waldo Lake Road north until it swings left (now called FR 5898) into North Waldo Campground. Stay right and look for the old Spur Road (514) that heads north and then west, 8 miles, to the campground at Taylor Burn. From the east, head for Little Cultus Lake and then continue west, past Irish and Taylor Lakes (see Central Zone) and on to Taylor Burn Campground. Beware the road into Taylor Burn, which is notoriously rugged.

Eddeeleo Lakes, Upper & Lower (Waldo Lake Wilderness)
hike-in

A pair of large hike-in wilderness lakes, Lower and Upper Eddeeleo offer fair-to-good fishing for brook trout that typically range from 5 to 11 inches. Both lakes produce a fair number of plump 12-inchers and an occasional wilderness trophy of 14 inches. The Eddeeleo Lakes are included in the Waldo Lake Wilderness Area north of Hwy 58 and sit about a mile northwest from the northwest corner of Waldo Lake. Currently there is no limit on the number of brook trout taken.

Any number of trail routes reach these lakes, but if you're comfortable and competent with cross-country trekking, you can reach Lower Eddeeleo (the northernmost of the pair) in less than 30 minutes from the nearest trailhead to the northwest. From Oakridge on Hwy 58, take the Salmon Creek Road (FR 24) east into the high Cascades. When FR 24 forks, stay left on FR 2417; it ends at the trailhead. Instead of following the trail south, take a due east or southeast course through the woods. You will cross a trail at the top of the ridge. Continue your course, climbing down the east side of the ridge (fairly easy going for the most part). At the bottom you will run into Long Lake (east from the trailhead), Lower Eddeeleo (southeast from the trailhead), or the trail connecting the two lakes.

If you prefer to stay on the trails, the hike to the Eddeeleo Lakes is three times longer. About a mile before the end of FR 2417, park at the first Winchester Trailhead (#3594), located a short distance up Spur Road 254. Follow this trail east for almost 1 mile, and then turn left at the trail junction. Continue north .5 of a mile and turn right at the next trail junction. After another mile, turn right again onto the Six Lakes Trail, which takes you past the Quinn Lakes and Long Lake before reaching Lower Eddeeleo after 3 miles. You can also reach the lakes from the east, starting at North Waldo Campground and following the trail along Waldo Lake's north shore. The distance is about the same.

Upper Eddeeleo Lake spans 63 acres; Lower Eddeeleo covers about 160 acres. They offer plenty of good bank fishing, though in many places you'll fight with the brush a bit. A float tube offers an advantage, but is not necessary. Generally the trails here are clear of snow by late June and the fishing holds up all summer. Autumn fishing can be especially good and you'll have the lakes to yourself.

Edna Lake (Three Sisters Lake Wilderness)
hike-in

A small cutthroat/rainbow trout lake located a short distance from the end of the Taylor Burn Road in the Three Sisters Wilderness Area, Edna generally offer fair action for 6- to 9-inch fish. From North Waldo Campground, head north on FR 514, and then west on FR 514. The trail, which goes on to the Erma Bell Lakes, passes Edna after about .25 of a mile.

Eileen Lake (Three Sisters Wilderness)
hike-in

Spanning about 6 acres and reaching depths of 14 feet, Eileen Lake sits a few miles southeast from popular Linton Lake in the northern portion of the Three Sisters Wilderness Area. The lake is lightly fished owing to the long hike required to reach it and offers good fishing for cutthroat and rainbow trout that reach 14 inches in length. The shortest route covers 9 miles, arriving from the west via the Substitute Point Trail (#3511) and then the Husband/Eileen Lakes Trail (#3547). To reach the trailhead, follow Hwy 126 east from Eugene or southwest from Santiam Junction. Two miles west from the Old McKenzie Highway turnoff (SR 242) and just east of the ranger station turn south on FR 2643 (the Foley Ridge Road) and follow it all the way to its end. At the 8-mile mark along Trail #3511, head north on Trail #3547 for 1 mile to reach Eileen. From the north, the ever popular, limited-entry Obsidian Cliffs Trail covers about the same distance to reach Eileen Lake.

Elbow Lake (Waldo Lake Wilderness)

hike-in

Generally slow for brook trout or cutthroat trout, 10-acre Elbo Lake sits adjacent to the northwest shoreline of Waldo Lake. The Waldo Mountain and Salmon Lakes Trails get you to the area from the west (using Salmon Creek Road out of Oakridge). Elbow itself is not worth the hike, but you can fish it in conjunction with quite a few other small lakes in the vicinity, including Sapphire, Kinglet, Zircon, and the Salmon Lakes. If you have a boat, simply launch at one of the campgrounds on Waldo's northeast corner and motor across to the west shore, cutting several miles off the hiking distances required to fish these small lakes.

Elf Lake (Mt. Washington Wilderness)

hike-in, cross-country

Located just 200 yards south of popular Benson Lake in the Mt. Washington Wilderness, diminutive Elf Lake is lightly fished and offers planted cutthroat that can reach about 14 inches. Most range from 8 to 12 inches. Only an acre and a half in size, Elf Lake reaches a maximum depth of 20 feet and its trout over-winter well. To find Elf, first consult a map of the Mt. Washington Wilderness. Then follow the trail to Benson Lake and hike around to the south shore. Look for the bushwhacker's trails heading south and a bit west. The area is dotted with small fishless ponds, so be sure to consult the map before heading off in search of Elf Lake or its nearby neighbors, Glaze Lake and Island Lake (see separate listings herein).

Elk Lake (Willamette National Forest)

campground, small boat recommended

Despite the rugged access road, Elk Lake is a popular summer destination located high in the mountains above the little town of Detroit. Brook trout, cutthroat trout, and kokanee salmon inhabit this scenic, 60-acre lake in good numbers. Most fish range from 8 to 12 inches with a few to 16 inches. The lake offers a nice, fairly informal campground and lots of shore fishing access. Regulars often bring car-top boats and rafts, but don't attempt hauling any kind of boat trailer over the steep, rough road. Likewise, this is no road for RVs.

To get there, head for the town of Detroit and then turn east on Breitenbush Road (FR 46). After 5 miles, take a left turn onto Humbug Road (FR 4696) and then take another left onto Elk Lake Road (FR 4697). The first 3 miles are easy going but full of big, deep potholes. The next 2 miles are steep, badly wash-boarded, rocky and rugged and the final mile, while flat, is full of big, sharp rocks and nasty potholes. Take your time getting there. The road is usually open all the way to the lake by around the third week in June.

Emma Lake (Waldo Lake Wilderness)

hike-in

Diminutive Emma Lake sits on the trail .75 of a mile south of the trailhead at Taylor Burn Campground north of Waldo Lake. Spanning 3.5 acres and reaching a maximum depth of 12 feet, Emma is stocked with cutthroat every other year. They range from 6 to 12 inches. Emma is a little too close to the trail but can be good at times. It's worth a few casts if you're in the area fishing Eastern Brook Lake a quarter mile to the west. See Eastern Brook Lake for directions to the area.

Erma Bell Lakes (Three Sisters Wilderness)

hike-in, float tube recommended

The popular and productive Erma Bell Lakes (Upper, Middle, & Lower) sit in lush forestlands above the headwaters of the North Fork of the Middle Fork Willamette about 6 miles due north of Waldo Lake in the Taylor Burn area. Upper Erma Bell is the southernmost of the three and called "Upper" because it is the highest of the three (not by much). It offers small, wild brook trout and some wild rainbows, covers 25 acres and reaches a depth of 25 feet.

The Three Sisters Wilderness offers countless trout lakes.

Lower and Middle Erma Bell Lakes offer naturally reproducing rainbows averaging pan-size, but reaching 14 inches or so. Lower Erma Bell spans 55 acres and reaches a maximum depth of 60 feet. More than 40 feet at its deepest, Middle Erma Bell covers 60 acres. Lower and Middle Erma Bell Lakes are the most popular and generally better than Upper Erma Bell but, despite heavy use, all three lakes hold up well throughout the season, in part owing to a special two-fish bag limit (on rainbows) and a late May opener designed to protect spawners. Snow often hangs in here until mid-June.

All methods produce here and anglers of all bents should consider fishing barbless, because all rainbows less than 8 inches in length must be released unharmed. Besides, barbless anglers can easily catch-and-release a lot of trout before keeping a couple for dinner. Fly anglers will find a daily hatch of *Callibaetis* (speckled-wing dun) mayflies during the summer. The hatch is best on still days and a No. 14-16 Compara-dun, Gulper Special, or Parachute Adams imitates the duns perfectly. Otherwise, small nymphs and streamers fished on a sink-tip or sinking line produce lots of action. These lakes drop off fairly quickly limiting wade fishing. Spin casters can fish from shore, but fly anglers may want to bring a float tube.

The Erma Bell Lakes lie adjacent to an easy trail (maintained as a barrier-free trail) and are approachable from both the north and south. The best road arrives from the north: Just west of Oakridge, turn north off Hwy 58 at the Oakridge Ranger District Station and follow FR 19 (Aufderheide Drive) through Westfir. Continue north and east on FR 19 all the way to a right turn on FR 1957 near Box Canyon Horse Camp (something like 30 miles). Forest Road 1957 takes you to diminutive Skookum Creek Campground, a great place to camp for day hikes into the Erma Bell Lakes. Alternately you can reach Skookum Creek Campground by following FR 19 south from Hwy 126 east of Springfield: A few miles east of Blue River, turn south toward Cougar Reservoir (this is FR 19) and head south until you reach the left-hand turn at FR 1957 (about 25 miles). From the campground, Lower Erma Bell is about a mile south by easy trail. Middle Erma Bell lies just south, also on the left-hand side of the trail and Upper Erma Bell lies a half mile south from Middle, but on the right-hand side of the trail.

From the east/south, the Erma Bell Lakes are reachable from Taylor Burn Campground. Follow Spur Road 514 north from North Waldo Lake Campground or west from Little Cultus Lake on Spur Road 600. These are rugged, bumpy, dusty roads and the trail into Upper Erma Bell covers 2 miles, but anglers from central Oregon often use this route instead of driving across the Cascades. Just beware of the road into Taylor Burn, which is notoriously rugged.

Ernie Lake (Waldo Lake Wilderness)
hike-in

In the Waldo Lake Wilderness Area, 3-acre Ernie Lake sits right next to much larger Lake Kiwa. Ernie is the small, deep lake sitting a hundred yards or so west of Kiwa's southwest end. Stocked every other year with cutthroat trout (sometimes rainbows), Ernie is a good float tube lake. The ranger district map labels Ernie Lake, but the Waldo Lake Wilderness Map does not. Nonetheless, Ernie Lake sits trailside so you can't miss it.

Fall Creek (Lane County)

A tributary to the Middle Fork Willamette River southeast of Springfield, Fall Creek is divided into two distinct fisheries by Fall Creek Reservoir. Below the dam, the stream supports fair numbers of hatchery-produced spring chinook salmon and summer steelhead, along with a handful of winter steelhead. This tailwater section also offers catch-and-keep trout fishing for hatchery rainbows. Jasper-Lowell Road follows the creek outside of Springfield. Above Fall Creek Reservoir, the creek flows through timbered slopes and provides decent trout fishing with harvest opportunities. Access to the upper creek is excellent along FR 18, which begins at the upstream end of Fall Creek Reservoir. A number of campgrounds are scattered along the creek. Proximity to Eugene/Springfield assures heavy use of the creek, especially during weekends. The best fishing is from June through September.

Fall Creek's major tributaries include Little Fall Creek, which joins the main creek downstream from Fall Creek Reservoir. Little Fall Creek offers fair-to-good trout fishing and harvest opportunities for spring chinook salmon and hatchery summer steelhead. The deadline for salmon and steelhead fishing is at the fish ladder, about 12 miles above the mouth. The trout-fishing season is currently split between a catch-and-release season from Nov. 1 through the beginning of the state-wide trout season in late April. During the general season, anglers can keep five trout per day. Little Fall Creek Road follows the stream, though private property excludes access in many places. Above the dam on Fall Creek, Winberry Creek feeds the south arm of Fall Creek Reservoir. Winberry Creek offers fair trout fishing during the general trout season and anglers are currently allowed a five-trout limit.

Fall Creek, Little (Lane County)
see Fall Creek

Fall Creek Reservoir (Lane County)
boat ramp, campground

A fair producer of stocked rainbow trout, crappie, and largemouth bass, Fall Creek Reservoir is a 1,800-acre impoundment southeast of Eugene, on the other side of Disappointment Butte from Foster Reservoir. To get there, follow I-5 south past Eugene to Hwy 58 and head east. Just east of Foster Dam, turn left on the causeway road heading across Foster Reservoir, then head north to Unity and Big Fall Creek Road. The road wraps around the north side of the impoundment along the Fall Creek Arm. The Winberry Creek Arm is on the south side. Both arms have boat ramps and campgrounds.

Faraday Lake (Clackamas River)

A small reservoir on the Clackamas River just south of Estacada, Faraday Lake is liberally stocked with legal-size rainbow trout and provides fair fishing during spring and summer. Bank fishing with bait is the usual method here and the reservoir draws quite a bit of pressure on weekends. Watch for the turn-off about 2 miles outside of Estacada on Hwy 224.

Fay Lake (Linn County)
float tube or small boat recommended

A pretty and popular little 7-acre lake just outside the Mt. Jefferson Wilderness Area, Fay Lake offers fair action on small brook trout and rainbow trout. Forest Road 2257, marked Big Meadows Road on the highway, turns off Hwy 22 just south of the North Santiam River Bridge near milepost 76 and leads through Big Meadows and on up to Fay Lake, which lies adjacent to the road. Fay offers good hatches of *Callibaetis* mayflies and caddisflies throughout the summer, making it fine fly-fishing water, especially if you have a float tube, raft, or canoe. Spin fishers do better from the brushy shoreline. Good campsites abut the shoreline on the roadside of the lake.

Fern Ridge Ponds (Lane County)

These small ponds lie just below the dam at Fern Ridge Reservoir west of Eugene. They feature largemouth bass, white crappie, and brown bullhead. To get there, head west out of Eugene on Hwy 126 and then at Veneta, turn north on Territorial Road. Drive along Fern Ridge to a right turn on Clear Lake Road. From Corvallis, head south on Hwy 99W. At Monroe, take the right-hand fork on Territorial Road and follow it south, past Cheshire and Franklin and down to a left turn on Clear Lake Road.

Fern Ridge Reservoir (Lane County)
boat ramp, campground

Covering almost 9,000 acres, Fern Ridge Reservoir west of Eugene serves as a multi-use recreational area. It draws lots of pleasure boaters and beach goers during the summer, lots of wingshooters during the fall and winter, and quite a few anglers who pursue a variety of warmwater fish. The reservoir is home to largemouth bass, crappie, and bluegill. The bass reach several pounds; crappie range from 6 to 10 inches and are abundant once you locate productive water. Favorite crappie haunts include the Fern Ridge Dam on the north side of the reservoir and the potholes and channels along Hwy 126 on the south side of the reservoir. Bluegill are common where appropriate structure exists along Hwy 126 and lots of anglers fish from shore along and near the highway, and at Perkins Peninsula Park.

The reservoir has lots of good bass-holding structure, ranging from stumps and snags to channels and points. When the reservoir is full, the numerous creek-mouth channels and coves are good bets for bass. A powerboat is handy for covering a lot of water and reaching offshore bass-fishing areas. Some anglers launch float tubes to fish the shoreline areas along Hwy 126. The water here is rarely, if ever, clear, so consistent success on bass generally requires that anglers fish not only the visible structure, but also submerged structures hidden by the murky water.

Fern Ridge Reservoir has several boat ramps, all of which can be used to reach good fishing areas. The ramp at Orchard Point Park is busy with water-sports enthusiasts during the summer and the park itself draws huge summer crowds, especially on weekends. Rental boats are available at the park. The ramps on the south side (Perkins Peninsula and Fern Ridge Shores) are ideal launch points for anglers until the reservoir gets low, at which time the north side offers more water and better fishing.

To reach Fern Ridge Reservoir from Eugene, take I-5 to the Beltline Road Exit and head west Florence/Santa Clara. Then take Exit 195B and go about 10 miles, turning right onto West

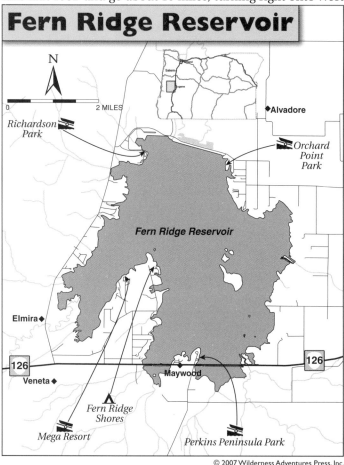

© 2007 Wilderness Adventures Press, Inc.

11th Avenue, heading west through town. When you leave town, this becomes Hwy 126. Continue west to reach the south side of the reservoir. Near the southwest corner of Fern Ridge, Hwy 126 intersects with Territorial Highway, which leads north along the west side of the reservoir and provides easy access to Richardson Park (boat ramp/camping) on the west side of the dam and Orchard Point Park on the east side of the dam. If you are heading directly to the dam and Orchard Point Park, take Beltline west to Hwy 99 and turn north toward Junction City and then turn left on Clear Lake Road, following the signs to Fern Ridge.

Bass fishing at Fern Ridge is best during spring and early summer. By mid-summer, search for the bass in slightly deeper water. Bluegill fishing is best during summer and crappie action can be good all year, depending on location. Even during winter, the fishery at the dam can provide good crappie fishing.

Fields Lake (Waldo Lake Wilderness)

hike-in

Tiny little Fields Lake is located near Taylor Burn on the north edge of the Waldo Lake Wilderness Area, immediately north of Whig Lake and right beside the trail. Not labeled on most maps, it is usually stocked every other year with several hundred brook or cutthroat trout. Fields Lake spans an acre and reaches a depth of 16 feet. Its trout usually range from 8 to 10 inches, but a few 14- to 16-inchers appear from time to time. Despite the heavily burned landscape throughout the area (from the Charlton Fire in 1996), Fields Lake offers a prime camp spot situated atop the adjacent rimrock. To reach Fields Lake, follow the Taylor Butte Trail south from FR 517, about a mile east from the end of the road. Follow the trail south around the west side of Taylor Butte and you'll reach Fields Lake after half a mile. Informal but well-used trails lead south a short distance to Whig and Torrey Lakes. The area is heavily used (somewhat less so since the '96 fire), but still a great place to wander around and sample half a dozen or more lakes.

Fig Lake (Waldo Lake Wilderness)

hike-in, cross-country, float tube recommended

Spanning just 3 acres, Fig Lake sits off-trail about 1 mile west of Waldo Lake. This lightly fished lake is stocked with cutthroat that can reach about 14 inches. The lake is 17 feet deep. Use the Koch Mountain Trail (#3576) to access Fig and nearby Photo, Last, and Cardiac Lakes, all of which require a bushwhacking cross-country course of upwards of 1 mile. In this case, bushwhacking serves as a precise description because some of this region grows dense stands of rhododendron. From Oakridge, head northeast on the Salmon Creek Road (FR 24) until you reach the junction where 24 becomes FR 2420 to the right (gated) and FR2421 to the left (the main branch). This is the Black Creek Road. Follow it half a mile to a left-hand turn onto FR 2422 and follow this road all the way to its end at the trailhead. From there, the shortest route to Fig follows a southeasterly compass course from the trailhead—consult you topo map first, but beware that Fig Lake and its neighbors are not labeled on the maps. The area is dotted with small ponds, all of which are smaller than the fishable lakes. Beware the incessant clouds of mosquitoes throughout the summer.

Fir Lake (Linn County)

hike-in

Fir Lake sits just outside the west edge of the Mt. Jefferson Wilderness and requires an easy 1-mile hike from the trailhead, which is located just north of Fay Lake on FR 2257. To reach the trailhead (which also takes you to Pika Lake), turn east off Hwy 22 at the Big Meadows sign immediately south of the North Santiam River bridge near mile marker 76. Follow the road less than a mile to the fork and head down the left-hand fork toward Big Meadows Horse Camp. Continue past Big Meadows another mile or so until you see Fay Lake on your right. The Pika-Fir Lake Trailhead is the next pullout on the right a few hundred yards past Fay Lake.

Fir Lake, covering 6 acres, used to support brook trout, but is now stocked with cutthroat trout. Fishing is generally good for 8- to 10-inchers. A few fish reach 13 inches. You can fish the lake effectively from shore, although a float tube is certainly handy. Some nice, flat camping sites occupy the south and east shoreline areas. Fir Lake fishes best in June and July and again in the fall. During June you often must pick your way through snow banks. Don't forget mosquito repellent.

Fir Lake (Lane County)

Diminutive Fir Lake sits just east of Alpine Lake near the road over Emigrant Pass in the extreme southeast corner of Lane County. This 1-acre pond is stocked yearly with brook trout (sometimes cutthroat). At 5,500 feet, Fir Lake and its neighboring lakes are accessible most years by late June.

To reach Emigrant Pass from the west, take Hwy 58 through Oakridge. Two miles east of town, turn south on the Kitson Springs Road (FR 21) towards Hills Creek Reservoir. Stay right and follow FR 21 south along the west side of the reservoir. Remain on FR 21 for about 32 miles until you reach a left turn on FR 2154. Follow 2154 about 5 miles to a left turn on FR 2160 and head north a1.5 miles to Alpine Lake. From the east side, head for the west shore of Crescent Lake, then follow the rugged route west over Emigrant Pass.

Firecamp Lakes

see Clagget, Crown and Sheep Lakes

Fish Lake (Clackamas County)

hike-in

A scenic cutthroat lake in the Olallie Lake area of the Mt. Hood National Forest, 20-acre Fish Lake is fairly productive and quite popular owing to the easy hike and the attractive setting. The lake sits about 2 miles northwest from Olallie Lake and a few hundred yards south of the power lines. Take the Clackamas River Highway (SR 224) south from Estacada up to Ripplebrook Ranger Station and then follow FR 46 south and then east to FR 4690. Follow FR 4690 about 3 miles to a right-hand turn on FR 4691, leading to Si Lake and the Fish Lake Trail, which covers about 1 mile. FR 4691 splits after about 1 mile, with the right-hand fork (Spur 120) leading to the trailhead and the rugged left-hand fork leading almost all the way to Fish Lake.

Fish Lake (Linn County)

Fish Lake is located along Hwy 126 a few miles south from Santiam Junction and 2 miles north of Clear Lake. Fish Lake grows small, wild cutthroat, but the lake often dries up by late summer so fishing is usually slow during the late-spring open season. The best action occurs after three or more consecutive high-snowpack winters.

Fisher Lakes (Three Sisters Wilderness)
hike-in

East and West Fisher Lakes are productive, deep 2-acre ponds located in the Horse Lake/Sunset Lake area of the Three Sisters Wilderness Area a few miles west from Elk Lake and Century Drive. East Fisher is stocked with rainbows and/or cutthroat trout; West Fisher is stocked with cutthroat and/or brook trout. The lakes are typically stocked every other year and both lakes produce a handful of 14-inch fish, though most are pan-size. Both lakes sit right beside the trail and several other nearby lakes make the area worthwhile for a multiple-day excursion. (See Herb, Aerial, Platt, and Mile Lakes). Plenty of nice camping areas are scattered all throughout the area.

You'll walk a lot of miles to reach these lakes from the south or west, so the easiest route is from Elk Lake Trailhead to the east, 33 miles from Bend on Century Drive. The southerly route, via the Pacific Crest Trail and McBee Trail, is slightly shorter than the more northerly route via the Horse Lake Trail. For the southerly route, use Trail #3 out of the trailhead (the Island Meadows Trail) and head 1.3 miles over to the Pacific Crest Trail. Follow the PCT 2.3 miles to a right turn on Trail #3517 (the western extension of Island Meadow Trail) heading northwest to meet up with the McBee Trail. When you hit the McBee Trail after another mile, turn north (right). The Fisher Lakes lie a quarter mile ahead on the left side of the trail.

The Fisher Lakes are easy to fish from shore as are most of the lakes in the vicinity, but a float tube sure won't hurt matters if you're willing to carry it in. At 6,224 feet, nearby Horse Mountain offers a splendid view of the surrounding area and of the Three Sisters. The Horse Mountain Trail heads up the ridgeline to the summit, starting at West Fisher Lake. The climb covers about .75 of a mile and the peak is a great place to catch a sunrise or sunset.

Foster Reservoir (Linn County)
boat ramp, campground

A fair stocked-trout fishery, with increasing opportunities for smallmouth bass, largemouth bass, and bluegill, 1,200-acre Foster Reservoir lies just east of Sweet Home on the South and Middle Santiam Rivers. Trout anglers predominately still fish with bait from the banks or troll, as the reservoir offers several boat ramps. Trout fishing is best from April through July, but can be fair to good just about any time. Increasing bass populations (from unauthorized stockings) are drawing more and more attention from anglers. A few miles east of Sweet Home, Hwy 20 skirts the reservoir's south shore, while North River Drive follows the north bank (out of Sweet Home). At the South Santiam Arm on the upper end of the reservoir along the highway, Quartzville Road heads north and reaches the north side. Foster Dam, which forms the impoundment, is the upstream extent of the South Santiam River's popular

run of hatchery summer steelhead. At the upstream end of the reservoir on the Middle Santiam Arm, Sunnyside County Park has a small campground. Another campground is located at Whitcomb County Park upstream to the northeast on Green Peter Reservoir. You can reserve camp spots by calling (541) 967-3917.

Frazier Lake (Clackamas County)
see Hideaway Lake

Freeway Lakes (Albany)

A pair of productive ponds sitting next to I-5 just south of Albany, Freeway Lakes are stocked annually with rainbow trout and also have good numbers of crappie and small bluegill, along with a few modest-size largemouth bass. The easternmost pond is the trout fishery and is fairly popular and fishable from shore or by small boat, float tube, or similar craft. The larger pond offers less shore access and is connected by channel under the freeway (Oak Creek) to a third lake on the west side of the freeway, accessible by boat. Trout fishing peaks between April and June; warmwater fishing is best from May through July. From I-5 southbound, take Exit 223 (Albany), head east past the stoplight, and turn south on Three Lakes Road leading to the ponds. From I-5 northbound, take Exit 228 and head west about .5 of a mile to a left-hand turn on Seven Mile Lane and head north. Just before crossing the freeway, turn right on Three Lakes Road to the pond.

French Creek (near Detroit)

French Creek flows into Detroit Reservoir adjacent to the Breitenbush Arm across the bridge from the town of Detroit. This small, forested stream offers fair fishing for small wild trout. The limit is currently five trout per day with an 8-inch minimum length. French Creek Road follows the creek fairly closely for 5 miles and the best fishing is found as far from the road as possible and well upstream from the reservoir. Try dry flies and small spinners for the creek's small, feisty wild rainbows and cutthroat trout.

Frog Lake Reservoir (Clackamas County)

Best known for kicking out a few large rainbows and an occasional large brown trout, Frog Lake Reservoir is a small storage reservoir near Ripplebrook Ranger Station on the Clackamas watershed. The fish range from 10 to 20 inches, but are few in number. Boat are not allowed, so most anglers still fish with bait. The reservoir sits just west of Timber Lake Job Corps Center. From SR 224 (Clackamas Highway), turn east on FR 4630, which leads to the reservoir.

Gales Creek (Tualatin River tributary)
no bait

Years ago, this little creek, northwester of Forest Grove along Gales Creek Road (state route 6), was a secret sleeper for winter steelhead and big searun cutthroat, and the fishery is still largely unknown owing to extensive private property. Access is still tricky, and the creek continues to offer fishing for a few cutthroat, and in recent years, coho salmon; steelhead still return to this stream after a circuitous journey up the Columbia, Willamette, and Tualatin rivers. However, check the current regulations before fishing here to make sure the stream remains open for your intended quarry. Currently the fishery is open from its mouth in Forest Grove up to NW Clapshaw Hill Road in the town of Gales Creek for coho and trout (check season dates).

Gander Lake (Waldo Lake Wilderness)
hike-in
A large, fairly productive lake in the Waldo Lake Wilderness Area, Gander Lake spans about 60 acres and is stocked with rainbow and/or brook trout. The fish typically range from 6 to 12 inches, with a handful of larger trout. Gander Lake is easy to reach via a short (1 mile) hike, so it is fairly popular and usually attracts a few campers, day hikers, and anglers on summer weekends. During autumn, you'll likely have it to yourself. From Oakridge, take the Salmon Creek Road (FR 24) east. When the road forks after about 10 miles, take FR 2417 until it ends at the trailhead. Follow the trail south and after .7 mile, turn right at the trail junction.

Gilbert River (Sauvie Island)
boat ramp, boat recommended
A fairly productive, slow, meandering river on Sauvie Island, Gilbert River connects Sturgeon Lake to Multnomah Channel and runs through the ODFW's Sauvie Island Wildlife Management Area. The river offers crappie, brown bullhead, yellow perch, bluegill, largemouth bass, and a few walleye and catfish. You can fish the river by foot, using a wide array of trails and roads on the wildlife area, but a small boat, kayak, or canoe offers the advantage of mobility. The launch site is near the river's mouth: Cross the bridge onto Sauvie Island, then head north to a right-hand turn on Reeder Road. Follow Reeder Road to the northern end of the island and then watch for the signs to the Gilbert Ramp. Sauvie Island requires a fee permit, available at the store near the bridge when you cross over from Hwy 30.

Glaze Lake (Mt. Washington Wilderness)
hike-in, cross-country
Glaze Lake is a 2-acre gem located just 200 yards or so southwest from the south shore of Benson Lake in the Mt. Washington Wilderness. Follow the trail from Scott Lake to Benson Lake (Scott Lake is located just off the Old McKenzie Highway on the eastern edge of Linn County). Consult a map of the Mt. Washington Wilderness and then look for the bushwhacker's trails leaving the south shore of Benson Lake. Glaze Lake offers fair-to-good fishing for cutthroat and/or rainbow trout, which are planted every other year. They over-winter here and three-year old trout can reach 15 to 18 inches, though smaller fish predominate. You can fish this one from shore, but a float tube comes in handy. The area is dotted with tiny ponds, but Glaze Lake (along with Elf Lake) is substantially larger than these marshy ponds.

Gnat Lake (Three Sisters Wilderness Area)
hike-in
One of the many small lakes in the popular Mink Lake Basin of the Three Sisters Wilderness Area, 3-acre Gnat Lake is usually stocked with cutthroat trout every few years and provides fair angling for 6- to 10-inch fish. It sits alongside the trail that connects the Pacific Crest Trail to the east with Porky Lake to the southwest. See Mink Lake herein for directions to the area. The Mink Lake Basin is usually accessible by late June.

Gold Lake (Lane County)
boat ramp, campground, no motors, float tube or boat recommended, fly only
A long-time favorite destination for Eugene-area fly anglers, Gold Lake's fly-only regulations—along with the lake's excellent fishing—now attract anglers from all around the state. Gold Lake sits just south from Waldo Lake in the high Cascades near Hwy 58 and Willamette Pass. The well-marked turnoff heads north off the highway about 3 miles east from the Waldo Lake turnoff and about a mile west from 5,126-foot Willamette Pass. The road into Gold Lake covers about 2 miles and leads to the lake's south end, where a nice campground and boat ramp await. Expect the campground to fill

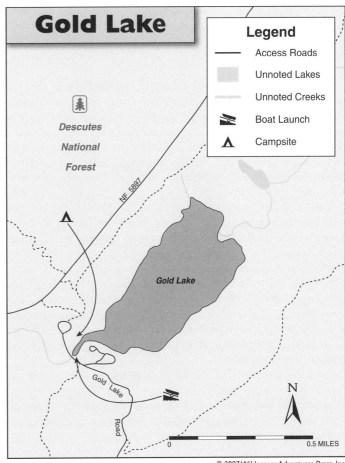

up early on summer weekends, but additional campgrounds are located a few miles away at Waldo Lake and at Odell Lake.

Gold Lake spans about 100 acres and reaches a maximum depth of 25 feet. As high Cascades lakes go, Gold is quite fertile and supports self-sustaining populations of both brook and rainbow trout. The rainbows provide the fishery of note, but the brook trout outbreed them and out-compete them, so ODFW has lifted the bag limit on brook trout. Anglers may harvest as many brook trout as they want with no size restrictions. All rainbows must be released. The brookies typically range from 5 to 9 inches, but some real trophies—brookies from 14 to 18 inches—swim these waters. The rainbows average larger and commonly reach 14 inches. Unfortunately you can fish all day at Gold, catch 20 fish and not one will be a rainbow. On the other hand, when you do find the rainbows—or the larger brookies—you'll understand why this lake carries such a lofty reputation.

No motors are allowed on Gold Lake, a fact that helps preserve the serenity of this beautiful locale. However, the best action occurs on the shallow north end of the lake, which lies almost half a mile distant from the formal boat ramp situated down the outlet channel from the main body of water. Thus float tubers face an arduous paddle to reach the far end. For that reason, rowboats, pontoon boats, or canoes are better options. If you're limited to a float tube, shorten your paddle by walking or driving north through the east-side camping area to reach the informal launch sites on the southeast end of the lake. In any event, you'll need a boat or float tube here because brushy shorelines and mucky bottom ooze makes for difficult bank fishing.

The shallow (north) end of Gold Lake features lush aquatic weed growth that harbors myriad trout foods, including damsel nymphs, *Callibaetis* mayfly nymphs, Chironomids, scuds, dragonfly nymphs, water beetles and leeches. Many different fly patterns prove effective on Gold. The mayfly hatch runs throughout the summer and follows the typical high-lake pattern of coming off between late morning and mid-afternoon, especially on still days. The intensity and duration of the hatch varies daily but a good hatch provides excellent dry-fly prospects on the north end of Gold Lake. Likewise, the early morning and evening midge (Chironomid) hatches bring plenty of trout to the surface.

During July, damsels hatch profusely around the northern shoreline. Try fishing damsel nymph patterns between mid-morning and mid-afternoon. Concentrate on the weedy shallows and fish these flies on an intermediate or slow-sinking line. Also keep an eye peeled for mid-summer flights of flying ants. When these ants end up on the water, they always bring trout to the surface.

During non-hatch periods, try the usual array of attractor wet flies, including the following: Prince Nymph, Zugbug, Partridge & Olive Soft Hackle, Pheasant Tail, and various leech patterns. Or try trolling around with a streamer pattern fished on a sinking or sink-tip line.

Gold Lake opens for the season during late May (check current synopsis for specific dates) and closes October 31.

Snow often blocks the access road on the opening weekend and the road is usually rough and wet through mid-June. October fishing is excellent, but beware the weather, which can change rapidly during mid-autumn. The fly-fishing stores in Eugene keep close tabs on Gold Lake and it's a good idea to call them to see if the road is open before you head up there during May or early June.

Goodfellow Lakes (Bullrun Watershed Management Area)
closed waters

Goose Lake (Marion County)
hike-in, float tube recommended

Covering about 6 acres and located in Willamette Mission State Park, Goose Lake offers fair-to-good action for bass and panfish. It is located by trail south from the entrance road. When you reach the entrance booth (day pass required), turn right and park at the adjacent lot. Head back towards the entrance booth and then veer right down the main road a short distance until you meet the trail. Turn left and then follow the trail along the edge of the field until you reach a section of wood-rail fence and a side trail heading left into the trees (and marked with a fishing sign). Best fishing occurs between late spring and late summer. See also Mission Lake herein. To get there, take I-5 to the Brooks Exit just north of Salem. Head west, crossing the railroad tracks and going straight through a four-way intersection at SR 219 to a right-hand turn on Wheatland Road and then watch for the signs to the park.

Goose Lake (Three Sisters Wilderness)
hike-in

Goose Lake is a big, shallow, swampy, mosquito-infested lake offering small, wild brook trout. It is located about a mile northeast from Mink Lake in the Three Sisters Wilderness. You'll want a float tube here, though many other nearby lakes offer better fishing.

Gordon Creek (Sandy River drainage)
no bait, catch-and-release

A small, scenic wild trout stream, nicely protected by a rather steep, forested canyon, Gordon Creek drains the west side of Larch Mountain and flows west to join the Sandy River on the east bank across from Oxbow Park. The creek's abundant trout typically range from 4 to 8 inches, with a rare fish reaching 10 or more inches. Access is from several forest road approaches off the Larch Mountain Road east from the Sandy River and south from Bridal Veil Falls on the Columbia. To get there, follow I-84 east from Portland to Exit 22 and then head east to Larch Mountain Road. You will need the ZigZag Ranger District Map to navigate the maze of roads and a rather stout sense of adventure to navigate the drainage by foot. Nearby Trout Creek and Buck Creek offer similar opportunities, but of the three, Gordon Creek is the best. Its headwaters are located within the Mt. Hood National Forest.

Gordon Lakes

hike-in, float tube recommended

Easy to reach off Hwy 20 east of Sweet Home, Upper and Lower Gordon Lakes offer small, wild cutthroat trout. Lower Gordon, the northernmost of the two lakes, spans 8 acres and reaches a depth of 21 feet. The upper lake is slightly smaller and shallower. The short walk into the lakes covers less than a quarter mile, so hauling in a float tube is a simple and worthwhile proposition. The lakes sit at about 4,000 feet and are usually reachable by early June, often by late May.

To get there, follow Hwy 20 east from Sweet Home or west from Santiam Junction until you see the signs for House Rock Campground. From there head south on FR 2044 (Latiwi Creek Road), crossing the South Santiam River after about 1 mile and continuing 3 more miles to a right-hand turn on Spur Road 230. Follow 230 for 2 miles to its terminus and then follow the trail west from the end of the road. Upper Gordon is south of the trail; Lower Gordon lies on the north side.

Green Peak Lake (Mt. Jefferson Wilderness)

hike-in, cross-country

A beautiful and remote 6-acre lake on Marion Flats in the Mt. Jefferson Wilderness Area, Green Peak, though stocked with brookies, usually proves fairly slow fishing; it seems to winterkill at times, though I can't confirm this. Nonetheless it is rarely visited, highly scenic, and might be worth checking out any given year. You will need a good topo map and a compass to find this one. I've reached Green Peak Lake by first taking the Pine Ridge Trail east to the Marion Mountain Trail, climbing Marion Mountain and following the high ridgeline south to the summit of Marion Peak and then dropping down to Green Peak Lake. It's a rather rugged but scenic route, requiring off-trail skills. I've also reached the lake via a difficult cross-country compass route from the Cleo Lake area. For an easier route, head to Blue Lake in Eight-Lakes Basin, walk to the backside of the lake (the west shore) and head due west through the woods, climbing the saddle between Marion Peak and Green Peak and then descending to the lake. The cross-country portion of the hike covers about 1 mile—do not attempt it without map and compass, and the skills to use them for backcountry navigation.

Green Peter Reservoir (Linn County)

boat ramp, boat recommended, campground

Primarily known for kokanee and stocked rainbow trout—and water skiing—Green Peter Reservoir is a popular and fairly productive 3,700-acre impoundment on the Middle Santiam River east of Sweet Home.

Quartz Creek is a major feeder stream. The reservoir also has populations of both smallmouth and largemouth bass. The bass fishery has gained increasing popularity in recent years, and anglers targeting smallmouth often find the best success using deep-jigging techniques. Trout and kokanee anglers have fair-to-good success trolling off the face of the dam, around the island, and at the upper end as far up as Fisherman's Bridge. At high water, the creek's mouths can be good places to look for trout and bass. Typically the fishing is best during the morning because most days the wind starts blowing by early afternoon. From I-5, head for Sweet Home and follow the signs to Green Peter Reservoir.

Green Point Reservoir

see Kingsley Reservoir

Grenet Lake (Mt. Jefferson Wilderness)

hike-in, cross-country

Located north of Duffy Peak in the Mt. Jefferson Wilderness, small and remote Grenet Lake is a great destination for the adventurous type. Its rainbows, planted every few years, reach 16 to 18 inches by their third year in the lake. Even though the trout are rarely numerous, their size and the pristine setting of the lake make Grenet well worthwhile for the hardy type.

Getting there is the catch. I've done it by two routes. The first is to take the Duffy Lake Trail 1.7 miles to its intersection with the Turpentine Trail, which heads north toward Turpentine Peak and Camp Pioneer Boy Scout Camp. After about a mile, the trail crosses Green Creek, which carries little or no water by late summer. Immediately after crossing the creek (or creek bed), watch for an easy-to-miss bushwhacker's trail heading off to the right (east). If you can't find the trail,

The Willamette Valley has many ponds and reservoirs teeming with bluegills.

just follow the creek bottom, which leads right to the lake. The lake lies about 1.5 miles up the creek, which alternately runs through nasty blow-down jungles and small, pristine meadows, often occupied by elk early in the morning. The elevation gain is 800 feet from the Turpentine Trail to Grenet Lake.

The other option is to hike to Duffy Lake, climb the saddle on the east flank of Duffy Peak and head north, downhill to Grenet Lake. If you try this route, be sure to consult map and compass, and be prepared for a steep climb in and out.

Grossman Pond (Polk County)

This small private pond in Independence is usually open to fishing by landowner permission and offers catch-and-release largemouth bass and bluegill fishing. In Independence, just west from Central High School, turn south from the main road onto Talmadge Road and follow it about .6 of a mile to the pond (on your right).

Hagg Lake
see Henry Hagg Lake

Haldeman Pond (Sauvie Island)

A small pond on Oak Island in the Sauvie Island Wildlife Management Area, Haldeman has blugill, some largemouth bass and stocked rainbow trout. Be sure to check with the current synopsis for season dates here.

Hampton Pond (Willamina)
see Huddeston Pond

Hand Lake (Mt. Washington Wilderness)
hike-in, float-tube recommended

A nice 25-acre rainbow and cutthroat lake, Hand lies less than a mile from the Old McKenzie Highway, just inside the Mt. Washington Wilderness. Look for the trailhead a mile northeasterly from the turn-off to Scott Lake. The trout here range from 8 to 15 inches. If you camp at Scott Lake, you can hike north to Hand Lake on Trail #3513A. The flat route covers about 1.7 miles and departs from the end of the spur road (west of the Scott Lake Campground) that heads north from the Benson Lake Trailhead (Trail #3513B). Much of the shoreline is brushy and swampy, but there is enough bank access for easy fishing, though a float tube is handy here.

Hanks Lake (Mt. Jefferson Wilderness)
hike-in

A good brook trout lake, also planted with rainbow, located at 5,200 feet in a scenic, forested enclave called Hunt's Cove, high above ever-popular Pamelia Lake in the Mt. Jefferson Wilderness Area. Hanks Lake spans 7 acres and reaches depths of 12 feet. Shoreline access abounds, but a float tube is helpful for reaching the deeper water, especially if you are fly fishing. Hunts Cove sits just west and downslope of the beautiful Cathedral Rocks and the Pacific Crest Trail. From Hwy 22 east of Idanha, turn left (or right if you are coming from Bend) on FR 2246, the Pamelia Creek Road. Don't leave any valuables in your car at the popular Pamelia Lake Trailhead. Hike past Pamelia Lake and follow the steep trail up Hunts Creek. Once the trail forks, head left a half-mile to Hanks Lake. The trail gains 1400 feet in the 3 miles between Pamelia Lake and Hanks Lake. Visitors to Hunts Cove are required to obtain a special limited-entry permit from the Detroit Ranger District Headquarters in Detroit. Call ahead with your requested dates and the number of people in your party. The headquarters can be reached at 503-854-3366.

Happy Lake (Diamond Peak Wilderness)
hike-in, float tube recommended

Happy Lake is a real gem located north of Blue Lake in the Diamond Peak Wilderness. It is stocked with rainbows and with cutthroat, and some natural reproduction may be occurring in this 8-acre scenic beauty. You can get there via the Blue Lake Trail, but the easier route (marginally speaking) arrives from the north on the Diamond Peak Trail (#3699), which leads an easy 2 miles south to a side trail (#3653) leading a few hundred yards west to the lake.

Nestled in a broad, marshy basin, Happy Lake is surrounded by forests of mountain hemlock and western white pine. Shallow bogs dominate the entire southern and eastern extents of the lake. The western end is the fishable end and a float tube comes in handy. The trout here can reach 16 inches or so and Happy Lake is not nearly so popular as nearby Blue Lake and Corrigan Lake. The bogs here attract elk and deer, but also provide ample breeding grounds for mosquitoes. Bring plenty of repellant. The lake is rarely accessible before mid-June and fishing seems to get better during September and October.

To reach the Diamond Peak Trailhead, follow Hwy 58 for 2 miles east of Oakridge and turn south onto Kitson Springs Road, which becomes FR 21. Continue about 28 miles to its junction with FR 23, which is 2 miles past Sacandaga Campground, and head up 23 about 7 miles to the trailhead (past the intersection with FR 2149). Some nice natural camp spots are located above the west shore and the outlet stream features a lovely waterfall (Happy Lake Falls).

Harriet Lake (Clackamas County)
see Lake Harriet

Hartman Pond (Multnomah County)
see Benson Lake

Harvey Lake (Waldo Lake Wilderness)
hike-in

A 22-acre rainbow trout lake north of Waldo Lake, Harvey usually holds up well throughout the season, its trout ranging from 6 to 14 inches or so. A 10,000-acre wildfire (the Charlton Burn) swept through the area in 1996 and since then visitation is down, but fishing continues to be good here. Harvey is easy to reach from either Taylor Burn to the north or North Waldo Campground to the southeast. The Taylor Burn route is 2 miles shorter. Head due south, past Emma Lake, and stay to the right at the trail junction at Wahanna Lake. Half a mile south from the trail junction, look for the bushwhacker trails leading off to the right. Harvey sits about 300 yards back from the trail.

Hawkum Lake
see Howkum Lake

Heart Lake (Linn County)
hike-in

Heart Lake is a lightly fished cutthroat lake off the beaten path high in the Santiam watershed just south of Hwy 20 and southwest from Santiam Junction. The fish range from 6 to 12 inches and respond well to all methods. Heart Lake was much easier to reach before the forest service gated the spur road that led to within half a mile of the lake. If you use the old route, you will add 3.5 miles of flat road to the journey (not so bad if you have a mountain bike, so directions follow).

Near Iron Mountain, look for a south turn of the highway onto FR 060 just east from the FR 15 turnoff (watch for the Sno-Park). Follow 060 east for about 3.5 miles, crossing two creeks. The second creek is the outlet from Heart Lake. From there, backtrack a short distance until you see the old trail on the uphill side of the road. The trail is very steep for the first quarter mile and then levels out as it skirts through thinned old growth.

Since the 060 Spur was gated, the usual route to Heart Lake now arrives from the south via a pleasant and scenic 3-mile trail up Browder Ridge. The main trail (#3409 from the west end or #3412 from the east end) leads to a half-mile-long side trail (#3407) that reaches the top of the ridge and from there you bushwhack an easy half-mile down to the lake. To find the trailhead, turn off Hwy 20 at FR 15 (just west of Tombstone Prairie Sno-Park) and head just over 2 miles to the trailhead on your left. If you don't mind a little uphill bushwhacking you can cut 2 miles off the hike by skipping the trailhead and instead turning left on Spur Road 080. Drive 1.5 miles up 080, park where you can and hike up the ridge to your left going due northeast until you hit the trail after about a quarter mile. Turn right and continue east until you find the left-hand turn leading out to the ridge south of Heart Lake.

Heart Lake offers ample shoreline fishing and covers about 12 acres. Last time I visited Heart Lake (probably around 1994) some gargantuan old-growth Douglas Firs clung to the steep canyon through which the outlet stream flows. If the trees have not since been harvested, the effort to get down into the upper half of the canyon (the west side) is well worth it: I found half a dozen trees boasting diameters of at least 10 feet.

Helen Lake (Three Sisters Wilderness)
hike-in

Six-acre Helen Lake reaches a depth of 20 feet and is capable of producing rainbows to 16 inches. Most of the fish range from 9 to 12 inches and they are usually stocked every other year. The lake is an easy quarter-mile walk north from FR 514, the road into Taylor Burn. Watch for the trailhead on your right, oppo-

Hagg Lake is a tremendous smallmouth bass fishery.

site Taylor Butte, a mile before you reach the camping area. If you're fly fishing, be sure to bring along a sinking line and a float tube for Helen Lake. Spin fishers do well from shore.

Henry Hagg Lake (Washington County)
boat ramp

One of western Oregon's top fisheries for bass and panfish, Henry Hagg Lake, or Hagg Lake is it is often called, attracts a lot of attention for its smallmouth and largemouth bass prospects. Covering 1,113 acres at full pool, this sprawling reservoir sits in the foothills southwest of Forest Grove. The reservoir has produced two state-record smallmouth bass over the years and holds largemouth bass in the 8-pound range. The lake yields quite a few 4- pound and larger smallies, but 1- to 3- pound fish are common. In addition to lots of smallmouth bass and fair numbers of largemouth bass, Hagg Lake also offers plenty of crappie, bluegill, yellow perch, and brown bullhead. Plus, ODFW stocks the lake liberally with trout and some of the carry-over rainbows reach 20 or more inches.

Anglers employ all methods on Hagg Lake, from still fishing with bait for a mixed-bag experience, to specifically targeting large bass with plugs or other lures. Once you figure out their depth and location, crappie are easy to catch on jigs or flies. The smallmouth bass congregate around structure and tend to occupy shallow water during the mid- to late-spring spawning season. During summer they prefer cooler water and can be found in the channels and deep along the face of the dam.

Though the dam ranks as the top smallmouth locale, other popular and productive haunts for bass and crappie include both of the long, narrow arms on the northeast side of the reservoir (the northernmost of these is the Tanner Creek inlet). The flooded snags outside the Tanner Creek Arm also produce smallmouth bass and crappie, along with a few largemouth bass. The Scoggins Creek Arm on the northwest corner is a popular trolling area for trout during spring and early summer and the Sain Creek Arm just to the south is a fair bet for the reservoir's oft-elusive largemouth bass. Trout anglers also troll along the southwest edge of the reservoir.

Henry Hagg Lake attracts lots of boaters, especially during late spring and summer. Bass and crappie anglers frequent the numerous arms and creek mouths, while trout anglers seem about equally divided between still fishing and trolling. Be sure to heed the lake's boating rules. Ramps are located on the east and west shores, as are day-use picnic areas and wheelchair-accessible fishing platforms. During spring and summer, get to the lake early if you intend to secure prime fishing locations. During late summer, the action at dawn and dusk can be fast and furious in certain places, and top-water plugs or streamer flies fished on floating line can tempt wild strikes from voracious bass. The reservoir quiets down noticeably by late September, a time when the fishing picks up again after late-summer doldrums.

Washington County Parks charge a $5 daily fee at Hagg Lake and over-night camping is not allowed. The park opens for the season on March 1.

To get to Henry Hagg Lake from I-5 south of the Portland area, you have two choices. You can exit the freeway at Woodburn (Exit 271) and follow SR 219 to Newberg. At Newberg, head west and take SR 240 to Yamhill, then SR 47 north to the turn-off up to Henry Hagg Lake (Scoggins Valley Road). Alternately, take I-5 north to Hwy 217 northbound (Beaverton Highway) and then take the Tualatin Valley Highway (SR 8) west to Forest Grove. At Forest Grove, turn south on FR 47.

Herb Lake (Three Sisters Wilderness)
hike-in

Herb Lake lies clustered together with several similar small lakes just south of Horse Lake in the Three Sisters Wilderness Area. Herb spans 3 acres and reaches a maximum depth of 9 feet. ODFW stocks cutthroat trout here every other year.

You'll walk a lot of miles to reach these lakes from the south or west, so the easiest route is from Elk Lake Trailhead to the east, 33 miles from Bend on Century Drive. The two routes to the area are about the same length, but a little cross-country

work cuts nearly a mile off the hike: From the Elk Lake Trailhead, take the Island Meadow Trail (#3) 1.3 miles west to the Pacific Crest Trail and then continue another 1.3 miles along the PCT to a right (north) turn on the Sunset Lake Trail. Next consult your map and, after passing the pond on the left side of the trail, cut over to the southern shore of Sunset Lake and then head (by compass) towards Aerial and Herb Lakes or to the Horse Mt./McBee Trail immediately north of them.

If you prefer to use the trails, continue past the Sunset Lake turnoff on the PCT until you reach the northwesterly turn onto Trail #3517 (the western extension of the Island Meadow Trail), which cuts a mile over to the McBee Trail. Head north to Herb Lake on the right side of the trail. The Fisher Lakes are on the left side before you get to Herb, and Platt Lake sits across the trail from Herb Lake. From the north, the Horse Lake Trail departs the Elk Lake Trailhead as Trail #2. After 4 miles, you'll reach the trail junction at Horse Lake. Turn south and then take the second right turn onto the Horse Mt./McBee Trail to reach Herb Lake.

Hideaway Lake (Mt. Hood National Forest)

Hideaway Lake is a convenient and thus popular drive-to lake near the upper Clackamas River north of Ripplebrook Ranger Station. The lake is stocked with rainbow and cutthroat trout and the fish usually range from 6 to 12 inches. Follow SR 224 up the Clackamas River to Ripplebrook, turn east on FR 57 and continue past Lake Harriet to Shellrock Creek Campground (you are now on FR 58). About 3 miles past the campground, turn left on FR 5830 leading up to the lake.

Less than a mile north of Hideaway by trail, Shellrock Lake offers good prospects for rainbow and brook trout, not to mention lots of late-summer huckleberries. Also north of Hideaway Lake, lightly fished 3-acre Frazier Lake usually supports a few small brookies. From FR 5830, about 1 mile before you reach Hideaway Lake, turn north on Spur 130 and follow it to the end. From there, hike the left-hand (north) spur about a mile up to the lake.

To the south, Cottonwood Meadows Lake usually offers fair-to-good prospects as well. To reach Cottonwood Meadows, follow the main road around Hideaway Lake and continue south, past the trailhead for the Mt. Mitchell Trail (on the right-hand side of the road), until you see a blocked-off old spur road on the left. Hike down this spur road until you reach the creek, then head upstream to the lake (about 1 mile total).

Shellrock Creek, the outlet from Hideaway, Shellrock and Frazier Lakes, flows for about 6 miles down to the Oak Grove Fork of the Clackamas River and offers fair catch-and-release fishing for small, wild cutthroat and brook trout.

Hills Creek Reservoir (Lane County)
boat ramps, campgrounds

Formed by a dam on the Middle Fork Willamette River a few miles from Oakridge and 45 miles from Eugene, Hills Creek Reservoir enjoys a long-standing reputation as one of the area's top off-season trout waters. The reservoir receives heavy annual stockings of legal-size rainbow trout and the winter and spring fishing can be as good as the summer action. Around the middle of September the reservoir is drawn down, making the formal boat ramps inaccessible, but opening up lots of shore fishing.

During the summer, this 2,800-acre reservoir serves not only as a popular trout fishery, but also as a playground for water skiers. Shore fishing is pretty easy along this 8-mile long reservoir, whose entire circumference is followed by good roads. You can launch boats at any of several ramps. The best launches are located at CT Beach Picnic Area on the Hills Creek Arm (on the north) and at Packard Creek Campground on the west shore. The campgrounds fill up frequently during the summer. Three are located on the reservoir itself and several more upstream, strung along the Middle Fork.

In addition to the good fishing for stocked trout, Hills Creek offers a few native cutthroat and some naturally spawned land-locked chinook salmon. ODFW trucks adult salmon upstream around the dams so they can spawn in the tributaries. The juveniles look like kokanee salmon and put up a spirited fight. The drainage is home to a precious few bull trout (I caught one in the reservoir during the spring of 1988) and consequently in an effort to better protect them all planted rainbows are fin-clipped and only these fish may be kept. Non-clipped fish must be released immediately.

Hills Creek Reservoir also offers a fishery for crappie and largemouth bass. Most are taken at the north end of the reservoir and in the adjacent Hills Creek Arm, which reaches off to the east. They also inhabit Larison Cove and a few other places (no motors allowed on Larison Cove).

The upper end of the reservoir is a fine winter and early spring fishery for fly anglers adept at nymph-fishing tactics. The water is drawn down then and the channel is easily accessible in the vicinity of the FR 21 bridge. Try a tandem rig comprised of a weighted No. 6 or 8 dark stonefly nymph pattern above a smaller pattern, such as a No. 12 beadhead Pheasant Tail. Work the flies through the deeper, slow runs and pockets.

To get to Hills Creek Reservoir, head for Oakridge on Hwy 58. About a mile-and-a-half east of town, follow the signs and turn south on Kitson Springs Road (FR 21). After half a mile, turn left to reach the dam and the Hills Creek Arm or turn right to follow FR 21 along the west side of the reservoir. The road crosses the reservoir's upper end and then a signed left turn follows the east bank, eventually connecting back to the Hills Creek Arm.

Honey Lake (Three Sisters Wilderness)
hike-in

The Honey Lakes cluster includes nine small ponds and one 15-acre lake situated southeast of 6,344-foot Substitute Point in the northern part of the Three Sisters Wilderness. The ponds are not stocked, but Honey Lake offers good fishing for fairly abundant pan-size cutthroat or brook trout (depending on the latest stockings by ODFW), stocked every other year. There is plenty of shoreline fishing, but a float tube would be handy. The hike to Honey covers 6.5 miles arriving from the west via the Substitute Point Trail (#3511). To reach the trailhead, follow Hwy 126 east from Eugene or southwest from Santiam Junction. Two miles west from the Old McKenzie Highway turnoff (SR 242) and just east of the ranger station turn south on FR 2643 (the Foley Ridge Road) and follow it to its end. From there, take the Substitute Point Trail 5 miles to a right (south) turn on the cut-off trail to Honey Lake (#3520). After climbing up a fairly steep incline for .75 of a mile, take the left-hand fork in the trail down to the lake. The lake's shoreline offers a nice, flat camping area close to the water.

Horse Creek (McKenzie River drainage)
no bait, C&R, campground

A small, swift tributary to the upper McKenzie River, Horse Creek originates in the Three Sisters Wilderness and reaches the McKenzie near McKenzie Bridge. The lower half of the creek provides fair catch-and-release fishing for small native trout. Forest Road 2638 follows the creek southeast from McKenzie Bridge. Inside the wilderness area the creek, along with its tributary Separation Creek, offers only sparse populations of small trout.

Horse Lakes (Three Sisters Wilderness)
hike-in, float tube recommended

The three Horse Lakes lie strung out along Horse Creek in the Three Sisters Wilderness Area to the west of Century Drive and Elk Lake. The largest, Horse Lake (or "Upper Horse Lake"), covers 60 acres and reaches a depth of about 24 feet. It's naturally reproducing brook trout range from 4 inches to 14 inches and they are usually quite plentiful. This is by far the best of the three lakes. If you are fly angling, take along a float tube and a sinking line and work the drop-offs with a tandem rig featuring a No. 6 olive or black Woolly Bugger and a No. 12 Pheasant Tail or Prince Nymph.

Middle and Lower Horse Lakes offer naturally reproducing brookies and cutthroat trout, most ranging from 4 to 8 inches in length. A float tube comes in handy on both lakes. Middle Horse spans 5 acres, Lower Horse covers 25 acres. Neither is deep. To reach Middle Horse Lake, follow the trail north from Horse Lake for a mile and then watch for a spur trail heading due south. From Middle Horse, head downstream half a mile (via the trail) to Lower Horse. Or continue west on the Horse Creek Trail and drop in from the north. Moist bogs and meadows surround the lower lake.

To reach Horse Lake, follow the Horse Lake Trail (#2) from the Elk Lake Trailhead just off Century Drive, 33 miles from Bend. The route covers about 4 miles.

Horsefly Lake
hike-in, float tube recommended

A little 4-acre lake near the south shore of Waldo Lake, Horsefly occasionally yields a 16- or 18-inch fish, though the cutthroat stocked in recent years seem to grow slower than the rainbows once planted here, and in 2009, ODFW stocked brookies instead of cutts. It is located on the west side of the Betty Lake Trail (#3664). The hike from the Betty Lake trailhead covers an easy mile, passing Betty Lake at the half-mile mark and Howkum Lake shortly thereafter. Horsefly Lake sits on the left side of the trail just beyond Howkum. If you're camped at mosquito-infested Shadow Bay Campground, you can reach these lakes just as easily by following the trail south. Otherwise, the Betty Lake Trailhead is located on the west side of Waldo Lake Road, 3 miles from Hwy 58. Take a float tube or small raft for this one as well as for Betty and Howkum Lakes.

Horseshoe Lake (Marion County)

Horseshoe is a private lake on French Prairie south of Newberg. No public access.

Howkum Lake (Waldo Lake area)
hike-in, float tube recommended

Howkum Lake (sometimes labeled Hawkum Lake) lies half a mile from the southeast shore of Waldo Lake, along the trail from Betty Lake immediately to the south. Howkum is stocked with cutthroat trout and is fairly popular owing to its close proximity to Shadow Bay Campground on Waldo Lake. Howkum covers about 4 acres and is only 10 feet deep. It can winter kill. The hike from the Betty Lake trailhead covers an easy .75 of a mile, passing the larger and much better Betty Lake at the half-mile mark. Howkum will be the next lake on your left. Horsefly Lake sits on the left side of the trail just beyond Howkum. If you're camped at mosquito-infested Shadow Bay Campground, you can reach these lakes just as easily by following the trail south. Otherwise, the Betty Lake Trailhead is located on the west side of Waldo Lake Road, 3 miles from Hwy 58. Take a float tube or small raft for this one as well as for Betty and Horsefly Lakes.

Huddeston Pond (Willamina)

A large millpond at Hartman Park in Willamina, Huddeston is stocked regularly during the spring with catchable size rainbow trout and also offers brown bullhead, crappie, yellow perch, and a few largemouth bass. Hartman Park lies adjacent to the South Yamhill River on Polk Street. No boats are allowed. Alternately this 5-acre pond has been called Hampton Pond and Willamina Pond.

Humbug Creek (Willamette National Forest)

A tributary to the Breitenbush River east of Detroit, Humbug Creek offers fair fishing for small, wild cutthroat and rainbows. The creek has two forks: The Elk Lake Road (FR 4697) follows Humbug Creek for 3 miles and Humbug Road (FR 4696) follows East Humbug Creek, the larger and better of the two forks, for about 5 miles. Follow Hwy 22 to Detroit, and then head east on Breitenbush Road. After crossing the Breitenbush River, watch for the left-hand turn on FR 4696.

Hunts Lake (Mt. Jefferson Wilderness)
hike-in

Hunts Lake offers good fishing in a scenic location in the Mt. Jefferson Wilderness Area. This 7-acre lake offers naturally reproducing cutthroat and stocked rainbows. Shore fishing is good here and all methods produce. From Hwy 22 east of Idanha, turn left (or right if you are coming from Bend) on FR 2246, the Pamelia Creek Road. Don't leave any valuables in your car at the popular Pamelia Lake Trailhead. Hike past Pamelia Lake and follow the steep trail up Hunts Creek. Once the trail forks, head left a half-mile to Hanks Lake. The trail gains 1400 feet in the 3 miles between Pamelia Lake and Hanks Lake. Visitors to Hunts Cove are required to obtain a special limited-entry permit from the Detroit Ranger District Headquarters in Detroit. Call ahead with your requested dates and the number of people in your party. The headquarters can be reached at 503-854-3366.

Indigo Lake (Lane County)
hike-in, float tube recommended

Truly one of the most beautiful of the high-Cascades lakes Indigo, as it name implies, radiates a brilliant bluish color with Sawtooth Mountain mirrored in its vibrant waters. This stunning setting invites anglers, hikers, photographers, and outdoor enthusiasts of many other interests. Still, angling pressure is usually light and the fishing is generally quite good. Indigo is planted with both rainbow and cutthroat trout, with rainbows predominating.

Reaching a maximum depth of almost 40 feet, this 17-acre gem over-winters its trout reasonably well considering the elevation of almost 6,000 feet. The typical trout range from

Many little streams in the Cascades offer small wild trout.

8 to 12 inches, but they reach at least 15 inches. All methods produce here and a float tube offers a distinct advantage, especially as it allows you to fish the drop-off area near the center of the lake where the bottom drops away quickly from the 8- to 12-foot deep shallows that dominate the north half of the lake. Scree fields from the slopes of Sawtooth Mountain reach all the way to Indigo's south shore. You can pick your way through the boulders and enjoy some fine shoreline action in deep water.

During the morning and evening, trout frequent the shallower areas of the north half of the lake, providing excellent fly-angling opportunity, especially during the mayfly hatches. Fly anglers need a sinking or sink-tip line to fish the lake effectively throughout the day.

Indigo Lake features a nice walk-in campground with five tent sites, though these can be tough to get on weekends. The hike into Indigo covers almost 2 miles and gains about 700 feet. The lake sits at 5,900 feet and is rarely accessible before mid-June and sometimes not until late June. To get there, take Hwy 58 through Oakridge. Two miles east of town, turn south on the Kitson Springs Road (FR 21) towards Hills Creek Reservoir. Stay right and follow FR 21 south along the west side of the reservoir. Remain on FR 21 for about 32 miles until you reach a left turn on FR 2154. Follow 2154 for 10 miles to the Timpanogas Lake Campground. The trail is at the end of the spur road into the campground.

For a spectacular view of the surrounding mountains, make an early morning climb up 7,301-foot Sawtooth Mountain, a steep, huge heap of rock and scree lined here and there with rugged sub-alpine fir and laced with snowfields during early summer. The easiest route heads up and over the east ridgeline to meet the Cowhorn Mt. Trail. From there, scramble up and over the south pinnacle to reach the main summit. Be sure to take a camera along.

Island Lake
(Deschutes National Forest near Suttle Lake)
see Central Zone

Island Lake (Mt. Washington Wilderness)
hike-in, cross-country

This 2-acre cutthroat trout lake is tricky to find, requiring skill with map and compass. It lies half a mile southwest of popular Benson Lake, right on the boundary of the Mt. Washington Wilderness Area. With a topo map and compass in hand (and the skills to navigate with them) you can get there easily from Benson Lake. The trout range from 8 to 12 inches with a few carry-over fish reaching 16 inches and generally, you'll have the place to yourself.

Island Lake (Three Sisters Wilderness)
hike-in

A mostly unproductive small lake in the northern part of the Mink Lake Basin, Island Lake is pretty enough, but its brook trout are small and usually few in number. It's worth sampling in conjunction with the myriad other fishable lakes in the area. See Mink Lake herein for directions to the area.

Island Lake (Warm Springs Reservation)
hike-in

A pretty lake in the Olallie Lake group, Island Lake is shallow, and stocked brook trout don't seem to over-winter in great numbers and don't grow very large. Try it in conjunction with the other lakes in the area, but be sure to obtain the tribal fishing permit before you go. Nearby lakes, also on the Warm Springs Reservation, include Dark and Long Lakes. You can drive to within half a mile of Dark Lake and from there it's a short jaunt to Island Lake and several others. However, if you are coming from western Oregon, it will take you substantially longer to drive to the trailhead on the east side than to drive to Olallie Lake and hike over to Island Lake (and the others in the group). Follow the trail along the north shore of Olallie Lake, and then follow the trail leading a short distance to Long and Dark Lakes. From Dark Lake, Island Lake is about half a mile to the south.

Island Lakes, Upper & Lower (Gold Lake area)
hike-in

Upper and Lower Island Lakes sit just south of Waldo Lake and northwest from Willamette Pass. Both can offer consistent action between June and September, though you won't find any trophy fish here. Both are stocked every other year, Lower Island with cutthroat or rainbows and Upper Island with brook trout and sometimes rainbows. They are fairly popular lakes with anglers, swimmers, and hikers. Both lakes feature some nice camping areas and lie within easy reach of the other fishable lakes in the immediate vicinity: Lorin, JoAnn, Birthday, and Verde Lakes.

The shortest walk to the Island Lakes covers about a mile-and-a-half from the Fuji Mountain Trailhead to the west. To reach the trailhead, follow Hwy 58 east from Oakridge or west from Willamette Pass. Between mileposts 50 and 51, just east from the train trestle, turn north onto Eagle Creek Road (FR 5883) and follow the road about 10 miles until it ends at the trailhead. Hike .2 of a mile to the first trail junction and stay to the right. After another .75 of a mile you will reach the South Waldo Trail. Head north (left) and hike a quarter mile to Lower Island Lake on your right and a bit further to Upper Island Lake on the left side of the trail.

Both lakes sit higher than 6,000 feet and the Fuji Mountain trailhead, at 6,200 feet, is rarely accessible before mid-June. Like the entire Waldo Lake region, the Island Lakes Basin is a haven for mosquitoes. The climb up 7,144-foot Fuji Mountain covers a fairly easy 1.5 miles and the summit provides a fine view of the surrounding peaks and of Waldo Lake.

Jefferson Park (Mt. Jefferson Wilderness Area)
hike-in

Jefferson Park is a scenic, heavily used lake basin sitting just below 6,000 feet at the foot of Mt. Jefferson in the northern portion of the wilderness area. Its five fishable lakes are covered individually herein. See Bays Lake for directions to all five lakes and see separate headings also for Park Lake, Rock Lake, Russell Lake and Scout Lake.

JoJo Lake (Willamette National Forest)
hike-in, float tube recommended

JoJo Lake is a deep pond spanning about an acre and located just above the North Santiam River a few miles beyond Idanha and almost directly across the river from Whispering Falls Campground. The lake is stocked with rainbows that can reach 18 inches, though they are generally few in number. A few years ago the old easy-to-find route into JoJo was basically plowed over by a clear-cut, so it's a little tricky now: From Hwy 22, cross the North Santiam River at the Bruno Mt. Road Bridge a few miles uphill from Idanha. Then with topo map in hand, park along the road and bushwhack over to the lake.

Jorn Lake (Mt. Jefferson Wilderness)
hike-in

The largest and most scenic of the lakes in Eight Lakes Basin, 35-acre Jorn Lake offers fair-to-good action for brook and rainbow trout; cutthroat trout are also stocked at times. Most range from 8 to 10 inches and a very few reach at least 16 inches. The lake is popular and its 16 designated campsites can prove hard to obtain during summer weekends. Still, it's a pretty place and makes for a nice base camp for exploring the other lakes in the area. The hike to Jorn covers 6.4 miles from the Duffy Lake Trailhead to the west.

The Duffy Lake Trailhead lies east of Hwy 22 immediately south of the North Santiam River Bridge near milepost 76. After crossing the river, watch for a left-hand turn to Big Meadows. The road forks a little more than half a mile in. The left-hand fork leads down to Big Meadows while the right-hand fork leads to the Duffy Lake Trailhead. Big Meadows offers a horse camp and horse trail that parallels the foot trail most of the way to Duffy Lake. (Horse packers frequent the Eight Lakes Basin area).

Junction City Pond (Lane County)

Regularly and heavily stocked from December through May, this small, popular pond south of Junction City tends to hold up fairly well during the spring for anglers still fishing with bait. In recent years, ODFW has stocked several hundred of its "trophy" size rainbows in the pond during December and January. The pond sits on the west side of Hwy 99, about 2 miles south of Junction City.

Kingsley Reservoir (Hood River County)
campground

Fairly popular with locals, 60-acre Kingsley Reservoir lies just minutes from the community of Hood River and is stocked liberally with legal-size rainbows. Many anglers still fish with bait from the dam during the spring and summer, though small boats are popular here. A nice campground sits nestled in the trees and is usually quiet. About half the campsites are right next to the water and these fill quickly on summer weekends. Though bank fishing is easy, a small boat, raft, pontoon, or float tube is convenient here. From I-84, take the westernmost Hood River exit (Exit 62). Take an immediate west turn and follow the frontage road along the freeway. This is Country Club Road. Stay on this road, following it around the corners, and watch for the signs that keep you headed in the right direction. At Oak Grove, Binns Hill Drive is signed to the reservoir. Kingsley is usually accessible by mid-April, but check ahead if you are headed there in the spring, as some years the snow lingers.

Kiwa Lake
see Lake Kiwa

Krag Lake (Three Sisters Wilderness)
see Nightshade Lakes

Lake Ann (Mt. Jefferson Wilderness)
hike-in, float tube recommended

This shallow, weedy 18-acre lake lies adjacent to the Marion Lake Trail in the Mt. Jefferson Wilderness Area and offers good fishing for small, naturally reproducing brook trout. The weedy shoreline makes for tough bank fishing, but float tubers can have a ball here with 6- to 10-inch brookies. A few fish reach 12 inches, but these are scarce. The mile-long hike is usually snow free by mid-June and the fishing holds up through the summer, peaking early and late (June and September). Lake Ann lies within the fire-ban zone established at Marion Lake, so only gas-powered stoves/lanterns are allowed.

Lake Harriet (Clackamas County)
campground

A power-generation impoundment on the Oak Grove Fork of the Clackamas River east from Ripplebrook, Lake Harriet is a consistently productive fishery for stocked rainbow trout. The reservoir also has a few good-size brown trout and a few small brook trout. Both trolling and bank fishing are popular. ODFW stocks the lake with lots of legal-size rainbows and also with some of its trophy-size fish. There's a nice campground here.

Lake Kiwa (Lane County)
hike-in

Covering about 40 acres, Lake Kiwa sits north of Waldo Lake in the Taylor Burn area and offers consistently fair-to-good fishing for rainbow and brook trout. The fish typically range from 8 to 12 inches with a few bigger. See Waldo Lake herein for direction from the area and, from North Waldo Lake Campground follow the trail along the Waldo's north shore. At the trail junction, turn north (right) and hike about 1.5 miles up to Kiwa. The short hike is conducive to carrying a float tube, though shoreline fishing is good. The trails are generally snow free by mid- to late June. This entire area bears the scars of being severely burned in 1996, but the wildflowers bloom profusely in places, and fishing remains productive. There are good camping sites around the lake, which offers a commanding view of Rigdon Butte.

Lake of the Woods (Mt. Jefferson Wilderness)
hike-in, float tube recommended

This fairly popular trailside lake offers fair-to-good action for rainbows and/or cutthroat, depending on which species has been planted in recent years. Dense shrubs and trees line most of the shoreline of this 5-acre lake, so a float tube comes in handy, especially for fly anglers. The lake offers five designated campsites and is usually accessible by mid-June. You can get there from the popular Marion Lake Trail, but the Bingham Ridge Trail is easier and quieter. Off Hwy 22, a mile south of Riverside Campground and 2 miles north of Marion Forks, turn east on Bingham Ridge Road (FR 2253) and follow it a few miles to the trailhead. Hike east on the Bingham Ridge Trail and then southeast on Lake of the Woods Trail (#3493). The route covers an easy 5 miles.

Lambert Slough (Willamette River)
boat recommended

Lambert Slough departs the Willamette River off a side channel behind Wheatland Bar, just north of Wheatland Ferry. The narrow slough winds its way north for 6 miles, forming so-called Grand Island before re-joining the Willamette at Lambert Bar. The slough, popular with duck hunters during winter, offers excellent prospects for bass and panfish during summer and early autumn. With no public bank access and little room to maneuver large craft, the slough is ideally suited to canoes and kayaks.

Unless you can get permission from a Grand Island land-owner, you have three options for accessing the slough, all of which require fairly strong kayak or canoe skills. For specific details on how to get to the launch sites mentioned below, see Willamette River, Salem to Oregon City herein.

One option is to launch a kayak or canoe on the cobble-stone bar on the Willamette's west bank immediately downstream from the Wheatland Ferry. Paddle down the bank and turn left into the side channel that forms the island known as Wheatland Bar—beware the row of pilings extending partway across the mouth of the channel (but fish these for smallmouth bass). About a mile down the channel, turn left into Lambert Slough. All of this is downstream work; so coming back up requires far more effort, especially in the channel behind Wheatland Bar. The next option is to launch at the Grand Island Access and paddle upstream on the side channel to reach the mouth of Lambert Slough. Lastly, you can access the mouth of the slough by launching at Wheatland Ferry, 7 miles upstream or at San Salvador Park, 8 miles downstream. Throw a canoe or kayak in the boat for paddling up the slough.

During the long days of summer, experienced paddlers can launch at Wheatland Ferry and then paddle down Lambert Slough to a pre-arranged pickup by boat. Arrange to have a friend pick you up by boat at Lambert Bar. Or make a two-day trip of it by packing some camping gear and spending the night at Lambert Bar or one of the islands downstream. Then paddle down to San Salvador Park. Paddlers might be well served to carry a camp saw or hatchet in case you encounter a brush jam or log jam in the channel.

Laying Creek (Lane County)

A nice little cutthroat stream southeast of Cottage Grove, Laying Creek joins Brice Creek to form the Row River near the tiny community of Disston. Laying Creek is open to catch-and-keep fishing during the general season (five-fish limit with an 8-inch minimum length), during which bait is allowed. For the rest of the year, the creek is governed by catch-and-release, artificials-only rules. To get there, take I-5 to Cottage Grove (Exit 174) and then head east toward Dorena Reservoir on Row River Road. Continue around the reservoir and then east through Dorena, Culp Creek, and Disston. After Disston, Brice Creek Road heads right and FR 17 heads left, following Laying Creek. Rujada Campground lies 2 miles upstream and two additional campgrounds lie alongside nearby Brice Creek.

Lenore Lake (Bull of the Woods Wilderness)
see Big Slide Lake

Leone Lake
hike-in, float tube recommended

Throughout the 1980s Leone Lake served as one of my favorite hideaway brook trout lakes. Nothing much has changed up there, save a few more clear cuts each year since. Leone is located in the Breitenbush River drainage above Detroit, east of Hwy 22. The brookies run 8 to 14 inches in this 5-acre lake, averaging around 9 or 10 inches.

You can get to Leone from either the Breitenbush Road (FR 46), which heads east out of Detroit, or from the Boulder Ridge Road (FR 2231), which heads east a few miles southeast from Detroit. Forest Road 2231 leads about 10 miles to a right hand turn on a steep spur road, FR 847. This road ends at the base of a steep hill clear cut about 20 years ago and a trail leads straight up the ridge and then turns to your left, following the ridge until it drops down to Leone Lake. You can reach this same trail by following the Breitenbush Road (FR 46) up towards Cleator Bend Campground and Breitenbush Hot Springs. Cross the river on FR 2231 just past Cleator Bend and head left, just a few miles up the hill to Spur Road 847. Alternately you can take a less steep route to the lake from the spur road on the south side (FR 850). Consult the forest map for particulars or, better yet, the Detroit Ranger District Map available from the district headquarters near Detroit.

Leone is often accessible as early as late April. All methods produce here and while shoreline fishing is fairly easy from several good spots (especially on the back corner of the lake), a float tube or raft comes in handy. Old records and persistent rumors suggest that the lake has a reproducing population of brown trout but I, nor anybody I fish with, has ever taken one there.

Linton Lake (Lane County)
hike-in, float tube recommended, campground

Unique for this part of Oregon because of its naturally reproducing brown trout, 70-acre Linton Lake occupies a scenic forest setting high on the McKenzie River drainage east of Springfield. Take Hwy 126 heading east up the McKenzie and then turn right onto the Old McKenzie Highway (Route 242). After about 9 miles, watch for the trailhead near Alder Campground. The easy trail covers about a mile, crossing over a lava field and through scenic and dense stands of conifers. Linton's brown trout typically range from 8 to 13 inches, but a few reach several pounds. Big fish are rare, but the lake has a fair number of 14-inch browns. Brook trout reach at least 14 inches, but most are 7 to 12 inches. Linton Lake is a popular destination during the summer; so if you want to avoid the crowds, fish on weekdays. Better yet, wait until early October when seemingly all the lake's trout hang out in the shallows and when few other anglers bother with them. A float tube or other small craft is handy here.

Little Cincha Lake
see Cincha Lakes

Little Duffy Lake
see Duffy Lake, Little

Little North Santiam River ("Little North Fork")
see Santiam River, Little North Fork

Long Tom River (Lane County)

Essentially two different rivers, the Long Tom provides fair trout fishing in its headwater reaches and fair-to-good fishing for warmwater fish and rough fish on its lower end. The dividing line is sprawling Fern Ridge Reservoir west of Eugene. The Long Tom emerges from the Coast Range foothills northeast from Triangle Lake and then flows south before reversing its course to double back into Fern Ridge. For several miles the river runs alongside SR 36, which connects Junction City and Cheshire to Triangle Lake. This section, as far down as Alderwood Wayside, offers modest opportunities for small trout. Downstream from the wayside, private property severely curtails access, but the entire stretch harbors cutthroat trout.

Below Fern Ridge Reservoir, the Long Tom hosts decent populations of bass, yellow perch, crappie, carp, and other species, along with lots of brown bullhead that provide a fairly popular fishery. Access to the lower river is difficult because it flows mostly through private lands. Be sure to ask permission. The city park in the little town of Monroe offers some bank access and the mouth of the river is accessible by boat from the Willamette.

Lookout Point Reservoir (Lane County)
boat ramps, boat recommended

The largest reservoir on the Willamette system in Lane County, Lookout Point ranks a distant second in popularity to its downstream neighbor, Dexter Reservoir. At full pool, Lookout Point covers 4,360 acres, but it retains full pool only for a few months each summer. Subject to frequent moderate to high winds, the reservoir offers slow fishing for trout and some juvenile chinook salmon. The more significant fishery for a handful of anglers "in the know" is the reservoir's modest fishery for large white crappie. They congregate around structure, mostly along the north bank. To get there from I-5 (just south of Eugene), follow Hwy 58 to Dexter Reservoir and turn left, crossing the causeway to the town of Lowell. Turn right on West Boundary Road, which accesses the two boat ramps. Near the dam, the Meridian Point ramp is only viable at or near full pool. The low-pool ramp is further east at Signal Point. Concentrate on the rock structure and the coves along the north bank between the two ramp areas. A fish finder is helpful and most crappie specialists rely on jigs.

Lost Creek (Lane County)

A tributary to the Middle Fork Willamette, Lost Creek is open to catch-and-keep fishing for a modest population of wild trout. The creek reaches the Middle Fork 3 miles below Dexter Dam and flows entirely through private property. You'll have to knock on doors to fish this water. Lost Creek Road turns south off Hwy 58 across from Dexter Dam.

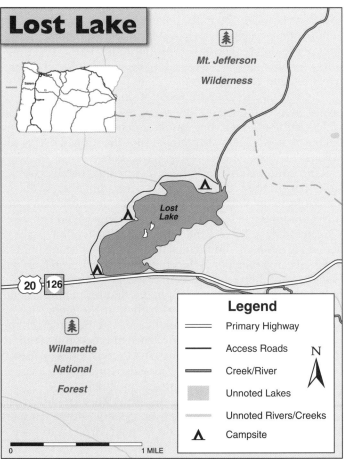

© 2007 Wilderness Adventures Press, Inc.

Lost Lake (Santiam Pass)
catch-and-release, no bait, float tube recommended, boat recommended

A popular and generally productive catch-and-release fishery, Lost Lake sits immediately adjacent to the highway 2 miles west of the Santiam Pass summit. Covering 50 acres when full, Lost Lake offers brook trout and rainbows. Both species can reach 18 inches, especially after two or more winters of higher-than-average snow pack. Lost Lake sits atop porous lava fields and the water leeches away all summer, leaving but a comparative puddle by August. If the Cascades get lots of snow pack and autumn rain for two years running, the lake retains enough water during the winter to allow lots of fish to over-winter. During drought years, the lake shrinks to just a handful of small over-wintering pools and big fish become rather scarce.

No matter when you fish Lost Lake—during early summer at high water or late summer at low water—you'll want a float tube, canoe, or small boat. During early summer you can

Lost Lake near Santiam Pass is a consistent producer of brook and rainbow trout.

quite literally catch trout right along the highway, but as the lake shrinks, the trout begin to migrate toward the holes on the north side. During drought years, many anglers forgo the fishing here because the trout are simply too vulnerable as they sweat out the summer in the confines of a couple deep holes. During high-water years, however, the September and October fishing can be especially good and the prospects of 14- to 18-inch brookies, in bright spawning colors, makes the effort worthwhile, though smaller rainbows predominate.

The lake offers an abundance of trout foods, including dense populations of *Callibaetis* mayflies, caddis, damsel nymphs, and Chironomids. Fly anglers enjoy ample opportunity for surface and near-surface action. Look for the mayflies to hatch virtually every day during summer and early autumn, especially when the wind stays down. Early and mid-summer brings a little-known hatch of "traveling sedges." These large caddisflies skitter about on the surface right at dusk and after dark, driving trout into frenzy. During non-hatch periods, fish a No. 6 Woolly Bugger (black or olive) in tandem with a No. 12 beadhead Pheasant Tail or Prince Nymph. Or try a peacock Carey Special. Gear anglers enjoy consistent success with small spoons and spinners and with bubble-and-fly combos.

You can't miss Lost Lake: Just follow Hwy 20, 126, or 22 east from the Willamette Valley or follow Hwy 20 west from Sisters. About 2 miles east of Santiam Junction and 2 miles west of Santiam Summit, watch for the lake on the north side of the highway. A spur road follows along the west bank and wraps around the backside of the lake to some nice camping spots (undeveloped). Use caution when you make the turn onto the access road, for it lies near a blind curve on the highway. Early in the season, the access road is often blocked by snow or standing water.

Lower Berley Lake
see Berley Lakes

Luckiamute River (Polk County)
boat recommended, boat ramp

A poor-to-fair trout stream in its difficult-to-access upper reaches, the Luckiamute River evolves into a good warmwater fishery by the time it reaches the Willamette River north of Albany. The mouth of the Luckiamute offers good prospects for smallmouth bass, crappie, bullhead, and catfish. This small, meandering farm-country river reaches the Willamette almost across from the mouth of the Santiam River and less than 2 miles upstream from the boat ramp at Buena Vista. Anglers often boat up to the mouth of the Luckiamute, though a large tract of public land lies between the Luckiamute and the Willamette and offers good public access for those wishing to canoe or kayak down from the drop point on Buena Vista Road. From I-5, take the Talbot Road exit (Exit 242) and head west to the Willamette River. Cross the river on the Buena Vista Ferry to Buena Vista Park and Ramp. Or head south along the west bank of the Willamette for about 3 miles down to the Luckiamute.

Lula Lake (Mt. Jefferson Wilderness)

hike in; cross-country

Lula Lake is among the most remote of the lakes on Marion Flats in the Mt. Jefferson Wilderness and you'll need cross-country skills and a sense of adventure to find it. Marion Flats also includes Cleo, Turpentine, Green Peak, Temple, and Davis Lakes. Lula lies east of Turpentine Peak. The route to the lake follows Turpentine Creek more than a mile from its juncture with the Pine Ridge Trail. Follow the Pine Ridge Trail about 1.5 miles to Turpentine Creek and then head uphill to the south. In places the going is easy; in other places fairly rugged due to dense stands of young evergreens (so dense in places that you cannot walk through them with a backpack). Stay close to the creek, but don't follow its course or you'll run into heavy brush in places. I've made this trek as early as mid-June without encountering more than a few snowfields. The reward for your effort is total solitude and brook trout all to yourself. Maude Lake is a stone's throw away (see listing herein) and Green Peak Lake lies a mile to the southeast by cross-country route. The best campsites are at Green Peak and Lula; the best fishing of the three—during the 80s at least—was at Lula. Use the Pine Ridge Trailhead, whose trailhead sits 5 miles up Twin Meadows Road, an east turn off Hwy 22 at milepost 70.

Mac Lake (Three Sisters Wilderness Area)

hike-in

A large, fairly productive lake in the Three Sisters Wilderness Area, Mac Lake sits about half a mile southeast of Mink Lake and right along the Pacific Crest Trail. The entire Mink Lake Basin is very popular with hikers and anglers, but don't be surprised to have Mac Lake to yourself during weekdays. The lake is accessible by July. Rainbow trout range from 6 to 12 inches. See Mink Lake for trail directions.

Marilyn Lakes (Lane County)

hike-in, float tube recommended

Close to popular Gold Lake near Willamette Pass, the two Marilyn Lakes (Upper and Lower) offer good fishing for small brook trout, with an occasional fish to 14 or more inches. The hike to the lake covers an easy mile and they are ideal for float tubes. Follow Hwy 58 to Willamette Pass and turn onto the Gold Lake Road. The trailhead for the Marilyn Lakes is along this road. The lakes are accessible by late June and fishing holds up all summer. Autumn fishing—as late as mid-October—can be very good here, especially if you're after the larger brookies in Upper Marilyn Lake.

Marion Creek (Linn County)

catch-and-release, no bait

The outlet stream from ever-popular Marion Lake, Marion Creek, flows through a scenic, forested canyon for about 6 miles down to its confluence with the North Santiam River at Marion Forks. Puzzle Creek, a major tributary, adds substantial volume to the creek, which offers fair catch-and-release fishing for small, wild rainbow and cutthroat trout. This is good dry-fly water, mostly from July through September. Follow Hwy 22 to Marion Forks and turn on the signed road to the Marion Lake Trailhead. The creek runs along the south side of the road, usually at a distance, over several waterfalls.

Marion Lake (Mt. Jefferson Wilderness)

hike-in

At 360 acres, Marion Lake is the largest lake in the Mt. Jefferson Wilderness Area. This scenic gem is also the best and most popular of the four dozen or so fishable lakes in the wilderness area, which spans more than 100,000 acres in the Willamette and Deschutes National Forests. Marion Lake sits at an elevation of 4,100 feet and requires a fairly easy hike covering 2.5 to 4 miles, depending on which end of the lake you decide to fish. The paved road leading to the trailhead follows Marion Creek east from the little town of Marion Forks, on Hwy 22 at milepost 70.

Marion Lake abounds in naturally reproducing brook trout and rainbows, their numbers bolstered by periodic stocking. The rainbows range from 9 to 20 inches with 12- to 14-inchers typical. The average brookie is smaller, but gets just as big in this lake, which reaches depths of 180 feet. Native cutthroat are less numerous and smaller, but are always a welcome catch. During early summer, look for spawning rainbows in

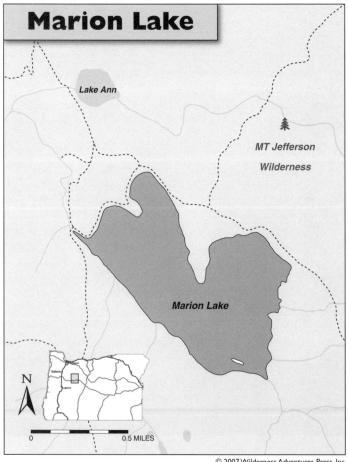

the outlet creek. You can stand atop a footbridge and spot them. Naturally, they are protected and the outlet stream is closed to all angling from the bridge to the markers placed by ODFW.

All methods produce at Marion. Many anglers opt for small Rooster Tails and other such spoons and spinners. Fly anglers can have a field day here, especially with the aid of a float tube. The *Callibaetis* mayflies hatch every day of the summer and early fall and Chironomids follow in the evening. During June, watch for "traveling sedges:" inch-long caddisflies that skitter about on the surface right at dusk. In the absence of hatch activity, try a two-fly rig with a Woolly Bugger in the lead trailed by a small beadhead Prince Nymph, Zugbug, or Carey Special. Fly anglers will need both floating and sinking lines.

Packing a float tube into Marion Lake is well worth the effort.

The front side (north side) of Marion Lake is the deepest and offers good fishing from shore. The better action occurs on the far side, where substantial shallow shoals feature aquatic weed growth and an abundance of both trout food and trout. The main trail leads to the north shore via two alternate routes that diverge about a quarter mile from the lake. The right-hand fork (Blue Lake Trail) takes you to the outlet and then heads south toward Eight Lakes Basin. The left-hand trail heads straight to the lake's north corner and then follows near the northeast shoreline for a mile. A popular shoreline trail connects this latter trail with the Blue Lake Trail by skirting along the lake's front (northwest) end.

Marion Lake's entire south half—almost 2 miles of shoreline—is devoid of formal trails, though fishermen's trails abound. This is the best half of the lake. If you look at a map of the lake you'll see a long peninsula jutting into the lake from the north and extending due south. Draw a line from the tip of this "finger" south to the opposite shore and you've lopped off the southeast half of the lake and, for my money, this is the best part of Marion. The far south corner (look for the island) features several inlet streams, the most significant of which is Eight Lakes Creek. The inlet area adjacent to the island ranks among the best areas on the lake and is the least crowded. You can get there by foot from either side of the lake—not an easy undertaking owing to dense brush, blowdowns, and swampy areas—or by raft or float tube. I like to camp back there and have the place all to myself, but doing so requires a somewhat arduous trek around the north and east shore to get my gear packed in.

Otherwise, the best campsites on the lake are scattered along the northeast shoreline, starting out on the peninsula and extending east to Mazama Creek and south to Mist Creek. Marion is generally accessible by mid-June. A few precautions are in order: First, don't forget mosquito repellent and second, don't leave anything valuable in your car at the trailhead. A permanent fire ban is in affect at Marion Lake and only stoves/lanterns powered by liquid or compressed gas are allowed.

Maude Lake (Mt. Jefferson Wilderness)
hike-in, cross-country, float tube recommended

A scenic and rarely visited small lake in the Mt. Jefferson Wilderness Area, Maude offers 8- to 12-inch brook trout and you'll have them to yourself. The price of admission is a fairly rugged mile of cross-country work. The route is not steep, but if you choose unwisely you can end up fighting through dense stands of young evergreens. Use the Pine Ridge Trail, which begins at the end of Twin Meadows Road (milepost 70 along Hwy 22, south of Marion Forks). Follow the trail 2 miles to the side trail leading left to Temple Lake. From there, strike off uphill to your right (south) about a mile to Maude Lake. Be sure to consult the topo map. Keep the outlet stream on your left and the Lula Lake outlet on your right and beware the swamp ponds just downhill from Maude Lake. Be sure to check out nearby Lula and Green Peak Lakes—both rarely fished—while you're there.

Maxwell Lake (Mt. Jefferson Wilderness)
hike-in, cross-country

A tiny, but deep brook trout lake in the Mt. Jefferson Wilderness, Maxwell Lake sits on the western flank of Maxwell Butte. The first 3 miles of the hike follows the Maxwell Butte Trail, but the last quarter mile is off trail. Be sure to consult the topo map. The Maxwell Butte Trailhead is located at the Maxwell Butte Sno-park, 3 miles west from Santiam Junction on Hwy 22.

McFarland Lake (Three Sisters Wilderness)
hike-in

This very pretty 39-acre wilderness lake offers consistently good fishing for stocked rainbow trout that can reach 2 pounds. Large fish are rare however, and most of the trout range from 8 to 12 inches. McFarland is a great place for camping if you want to stay a few days to explore the other lakes in the area. McFarland and several other smaller lakes sit on a high, rugged plateau north of Irish Mountain. As a map reference, Cultus Lake lies several miles to the southeast. McFarland is deep and its trout over-winter easily, so this lake is a reliable year-to-year producer. Generally the trails are clear of snow by late June or early July. The shortest route—nearly 6 miles—arrives from the north via the Crossing Way Trail (#3307). From Blue River to the north (Hwy 126) or Westfir to the west (Hwy 58), take Forest Primary Route 19 to FR 1958. Follow FR 1958 to FR 380 and watch for the trailhead just past the junction of the two roads.

McKenzie River, Lower (Lane County)
boat ramps, boat recommended, services, campground

A river of multiple personalities, Oregon's famed Lower McKenzie ranks among the region's best combination trout, salmon, and steelhead fisheries. Native cutthroat and wild rainbows inhabit the lower river alongside strong runs of hatchery-produced summer steelhead and spring chinook salmon.

The Lower McKenzie begins at Leaburg Dam, east of Springfield, and flows about 35 miles westerly through Springfield, past I-5 and down to its confluence with the Willamette River. The lower river is managed for wild trout, while offering a top-notch spring/summer fishery for steelhead and salmon. The McKenzie's beautiful wild rainbows—called "redsides"—can reach 20 inches in length and 12- to 14-inch specimens abound. Moreover, these strong, healthy rainbows, along with native cutthroat, thrive in what is essentially an urban fishery: The McKenzie's best trout water flows through and adjacent to the cities of Springfield and Eugene.

From its mouth upstream to Hayden Bridge in Springfield, the river is open year-round for catch-and-release fishing with flies or artificial lures. Hayden Bridge is located off Marcola Road and offers bank access on both sides of the river. Above Hayden Bridge, all wild trout must be released during the year-round season, but during the general season, ODFW plants the river with legal-size rainbows. Bait is allowed after the season opener in April.

Noted for its prolific hatches, the Lower McKenzie offers miles of prime dry-fly water. By late February, Eugene-area fly anglers start feeling antsy, for they know that any day the trout will begin rising to the river's inaugural emergences of March Brown mayflies (*Rithrogena morrisoni*). By mid-or late March, the mayfly hatch gathers full steam and when water levels remain reasonable, any warm, muggy day offers the promise of an hour or so of exceptional dry-fly action.

The March Browns are easily imitated by any of several popular patterns. My typical preferences include the March Brown Sparkle-dun and Compara-dun, both tied on No. 12 and 14 hooks and dressed with a light tan body. Although more time-consuming at the vice, the extended-body Paradrake works well on choppy water. Many anglers fish soft-hackle emergers just below the surface, sometimes as a trailing fly behind a dry fly.

The McKenzie River is prized for its wild rainbow trout.

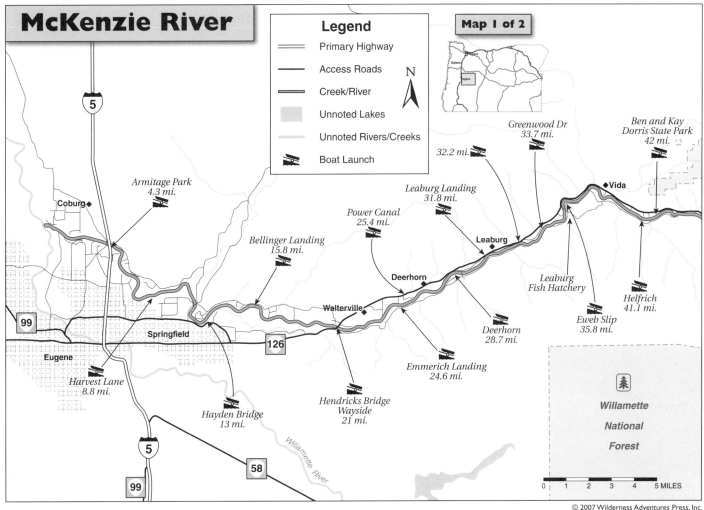

McKenzie River

Legend

Primary Highway
Access Roads
Creek/River
Unnoted Lakes
Unnoted Rivers/Creeks
Boat Launch

Map 1 of 2

N

Armitage Park
4.3 mi.

Coburg

Bellinger Landing
15.8 mi.

Power Canal
25.4 mi.

Leaburg Landing
31.8 mi.

32.2 mi.

Greenwood Dr
33.7 mi.

Ben and Kay
Dorris State Park
42 mi.

Vida

Leaburg

Deerhorn

Walterville

Leaburg
Fish Hatchery

Helfrich
41.1 mi.

Eweb Slip
35.8 mi.

Deerhorn
28.7 mi.

Springfield

Eugene

Harvest Lane
8.8 mi.

Hayden Bridge
13 mi.

Hendricks Bridge
Wayside
21 mi.

Emmerich Landing
24.6 mi.

Willamette
National
Forest

Willamette River

0   1   2   3   4   5 MILES

© 2007 Wilderness Adventures Press, Inc.

Riffles and runs of shallow to moderate depth offer prime locations for hatches of these large mayflies. Expect the hatch to begin during early afternoon and don't be surprised if seemingly lifeless water suddenly springs to life with surprisingly large trout as the hatch gains momentum.

While the March Brown emergence ranks as the most significant early season hatch, the McKenzie offers increasing insect activity as spring transitions to summer. Large stoneflies hatch sporadically during this time and evening caddis activity begins as water levels stabilize during early summer. Most significant of the river's myriad caddis hatches is the famed summer emergence of the so-called McKenzie Green Caddis (*Arctopsyche grandis*). These large, green-bodied caddis hatch profusely during summer evenings and often draw large trout into shallow water around dusk.

Caddis hatches dominate the summer months, but many other insects hatch at least sporadically, including green drakes, whose unheralded June hatch lasts about a week but often provides good surface action during overcast days. Blue-winged olives (*Baetis*) and pale morning duns (*Ephemerella*) hatch during spring and summer, along with yellow sallies

and a few golden stoneflies. During the fall, huge October caddis (*Dicosmoecus*) begin their annual emergence and Baetis mayflies often continue daily emergences until the first heavy rains of mid-autumn.

The Lower McKenzie offers several public access points, some easily located and others somewhat more secret and guarded. The best bank fishing occurs at the boat ramps and parks. Hendrick's Bridge (just past Springfield), Hayden Bridge and Armitage Park (immediately adjacent to Interstate-5) rank as the most popular access points for trout anglers. Steelhead anglers converge on the first 2 miles of river below Leaburg Dam. Most of the lower river flows through private lands, so a drift boat offers access to many reaches of the river otherwise un-fishable. If you are new to the McKenzie, consider hiring a drift-boat guide for your first excursion. If you prefer wild trout, steelhead, or salmon, be sure to tell your guide that you want to fish the lower river.

Boat access begins below Leaburg Dam, where several popular and productive steelhead runs await. You can choose from myriad float segments. The uppermost drift (the dam down to Greenwood Lane or Lower Greenwood) draws the

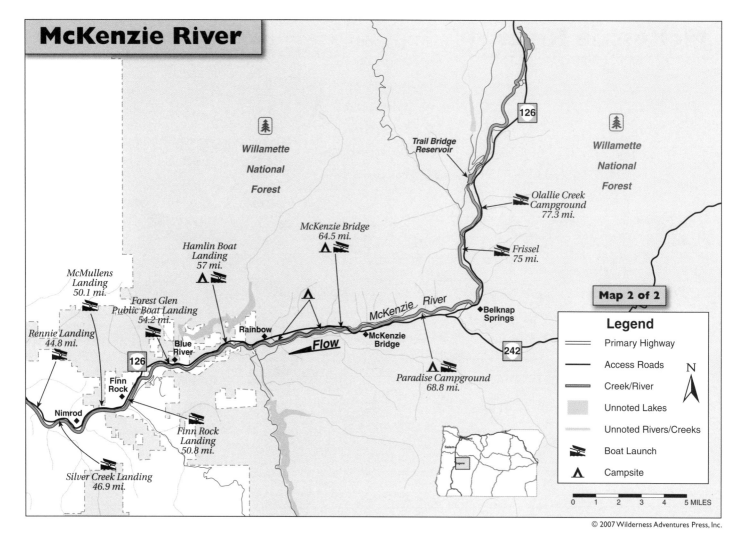

McKenzie River

Willamette National Forest

Willamette National Forest

Trail Bridge Reservoir

Olallie Creek Campground 77.3 mi.

Frissel 75 mi.

McKenzie Bridge 64.5 mi.

Hamlin Boat Landing 57 mi.

McMullens Landing 50.1 mi.

Forest Glen Public Boat Landing 54.2 mi.

Rennie Landing 44.8 mi.

Blue River

Rainbow

McKenzie River

Flow

McKenzie Bridge

Belknap Springs

Map 2 of 2

Finn Rock

Nimrod

Finn Rock Landing 50.8 mi.

Paradise Campground 68.8 mi.

Silver Creek Landing 46.9 mi.

Legend

═══	Primary Highway
────	Access Roads
═══	Creek/River
▒▒	Unnoted Lakes
┈┈	Unnoted Rivers/Creeks
	Boat Launch
▲	Campsite

N

0 1 2 3 4 5 MILES

© 2007 Wilderness Adventures Press, Inc.

most use from steelhead and salmon anglers, but also includes lots of perfect water. The lower-river ramp sites are as follows, with mileage given from the uppermost ramp below the dam:

- Leaburg Dam
- Greenwood Lane (3 miles)
- Lower Greenwood (4.5 miles)
- Near Leaburg Store (7 miles)
- Bridge at Deerhorn Gold Course (11 miles)
- Primitive launch at Partridge Lane (15 miles)
- Hendrick's Bridge Wayside (19 miles)
- Bellinger Landing (23 miles)
- Hayden Bridge (28 miles)
- Harvest Lane (31 miles)
- Armitage Park (36 miles)

While its trout fishing attracts the most attention, the McKenzie's summer steelhead fishery ranks among the state's best during years of strong runs. The steelheading begins during May, peaks in June and lasts through September. Chinook salmon arrive as early as February, but the fishing peaks between April and June.

The McKenzie seems custom designed for classic dry-line steelheading and such tactics predominate among fly anglers. Popular flies include such classics as the Green-butt Skunk, Purple Peril, and Purple Muddler. All other methods produce good results; anglers here use bait, spinners, spoons, and jigs to entice the river's 5- to 12-pound steelhead. The fish are easily identified as hatchery steelhead by their missing adipose fin and, because they don't reproduce, you needn't feel awkward about killing one for the barbecue. Non-clipped steelhead and salmon must be released. The Lower McKenzie's wild rainbows and cutthroat are available only for catch-and-release fishing.

McKenzie River near Leaburg

McKenzie River, Upper (Lane/Linn Counties)
campground, boat ramp

Above Leaburg Dam, the upper half of the McKenzie River is the state's most heavily stocked trout river. ODFW stocks legal rainbows weekly during the season, providing a productive fishery on this popular, scenic river. Between the uppermost reaches and Leaburg Dam, the McKenzie flows for many beautiful miles. The upper river, very popular with rafters and anglers alike, offers lots of bank access. Highway 126 follows closely along the river and various side roads cross the flow. Along the way, you can choose from many easy-to-fish and popular roadside access points or you can find more out-of-the-way access points along the south bank, using local roads and bridges to get to the water.

An additional wild-trout fishery exists in the headwaters region of the McKenzie, where cold, rushing flows cascade violently down a precipitous path through elegant conifers. State Hwy 126 leads east out of Springfield, following the McKenzie River from the outskirts of town all the way to the headwaters not far from the summit of the Cascade Range. This uppermost reach of the McKenzie, upstream from a couple of diversion reservoirs, offers small vibrantly-marked wild trout accessible only to those willing to brave steep and often treacherous banks. Beware the waterfalls. Trails follow both banks from Carmen Reservoir upstream to the two elegant waterfalls (Koosah and Sahalie).

Melakwa Lake

Melakwa Lake is the playground for Melakwa Boy Scout Camp, located off the Old McKenzie Highway southwest of Scott Lake. The lake is stocked annually with rainbows and cutthroat to provide a fishery for the scouts, though it is open to public use as well.

Melis Lake (Mt. Jefferson Wilderness)
hike-in

Five-acre Melis Lake, situated north of Marion Lake, offers fair fishing for planted rainbow trout that can reach 14 inches or more if you happen to be there the right year. The easiest route covers 4.5 miles from the Pine Ridge Trailhead. At milepost 70, turn east off Hwy 22 at Twin Meadows Road (watch for the Camp Pioneer sign). Follow the road uphill 5 miles to the trailhead and head east an easy 3.4 miles to a right-hand turn on the Blue Lake Trail (#3422). Watch for Jenny Lake on your left after about 1 mile. Melis Lake sits behind Jenny. Melis Lake goes through cycles of fair-to-good fishing balanced against years of slow-to-no action, depending on how long it's been since the last stocking.

MHCC Ponds (Multnomah County)

The small ponds on the Mt. Hood Community College Stark Street Campus in Gresham are stocked during the spring with rainbow trout. Fishing holds up during April and May but slows considerably as the summer weather sets in.

Mickey Lake (Waldo Lake Wilderness)
see Brittany Lake

Mildred Lake (Mt. Jefferson Wilderness)
hike-in, cross-country, float tube recommended

Well off the beaten path, Mildred Lake is a lightly fished lake in the northern tip of the Mt. Jefferson Wilderness Area, east from the Firecamp Lakes. Mildred spans just 3 acres and reaches a depth of 11 feet. It has been stocked in past years with brookies, cutthroat, and rainbows, most recently with the latter. At 4,880 feet, it is accessible most years by mid-June. The route to Mildred (and Slideout Lake) begins at the Roaring Creek Trail that leads to Crown Lake and the other Firecamp Lakes: From the town of Detroit, head east on Breitenbush Road for about 11 miles to a right-hand turn onto FR 4685. The trailhead is at the end of the road and heads 1 mile to Crown Lake. A faint bushwhacker's trail departs the north end of Crown Lake and heads east, up and over the ridge-line and down to Mildred Lake. You can pretty easily choose a cross-country route to traverse the ridge, but consult your map. The cross-country hike covers about 2 miles.

Mile Lake (Three Sisters Wilderness)
hike-in

Seven-acre Mile Lake offers fair-to-good fishing for stocked rainbows and cutthroat trout in an area rich in good hike-in lakes. The fish average pan-size but a few reach 14 to 16 inches. Shoreline fishing is pretty easy here, but a float tube is ideal if you're fly angling. The lake sits right on the trail and sees a fair amount of pressure, but serious hikers always seem to outnumber serious anglers.

Mile Lake sits southwest from Horse Lake near the eastern edge of the Three Sisters Wilderness Area, not too far from Elk Lake and Century Drive. The shortest route is from the east on the Horse Lake Trail from Elk Lake Trailhead. Head 4 miles to Horse Lake and turn south at the trail junction. Follow McBee Trail south to a right turn on the Park Trail (#3530), which takes you to Mile Lake after 1 mile.

Milk Creek (Polk County)
no bait, catch-and-release

A nice little forested trout stream 20 miles west of Salem, Mill Creek has only gotten better since the timber company (Willamette Industries) gated the road leading to the upper reaches. Highway 22, leading west from Salem, crosses the creek and immediately thereafter Mill Creek Road turns to the left (south) and heads a few miles up to Mill Creek Park. Shortly thereafter the road turns to gravel and is gated. Hike or bike from there to enjoy the best section of the small creek, a 6-mile-long, shaded reach home to wild cutthroat trout ranging from 4 to 10 inches with a few rare 12- to 14-inch fish. Fishing is best from mid-June through mid-autumn. By late July the water gets very low, at which time the trout congregate in quiet, gin-clear pools.

Mink Lake (Three Sisters Wilderness)
hike-in

Ever-popular Mink Lake is the largest lake in the 242,000-acre Three Sisters Wilderness Area. Mink Lake offers good fishing for stocked rainbows, cutthroat, and brook trout. A few rainbows and brookies reach 14- to 18 inches; most fish range from 8 to 12 inches. All methods produce here and fly anglers can enjoy excellent dry-fly action on still summer evenings when large, skittering caddis hatch around dusk. Likewise, daily hatches of speckled-wing dun mayflies (*Callibaetis*) and Chironomids ("midges") provide fun dry-fly opportunities all summer.

A float tube or other small craft comes in handy despite the long hike, but ample shoreline fishing awaits also. The lake is surrounded by verdant forest and numerous fine, mosquito-infested campsites surround the lake's lengthy shoreline. Surrounding the lake are 2.5 miles of trails, offering easy access.

Mink Lake makes a fine base camp for exploring the myriad other fishable lakes in the immediate vicinity.

Trails arrive from all directions. From central Oregon, the shortest route covers nearly 9 miles and begins at the Doris Lake Trailhead a mile south of Elk Lake on Century Drive. This route takes you for a mile through pine forest before heading into deeper, darker stands of mountain hemlock. The trail is popular with horse-packers as is typically evident by the parking lot full of horse trailers. From the west side of the Cascades, the shortest route to Mink Lake covers about 8 miles on the Crossing Way & McBee Trails. From Blue River, take Hwy 126 east for 3.5 miles and turn right on FR 19 (Aufderheide National Scenic Byway). Continue on for 25 miles to FR 1958, half a mile before you reach Box Canyon Campground. Follow FR 1958 east about 5 miles to a right turn on Spur Road 380. The trailhead for trail #3307 (Crossing Way Trail) is a quarter mile down this spur road on the right, but you can take a mile off the hike by driving to the end of Spur Road 380 and then walking due south cross country (by map & compass) for a half mile until you intercept the McBee Trail. Head east from there.

The campground at Box Canyon is a horse camp and so, not a particularly pristine place to camp when lots of horses are around. If you're horse packing however, the setup is ideal. The trailhead for horse packers is located across the road from the campground, adjacent to the south side of the Box Canyon Guard Station.

Minto-Brown Island Park (Salem)

A 900-acre park adjacent to the Willamette River in Salem, Minto-Brown features myriad sloughs and ponds that are home to a variety of warmwater species. Foot and bicycle access is good on the park's 11 miles of trails and you can fish a lot of untouched water by carrying a canoe or similar small craft by foot over to the sloughs, especially those located at the back parking lot adjacent to the picnic area. Also, power boaters can launch downstream on the Willamette River at Wallace Marine Park and access the largest slough from the river.

The ponds (most are old gravel pits) and sloughs at Minto-Brown offer largemouth bass, crappie, bluegill, catfish, bullheads, and an occasional yellow perch, smallmouth bass, or green sunfish. Smallmouth bass are more common at the mouths of the sloughs and along structure-filled banks along the river (a trail leads along the river for a short distance at the north end of the park).

The main entrance to Minto-Brown Park turns right off River Road South in Salem: From the I-5, take the Hwy 22/Mission Street exit and head west into Salem. Follow Mission Street all the way to a left turn on Commercial Street and after three blocks turn right onto Owens Street/River Road. Follow River Road to the next traffic signal and turn right into the park. Another entrance (Homestead Road) is located another few miles south on River Road.

Minto-Brown Park is a good place to introduce young-sters to fishing as several of the ponds and sloughs offer easy bank fishing opportunity. The fishing is best from late spring through fall, when the Willamette runs at low flows, but during late summer, the sloughs are so low and weed-choked that fishing becomes troublesome.

Mirror Lake (Mt. Hood National Forest)
hike-in
A better scenic attraction than fishery, popular and pretty Mirror Lake sits just off Hwy 26 near Yokum Falls, west of Ski Bowl and Multorpor and Summit Ski Areas. Watch for the trailhead after you come around the last sweeping bend in the highway, heading east toward the mountain. The hike covers 1.4 miles and draws lots of visitors during the summer months. Mirror Lake spans 8 acres and is stocked annually with cutthroat trout or rainbow trout, sometimes both. The fish reach 12 inches, but most are 8 to 10 inches.

Mission Lake (Marion County)
boat ramp, boat or float tube recommended
Mission Lake is one of the long, narrow "oxbow lakes" formed when the Willamette River often changed course prior to the installation of flood-control measures and dams on all major tributaries. Mission Lake is located mostly within Willamette Mission State Park on the east side of the river near Wheatland Ferry, 10 miles north of Salem. Jason Lee founded his Method-ist mission here in 1834 before moving to Salem in 1840.

The fishery covers 20 acres and offers largemouth bass, bluegill, crappie, and bullhead. Only electric motors are allowed and fishing is best during early summer. To get there, take I-5 to the Brooks exit just north of Salem. Head west, crossing the railroad tracks and going straight through a four-way intersection at SR 219 to a right-hand turn on Wheatland Road and then watch for the signs to the park. Follow the entry road (daily fee required) all the way into the main park and watch for boat ramp signs. (See also Goose Lake herein).

Mohawk River (Lane County)
The Mohawk River empties into the McKenzie on the north-eastern outskirts of Springfield. Traditionally it provides about 10 percent of the McKenzie's flow. Dominated by private property, the Mohawk offers limited access for mostly limited fishing for wild cutthroat and rainbow trout. The best fishing occurs during early summer and by late July, the stream flows drop drastically and the water warms substantially. The lower half of the river, essentially all on private land, serves as rearing habitat for cutthroat trout, many of which drop down to the McKenzie. The Mohawk is closed to fishing for its remnant and rare salmon and steelhead. The diminutive upper reaches of the Mohawk can provide good late-season fly fishing for small trout in skinny water.

Marcola lies about halfway up the river, 14 miles from Springfield. All of the river's public access —along with two at-tractive 1930s-vintage covered bridges—lies upstream of the small town. The BLM's Shotgun Creek Recreation Site lies 5 miles upstream and then off to the west on Shotgun Creek.

Molalla River (Clackamas County)
boat ramp
Once an excellent producer of hatchery-produced summer steelhead, the Molalla River is no longer stocked with these fish, so angling is limited to a rather sparse run of native winter steelhead, a small run of spring chinook salmon, resident trout and, in the river's lower-most reaches, smallmouth bass. Most of the salmon-fishing effort occurs on the Molalla's lower few miles during May and June. Winter steelhead arrive between January and April, with the run peaking in March (be sure to check current regulations for open seasons). Though the steelhead-stocking program has long been discontinued, the Molalla continues to produce a fair number of fin-clipped fish, including summer runs. These are strays origi-nally headed for the Willamette's other tributaries. The upper third of this small, 45-mile-long river offers fair-to-good catch-and-release fishing for wild trout.

Salem's Minto-Brown Park offers secluded fishing for warmwater species.

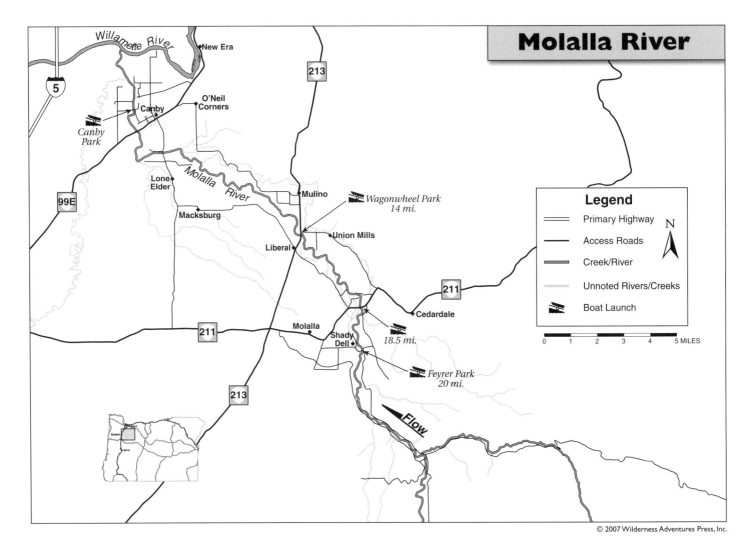

Molalla River

Legend

Primary Highway

Access Roads

Creek/River

Unnoted Rivers/Creeks

Boat Launch

0 1 2 3 4 5 MILES

© 2007 Wilderness Adventures Press, Inc.

Access is quite good on the Molalla, even though most of the river flows across private lands. The Molalla Forest Road closely follows the upper river, upstream from the town of Molalla. This upper portion of the river produces quite a few small, wild trout that love to smack dry flies. Both winter steelhead and stray hatchery summer steelhead occur well into the river system. The North Fork likewise offers good catch-and-release trout fishing. Downstream from Molalla, the river is easily floatable by drift boat all the way to its mouth on the Willamette River upstream from Oregon City. Just east of the town of Molalla, Feyrer Park serves as the upper launch site. At the junction just east of town, turn south at the signs indicating the park. From there, it's 6 miles down to the gravel bar takeout/launch at Wagonwheel Park. Wagonwheel to Canby Park covers about 12 miles and Canby Park to the mouth (Molalla River State Park) covers about 4 miles.

Salmon anglers catch quite a few springers around the mouth of the Molalla and as the salmon fishing slows down during June, fishing the area for smallmouth bass picks up. Crappie are also found off the mouth of the Molalla and the confluence is a popular and productive spot for catfish and brown bullheads. To reach the mouth of the river at Molalla State Park, take I-5 to Exit 278 (Aurora) and head east on Ehlen Road to Aurora. Follow Hwy 99 north to Canby and turn north on Holly Street. Wagonwheel Park is located near the Hwy 213 Bridge north of Molalla.

Moolack Lake (Waldo Lake Wilderness)
hike-in, float tube recommended
Moolack Lake is a scenic, lightly fished 12-acre lake stocked with cutthroat trout. A few fish reach 14 inches, but they average pan-size. The lake sits on a bench south of Moolack Mountain, right on the divide between the Fisher Creek drainage that drops steeply off to the west and the North Fork of the Middle Fork Willamette drainage that plunges off to the east.

From the west (Eugene, etc) head up Salmon Creek Road out of Oakridge and watch for the Y-intersection where FR 2417 heads off to the left. Follow FR 2417 all the way up to a left turn on Spur Road 254, which leads a quarter mile to the Winchester Trailhead (#3594). If you are comfortable with a bit of cross-country travel, take the Winchester Trail (map and compass in hand) east to its junction with Trail #3596 (1.4

miles). From the junction continue due east cross-country until you run into the Blair Lake Trail after about half a mile. This route saves you half a mile, but if you'd prefer to stay on the trails, turn north at the trail junction and follow the route to the next trail junction and turn right (east). Walk another 1.2 miles to the junction with the Six Lakes Trail and continue east. After about a quarter mile, watch for an easy-to-miss trail heading due north to Moolack Lake (if you reach the junction of Trail #3567, Shale Ridge Trail, you have walked too far east).

If you're coming from central Oregon, head for Taylor Burn and head due west on the Blair Lake Trail. At the 2-mile mark you'll reach the Shale Ridge Trail, which heads north. Continue east for a quarter mile watching for the trail heading north to Moolack Lake.

Moonlight Lake (Three Sisters Wilderness)
hike-in, float tube recommended

This trailside lake offers fair-to-good fishing for pan-sized rainbows in a little-used area of the Three Sisters Wilderness Area. The shortest route is from the east side of the wilderness via the Horse Lake and Horse Creek Trails. The trail begins at Elk Lake Trailhead just off Century Drive, 33 miles from Bend. Follow the Horse Lake Trail 4 miles to Horse Lake and then continue north on Horse Creek Trail (#3514) for 2 miles. The lake sits just off the trail, downhill to your left. You can camp at Horse Lake and fish Moonlight and the myriad other productive small lakes in the area (see Aerial, Fisher, Marten, Mile, Platt, Sunset Lakes).

Mowich Lake (Mt. Jefferson Wilderness)
hike-in

Mowich Lake is a large, popular and scenic lake north from Duffy Lake in the Mt. Jefferson Wilderness Area. Spanning 54 acres and reaching a depth of 45 feet, Mowich offers lots of easy shoreline fishing and 19 designated campsites. The hike covers 4.5 miles on the Duffy Lake and Blue Lake Trails. The lake is stocked with brook, cutthroat and rainbow trout and fishing usually holds up fairly well throughout the season, though the action may slow during August. Fall is the best time and the lake yields a handful of 16-inch fish each season.

Mud Lake (Waldo Lake Wilderness)
hike-in

Mud Lake lies just half a mile southeast of Upper Erma Bell Lake in the Three Sisters Wilderness Area north of Taylor Burn. Covering a shallow 6 acres, Mud Lake offers naturally reproducing brook trout, most of which are pan-size or smaller. From the south (Taylor Burn Camp) the hike covers an easy .8 mile, north on Williams Lake trail for a quarter mile and then left on a spur trail leading to the lake. From the north, the trail travels about 3 miles south from Skookum Campground. Stay right at the first trail junction and then left after you pass by the three Erma Bell Lakes. For directions to Taylor Burn and Skookum Campground, see Erma Bell Lakes herein. You'll find ample shore access, but fly anglers might want a float tube

here. The lake offers a strong hatch of both Callibaetis mayflies (speckled-wing duns) and caddisflies throughout the summer. It's usually accessible by mid-June.

Multnomah Channel (Portland)
boat recommended, boat ramp

A 20-mile-long channel branching off from the Willamette River and connecting to the Columbia well to the north, Multnomah Channel forms the western boundary of Sauvie Island, separating the island from the mainland. Multnomah Channel offers a variety of angling opportunities, but is best know for its productive spring chinook salmon fishery that peaks during April and May. Most of the fishing is done by boat, with trolling the primary strategy. The fish range from 12 to 40 pounds, with 15- to 25-pound salmon being typical. Be sure to check current regulations related to salmon angling.

In addition to the salmon fishery, Multnomah Channel offers fair-to-good prospects for bass (smallmouth and largemouth), crappie, yellow perch, walleye, and catfish. The channel abounds in excellent habitat for warmwater fish and anglers fishing by boat and from shore often enjoy fast action. Bank access is fairly good, especially on the Sauvie Island side of the channel, where lots of public land is included in the state wildlife management area. Several boat ramps, indicated by signs along Hwy 30, serve Multnomah Channel.

Nan-Scott Lake

Nan-Scott appears on most maps of the area and is a private lake hidden in the woods behind the town of Marion Forks. No public access.

Nash Lake (Three Sisters Wilderness)
hike-in

A good producer of small brook trout, 33-acre Nash Lake sits toward the northern end of the Three Sisters Wilderness Area. The oft-photographed Sisters Mirror Lake lies a few miles to the east along the same trail. The shortest route, covering more than 7 miles, arrives from the trailhead at Devils Lake on the Cascade Lakes Highway west of Bend.

Neet Lake (Diamond Peak Wilderness)
hike-in

Neet Lake sits just inside the southwest corner of the Diamond Peak Wilderness Area near Emigrant Pass and immediately northeast from Ruth Lake. Stocked with rainbow trout every other year, Neet Lake is 10 feet deep and spans only an acre. At 5,500 feet, the area is accessible most years by late June or early July. Be sure to consult the topographical map to find this tiny lake.

To reach Emigrant Pass from the west, take Hwy 58 through Oakridge. Two miles east of town, turn south on the Kitson Springs Road (FR 21) towards Hills Creek Reservoir. Stay right and follow FR 21 south along the west side of the reservoir. Remain on FR 21 for about 32 miles until you reach a left turn on FR 2154. Follow 2154 about 5 miles to a left turn on FR 2160, which leads north 1.5 miles to Emigrant Pass. From the east side, head for the west shore of Crescent Lake, then follow the rugged route west over Emigrant Pass.

Nekbobets Lake (Olallie Lake Scenic Area)
hike-in

A pretty little lake in a very scenic area, Nekbobets is one a maze of small lakes west from Olallie Lake in the Mount Hood National Forest. The lake (about 2 miles due west from Olallie Lake) is stocked with brook trout and can provide quite good fishing when the trout reach reasonable size after a couple years. To get there, first consult a good map of the area, then take the Pacific Crest Trail west from the trailhead near Olallie Lake Resort or from the Red Lake Trail (#119) departing the road along the west edge of Olallie Lake. Nekbobets Lake sits just off to the west of the junction between the two trails. Its immediate neighbor to the south, Ring Lake, is not stocked.

Nightshade Lakes (Three Sisters Wilderness)
hike-in, cross-country

The two small Nightshade Lakes sit on a broad bench along with Sandy Lake in the northern part of Mink Lake Basin. Both lakes span about 3 acres and reach depths of 16 feet. Fishing depends on how recently the lakes have been stocked. West Nightshade has been stocked with brook trout in the past and more recently with cutthroat while East Nightshade has most recently been stocked with brookies and cutthroat. The two lakes lie immediately west from Krag Lake and just south of Sandy Lake. An un-maintained, informal trail heads west from the main trail north of Dumbell Lake. This route heads for Krag Lake and continues to the Nightshade Lakes. Or just make the trek cross-country after consulting the topo map. The area is dotted with smaller ponds, but the fishable lakes are all larger. All these lakes, including the Nightshades, Krag, Sandy, and April receive little angling pressure owing to the absence of formal trails leading to them. Krag, Sandy, and April are likewise stocked with brookies and/or cutthroat and/or rainbows.

North Fork Reservoir (Clackamas River)

The productive stocked-trout fishery attracts quite a bit of pressure to this 350-acre reservoir located on the Clackamas River south of Estacada. The fishing holds up well from late spring through most of the summer as the impoundment is liberally stocked with legal rainbows by ODFW. A boat is handy, but not necessary and the reservoir has several boat ramps, along with boat rentals and a campground.

North Santiam River
see Santiam River, North

Notch Lake (Diamond Peak Wilderness)
hike-in

Notch Lake is a stunning little jewel nestled into a rocky enclave surrounded by spire-like sub-alpine fir. It lies in the northwestern corner of the Diamond Peak Wilderness. The lake is stocked every other year, generally alternating between cutthroat and rainbow trout, which reach 14 inches. The hike covers an easy mile. Follow Hwy 58 just past Oakridge and turn south toward Hills Creek Reservoir on FR 23. Follow FR 23 all the way up Hills Creek and then up Pinto Creek until you reach the trailhead on your left, across from Hemlock Butte. The trail (#3662 on the left-hand side of the road) starts just past Spur Road 425, which heads west (right) from the main road.

Opal Creek (Marion County)
hike-in, catch-and-release

Opal Creek, a major tributary to the Little North Santiam, offers good catch-and-release fishing for small, wild cutthroat and rainbow trout, along with a few brook trout. Opal Creek is hike-in only: Follow the easy 3-mile-long trail along the Little North Santiam River up to Jawbone Flats and from there head south along Opal Creek. You can also hike down from Opal Lake, though it's brushy and nasty most of the way. (See Santiam River, Little North).

Opal Lake (Detroit area)
hike-in, float tube recommended

This scenic 11-acre lake occupies a timber-clad bowl over the highest ridge north of the town of Detroit. The lake offers small, naturally reproducing brook trout and requires a steep 500-yard hike from the road above, from which it is visible. The fishing can be good, especially if you have a float tube. You can reach Opal from Detroit or from Mehama via the Little North Fork Road. The former route requires a longer drive on gravel but is smoother: Follow the North Fork Road past the community of Elkhorn and then take the right-hand fork on FR 2207. Continue on FR 2207 at each fork thereafter, heading up a steep ridge and then following that ridgeline until you wrap around a corner at a small summit. Look for the lake on the downhill side to your left. The more rugged route begins on the paved French Creek Road just across the bridge from the town of Detroit. When the pavement ends, take the right-hand fork on FR 2207. Follow this road over its rugged, rocky course up, over, and around the ridge until you see the lake downhill on your right.

Opal Lake (Oakridge Ranger District)
hike-in

A fairly good stocked rainbow trout lake, Opal covers about 9 acres and reaches a depth of 30 feet. It is easy to get to via a short hike down from an adjacent forest road and offers a single nice semi-developed campsite featuring a picnic table, fire ring, and pit toilet. This is a pleasant place for a float tube, canoe, or raft on a quiet, cool autumn day. The lake is located just northwest from popular Timpanogas Lake above the headwaters of the Middle Fork Willamette River. To get there, follow Hwy 58 about 2 miles east of Oakridge and turn south onto Kitson Springs Road, which becomes FR 21 and leads about 33 miles to a left turn at FR 2154, about 3 miles past Indigo Springs Campground. Follow 2154 toward Timpanogas Lake. Opal Lake Trail is on your right just before you reach Timpanogas. From the east side (central Oregon) you can get there via the Summit Lake road departing the west end of Crescent Lake. It's not much of a road, but neither is it very far—about 12 miles.

Otter Lake (Three Sisters Wilderness)
hike-in, float tube recommended
This 17-acre rainbow lake sits a stone's throw from the popular Erma Bell Lakes (see listing herein) in a little corner of the Three Sisters Wilderness Area north of Waldo Lake. Otter offers lots of pan-size trout, planted every year, and a few that reach 16 inches, especially for anglers who carry in a float tube to get out away from the brushy shoreline. The lake hosts plenty of anglers, but is usually a quiet, peaceful place during the week. From Skookum Creek Campground to the north, Otter Lake is an easy mile-long walk. See Erma Bell Lakes for directions to the campground at Skookum Creek, then head south on Trail #3563 for .3 of a mile to a left turn on Trail #3589, which takes you right by Otter Lake after half a mile. Alternately you can get there from Taylor Burn Campground to the south via the Williams Lake Trail (3589). See Eastern Brook Lake for directions to Taylor Burn and be sure to consult the maps.

Palmer Creek (Yamhill County)
catch-and-release, no bait
Palmer Creek, highly denuded by residual pesticides, flows entirely through private agricultural property in the flat lands a few miles west of the Willamette River, southeast of McMinnville. After its south-to-north run, Palmer Creek feeds into the South Yamhill at Dayton. Where suitable habitat exists, the creek has a few small native cutthroat.

Pamelia Lake (Mt. Jefferson Wilderness)
hike-in
Pamelia Lake ranks among the most popular destinations in the Mt. Jefferson Wilderness and its naturally reproducing cutthroat are stunted due to over-population. In years past the ODFW allowed an expanded bag limit, but it didn't help much in reducing the trout numbers to foster better growth rates. Nonetheless, Pamelia is a pretty place and a nice place to introduce kids to hike-in lake fishing. The easy walk covers about 2.5 miles and gains about 800 feet in elevation. The signed turnoff (FR 2246) is on the east side of Hwy 22, about half way between Idanha and Marion Forks. Don't leave any valuables in your vehicle at the trailhead.

From Memorial Day weekend to October 31, visitors to Pamelia Lake are required to obtain a special limited-entry permit from the Detroit Ranger District Headquarters in Detroit. Call ahead with your requested dates and the number of people in your party. The headquarters can be reached at 503-854-3366. The lake features 13 designated campsites and fires are banned within 100 feet of the shoreline.

Panther Creek (Yamhill County)
no bait, catch-and-release
Flowing west from the foothills of the coast range, Panther Creek is a fair cutthroat producer, but you'll need permission from landowners to fish this small stream. Panther Creek flows entirely through private properties northwest of McMinnville. There is a minimal amount of road right-of-way at the three crossings, but not enough to warrant the effort. You are better served to seek permission to fish more lengthy sections.

Park Lake (Mt. Jefferson Wilderness)
hike-in
A pretty little 2-acre lake in Jefferson Park in the Mt. Jefferson Wilderness, Park Lake has in the past been stocked with brook trout that don't generally fare well over the winter. For directions, see Bays Lake. Regulations require that visitors to Jefferson Park use only established campsites, and a permanent fire ban is in effect for the area. Only stoves/lanterns using liquid or compressed gas are allowed.

Parish Lake (Willamette National Forest)
hike-in, float tube recommended
A deep, scenic 7-acre lake near Hwy 22 southwest from Marion Forks, Parish Lake offers good fishing for mostly small, naturally reproducing brook trout. The hike down to the lake covers an easy half mile, making Parish a nice place to visit for a little peace and quiet and for a chance at willing brook trout. A few fish reach 14 inches, but most are tiny (from 4 to 8 inches), and in recent years, the fish seem to be few in number. All methods produce here, and while Parish is a great place for youngsters armed with spinning rods, the sparse fish population suggests kids would have more fun at other lakes in the general area. To get there, head east from Salem or west from Sisters toward the town of Marion Forks.

At milepost 74, turn west off the highway onto Parish Lake Road and head west into the woods for about 5 miles to the Parish Lake trailhead on the left side of the road. At 3,300 feet elevation, Parish Lake is usually accessible sometime between early and mid-May, depending on snow pack.

Patjens Lakes (Mt. Washington Wilderness Area)
hike-in
Two of the three small Patjens Lakes offer fair fishing for small trout. Upper Patjens has brookies or cutthroat (depending on the most recent stocking) and covers about 3 acres. Middle Patjens is usually stocked with rainbows. The third lake is too shallow for stocking. This group of lakes sits near the crest of the Cascade Range south of Santiam Summit. The lakes are easy to reach by trail from Big Lake. At the top of the Santiam Pass on Hwy 20/22/126, turn south at the signs for Hoodoo Ski Area and continue past the ski area to Big Lake. The trailhead is past the campground on the lake's west side. From there, the hike to the Patjens Lakes covers 1.4 miles.

Penn Lake (Three Sisters Wilderness)
hike-in

Penn Lake is a large, shallow lake in Cabin Meadows north of Mink Lake in the Three Sisters Wilderness. The lake contains small, wild brook trout and is generally less popular among anglers than the myriad better lakes in the vicinity. Trails lead in from all directions. Penn Lake alone is hardly worth the effort, but many other lakes in the area offer very good fishing.

Photo Lake (Waldo Lake Wilderness)
hike-in, cross-country, float tube recommended

A fairly productive 5-acre rainbow trout fishery, Photo Lake sits off-trail about 1 mile west of Waldo Lake. Lightly fished, the lake is 26 feet deep and capable of growing some impressive fish. Use the Koch Mountain Trail (#3576) to access Photo and nearby Fig, Last, and Cardiac Lakes, all of which require a bushwhacking cross-country course of upwards of 1 mile. In this case, bushwhacking serves as a precise description because some of this region grows dense stands of rhododendron. From Oakridge, head northeast on the Salmon Creek Road (FR 24) until you reach the junction where 24 becomes FR 2420 to the right (gated) and FR 2421 to the left (the main branch). This is the Black Creek Road. Follow it half a mile to a left-hand turn onto FR 2422 and follow this road all the way to its end at the trailhead. From there, the shortest route to Photo follows a southeasterly compass course from the trailhead—consult you topo map first, but beware that Photo Lake and its neighbors are not labeled on the maps. Note their locations from the map herein. The area is dotted with small ponds, all of which are smaller than the fishable lakes. Beware the incessant clouds of mosquitoes throughout the summer. Photo Lake sits at 5,700 feet and is rarely accessible before mid-summer.

Pika Lake (Willamette National Forest)
hike-in, float tube recommended

This little 3-acre pond is the smallest of the four lakes in the Widgeon-Fir-Pika-Fay chain. The trail to Fir Lake takes you right along the shore of Pika (see Fir Lake for directions). Small stocked cutthroat trout occupy the lake and fishing can be fair to good if you have a float tube. Rainbows have been stocked some years. Camp at Fir Lake or Fay Lake or down at Big Meadows.

Pine Ridge Lake (Willamette National Forest)

This is the lake at Camp Pioneer Boy Scout Camp, south of Marion Forks. ODFW plants the 5-acre lake with either cutthroat or brook trout and rainbow, mostly to entertain the scouts during their summer season. Wait until late September (after the camp closes) and sneak into the lake with a float tube. Camp Pioneer surrounds Pine Ridge (or Pineridge) Lake at the top of Pine Ridge Road (FR 2261). From Hwy 22, watch for the sign pointing east to Camp Pioneer about 5 miles south of Marion Forks.

Pinet Lake (Mt. Jefferson Wilderness)
hike-in, cross-country

A 4-acre brook trout lake on the edge of the Mt. Jefferson Wilderness, Pinet is lightly fished owing in part to the lack of a formal trail. Nonetheless, Pinet is easy to find via a cross-country hike covering about a quarter mile starting at the end of a spur road. Blazes in the form of ribbons hang from some of the tree branches, marking the route to Pinet. From Hwy 22, at the south end of Marion Forks just past the fish hatchery, turn east on Horn Creek Road (FR 2257) and then take a right on Spur Road 515. Follow 515 past Presley Lake (on your left near the top of the ridge). If the road is gated just past Presley Lake, you'll have to walk the remaining 1.5 miles to the end of the road. From the end of the spur, head southwesterly to the lake. A slightly larger lake lies just to the west—informally called Bear Lake and too shallow to support fish. Be sure to consult the topo map.

Platt Lake (Three Sisters Wilderness)
hike-in

Located trailside south of Horse Lake, scenic, 8-acre Platt Lake is stocked every other year with rainbows and/or cutthroat trout. They reach at least 14 inches, but the majority of the fish range from 8 to 11 inches. Platt sits just across the Horse Mt./McBee Trail from Herb Lake. To get there, take the Horse Lake Trail west from the Elk Lake Trailhead, located 33 miles from Bend on Century Drive. At the 4-mile mark, turn south and then take the second right turn after half a mile. Another 1.2 miles takes you to Platt Lake on the right-hand side of the trail. Other good lakes in the immediate area include Aerial, West Fisher, East Fisher, Herb, Marten, and Mile Lakes. (See separate listings).

Plumb Lake (Three Sisters Wilderness Area)
hike-in

A fairly large, productive lake in the Mink Lake Basin, Plumb Lake offers a fairly dense population of small brook trout, ranging from 5 to 10 inches. Plumb Lake, spanning about 12 acres, lies about 1 mile northwest of Mink Lake, adjacent to Trail #3523. Mink Lake Basin is very popular with hikers and trails arrive from all sides. See Mink Lake herein for directions.

Pope Lake (Sauvie Island)

A fairly productive warmwater fishery on Sauvie Island, 10-acre Pope Lake offers brown bullhead, crappie, and a few largemouth bass. The short hike, heading south from the hunter's check station, covers about half a mile. Take Hwy 30 north from Portland and cross over to Sauvie Island on the bridge. Turn right on Reeder Road and follow it around until you reach the check station.

Porky Lake (Three Sisters Wilderness Area)
hike-in

A popular and productive 30-acre lake in the Mink Lake Basin, Porky Lake offers lots of small, naturally reproducing brook trout, along with very nice campsites. The area attracts a lot of visitors during the summer backpacking season, so serious anglers might want to wait until after Labor Day, when the crowds thin and the brook trout fishing picks up. See Mink Lake herein for directions to the area.

Presley Lake (Willamette National Forest)

A 2-acre pond surrounded by clear-cuts, Presley Lake lies just a few miles from the tiny town of Marion Forks along Hwy 22. You can drive right to the lake for fair-to-good action on pan-sized planted rainbows. Half a mile south of Marion Forks, turn left on Horn Creek Road (FR 2257) and stay on the road as you ascend a steep ridge. About a mile after the road switches back after climbing the steep part of the ridge, watch for Spur Road 515 on your left. Follow 515 half a mile to the lake.

Prill Lake (Mt. Jefferson Wilderness)
hike-in, cross-country

Prill Lake is a beautiful little brook trout lake situated near the edge of a big lava flow a thousand feet above the east shore of Marion Lake in the Mt. Jefferson Wilderness. Prill doesn't get much pressure because neither route up to the lake is particularly fun. One route, the easier of the two if you don't mind a steep climb, ascends the ridge where Mist Creek dumps down into Marion Lake: Follow the Minto Pass Trail around the eastern extent of Marion Lake (see Marion Lake for details on how to get there). The main trail swings close to Marion Lake at Mazama Creek and follows fairly close to the shore for a quarter mile. Then the trail swings away from the lake and after about another quarter mile crosses Mist Creek. If you cross the Mist Creek streambed (the next streambed after Mazama Creek), you've just missed the bushwhacker trail that climbs up to Prill Lake.

The second route to Prill Lake is rougher but not nearly so steep. First consult the directions herein to Marion Lake. After you pass Lake Ann on the trail into Marion Lake, take the left-hand fork at each of three trail junctions. The first junction is a quarter mile past Lake Ann. The second is at the northwest corner of Marion Lake and the third is the signed junction with the Whiskey Lake/Lake of the Woods Trail. After taking a left at the Whiskey Lake Trail, head northeast a little more than a mile until you cross a streambed. This is the outlet from Prill Lake. Follow the stream's course southeast (uphill to your right) a little over a mile to Prill Lake, but don't mistake Prill for the 2-acre pond that lies along the streambed adjacent to the main lake.

Prill Lake covers a scenic 8 acres and its brook trout range from 8 to 16 inches. All methods produce here and the lake offers two nice campsites, one at each end. Or you can camp down at Marion Lake and carry just enough gear for half a day's fishing up at Prill, which makes the climb a lot easier than with a full pack. Either way you're likely to have the lake all to yourself.

Pyramid Creek (Willamette National Forest)

A lengthy tributary to the Middle Santiam River, Pyramid Creek offers fair-to-good fishing for small, wild trout assuming you're tough enough to get at them. The best part of the creek, below its confluence with Single Creek, runs through a steep-sided, forested gorge. Logging roads approach both sides of the creek near its mouth; otherwise you must climb down from roads running somewhat parallel to the creek. Pyramid Creek lies west of Parish Lake. Consult the Detroit Ranger District Map for specific directions.

Pyramid Lake (Mt. Hood National Forest)
hike-in

A fair-to-good producer of cutthroat trout, easy-to-reach 4-acre Pyramid Lake is located on the Clackamas drainage in the High Rocks area. Head south up the Clackamas River on SR 224, past Ripplebrook Ranger Station and up to FR 58. Follow FR 58 past Shellrock Campground to FR 140, which ends at the Pyramid Lake Trailhead. The lake is usually accessible by June and produces cutthroat to 12 inches, with most ranging from 7 to 10 inches.

Quartzville Creek (Linn County)
campgrounds

A major tributary to Green Peter Reservoir near Sweet Home, Quartzville Creek is stocked with catchable rainbow trout, providing a productive and scenic put-and-take fishery. The creek runs for many miles through public property and is followed virtually all the way by FR 11, the Quartzville Scenic Route. Quartzville Creek also offers some native cutthroat and wild rainbows, which become increasingly common—though never abundant—as you progress upstream.

The creek features a broad spectrum of water types, from gin-clear, bubble-shot pools to swift, rushing cascades. Stocked several times each year the creek holds up well all season (late April through October). This is beautiful, forested country and a great place to take the family for some catch-and-keep stream fishing. A nice BLM campground (Yellow Bottom) sits streamside about 10 miles past Green Peter Reservoir and informal campsites abound.

You can reach Quartzville Creek from the west via Sweet Home and Hwy 20 or from the east via Hwy 22. From Hwy 22, 3 miles south of Marion Forks, head west on the Straight Creek Road (gravel), which reaches the upper stretch of Quartzville Creek after about 15 miles. From Sweet Home, head east on Hwy 20. At the east end of Foster Reservoir watch for a left-hand turn to Green Peter Reservoir. Continue northeasterly, winding your way along the north shore of Green Peter, up the Quartzville Arm of the reservoir and up to the creek itself.

Questionmark Lake (Three Sisters Wilderness)
hike-in

A popular and productive lake at the northeast corner of the Mink Lake Basin, Questionmark spans about 10 acres and offers good fishing for small rainbows trout and sometimes for cutthroat trout (depending on recent stockings). Easiest access is from the trail leading in from the east, heading across the Cascade Lakes Highway from Elk Lake. The trails are usually passable by mid-June.

Quinn Lakes (Waldo Lake Wilderness)
hike-in, cross-country, float tube recommended

Upper and Lower Quinn Lakes, 20 acres and 25 acres respectively, are fairly popular with anglers, but often deserted, especially if you visit them mid-week or if you wait until late September. Lower Quinn, the northernmost of the two, offers rainbows and Upper Quinn has been stocked most recently with cutthroat and brook trout. Both lakes occasionally kick out 15-inch fish.

Trails lead to the Quinn Lakes from several starting points. From the west, the easiest route (in my opinion) to Lower Quinn is to take the Winchester Trail (#3594) heading east for 1.4 miles to its junction with the Winchester Ridge Trail (#3596). From the junction, take off cross-country for half a mile on an east-by-southeast heading. If you cross a second trail along your route, you've walked right by Lower Quinn, but that's not likely if you have a little experience with map & compass. Otherwise, take a left at the trail junction and walk a quarter mile to Trail #3553. Turn right and walk a mile. Lower Quinn will be on your left.

Likewise, the easiest way to reach Upper Quinn is by a 1-mile cross-country walk northeast from FR 2417. See Long Lake for directions to the area. From the end of FR 2417, stay left of the summit of 5,848-foot Winchester Ridge. You'll gain about 250 feet elevation over the first quarter mile and then lose about 600 feet between the ridge and the lake, crossing the Winchester Ridge Trail along the way.

From the east, head west on the Blair Lake Trail from the campground at Taylor Burn. After 2.5 miles, turn left on the Six Lakes Trail, which skirts within a few hundred yards of Lower Quinn and passes right by Upper Quinn and then Long Lake. Beware the road into Taylor Burn, which is quite rugged.

Rainbow Lake (Idanha)

A private lake near Idanha with no public access.

Ralph's Lake (Mt. Jefferson Wilderness)
hike-in, cross-country

A 2-acre cutthroat trout lake in the Duffy Lake area, Ralph's Lake kicks out a few 15-inch brookies, though most fish are much smaller. Take the Duffy Lake Trail to its junction with the Lava Trail (#3433). From the junction, make a quarter-mile compass course to the lake. Alternately, from the same trail junction or from Santiam Lake, just follow the diminutive North Santiam River headwaters directly to Tom's Lake and then head westerly about 200 yards to Ralph's Lake. See Duffy Lake for directions to the trailhead. Generally you'll have Ralph's Lake to yourself and a float tube is handy here. The lake is generally accessible by mid-June.

Rat Creek (Lane County)

A short tributary to Dorena Reservoir, Rat Creek offers limited opportunities for harvesting wild trout during the general season, during which bait is allowed. Catch-and-release, artificials-only rules apply during the rest of the year. Rat Creek flows into Dorena on the north side at Harms Picnic Area. Brice Creek, Sharps Creek, and Laying Creek—all tributaries to the Row River above Dorena Reservoir—are the better fisheries if you're in the area and looking for some stream fishing.

Red Lake (Olallie Scenic Area)

Usually planted with brook trout every other year, 4-acre Red Lake sits atop a steep ridge at the west edge of the Olallie Scenic Area northeast from Detroit and southeast from Estacada. Popular Averill Lake (see separate listing) lies just to the northeast along the same trail. The shortest route arrives via the Breitenbush Road (FR 46) east of Detroit. Follow FR 46 all the way to the Mt. Hood National Forest border and turn right on FR 4220, which heads east toward Breitenbush Lake. After half a mile turn left on Spur Road 380 and follow it to the trailhead (#719) a few hundred yards north of the overhead power lines. From the north (Estacada), follow FR 46 south and then you can turn left onto Spur Road 380. It's .7 of a mile to the trailhead. The hike covers an easy 1.2 miles.

Red Butte Lake (Mt. Jefferson Wilderness)
hike-in

Deep and capable of growing brookies to respectable size (I've taken a few 14-inchers here in years past), Red Butte Lake is simply too close to the trail leading through ever-popular Eight-Lakes Basin in the Mt. Jefferson Wilderness Area. Its planted brookies average about 9 inches. Spanning 6 acres, Red Butte is located halfway between Mowich Lake and Jorn Lake, just off to the west side of the trail connecting the two larger lakes. The lake is named for Red Butte, which provides a nice overview of the area. From Alice Lake or Red Butte Lake, the short climb to the top of Red Butte gains about 700 feet.

Rigdon Lakes (Waldo Lake Wilderness)
hike-in

Fairly popular with anglers, the two 50-acre Rigdon Lakes offer fair-to-good fishing for planted rainbows and brook trout (Upper Rigdon) and planted rainbows and cutthroat trout (Lower Rigdon). In both lakes the trout range from 9 to 13 inches or so. The entire area was burned by a large wildfire in 1996, so visitation is down. From North Waldo Campground, the trail into Upper Rigdon (the southernmost of the two lakes) covers an easy 2.7 miles. Lower Rigdon is a quarter mile further north along the trail. From the north, the trail from Taylor Burn Campground covers about 3 miles to Lower Rigdon. The Rigdon Lakes sit at an elevation of about 5,500 feet, making them inaccessible before mid-June.

Riggs Lake (Willamette National Forest)
hike-in, float tube recommended

Riggs Lake is a lightly fished 3-acre beauty located about 1.5 miles northwest from Parish Lake, west from Hwy 22 in the Willamette National Forest. At milepost 74, turn west off the highway onto Parish Lake Road and head west into the woods for about 5 miles to Parish Lake Trailhead. Drive about a mile past this trailhead until you cross the second of two stream-beds (the road makes a wide bend). After another .3 of a mile, watch closely for a signed trail on the right side of the road (parking is just a wide shoulder on the gravel road). The easy hike covers less than half a mile. The lake has been alternately stocked with brookies, rainbows, and cutthroat, with the latter species apparently the fish of choice these days. They grow to at least 13 inches here, sometimes bigger, and most range from 8 to 12 inches. The lake offers outstanding summer hatches of *Callibaetis* mayflies. However, catch this little lake on an off year, and it holds few or no trout. Though extremely brushy, the shoreline is fishable by foot because on one side of the lake, large boulders allow good access, and on the other, several large logs jutting into the lake make nice casting perches. A float tube is a nice luxury here, but beware the many submerged stick-ups. One nice little campsite sits on the far side of the lake—just follow the trail around to the inlet. (See also Don Lake).

Robinson Lake (Mt. Washington Wilderness)
hike-in

Popular and productive Robinson Lake sits on the western border of the Mt. Washington Wilderness Area a few miles southeast from Clear Lake and Hwy 126. Its stocked cutthroat and rainbows range from 8 to 18 inches, with most being pan-size. To get there, follow Hwy 126 south from Santiam Junction or northeast from McKenzie Bridge. About 2 miles south from Carmen Reservoir and 3 miles north from Trail Bridge Reservoir, FR 2664 (Robinson Lake Road) heads east from the highway near milepost 8. This good gravel road leads about 4.5 miles up to the quarter-mile trail into Robinson Lake. Robinson covers about 6 acres and reaches a depth of 18 feet.

Rock Lake (Mt. Jefferson Wilderness)
hike-in

Rock Lake is a beautiful, small lake in Jefferson Park (See Bays Lake for directions). Covering 8 acres, but only 6 feet deep, Rock Lake suffers winterkill problems so, when present, the fish rarely grow large. They tend to be few in number and are stocked infrequently. A few perhaps escape nearby Scout Lake to find their way into Rock Lake. Nonetheless, it's an awfully pretty place and worth a look if you're fishing nearby Bays Lake and Scout Lake. Regulations require that visitors to Jefferson Park use only established campsites and a permanent fire ban is in effect for the area. Only stoves/lanterns using liquid or compressed gas are allowed. Rock Lake offers three designated and highly scenic campsites.

Rockpile Lake (Diamond Peak Wilderness)
hike-in

This beautiful cutthroat lake offers good fishing between mid-June and mid-autumn. It is fairly popular during summer, but virtually deserted by mid-September. Rockpile covers about 5 acres and reaches a depth of 25 feet. Cutthroat trout, usually stocked each year, over-winter successfully but don't grow very quickly in this relatively infertile, 6,100-foot lake. Most fish range from 8 to 10 inches with a few that reach 14 inches.

The Rockpile Lake Trail (#3632) covers an easy 2.5 miles. To reach the trailhead, follow Hwy 58 about 2 miles east of Oakridge and turn south onto Kitson Springs Road. Follow this road (FR 21) about 30 miles to its junction with FR 2149, just past Indigo Springs Campground. Turn left onto 2149 and continue about 4 miles to a right-hand turn onto FR 2160. Follow 2160 uphill 2.5 miles to the trailhead.

Rockpile Lake (Mt. Jefferson Wilderness)
see Central Zone

Rooster Rock Slough (Multnomah County)
boat ramp, boat recommended, float tube recommended

Located in Rooster Rock State Park along I-84 east of Portland, this narrow slough houses a protected boat launch used by anglers fishing the adjacent Columbia River. The slough itself is a good bet for crappie, bass, and other Columbia River species. The state park offers ample parking for a modest fee and ready access to the ramp. Fishing is best between mid-spring and mid-autumn and the slough has been known to yield some large smallmouth bass, walleye, and even a few

The author holds a brook trout from a lake in the Three Sisters Wilderness.

sturgeon. It's small enough for a float tube or similar craft, but plenty big enough for a boat.

Round Lake (Mt. Hood National Forest)
hike-in, float tube recommended, no bait

Once home to some impressive-sized brown trout, Round Lake rarely if ever produces such fish anymore. Instead it offers mostly small brook trout, along with a few browns in the 8- to 13-inch range, and is restricted to flies and artificial lures. The lake has a two-fish limit with an 8-inch minimum length. Round Lake spans 9 acres and reaches a depth of about 20 feet. It sits high above the upper reaches of the Collawash River in the southern end of the Mt. Hood National Forest. Severe landslides wiped out the old access road some years ago, so the easiest route now is to follow Hwy 22 east from Salem to Detroit. At Detroit, turn left onto Breitenbush Road and then left again (after crossing the Breitenbush River) onto Humbug Road (FR 4696). Follow FR 4696 all the way to the top, where three roads converge. Turn left on FR 6370, which crosses the headwaters of the Collawash and then leads a few miles to the Round Lake Trailhead. The hike covers about a quarter mile.

Round Lake (Waldo Lake Wilderness)
hike-in

Round Lake is located adjacent to the popular Eddeeleo Lakes just northwest from Waldo Lake and just outside the Charlton Burn that scorched the area in 1996. Rectangular in shape, Round Lake spans 22 acres and usually offers good fishing for small, wild brook trout and stocked rainbows that can reach 16 inches. The trail heading west from North Waldo Campground reaches Round Lake after about 3 miles. From the east, the easiest route is a cross-country hike from the Swan Lake Trailhead at the end of FR 2417. Check the map and then head southeast over Winchester Ridge for about a mile to pick up the Six Lakes Trail at Lower Eddeeleo Lake and head uphill another mile or so to reach Upper Eddeeleo and Round Lakes. If you'd prefer to stay on the trails, take the Six Lakes Trail south from its junction with the Blair Lake Trail, which heads at Taylor Burn to the east and off Spur Road 254 (from FR 2417) on the west. It's a long walk.

Row River (Lane County)

The Row River is a short tributary to the Coast Fork Willamette near Cottage Grove. The river is dammed to form popular Dorena Reservoir, effectively dividing the Row into two different fisheries. Above the reservoir, the river offers wild trout, mostly cutthroat, but access is tight owing to extensive private property. Always ask permission before crossing private land.

Rainbows and a few cutthroat inhabit the river below Dorena Reservoir, where access remains problematic. One popular spot is Schwartz Park just below the dam, where anglers find a few big rainbows along with an occasional chinook salmon or steelhead. The other popular spot is the mouth of the river at the confluence with the Coast Fork, near Riverside Speedway.

During the general season, bait is allowed on the Row River and a five-fish limit applies. Throughout the rest of the year, the creek is governed by catch-and-release rules and no bait is allowed.

Russell Lake (Mt. Jefferson Wilderness)
hike-in

Russell Lake, located in Jefferson Park in the northern portion of the Mt. Jefferson Wilderness, offers splendid views of the mountain and good fishing for stocked rainbows and brook trout. Cutthroat trout have been stocked in the past. The lake spans about 10 acres and reaches depths of 27 feet. The fishing holds up fairly well, though the fish grow slowly and average pan-size. For directions to Jefferson Park, see Bays Lake. Regulations require that visitors to Jefferson Park use only established campsites and a permanent fire ban is in effect for the area. Only stoves/lanterns using liquid or compressed gas are allowed. Russell Lake offers four designated campsites; if they are already taken, camp at least 250 feet away from the lake shore. Shoreline fishing is easy at Russell Lake, which features minimal casting obstacles for fly anglers and myriad rocks that serve nicely as casting platforms. The lake is accessible by late June.

Ruth Lake (Diamond Peak Wilderness)
hike-in

Ruth Lake sits just inside the southwest corner of the Diamond Peak Wilderness Area near Emigrant Pass. The lake is 15 feet deep and spans less than 2 acres. ODFW stocks it with either brook or cutthroat trout usually every other year. At 5,500 feet, Ruth Lake is accessible most years by late June. Be sure to consult the topographical map to find this tiny lake.

To reach Emigrant Pass from the west, take Hwy 58 through Oakridge. Two miles east of town, turn south on the Kitson Springs Road (FR 21) towards Hills Creek Reservoir. Stay right and follow FR 21 south along the west side of the reservoir. Remain on FR 21 for about 32 miles until you reach a left turn on FR 2154. Follow 2154 about 5 miles to a left turn on FR 2160, which leads north to a mile and a half to Emigrant Pass. From the east side, head for the west shore of Crescent Lake, then follow the rugged route west over Emigrant Pass.

Sad Lake (Mt. Jefferson Wilderness)
hike-in, cross-country

Seldom-fished Sad Lake sits at 5,100 feet just off the Swallow Lake Trail in the Mt. Jefferson Wilderness Area. Spanning 2 acres and reaching a depth of 10 feet, Sad Lake is stocked with brookies every few years. The hike covers about 4.5 miles. Take the Marion Lake trail to the Lake of the Woods Trail and onto the Swallow Lake Trail. Offering splendid views of the mountains, Sad Lake sits off to the south side of the trail half a mile east from the Swallow Lake/Lake of the Woods Trail. See Marion Lake for driving directions.

St. Louis Ponds (Marion County)

A group of seven small man-made ponds near I-5 south of Woodburn, St. Louis Ponds offer good fishing for a variety of warmwater species, including bluegill, redear sunfish, crappie, brown bullhead, and largemouth bass. The area is very popular and the ponds were designed and dug out in a maze-like pattern to provide maximum shoreline for angling. No floating devices are allowed and none are needed. The area offers a large central parking area, a wheelchair-accessible path at pond #3, and a separate dog training area. From I-5, take Exit 271 (Woodburn) and head west to a left-hand turn on Butteville Road. Follow Butteville Road south, over the freeway. About 1.5 miles past the freeway, take the right-hand turn leading due west, and then turn right again on St. Louis Road, again crossing the freeway. Turn left on Tesch Road, leading to the ponds.

Salmon Creek (Lane County)

campground

This large, scenic creek near Oakridge offers fair-to-good trout fishing with harvest opportunity. Access is good and the creek is popular during summer, especially on weekends. The best fishing occurs from July through mid-October. In Oakridge, turn north on Crestview Street and then take a right on 1st Street, which becomes Salmon Creek Road (FR 24). Forest Road 24 follows the creek for about 10 miles and Salmon Falls Campground lies about 3 miles upstream from Oakridge.

Salmon River (Mt. Hood National Forest)

catch-and-release, no bait, campgrounds

A very pretty tributary to the Sandy River, the Salmon River once hosted a popular run of hatchery summer steelhead. Few of these fish reach the Salmon River since the decision was made to intercept the hatchery fish at Marmot Dam on the Sandy. But the Salmon still hosts a small run of wild winter steelhead, along with a few salmon, and also has fair populations of wild trout. The river's salmon and steelhead are now protected and there is no open season for them. Trout fishing is catch-and-release, artificials-only. Forest roads provide good access to the river between the community of Welches and Green Canyon Campground to the south, but the Salmon River's real treasure is a verdant, waterfall-laden wilderness reach accessible only by trail. The upper half of the river is the centerpiece of the Salmon-Huckleberry Wilderness Area and those willing to hike the trail along the river are treated to spectacular forest scenery and good fishing during the summer for small native trout. The fishing here can be a bit on the physically demanding side, with lots of steep descents to the river and plenty of swift, rugged water. The trail begins near Green Canyon Campground on FR 2618. From Hwy 26, east of Brightwood, turn south on Salmon River Road, which is just east of the fire station and Territory Restaurant.

Salt Creek (Yamhill/Polk Counties)

This small stream meanders entirely through private lands for 32 miles between Hwy 22 (west of Salem) and its confluence with the South Yamhill near Amity. Where suitable habitat exists, small native cutthroat trout inhabit Salt Creek, but you'll need landowner permission to pursue them (catch-and-release only).

Sandy Lake (Three Sisters Wilderness)

hike-in, cross-country

Sandy Lake occupies a broad, forested bench, along with the Nightshade Lakes, in the northern part of Mink Lake Basin. Fishing on this remote lake depends on how recently it has been stocked, but there always seems to be a few large fish available. In recent years Sandy has been stocked with both brook trout and rainbows. No formal trails reach Sandy Lake, but it's quite easy to find by compass course from the McBee Trail to the west or the Pacific Crest Trail to the east. Also, an informal trail that is not maintained, heads west from the main trail north of Dumbell Lake. This route heads for Krag Lake and continues to the Nightshade Lakes. Consult the topo maps. The area is dotted with smaller ponds, but Sandy spans about 12 very attractive acres. All these lakes in the immediate vicinity—the West Nightshade, East Nightshade, Krag, Sandy, and April—receive little angling pressure owing to the absence of formal trails leading to them. Be sure to consult the topo map.

Sandy River

boat ramp, campground

The Sandy River is a rather remarkable stream in the sense that it produces consistently good fishing for steelhead and salmon despite its immediate proximity to the Northwest's second-largest metropolitan area. The Sandy drains a sizeable portion of the Mt. Hood area, gathering several important tributaries, before flowing into the Columbia at Troutdale, a few miles east of Portland. Interstate-84 crosses the Sandy near the river's mouth and local roads access the river along its northwesterly course north of Hwy 26 and east of Gresham.

The Sandy is perhaps best known for its strong runs of winter steelhead, which enter the river as early as late November and as late as April. Both wild and hatchery fish are available. The peak season extends from late December through March. The Sandy's wild steelhead range from 6 to more than 20 pounds. Truly huge steelhead are rare, but the river kicks out quite a few 10- to 14-pound fish each year. Each year the precise peak of the run varies, but steelhead swim the Sandy every month of the year and are available in good numbers throughout the winter season.

Smaller runs of hatchery-produced summer steelhead enter the Sandy River as early as late March, but most arrive between May and July, with a later and much smaller push of fish during early autumn. Because of its glacial sources, however, the Sandy runs off-color from early to mid-summer through September or later. Warm weather on Mt. Hood is the culprit and the glacial till makes the river essentially unfishable. So for summer steelhead, May, June, and November tend to be the top months and from mid- to late November, summer and winter fish tend to occupy the river side-by-side.

A few years ago, Marmot Dam, at river mile 30 on the Sandy River, was decommissioned and removed, opening many miles of spawning habitat to salmon and steelhead. Despite many opinions to the contrary, the old river channel began to stabilized and flush itself very rapidly and anadromous fish began using the newly available river and tributaries virtually overnight. Naturally, in response to such an historic achievement in the removal of the dam, the ODFW had to re-evaluate all management plans for the river and its fisheries. Management highlights include the following:

For winter steelhead, ODFW initiated the conversion to a hatchery stock native to the Sandy Basin in 2001. Beginning in 2004, all returning winter steelhead were Sandy stock. In addition, ODFW shifted the annual release locations of the 160,000 smolts away from Marmot Dam to ODFW's Sandy Hatchery in the lower river. This shift was made to acclimate the fish to a lower section of the river and helps maintain the wild fish sanctuary in the upper river. The conversion to a local brood stock reduces risks to the wild population by more closely mimicking the habits of wild fish.

With spring chinook salmon, ODFW also shifted to a new brood stock from wild fish. By 2007, the brood conversion was completed and out-of-basin stocks removed. Like the winter steelhead, the annual release site for the 300,000 smolts was moved to the lower river.

The ODFW continues to stock the river annually with some 700,000 Sandy Basin coho salmon smolts, releasing them at Sandy Hatchery on Cedar Creek. Less than 2 percent of hatchery coho currently attempt to spawn above Marmot Dam, which meets recovery goals for the species.

Summer steelhead did not historically spawn in the Sandy Basin, so the sport fishery there is the product of hatchery-produced stock. The usual stocking allotment for the Sandy is 75,000 smolts, released at Cedar Creek on the lower river, though ODFW may decide to use additional acclimation sites to minimize straying into the wild fish sanctuary on the upper river.

The Sandy is rich in ideal spawning habitat for anadromous fish and is fortunate to avoid the Portland area's industrialized areas. Consequently the river boasts upwards of 20,000 returning steelhead annually, including both winter and summer fish, hatchery and wild. Several thousand wild winter steelhead spawn in the Sandy.

Anglers on the Sandy use virtually every conceivable steelhead fishing method. The river offers a full spectrum of water types conducive to everything from plunking and drift fishing to jig-and-bobber fishing and traditional fly angling. The extreme lower river—from the Troutdale Bridge to the mouth—is especially popular with plunkers and jig anglers and offers plenty of bank access. Boat anglers enjoy consistent success pulling plugs, free drifting, and fishing conventional drift gear.

Power boats are allowed as high as Dabney Park and fishing from a boat is not permitted upstream from the power lines located about 1 mile below Oxbow Park. All told, the lower half of the Sandy offers about 30 miles of fishable water from the mouth upstream to Marmot Dam. The popular drift segments include the upper drift from Dodge (river mile 18.5) to Oxbow Park and on this stretch you must get out of the boat to fish. Oxbow to Dabney Park is a very popular daylong run covering a wealth of excellent water and the Dabney Park-to-Lewis & Clark State Park run is equally popular and productive.

Lewis & Clark State Park is located at Troutdale, south of I-84. Take Exit 18 and follow the signs. Exit 18 also delivers you to Dabney Park and Oxbow Park. Just continue south for 4 miles along the old highway that follows the river's east bank

The Sandy River offers excellent steelhead prospects just minutes from Portland.

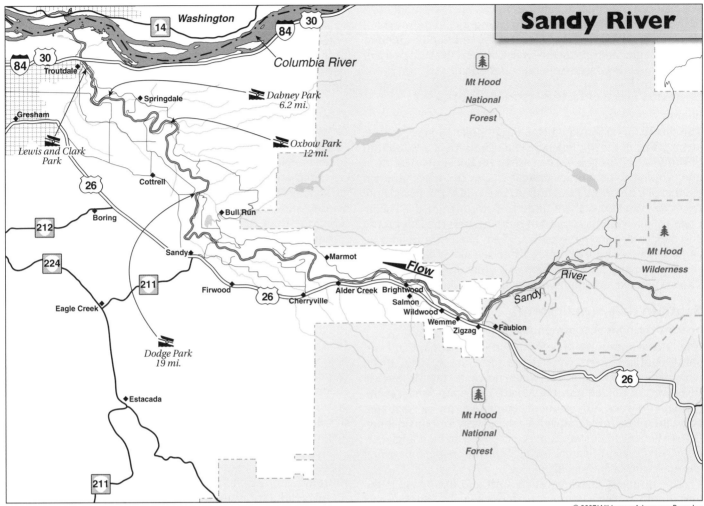

© 2007 Wilderness Adventures Press, Inc.

to reach Dabney Park (river mile 6-7). Continue past Dabney Park to Springdale and take the signed right-hand turn to reach Oxbow Park (river miles 10-14). To reach Dodge Park, follow Hwy 26 heading east from Gresham and turn left onto Powell Valley Road. Follow the signs to the park (at the end of Dodge Park Boulevard). Or from Oxbow Park, follow Hosner Road south to Oxbow Park Boulevard.

Upstream from the old Marmot Dam site, wild winter steelhead provide a fair catch-and-release fishery near the communities of Brightwood and Welches. This stretch of the river is traditionally known as Messinger Bottom. These wild fish are bigger than their hatchery brethren, with some surpassing 20 pounds. The catch-and-release fishery is fairly popular with fly anglers, who enjoy fairly consistent success when water levels cooperate. The general upper angling cutoff is the mouth of the Salmon River, located downstream from Welches. However, more recently ODFW opened even more of the river for artificials-only (no bait) summer steelhead fishing: The mainstem and tributaries upstream of the ODFW markers at the mouth of the Salmon River, including the Salmon River, are open to clipped and non-clipped summer

steelhead from July 1 through Aug. 31. Angling in this area is restricted to artificial flies and lures with a single-point hook no larger than 0.5-inch gap (size 1) and multiple-point hooks no larger than 0.375-inch gap (size 4).

The Sandy River's spring chinook fishery has become increasingly productive and popular. The run typically comprises 5,000 to 10,000 fish and peaks during May and June. These springers typically range from 18 to 22 pounds, with a few fish reaching the 30- to 35-pound mark. Chinook salmon are available up to the angling deadline at the mouth of the Salmon River. Most salmon anglers rely on plugs or divers tipped with shrimp; spinners are popular with bank anglers. Hatchery-produced coho salmon enter the river during late summer and autumn and are available for harvest from August through October. At the same time, fall chinook salmon enter the river in modest numbers, providing another harvest opportunity for fin-clipped fish. These fall chinook darken quickly and are generally limited to the river's lower 20 miles.

The Sandy River, with its fairly stable and healthy riparian habitat, tends to clear quickly after the frequent winter rain events. Ideal fishing flows range from about 700 to as high as 4,000 cubic feet per second, so the Sandy is fishable most of the time. Area tackle stores, including fly-fishing shops in Gresham and Welches, keep close tabs on the Sandy and offer or arrange guided trips on the river. Contact ODFW for a list of fishing guides licensed to operate on the Sandy.

Santiam Lake (Mt. Jefferson Wilderness)
hike-in

The source of the Santiam River, this popular 16-acre gem sits at 5,200 feet in the Mt. Jefferson Wilderness Area, a mile south of Duffy Lake. Santiam is a consistent producer of brook trout and rainbows, some of which reach 12 to 16 inches. You can get there by following the Santiam Lake Trail south from Duffy Lake (see directions there under) or north from the Pacific Crest Trailhead at the summit of Santiam Pass. The latter route covers 5.5 miles and gains only 377 feet. The Duffy Trail Route gains 1,125 feet over 4.5 miles. Santiam Lake is generally accessible by early June and features a great view of 7,841-foot Three-Fingered Jack along with 14 nice designated campsites.

Santiam River (mainstem)
boat ramp, boat recommended

Near the community of Jefferson, the North Santiam and South Santiam Rivers converge to form the Santiam River, which then flows about 12 miles down to the Willamette River west of I-5 and north of Albany. Interstate-5 crosses the Santiam between Albany and Salem, and a freeway rest area adjacent to the bridge provides good access for bank fishing. Otherwise, the mainstem is most accessible to boat anglers—especially power boaters—who fish the river for spring chinook salmon and steelhead.

The springers arrive between April and June. May is the best month, but watch the counts for Willamette Falls because during some years, lots of fish enter the system during April. Lots of steelhead are taken incidentally by salmon anglers. Wild winter fish (no fin clip) must be released immediately. Hatchery summer steelhead are available as early as April and quite common most years by mid-May. Both winter and summer steelhead tend to move quickly through this stretch of the Santiam system, but during years with strong runs, the river is a good producer for anglers pulling plugs. Boat ramps are available at Jefferson, the I-5 rest area, and down on the Willamette at Buena Vista.

Santiam River, Little North Fork
catch-and-release

Locals and Salem-area residents refer to this small river simply as the "Little North Fork." It reaches the North Santiam River at Mehama, about 8 miles west of Mill City and almost directly across the river from popular John Neal Park (see Santiam River, North). The little North Fork abounds with small, wild trout and with private property. A modest run of native winter steelhead ascends the river between late autumn and mid-spring and a few hatchery summer steelhead stray up from the North Santiam during May and June.

By late July and often earlier, the Little North Fork shrinks to a comparative trickle, but its deep pools attract lots of swimmers until school begins in the fall. Most of the river's best water flows through private property and you'll need permission to fish. A few miles of the Little North Fork flow through BLM-administered lands and the BLM operates two campgrounds on the river. Canyon Creek Campground is at mile 7.3 and Elkhorn Valley Recreation Site is at mile 8.5 on North Fork County Road. Marion County operates North Fork Campground 3 miles upstream from Hwy 22, along with Bear Creek and Salmon Falls Campgrounds further upstream.

Catch-and-release fishing for wild cutthroat and rainbow trout peaks from June through early July and also during September and early October, when large October caddis hatch along the river. Access for steelheading is best at the campgrounds and bridges unless you're willing to knock on some doors and lucky enough to get permission to fish.

The river's uppermost reaches flow through about 8 miles of national forest land and offer fair-to-good fishing for small, wild trout during early summer and autumn. Shady Cove Campground, run by Willamette National Forest, lies along the upper river, just below the confluence of Cedar Creek, off FR 2207. For 2.5 miles upstream from Shady Cove, the river is tough to get to via a very steep descent from FR 2209 (or by hiking up from the campground). Forest Road 2209 ends at the trailhead for the headwaters up to Jawbone Flats and the confluence with Opal Creek. (See separate headings herein for details on Opal Creek and Cedar Creek). The trail is a gated old logging road and is easy walking.

North Fork Road turns north off Hwy 22 about 1 mile east of Mehama and 24 miles east of Salem. Exit I-5 at the Stayton-Detroit Lake exit (253) and head east. Use extreme caution on this road during summer, especially on the gravel section, where heavy traffic makes for some dangerous corners.

Santiam River, Middle

The Middle Fork Santiam, upstream from Green Peter Reservoir, offers catch-and-keep opportunity in a truly beautiful setting. This difficult-to-access, steep-gradient, mountain river is characterized by rugged canyon reaches interspersed with opulent pools and glides. By mid-summer it flows at low levels ideal for dry-fly angling, but all methods produce here on the river's wild rainbow and cutthroat.

Fishing the Middle Santiam is a bit of an adventure owing to access issues created by gated private timber company roads in the lower reach, roadless wilderness in the middle reach and long, rugged forest roads leading to the upper reach. Of the three sections, the headwaters are easiest to get to, but generally produce only small trout. Nonetheless, this is pretty country and lightly fished: From Hwy 22 south of Marion Forks, turn west across the North Santiam on the Parish Lake Road. Follow this road 3 miles to a left turn on FR 2047, which leads southwest, eventually following the headwaters of the Middle Santiam. Alternately (and for fewer miles on gravel), head north from the southern terminus of FR 2047, which turns north off Hwy 20 about 2 miles east of House Rock Campground.

The wilderness section of the Middle Santiam flows through rugged, scenic timberlands south of the Quartzville Creek headwaters and north of Hwy 20. The 7,500-acre Middle Santiam Wilderness Area, designated as such in 1984, includes substantial tracts of old-growth hemlock, Douglas fir, and fir. Through the wilderness, the Middle Santiam ranks among the truly beautiful trout streams in the Willamette region. It is very lightly fished because the wilderness trail runs high above the river more than a mile to the north. To access the wilderness reach from the trail, you will need strong wilderness skills and a willingness to plunge downhill, cross-country, through all manner of undergrowth and treachery. To find the trail, head 4 miles east from Sweet Home on Hwy 20, then turn left on Quartzville Road. Follow the road 25 miles. Follow FR 11 into the national forest and then, after 2.5 miles, turn south (right) on FR 1142, which leads 4 miles to the McQuade Creek Trailhead. Having said all that, I suggest you don't bother unless you simply want to hike this beautiful country.

The more prudent choice and the easiest access for fishing is from the old forest road (#2041) that used to reach the stream at the east end of the wilderness. A major slide blocked the road during the floods of 1996, so now you must hike the last 2 miles. Head east on Hwy 20 and then turn north (left) on FR 2041, about a mile past Fernview Campground. Follow FR 2041 to its end (at the slide). The new trail begins nearby.

Downstream from the Middle Santiam Wilderness, the river flows 7 miles down to Green Peter Reservoir. This reach flows entirely through private timberland and has traditionally been open only on weekends for deer and elk hunters. So check with the Sweet Home Ranger District or with the landowners (Giustina Resources) before heading up there. To reach the lower section, turn left on the Quartzville Road, just past Dexter Reservoir. Turn right, across the dam, when you reach Green Peter Reservoir.

Santiam River, North (below Big Cliff Dam)
boat ramp, campground, services

A fair-to-good producer of spring chinook salmon and summer-run steelhead, the North Santiam River is a beautiful, medium-gradient, mid-size river flowing westerly from the Cascade Mountains and joining the South Santiam near the small town of Jefferson near Albany. The anadromous fish passage is blocked by Big Cliff Dam on the North Santiam, located a few miles upstream from Mill City.

With lots of private property surrounding the river, bank fishing on the North Santiam is generally limited to the public access points, as follows (starting downstream and moving up): Jefferson, Green's Bridge, Shelburn, Stayton Bridge, Mehama Bridge, John Neal Park, North Santiam State Park, Fisherman's Bend Campground, Mill City, Gates Bridge, Packsaddle Park. However, these public access areas are located along some of the river's prime salmon and steelhead reaches.

State Highway 22 follows the river from just downstream of Mehama all the way to Big Cliff Dam. For the lower river, access is from side roads leading off the two major routes between Stayton and Jefferson, one of which follows the south

bank (the Scio Road) and one of which follows the north bank (the Marion Road). Neither road approaches close to the river except at Green's Bridge, just east of Jefferson on the route to Scio.

To reach Stayton Bridge, exit Hwy 22 (east of Salem) at the second Stayton exit. Head south and drive straight through town until you reach the bridge. Mehama Bridge is half a mile south of the highway at the tiny town of Mehama. Steelhead anglers often fish directly off the bridge and on those occasions when a bridge angler hooks a fish the circus act begins. You're better off fishing the bridge pool from the south bank above or below the boat launch. To reach Neal Park, cross Mehama Bridge and continue south a short distance to a left turn on SR 226. Then watch for another left turn with signs to Neal Park. Upstream from Mill City and Gates, Packsaddle Park is a clearly marked right-hand turn off the highway. Be sure to note and obey the angling closure extending upstream from a sign just below the boat ramp. Never launch at Packsaddle without first going with someone familiar with the serious rapids in this section.

To reach the river at Mill City, turn right at the Circle K store and follow the road down to the Mill City Bridge, where a popular salmon pool awaits (check current regulations here). Mill City offers two boat launches: The first is a pole slide at Kimmel Park on the south bank, but is only usable at high water and is thus not used during the summer season. The more popular choice is the launch a quarter mile upstream from Mill City Bridge (turn left just before you reach the bridge, and then take the first right and then another right). Be sure to scout the falls below the bridge before using this launch and if you have any doubts, speak with someone who knows how to boat these falls.

A fairly straightforward float in most sections, the North Santiam is popular with drift-boat anglers, especially during June and July when salmon and steelhead fishing peaks. The easiest float is the half-day (or less) run from Fisherman's Bend to North Santiam State Park. For a full day on the water, many floaters continue down to Neal Park or Mehama Bridge, but don't drift this section without first going with someone familiar with the route. The upper drift, from Packsaddle Park to Mill City, is the most hazardous.

Below Mehama, the river's speed lessens. During low-water periods, the Mehama-to-Stayton drift is difficult owing to the portage required over Bennet Dam at Stayton. If you float this reach during summer, you'll need the key (from the city police department) to access the bridge on the north channel. Meanwhile, the ramp at North Santiam State Park is a fairly steep, unimproved cobblestone bar, which requires 4-wheel drive vehicles. Shuttle service is available for the upper river—contact the tackle shop in Mill City (Santiam Sports Center).

The river's spring chinook salmon, which range from 10 to 30-plus pounds, enter the river between April and early July. The fishing peaks during May and June. Hatchery produced summer steelhead arrive between May and September. They range from 5 to 18 pounds, averaging about 8 or 9 pounds. The steelhead fishing peaks during June and July and contin-

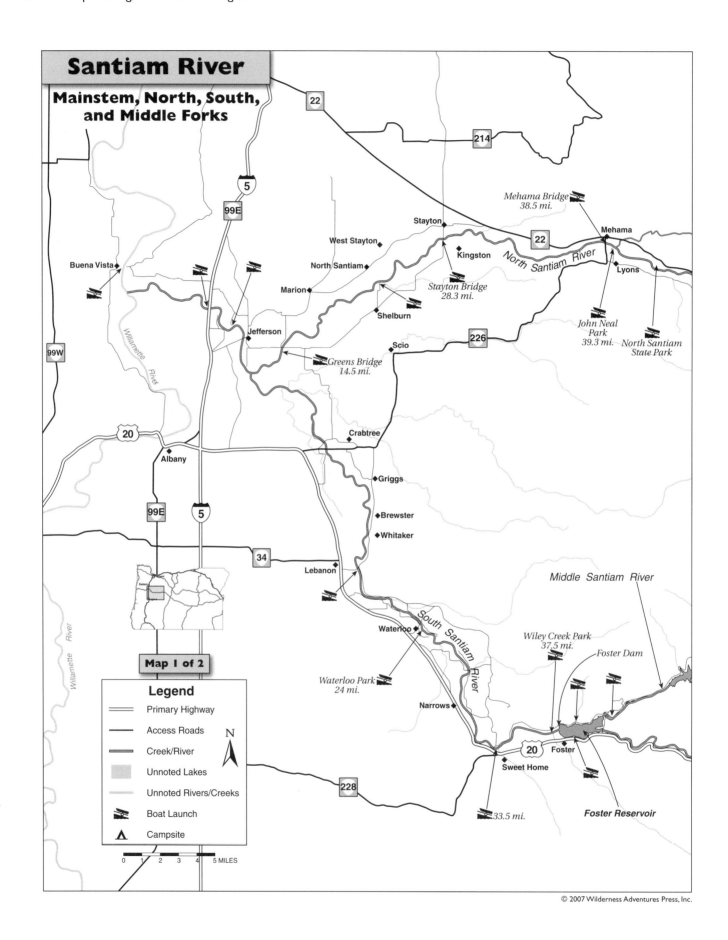

Santiam River

Mainstem, North, South, and Middle Forks

Mehama Bridge 38.5 mi.

Mehama

Stayton

West Stayton

Kingston

Lyons

North Santiam River

North Santiam

Buena Vista

Marion

Stayton Bridge 28.3 mi.

Shelburn

John Neal Park 39.3 mi.

North Santiam State Park

Jefferson

Scio

Greens Bridge 14.5 mi.

Willamette River

Crabtree

Albany

Griggs

Brewster

Whitaker

Middle Santiam River

Lebanon

Wiley Creek Park 37.5 mi.

Foster Dam

Waterloo

South Santiam River

Map 1 of 2

Waterloo Park 24 mi.

Narrows

Foster

Willamette River

Sweet Home

Foster Reservoir

33.5 mi.

Legend

Primary Highway	
Access Roads	N
Creek/River	
Unnoted Lakes	
Unnoted Rivers/Creeks	
Boat Launch	
Campsite	

0 1 2 3 4 5 MILES

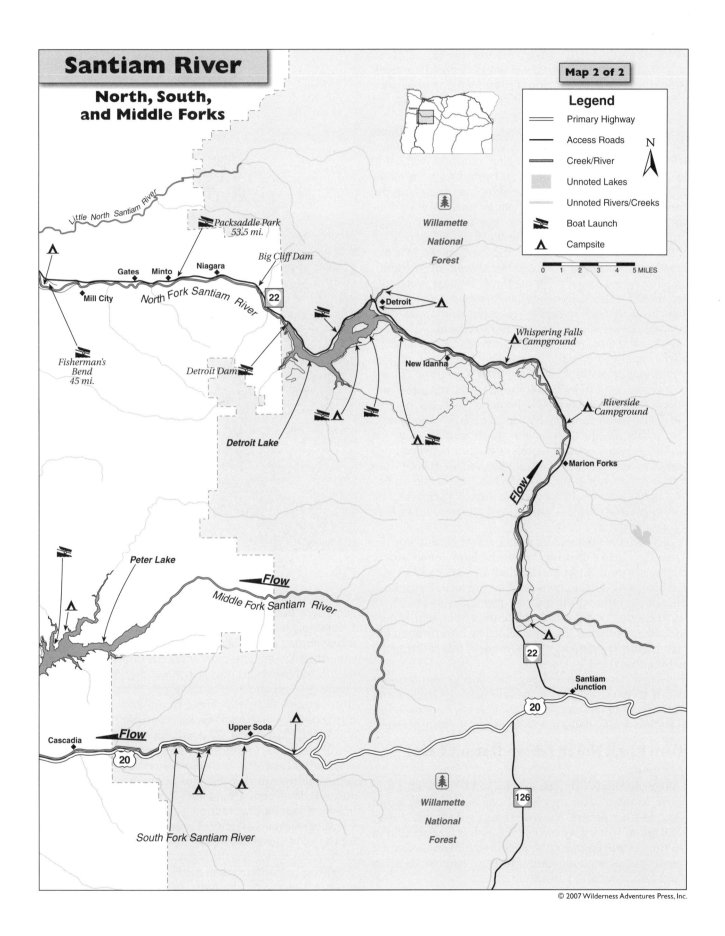

Santiam River

North, South, and Middle Forks

Map 2 of 2

Legend

Primary Highway
Access Roads
Creek/River
Unnoted Lakes
Unnoted Rivers/Creeks
Boat Launch
Campsite

N

0 1 2 3 4 5 MILES

Willamette National Forest

Little North Santiam River

Packsaddle Park
53.5 mi.

Big Cliff Dam

Gates
Minto
Niagara

Mill City

North Fork Santiam River

22

Detroit

Whispering Falls Campground

New Idanha

Detroit Dam

Fisherman's Bend
45 mi.

Detroit Lake

Riverside Campground

Marion Forks

Flow

Peter Lake

Flow

Middle Fork Santiam River

22

Santiam Junction

20

Flow

Upper Soda

Cascadia

20

Willamette National Forest

126

South Fork Santiam River

© 2007 Wilderness Adventures Press, Inc.

ues into early autumn. ODFW traps the summer fish at Minto, above Packsaddle Park and trucks them back down the river, releasing them for another run up from Mehama or various other release points. Re-run fish are marked with a thin red dorsal tag.

All methods produce for steelhead, and the river attracts quite a few fly anglers during the summer. During May, when the water runs fairly high, gear anglers do quite well using spoons, jigs, Corkies, plugs, and bait. By mid-June the water drops into prime condition for fly angling and throughout the summer most fly anglers opt for floating lines. Popular flies include traditional favorites like the Green-butt Skunk, Purple Peril, and Silver Hilton, along with several flies of local origins, including Maxwell's Purple Matuka and the Spawning Purple. *The Statesman Journal* (Salem) and *The Oregonian* (Portland) publish river flow data daily. For the North Santiam, watch the reading listed for the Mehama gauge. Anything under 3.2 feet provides ideal fly-angling flows. At 3.8 feet and above, gear anglers enjoy better success on summer steelhead.

Likewise, the *Statesman Journal* generally publishes fish-count information for Willamette Falls at Oregon City. The same information is available on the ODFW website. During the best years, more than 25,000 summer-run steelhead and more than 60,000 salmon pass Willamette Falls, destined for the North and South Santiam, McKenzie and the Willamette.

Wild winter steelhead enter the North Santiam between December and April, with the peak of the run between mid-February and mid-March. Many anglers pursue them in the lower river, between Stayton and Jefferson. Beware the sweepers, log jams, and braided channels below Shelburn. The Stayton-to-Shelburn drift is more straightforward and offers plenty of good water.

In 1996, ODFW changed its management scheme for the North Santiam below Big Cliff Dam and thus no longer stocks the river with trout. Instead, the river is managed for wild trout, which are available on a catch-and-release basis. Both rainbows and cutthroat inhabit the river and a few reach 18 inches in length. They feed on a relatively abundant supply of caddisflies, stoneflies, and mayflies. The best trout action occurs on summer evenings when swarms of insects bring the fish to the surface.

The small communities along the North Santiam offer all needed services. Mill City is the hub for most anglers and offers a handful of restaurants, stores, and gas stations. Additional choices are located 2 miles east at the tiny burg of Gates.

Santiam River, North (above Detroit Lake)
campgrounds

With all anadromous fish passage blocked by Big Cliff Dam, the North Santiam River upstream from Detroit is managed as a stocked-trout fishery. The river flows right alongside Hwy 22 for 20 miles. This upper section of the river flows clear and cold during summer and is so serenely beautiful in its verdant surroundings that even die-hard wild-trout enthusiasts often stop for a few hours of dry-fly action.

Rich Youngers fishes the North Santiam River.

Quite small and intimate in its upper reaches, the river gains size fairly rapidly below the hamlet of Marion Forks. Several major tributaries join the North Santiam in just a few miles, among them Marion Creek, Pamelia Creek, and White-water Creek. This latter stream feeds directly off the glaciers on Mt. Jefferson and during hot weather invariably contributes a gray-green tinge to the river. Except during autumn storm events, the glacial water from Whitewater Creek melds into the gin-clear flows of the river and hardly affects the color a mile and more below the confluence.

All methods produce on this section of the river. Fly anglers, bait anglers, and spin-fishers are all well represented on the river during the summer months. Two nice campgrounds, Whispering Falls and Riverside, sit beside the river between Idanha and Marion Forks. They tend to fill up on summer weekends. Plenty of unimproved campsites are there for the taking for those willing to drive a short distance up any of the side roads along the highway.

The uppermost reach of the North Santiam emanates from its source, Santiam Lake, and flows for a few miles through the

Mt. Jefferson Wilderness Area before arriving at Big Meadows Horse Camp. From the lake down to Big Meadows, the tiny river offers small pools and pockets with resident, wild cutthroat, rainbows and a few brook trout. The Duffy Lake trail offers good access to this section and adventurous types can hike down the river below the horse camp and fish the remaining mile-and-a-half of river flowing down to Hwy 22.

Santiam River, South
boat ramps, campground

Despite limited bank access, the South Santiam is a very good producer of hatchery summer steelhead and spring chinook salmon. The salmon fishery peaks during May and June; steelhead fishing lasts from May through September. The steelhead typically range from 6 to 9 pounds, with a few 10- to 14-pound fish available. All methods produce on the river. The upstream extent of the fishery is Foster Dam, upstream from Sweet Home. Below the dam, Wiley Creek Park offers good bank access and is the most popular spot on the river, often attracting substantial crowds of steelhead anglers. Additional bank access is available at and below the boat ramp at Pleasant Valley Bridge in Sweet Home, at Lebanon Dam, and at Waterloo County Park upstream from the town of Lebanon.

The most popular drift on the South Santiam goes from Foster Dam (Wiley Park) down to Sweet Home or down to the fee ramp at McDowell Creek. Waterloo County Park lies 18 river miles below the put-in at Wiley Creek Ramp, making it too long a run for one day. The new Linn County Parks Department ramp at Waterloo allows boaters easy access to the river above Lebanon Dam and below Waterloo Falls. The McDowell Creek-to-Waterloo (or Lebanon Dam) run covers some good salmon water.

Hatchery summer steelhead are recycled on the river. The fish are trapped at Foster Dam and then trucked downstream for release at the boat ramps as far down as Waterloo. In recent years, quite a few steelhead have been recycled at Wiley Creek, just downstream from the dam. Be forewarned, however, that the recycling efforts tend to attract hordes of anglers to the release sites.

To reach the South Santiam River, follow I-5 to the Hwy 20 exit (Exit 233) or the Corvallis/Lebanon Exit (Exit 228). Head east toward Lebanon. Lebanon Dam is located on the east edge of town off Berlin Road (via Brewster Road) and a multitude of vehicles parked along the road below the dam assures that the salmon run is in full swing. Continue east on the highway toward Sweet Home to reach Waterloo Park. Upstream (east) from Waterloo, McDowell Creek Road leads down to the fee launch at McDowell Creek. In Sweet Home, Pleasant Valley Drive crosses the river (and accesses the Sweet Home ramp) and heads back down the north bank to meet up with McDowell Creek Road. After crossing the river on Pleasant Valley Drive in Sweet Home, turn right on North River Drive to reach Wiley Creek Park and Foster Dam.

Sapphire Lake (Waldo Lake Wilderness)
hike-in, cross-country, float tube recommended

Usually not labeled on the maps, 6-acre Sapphire Lake is a good cutthroat trout fishery sitting off the trail about 1 mile west of Waldo Lake. You can fish it from shore, but Sapphire, which reaches a depth of 20 feet, is an ideal float tube lake. Sapphire Lake lies west-by-southwest from Elbow Lake and less than a quarter mile from Zircon Lake (see listing herein). Zircon and Sapphire make for a fine day's fishing and you won't likely see any other anglers, especially if you go midweek.

The Koch Mountain Trail (#3576) provides easiest access to Saphire Lake, along with nearby Zircon. From Oakridge, head northeast on the Salmon Creek Road (FR 24) until you reach the junction where 24 becomes FR 2420 to the right (gated) and FR 2421 to the left (the main branch). This is the Black Creek Road. Follow it half a mile to a left-hand turn onto FR 2422 and follow this road all the way to its end at the trailhead. Follow the trail east less than a mile to Waldo Lake and then head north 2 miles to Elbow Lake. Follow the trail past Elbow and then head off cross-country to the southwest after you pass a small pond on your left. Keeping the rim on your right, head past Zircon to find Sapphire. Reference the map herein. Beware the incessant clouds of mosquitoes throughout the summer.

Sardine Creek (Willamette National Forest)

This short tributary to Big Cliff Reservoir offers a few small, wild trout for those willing to scramble over slippery boulders and bust through the brush to get to the water. It empties into Big Cliff Reservoir along Hwy 22 west of Detroit. Watch for the large pullout and the gravel road that leads up along the creek for a short distance. (See Big Cliff Reservoir).

Scout Lake (Mt. Jefferson Wilderness)
hike-in

There are two Scout Lakes in the Mt. Jefferson Wilderness, but only this one is named such on the maps. It spans 7 acres, offers planted brookies, including a few 14- to 16-inchers and lies adjacent to Bays Lake in ever-popular Jefferson Park. The trails into this lake basin cover about 6 miles. You can get there by any of several routes. See Bays Lake for specifics. If you dare chance the weather in early October, you'll find Jefferson Park devoid of people and the Scout Lake brookies in beautiful spawning colors. Check the weather forecast first and be prepared for snow at any time during autumn. Fires are banned in Jefferson Park and campers are required to use the established campsites. Scout Lake offers eight of these sites. The lake is easy to fish from shore and all methods produce here.

Separation Lake
(Three Sisters Wilderness Area)
hike-in

A very attractive and fairly productive 5-acre lake in the Three Sisters Wilderness Area, Separation Lake is aptly named: Plenty of geography, and hence legwork, separates it from any other lakes in the wilderness. Nonetheless, the lake's isolation is its saving grace, perhaps, as it is lightly fished. Brook trout range from 6 to 14 inches. From Hwy 126, just east of McKenzie Bridge Ranger Station, turn south onto FR 2643 (Foley Road) and follow it 8.5 miles up to a right-hand turn on FR 480, which leads about 2 miles to the trailhead. The hike covers about 6.5 miles, climbing down into Separation Creek. Stay right at both trail junctions (at the 1-mile mark and along the creek at the 5.5-mile mark). The lake is usually accessible by early June, but bring your mosquito repellent.

Serene Lake (Clackamas County)
hike-in

As its name implies, this 20-acre hike-in lake generally offers peace and quiet, especially mid-week, and also offers good fishing for 6- to 12-inch brook and rainbow trout. The lake is located northeast from Ripplebrook Guard Station. You can reach the trailhead at Frazier Forks Campground from the south via FR 58 or from Timothy Lake to the east. Be sure to consult the map. The scenic, 3-mile hike takes you first through the Rock Lakes Basin. All three of the Rock Lakes offer fair-to-good fishing prospects. They are fairly heavily fished on summer weekends.

Shale Lake (Mt. Jefferson Wilderness)
hike-in

Shale Lake is a 1-acre pond traditionally stocked with brook trout and located along the Pacific Crest Trail in the Mt. Jefferson Wilderness Area. The lake lies just to the northwest of Cathedral Rocks and is on the east side of the trail. It offers ample, easy shoreline fishing, though tends to be rather slow most of the time. Mudhole Lake lies immediately north and is larger, but is not stocked. Coyote Lake, another 1-acre brook trout pond, lies 300 yards to the west, on the other side of the trail. Both lakes sit on the rim above Hunts Cove and an old bushwhacker's trail leads from Shale/Mudhole over to Coyote and then descends the steep ridge to Hunts Lake.

If you use the Pamelia Lake/Hunts Cove Trail to access these lakes, you must first obtain a limited-entry permit from the Detroit Ranger District headquarters in Detroit (503-854-3366). Save yourself the trouble and hike in on the Woodpecker Ridge Trail (#3442), which takes you to a north turn onto the Pacific Crest Trail. Trail #3442 is at the end of Woodpecker Road, which turns east off Hwy 22 near milepost 61. There are several scenic campsites at and around Shale/Mudhole/Coyote Lakes with commanding views of nearby Mt. Jefferson.

Sharps Creek (Lane County)

A nice little trout stream dumping into the Row River above Dorena Reservoir, Sharps Creek offers small native cutthroat trout along with a few wild rainbows. During the general season, bait is allowed and a five-fish limit applies. During the rest of the year, the creek is governed by catch-and-release, artificials-only rules. A small BLM campground is located about 2 miles up the creek and a small primitive campground sits further upstream. From I-5, take Exit 174 at Cottage Grove and head east on Row River Road. Follow the road around Dorena Reservoir and up to a right turn on Sharps Creek Road.

Sheep Lake (Mt. Jefferson Wilderness)
hike-in, float tube recommended

Sheep Lake is one of the so-called "Firecamp Lakes" in the northern portion of the Mt. Jefferson Wilderness Area. Sheep Lake, which spans about 2 acres, offers stocked brook trout that rarely grow beyond a foot in length. They usually run 8 to 9 inches. This is a shallow, brushy lake conducive to float tube fishing. To reach the Firecamp Lakes, turn east at Detroit onto Breitenbush Road and continue about 11 miles up to a right turn onto FR 4685 (South Fork Breitenbush Road), 2 miles past Cleator Bend Campground. Follow FR 4685 up the South Fork and then up a steep ridge. The trailhead is at the end of the road. Crown Lake is a mile in; Sheep and Clagget Lakes are a quarter mile to the southeast. The lakes are accessible by mid-June.

Shellrock Creek (Clackamas County)
see Hideaway Lake

Shellrock Lake (Clackamas County)
see Hideaway Lake

Shining Lake (Clackamas County)
hike-in

Usually very good for rainbow trout, including a few fat 14-inchers, Shining Lake is located at the west end of Indian Ridge on the Roaring River drainage. The hike covers about 3.5 miles, beginning at Frazier Fork Campground to the east. From Ripplebrook Guard Station on the Clackamas (Hwy 224) or from Timothy Lake to the east, pick up FR 58 and head for High Rock Spring Campground. From there follow the rugged spur road 240 up to Frazier Fork and take Trail 510 to Shining Lake.

Shorty's Pond

Located in Ivor Davies Park in Molalla, Shorty's Pond has been stocked with catchable-size rainbow trout by ODFW in recent years. As of this writing the small pond is still very brushy, leaving room for only a few anglers at a time, but rumors persist of brush-clearing operations to make the pond more user friendly.

Silver Creek (Marion County)
hike-in

Famous for its stunning waterfalls, Silver Creek cascades through a scenic gorge 26 miles east of Salem. Silver Creek Falls State Park offers miles of trails leading to superb close-up views of the towering waterfalls. Despite the stifling crowds that walk the trails, few people bother to sample the small creek for trout. It harbors a fair population of small, wild rainbows and cutthroats, with the larger fish often living in the large plunge pools beneath the various waterfalls. This is good fly water. Dry flies draw rises from the shallow portions of the creek, while wet flies, fished on sink-tip lines, produce strikes from the trout living in the deep plunge pools. A 10-inch trout is a trophy here, but you'll rarely encounter another angler, despite the constant parade of waterfall watchers on the trails. Much of the fishing on Silver Creek is rather physically demanding, requiring you to negotiate steep, slippery inclines to

Scenic Silver Falls State Park offers small wild trout.

reach the creek in places. From Salem, head east on Hwy 22, exit at SR 214 (Silver Falls Highway) and then follow the signs to Silver Falls State Park. A use fee is required at the parking lots.

Silver King Lake (Bull of the Woods Wilderness)
see Twin Lakes

Sitton Lake (Mt. Jefferson Wilderness)
hike-in, cross-country

If you're looking for a combination of solitude and scenery, Sitton Lake is a fine choice, located deep in the Mt. Jefferson Wilderness and requiring almost 2 miles of cross-country trekking after more than 5 miles on the trails. Stocked with brookies or rainbows every other year, Sitton covers just 2 acres and reaches a depth of 15 feet. At 5,760 feet it is accessible most years by early July.

The Bingham Ridge Trail offers the shortest, easiest route. From Hwy 22, turn east on Bingham Ridge Road, a mile south of Riverside Campground. The trailhead is at the end of the road. Follow Bingham Ridge Trail east about 4 miles to a south turn on the Lake of the Woods Trail (#3493). From the north shore of Lake of the Woods, head east, more or less following the drainage uphill first to Enelrad Lake and then up to Sitton Lake. Be sure to consult the map.

Slide Lake, Big
see Big Slide Lake

Slideout Lake (Mt. Jefferson Wilderness)
hike-in, cross-country, float tube recommended

Well off the beaten path, Slideout Lake is a lightly fished brook trout lake in the northern tip of the Mt. Jefferson Wilderness Area, east from the Firecamp Lakes. Slideout spans 6 scenic acres and reaches a depth of 20 feet. Very scenic, the lake is surrounded by dense conifers that crowd right down to the water's edge; shallow shoals on one side give way to the deep center of the lake. At 4,760 feet, it is accessible most years by late June. The route to Slideout begins at the Roaring Creek Trail that leads to Crown Lake and the other Firecamp Lakes: From the town of Detroit, head east on Breitenbush Road for about 11 miles to a right-hand turn onto FR 4685. The trailhead is at the end of the road and heads 1 mile to Crown Lake. A faint bushwhacker's trail departs the north end of Crown Lake and heads east, up and over the ridgeline and down to Mildred Lake and then south to Slideout. You can pretty easily choose a cross-country route to traverse the ridge, but consult your map. The cross-country hike covers about 2 miles. A nice campsite occupies the southeast shore of Slideout Lake.

Smith Lake (Three Sisters Wilderness)
hike-in

One of several fishable lakes in the McFarland Lake area southwest of Mink Lake Basin and north of Irish Mountain in the Three Sisters Wilderness Area, Smith Lake offers fair fishing for small brook trout. See McFarland Lake herein for directions. Smith sits along the trail a few hundred yards southwest from much larger McFarland.

Smith Reservoir (Linn County)

Also called "Smith River Reservoir," this 170-acre reservoir serves as the storage for the Carmen Power Plant and is part of the Carmen-Smith Hydroelectric Development on the upper McKenzie River. Upstream at Carmen Reservoir, the McKenzie is diverted through a buried tunnel, 9.5 feet in diameter, which stretches for more than 11,000 feet to reach Smith Reservoir. Smith is stocked with legal rainbows and the fishing usually holds up well through the summer and early autumn. A boat ramp and camping area are located at the upstream end of the reservoir. Watch for the turnoff from Hwy 126 near the upper end of Trail Bridge Reservoir (see separate listing herein).

Spinning Lake (Olallie Scenic Area)
hike-in

Just off the rugged western end of the Oregon Skyline Road (FR 4220) west of Breitenbush Lake, 3-acre Spinning Lake is stocked periodically with brook trout. They range from 9 to 13 inches with an occasional 16-inch fish. To get there from Detroit, follow the Breitenbush Road (FR 46) all the way to the Willamette/Mt. Hood National Forests boundary, then turn right on FR 4220. Follow FR 4220 until you cross the North Fork Breitenbush twice. The trail leads a quarter mile to the lake. From Estacada, follow SR 224 south, pick up FR 46 and continue south to the national forest boundary and a left turn onto FR 4220.

Spirit Lake (Lane County)
hike-in

Spirit Lake is a pretty and productive 12-acre lake east of Oakridge, accessed via the Salmon Creek Road. The brook trout here reproduce naturally and most range from 6 to 10 inches with a few larger fish around to keep things interesting. One side of the lake borders a lush meadow, decorated with myriad wildflowers. The other side meets verdant timber stands. To get there, follow Salmon Creek Road (FR 24) east out of Oakridge until you reach the junction where 24 becomes FR 2420 to the right (gated) and FR 2421 to the left (the main branch). Take FR 2421 half a mile to a left turn onto FR 2422 and follow 2422 about 7 miles up to the Spirit Lake Trail, which covers an easy 500 yards to the lake.

Spring Lake (Three Sisters Wilderness)
hike-in

A deep, little cutthroat lake in the northwest corner of the Three Sisters Wilderness, Spring Lake offers good fishing for trout ranging from 6 to 12 inches. Only 3 acres in size, Spring Lake reaches 21 feet in depth and is a good place for a float tube. The lake lies just south of the popular Frog Camp Campground & Picnic Area half a mile south from the turnoff to Scott Lake along the Old McKenzie Highway. The popular Obsidian Cliffs Trail heads south from Frog Camp for .75 of a mile before reaching the spur trail heading half a mile west to Spring Lake, which sits at the base of Sims Butte. At 5,150 feet elevation, this area is rarely accessible before late June.

The trout-rich Ollalie Lake Scenic Area is well named.

Spy Lake (Three Sisters Wilderness)

hike-in

A deep, scenic, little, rock- and tree-lined 3-acre cutthroat/brook trout lake in the Three Sisters Wilderness Area, Spy Lake sits just far enough off the beaten path to escape attention. The lake reaches a depth of 20 feet and the trout reach about a foot in length and average 8 or 9 inches. From Cabin Meadows at the north edge of the Mink Lake Basin, follow the McBee Trail (#3523) north. After the trail climbs a steep ridge, gaining about 350 feet, watch for the lake off to the right. From the trail junction at Corner Lake, the route to Spy Lake covers 1.7 miles.

Squaw Lakes (Clackamas County)

hike-in

A group of three small mountain lakes easily reached from Estacada, the Squaw Lakes offer fair-to-good fishing for small brook trout. From Estacada, head south on SR 224 to North Fork Reservoir. Turn east on FR 4610 and follow it about 15 miles to Squaw Meadows. The lakes sit off to the left (north) side of the road and a short spur road makes a good hiking trail.

Staley Creek (Lane County)

Rugged little Staley Creek, a tributary to the Middle Fork Willamette River, offers fair-to-good action for small, wild cutthroat and rainbows. The creek draws its headwaters from the Calapooya Mountains and flows north about 10 miles to meet the Middle Fork above Hills Creek Reservoir. Staley Creek Road (FR 2134) follows the lower end of the creek closely and provides ready access before yielding to FR 2136, which follows the creek deeper into the drainage. Sections of the creek flow through steep-sided gorges that are difficult to negotiate. Two miles past Oakridge, turn south on Kipson Springs Road (FR 21) and follow the road around the west side of Hills Creek Reservoir. Just past Campers Creek Campground, FR 2136 turns off to the south and heads up Staley Creek.

Stewart Reservoir (Yamhill County)

Private reservoir. No public access.

Sturgeon Lake (Sauvie Island)

A very large natural lake on Sauvie Island, Sturgeon Lake offers fair prospects for various warmwater species, including crappie, brown bullhead, yellow perch, and largemouth bass. Some decent-sized fish live in the lake, though the largest bass and crappie are frequently taken by anglers fishing by boat. Boaters can launch at the ramp at the mouth of Gilbert River (on Multnomah Channel) and motor up to the lake. From Hwy 30 north of Portland, cross the Sauvie Island Bridge and head north to a right-hand turn on Reeder Road, which accesses the Oak Island area and the Coon Point access. To reach the boat launch at the mouth of the Gilbert River, follow Reeder Road all the way to the north end of the island.

Sunrise Lake (Emigrant Pass)

float tube recommended

Sunrise Lake sits at the summit of Emigrant Pass in the southeast corner of Lane County, just west of Summit Lake. Two-acre Sunrise Lake is 22 feet deep and is stocked with rainbow trout, usually every year. At 5,500 feet, Sunrise Lake is accessible most years by late June. Most of the tiny lakes on Emigrant Pass, including Sunrise, are not labeled on forest service maps, but Sunrise sits right on the road.

To reach Emigrant Pass from the west, take Hwy 58 through Oakridge. Two miles east of town, turn south on the Kitson Springs Road (FR 21) towards Hills Creek Reservoir. Stay right and follow FR 21 south along the west side of the reservoir. Remain on FR 21 for about 32 miles until you reach a left turn on FR 2154. Follow 2154 about 5 miles to a left turn on FR 2160, which leads north a mile and a half to Emigrant Pass. From the east side, head for the west shore of Crescent Lake, then follow the rugged route west over Emigrant Pass.

Sunset Lake (Emigrant Pass)

float tube recommended

Sunset Lake sits immediately east of Sunrise Lake at the summit of Emigrant Pass in the southeast corner of Lane County, just west of Summit Lake. Two-acre Sunset Lake is 16 feet deep and is stocked with cutthroat trout, usually every year. At 5,500 feet, Sunset Lake is accessible by late June most years. Most of the tiny lakes on Emigrant Pass, including Sunset, are not labeled on forest service maps, but Sunset sits right on the road.

To reach Emigrant Pass from the west, take Hwy 58 through Oakridge. Two miles east of town, turn south on the Kitson Springs Road (FR 21) towards Hills Creek Reservoir. Stay right and follow FR 21 south along the west side of the reservoir. Remain on FR 21 for about 32 miles until you reach a left turn on FR 2154. Follow 2154 about 5 miles to a left turn on FR 2160, which leads north a mile and a half to Emigrant Pass. From the east side, head for the west shore of Crescent Lake, then follow the rugged route west over Emigrant Pass.

Sunset Lake (Three Sisters Wilderness)

hike-in

Sunset Lake is a scenic 40-acre rainbow and brook trout fishery in the Three Sisters Wilderness Area just west from Elk Lake and Century Drive. The fish range from 8 to 14 inches and the lake is generally stocked every other year. The shortest route to Sunset Lake begins at Elk Lake Trailhead, on the west side of Century Drive opposite Elk Lake, 33 miles from Bend. Take the Island Meadows Trail (#3) west 1.3 miles to its intersection with the Pacific Crest Trail and turn left, following the PCT another 1.3 miles until you reach a right (north) turn leading .75 of a mile to Sunset Lake, on the left side of the trail. The lake offers some nice camping areas, but stay well back from the shoreline to preserve the heavily trodden riparian area.

Swallow Lake (Mt. Jefferson Wilderness)
hike-in

A tiny trailside lake in the Mt. Jefferson Wilderness Area, Swallow Lake generally offers slow-to-fair fishing for planted brook trout, including the occasional 14-incher. From the west side (Hwy 22), follow the Marion Lake Trail (see Marion Lake for directions) 3 miles to its junction with the Lake-of-the-Woods Trail and from there head left towards Lake-of-the-Woods. After about 1.5 miles, watch for the next trail junction and take the right-hand fork about 2 miles to Swallow Lake (on the right-hand side of the trail).

Swan Lake (Waldo Lake Wilderness)
hike-in, float tube recommended

Swan Lake lies on the west edge of the Waldo Lake Wilderness Area and offers fair-to-good fishing for cutthroat or rainbow trout, depending on when you happen to be there. It is stocked every other year, sometimes with 'bows, sometimes with cutts. From Oakridge, head northwest on the Salmon Creek Road, FR 24. When FR 24 forks, follow FR 2417 all the way until it ends at the trailhead to Swan Lake, which is an easy half-mile walk due south. Swan covers 10 acres and reaches a depth of about 15 feet.

Tanner Creek (Multnomah County)

A popular spot for bank anglers targeting shad on the Columbia River, the mouth of Tanner Creek also hosts a small run of winter steelhead. Only adipose-fin-clipped fish may be kept and the creek is open only above the mainline railroad bridge. The shad fishery peaks in May and often draws quite a crowd to the mouth of Tanner Creek because this area is one of just a few good bank-fishing spots for shad anglers. Tanner Creek reaches the Columbia just downstream from the hatchery facilities below Bonneville Dam.

Temple Lake (Mt. Jefferson Wilderness)
hike-in, float tube recommended

Temple Lake is a quiet, pretty, lightly fished brookie and rainbow lake in the Mt. Jefferson Wilderness Area about halfway between Marion Lake and Camp Pioneer Boy Scout Camp. To reach Temple, follow Hwy 22 to the Camp Pioneer turnoff about 5 miles south from Marion Forks and then ascend the Twin Meadows Road (FR 2261) up to the Pine Ridge Trailhead. Hike east on Pine Ridge Trail for just over 2 miles and keep a sharp eye out for a secondary trail heading off to your left. In a few places along the Pine Ridge Trail, the trail heads through stands of fairly young lodgepole pines instead of the usual mix of firs, Douglas fir, and hemlock. The trail to Temple departs the main trail in one of the stands of lodgepole and the tree marking the trail is blazed. From the junction, Temple is just a quarter mile from the Pine Ridge Trail. Temple offers a nice view of Mt. Jefferson and features some nice, flat, shaded camp spots.

Tenas Lakes: Upper, Middle & Lower (Mt. Washington Wilderness)
hike-in

The three tiny and popular Tenas Lakes—Upper, Middle and Lower—offer fair-to-good fishing for mostly small trout. They are easy to reach via a short walk from the trailhead at Scott Lake just off the Old McKenzie Highway on the eastern edge of Linn County (see Scott Lake for directions). The Tenas Lakes are stocked with rainbow and cutthroat trout. The usual allotment for each lake ranges from 250 to 600 fish, but the lakes range from 14 to 20 feet in depth, so carryover is no problem.

Lower Tenas, the largest at 2.6 acres, offers rainbow trout and is the first you will come to via the route from Scott Lake. Middle Tenas (1.3 acres) lies due west of the north half of elongated Lower Tenas and offers rainbow and cutthroat trout. Upper Tenas lies immediately northwest of Middle Tenas and covers only 1 acre. It is planted with cutthroat trout.

From Scott Lake, follow the Trail to Benson Lake and continue .6 of a mile north from Benson until you see the left-hand fork that leads about 200 yards over to Lower Tenas. Upper and Middle Tenas are located on the far side of Lower Tenas. A float tube is handy here but certainly not required.

Teto Lake (Mt. Jefferson Wilderness)
hike-in

Guarded to the immediate south by a monolithic rock dome, Teto Lake sits at the north edge of Eight Lakes Basin, north from Marion Lake in the Mt. Jefferson Wilderness Area. Teto's naturally reproducing brook trout tend towards the small size, but the lake makes a nice home base for fishing the other nearby lakes. Teto spans 11 acres and reaches a depth of 45 feet. A float tube comes in handy here, though shore fishing is easy.

Thomas Creek (Linn County)
no bait, catch-and-release

A fine little catch-and-release trout stream in the Cascade foothills southeast from Salem and Stayton. Access is difficult throughout much of the drainage, but the upper stretch flows through a forested canyon accessed by Thomas Creek Road south of the community of Lyons, which lies on the south side of the North Santiam River off Hwy 22. From Salem, follow Hwy 22 east until you reach Mehama, then turn south across the river and through Lyons. From Lyons, turn right (west) and follow the Lyons-Albany Road (SR 226) about 5 miles to a left-hand turn on Thomas Creek Road. A trail follows the uppermost end of the creek. The lower part of Thomas Creek has modest populations of cutthroat trout and smallmouth bass, but you'll need landowner permission to try for them.

Timothy Lake (Clackamas County)
boat ramp, campground

A popular and scenic 1,400-acre reservoir on the Clackamas River's Oak Grove Fork, Timothy Lake offers good fishing for stocked rainbow trout, along with brook trout and kokanee salmon. The stocked bows range from 9 to 16 inches. Brook trout are usually small, but the reservoir kicks out a few 14- to 19-inch fish. The reservoir gets rather warm by mid-summer, so most angling pressure occurs during May and June. September and October can also be very good here. The lake offers five campgrounds and several boat ramps. A boat comes in handy. Trails circle the lakeshore and many anglers enjoy consistent success fishing from the banks. To reach Timothy Lake, follow Hwy 26 east from Portland and up to the Skyline Road near Mt. Hood. Turn south onto the Skyline Road and follow it to FR 42 at Clear Lake. Forest Road 42 leads to several turn-offs that take you to Timothy Lake, with FR 4280 being the usual route.

Timpanogas Lake (Lane County)
campground

Popular Timpanogas Lake sits near the headwaters of the Middle Fork Willamette River and offers good fishing for naturally reproducing brook trout from 6 to 16 inches. Cutthroat trout have also been planted during some years. A nice campground occupies the south shore and trails circle the 43-acre lake, which reaches a maximum depth of more than 100 feet. The campground offers ten sites with well water, fire pits, tables, and pit toilets. At 5,300 feet, Timpanogas doesn't usually open until late June. Lower Timpanogas Lake sits just to the south and offers similar fishing. It spans about 8 acres.

To get there, follow Hwy 58 about 2 miles east from Oakridge and turn right (south) on Kitson Springs Road. After half a mile head to the right on FR 21 and continue for 32 miles to the junction with FR 2154. Turn left at 2154 and head 10 miles up to the lake. If you are arriving from central Oregon, you can get to Timpanogas Lake from Crescent Lake via a very rugged road leading past Summit Lake. The road departs the west end of Crescent, heads west to Summit Lake and turns south to meet FR 2154 a few miles north of Timpanogas.

Tom's Lake (Mt. Jefferson Wilderness)
hike-in, cross-country

Two-acre Tom's Lake offers stocked brook trout and you'll generally have the place to yourself. To get there, follow the Duffy Lake Trail 3.5 miles east to its junction with the Lava Trail and follow a compass course to Tom's Lake. Alternately, from the same trail junction or from Santiam Lake, just follow the diminutive North Santiam River headwaters directly to the lake. Check out Ralph's Lake while your there (see separate listing herein).

Top Lake (Three Sisters Wilderness)
hike-in

A trailside lake south of the Mink Lake Basin, Top Lake has been stocked in the past, but is so shallow that the fish often winterkill. Don't mistake this one for the much better Burnt Top Lake farther north (see listing herein).

Torrey Lake (Waldo Lake Wilderness)
hike-in, float tube recommended

A productive 67-acre lake in the Taylor Burn area north of Waldo Lake, Torrey offers planted cutthroat and rainbow that average about 10 inches. Torrey Lake is an easy 1-mile hike from a trailhead 3 miles north of North Waldo Campground, on FR 514. Alternately you can get there from Taylor Butte to the north, following Trail #3579 to Fields and Whig Lakes and then continuing on the un-maintained trail down to Torrey. The lake sits at an elevation of 5,300 feet and is accessible by early or mid-June. Mosquitoes run rampant here, as they do throughout the Waldo Lake area.

Torrey Lake, North (Waldo Lake Wilderness)
hike-in, cross-country, float tube recommended

Sitting a quarter mile east-by-northeast from its much larger neighbor Torrey Lake, North Torrey Lake offers a shot at large brook trout planted every few years. If they survive several winters in a row, the fish can reach 14 to 16 inches in this 8-acre elongated pond. Check the map and find North Torrey by cross-country route or look for the bushwhacker trail departing the easternmost end of Torrey Lake and heading uphill. The lake is not named on most maps, but shows up as a small, elongated pond surrounded by several much smaller ponds. Take along a float tube and ample mosquito spray.

Trail Bridge Reservoir (Linn County)

A re-regulating reservoir on the upper McKenzie River, 120-acre Trail Bridge Reservoir sits right alongside Hwy 126 about 12 miles from Santiam Junction. Stocked annually with about 30,000 legal-sized rainbow trout, Trail Bridge holds up well through the summer and into early fall. A campground sits adjacent to the reservoir. All methods produce here, though regulars seem to prefer bait to all other methods.

Trillium Lake (Clackamas County)
campground

With a stunning view of Mt. Hood, Trillium Lake ranks among the most oft-photographed lakes in the region. It sits due south of the mountain and on the south side of Hwy 26. Trillium Lake, covering about 60 acres, is very popular and usually crowded during the summer. It is heavily stocked with rainbow trout, including some of ODFW's trophy-size fish. The campground fills quickly on weekends. Follow Hwy 22 up to Mt. Hood and then turn south at the signed road (FR 2656) east from Summit Ski Area and adjacent to Snow Bunny Ski Area.

Tualatin River
boat ramp, boat recommended

A lengthy tributary to the Willamette, the Tualatin River is largely urban, its lower half flowing though the southern end of the Portland-metro area. It heads easterly through Tualatin and reaches the Willamette River above Oregon City. Long abused, first by valley agriculture and later by rapid urbanization of the watershed, the slow, meandering Tualatin nonetheless offers some opportunity for warmwater species, including crappie, smallmouth bass, largemouth bass, bullhead, and catfish. Access is difficult and the river is best fished by canoe, kayak, or other small craft. The mouth is accessible by powerboat from the Willamette (Bernert Landing) and is a good bet for smallmouth bass. Canoes and kayaks can be launched at Tualatin City Park and at various bridges and road easements, including the sites established by Portland Metro with help from other organizations.

The westernmost access point is a 5-acre site at the Farmington Road Bridge—also known as the Harris Bridge—near the intersection with River Road. It is about a two- to three-hour canoe trip from Hillsboro's Rood Bridge Park. Downstream, 1 mile south of the Scholls Bridge on Scholls Ferry Road, Metro purchased a second potential access point with 114 acres and more than a half-mile of frontage on the river. In 2002, the Gotter family donated a conservation easement over an adjacent 6-acre property.

Off Scholls-Sherwood Road and Munger Lane, Metro acquired a third potential access point with 91 acres and more than a mile of frontage on the south bank of a large oxbow. Across the river from the Tualatin River National Wildlife Refuge, the parcel is teaming with wildlife such as beaver, nutria, black-tailed deer, red-legged frogs, green herons, and a host of songbirds. In 2001, Metro planted 5,340 trees to further enhance the site.

Moving 13 miles down the river, Metro acquired 148 acres and nearly a mile of river frontage in Sherwood, off Hwy 99W near Beef Bend Road as another potential new access point. Just 3 miles upstream from Cook Park, the site is well situated for a leisurely paddle. Recently the US Fish and Wildlife Service agreed to restore and manage the floodplain portion of the property.

The fifth potential access point is south of Lake Oswego off Borland Road, near its intersection with Stafford Road at Wanker's Corner. With an existing boat dock, the 18-acre site has already been used by the Tualatin Riverkeepers as a take-out site for Discovery Days, an annual paddle with more than 250 participants.

Tule Lake (Willamette National Forest)
float tube or small boat recommended

Adjacent to a gravel road not far from Hwy 22, this 5-acre lake offers fair fishing for rainbow and a few cutthroat trout and is generally lightly fished. Some of the rainbows reach 14 to 16 inches, though pan-size trout prevail. The lake is easily fished from shore, especially if you use bait or spin-casting gear. Fly anglers might consider bringing a float tube or small boat.

Located southwest of Marion Forks in the Willamette National Forest, Tule Lake is easy to find: Head south (upstream) past Marion Forks, watch for the second bridge crossing the North Santiam River on your right. The first bridge is Bugaboo Road and the second, about 4 miles from Marion Forks, is

Straight Creek Road (FR 11). Turn right (left if you're coming from central Oregon) on Straight Creek Road and head uphill about 3 miles to a left turn on FR 1164. Follow FR 1164 downhill and across Straight Creek, then up the other side until you see the right turn on FR 1162 at a major intersection. Follow FR 1162 a short distance to the lake.

Alternately you can take the third bridge over the river south of Marion Forks, which is signed as the Parish Lake Road. If you're arriving from Bend/Sisters, this is the shortest route to Tule Lake. Just past Big Meadows Road on your right, you will cross the North Santiam River on Hwy 22. Go another 2 miles to the signed left-hand turn to Parish Lake. This is FR 2266. Follow 2266 about 2 miles to a right-hand turn onto FR 1164. Follow 1164 almost 3 miles to the intersection with FR 1162 and follow 1162 a few hundred yards to the lake.

Tumble Lake (Willamette National Forest)
hike-in

A scenic 20-acre gem located in the mountains north of Detroit, Tumble Lake offers good fishing for small, wild brook trout. Despite the steep climb in and out, Tumble Lake is fairly popular on summer weekends. To get there, follow Hwy 22 to Detroit and turn onto the French Creek Road (FR 2223) just across the bridge north from town. When you reach a Y-intersection, stay left on 2223, winding up the mountain until you get to the top of the ridge (about 7 miles). The trailhead is on your left just before you reach the junction of FR 2223 and Spur 520. The trail zigzags down the steep incline to the lake.

Turpentine Lake (Mt. Jefferson Wilderness)
hike-in, cross-country

Covering about 9 acres, Turpentine Lake, in the Mt. Jefferson Wilderness near Camp Pioneer, is a little tricky to reach by way of a couple different informal routes. The easiest route takes you to "Scout Lake," a small, shallow pond along the informal trail to Cleo Lake (see directions hereunder). Just past Scout Lake watch for a spur leading off to your right (south) and simply walk a quarter mile over the low, timbered rise to reach Turpentine Lake. Or you can take the Turpentine Trail south from the Pine Ridge Trail (these are marked), go about a mile and then head due east half a mile to the lake. Consult map and compass for this route.

Owing to the absence of a formal trail, Turpentine is lightly fished. It holds up well throughout the season. It offers stocked rainbow trout and cutthroat trout that reach 16 inches (at times it has also been stocked with brook trout). Typical fish range from 8 to 12 inches and they are responsive to all methods. The lake covers 8 acres and offers lots of shoreline fishing and plenty of nice, primitive campsites, especially along the north and west sides. Snow hangs in late in this area, often blocking easy access until late June.

Twin Lakes (Bull of the Woods Wilderness)
hike-in

Upper and Lower Twin Lakes, both covering about 12 acres and offering good fishing for brook trout, are located in rugged wilderness north of Elk Lake in the Bull of the Woods Wilderness. This small wilderness area sits in the high Cascades on the Collawash River watershed. Its southern boundary skirts popular Elk Lake near Detroit and its northern boundary lies south of Fan Creek and Kingfisher Campgrounds on the Collawash. To reach the northern trailheads from the Portland area, head southeast up the Clackamas River to Ripplebrook and then head south on FR 46 and at River Ford Campground, turning right on FR 63. Follow FR 63 about 6 miles south to a right-hand turn on FR 6340. To reach the southern trailheads at Elk Lake, follow Hwy 22 to Detroit, turn left on the Breitenbush Road and then watch for the signs leading to Elk Lake (see listing herein).

The shortest (and steepest) trail to Twin Lakes is the highly scenic Battle Axe Trail from Elk Lake. The Battle Axe Trail (#544), after climbing up and over the peak for which it is named, heads north along the ridgeline toward Silver King Mountain. At the 3-mile mark, Trail 573 heads off to the right and down to Twin Lakes, while the main trail continues north another 1.5 miles to 4-acre Silver King Lake. This lake also offers fair-to-good prospects for brook trout, but the shoreline is very brushy. It would be ideally suited to a float tube.

Upper Berley Lake
see Berley Lakes

Verde Lake (Lane County)
hike-in

Verde Lake sits beside the Fuji Mountain Trail in the Island Lakes Basin a few miles south of Waldo Lake and a few miles north of Hwy 58. Unlike its neighbor Birthday Lake, Verde is stocked with cutthroat and rainbow trout and they over-winter well, so 12- to 14-inch fish sometimes complement the usual 8- to 10-inchers. Verde sits at about 6,000 feet elevation and is rarely accessible before late June. The trail to Verde covers less than 1.5 miles. The lake, very pretty, is surrounded by conifers, with lots of sunken deadfalls that like to snag fishing tackle. A float tube us advantageous, especially for fly anglers. For directions, see Birthday Lake herein.

Vivian Lake (Diamond Peak Wilderness)
hike-in, float tube recommended

A scenic 24-acre cutthroat- and brook-trout fishery near the headwater tributaries of Salt Creek, Vivian Lake usually provides good fishing for 8- to 12-inch fish and is easy to reach via a scenic trail near Hwy 58. The lake is fairly popular, but holds up well throughout the season. The lake sits at 5,450 feet and snow lingers through May here. Still, early summer and mid-autumn rank as the best time to fish Vivian, whose north shore provides a nice view of Mt. Yoran to the south. A float tube is handy here if you're fly angling, but the lake offers some nice, sandy/gravelly beach areas as well.

You can reach Vivian from the north or from the west. Both routes cover about 2.5 miles. From the north, follow Hwy 58 to Salt Creek Falls, a few miles west from Willamette Pass. Drive down the access road to the falls and turn left on Spur Road

420, which leads to the trailhead. The trail heads due south along Fall Creek, gaining 1,200 feet of elevation along the way and passing right by Fall Creek Falls. The western route actually descends to Vivian Lake after gaining about 250 feet over the first mile. To reach this trailhead, follow Hwy 58 about 2 miles east of Oakridge and turn south onto Kitson Springs Road. Stay left at the first intersection and head east on Hills Creek Road (FR 23) until you reach a left turn on FR 2316. Follow 2316 past Wolf Mountain to a left turn on FR 510. The Vivian Lake Trailhead is at the end of this road.

A faint, non-maintained cross-country trail leads north along Vivian Lake's outlet stream and reaches lightly fished Lopez Lake. You can easily fish both lakes in a day.

Vogel Lake (Three Sisters Wilderness)
hike-in

Located just south of Cliff Lake in the Three Sisters Wilderness, 25-acre Vogel Lake is usually stocked with either brook trout or cutthroat. You won't find any big fish, but neither will you find many people. Follow the trail along the west shore of Cliff Lake and continue a quarter mile down to Vogel. See Cliff Lake for directions to the area.

Wahanna Lake (Waldo Lake Wilderness)
hike-in, float tube recommended

One of the dozen-odd fishable lakes immediately north of Waldo Lake, Wahanna offers rainbow trout, stocked en masse every other year. They typically range from 9 to 12 inches, but sometimes grow substantially larger. The lake is deep enough to easily over-winter its trout, so three-year-olds commonly reach 14 to 18 inches. Bring along a float tube to escape the shoreline brush and try wet flies on a sinking line or small spoons and spinners fished around the drop-offs. Wahanna Lake lays a 1.5 miles by trail south from Taylor Burn Campground or west from the Whig & Torrey Trailhead 2 miles north from North Waldo Campground on FR 514 (which leads about 8 miles up to Taylor Burn). Fifty-acre Wahanna Lake sits at an elevation of 5,200 feet and is accessible by mid- to late June. The area is quite popular, though visitation is not so heavy since the 1996 wildfire that burned most of the area.

Wahkeena Pond (Multnomah County)
see Benson Pond

Waldo Lake (Lane County)
campgrounds, boat ramps, boat recommended

Waldo Lake, Oregon's second or third largest natural lake (depending on how much water is present in Malheur Lake any given year), offers poor-to-fair fishing for naturally reproducing brook trout. Waldo is so pure that it is largely infertile and thus incapable of supporting a high population density of fish, even though the lake was stocked for decades. These days only the wild brookies, and some remnant kokanee, reside in the amazingly clear, clean waters of this 6,400-acre gem.

No permanent inlet streams feed nutrients to Waldo Lake and consequently no aquatic plant life lives here. In fact, only two indigenous forms of moss thrive in Waldo. The lake's exceptional purity gives Waldo its remarkable indigo color as all sunrays save blue are absorbed.

Certainly you can enjoy good brook trout fishing on Waldo, especially during October, but day in and day out the action is rather slow. The fish range from 5 inches to 5 pounds with a preponderance of skinny 8- to 12-inchers. They occupy the lake's shallow margins, so anglers need not venture into the middle, where depths reach more than 400 feet. In fact, on a still, sunny day you can see the bottom in 80 or more feet of water. High winds usually blow across the lake daily, making the middle of Waldo a dangerous place to venture in any kind of small watercraft, and a 10 mph speed limit discourages power boaters.

Sitting at 5,414 feet elevation, Waldo is usually accessible by late May or early June, but most people avoid the area during June owing to an infamous mosquito population. Waldo Lake is surrounded on all sides by dozens upon dozens of small forest ponds and marshes that serve as prime breeding grounds for mosquitoes, and they get so thick during summer that some days remind one of June on the Alaska tundra. They dissipate by fall and, with the brookies in spawning mode (and spawning colors), late September and October are the prime times to fish Waldo.

Ample shoreline fishing awaits, especially if you don't mind hiking (trails circle the lake), but a small boat, canoe, or float tube comes in handy. When you fish Waldo, forget about its intimidating size. Just choose one small cove or promontory and concentrate your efforts there. The brookies invariably occupy these near-shore areas; especially if cover is available in the form of channels, rock piles, logs, or drop-offs.

Waldo's east shoreline is accessible by road at both the north and south ends, both of which offer nice campgrounds and boat launches. More than 200 developed campsites are available along the east shore and all three campgrounds offer good boat ramps, flush toilets, and tables. The west shoreline forms the boundary of the 37,162-acre Waldo Lake Wilderness Area and is reachable only by foot or by boat, making the campgrounds on the east shore great base-camp areas for excursions to the myriad small trout lakes in the wilderness area. Primitive campsites abound on the west side of the lake, so boaters can enjoy total solitude, though crowds rarely assemble on Waldo anyway.

Wall Lake (Olallie Lake Scenic Area)
hike-in

Stocked with brook trout, Wall Lake lies almost half a mile east of popular Averill Lake on the western edge of the Olallie Lake Scenic Area in the southeast corner of the Mt. Hood National Forest. The hike in covers 2 miles on the Red Lake Trail (#719). From Estacada, follow SR 224 and then FR 46 south to the boundary of the Willamette National Forest. From Detroit, just head east on FR 46 (Breitenbush Road) to the Mt. Hood National Forest Boundary. Turn east on FR 4220 (Oregon Skyline Road) for about .75 of a mile and then turn north (left)

on Spur Road 380. Pass under the power lines and then watch for the signed trailhead. The brookies typically range from 8 to 10 inches.

Walling Pond (Salem)

An old gravel-pit pond located within the Salem city limits, Walling Pond is popular with bait anglers and produces stocked rainbow trout, including brood stock fish up to at least 8 pounds, along with some bass and a few panfish. The pond is located at the corner of McGilchrist and 16th Streets, west from the Salem airport. Follow Mission Street east from downtown or west from the freeway (Hwy 22 Exit) and turn south at 25th Street. Follow 25th to a right turn on McGilchrist.

Walter Wirth Lake (Salem)

Walter Wirth Lake is the larger of the two ponds located in Salem's Cascade Gateway Park, right next to I-5 and the Salem Airfield. This 20-acre lake offers stocked rainbow, including some brood stock fish, along with wild sunfish, crappie, bullheads, and a few bass. Trout, including brood stock fish up to about 8 pounds, are planted throughout the year. Shore fishing is easy here and most people prefer bait, though all methods produce. It's a good place for kids, but keep an eye on them because drownings have occurred here and some of the people that show up can be a little unsavory. To get there from I-5, take the Hwy 22/Mission Street Exit and head west towards town. Take the left turn at the next stoplight onto Turner Road. The entrance to the park is about a quarter mile south, on the left. The park includes picnic areas, restrooms, and garbage cans, though this latter amenity seems lost on some of the anglers who show up here.

Waverly Lake (Albany)

A popular city-owned lake in Albany, just off I-5, Waverly Lake offers fair-to-good fishing for small bluegill, stocked rainbow trout, and a few other warmwater species. Take Exit 234 from I-5 and head west. The lake sits in a small park on your right.

Welcome Lakes (Bull of the Woods Wilderness)
see Big Slide Lake

West Lake (Bull of the Woods Wilderness)
see Big Slide Lake

Whig Lake (Waldo Lake Wilderness)
hike-in

Whig Lake is a productive and fairly popular brook trout lake spanning 15 acres and situated a mile by trail from the road into Taylor Burn north of Waldo Lake. The planted brookies generally range from 6 to 12 inches. The Taylor Butte Trail (#3579) departs south from the Taylor Burn Road (FR 514) about a mile east from the road's end near Taylor Burn Campground. Follow the trail south less than a mile to reach 1-acre Fields Lake (see listing herein) and then the north end of elongated Whig Lake. Nearby Torrey Lake, Wahanna Lake, and several others offer fair-to-good trout fishing as well (see listings herein).

Whiskey Lake (Mt. Jefferson Wilderness)
hike-in, cross-country

A 3-acre brook trout/cutthroat trout lake (depending on the most recent species stocked by ODFW) northeast from Marion Lake, Whiskey usually offers fair-to-good action on mostly small fish. See the directions to Marion Lake. After skirting the northeast corner of Marion Lake, watch for a signed trail heading northeast to Lake-of-the-Woods. The hike from Marion Lake covers an easy 2-plus miles and gains about 700 feet. Whiskey Lake is situated about 300 yards behind (east from) Lake-of-the-Woods. Both lakes offer some nice camping areas in scenic settings.

Whitewater Lake (Mt. Jefferson Wilderness)
hike-in, cross-country

Whitewater Lake supports small, wild cutthroat and is located just inside the west edge of the Mt. Jefferson Wilderness east of Idanha. Whitewater Lake draws water from the glaciers on Mt. Jefferson and typically ranges in color from green to glacial-gray, making it un-fishable most of the time. You can get there from the end of either of two nearby forest roads. Be sure to consult map and compass.

Widgeon Lake (Mt. Jefferson Wilderness)
hike-in, cross-country, float tube recommended

Three-acre Widgeon Lake offers fair fishing for brook trout that reach 16 inches. Located just a few hundred yards south of a little-used trail on the west edge of the Mt. Jefferson Wilderness Area, this small, secluded lake is lightly fished. A bushwhacker's trail leads to Widgeon from more popular Fir Lake, but this is hardly the easiest route unless you happen to be fishing Fir Lake anyway. The Pika-Fir Lake Trailhead is located immediately north of Fay Lake, which is accessible by vehicle from the Big Meadows Road. Look for the Big Meadows sign on the east side of Hwy 22, immediately south of the North Santiam River Bridge at about Milepost 76.

The easier route to Widgeon requires a little map-and-compass work, but saves a lot of bushwhacking. Follow the gravel road north past Fay Lake and past the Pika-Fir Lake Trailhead. Shortly thereafter watch for a closed and gated logging road on your right. Park here and hike the road until it ends and becomes an eastbound trail. The trail soon reaches the wilderness boundary, but this boundary was unmarked last time I was in there. So you'll need a little map and compass (or GPS) work to find the lake, which resides exactly on the boundary line just a couple hundred yards south of the trail. If you know where to look, you can just barely see the lake from one spot on the trail. (In 2003, firefighters dozed a fire line through this area near the wilderness boundary and the aforementioned roadway runs into it, making finding the trail somewhat troublesome: at the end of the road, continue walking along the right-hand side of the fire break and just watch carefully for the trail.)

The Willamette River is home to fat smallmouth bass.

Willamette River, Coast Fork (Lane County)

Only marginally productive—for a few wild trout in its upper reaches and some hatchery trout in its lower stretch—the Coast Fork Willamette feeds Cottage Grove Lake before running through Cottage Grove and north along I-5 to meet the Middle Fork Willamette. Most of the trout fishing takes place below the dam on Cottage Grove Lake. Take Exit 170 from I-5 and follow the signs.

Willamette River, Middle Fork (upper)
campgrounds

The Middle Fork Willamette above Hills Creek Reservoir is a fine trout stream offering mostly small, wild cutthroat trout along with planted rainbows (mostly in the lower 8 miles). You won't find many big trout, but the scenery and the frequent bouts of fast action more than atone for the small fish. In fact, most years during the summer and early autumn the first 10 miles of the river above the reservoir come alive with rising trout looking for the abundant grasshoppers. The smaller uppermost reaches hold lots of small natives, equally eager to pounce on dry flies.

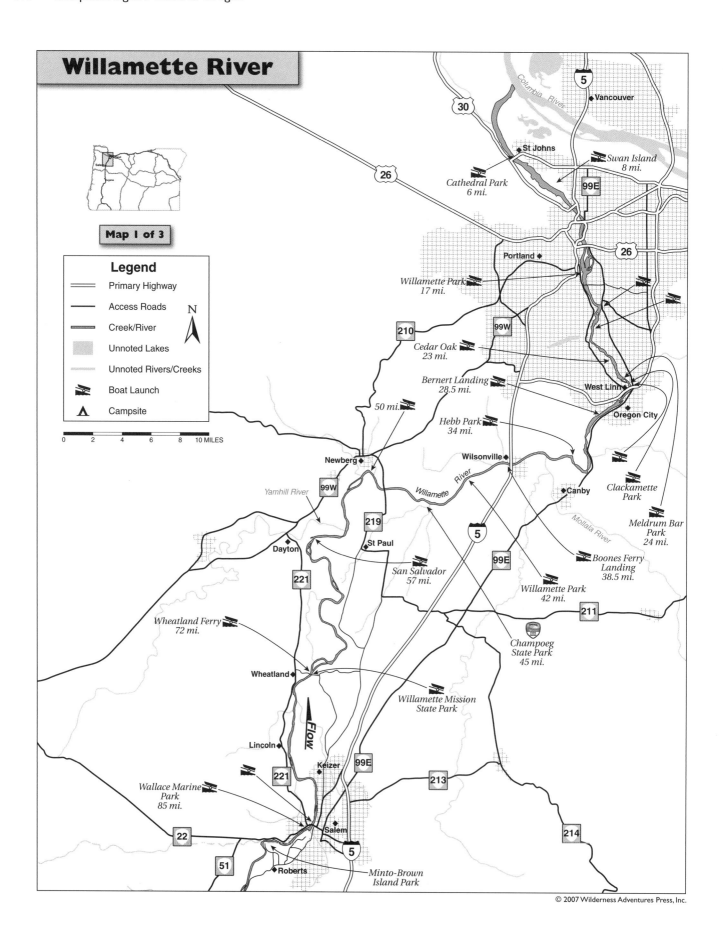

Willamette River

Map 1 of 3

Legend
	Primary Highway
	Access Roads
	Creek/River
	Unnoted Lakes
	Unnoted Rivers/Creeks
	Boat Launch
	Campsite

N

0 2 4 6 8 10 MILES

Columbia River

Vancouver

St Johns

Swan Island
8 mi.

Cathedral Park
6 mi.

Portland

Willamette Park
17 mi.

Cedar Oak
23 mi.

Bernert Landing
28.5 mi.

West Linn

Hebb Park
34 mi.

Oregon City

50 mi.

Newberg

Wilsonville

Clackamette
Park

Yamhill River

Willamette River

Canby

Meldrum Bar
Park
24 mi.

Dayton

St Paul

San Salvador
57 mi.

Mollala River

Willamette Park
42 mi.

Boones Ferry
Landing
38.5 mi.

Wheatland Ferry
72 mi.

Champoeg
State Park
45 mi.

Wheatland

Willamette Mission
State Park

Flow

Lincoln

Keizer

Wallace Marine
Park
85 mi.

Salem

Roberts

Minto-Brown
Island Park

© 2007 Wilderness Adventures Press, Inc.

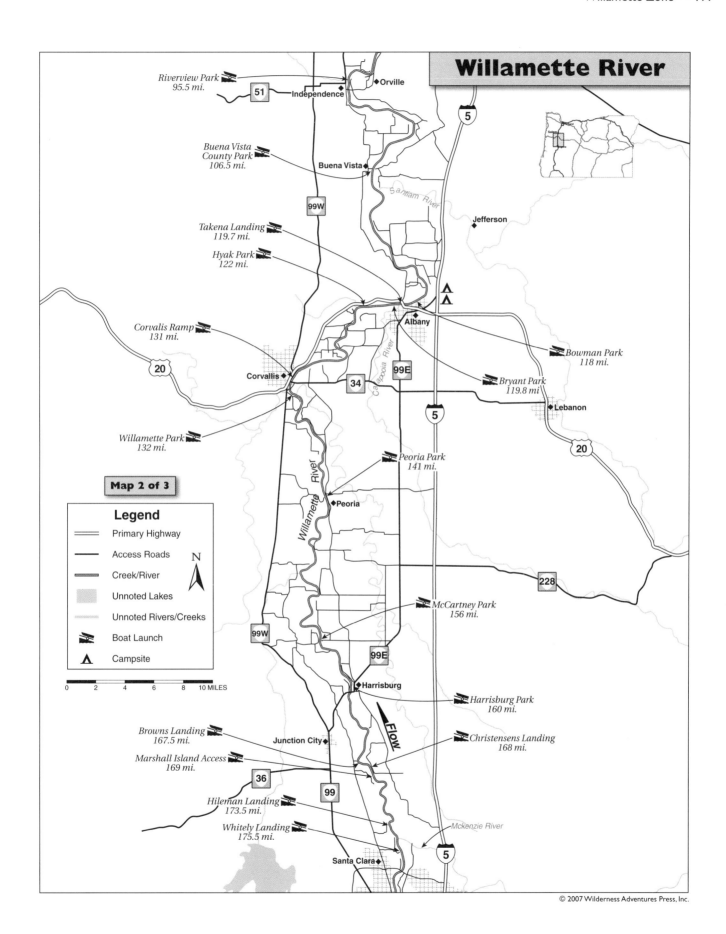

Willamette River

Riverview Park
95.5 mi.

51

◆Orville
◆Independence

5

Buena Vista
County Park
106.5 mi.

Buena Vista◆

Santiam River

99W

◆Jefferson

Takena Landing
119.7 mi.

Hyak Park
122 mi.

Λ
Λ

◆Albany

Corvalis Ramp
131 mi.

Calapooia River

99E

Bowman Park
118 mi.

20

Corvallis◆

34

Bryant Park
119.8 mi

5

◆Lebanon

Willamette Park
132 mi.

20

Peoria Park
141 mi.

Map 2 of 3

◆Peoria

Willamette River

228

Legend

	Primary Highway
	Access Roads
	Creek/River
	Unnoted Lakes
	Unnoted Rivers/Creeks
	Boat Launch
Λ	Campsite

N

McCartney Park
156 mi.

99W

99E

0 2 4 6 8 10 MILES

◆Harrisburg

Harrisburg Park
160 mi.

Browns Landing
167.5 mi.

Flow

Junction City◆

Christensens Landing
168 mi.

Marshall Island Access
169 mi.

36

99

Hileman Landing
173.5 mi.

Whitely Landing
175.5 mi.

Mckenzie River

5

Santa Clara◆

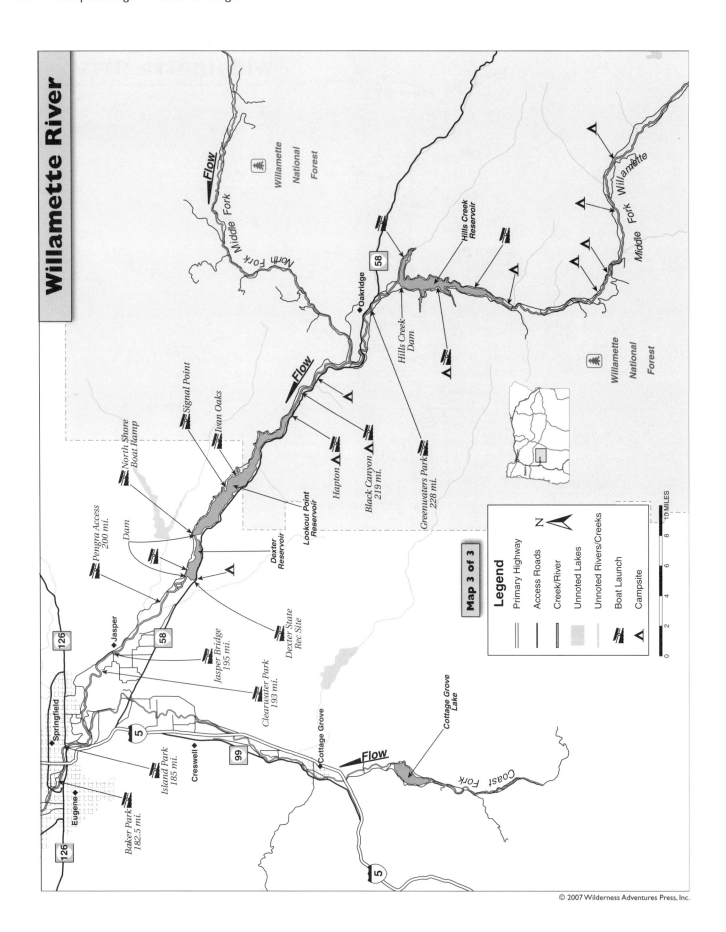

Middle Fork Willamette River

Middle Fork Willamette
(Hills Creek Dam to Lookout Point Reservoir)
no bait, catch-and-release

Between Hills Creek Dam and the top end of Lookout Point Reservoir, the Middle Fork Willamette offers fair fishing for wild rainbow trout, including some fish in the 14- to 20-inch range. Less abundant wild cutthroat trout also inhabit the river. Good hatches of caddisflies and stoneflies make this stretch popular with fly anglers. The river is open year-round and can produce good fishing just about any time unless the water is too high. Most fly anglers target this reach of the Middle Fork from late spring through early autumn, but the mid-winter fishing can be quite productive. Access to this portion of the Middle Fork is good from Hwy 58 and from several local roads on both sides of the river. Few anglers drift the Middle Fork here, but you can do so by launching at Greenwater Park (pole slide) and taking out at Black Canyon.

Middle Fork Willamette (below Dexter Dam)
boat recommended, boat ramp

Below Dexter Dam, the Middle Fork Willamette is a popular and productive chinook salmon fishery and also fairly good for hatchery summer-run steelhead. Spring chinook arrive as early as April and the fishery peaks during May and June. Hatchery summer steelhead show up between May and July. The Middle Fork is most productive for anglers fishing by boat and the river hosts quite a bit of traffic in the form of drift boats and jet sleds. The usual drift goes from Dexter Dam or Pengra down to Jasper Bridge or from either of those points down to Clearwater Park in Springfield. The upper drift is a good one for summer steelhead and is popular with drift boat anglers. To reach the launch site, take Hwy 126 heading east into Springfield and turn right on 42nd Street, then left on Jasper Road. Follow the signs to Dexter Dam. Before you reach the dam, a signed gravel road leads to the ramp.

The Pengra Access is very popular with power boaters, who run both directions from the launch. Drift boaters enjoy consistent success on this stretch, mostly by pulling plugs and bait fishing. Keep an eye peeled for stumps, logs, and other obstacles. As you approach the Jasper Bridge, the takeout is on your left. Jasper Bridge is accessible from both directions (Springfield or Hwy 58) and the popular drift from the bridge down to Springfield covers a lot of shallow water ideal for fishing flies for summer steelhead. The takeout is at Clearwater Park, accessible from 42nd Street in Springfield.

Generally speaking, pressure on the Middle Fork diminishes as you move downstream, namely because the upper drifts are so productive for salmon and because jet boaters seem to prefer the Pengra Launch, which allows them to fish more than enough prime water in both directions. Steelhead fishing, however, can be good all the way down to Whitely Landing in Eugene. The stretch from Clearwater Park to Eugene offers plenty of good steelhead water for all angling methods and receives a fairly heavy allotment of smolt plants.

Obviously fly anglers do especially well here, as the trout frequently prove eager to rise for basic attractor-style dry flies. In addition to hopper patterns for late summer, carry Stimulators, Royal Humpies, Madam-X's, and Parachute Adams. On those rare occasions when dry flies don't work, try beadhead nymph patterns drifted through the deeper pools and runs. Spin fishers often enjoy fast action on small Panther Martins, Rooster Tails, and similar lures.

The river runs for many miles through a scenic, forested canyon. Forest Road 21 follows the river above Hills Creek Reservoir and all the way to the headwaters. Four campgrounds are located riverside along the way. About 2 miles east of Oakridge, turn south on Kitson Springs Road (FR 21) and follow it around the west side of Hills Creek Reservoir.

Willamette River, North Fork of the Middle Fork
fly-only, campgrounds

This highly scenic and surprisingly lightly fished river is reserved for fly fishing and is open all year with a catch-and-release-only season from November through April. The beautiful North Fork offers fairly abundant wild cutthroat and rainbow, most of them ranging from 4 to 9 inches, but with a few picture-perfect 12- to 16-inchers, which usually come from the deeper pools and runs in the river's lower reaches, just above the confluence with the Middle Fork. Brook trout occur in the river's seldom-fished uppermost pools. Throughout its run, the North Fork's little natives love dry flies during summer and fall, and a No. 8 Stimulator or Madam-X works perfectly and offers the added attribute of being too big for the 4-inch fish to impale themselves upon.

The North Fork of the Middle Fork begins as a swift-moving creek flowing from the northwest corner of Waldo Lake. The river drops 2,400 feet in its first 3 miles, pouring over 34 separate waterfalls and flowing north through the Waldo Lake Wilderness. This is cross-country work for anglers willing to bushwhack through some heavy brush, but the 1996 Charlton Fire burned a lot of the drainage here and made for easier walking in many places. The Blair Lake Trail crosses the river, which then begins a tumultuous plunge through a virtually inaccessible canyon at the eastern foot of Moolack Mountain.

Emerging from the gorge, the North Fork then meanders briefly through narrow, scenic meadows. Cutthroat trout prevail and rainbow become increasingly common. The river's native cutthroat are heavily marked with big, black spots. The Shale Ridge Trail (#3367) follows the river upstream for more than 2 miles from FR 19, south of Box Canyon Guard Station. Watch for the brown and white hiker sign just before you head around a 35-mph corner, near milepost 30. These upper reaches are accessible by June and fish best between mid-July and October. The river wraps around the north slope of Moolack Mountain and begins its 25-mile run down to Westfir, gaining size from myriad tributaries that drain the rugged timber-clad escarpments climbing high above the road.

All told, the North Fork of the Middle Fork flows for 43 miles. It changes gradually from a plunging alpine cascade to a scenic, high- to medium-gradient freestone river surrounded by lush temperate forest. The lower half of the river is strewn with boulders, especially in the steep sections; rugged pocket water stretches alternate with cobble glides and pools. A few miles upstream from Westfir, the river flows through an area called "The Gorge," where sheer rock cliffs descend right to the water.

The upper river flows through dense forest and the best way to access it is to get into the riverbed at a side-road, bridge, or trail and then wade up or down the channel. Often you'll be wading through a tunnel of impenetrable alders, maples, evergreens, and underbrush. You won't need waders during late summer, but be sure to wear cleated or felted wading boots.

The river swells with heavy rain, but winter dry spells allow for windows of good nymph fishing on the lower few miles near Westfir. During May, the flows run with a tinge of snowmelt color, which subsides by July. Optimal low flows predominate from July through October, when caddis and stoneflies dominate the insect activity. The trout are rarely fussy over a specific pattern, but anglers who seek out-of-the-way reaches enjoy the most consistent action.

Forest Road 21—the Aufderheide Scenic Road—follows the North Fork for 26 miles, sometimes right alongside the river and sometimes at a distance. A paved, well-maintained mountain highway, FR 21 begins at Westfir, near Oakridge, off Hwy 58. Before you reach Oakridge, watch for the left-hand exit to Westfir at milepost 31 (across the highway from the ranger station). Cross the Middle Fork at the RV park and turn left at the east side of the bridge. Continue straight ahead when you reach the four-way stop at Westfir. On your left is the largest covered bridge in Oregon, built by the Westfir Lumber Company in 1944 and spanning 180 feet. Kiahanie Campground is located about mid-way up the river.

North Fork of the Middle Fork Willamette River

Willamette River, Eugene/Springfield
services

One of the state's most intriguing urban fisheries exists within the city limits of Eugene. Here the Willamette River offers good fishing for wild trout and whitefish along with fair action for hatchery summer steelhead and spring chinook salmon. Fly anglers especially relish the easy-access opportunity to fish dry flies to rising fish during a March brown mayfly hatch that rivals that of the Willamette's more famous neighbor, the Lower McKenzie. And in the past decade, the river within the city limits has become very popular for hatchery summer steelhead. The so-called "town run" was started by ODFW when the agency started stocking steelhead smolts in the Willamette within Eugene/Springfield, hoping the fish would hang around town, so to speak, when they returned as adults. The program started working and now anglers enjoy consistent success. Drift boats can use any number of ramps between Dexter Dam and the city itself (see map).

For trout fly fishers, the mayflies first appear during February and the hatch continues through early or mid-April. At its peak, the hatch offers daily dry-fly action that can last for an hour or more around mid-day. The river's native cutthroat trout and whitefish typically range from 8 to 12 inches. Wild rainbow trout in this section reach at least 18 inches, but most range from 9 to 13 inches. Access to good trout water is available by footpath throughout town and behind the Valley River Center Mall. Additional access to good trout and steelhead water is available from extensive Alton Baker Park, which stretches from the Interstate-5 bridge area over the river downstream to Coburg Road, just west of Autzen Stadium.

Willamette River, Eugene to Salem
boatr ramps, boat recommended, services

From Eugene north to the Santa Clara area, the Willamette River offers good fishing for wild trout, along with decent prospects for spring chinook salmon that arrive between April and June. The salmon fishery is mostly a boat show, with good launch points in Eugene and downstream as far as the Lane County line. During the spring salmon season, the Willamette carries enough flow that drift boats are viable options. You can launch at Alton-Baker Park, Island Park, or West D Street in Eugene and drift through the city down to the take-out at Whitely Ramp north of Santa Clara. This float covers about 10 miles and is a good choice for the long days of May and June, when both salmon and summer steelhead are in the river.

Most serious Willamette River salmon anglers, however, prefer power boats to fish the water below Eugene and down to Corvallis. Popular launch/access sites include Marshall Island (river mile 169), Harrisburg Park (rm 160) and McCartney Park (rm 156). The stretch from Eugene to Harrisburg presents few obstacles except for the shifting nature of the riverbed itself. From Eugene to Corvallis, the river changes course frequently. Salmon tend to move quickly through the Willamette, so success usually depends on locating the deeper slots and runs where the fish tend to slow down and hold for brief periods.

By mid-summer, the Willamette drops to significantly lower levels and in several segments becomes a popular playground for pleasure boaters, including canoeists and kayakers. From July through September, the river is a fair-to-good bet for both trout and smallmouth bass, depending on where you want to fish. The trout fishing can be quite good between Eugene and Harrisburg, with the best action in the Santa Clara area. Fly anglers will enjoy the morning and evening hatches. Indeed, very few fly anglers realize that this stretch of the Willamette offers localized but dense morning hatches of Trico mayflies, a species widely known for its presence on famous spring creeks.

A fine trip for trout—any time from early spring (water levels permitting) through mid-autumn—is to launch at Armitage Park on the lower McKenzie River and take out on the Willamette at Beacon Road or at Marshall Island. The Beacon Road access is suitable for pontoons and other such personal craft. For drift boats, use the Marshall Island ramp. Powerboat anglers can launch at Marshall and run up the Willamette and then up the McKenzie and fish back down.

Below Marshall Island, trout become increasingly less common, but smallmouth bass become more abundant. The Harrisburg-to-Corvallis section (30 miles) offers several possible float segments that are good for drift boats, pontoons, canoes, and other such craft. Be advised of the hazards, however, which include the shifting channel that creates new side channels, along with shallows, logs, swift currents around the islands, and a variety of other potential pitfalls. Throughout this stretch, various channels, inlet mouths, islands, and other structures create holding water for bass, along with a few crappie and other species.

Downstream from Corvallis, the smallmouth fishing steadily improves. In fact, in addition to producing quite a few spring chinook salmon and a few summer steelhead, the Willamette River between Albany and Salem offers some top-notch fishing for bass. Smallies of several pounds inhabit these waters and a handful of anglers specialize in pursuing them. They guard their secret spots closely for good reason. Some of the best bass haunts lie in the stretch from Salem's Minto-Brown Park upstream (south) to the mouth of the Luckiamute River, a reach of 22 miles that encompasses a wide variety of bass structure.

River mileage and estimated float times for the Willamette upstream from Salem are as follows:

- Dexter Dam to Springfield: 18 miles/4 hours
- Armitage State Park to Harrisburg: 21 miles/5 hours
- Harrisburg to Corvallis: 30 miles/8-10 hours
- Corvallis to Albany: 11 miles/5 hours
- Albany to Buena Vista: 15 miles/6 hours
- Buena Vista to Independence: 11 miles/5 hours
- Independence to Salem: 12 miles/5 hours

Willamette River, Salem to Oregon City
boat ramps, services

From Salem downstream to Oregon City, the Mainstem Willamette is the haunt of anglers in search of spring chinook salmon along with warmwater species. The salmon, a majority of which are of hatchery origin, pass over Willamette Falls between April and June. They range from 10 to more than 30 pounds. In the Willamette River, the fishery peaks in May. The exact timing of the best fishing varies from year to year, but late April through late May is best. Keep an eye on the counts at Willamette Falls. The salmon fishery is almost entirely a boat show, though bank-fishing access is available at most of the launch sites.

Tactics on the river range from bank fishing with Corkies, Birdies, spoons, and spinners to trolling the broad, slow-moving water that predominates from Newberg to Oregon City. During late spring, salmon anglers account for most of the summer steelhead taken on the Willamette below Salem and they usually tag quite a few of these hatchery produced one- and two-salt fish, which typically range from 7 to 12 pounds.

While this section of the river presents no technical water per say, boaters must always exercise caution during the elevated flows of spring. Generally the flows remain stable, but storm events on the up-river tributaries—especially the Santiam Rivers and the two upper-most forks of the Willamette—can result in fairly substantive and rapid increases in water height. More significantly perhaps, anglers must keep a constant eye peeled for flotsam, often in the form of logs and trees. Likewise, beware the shallow gravel bars.

The salmon fishing ends during early June, after which warmwater species steal the show. Bass and crappie, along with catfish, bluegill, and a few incidentals, abound in the river. Crappie and smallmouth bass inhabit the main channel where proper habitat exists in the form of some kind of structure. Look for rock piles, back-eddies, steep drop-offs, riprap, and even cobblestone bars in slow water. Also study the downstream end of the islands, where deflected currents often form seams that concentrate baitfish and smallmouth bass that prey on them. The largemouth bass and bluegill invariably inhabit the sloughs and slack-water sections. The less current, the better; and no current is best. Both species tend to seek structure: snags, pilings, stumps, stick-ups, logjams, cut banks, brush piles, and so on.

Throughout this reach, whether you fish for salmon or for bass and panfish, boat access is better than bank access, though bank anglers can enjoy good sport at various locales. During the summer, beware the heavy use by recreational boaters, including jet skiers and water skiers. Non-motorized craft are fine here, especially between Salem and Wheatland Ferry. Below the ferry, the current begins to slow and the next boat landing is 15 miles downstream. Downstream from St. Paul and Newberg, slow-moving water makes non-motorized craft best suited to localized use rather than lengthy trips.

Some of the popular fishing holes for salmon, bass, panfish, and catfish include the mouths of both the Yamhill and Molalla Rivers. The Molalla confluence, which offers good bank access at a state park on the south bank, is also a good salmon hole and the entire lower end of the Yamhill River offers a productive smallmouth bass fishery. The Molalla meets the Willamette at river mile 36, east of Wilsonville and the Yamhill dumps into the Willamette at river mile 55, south of Newberg. Rock Island, at river mile 30 (5 miles upstream from Oregon City) is a popular bass fishing and boat-in camping spot.

Additional bank access includes a variety of state, county, and city access points. Salem offers good access at Wallace Marine Park on the west side of the river in Salem and just upstream at Minto-Brown Island Park (see listing herein). The latter park offers access to a lengthy slough and a series of ponds, all of which have bass, crappie, bullheads, and bluegill. To get to Minto-Brown by powerboat, launch downstream at Wallace-Marine Park and run across the river and up into the mile-long slough. Otherwise, fish the east bank (for smallmouth, along with a few trout and salmon) by foot from the trail in the park or fish the ponds by foot, float tube, or canoe.

To the north, Salem merges into the city of Keizer, which owns several small parks along the river; all accessed off side roads leading west from River Road, the main artery running through town. River's Edge Park is at the end of Garland Way, but access is only by foot and can be troublesome (plus I wouldn't leave a vehicle unattended there). Sunset Park lies off Sunset Drive and offers a fair amount of bank access and even more for anglers who ask permission from the landowners who own property adjacent to the park. Palma Ciea Park sits at the end of Cummings Lane, but offers no meaningful access to the water. Just downstream from Keizer, Oregon State Parks owns two boat-accessible landings, one on each bank near river mile 80. Spong's Landing, at the end of Windsor Island Road north of Keizer, offers good access to the east bank.

The Middle Fork Willamette River near Eugene/Springfield produces beautiful wild rainbows.

Across the river, accessible from SR 221 (Wallace Road) through West Salem, is Lincoln Access along with Darrow Bar Access (milepost 16), Lincoln Access (immediately north of Lincoln) and Spring Valley Access (milepost 12 across from the Mennonite Church). A small side channel at the Lincoln Access is easy to ford at low summer flows and allows access to the adjacent island. Any craft you can carry to the water's edge can be launched at these points, but none offer boat ramps. To reach them from Salem, cross the river on the Marion Street Bridge, taking the first exit to West Salem. Swing right at the bottom of the ramp and head straight out of town on SR 221. Lincoln is a tiny town a few miles outside of Salem.

Also on the west side and a few miles north from Spring Valley Access, Grand Island offers a state access point that is fairly popular with waterfowl hunters. This public easement allows good access to some fine prospects for bass, crappie, bluegill, and catfish. On SR 221, continue north from Lincoln or south from Dayton. Watch for the east turn onto Grand Island Road, across from the gas station. Head east to a right-hand turn on Upper Island Road and follow this road about 2 miles to the public access point on your right. Some shoreline fishing is available from the informal trails leading through the woods, but the best action is by canoe or kayak.

The launch site—a hundred yards straight ahead from the parking area—lies on a side channel off the main river. Turn right, heading up current, to reach the mouth of Lambert Slough along with several cover-filled side sloughs and cut banks. The mouth of Lambert Slough (see separate listing herein) lies about a mile upstream. At its upstream end, the main side channel departs the main river just downstream from Wheatland Ferry—you'll fight the current all the way, but it's not too bad during the summer. If you turn left off the launch site at Grand Island Access, the main Willamette lies just a few hundred yards downstream. The island formed by the channel is called Wheatland Bar.

Six river miles to the north, Grand Island ends at the mouth of Lambert Slough. Boaters can fish this productive area for salmon and warmwater fish. Half a mile of bank to the south of the slough's mouth is owned by the state for public access. The nearest launch sites are 7 miles upstream at Wheatland Ferry and 8 miles downstream at San Salvador Park (both on the east bank).

Windsor Island, owned by the Division of State Lands, is a fairly popular fishing and camping spot, accessible by boat, at river mile 76, a few miles north of Keizer. Most people get to Windsor by launching at Wallace Marine Park in Salem or at one of the downstream launches, such as Wheatland Ferry.

Just below Windsor Island, Wheatland Ferry (an active ferry that charges $1 per car) and adjacent Willamette Mission State Park, along with the aforementioned Spring Valley Access on the west bank, offer a combined 4 miles of bank access, including lots of good fishing water. To get to Wheatland Ferry and Willamette Mission State Park, exit I-5 at Brooks, north of Salem, and head due west until you hit a forced right-hand turn on Wheatland Road. Watch for signs to Willamette Mission State Park and the ferry. (See separate list-

The Willamette River below Wheatland Ferry

ings for Mission Lake and Goose Lake).

Downstream from the Wheatland Ferry, boaters enjoy a distinct advantage because bank access is essentially non-existent for the next 15 river miles, save for the Grand Island Access on the west bank. The next public access is San Salvador Park near St. Paul on the east (south) bank. From St. Paul, follow Blanchet Road heading west until you reach the park, which offers a good ramp and some good water for salmon angling. Two miles downstream is the mouth of the Yamhill River, entering from the west. Under normal flows, the Yamhill is navigable up to the town of Dayton, 6 miles upstream. The entire lower reach of the Yamhill offers good fishing for small-mouth bass (see listing herein).

The Willamette's current dissipates substantially as you progress downstream from Newberg, and from there to Oregon City, salmon fishing is mostly done by trolling or by casting to known holding areas at the mouths of the major tributaries, including the Mollala River. The Molalla's mouth

Spring Valley Access on the Willamette River

also offers fair chances for winter steelhead from January through March and has a good population of smallmouth bass and crappie. The Newberg-to-Oregon City stretch also produces some sturgeon, though not as consistently as the river below Willamette Falls. Boat launching facilities are available in Newberg, near I-5 (Boones Ferry Landing), at the mouth of the Molalla, and at Hebb Park, Bernert Landing, and Oregon City Landing.

River mileage and estimated float times for the Willamette upstream from Salem are as follows:

- Salem to Wheatland Ferry: 12 miles/5 hours
- Wheatland Ferry to San Salvador Park: 15 hours/6-7 hours
- San Salvador Park to Champoeg State Park: 11 miles/5 hours
- Champoeg State Park to West Linn: 17 miles/8 hours
- West Linn to Willamette Park: 12 miles/7 hours
- Willamette Park to Kelley Point Park: 18 miles/10 hours

Willamette River, Oregon City to Columbia
boat ramp, boat recommended, services

One of Oregon's most popular river fisheries occurs each spring on the Willamette River in Oregon City and Gladstone, downstream from Willamette Falls. Boats crowd in tight for a chance at spring chinook salmon—along with steelhead and shad—that congregate below the falls and at the mouth of the Clackamas River. Clackamette Park is the site of "hog-line" fishing, defined by boats lining up side-by-side throughout the prime spots. The pattern repeats itself just upstream, and below Clackamette, both still fishers and trollers work the river intensively and enjoy consistent success on salmon and steelhead. Bank anglers get in on the action at any of several easy-access areas, including the breakwater on Hwy 99 in Oregon City downstream from the falls and the ever-popular Meldrum Bar.

The remainder of the lower river offers trolling opportunities for salmon, fair fishing for sturgeon and shad, and good prospects for smallmouth bass and other warmwater species. The many bridge footings, pilings, breakwaters, docks, and other structures provide lots of good bass structure and anglers take quite a few 1- to 3-pound smallies from the lower river. The best smallmouth fishing occurs from Milwaukee, through downtown Portland (both sides of the river, but especially Oak Bottoms on the east bank), down to Swan Island. Largemouth bass become increasingly common as you approach the river's mouth, but they can be found anywhere that offers suitable habitat.

The Willamette offers a handful of decent bank-access fishing areas, but boaters have the advantage for all species. Boat ramps are scattered the length of the lower river, from Oregon City down to Multnomah Channel. Motorized craft are the norm, but in several places anglers use canoes, kayaks, pontoon boats, and even float tubes to fish for warmwater species. Bill Egan, director of the Oregon Bass & Panfish Club (http://obpc0.tripod.com/), once compiled for the local newspaper a list of accessible Portland bank fishing spots as follows:

"Cathedral Park: A long fishing pier extends beneath the east bank of the St. Johns Bridge; expect a few smallmouth bass and occasional walleye, but the area below the dock is silted. Cast long into the Willamette River for a good chance at sturgeon in a popular area for boat angling.

Swan Island Lagoon: Follow the signs to the boat ramp. The shoreline around the ramp is rocky and a good location for bass and crappie. Many anglers fish there at night, mostly with lanterns on the dock. Crappie hang out near the pilings. Hike to the opposite shoreline for smallmouth bass among the submerged pilings.

Downtown Portland: The river's east shoreline is a gold mine for smallmouth bass anglers. From the Esplanade, cast to the rocks, not the river. Crappie also hang out on the down-current side of the steel pilings. Bank fishing beneath the Hawthorne Bridge is accessible from OMSI.

Willamette Park: Boats might come and go for spring chinook, but the park's shoreline is good habitat for bass. Cast a worm to the bottom a little farther out for bullhead catfish.

Sucker Creek: Water backs up in May and June in a small bay where the creek enters the Willamette River, giving bass, crappie and bluegill good spawning cover. A public park offers good access for fishing.

Gladstone: Meldrum Bar Park's boat launch is a lagoon protected from the river by a large gravel bar. On the east side, fish for bass and crappie in the morning before the boats make a lot of noise or the evening after they've gone home.

Oregon City: Clackamette Park has structure and access on both the Clackamas and Willamette Rivers. Smallmouth bass and some walleye are caught from the shoreline, but the park becomes very popular in May when tightly schooled shad surge close to the bank. It's one of the area's best smallmouth bass shoreline fisheries through most of the summer.

West Linn: Bank access is good in Cedaroak Park, and smallmouth bass hang out throughout the area. When the water rises sometime after April 15, the city will swing a bridge from the shoreline at Mary S. Young Park to Cedar Island, where there are several fishing platforms. The Bass and Panfish Club anchored Christmas trees on the bottom of the lagoon two decades ago for crappie habitat."

Willamina Creek (Yamhill County)
catch-and-release, no bait

Probably the best wild cutthroat streams in Yamhill County, Willamina Creek offers a fair amount of access for those seeking a quiet day of catch-and-release action. The trout range from 4 to 12 inches. Most of the accessible water lies on the upper portions of the creek, though you can often find a few trout at Blackwell Park, 4.5 miles north of the town of Willamina. To get there, follow SR 18 south from McMinnville to the Sheridan Junction. Head through Sheridan to Willamina and turn north on Willamina Creek Road. Alternately from Salem, follow Hwy 22 west to Hwy 18 and then follow the signs to Willamina.

Willamina Pond

Willamina Pond is no longer stocked and is now closed. See Huddeston Pond herein.

Williams Lake (Lane County)
hike-in

Easy to reach from Taylor Burn north of Waldo Lake, Williams Lake offers decent fishing for stocked brook trout or cutthroat trout (depending on which species has been stocked most recently) and is not nearly so popular as its much larger neighbors to the northwest, the Erma Bell Lakes. Williams is a good float-tube lake, but also offers ample room to fish from shore. It spans about 4 acres. From Taylor Burn, follow the Williams Lake Trail (#3589) north .8 of a mile to the lake, which sits on the right side of the trail. From Skookum Campground to the north it's about 3 miles down to Williams Lake, which is usually accessible by mid-June. See Erma Bell Lakes for directions to the area.

Winberry Creek (Lane County)
see Fall Creek

Windfall Lake (Lane County)
hike-in, cross-country

A remote lake with small wild cutthroat trout, Windfall Lake occupies a narrow bench at the bottom of a steep canyon a few miles west from the Middle Fork Arm of Hills Creek Reservoir. There is no easy approach to 2-acre Windfall Lake and consequently it is rarely visited. Logs and brush litter Windfall Creek, making it a tough way to get to the lake so you are better off climbing down the steep slope from a logging road on the south side that approaches to within about a quarter mile of the lake. Study a topo map carefully and then head south from Oakridge along the west side of Hills Creek Reservoir. When FR 21 crosses over the upper end of the reservoir, head right instead on FR 2117 and follow it all the way up to the ridge above Windfall Lake.

Wirth Lake
see Walter Wirth Lake

Yamhill River (Yamhill County)
boat ramp, boat recommended

The Yamhill River is a tributary to the Willamette, with the confluence located east of Dayton. The Yamhill is a small, slow-moving, and meandering river that offers fair-to-good prospects for a variety of gamefish, including smallmouth bass, crappie and catfish, and also a chance for catch-and-keep angling for stocked rainbow trout on the upper river and the forks (no bait above the forks). The best warmwater fishing is near the river's mouth, which is accessible by powerboat from San Salvador Park on the Willamette. To reach San Salvador Park, follow River Road north from Salem or SR 219 south from Newberg to the little town of St. Paul and turn west on Blanchet Avenue, following the signs about 3 miles to the park. From the boat ramp, the mouth of the Yamhill is about 2 miles downstream and on your left. The river is open to fishing, up to the forks, from March 1 through October 31 for warmwater fish.

Powerboats can motor up as far as Dayton and drifting anglers can float down from Dayton and then continue down to the Willamette to Newberg. The total distance is about 13 miles, leaving only minimal time to make a serious effort out of the fishing. Hence the powerboat option makes more sense. Regardless of how you access the river, beware the potential for debris in the form of logs, sweepers, and other hazards.

Upstream from Dundee, the Yamhill flows mostly through private lands and access is difficult to impossible. Bass, cutthroat trout, and a few other fish inhabit the river as it meanders through the wine country, splitting into two forks east of McMinnville. The South Yamhill River and the North Yamhill River both offer fair catch-and-release fishing for small, wild trout in their uppermost reaches. For my money, the South Yamhill is the better of the two, mostly in its headwaters upstream from Grande Ronde. Like the upper stretch of the South Yamhill, the North Yamhill also offer only limited access, with the best fishing upstream from the tiny wide spot called Pike, northwest from the town of Yamhill.

The stocked-trout opportunity is on a short stretch of the South Yamhill, from Gold Creek near Valley Junction, downstream to the U.S. Highway 22 bridge, with access from pullouts along Yamhill River Road. All told, the 20-mile stretch from the forks upstream on the South Yamhill to Rock Creek near Grande Ronde is open to catch-and-keep fishing for hatchery trout. The catch-and-keep trout season runs from late May (check season dates) to the end of October.

Yoncalla Creek ("Yoncalla River")
see Agency Creek

Zigzag River (Mount Hood area)
catch-and-release, no bait

A very pretty and swift little mountain river, the ZigZag offers slow to fair catch-and-release fishing for small wild trout. The river flows more-or-less alongside (often out of view) Hwy 26, upstream from the town of ZigZag. Fishing is best during the summer and early fall.

Zircon Lake (Waldo Lake Wilderness)
hike-in, cross-country, float tube recommended

Usually not labeled on the maps, 4-acre Zircon Lake sits just west of Waldo Lake, a short distance off the Salmon Lakes Trail near Elbow Lake. Zircon is stocked every other year with rainbows. They average pan-size, but this deep lake grows a few big fish. You can fish it from shore, but Zircon is an ideal float tube lake.

The Koch Mountain Trail (#3576) provides the easiest access to Zircon Lake, along with nearby Sapphire Lake (see listing herein). From Oakridge, head northeast on the Salmon Creek Road (FR 24) until you reach the junction where 24 becomes FR 2420 to the right (gated) and FR 2421 to the left (the main branch). This is the Black Creek Road. Follow it half a mile to a left-hand turn onto FR 2422 and follow this road all the way to its end at the trailhead. Follow the trail east less than a mile to Waldo Lake and then head north 2 miles to Elbow Lake. Follow the trail past Elbow and then head off cross-country to the southwest after you pass a small pond on your left. Reference the map herein. Beware the incessant clouds of mosquitoes throughout the summer.

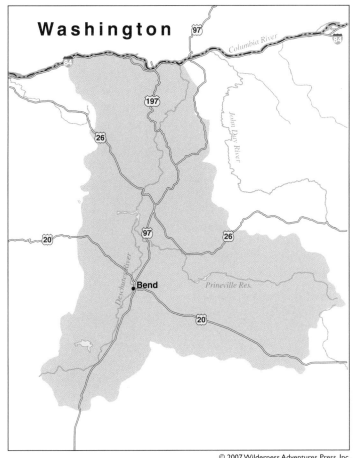

Washington

Columbia River

John Day River

Bend

Prineville Res.

Deschutes River

© 2007 Wilderness Adventures Press, Inc.

Central Zone

O regon's Central Zone might very well be called the state's "famous zone," for central Oregon is home to many of the state's most famous and productive fisheries. The names are familiar: The Deschutes, Metolius and Crooked Rivers; Crane Prairie, Wickiup and Prineville Reservoirs; Davis, Paulina, and Odell Lakes. And that's just the tip of the iceberg. Most of the region's fisheries fall within the Deschutes River watershed and indeed, this amazing river system is the life-blood of the entire region, not just from an angling perspective, but also in terms of the area's geography, ecology, and economy.

The ODFW's Central Zone is managed from the High Desert Regional Headquarters in Bend. The zone includes most of Deschutes, Jefferson, and Wasco Counties along with much of Hood River County on the east-draining side of the Cascade Range. This comprehensive zone stretches from the Columbia River (Hood River and Wasco Counties) south into Klamath County on the Crescent Creek and Little Deschutes River drainages. It stretches east to the Ochoco Mountains east and southeast of Prineville.

The region's most famous waters deserve their lofty reputations, for this is big trout country and many state record fish have come from the waters of central Oregon. Anglers on the famous lakes and reservoirs near Century Drive don't even get excited over a 14-inch trout. Moreover, the region's flagship river—the Lower Deschutes—has no rival in that it offers a unique combination of a world-class trout fishery with a superb summer steelhead fishery.

Central Oregon is especially renowned as a destination for fly anglers. Famous fly waters include not only the Deschutes, but also places like the beautiful Metolius River, the rugged Crooked River, super-fertile Davis Lake, and scenic and serene Hosmer Lake, long revered for its land-locked Atlantic salmon fishery.

Naturally all these famous fisheries attract lots of attention and draw lots of people. If you prefer solitude in your fishing, you can pursue one of two strategies in central Oregon: Fish the well-known waters at the margins of the seasons, especially late in the fall when many of these waters are both comparatively deserted and highly productive. Or you can seek the many out-of-the-way, out-of-the-limelight lakes and streams throughout the region. For example, anglers who don't mind hiking can find many dozens of wilderness lakes teeming with eager trout.

Certainly the trout—and the steelhead of the Deschutes River—attract most of the attention in this zone, but don't forget about the superb warmwater possibilities. Some of the state's best bass and pan fish action occurs at places like Prineville Reservoir, Davis Lake, and the lightly fished ponds and sloughs along I-84 and the Columbia River. All told, Oregon's Central Zone delivers outstanding prospects for a wide array of fish and a broad spectrum of waters and angling opportunities.

Central Zone Contact Information

**Oregon Department of Fish & Wildlife
High Desert Regional Office**
61374 Parrell Road
Bend, OR 97702
541-388-6363

ODFW, Madras-Trout Creek Field Station
1950 Mill Street
Madras, OR 97741
541-475-2183

ODFW, Prineville Field Office
2042 SE Paulina Highway
Prineville, OR 97754
541-447-5111

ODFW, The Dalles Field Office
3701 W. 13th Street
The Dalles, OR 97058
541-296-4628

ODFW, White River Wildlife Area
78430 Dodson Road
Tygh Valley, OR 97063
541-544-2126

BLM Prineville District Office
3050 NE Third Street
Prineville, OR 97754
541-416-6700

Deschutes National Forest
1645 Hwy 20 E.
Bend, OR 97701
541-383-5300

Bend-Fort Rock Ranger District
1230 NE 3rd St., Ste. A-262
Bend, OR 97701
541-383-4000

Crescent Ranger District
P.O. Box 208
136471 Hwy 97 N
Crescent, OR 97733
541-433-3200

Sisters Ranger District
P.O. Box 249
Pine Street & Hwy 20
Sisters, OR 97759
541-549-7700

Ochoco National Forest
3160 NE 3rd Street
Prineville, OR 97754
541-416-6500

Paulina Ranger District
7803 Beaver Creek Road
Paulina, OR 97751
541-477-6900

Crooked River National Grassland
813 SW Hwy 97
Madras, OR 97741
541-475-9272

Mt. Hood National Forest
16400 Champion Way
Sandy, OR 97055
503-668-1700

Barlow Ranger District
780 NE Court Street
Dufur, OR 97021
541-467-2291

Hood River Ranger District
6780 Hwy 35
Parkdale, OR 97041
541-352-6002

Allen Creek Reservoir (Crook County)
float-tube recommended, hike-in

An irrigation-storage impoundment in the hills east of Prineville, Allen Creek Reservoir is a solid producer of nice redband trout, along with a few brook trout. The redbands typically range from 7 to 12 inches, but every once in a while a lucky angler tangles with fish up to 18 inches. The brook trout are similar in size and Allen Creek has produced a few fat 16-inch brookies.

Except for a 200-yard-long BLM easement, the reservoir's shoreline sits on private land. Anglers should respect the private property and stay off the banks except at the BLM site. For this reason, a boat or float tube is well worthwhile on this 80-acre lake, with car-toppers, canoes, rafts, pontoons, and float tubes being ideal. However, the road into the lake is traditionally open only from May 15 to September 15 and gated at all other times. When the road is closed, you'll have to walk about 1.5 miles into the reservoir. The primitive boat launch and BLM access lie along the southeast shore.

Both trolling and bank fishing are popular and productive here and the lake is open to bait fishing. Many anglers rely on the old standbys, including Power-bait, worms, and eggs, but spinners and spoons are effective and trollers often do quite well. Increasingly, fly anglers have discovered Allen Creek Reservoir and they enjoy consistent success using sink-tip and sinking lines coupled with various wet flies.

Allen Creek Reservoir is about 45 miles east of Prineville, on the edge of Big Prairie. There are no facilities, but you can camp on the BLM property or at nearby Scotts Campground or Allen Creek Horse Camp. To get there; follow the highway east out of Prineville to a right-hand turn on CR 23. Follow 23 (Ochoco Creek Road) up into the national forest, where it becomes FR 22. Follow FR 22 past Walton Lake, past Allen Creek Horse Camp, and then turn right on FR 3010 and then right again on FR 3010-019. Carry the forest map with you.

Antelope Flat Reservoir (Crook County)
campground

Relatively remote, Antelope Flat Reservoir (aka Antelope Reservoir) is far enough from Bend/Redmond/Prineville to avoid the crowds that gather at the area's other stillwater fisheries. In addition, Antelope's rainbow trout, stocked as fingerlings to assure good winter survival, grow faster and fatter than those in Prineville Reservoir, Haystack Reservoir, or Walden Lake. During years of good water supply, the fish average a fat 12 or 13 inches. Stack together three wet winters and this reservoir grows lots of fish to 16 inches, and a few reach 18 or more inches. Antelope was chemically treated to remove brown bullheads in 2009, and subsequently restocked.

All methods produce here, and the reservoir is open all year, but road conditions can limit access during the off-season. The drawdown occurs during late spring and summer and can severely affect the water table and the fishing during low-water years. Almost always turbid, Antelope Flat spans 170 acres at full pool; so many anglers haul a small boat over the lengthy route into the reservoir. Maximum depth is about 25 feet and the reservoir sits at an elevation of almost 5,000 feet. Because of its elevation, Antelope Flat generally gets snowed in for the winter and the roads can be sloppy during spring. Before heading out, check road conditions by calling the Prineville Ranger District at 541-416-6500.

Antelope Flat Reservoir is popular with central Oregon's fly-angling crowd and the fly anglers usually fish by pontoon boat and float tube. Sinking or sink-tip lines and general-use wet flies account for most of the action. Productive patterns

This fine smallmouth bass came from the John Day River, one of the state's best "smallie" rivers.

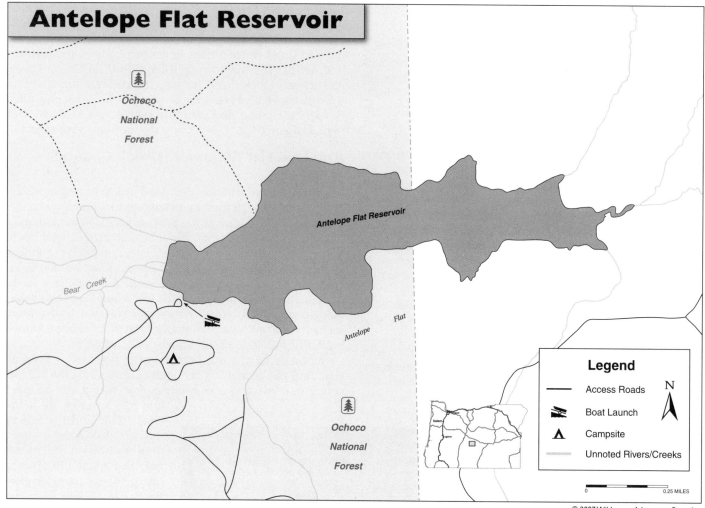

Antelope Flat Reservoir

include Woolly Buggers, bead-head Prince and Pheasant-Tail Nymphs, marabou damsel patterns, Carey Specials, and Chironomid patterns. The lake abounds in all the usual trout foods, including scuds, leeches, and water beetles.

A large campground sits adjacent to the west side of the reservoir and offers all amenities except water. An improved cement boat ramp — for small and medium-sized boats — also occupies the west shore near the dam, but can be rendered unusable when the water is drawn down in summer. Bank anglers congregate in the vicinity of the ramp and dam and usually fare quite well when the trout are on the bite.

To reach Antelope Flat Reservoir from Prineville, follow SR 380 (Post-Paulina Highway) southeast to milepost 30, where a right-hand turn on FR 17 announces "Antelope Reservoir." Follow FR 17 about 12 miles to a left-hand turn on Spur Road 600, leading to the reservoir.

Badger Creek (Mt. Hood National Forest)
hike-in

A fair mountain trout stream, Badger Creek begins as the outlet from Badger Lake, located near the headwaters of the Hood River east of Mt. Hood. The creek runs for many miles, heading east into Tygh Valley. The stream's upper 10 miles are road less and followed by the Badger Creek Trail between Badger Lake and Bonney Crossing Campground. See Badger Lake for directions to the uppermost watershed. To reach Bonney Creek Campground from Portland, follow Hwy 26 to Hwy 35 heading towards Hood River. Turn right on FR 48 and then turn left just east of Rock Creek Campground on FR 4810. Next take a right on FR 4811 and then the next right on FR 2710. This small campground offers eight sites and serves as a nice base for hiking up Badger Creek.

Badger Lake (Mt. Hood National Forest)
campground

A fairly popular and productive high-elevation reservoir on the southeast slope of Mt. Hood, Badger Lake spans about 40 acres. The lake is regularly stocked with legal rainbows, which range from 9 to 13 inches. Brook trout reach 16 inches, though most range from 6 to 11 inches. The last leg of the journey to Badger Lake covers 3 miles on a very rough mountain road. Trailers are prohibited for good reason and only high-clearance vehicles are appropriate. Boats are therefore limited to car-toppers and other small craft.

To reach Badger Lake from Hood River or from Portland, head for Bennett Pass on Hwy 35 (Hood River Highway) and then head east on FR 3550. After a few miles, turn left on FR 4860 and then left again on FR 140 (this is where it gets rugged), leading to the lake. From the east side of the mountains, head for Tygh Valley and then take FR 48 heading west to the National Forest boundary. Then after another 8 miles, bear right onto FR 4860, which leads about 7 miles to a right-hand turn on FR 140. The final leg of the route into Badger Lake may be snowbound until the first week in July, so check ahead by calling the Barlow Ranger District office.

Bakeoven Creek
closed water

Baker Pond (Wasco County)
Baker Pond is a small, stocked trout pond located on the White River Game Management Area northwest from Tygh Valley. The pond spans only 1 acre and is open during the general trout season; ; ODFW stocks about 1,000 rainbows in the pond before the April opener. From Tygh Valley turn west on Wamic Market Road and at Wamic turn south on the road to Rock Creek Reservoir. Then take the first left turn onto Miller Road, leading to a right-hand turn on Driver Road. Follow Driver Road to a right turn on Smock Prairie Road and watch for the short trail to the pond about a mile-and-a-half down the road.

Barbie Lakes (Three Sisters Wilderness)
see Brahma Lake

Barnes Butte Pond (Crook County)
fee fishery, flyfishing only

A private, fee fishery near Prineville, Barnes Butte Lake is widely known in fly-fishing circles for its ability to produce trophy-class rainbow trout, bluegill, and largemouth bass. Fly shops throughout the state host trips here, so call your local shop for details.

Big Marsh Creek (Klamath County)
no bait

A tributary to Crescent Creek in the Little Deschutes River watershed, Big Marsh Creek is aptly named: It meanders through an extensive marshy bog that sprouts an impressive array of spring wildflowers. Small brook trout are fairly common and the stream also supports a sparse population of native redband trout. You'll catch 10 or 15 brookies for every redband trout, and you will need plenty of mosquito repellent. A federally designated Wild & Scenic River, Big Marsh Creek suffered decades of dewatering for grazing purposes and by the middle of the 20th Century the marsh had been turned into a giant pasture.

In recent decades, however, the Forest Service and allied agencies have worked to restore the marsh to a more natural state. The project included repairing and rebuilding some of the original streambed, including a 600-foot section that was essentially built from scratch. The creek is 17.5 miles long in total and the lowest 3.5 miles flow across private property.

The fishing is fair-to-good for brook trout from 5 to 10 inches. June and July are prime and autumn can be even better. Some reaches of the stream, especially the upper half, are somewhat difficult to fish owing to the marsh itself and extensive vegetation and just getting to the creek can prove problematic in places. But you'll usually have the place to yourself except for the abundant wildlife. Most of the actual marsh (the upper length of the creek) is contained within the Oregon Cascades National Recreation Area. The creek is fairly accessible as it flows close to the access road for much of its length.

To get there, follow Hwy 58 to a south turn onto FR 5825. Take FR 5825 westerly and down a steep ridge west of Beales Butte. When you reach the bottom of the ridge, the creek and the marsh are due west. Follow FR 5825 left (south) to head for the upper section, or turn right onto FR 541 to head downstream. The middle section of the creek, from the north end of the marsh downstream to the private property, is hike-in-only and is crossed by FR 6020, which leads to nearby Crescent Lake. Be sure to carry a map with you.

Bikini Pond (Columbia River/I-84)
A small pond covering just a few acres and offering bass, perch, bullhead, and panfish, Bikini Pond sits adjacent to I-84 just west of milepost 76 and near Mayer State Park. Hood River is 11 miles to the west. Some anglers use the wide gravel pull-offs away from the freeway shoulder (westbound lanes), but the more prudent option is to depart the Interstate at Exit 76 and access the pond from the park.

Billy Chinook
see Lake Billy Chinook

Black Lake (Hood River County)
hike-in

A diminutive lake offering 6- to 12-inch brook trout, Black Lake is located in the Hatfield Wilderness. Follow the road to Rainey Lake (see directions herein), but continue about a mile past Rainy. The lake sits off to the left-hand side of the road. The road is usually free of snow by Memorial Day weekend. If not, just park at the snowline and walk in from there, or hike down to North Lake (see listing herein). For road directions from Hood River, see Rainy Lake herein.

Blow Lake (Deschutes National Forest)
hike-in

A fairly popular 45-acre brook trout fishery, Blow Lake lies about a mile southwest of Elk Lake near Century Drive west of Bend. Follow Century Drive past Elk Lake and watch for the turn-off at the Six Lakes Trailhead. Blow Lake is about 1 mile in.

Blowdown Lake (Deschutes National Forest)
hike-in, cross-country, float tube recommended

A fair brook trout lake with fish up to 12 inches, Blowdown sits on a forested bench at 5,556 feet about a mile southeast from Taylor Lake, west of Cultus Mountain. The rugged Taylor Burn Road (FR 600) gets you within a few hundred yards of Blowdown Lake. Consult your topo map and then head a mile east from the campground at Taylor Lake and strike off to the south. Blowdown spans only 4 acres and is fairly shallow.

Blue Lake (Jefferson County)

A deep, beautiful lake located just west from Suttle Lake below the Santiam Highway, Blue Lake sits mostly on private property and is thus not stocked by ODFW.

Blue Lake (Warm Springs Reservation)
closed waters

Bobby Lake (Deschutes National Forest)
hike-in

A large. scenic, deep high-mountain lake near the north flank of Maiden Peak, Bobby is stocked periodically with both brook trout and rainbows. Both species typically reach 12 inches, averaging 9 or 10 inches, but the lake does produce a few 14- to 18-inch fish. Bobby spans 86 acres and reaches a depth of more than 70 feet. Its shoal areas drop off steeply in places, providing ideal cover for trout during late summer. During July and August, concentrate on these areas at mid-day. Otherwise look for fish in the shallower margins fairly close to shore. Much of the shoreline is accessible for bank fishing, especially later in the year when a narrow apron of shoreline emerges on those stretches of the shore fronted by timber. Still, a float tube is great here.

Bobby is fairly popular during the summer, but the crowds disperse by mid-September if not sooner and autumn fishing is usually very good here with all methods producing. Wet flies and streamer patterns fished on sink-tip or sinking lines are especially effective. If you have a float tube, try trolling or casting and retrieving a Mickey Finn or Woolly Bugger as the lead fly in a tandem-fly set-up. For the second fly, try a bead-head Pheasant Tail or Prince Nymph. Spin casters enjoy consistent success with small spoons and Rooster Tails.

The trail covers an easy 2 miles, departing the trailhead on Waldo Lake Road just to the west. Follow Hwy 58 east from the valley or west from Hwy 97 and then turn north on the road to Waldo Lake. After about 5 miles, watch for the Bobby Lake Trail.

Booth Lake (Mt. Jefferson Wilderness Area)
hike-in

A fair-to-good bet for small brook trout (and sometimes rainbow or cutthroat, depending on the most recent stockings), 8-acre Booth Lake lies in the southeast corner of the Mt. Jefferson Wilderness Area, a few miles from Santiam Summit. Consult the wilderness map and then use either the Round Lake Trailhead or the Square Lake Trail. It's about 3.5 miles either way. Booth Lake is rather lightly fished and nearby Martin Lake (see listing herein) is very lightly fished. This area was burned over during the 2003 B&B Complex Fire.

Boulder Lake (Warm Springs Reservation)
hike-in

A good bet for brook trout from 8 to 14 inches, 50-acre Boulder Lake lies a few miles east from Olallie Lake. You'll need the tribal fishing permit to fish this lake and the others nearby, including Trout, Island, Dark, and Long Lakes. Permits are available from fishing tackle retailers and from the Warm Springs Market, or call 541-553-2000. The latter four lakes are interconnected by Mill Creek, while Boulder Lake sits half a mile southeast from Trout Lake (see listing herein). Boulder is deep and reasonably productive for a lake at 4,800 feet. The lake's bottom is littered with large boulders. A float tube is a good idea here, especially for fly anglers.

The other lakes are accessible by trail from Trout Lake and all offer good fishing for brookies from 8 to 12 inches, sometimes larger. You can also reach them from the west by taking the Long Lake Trail east from the east shore of Olallie Lake (see Olallie Lake herein). To reach Trout Lake and the trail to Boulder Lake, Take Hwy 26 over Mt. Hood and easterly to the reservation, watching for Road P-600 leading 19 miles up to Trout Lake. The trail into Boulder Lake begins about a quarter mile east from Trout Lake Campground.

Boulder Lake (Mt. Hood National Forest)
hike-in

Twenty-acre Boulder Lake and nearby Little Boulder Lake both offer fair-to-good action on small brook in beautiful settings. They are located southeast from Bennett Pass near Mt. Hood. The hike to Boulder covers about .75 of a mile and another quarter mile brings you to Little Boulder. Follow Hwy 35 (Hood River Highway) north from Hwy 26 or south from Hood River. At Bennett Pass (adjacent to the entrance to Mt. Hood Meadows Ski Area), turn east on FR 3550 and head for Bonney Campground, where the trails begin. Snow lingers late here and the lakes are usually inaccessible until sometime between Mid-June and early July.

Brahma Lake (Three Sisters Wilderness)
hike-in

An easy 2-mile hike on the Pacific Crest Trail delivers you to this productive 10-acre brook trout lake located in the Three Sisters Wilderness north of Irish and Taylor Lakes. Brahma's brookies, stocked periodically, reach 13 or 14 inches and average pan-size. For a fine day of adventurous hiking and fishing, get out the topo map and compass and explore the myriad small lakes in the immediate vicinity. Hike up to Brahma first thing in the morning and then make a cross-country loop back to the east and south to fish Pocket, Red Slide, Lady, Timmy, and other small lakes in the basin. The campground at Irish and Taylor Lakes makes the perfect base camp for exploring the region.

Most of these little potholes are stocked periodically with brook trout or rainbows. Cross-country travel in this area is for the experienced hiker only because the landscape is dotted with small ponds and you can get a bit bewildered without careful map-and-compass work. The lakes that have been stocked in the past include the aforementioned Lady (2 acres, 15 feet deep), Pocket (1 acre, 6 feet deep), Red Slide (2 acres, 15 feet deep) and Timmy (3 acres, 15 feet deep) along with Gleneden Lake (1 acre, 14 feet deep), Cathy Lake (2 acres, 18 feet deep), Copper Lake (1 acre, 10 feet deep), Simon Lake (2 acres, 10 feet deep), Tranquil Lake (1 acre, 10 feet deep), Pygmy Lake (1 acre, 12 feet deep), Barbie Lake (3 acres, 17 feet deep) and Clark Lake (1 acre, 12 feet deep).

Not coincidentally the deepest and largest of these lakes generally offer the best prospects for the occasional 14- to 18-inch brookie or rainbow. A float tube comes in handy because many of the lakes have rather brushy, inaccessible shoreline margins. This entire area, abounding in ponds, lakes, and small marshes is infamous for its mosquito populations, which peak during June and July. The entire basin sits above 5,000 feet and is usually accessible by June. For other nearby lakes, see Merle Lake, Navajo Lake, and Taylor Lake herein.

Browns Creek (Wickiup Reservoir tributary)
closed waters

Buck Hollow Creek and tributaries (Wasco County)
closed waters

Cabot Lake (Mt. Jefferson Wilderness Area)
hike-in

Located near Carl Lake on the eastern edge of the Mt. Jefferson Wilderness Area, Cabot Lake rarely supports more than a few small cutthroat trout, and is shallow and rarely very productive. Give it a few casts if you're heading into the wilderness on the adjacent trail, which begins at the end of FR 1230, off FR 12 (watch for the turn-off heading north from Hwy 20) a mile-and-a-half east of Suttle Lake. The lower end of Cabot Creek produces small, wild cutthroat. The entire area suffered heavily during the B&B Complex fire of 2003.

Cache Lake (Jefferson County)

One of the Corbett State Park lakes south of Suttle Lake, Cache is more of a bog than a lake and too shallow to over-winter trout. It has been stocked with cutthroat trout in years past. See Link, Hand, Island and Meadow Lakes herein.

Camp Creek (Crook County)
no bait

A small stream feeding the upper reach of the Crooked River near Paulina Guard Station, Camp Creek offers a few small redband trout. Only a few miles of the stream flow across public lands. At the east edge of Prineville, head east towards Paulina and Post on the Paulina Highway. Camp Creek Road heads south from the highway about 15 miles east from Post.

Candle Creek (Metolius River drainage)
closed waters

Canyon Creek (Metolius River drainage)
closed waters

Carl Lake (Mt. Jefferson Wilderness)
hike-in

An attractive and fairly popular lake on the eastern edge of the Mt. Jefferson Wilderness, Carl was lucky to largely escape the huge B&B Complex fire that swept over the area during the summer of 2003. The lake offers slow to fair fishing for small, stocked cutthroat. Easiest access is via the Cabot Lake Trail: Just east of Suttle Lake, turn north off Hwy 20 onto FR 12 and continue to a left-hand turn onto FR 1230, which ends at the trailhead. The hike to Carl covers about 4 miles and gains nearly 1,500 feet. The shoreline is rugged in places, but it's easy enough to pick your way along and fish from the banks, although a float tube would certainly be handy for those willing to pack one in.

Cathy Lake (Three Sisters Wilderness)
see Brahma Lake

Charlton Lake (Deschutes National Forest)
hike-in

Offering fair fishing for stocked brook trout to 14 inches (averaging about 9 inches), Charlton Lake lies about a mile east of the northeast shore of Waldo Lake. Charlton spans 200 acres and reaches a maximum depth of about 60 feet. The trail covers an easy quarter mile; so many anglers carry a raft or other craft into the lake. To reach Charlton Lake follow Hwy 58 east from Oakridge or west from Hwy 97 to the Waldo Lake turn-off (FR 5897). Follow the road north about 10 miles, watching for a right-hand turn 1 mile before you get to Harrelson Horse Camp. Half a mile east from the road junction, watch for the Pacific Crest Trail, which leads down to the lake and flanks its west shoreline. Charlton sits at 5,692 feet and is usually accessible by June. You can camp at the lake or at the nearby, established campgrounds on Waldo Lake.

Less popular and lightly fished than Charlton, nearby Found Lake and Hidden Lake offer fair-to-good brook trout action for fish ranging from 6 to 10 inches. Though the fish are small, you'll usually have them to yourself and both lakes are quite scenic. They sit on the flanks of 6,591 Gerdine Butte, about 1 mile south of Charlton's south shore. To reach these lakes, follow the Pacific Crest Trail around the west shore of Charlton, but stay to the left when the PCT departs the lake heading south. Trail #19 continues along Charlton Lake and then heads off to the southeast, leading about 2 miles down to Found Lake (9 acres). Stay to the right at the next two trail junctions. Eleven-acre Hidden Lake lies a quarter mile to the west, right at the base of Gerdine Butte. Both lakes are easy to explore during a day trip.

Chenoweth Creek (Wasco County)
catch-and-release, no bait

A rather unproductive trout stream near The Dalles, Chenoweth Creek flows entirely through private property on its 10-mile journey to the Columbia River. Interstate-84 crosses the mouth of Chenoweth Creek just east of the Columbia Discovery Center at the west end of The Dalles.

Clark Lake (Three Sisters Wilderness)
see Brahma Lake

Clear Creek (Mt. Hood National Forest)
no bait

The outlet from Clear Lake, this mountain stream offers fair prospects for brook trout and rainbow trout from 5 to 12 inches. The Creek flows along Hwy 26 southeast from Clear Lake and then heads off to the east. Best fishing is in this upper section. The creek fishes best during the summer and early autumn. A map of the Mt. Hood National Forest will help you decipher the back-roads in the area.

Clear Lake (Mt. Hood National Forest)
campground, boat ramp

Regularly and liberally stocked with rainbow trout, Clear Lake near Mt. Hood is a consistent producer of fish ranging from 9 to 13 inches. In addition, ODFW also stocks the lake with a few brook trout from time to time and they reproduce naturally in Clear Lake. Actually an irrigation-storage reservoir, Clear Lake spans 550 acres at full pool, but is drawn down enough by late summer that the boat ramp may not be usable. The reservoir is easy to fish from the bank and many anglers still fish with bait. Fly anglers can look forward to a prolific hatch of Callibaetis mayflies between June and August.

Overall, Clear Lake is a good family destination offering a fairly high catch rate most of the time. To reach Clear Lake, follow Hwy 26 east over Mt. Hood. Watch for the well-signed turnoff to Clear Lake about 10 miles east from Government Camp and 2 miles past Frog Lake. Clear Lake generally attracts a lot of people on spring and summer weekends, but the fishing tends to hold up well despite the pressure.

Cliff Lake (Columbia River/I-84)

Located adjacent to the eastbound lanes of I-84 near milepost 75, Cliff Lake is a small, fairly deep pond offering any number of warmwater species. It can be productive at times. Parking is at a gravel pull-off immediately past the guardrail on the east end of the pond. Be very carefully when pulling off of or back onto the freeway here. You can fish the lake from shore adjacent to the parking area, but a float tube allows you to fish the far side of the pond.

Cody Ponds (Wasco County)

Three small ponds located on ODFW's White River Game Management Area, the Cody Ponds offer fair-to-good fishing for smallmouth bass and bluegill. They range in size from 2 to 6 acres and are located adjacent to Rock Creek Reservoir. From Tygh Valley, head west on Wamic Market Road, following the road to Wamic and Rock Creek Reservoir. Four miles west of Wamic and a mile-and-a-half short of reaching Rock Creek Reservoir, watch for the access road turning north to the first pond (Cody Pond #1). Cody Pond #2 and #3 are located near the reservoir.

Copper Lake (Three Sisters Wilderness)
see Brahma Lake

Cottonwood Pit (Crook County)
campground

An abandoned rock quarry, Cottonwood Pit retains water year-round and is stocked annually with redband trout. The fish over-winter successfully in the pond. Cottonwood Pit is located in eastern Crook County. You can get there from Mitchell or from Paulina, the former route being a bit easier: Follow Hwy 26 east from Mitchell for about 13 miles to a right turn on FR 12. Head south 15 miles to FR 4274 and head west a quarter mile to the short access road to the pond and adjacent tiny campground.

Cove Palisades (Jefferson County)
see Lake Billy Chinook

Crane Prairie Reservoir (Deschutes County)
boat recommended, campgrounds, boat ramp, services

Traditionally one of the best trophy trout lakes in the Northwest, Crane Prairie Reservoir has suffered the indignity of being illegally stocked with warmwater species, first with largemouth bass and later with panfish and stickleback minnows. The bucket biologists succeeded not only in creating a good bass fishery on Crane Prairie, but also in undermining the wild trout population and the viability of all the lake's fisheries.

After years of glorious trophy trout action on the reservoir, today's Crane Prairie is a different place for those who have fished it for several decades. Gone are the days when massive hatches of damselflies, *Callibaetis* mayflies, and dragonflies assured superb surface-oriented action for fly anglers. And gone are the days when Crane produced trophy after trophy after trophy. Recent surveys suggest that entire year classes—in fact several consecutive year classes—of trout and bass are missing from the lake, indicating failed spawning and/or heavy predation on juvenile fish.

The good news is that, because of its inherent fertility and because of supplemental stocking by ODFW, this 3,400-acre fishery still ranks among the state's better destinations for rainbow trout ranging from 14 inches to 15 pounds. Located southwest of Bend along Century Drive, the lake also produces brook trout to at least 6 pounds, but these beauties are not nearly as common as they were 20 years ago. Meanwhile, the introduced largemouth bass grow to near-trophy size and Crane's long-time trout enthusiasts are annually subjected to

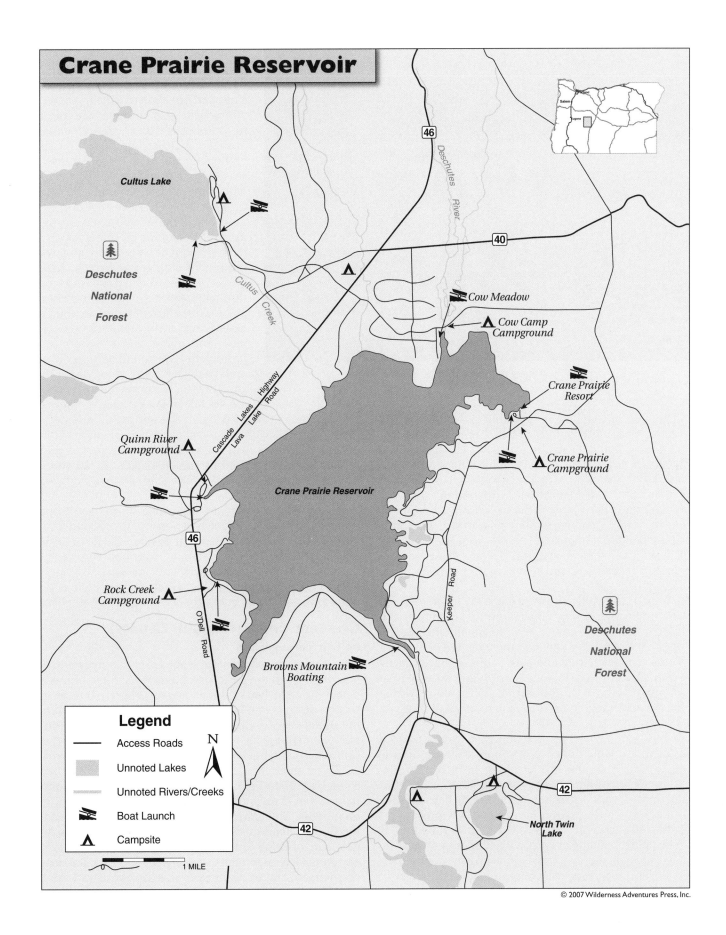

Crane Prairie Reservoir

Cultus Lake

Deschutes
National
Forest

Cultus Creek

Cow Meadow

Cow Camp
Campground

Crane Prairie
Resort

Quinn River
Campground

Crane Prairie
Campground

Crane Prairie Reservoir

Rock Creek
Campground

Keeper Road

Deschutes
National
Forest

O'Dell Road

Browns Mountain
Boating

North Twin
Lake

Cascade Lakes Highway
Lava Lake Road

Deschutes River

Legend

———	Access Roads
░░░	Unnoted Lakes
┈┈┈	Unnoted Rivers/Creeks
⛴	Boat Launch
⛺	Campsite

N

0   1 MILE

Crane Prairie Reservoir

the indignation of watching bass-fishing clubs hold tournaments here—apparently with the tacit approval of ODFW—that serve as a reminder of the extensive damage done to central Oregon fisheries by so-called "Johnny Bass-Seed."

Since ODFW seems more or less powerless to do anything about the bass/panfish/stickleback infestation at Crane, anglers might just as well enjoy the bass fishing. Commonly reaching 5 pounds, Crane's bass stick close to structure in the form of the flooded timber stands, large weed beds and reed stands in the lake's shallow margins. They eat just about anything, from plastic worms and spinner-baits to popping bugs and diving plugs.

The trout, meanwhile, no longer enjoy the luxury of foraging on damsel and dragonfly populations that used to exist in unbelievable densities. These insects still inhabit the lake and their seasonal emergences still draw the attention of the trout, though the hatches hardly compare to those that occurred yearly through the 1980s. Today's Crane Prairie fly angler had better be prepared to fish Chironomid pupae along with an array of wet flies ranging from streamers to small scud and mayfly nymph patterns.

Bait and gear anglers rely on time-tested trolling and still fishing methods, which often prove more effective than fly angling, especially on the smaller 14- to 18-inch trout. Bait anglers use night crawlers, Power-bait, and many other offerings and they all work. The classic Crane Prairie bait—in short supply these days owing to over-harvest and over-predation—is the dragonfly nymph, often called a "hellgrammite" by old-timers. Most bait anglers pick a likely spot in or near the channels or just off the snag stands and still fish with bobbers. Trollers do fairly well, especially early and late in the season.

Recent regulation changes dictate that anglers may keep five rainbow trout, of which only one may be a non-fin-clipped trout and only one of which may be over 20 inches. Also, despite the presence of warmwater fish, Crane is not open at night; it closes one hour after sunset and opens one hour before sunrise. The season goes from late April (check specific date in ODFW angling synopsis) through October 31.

Crane Prairie offers an intriguing array of hot spots, all of them bolstered by lush aquatic vegetation and several prominent old river and creek channels. The Deschutes Channel runs more or less through the eastern part of the reservoir. To the west and southwest are the Cultus River, Quinn River, and Rock Creek Channels (and inlets) and there are several prominent bays and fingers on the south and southeast side; these latter being good bets for warmwater fish. Boat ramps are found at Rock Creek, Quinn River, and at Crane Prairie Resort on the northeast corner. Campgrounds are likewise located at each of these places and also on the Deschutes Arm (Cow Camp). The resort offers boat rentals, supplies, and an RV park (541-383-3939/www.crane-prairie-resort-guides.com). You can also arrange guide service through the resort.

Crane Prairie is usually accessible by the April opener, though you must drive down to Sunriver or Wickiup Junction because the route from Bend up past Mt. Bachelor is always snowbound until at least late May. May and June are prime months here for trout anglers and the bass fishing peaks between June and September. Often the reservoir is drawn quite low by autumn, but October fishing can be excellent.

Crescent Creek (Klamath County)
no bait, campground

The outlet from popular Crescent Lake, this forested stream is a tributary to the Little Deschutes River. Most of the lower half of the creek flows through private property, but the upper section downstream from the lake offers a few small trout and the middle section flows through a steep-sided canyon and offers redband trout reaching 14 inches. They are not especially abundant, but you'll often have the canyon to yourself.

To get there, first consult a good map. Then follow Hwy 58 or Hwy 97 to the Crescent Cut-off Road, which connects the town of Crescent along 97 to Hwy 58 southeast of Willamette Pass. The canyon section of Crescent Creek parallels the Cut-off Road for a little more than a mile on the northwest side of Odell Butte. The canyon begins about 1.5 miles east from Hwy 58 (on the Cut-off Road, Route 61) and extends downstream almost as far as the Davis Lake/Lava Lake Road

(Route 46), which heads north. Park along Route 61 and scramble down into the gorge from the top or bottom end, or from a few places along the side. Or you can walk up from the small campground downstream from the gorge.

Additional public access is available where Crescent Creek flows under Hwy 58. Upstream (south) from the highway, the creek meanders through a quarter mile of national forest land and on the downstream (north) side of the highway, you can hike a mile down to the aforementioned gorge. The creek is alternately brushy and marshy in many places, so it can be slow going, especially when the water is high during spring and summer. During late summer and autumn however, flows subside quite a bit and you can walk the creek-bed.

The final stretch of productive public water on Crescent Creek is just west of Crescent, where low-gradient meanders approach the creek's confluence with the Little Deschutes River. Here you'll catch an occasional brown trout. Watch for Road 62 heading west to Davis Lake from Hwy 97 (5 miles north of the Crescent Cut-off Road). After crossing over the Little Deschutes, Road 62 follows the south bank of the creek at a distance. After 2 miles, the road crosses the creek, but this is private property. Across the bridge, a secondary road heads up the north bank. Be sure to carry the national forest map and the ranger district map to figure out access.

Crescent Lake (Deschutes National Forest)
boat recommended, boat ramp, campground, services

A large, scenic lake in the Cascade Mountains southwest from Bend, Crescent Lake is well known for its productive Mackinaw fishery (one fish per day, 30-inch minimum length). The Macs here range from 6 to at least 30 pounds with 8- to 12-pound fish being typical. During summer they haunt the lake's depths and you'll need down-rigging gear (or deep-working jigs designed specifically for Macs) and fish-finding electronics to enjoy consistent success on fish living from 80 to 180 feet deep.

However, Crescent Lake also offers a unique and productive late fall and winter fishery. By November the Mackinaw are cruising the shallows and you can catch them in 8 to 15 feet of water right along the shoreline. This off-season fishery has become popular enough that both the Forest Service and the owners of the Crescent Lake Resort keep the boat ramp clear enough of snow so that anglers can launch small boats. In fact, some of the best winter fishing occurs along the shorelines adjacent to the lodge on the lake's east and north edges.

No matter when you fish for them, Crescent's Mackinaw prefer big meals. One of the most popular local lures is a brown-trout-colored Rapala in size 15. Many other lures are equally productive, ranging from plugs and spoons to large jigs and even big streamer flies. In fact, a few hardy fly anglers venture to the lake during winter and spring for a chance at hooking big Mackinaw on fly tackle. For this effort you'll need fast sinking lines, flies in the 4- to 6-inch range and a boat or pontoon craft. Even with flies, trolling is the way to go. Bank anglers catch a few Mackinaw between November and April by casting spoons, plugs, and streamer flies from the beach (Simax Beach) on the east shore.

Crescent Lake freezes during hard winters, but generally thaws by late March. During years of heavy snowfall, the road may be closed. If the road is snowed in before the lake freezes or if it remains closed after the thaw, some anglers access the lake by snowmobile. Typically the road is plowed and the lodge remains open throughout the winter.

Crescent Lake also offers fair-to-good fishing for both brown trout and rainbow trout, along with kokanee. The kokanee range from 9 to 18 inches and comprise a very popular summer fishery. Rainbows reach several pounds but usually range from 12 to 16 inches. The brown trout here reach at least 10 pounds with typical fish ranging from 14 to 20 inches. Though Crescent is a popular summer playground, trout fishing at the lake is better from late September through December. The browns are especially prone to take the same lures fished for Mackinaw.

Crescent Lake is easy to get to as it lies just south of Hwy 58 and just east from Willamette Pass. Watch for the signs a few miles south from Odell Lake. The resort lies on the north shore just as you reach the lake and offers rental boats, tackle, food, rental cabins, and more. You can book a guide for Crescent Lake by calling the resort at 541-433-2505. Campgrounds are located on the southwest end of the lake.

Crooked River (Crook County)

One of Oregon's most popular fly-fishing streams, The Crooked River forms a veritable fish factory below Bowman Dam, the impoundment that forms Prineville Reservoir. For about 8 miles below the dam, the Crooked River meanders through a steep, scenic, juniper-clad canyon. The river's rocky course provides ample trout habitat and owing to the perpetually cold, nutrient-rich releases from the dam, the river offers something like 2,000 trout and up to 5,000 whitefish per river mile.

The water here flows off-color all the time, ranging from muddy at higher flows to tainted at lower flows. The river is so rich in aquatic life—scuds, mayflies, caddis, and midges—that the trout rarely need rise for dry flies. Thus most anglers fish small nymph, scud, and egg patterns unless the fish start rising for a hatch. Open all year, the Crooked River has become an extremely popular wintertime fishery. Don't be surprised to find the road and the off-highway access points filled with vehicles between January and April.

Typically the winter flows are modest, making fishing and wading fairly easy. Spring and summer flows range from unfishable to moderate as the reservoir above delivers stored water to regional agriculture. By autumn, the flows again subside. Numerous fly shops and websites track the flows from Bowman Dam, and the river is at its best below 300 cubic feet per second. Ideal flows are below 150 cuffs.

Though sub-surface tactics prevail on the Crooked, the river does offer several good hatches. Tiny blue-winged olive (*Baetis*) mayflies can emerge just about any time, with the best

Crooked River

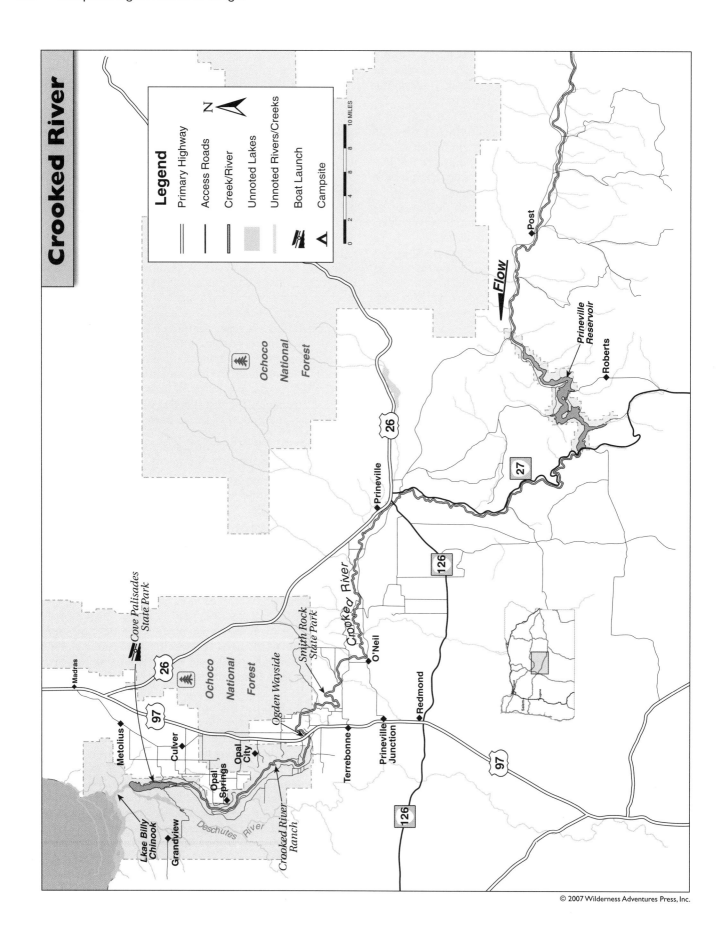

Legend

Primary Highway	
Access Roads	
Creek/River	
Unnoted Lakes	
Unnoted Rivers/Creeks	
Boat Launch	
Campsite	

N

10 MILES
0 2 4 6 8

Flow

Post

Prineville Reservoir

Roberts

Ochoco National Forest

US 26

27

Prineville

126

Crooked River

Smith Rock State Park

O'Neill

Redmond

126

Ogden Wayside

Cove Palisades State Park

US 26

Ochoco National Forest

US 97

Madras

Metolius

Culver

Opal City

Opal Springs

Lkae Billy Chinook

Grandview

Deschutes River

Crooked River Ranch

Terrebonne

Prineville Junction

US 97

Salem

© 2007 Wilderness Adventures Press, Inc.

hatches happening between March and May. Chironomids typically hatch alongside the mayflies. Late winter and early spring also offers sparse hatches of little brown stoneflies, *Skwala* stoneflies, and a smattering of March brown mayflies. By mid-May, caddisflies appear, sometimes in tremendous densities and they continue throughout the summer, with peak activity near dusk. Summer days tend to be terribly hot in the canyon. But the water, drawn off the bottom of the reservoir, usually remains cool enough for decent fishing, depending on flows.

In the stretch of popular water below Bowman Dam, native redband trout typically range from 6 to 10 inches. Fish hard and get a little lucky and you'll find a trout or two in the 14- to 20-inch range. The Crooked has been called the state's best 9-inch trout fishery and the label is quite accurate. Whitefish abound and if you find a school of them in a deeper pool you might catch a dozen or more in short order. They range from 8 to 14 inches.

This tailwater section of the Crooked River is located south of Prineville and the route begins as a well-marked turn from downtown Prineville. As the river reaches the end of the canyon it flows onto private lands. Private property dominates all the way down to its confluence with Lake Billy Chinook at Cove Palisades State Park. Smith Rocks, the popular rock-climbing reserve north of Redmond, offers good access to the river. The fishing here doesn't compare to the famous section upstream, but you can usually find a few trout during the spring.

Soon after departing the Smith Rocks area, the Crooked River plunges into one the state's most impressive and dramatic river gorges. Ogden Wayside, located along Hwy 97 north of Terrebonne, offers a superb view down into the gorge—a view that certainly underscores the inaccessibility of this reach of the river. Access to the gorge downstream from Ogden Wayside is limited primarily to a couple of private right-of-ways that are traditionally open to public access. One is at Opal Springs on the east bank and the other is on the other side at Crooked River Ranch, behind the golf course (turn west at Terrebonne on the Lower Bridge Road and watch for signs pointing north to Crooked River Ranch).

The gorge area offers fair fishing for redband trout, quite a few whitefish, and increasing numbers of smallmouth bass and other reservoir species once you drop below the Opal Springs area upstream from Cove Palisades State Park (see Lake Billy Chinook herein). Adventurous types can boat up the Crooked River arm of the reservoir and then hike the rugged canyon upstream. And even more adventurous types can float the lower Crooked River by kayak, starting at Smith Rocks and ending at Cove Palisades. Only highly skilled white-water kayakers need apply; and only when flows are essentially too high for productive fishing.

Upstream from Prineville Reservoir, stream-channel habitat on the Crooked River is generally and historically degraded. The river here offers only poor fishing and is inhabited by more bullhead, smallmouth bass, and non-game fish than trout. Besides the poor fishing, public access is essentially

Brent Snow lands a larger-than-usual Crooked River redband trout.

non-existent. The river's two headwater forks, however, offer fair fishing for rainbow and redband trout (see separate listings herein). Be sure to consult the fishing regulations before heading for the Crooked River. Currently the river is open to bait fishing from late May through October and open to flies/lures only the remainder of the year.

Crooked River, North Fork (Crook County)
no bait, hike-in, campground

The North Fork Crooked River heads on private ranchland at Summit Prairie high in the Ochoco Mountains. Picking up flows from myriad small tributaries, the North Fork heads east and then circles back to the south, eventually joining the South Fork near the Les Schwab Ranch, 12 miles east of the tiny community of Post along the Paulina Highway east of Prineville. A federally designated Wild & Scenic River, the North Fork Crooked offers fair-to-good prospects for redband

The Crooked River below Prineville Reservoir ranks among the state's most fertile trout streams.

trout from 6 to 12 inches with a few larger trout.

Difficult access no doubt contributes to the quality of the trout fishery on the North Fork. The river flows mostly through rugged canyon lands and the best stretches require anglers to hike the canyon. The best access to the North Fork is from Deep Creek Campground east of Summit Prairie: From Prineville, follow Hwy 26 east past Ochoco Reservoir to a right-hand turn onto CR 123/42 (the road to Walton Lake). After 8 miles, when you reach the guard station, bear right onto FR 42 and follow it east all the way to Deep Creek Campground. The road follows along the river for the last 4 miles of the drive.

The North Fork is best from June through early July and again during the fall. This is good dry-fly water, especially during the autumn and also well suited to small spinners. Near the campground, fishing pressure is moderate, but few anglers bother to hike far downstream or hike in from the more remote access roads. Deep Creek Campground is a rather primitive affair with six tent/camper sites and drinking water. The area offers quite a few informal hunters' campsites as well. Be sure to carry drinking water when you hike down the river.

Crooked River, South Fork (Crook County)
no bait

A poor-to-fair rainbow trout/redband trout stream southeast of Prineville, the South Fork Crooked River mostly produces fish in the 8- to 13-inch range. Most of the river flows across private property and across BLM tracts blocked by private property. Luckily, ODFW has been working with landowners to provide improved habitat conditions and better public access. In 2004, for example, landowner Otto Keller received a grant from ODFW's habitat and access program, which will improve conditions on his 1,200 acres and 2.5 miles of river. In return for the grant money, Keller provides by-permission access to the river and walk-through access to adjoining public lands.

Access to the South Fork's public-land stretches is very limited and only available by primitive roads. Most of the BLM land lies south of the Post-Paulina Highway and 6 miles of the river flow through the South Fork/Sand Hollow Wilderness Study Area. The most popular access site south of the highway is the Congleton Hollow Access: From Prineville, follow the Post-Paulina Highway east towards Paulina. At milepost 51, watch for a right-hand turn onto a primitive but well-traveled road leading 5 miles to the access area. When you reach the bottom of a steep grade near the end, take the right-hand fork down to the camping area.

The diminutive river here is glassy-smooth and gin-clear. Small squawfish predominate and are happy to take dry flies. The trout average larger than the course fish, so you can usually sneak along and either look for trout in the clear water or study the rise forms to decipher whether you might be casting to a 12-inch trout or a 6-inch squawfish. This is perfect dry-fly water and grasshopper patterns work as early as the first week of June.

Crystal Creek (Odell Lake tributary)
closed waters

Cultus Lake (Deschutes National Forest)
campground, boat ramp, boat recommended, services

Cultus Lake, sometimes called Big Cultus Lake, is a popular and productive 785-acre natural lake located off Century Drive about 40 miles southwest from Bend. Crane Prairie Reservoir is located across the highway from Big Cultus. This attractive lake offers good fisheries for both rainbow trout and Mackinaw. The Macs here range from 4 to 20 pounds and are primarily taken by anglers using downriggers or deep jigs (one fish per day). The rainbows range from 8 to 18 inches and a few small brook trout also inhabit the lake.

Exceptionally clear and very deep, Cultus sits at 4,668 feet and is usually fishable by late May. As is typical for the species,

Mackinaw follow their prey into shallow water during spring and late fall. In this case, whitefish provide the primary forage for the lake trout. When the lake opens in May, anglers sometimes find Macs in the shoreline shallows, especially early in the morning. Soon thereafter, however, the fish head deep and anglers must fish the depths. Most Mackinaw specialists rely on fish-finding electronics and do most of their fishing during the morning. By afternoon, at least during July and August, the lake can get a little busy with recreational watercraft.

The camping and boating crowds tend to disperse after Labor Day and the fishing often improves, especially for rainbows. A pleasant campground occupies the east end of the lake and nearby Cultus Lake Resort offers food, services, lodging, and rental boats. Remote campgrounds are located on the west side of the lake and accessible only by hiking or boating. A good trail wraps around the north shore.

From Bend, follow Century Drive into the Cascade Mountains, heading west and then south toward Crane Prairie. From the south, take South Century Drive from Wickiup Junction or Sunriver, heading west. The well-signed turn-off to Cultus Lake is located about 3 miles north of Quinn River Campground (Crane Prairie Reservoir).

Cultus Lake, Little (Deschutes National Forest)
campground, boat ramp
Little Cultus Lake offers fair-to-good fishing for rainbows and a few brook trout. Both species reproduce naturally here and can reach 18 inches. Typical fish range from 9 to 12 inches and they respond to all methods. Because of the lake's size (170 acres), many anglers launch boats and troll. Shoreline access is good and a nice, fairly secluded campground sits on the south shore (no hookups). Dirt roads follow the south and north shorelines, but the back (west) side of the lake is rather remote and also productive, owing to the spring-fed creek that enters there after meandering through an extensive bog. The shallow shoals near the bog produce good hatches of *Callibaetis* mayflies and caddisflies, along with Chironomids and damsels. Little Cultus lies just south of the better-known Cultus ("Big Cultus") Lake. See Big Cultus Lake for directions to the area.

Cultus River (Deschutes National Forest)
A short, very shallow, spring-fed river feeding Crane Prairie Reservoir, Cultus River offers few trout of any size. Crane Prairie's fish use it for spawning.

Dark Lake (Warm Springs Reservation)
see Trout Lake

Darlene Lake (Deschutes National Forest)
see Suzanne Lake

Davis Lake
boat or float tube recommended, boat ramp, campground, fly-only
One of Oregon's top still-water fly-angling destinations, Davis Lake carries a well-earned reputation for producing large rainbow trout. The 'bows here range from 14 inches to more than 10 pounds and 16- to 20-inch fish are typical most years. Davis Lake is very fertile and rich in aquatic vegetation. The trout feast on all the usual lake foods, including damsels, leeches, scuds, water beetles, mayfly nymphs, dragonfly nymphs, Chironomids, and snails. Moreover, they grow fat on the lake's dense population of illegally or accidentally introduced tui chub. All fishing, including for bass, is fly-fishing only.

Some years ago, in fact, ODFW began stocking Klamath Lake-strain rainbows in Davis Lake because these trout, of redband trout genetic stock, grow very large and tend to feed

Illegally introduced largemouth bass now thrive in Davis Lake.

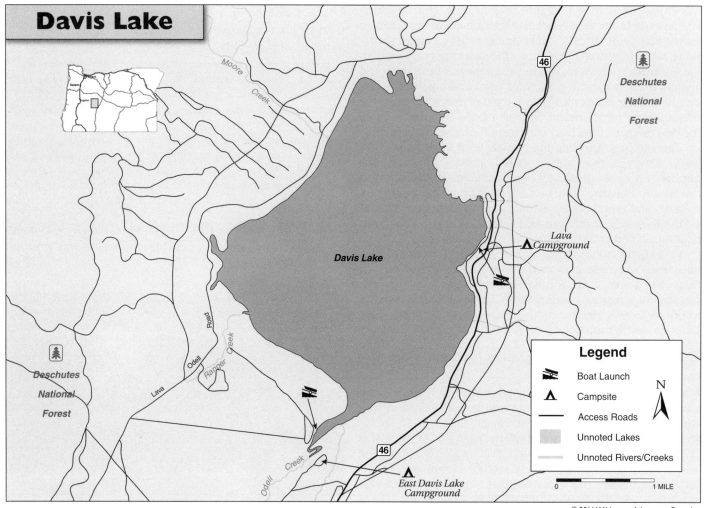

voraciously on smaller fish. The trout are self-sustaining, with their numbers bolstered every once in a while when the usual drought cycles take a heavy toll on Davis Lake. Every decade or thereabouts, Davis seems to go through a difficult low-water phase where it has trouble maintaining water levels and quality through the summer. Davis, formed several thousand years ago by a huge natural lava dam, loses water through the porous lava.

When water levels remain stable, however, Davis Lake's Klamath-strain redbands grow to enormous sizes. Fish in the 4- to 10-pound class are reasonably common. Most of the time they respond best to large flies that mimic the chub minnows, leeches, dragons, and damsels. Chub flies should be tied in lengths from 3 to 5 inches. A gold/olive Zonker is a fine choice, but many effective patterns are available for imitating the chub. Leech patterns should be dressed fairly sparse and natural shades of olive or brown are most popular.

Davis Lake's under-appreciated damsel hatch begins in late April or early May, but doesn't reach full strength until June. Even before the hatch gathers steam, however, the trout begin keying on the nymphs around mid-morning. Some days

during May, an olive damsel nymph, fished on a sink-tip line near the top of the weedbeds, can produce excellent results. By June, anglers should anticipate damsel-nymph activity almost every day, usually between 10:00am and noon. At the same time of year, Davis offers a rare opportunity to fish dragonfly nymph patterns during one of the West's best such hatches.

Like damselfly nymphs, the dragonfly nymphs migrate shoreward to emerge by crawling out on vegetation or shoreline rocks. On Davis Lake they do so en masse and the fish take notice. The most exciting and often the most effective way to fish the dragonfly hatch is to combine a sinking line with a long leader and a floating dragonfly nymph pattern constructed of spun, olive-dyed deer hair. The central Oregon fly shops sell these flies. The trick is to allow the line to sink towards the bottom while the fly remains afloat. Once the sinking line begins to tug at the fly, begin retrieving with quick, short pulls. Make five or six quick strips of line and then pause for about five seconds and repeat.

The dragonfly fishing, which peaks in June, is best on the south side of Davis along the lava flow and adjacent weed beds. The same goes for the damsel hatches. This part of the lake is also best for targeting the abundant and sometimes very large bass that were illegally introduced into the lake sometime during the 1990s. Some of these bass now top 10 pounds and lots of them range from 4 to 6 pounds. With luck, they won't prove too taxing on the trout population, but if nearby Crane Prairie Reservoir is any indication, anglers should be worried. Meanwhile there seems little to be done about the bass except fish for them, enjoy it and take as many home as you want for table fare.

The bass feed heavily on chub minnows, but also prey on damsel and dragonfly nymphs, leeches, and other invertebrates. They abound along the lava flow and each little cove therein seems to hold several nice bass. Creep along by boat and cast streamers or poppers into the coves.

Davis Lake spans about 3,500 acres when full and reaches a maximum depth of only 25 feet. Most years you can drive to the lake by early April, but call the ODFW or the local fly fishing shops in Bend before heading out in the spring. The April fishing centers mostly on leech and chub patterns, along with Chironomids. Both sides of the lake are productive during spring, but the lava flow on the south side seems to offer slightly warmer water and the largest rainbows tend to be more numerous there.

As the water warms during May and June, the Odell Creek channel on the lake's south side becomes highly productive and will remain so well into summer. When lake temperatures get too warm for the trout, many of the fish seek relief well up into the channel and good ethics dictate that they are left alone. With the onset of autumn, the trout disperse throughout the lake once again and the October through early November fishing often proves the best of the year.

Bank fishing is quite limited on Davis. You can fish from the south shoreline at East Davis Campground and from a few places on the east shore. Sometimes brave anglers will negotiate the brutal lava flow to fish from the bank on the north end of the lake, but I wouldn't recommend doing so. A boat is the way to go and if you don't have a boat, take your float tube or pontoon craft. You can launch boats at any of the three campgrounds on Davis, except that the Lava Flow Campground on the north shore has for many years been closed during spring and summer to protect nesting bald eagles. The Lava Flow ramp is an informal sand bank, but plenty serviceable and it leads to a narrow channel through the reed stands and out into the main lake (The weeds don't grow out of the water until late spring). Motors are allowed for transport, but not for fishing.

All told, Davis Lake usually ranks among the best lakes in the state for both the quality of the fishery and the size of the trout. With lots of remote corners to explore, fly anglers can enjoy solitude here even on crowded days. The fly-fishing shops in Bend and Sunriver keep close tabs on the conditions and can provide up-to-date reports just about any time.

Current regulations allow anglers to keep two trout per day between 10 and 13 inches, and there is no limit on the number of bass and other warmwater fish taken.

Deep Creek (Ochoco National Forest)
no bait, campground
A fair wild trout fishery, Deep Creek is a small tributary to the North Fork Crooked River. The entire creek lies above 4,000 feet, so it is generally inaccessible until late spring. You can walk up the creek from Deep Creek Campground or follow it upstream on FR 4250. Trout range from 5 to 9 inches. From Prineville, follow Hwy 26 east past Ochoco Reservoir to a right-hand turn onto CR 123/42 (the road to Walton Lake). After 8 miles, when you reach the guard station, bear right onto FR 42 and follow it east all the way to Deep Creek Campground.

Deer Lake (Deschutes National Forest)
hike-in
Tucked away on the west side of Cultus Butte, halfway between Cultus and Little Cultus Lakes, Deer Lake offers fair-to-good prospects for

The author lands a fine rainbow from Davis Lake.

planted cutthroat and brook trout. The easy quarter-mile hike makes this lake a good choice for a canoe, raft, pontoon, or float tube. The wind can get fierce during summer afternoons. Trout here range from 6 to 14 inches. Take Century Drive to the Cultus Lake turn-off and then head for Little Cultus Lake. When you reach Little Cultus, follow the dirt road around the north shore, which leads to the trailhead for Deer Lake. The lake spans 70 acres and reaches a maximum depth of 20 feet. Prolific hatches of *Callibaetis* mayflies create some great dry fly fishing here on calm summer days.

Dennis Lake
(Three Sisters Wilderness)
see Lindick Lake

Deschutes Ponds (Columbia River/I-84)

This series of five productive warmwater ponds lies alongside I-84 west from the mouth of the Deschutes River. Exit the Interstate at Celilo Park and then follow old Hwy 206 east to the ponds. If you are arriving from the east, exit the freeway at Biggs, turning left off the off ramp and then turning right (west) at the intersection next to the truck stops. Follow this road past the Deschutes River and from there you'll find the ponds in the reverse order as described here.

Deschutes Ponds

In any event, the first pond (Miller Pond) lies on your left, between the railroad tracks and the freeway, as you head east from the Celilo Exit. Parking is along the gravel pullouts just off the shoulder of the road or you can park and walk from the gravel lot located at the Celilo Exit. This large pond offers perch, bluegill, pumpkinseed, bullhead, bass and other species, and holds lots of carp.

Just around the corner on your right are the so-called Deschutes Pond #1 and Deschutes Pond #2, respectively. Parking is available at both ends of the first (and larger) of these two ponds and at the north end of the smaller pond (#2). An old paved roadbed bisects each of these ponds, making a convenient walkway for anglers and the perfect place to kick back in a chair if you are still fishing with bait. Pond #1 has a cut running through the old roadbed, so you can't walk all the way across. So, if you want to fish from the pavement here, park at the south end and walk back to the north along the old roadway. This pond offers some large bass, along with a smattering of all the other usual warmwater fish common to the Columbia backwaters and is also inhabited by lots of big—and strong—carp.

Deschutes Pond #2 is actually bisected by the old roadbed into two separate ponds. Bluegill of modest size dominate, but myriad species inhabit the pond. The half of the pond on the backside of the old roadway gets an occasional subtle flush of fresh water from a culvert and tends to avoid the heavy algae blooms that often plague its neighbors. This pond, which abuts the steep, rocky bank on the hillside, is the best bet for bluegill and also has some decent largemouth bass. It's a good place to take kids for some fun with small sunfish.

The fourth of the Deschutes Ponds (West Deschutes Pond) lies just a bit further south, but on the left-hand side of the road across the tracks. It stretches nearly to the mouth of the Deschutes River. This pond is a good producer of nice largemouth bass, especially if you take a float tube. Its shores are brushy and numerous snags and islets provide prime cover for bass and bluegill. Parking is on the gravel pullouts along the road or you can walk from nearby Heritage Landing on the Deschutes. The same goes for much smaller East Deschutes Pond on the other side (east) of the Deschutes River.

You can fish any of these waters from shore, but the three larger ponds are certainly conducive to a float tube or carryable boat. These ponds fish best from late spring through mid-autumn. From late May through summer, the best action occurs morning and evening, although still fishing with bait can produce any time. Beginning in May, aquatic weeds begin to sprout and by summer they pretty much choke out any possibility of fishing on parts of the ponds. Until that occurs, the best bet for a large bass is to try plugs and spoons fished above the weeds—even at the surface—during the evening when baitfish are active.

There are a handful of primitive campsites here, but heed any and all "No Camping" signs. The better choice, by far, is to camp a bit further east at Heritage State Park at the mouth of the Deschutes River.

Deschutes River, Lower (Pelton Dam to mouth)

boat ramp, campground, services

The Lower Deschutes River, Oregon's premier combination trout/summer steelhead river, runs south to north for about 100 miles, reaching the Columbia River east of The Dalles, an hour and a half east of Portland. Gouging out a deep, dramatic canyon, this massive river offers boundless opportunity for year-round fishing for native trout and several months of summer-run steelhead ranging from 4 to 20 pounds. Typical steelhead here run from 5 to 8 pounds with both native and hatchery fish in abundance. The river's native "redside" trout commonly reach 16 inches and most range from 10 to 14 inches. Prospects are always good for trout in the 16- to 20-inch range. The river is also home to abundant whitefish and a solid run of chinook salmon.

The Lower Deschutes River is one of the best steelhead and wild trout streams in the country.

Throughout most of its run, the Lower Deschutes is restricted to flies and artificial lures and while quite a few anglers fish lures for steelhead, the vast majority of the trout-angling effort comes from fly anglers. In that regard, the Deschutes offers something for fly anglers of every description. Given a decent hatch—of which the river boasts many—even beginning fly anglers can enjoy excellent dry fly action. Likewise, newcomers to the sport often find great success drifting nymph patterns with the aid of a strike indicator and many guides use this technique with clients who have little practice casting a fly rod.

But the Deschutes also offers lots of technical fishing to test the skills of even the most experienced anglers. Such challenges often arrive in the form of large trout feeding selectively on emerging caddis or mayflies in places where a drag-free drift is difficult to achieve. These big trout often feed in swirling back eddies and tight against the banks with a canopy of alder branches hanging overhead.

On the Lower Deschutes, river access proves tedious in many stretches, especially the 25 miles of roadless water from Macks Canyon to the mouth. This reach is the domain of jet boats running up from the mouth and drift boats departing from the launch at Macks Canyon. Above Macks Canyon, 17 miles of rough gravel road parallels the east bank. Above the gravel road, 8 miles of paved road follow the river to the little town of Maupin and 6 more miles of gravel reach upstream to the "Locked Gate." The upper reaches of the river can be accessed at Warm Springs, Trout Creek, and South Junction. Drift boats reign from throughout this upper half of the river, but throughout its run the Lower Deschutes requires strong skills at the oars.

Renowned for its treacherous wading, the Deschutes demands cleated boots. The water, frequently just slightly off color and running over dark-colored rocks, is difficult to see through. Many steelhead pools are carved from bedrock, whose reefs and ledges create uneven wading. For a few steps you fish from atop a ledge, the water barely reaching your knees, only to step off into cold neck-deep flows at the downstream end of the rock. The steelhead, however, find ample holding water amidst the ledges, boulders, and seams that abound in this broad, muscular river.

All told, the Lower Deschutes River ranks among the greatest fisheries in the West and nowhere else does a river combine such superb trout action with a voluminous run of aggressive summer steelhead. Naturally the river can be incredibly busy at times, especially during the famous hatch of salmonflies and golden stoneflies during May and June and also during the peak of the steelhead run during autumn.

Deschutes River Hatches

So famous is the stonefly hatch on the Lower Deschutes River that anglers arrive from all quarters between mid-May and mid-June to cast huge dry flies to free-rising trout. At times the river resembles a parade of boats, especially between Warm Springs and Maupin. The hatch is actually composed of two different insects, the inch-long golden stonefly and the even larger salmon fly. Both insects require imitations in sizes 2, 4, and 6. Stonefly nymphs crawl to the shore and climb out of the water to emerge into adults. Most of this hatch activity occurs during the morning hours. Later, the female stoneflies fly out over the water to deposit egg clusters and when the action is at its zenith, the river corridor fills with huge bugs buzzing about in the sky above the water.

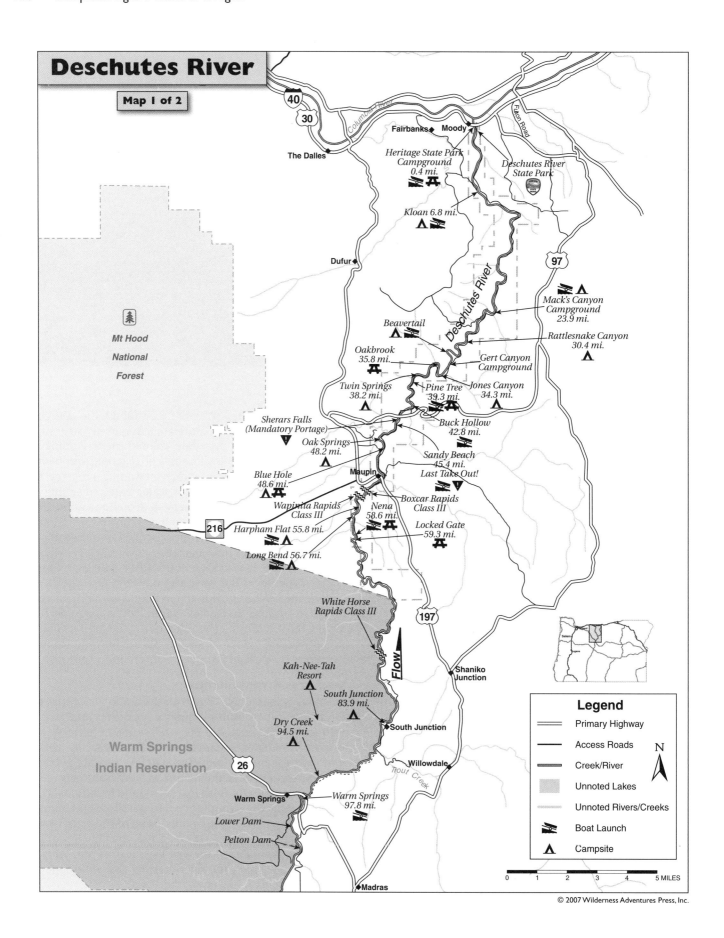

Deschutes River

Map 1 of 2

Fairbanks Moody

The Dalles

Heritage State Park Campground 0.4 mi.

Kloan 6.8 mi.

Deschutes River State Park

Dufur

Mack's Canyon Campground 23.9 mi.

Rattlesnake Canyon 30.4 mi.

Beavertail

Oakbrook 35.8 mi.

Gert Canyon Campground

Twin Springs 38.2 mi.

Pine Tree 39.3 mi.

Jones Canyon 34.3 mi.

Mt Hood National Forest

Sherars Falls (Mandatory Portage)

Buck Hollow 42.8 mi.

Oak Springs 48.2 mi.

Sandy Beach 45.4 mi. Last Take Out!

Blue Hole 48.6 mi.

Maupin

Wapinitia Rapids Class III

Nena 58.6 mi.

Boxcar Rapids Class III

Locked Gate 59.3 mi.

Harpham Flat 55.8 mi.

Long Bend 56.7 mi.

White Horse Rapids Class III

Flow

Shaniko Junction

Kah-Nee-Tah Resort

South Junction 83.9 mi.

South Junction

Dry Creek 94.5 mi.

Warm Springs Indian Reservation

Willowdale

Warm Springs 97.8 mi.

Warm Springs

Lower Dam

Pelton Dam

Madras

Legend

Primary Highway

Access Roads

Creek/River

Unnoted Lakes

Unnoted Rivers/Creeks

Boat Launch

Campsite

N

0 1 2 3 4 5 MILES

© 2007 Wilderness Adventures Press, Inc.

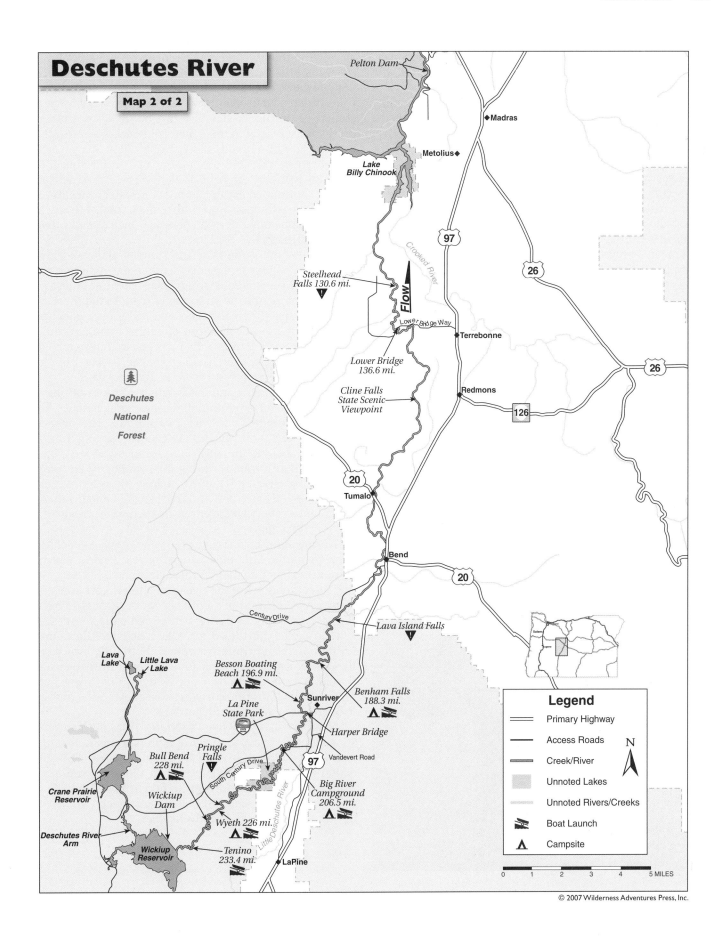

Deschutes River

Map 2 of 2

Pelton Dam

◆Madras

Metolius◆

Lake
Billy Chinook

Crooked River

97

26

Steelhead
Falls 130.6 mi.

Flow

Lower Bridge Way

Terrebonne

Lower Bridge
136.6 mi.

26

Cline Falls
State Scenic
Viewpoint

Redmons

126

Deschutes

National

Forest

20

Tumalo

Bend

20

Century Drive

Lava Island Falls

Lava
Lake

Little Lava
Lake

Besson Boating
Beach 196.9 mi.

Sunriver

Benham Falls
188.3 mi.

La Pine
State Park

Harper Bridge

Bull Bend
228 mi.

Pringle
Falls

South Century Drive

97

Vandevert Road

Big River
Campground
206.5 mi.

Crane Prairie
Reservoir

Wickiup
Dam

Little Deschutes River

Wyeth 226 mi.

Deschutes River
Arm

Wickiup
Reservoir

Tenino
233.4 mi.

LaPine

Legend

	Primary Highway
	Access Roads
	Creek/River
	Unnoted Lakes
	Unnoted Rivers/Creeks
	Boat Launch
▲	Campsite

N

Salem
Eugene

0 1 2 3 4 5 MILES

© 2007 Wilderness Adventures Press, Inc.

The stonefly emergence begins on the lower end of the river and then progresses upstream daily. Thus anglers who fish below Maupin may encounter dense hatches a week or two before the stoneflies appear upstream in the popular reach between Warm Springs and Trout Creek. In fact, the most under-rated, little-known trout action on the river occurs on the lower 25 miles below Mack Canyon when the stoneflies begin to appear as early as April.

The early morning nymph migrations provide opportunity for good nymph fishing using large, dark, weighted stonefly nymph patterns. These are especially productive when fished near shallow riffles and along the banks. As the morning sun begins to warm the air, the adults begin to emerge and adults that emerged on previous days still cling to the riparian vegetation. Trout often wait along the banks to pick off the winged insects that fall into the river. Often the best way to fish these areas is to wade out into the river just far enough that you can cast dry flies back in towards the bank and under the overhanging branches.

Deschutes guide Brad Staples hefts a big Deschutes steelhead.

Later in the day, breezes help dislodge stoneflies from the trees and brush and throughout the afternoon—and increasingly towards evening—adult stoneflies take flight over the water. Even at mid-river trout will eagerly chase down adult stoneflies. During the first few days of the hatch, trout gorge on the huge bugs, but after that, some fish seem to get both satiated and bored with them, while other fish get hooked enough times that they give up on large surface bugs. These selective fish can often be fooled with a "drowned adult" pattern (a trimmed dry fly, soaked with water so it sinks a few inches below the surface) or with a much smaller fly, such as a size 16 sparkle dun. Many anglers use small nymphs dangled below a large dry fly.

At about the same time the stonefly action begins, the river offers its first emergences of pale morning dun (PMD) mayflies (*Ephemerella*). During dense hatches of these pretty mayflies, many trout seem to prefer them to the much larger stoneflies. The aforementioned sparkle-dun is a good choice for imitating the mayflies, but of course there are countless other effective fly patterns. In a few places, huge green drake mayflies (*Drunella*) hatch alongside the PMD's. The drakes appear most frequently on overcast, blustery days.

Once the stonefly and PMD action subsides during June, the Deschutes River is dominated by caddis hatches for the rest of the summer and well into autumn. The river offers myriad genera and species of caddis, ranging from tiny "micro-caddis" to the inch-long, orange-colored "October Caddis" of late autumn. During the summer, when temperatures in the Deschutes Canyon frequently reach or surpass 100 degrees, all hatch activity is compressed into the dusk and dawn hours. Don't be surprised to encounter clouds of caddisflies at last light.

During autumn, a variety of mayflies appear, chief among them being the little blue-winged olives (*Baetis*), which will continue to hatch all the way through winter and spring. These tiny insects abound in the river and often trigger outstanding rises between November and May. Many fly anglers head for the Lower Deschutes during winter and early spring specifically to target short-lived mid-day hatches of these insects. Chironomids and winter stoneflies (both little brown stoneflies and *Skwalas*) appear in sufficient quantities to create dry fly action from time to time during the spring. These hatches tend to be highly localized. Otherwise, most winter and spring fishing is done with nymph patterns.

Nymph-fishing on the Deschutes runs the gamut from slinging huge, heavy stonefly-nymph patterns to fishing tiny size 16 and 18 patterns on long, light tippets. Sub-surface action is almost always effective on this river and at times fishing nymphs is the only way to find fish. Additionally small soft-hackle flies, fished just below the surface, can be deadly during both mayfly and caddis hatches.

Deschutes River Steelhead

By August, summer-run steelhead enter the Lower Deschutes River in numbers sufficient to motivate the river's many fishing guides to get started on a long and busy season. The late summer fishing is always best from Macks Canyon down to the river's mouth, so the river gets terribly busy with jet boats, along with drift boats launching at Macks Canyon. Fishing on the lower end of the river gets better and better as the season progresses.

As late August yields to September, ample numbers of steelhead pass upstream of Sherar's Falls and by mid-September the fish are well distributed throughout the river. September and October are the prime months and the fishing continues until the end of the year. By mid-November, many of the fish have regained their trout-like colors and by December, many of them are too dark and too tired to be considered fair sport. Nonetheless, many anglers find excellent steelhead fishing right on through January.

On the lower end of the river, from Macks Canyon to the mouth, the steelhead angling effort is about equally divided between fly fishers and anglers using spinning and casting gear. Gear anglers enjoy excellent results with a wide range of spoons and spinners and in recent years, anglers using float-and-jig setups have more than proven the efficacy of the technique. No matter what method you employ, the key is to recognize and fish the right kind of water. Good steelhead water abounds on the Deschutes and the general rule is to look for water of moderate speed and depth. Steelhead prefer water moving at about the pace a person can walk and ranging in depth from 3 to 6 feet, sometimes a bit deeper.

As you progress upriver, fly anglers become increasingly prevalent. The Deschutes rewards anglers with lots of skill and experience, yet at the same time this river ranks among the best for first-time steelhead fly anglers. If you're brand new to this game, hire a qualified Deschutes fly-fishing guide and chances are good that you'll hook your first fly-caught steelhead.

The river has long ranked among the best fly-rod steelhead waters in the Northwest because the fish are both abundant and eager. They enjoy ideal water temperatures for several months and are perfectly suited to dry-line tactics. This river has spawned a plethora of river-specific flies, the most famous of which is the Max Canyon pattern devised in the 1970s by Doug Stewart of Portland. Don't worry over specific fly patterns, however, because the fish are not at all particular. Locating and then properly fishing the best water is the key. For more specific on steelhead fly angling on the Deschutes, see *On the Fly Guide to the Northwest* by John Shewey and *Fly Fisher's Guide to Oregon* by John Huber, both published by Wilderness Adventures Press, Inc.

Steelhead in the Deschutes River come from several sources. The river boasts its own sizeable run of natives, most of which range from 4 to 7 pounds. These are supplemented by a generous allotment of hatchery fish ranging from 4 to 14 pounds. In addition, steelhead originating from many other rivers regularly ascend the Deschutes. These include both wild and hatchery fish, many from upper Columbia and Snake River tributaries. Among them are a few 15- to 20-pound giants from Idaho's Clearwater River.

Access: Warm Springs to Trout Creek

Spanning about 9 miles in length, this stretch is the most heavily fished section of the river during most of the year. The big draw here is the excellent trout action combined with good access and a minimum of difficult white water. Highway 26 crosses the Deschutes at Warm Springs, connecting Portland to Madras and the rest of central Oregon. The boat ramp and large parking area—always very busy during the stonefly hatch season—sits on the east bank a quarter mile upstream from the highway bridge. The Warm Springs Market sells tribal fishing permits, but obtaining both permits and boating passes ahead of time is a good idea (see Need to Know below). The float down to Trout Creek is fine for boaters of intermediate experience, but it's always a good idea to go first with someone who knows the river.

Foot access is available for about a mile along the highway upstream from the boat launch area. Downstream from the bridge, there is public bank access on the east bank at Mecca Flat. This is a popular camping area, offering public access for a short distance upstream and trail access leading all the way downstream to Trout Creek. You can drive down to Mecca: Just east of the highway bridge at Warm Springs, watch for the turn-off adjacent to the market. Follow the road's third fork for about 2 rugged miles down to Mecca. This road is best suited to high-clearance vehicles.

Throughout the run down to Trout Creek, the river's west bank is located on tribal property (Confederated Tribes of Warm Springs) and anglers fishing or camping on this side must have a valid permit. The designated camping spot on the west bank is at Dry Creek Campground about a mile-and-a-half below Mecca. You can drive to Dry Creek by turning north off Hwy 26 on the west side of the river—follow the signs to Kah-Nee-Tah Resort and after 3 miles, turn right at the signed road to Dry Creek Campground. There is no formal boat launch here and no drinking water. The only section of the reservation-side of the river runs from Dry Creek Campground about 6 miles to a signed boundary across from Trout Creek. Along the east bank there are about half a dozen popular boat-in (or walk-in/bike-in) campsites between Mecca and Trout Creek.

Trout Creek itself is a sprawling, busy access site with a large campground and popular put-in/take-out site. The campground can accommodate RVs. There is no drinking water. This is the last boat ramp for the next 30 miles and is thus the last chance to exit the river upstream of some of the most notorious rapids on the river. To drive to Trout Creek, follow Hwy 26 or Hwy 97 to Madras and then continue northeasterly on Hwy 97 leading out of town. Two miles east of town, watch for the signs announcing Trout Creek and Gateway Recreation Site. Follow the signs for Deschutes River and Trout Creek. The last 3 miles of the Trout Creek Road are rugged and rocky. Take it slow or you'll loose a tire in the process.

Access: Trout Creek to Harpham Flat

Below Trout Creek, the Deschutes becomes the domain of experienced oarsmen. Even good boaters should not float this section without first going with someone who knows the best passage through several heavy rapids. The most famous and treacherous of these is Whitehorse Rapids, a lengthy, rugged Class IV rapid that has eaten many boats over the years. Whitehorse looms 12 miles downstream of Trout Creek. The only drive-in access between Trout Creek and Whitehorse Rapids is at South Junction on the east bank, where a limited amount of public bank access offers good fishing: Just north of Shaniko Junction (the Hwy 97/Hwy 197 Junction north of Madras and southeast from Maupin) watch for a gravel road heading west with a sign pointing to South Junction. The road heads about 10 rugged miles down to the river, where a small campsite sits amidst about 1.5 miles of public bank access.

Along the drift from Trout Creek heading downstream toward Maupin, there are plenty of good BLM boat-in campsites. These can fill up quickly on busy weekends. For advice on camping spots, contact the BLM office in Maupin. The Warm Springs Reservation property ends at river mile 69, which is also the up-river deadline for powerboats. From this point all the way down to the mouth, anglers may fish and camp on both banks except where private property excludes bank access. Also, below the powerboat deadline, the river is open to year-round fishing while general regulations apply upstream from this marker.

As you progress downstream from Trout Creek, more and more of the east bank becomes private property, limiting access to the few public segments. Be sure to heed the signs. Anglers often hike upstream from the end of the road leading up from Maupin. The end of this road is appropriately called "Locked Gate." A mile below Locked Gate you can take out at Nena Creek or a little further down at Long Bend, though many floaters continue a short distance down to the sprawling Harpham Flats access.

Harpham Flats offers lots of camping space, a large boat ramp area (gravel) and outhouses. From Maupin, you can drive to Harpham Flats and all the way to Locked Gate. The turn-off is on the south end of town on the east bank, just before the highway begins to climb up the hill. This road is paved to Harpham and rugged rock/gravel the remaining 3 miles up to Locked Gate. There are several designated camping areas between Harpham and Locked Gate and lots of good steelhead and trout water.

Access: Harpham Flat to Sherar's Falls

The entire stretch of river from Harpham Flats to Maupin and then about 25 miles down to Macks Canyon is accessible by road. Halfway through this stretch is the un-floatable Sherar's Falls. From Maupin you can drive upstream for about 8 miles to Locked Gate. Harpham Flats is about 5 miles up by paved road and serves as a very popular put-in and take-out point for anglers and for the splash-and-giggle crowd that dominates the river during the hot summer months. The float

from Harpham down to Maupin takes in some serious and potentially dangerous rapids, including Wapinitia Rapids and Boxcar Rapids. You can scout this entire stretch from the road, but be sure you know the correct line through these rapids. If Harpham Flats is too busy, drop down to Wapinitia and launch there instead.

Maupin City Park offers the next ramp and, again, this stretch gets terribly crowded during the summer rafting season and is best avoided by anglers. During the spring or fall, however, Maupin makes a convenient take-out or launch for day trips. The city park is on the east bank, just downstream from the highway bridge. Maupin offers all services, including shuttles, markets, service station, restaurants, and two fly-fishing specialty shops, both offering guide service for trout and steelhead anglers.

The 8-mile stretch of river from Maupin down to Sherar's Falls offers some of the most popular and easy-to-access steelhead runs on the entire river because a nice paved road leads down the east bank. The west bank, far less accessible, has a mix of private and public property and many anglers use inflatables or drift boats to fish from that side. A nice wheelchair-accessible fishing platform is situated adjacent to good steelhead water near the Blue Hole just upstream from Oak Springs. Plenty of challenging water confronts floaters on this segment, the most hazardous being Oak Springs Rapids. The take-out—the last take-out—is Sandy Beach. You must exit the river here, as the falls below is impassable.

Access: Sherar's Falls to Macks Canyon

Below Sherar's Falls, a rugged gravel road follows the river for 17 miles down to Macks Canyon, providing good bank access. This section is frequented by steelhead anglers, but trout fishing can be excellent here as well. The first launch site below Sherar's Falls is the primitive ramp at Buck Hollow, half a mile down the access road from the pavement. Next is Pine Tree, 3 miles from the pavement, but Pine Tree was hammered hard by the flood of 1996, so BLM established Twin Springs Campground/Launch to replace Pine Tree. Twin Springs is half a mile further downstream.

A popular float segment goes from Twin Springs about 6 miles down to the large campground at Beavertail. Along the way there are additional campsites at Oakbrook, Jones Canyon, and Gert Canyon. Below Beavertail, camping areas are located at Rattlesnake Recreation Site and down at Macks Canyon. The Macks Canyon site is the largest campground on this segment of the river and is popular as a take-out point and as a launch point for trips down to the mouth of the river. The gravel road that leads from Sherar's Falls all the way to Macks Canyon is notorious for eating tires, so carry one or more spares and drive slowly.

Access: Macks Canyon to Mouth

Below Macks Canyon, the Deschutes River enters a remote 25-mile stretch leading eventually to the Columbia River. The only drive-in access to this section is at a site known as Klone, located 7 miles above the mouth. The road into Klone is always somewhat dangerous and is treacherous during wet weather. Do not drive down this road after or during a rain or snow shower. Also, do not drive this road in anything other than a capable 4-wheel-drive vehicle with low-range gears. If that's not enough to scare you away from this access, then be sure to stop at the top and take a look at the narrow primitive road as it hangs precariously to an impossibly steep canyon that plunges about a thousand feet to the river. One wrong driving maneuver and you're never heard from again. Consult your map and, from The Dalles, follow Fifteenmile Road heading east and then southeast heading toward Peterson School and Fairbanks. About 12 miles, turn left on Fulton Road. When the road forks, stay right and continue 2 miles to the rim of the canyon. From there you can ponder the precariousness of the situation.

With Klone being the only drive-to access on the lower 25 miles of the river, this section of the Deschutes is reserved for the boating crowd, although many anglers hike up both banks from the mouth and a few hike down the old railroad grade from Macks Canyon. This latter path is rugged going for several miles because you must negotiate several slides and washouts. Otherwise the old roadbed makes for easy walking or mountain biking and provides excellent access to lots of great steelhead water. If you choose to bike this road, be sure to carry plenty of supplies for patching tires because of the abundant "goat's head" thistle seeds.

Don't float or powerboat this segment of the river without first learning the rapids by going along with an experienced Deschutes boater. The lower river is rife with hazardous rapids and also presents lots of shallow bedrock reefs and ledges. Currently the BLM manages the lower river in a manner that allows a few days each month during the steelhead season when powerboats are not allowed to run the river. This gives other users a respite from the boat traffic. Check with ODFW or the BLM to get the current schedule.

At the mouth of the river, Heritage State Park Campground occupies the east bank, providing a pleasant, shaded camping area on the river's edge. From there you can hike upriver or you can park at the gated entrance to the road near the entrance to the campground. Across the river on the west bank is Heritage Landing, the busy boat ramp and large parking area that serves boaters arriving from Macks Canyon or departing for trips upstream. A few miles to the east is the little town of Biggs Junction that offers all services, including motels.

Deschutes River Need To Know

The Deschutes River is a very busy place and no one can envy the task of the BLM and ODFW in managing the resource. So visitors here must familiarize themselves with the rules and regulations not only for the actual fishing, but also for boating and camping. Because of the dynamic nature of Deschutes River management, be sure to consult the BLM for current rules and check the fishing synopsis for angling regulations. Below is a general framework of some of the rules and regulations. But be sure to consult the BLM and ODFW for a complete list of these rules (BLM Prineville, 541-416-6700).

Drift boats are extremely popular on the Lower Deschutes River.

Special Angling Regulations:

From the mouth upstream to the northern boundary of the Warm Springs Reservation, including the White River up the first falls, the river is open to trout year-round. From the northern boundary of the reservation up to Pelton Dam, the river is open for trout during the general statewide trout season and open to steelhead fishing from late April through Dec. 31.

- Anglers may keep two trout per day with a 10-inch minimum length and a 13-inch maximum length.
- Only adipose-fin-clipped steelhead may be kept.
- No angling from a floating device.
- Restricted to artificial flies and lures, except that bait may be used from Sherar's Falls downstream to upper trestle (about 3 miles).

- Closed to angling from Sherar's Falls down to Buck Hollow Creek from April 1 to July 31.
- Closed to angling from Pelton Dam downstream 600 feet to ODFW markers.
- Warm Springs Reservation (west bank) waters closed to angling except from Dry Creek Campground down to markers and only with valid tribal fishing permit.

Boating Regulations:

Boater's Pass—everyone in the boat or other floating device must possess a valid boater's pass. These are available by the day or for the season. They are widely available at tackle and outdoor stores throughout the region and at www.boaterpass.com.

- No angling is allowed from a floating device.

Camping Regulations:

All over-night boaters in the section from Warm Springs to Locked Gate are required to camp at BLM-designated campsites, which are marked by a brown post stating the river mile and the maximum number of persons allowed to camp at that site. A complete list of the many campsites is available from the BLM.

- Campsites are available on a first-come, first-served basis and may not be held or reserved by leaving unattended gear.
- From Locked Gate to Buck Hollow Recreation Site, camping is allowed only in designated sites.
- From Buck Hollow to Macks Canyon, campers on the east bank must use designated camp sites.
- Once a campsite is taken, other boaters must float on until they find a vacant site.
- Except for the segment from Locked Gate to Sherar's Falls, group size may not exceed 16 people (24-person maximum on the aforementioned segment).
- Campfires are not allowed between June 1 and October 31. Only white gas and propane are allowed. During the season when fires are allowed, use fire pans.
- Portapotties are required on the segment from Warm Springs to Locked Gate and must be set up at the campsite even when an outdoor toilet is available at the site.
- At developed campsites (drive-in) a camping fee is charged.

Deschutes River, Middle
(Bend to Lake Billy Chinook)
no bait, services

The Middle Deschutes River extends from Bend downstream to the slack water at the Deschutes River Arm of Lake Billy Chinook. Throughout this run, much of the river flows through a scenic juniper-clad canyon and access is somewhat restricted by extensive private property. Popular public access points include Tethrow Crossing downstream from Tumalo, Cine Falls State Park west of Redmond, Lower Bridge west of Terrebonne, and the "Foley Waters" near Steelhead Falls west of Crooked River Ranch. Each of these access points gets you to excellent water and a little map reading will reveal additional access areas.

Wild brown trout, rainbow trout, and whitefish inhabit the Middle Deschutes in good numbers, with the relative abundance of each varying from place to place. This part of the Deschutes is heavily drawn upon by the canal system that feeds local agriculture, so by late spring the river is but a trickle. The trout survive the summer by taking refuge in deep pools and in spring-fed areas. Summertime fishing is largely restricted to these locations.

During the winter and early spring, however, the Middle Deschutes flows full and fast. By all appearances it would seem to be flooded over its banks, but in reality the winter flows are the normal flows. The river looks flooded only because it inundates the trees and brush that grow along the low-water banks during summer. From late January through May, the Middle Deschutes is a fine fly-angling stream, offering regular and predictable hatches.

The Middle Deschutes River near Redmond

The daily dry fly activity begins by early February with mid-afternoon hatches of little brown stoneflies along with a smattering of the much larger *Skwala* stoneflies. By March, blue-winged olive mayflies begin hatching and by late March or early April, certain stretches of the river boast one of the state's most prolific and little-known hatches of western March brown mayflies. The March brown hatches continue through early May and then yield to decent hatches of golden stoneflies, along with a few salmon flies and caddisflies.

Flyfishing is the most productive way to fish the Middle Deschutes between January and April. The dry fly action occurs virtually every afternoon, at least somewhere on the river. Nymph fishing is usually productive and the river's whitefish are especially responsive to small bead-head patterns. As the water drops during May and the trout begin to seek refuge in the deep pools, spin fishing with spoons and spinners or casting with plugs becomes very effective.

The brown trout and rainbows here typically range from 9 to 13 inches, but the river offers quite a few 14- to 20-inch browns. Whitefish range from 6 to 16 inches and abound in the deeper, well-oxygenated runs. In the river's final and most remote leg, from the Squaw Creek confluence down to Lake Billy Chinook, rainbows and whitefish predominate and large bull trout are fairly common. This stretch is fast and rugged, requiring a stout sense of adventure, but the fishing can be good and you won't have much company. This lower section fishes best from May through October and is accessible by hiking down along Squaw Creek or by hiking up from the Deschutes Arm of Lake Billy Chinook.

Deschutes River, Upper (Little Lava Lake to Wickiup Reservoir)

no bait, campground, services

The spirited little stream emerging from Little Lava Lake off Century Drive hardly seems capable of producing the massive Deschutes River, but this is the river's source. From here it will flow almost 250 miles through central Oregon on its northerly journey to the Columbia River. Between Little Lava Lake and Crane Prairie Reservoir, the Upper Deschutes supports good populations of rainbow and brook trout, along with whitefish and, in season, spawning kokanee salmon. Between Crane Prairie Dam and Wickiup Reservoir, the river also supports brown trout.

While small trout predominate (except for the large spawners from the reservoirs), a few rainbows and browns reach 14- to 18 inches in the upper river. Most of the trout typically range from 6 to 10 inches. Both flies and spinners produce on this section of the river, but be sure to consult the most current regulations pamphlet. Fly anglers will enjoy lots of good hatch action throughout the summer. The river here seems to change character around every bend, from glass-smooth flat water reminiscent of a spring creek to gurgling mountain stream to pond-like stretches littered with logs. Trails more-or-less follow both banks, but often you must negotiate through streamside brush to get into or near the water. You can wade back and forth easily in many stretches.

Downstream from Sheep Bridge on South Century Drive, the river gains size and depth as it approaches the Deschutes Arm of Wickiup Reservoir. Sheep Bridge lies between Crane Prairie and Wickiup Reservoirs along South Century Drive. The campground here is quite popular. Additional campgrounds are located between Crane Prairie Reservoir and Little Lava Lake: Cow Meadows Campground sits on the Deschutes Arm on the north end of Crane Prairie; Deschutes Bridge Campground sits on FR 4270 about halfway between Crane and Little Lava Lake. Many other campgrounds are located at the myriad lakes and reservoirs in the area.

To reach the Upper Deschutes between the reservoirs, follow Hwy 97 to the Sunriver Exit and head west past the entrance to Sunriver. Continue around the bend and then stay westbound on Spring River Road (Road 40) heading about 20 miles to the river north of Cow Meadows. A mile further west, Road 40 meets the Cascade Lakes Hwy (Lava Lake Road): Turn north (right) to reach Little Lava Lake. In places you can park along the highway here and walk east to the river. Otherwise,

Tim Blount fishes streamer flies for brown trout on the Upper Deschutes.

Middle Deschutes brown trout

hike up or downstream from the bridges and campgrounds. To find the outlet of Crane Prairie Dam, turn left instead of right on the Cascade Lakes Highway (FR 46), heading south along the west side of Crane Prairie Reservoir. Turn left on Road 42 (South Century Drive), which leads about 3 miles to the river.

Deschutes River, Upper (Wickiup Reservoir to Bend)
boat ramp, campground, services

A good bet for wild brown trout, along with some rainbows and a few brook trout, the Deschutes River below Wickiup Dam flows through a highly varied landscape and produces numerous angling possibilities. The uppermost section is easy to float and throughout most of its run, the Upper Deschutes is best accessed by boat. The upper drift begins at Tenino Launch, just downstream from Wickiup Dam and ends at Wyeth Campground 6.5 miles downstream. This is easy water, suitable for most watercraft. However, do not float beyond Wyeth Campground as impassable Pringle Falls looms half a mile below.

Rafters, kayakers, and canoers often portage the falls to continue the float downstream, but doing so means you must then portage around the Tetherow Log Jam 2.5 miles below the falls. Once you get around the logjam, you have smooth, easy drifting all the way to Sunriver, a stretch of about 20 miles. Because the river moves slowly between Tetherow Log Jam and Sunriver, you should break the float into smaller segments. Ramps are located at LaPine State Park (15 miles to Sunriver) and at Big River Campground (7 miles to Sunriver). Be sure to scout the put-in and take-out locations. Drift boats should depart the river at Big River Campground or drift

past Harper Bridge down to the ramp at Besson Camp, 1.5 miles downstream from Harper Bridge. The take-out at Harper Bridge near Sunriver is suitable only for canoes and other small craft.

Many anglers fish this part of the Deschutes specifically to target large brown trout. These browns range from 12 inches to more than 10 pounds, with 14- to 20-inch fish being typical. They are not numerous, but anglers adept at working the under-cut banks and the deeper slots and pools enjoy consistent success using plugs, spoons, and large streamer flies. The browns respond best during the low-light hours.

Four campgrounds are scattered along this section of the river. To get to the uppermost launch below Wickiup Dam, follow Hwy 97 to Wickiup Junction, just north of LaPine. Head west from Wickiup Junction on Route 43, which crosses the river above Pringle Falls. Before you cross the river, turn left on East Deschutes Road, which follows the river up to the launch. Bull Bend Campground and raft launch lies on the other side of the river, 3 miles downstream. Wyeth Campground lies a mile further downstream: Remember to exit the river here unless you are prepared to portage Pringle Falls. There is a raft/canoe launch below the falls and a boat ramp below the Tetherow Log Jam.

To reach LaPine State Recreation Area (primitive boat launch and campground), watch for the signs on Hwy 97 about halfway between LaPine and Sunriver. Big River Boat Ramp (and group camp) is located 8 river miles north of LaPine State Park. To get there, follow Hwy 97 south of Sunriver or north from LaPine and turn west at Vandevert Road.

Below Sunriver, one last float segment—and a very scenic one—runs from Besson Camp down to the take-out above Benham Falls, a stretch of about 8 river miles. Do not float beyond the ramp above the falls and be sure to scout the take-out location before you make the float. This falls has killed unwary boaters in the past. Downstream from Benham Falls, the Deschutes River plunges through a rugged lava-filled whitewater corridor. This area is rich in good brown trout fishing, but access is limited to a few hike-in spots and a few drive-in spots near the launches used by experienced whitewater enthusiasts.

While floating the river is the best way to access the Upper Deschutes from Wickiup to Benham Falls, bank anglers willing to do a little searching can find plenty of access sites. The easiest bank access is on the upper section of the river within the Deschutes National Forest and on the lower section where public lands predominate from above Benham Falls to Lava Falls—a stretch of about 8 river miles. In this lower reach, the river is very swift and dangerous to wade. To get there, head west from Bend on Century Drive, following the signs leading toward Mt. Bachelor. A few miles from town turn left on the gravel road adjacent to the east end of the gold course at Inn of The 7th Mountain. From here you can drive down to the river and then use a network of trails to hike along the banks.

Deschutes River, Little (Deschutes/Klamath Counties)

The Little Deschutes River springs to life high on the slopes of Mule Peak in the Mt. Thielsen Wilderness, where several tiny rivulets join to form the makings of a small river. The Little Deschutes then joins with Clover Creek and flows through a broad, 1,000-foot deep canyon on its northeasterly journey. After about 10 meandering miles the river reaches Hwy 58 and a few miles later begins a lengthy flow through mostly private lands west of Hwy 97.

Along the way, the Little Deschutes creates two different fisheries. The headwater reaches offer fair fishing for small, wild trout in Deschutes National Forest. Then, as the river's gradient slackens, it begins to meander and, in full, spans more than 90 miles in length. In the river's lower 70 miles, trout populations are somewhat sparse overall, but fishing can be good in places. Some large brown trout and rainbows inhabit the river, especially in stretches where the banks retain lush riparian vegetation and where structure provides cover. Otherwise, smaller fish dominate the catch. The river's largest brown trout reach at least 6 pounds, but they are uncommon.

Generally the river's best reaches are located on private property, so if you can gain permission to access prime water, you'll stand a better chance of finding the 14- to 24-inch browns that hide below undercut banks. The stream flows through limited public lands west of Crescent and this stretch can produce some fair fishing for both browns and rainbows. Additional public land stretches are found both south and north of LaPine. The northernmost public access is located at Rosland Campground, off FR 43, about 30 miles south of Bend. Access to all reaches of the river is by a maze of county and forest service roads, so if you're serious about unlocking the secrets of the Little Deschutes, you'll need the Crescent Ranger District Map.

Devils Lake (Deschutes County)
campground

The first roadside lake you'll encounter when traveling from Bend west along Century Drive, 40-acre Devil's Lake is a gin-clear scenic beauty a few miles past Mt. Bachelor. The lake has small, wild brook trout and is regularly stocked with legal-size rainbows during the summer months. The lake's remarkable clarity belies its infertility and trout here haven't enough natural food on which to grow fat. Any method will work and a canoe, pontoon, or float tube helps quite a bit during those times when the fish stick to the deeper water. Otherwise there is ample shore fishing. Summer weekends attract lots of people to the Century Drive Lakes, so get there early to grab a campsite. Other campgrounds are located nearby at Elk and Hosmer Lakes.

Doris Lake (Three Sisters Wilderness)
hike-in

A large and scenic brook trout lake on the eastern edge of the Three Sisters Wilderness Area, Doris Lake lies along a fairly busy trail, so lots of people visit during the summer hiking season. The fishing, however, is marginally productive and the lake's brook trout generally range from 6 to 10 inches. The shoreline is rugged, but rocky shoals in some areas are easy to wade. Access is from the Six Lakes Trailhead about 2 miles south of Elk Lake on Century Drive. The easy hike covers 2.7 miles at a very gentle incline. Doris Lake spans 90 acres and reaches a maximum depth of 71 feet. It sits at 5,350 feet and is usually accessible by early June.

Eagle Creek (Hood River County)

The lower end of Eagle Creek is a popular salmon and steelhead angling location just upstream from Bonneville Dam on the Columbia River. The creek enjoys a fair run of chinook salmon during late summer and fall and a modest, but fishable run of winter-run steelhead from December through March. Be sure to check the current regulations for open seasons and dates. The upper reaches of Eagle Creek offer good fishing for small wild cutthroat and rainbow trout, but only if you are willing to hike the trail, which provides fantastic scenery of the gorge through which the creek flows. The trail leads south for many miles, following the creek deep into the Hatfield Wilderness Area. Trout angling is catch-and-release only with flies and artificial lures.

East Lake (Deschutes County)
boat recommended, boat ramp, campground, services

A beautiful and popular natural lake southeast from Bend, East Lake fills an ancient volcanic crater and offers good prospects for rainbow and brown trout along with kokanee and Atlantic salmon. The brown trout here typically range from 14 to 24 inches in length and the lake record weighed 22.5 pounds (note that a new regulation enacted in 2010 dictates that browns over 16 inches must be released). They feed on large prey, including kokanee and chub minnows, so most anglers target the big brown trout with large lures.

Popular brown trout lures include Rapalas, Power Minnows, Needlefish, and Krocodiles, all in the 3- to 4-inch range. Both trolling and casting are popular methods for targeting brown trout on East Lake, especially during the early part of the season when the browns tend to congregate along the southeast shoreline. Underwater springs here melt the ice faster than on the remainder of the lake, making this spot the best bet during May and early June. If the lake remains partially ice-covered, try trolling back and forth from the south end of Cinder Hill Campground, past East Lake Resort and over to the cliffs on the south shore just east from East Lake Campground. Also move out towards the edge of the ice to try for rainbows, which range from 10 to 20 inches here.

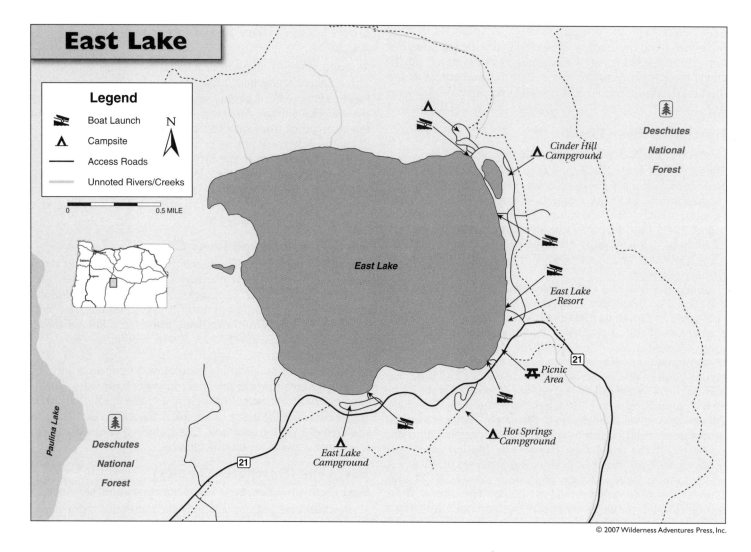

© 2007 Wilderness Adventures Press, Inc.

After the ice melts, the fish tend to disperse, but the east and southwest shoreline areas remain the best bet for big brown trout, especially early and late in the day. Even fly anglers enjoy success trolling large flies for brown trout. One of the best areas for fly fishing is just out from the large boulders and cliff immediately east of East Lake Campground. Find the drop-off here and troll or cast-and-retrieve a large Woolly Bugger, leech pattern, or Zonker on a sinking line. This area is also a good bet for targeting the lake's rainbows and Atlantic salmon with small nymphs and even dry flies when flying ants and *Callibaetis* mayflies cause surface activity.

Other good areas for targeting rainbows and Atlantic salmon include the entire south shoreline out from Cinder Hill Campground and the rock cliffs on the north bank, just west from Cinder Hill Campground. The northwest shoreline offers good prospects as well and often enjoys a bit of protection from the afternoon winds.

During mid- and late summer, both brown trout and kokanee frequent the deeper drop-offs and shoals near the lake's center and one popular trolling path is to circle the deep

central pool of the lake, which drops down to a maximum depth of 180 feet. The south edge of the deep water is a popular and productive spot: Line up the white pumice slide on the west shore with the north side of the resort on the east shore and troll along that path.

Bait anglers enjoy consistent success on East Lake, especially with the rainbow trout. Bank fishing with bait can be good just about anywhere, but the usual hotspots include the rocky bank just west from Cinder Hill Campground, the shoreline east of the boat ramp at East Lake Campground, and the shallow cove north of the white pumice slide. You can also bait fish by boat, especially along the east shoreline.

If you are specifically fishing for kokanee at East Lake, fish-finding equipment comes in handy because these schooling fish frequently change depths and locations. The drop-offs near the center of the lake always seem to have schools of kokanee and most anglers fish small bits of bait behind flasher rigs.

East Lake features three nice USFS campgrounds along with the ever-popular East Lake Resort, which offers a store, tackle shop, good fishing advice, cabins, RV park, and rental boats. They open in late May and remain open until the end of September (541-536-2230/www.eastlakeresort.com). To reach East Lake, head south from Bend on Hwy 97 about 24 miles to a signed left-hand turn on FR 21, leading 16 miles up to the lake. East Lake sits at 6,400 feet. Both East Lake and Paulina Lake are included in the New-berry Volcanic National Monument and an entry fee is required (currently $10 for three days).

Elk Lake (Deschutes County)
campground

Brook trout and kokanee inhabit this scenic lake located along Century Drive west of Bend. The fishing can be quite good early and late in the season, with autumn being prime because of the absence of the summer time throngs of water-sports enthusiasts that as-semble here. Offering the requisite views of the surrounding snow-capped peaks, Elk Lake spans about 250 acres and sits adjacent to better-known Hosmer Lake. The brook trout range from 5 to 20 inches, with

East Lake is one of central Oregon's prettiest fisheries.

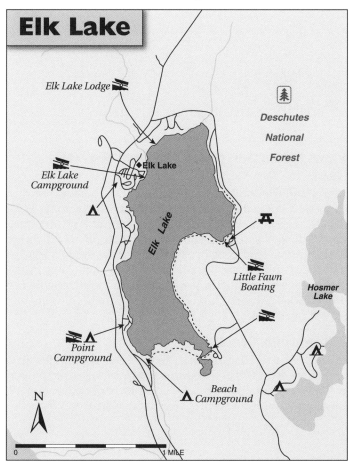

Elk Lake

Elk Lake Lodge

Deschutes
National
Forest

Elk Lake

Elk Lake
Campground

Little Fawn
Boating

Hosmer
Lake

Point
Campground

Beach
Campground

N

0   1 MILE

© 2007 Wilderness Adventures Press, Inc.

8- to 12-inch fish being typical. Kokanee abound, but most are 10 inches or less in length.

It offers several campgrounds and boat launches, and Elk Lake Resort (541-480-7228/www.elklakeresort.net), which offers lodging, food, and rental boats. The resort remains open during winter, catering to snowmobilers and cross-country skiers. To reach Elk Lake, head west from Bend toward Mt. Bachelor. About 36 miles from town, watch for the signs an-nouncing Elk Lake.

Fall River (Deschutes County)
fly-only

The scenic little Fall River is a spring-fed beauty that mean-ders through pine forests southwest of Sunriver, meeting the Upper Deschutes near LaPine State Recreation Area. The most popular access site and fishing area on Fall River is at the state fish hatchery about halfway up the stream. Fall River is home to wild brown, rainbow, and brook trout and is also liberally stocked with legal-size rainbows. Heavily fished by fly anglers of all skill levels, the small river offers something for everyone. The fish typically range from 6 to 12 inches, but big trout are always lurking around, especially in the harder-to-fish areas.

Fall River offers excellent prospects for challenging flat-water dry fly action during strong hatches of Blue-winged Olive (*Baetis*) and Pale Morning Dun (*Ephemerella*) mayflies, various caddisflies and Chironomids. Even the stocked hatch-ery trout soon learn to feed carefully and selectively on the flat-water sections of the creek so, long leaders, light tippets, and gentle presentations are a must. Sub-surface fishing is equally productive whether you fish tiny nymph patterns, small soft-hackle flies or streamer flies.

Access to the Fall River is fairly good, with a large public stretch at the hatchery and mostly public (Deschutes Nation-

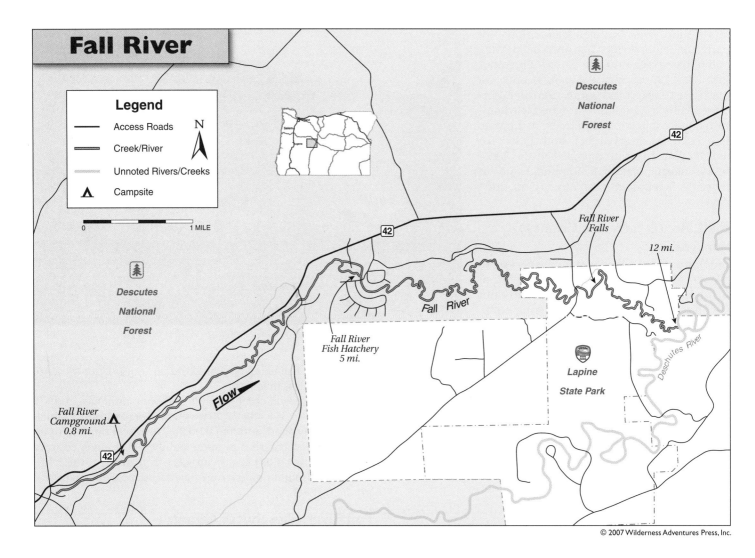

Fall River

Legend

— Access Roads

═ Creek/River

⋯ Unnoted Rivers/Creeks

⋀ Campsite

N

0   1 MILE

Descutes National Forest

Descutes National Forest

42

42

Fall River Falls

12 mi.

Fall River

Fall River Fish Hatchery 5 mi.

Lapine State Park

Deschutes River

Fall River Campground 0.8 mi. ⋀

42

Flow ►

© 2007 Wilderness Adventures Press, Inc.

al Forest) land upstream from the hatchery for about 4 miles to the springs. A nice campground sits near the headwaters. The lower end of the river is more difficult to access owing to extensive public property and gone are the days when one could hike the stream from the lower access road down to the mouth because a large housing development, complete with no-trespassing signs—now fills the area.

Currently most of the river (upstream from the falls) is open year-round, but the lower end below the falls opens in late May and closes at the end of September. The closure protects spawning trout from the Deschutes River. To get to Fall River, follow Hwy 97 south from Bend for about 18 miles or north from LaPine about 14 miles to the Fall River Exit. From there, head west on South Century Drive and watch for the signs to the river.

Farrell Lake (Deschutes National Forest)
see Snell Lake

Fawn Lake (Deschutes National Forest)
hike-in

A large and scenic hike-in lake situated about halfway between Crescent Lake to the south and Odell Lake to the north, Fawn Lake is a good producer of brook trout from 6 to 14 inches. Bank fishing is good, but you won't be disappointed if you go to the trouble of hauling in a float tube. Fawn sits at 5,700 feet and the trails here are usually passable by mid- to late June. Trails arrive from both Crescent Lake Resort and from the east end of Odell Lake and both routes cover about 2.7 miles and gain about 800 feet.

Fifteenmile Creek

Fifteenmile Creek is a tributary to the Lower Deschutes River and offers no public access owing to extensive private property. The creek supports a sparse population of native redband trout, and fishing for them is catch-and-release only

Fall River is a scenic fly-only stream in central Oregon, south of Bend.

Found Lake (Deschutes National Forest)
see Charlton Lake

Frog Lake (Mt. Hood National Forest)
campground

A super-popular trout lake near Mt. Hood and nearly adjacent to Hwy 26, Frog Lake is heavily and continually stocked with rainbows, including a few brood-stock fish. Fishing tends to hold up fairly well throughout the season, but the lake gets crowded on summer weekends. Watch for the signs announcing Frog Lake 7 miles southeast from Summit Meadows and about a mile north from Blue Box Pass.

Gleneden Lake (Three Sisters Wilderness)
see Brahma Lake

Government Cove (Columbia River/I-84)
boat ramp

A broad, shallow cove immediately east of Cascade Locks, Government Cove serves both as a launch site for anglers fishing the Columbia River and also as a destination in its own right. The cove is home to a wide array of warmwater species, including bass, sunfish, bullheads, crappie, and yellow perch along with lots of non-game fish and an occasional sturgeon. A nice cement boat ramp and park allows for easy access and shore fishing is fairly plentiful. Take the Herman Creek Exit from the Interstate. At high water the cove spans about 100 acres.

Green Lakes (Three Sisters Wilderness)
hike-in

Because of the inherent beauty of this lake basin, the Green Lakes area is heavily used during the summer hiking season, so don't expect to find solitude here unless you wait until October. In fact, the lake's designated campsites usually fill up by Friday evening every summer weekend and the Deschutes National Forest itself says that the trail into Green Lake "is one of the most over-used in the Three Sisters Wilderness, thus users are strongly encouraged to seek less visited trails, especially on weekends."

Nonetheless, should you wish to fish these lakes for average-size brook and rainbow trout, the action usually ranges from poor to good depending on angling pressure, recent stockings, and weather. The middle of the three lakes is by far the largest and most productive and spans 85 acres. North and South Green Lakes span about 8 acres each. My advice here is to forget about the summer season and wait until late September and early October, weather permitting. The shortest routes arrive from the south and cover about 5 miles. The super-popular trail from Devil's Lake on Century Drive is easy, though steep in a few spots and a somewhat lesser used trail originates to the northeast at Todd Lake.

Green Point Reservoir
see Kingsley Reservoir

Grindstone Lakes (Crook County)
fee fishery, fly fishing only

A popular fee fishery on a private ranch in eastern Crook County, the Grindstone Lakes are well known for their propensity to produce trophy-class rainbow trout. Trips here are arranged by fly shops throughout the region. For current information, contact your local fly-angling retail store.

Hand Lake (Jefferson Lake)

A fair-to-slow fishery for stocked cutthroat trout, Hand Lake is a 4-acre lake located close to Santiam Pass in the southwest corner of Jefferson County. The area has become popular with ATV enthusiasts, who tend to stir up lots of dust during warm summer weekends. This area was partially burned over by the Link Fire and by the B&B Complex fire in 2003. Follow Hwy 20 northwest from Sisters or easterly from Santiam Pass and turn south on FR 2068 about 3 miles east of Suttle Lake. Follow FR 2068 to a right-hand turn on FR 600.

Hanks Lakes (Three Sisters Wilderness)
hike-in, float tube recommended

The three Hanks Lakes lie close to the Merle Lake Trail, just east of popular Irish and Taylor Lakes northeast from Waldo Lake. All three are periodically stocked with brook trout or rainbow (cutthroat have been used in Middle Hanks). East Hanks Lake spans 10 acres and is 22 feet deep. Middle Hanks, covering 6 acres, also reaches a maximum depth of 22 feet and West Hanks spans 8 acres and is 10 feet deep. Typical trout here range from 8 to 10 inches with an occasional 14-incher to keep things interesting.

Despite the short, easy hike to the lakes and despite their proximity to Irish and Taylor Lakes, these pleasant fisheries are rarely over-run by people and solitude is possible even on summer weekends. Still, fishing is best in September and early October and the lakes are usually accessible by June. The trail departs FR 600 about 1.5 miles east from the campground at Taylor Lake. You'll reach Middle Hanks Lake first after less than a quarter mile. See Taylor Lake herein for directions to the area.

Harlequin Lake (Three Sisters Wilderness)
see Merle Lake

Harvey Lake (Warm Springs Reservation)
hike-in

One of the most starkly scenic of the lakes in the Olallie Lake area, Harvey Lake is located southeast from Breitenbush Lake. A 3-mile trail takes you to this 25-acre gem, which offers brook trout from 6 to 16 inches. Most of the brookies range from 8 to 12 inches and a few cutthroat trout may still show in the catch as well.

Harvey Lake sits within the Warm Springs Indian Reservation, so you'll need the tribal fishing permit to fish this lake and the other nearby including Trout, Island, Dark, and Long Lakes. Permits are available from fishing tackle retailers and from the Warm Springs Market, or call 541-553-2000. To reach Harvey, head south from Olallie Lake or east on Breitenbush Road from the town of Detroit. Follow the signs to Breitenbush Lake. The trail to Harvey Lake begins at the campground. At 5,400 feet, Harvey is accessible most years by late June.

Haystack Reservoir (Jefferson County)

A popular and generally productive mixed-bag fishery near Madras, Haystack Reservoir is best known for its crappie fishery, but also produces lots of kokanee, along with stocked rainbow trout, wild largemouth bass and bullhead, along with an occasional large brown trout. Drawing its flow from the canal system on the Deschutes River, Haystack spans 233 acres at full pool, but it fluctuates often because it was built as a storage facility for the North District Irrigation Unit.

Increasingly the reservoir has become a popular destination for water-sports enthusiasts, so water skiers, jet skiers and swimmers abound during summer, especially on weekends. Despite the crowds, summer fishing can be quite good. You can catch all species, including kokanee, from shore. Many anglers fish from the area adjacent to the dam and from the campground on the east side of the lake. Nonetheless a boat is handy here, especially for kokanee fishing, wherein the usual trolling techniques work best. Experiment with depth (or use a fish-finder) until you locate the schools of kokanee. The stocked rainbows respond equally well to trolling and a few of them carry over each year, reaching 13 to 16 inches.

For crappie, try small grub-colored or chartreuse jigs and search for structural elements in the form of shoals and steep drop-offs. The channels along the reservoir's south shoreline are always good bets for crappie and for largemouth bass and they are easy to fish from shore or by boat. At full pool, the reservoir offers lots of flooded brush on the south shoreline, especially in the southeast corner. These areas are prime locations for bass, some bluegill, and large black crappie. You can fish the shallows by boat, from shore or by wade fishing. The same channels and shoals on the south and southwest shores sometimes come alive with rising trout during summer evenings.

To reach Haystack, follow Hwy 97 north from Redmond or south from Madras. About 8 miles south of Madras and about 15 miles north of Redmond watch for the signed turn-off leading east to Haystack. The reservoir freezes over during prolonged cold spells, sometimes offering good ice-fishing prospects. The water skiers tend to disperse with the onset of autumn weather and the fishing can be quite good during October, with kokanee coming into the shallows.

Herman Creek (Hood River County)

A small, scenic tributary to the Columbia at Cascade Locks, Herman Creek is best known for its salmon hatchery, which produces fall-run chinook. Below the hatchery, the creek is closed during the late-summer-through-autumn run of hatchery-bound salmon. Herman Creek produces a few winter steelhead between January and March and a few summer-run steelhead from June through September. Even a few coho salmon enter the creek. All wild fish must be released (hatchery fish are marked by a clipped adipose fin). Herman Creek also offers good fishing for small, wild trout during the summer. The trout fishing is hike-in only via a good trail system. Be sure to check current regulations before fishing for anything in Herman Creek.

Hidden Lake (Deschutes National Forest)
see Charlton Lake

Hood River (Hood River County)

Hood River, as the name suggests, originates on the flanks and glaciers of Mt. Hood as myriad small streams and forks. Eventually all of the forks and their tributaries converge to from Hood River proper about 15 miles south of the city of

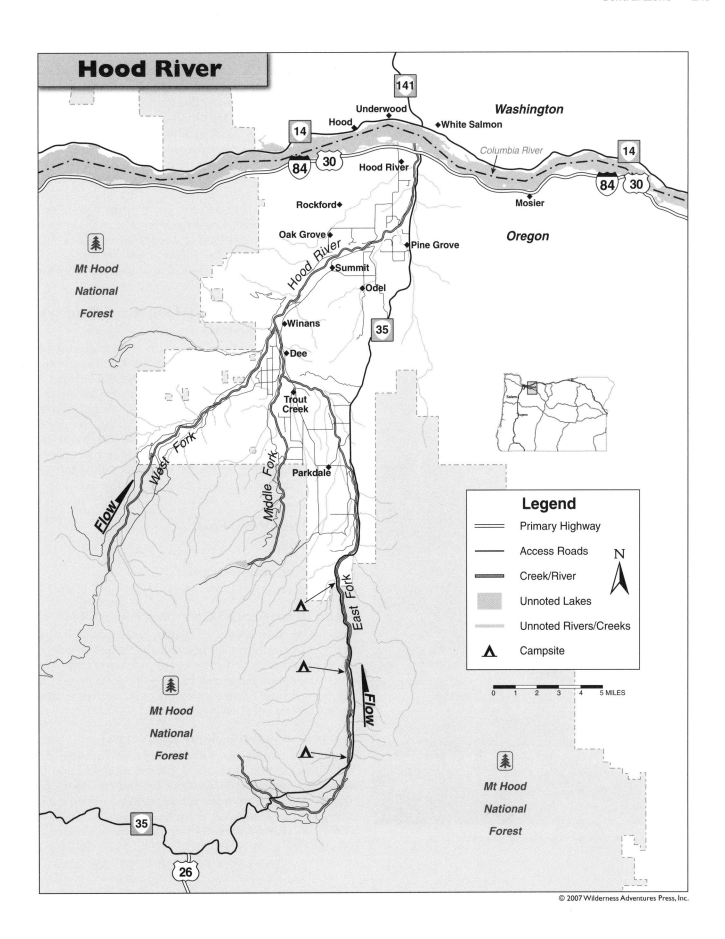

Hood River

Washington

141

Underwood

14

Hood

♦White Salmon

Columbia River

14

84 30

Hood River

84 30

Mosier

Rockford♦

Oregon

Oak Grove♦

♦Pine Grove

Hood River

♦Summit

♦Odel

♦Winans

35

♦Dee

Salem

Eugene

Trout Creek

West Fork

Middle Fork

Parkdale

Legend

═══	Primary Highway
───	Access Roads
▭▭▭	Creek/River
▨	Unnoted Lakes
▨	Unnoted Rivers/Creeks
Λ	Campsite

N

Flow

East Fork

Λ

Λ

Flow

🌲
Mt Hood National Forest

Λ

0 1 2 3 4 5 MILES

🌲
Mt Hood National Forest

35

26

🌲
Mt Hood National Forest

the same name. Hood River is primarily known for its runs of salmon and steelhead. Currently the river is open to angling for both chinook and coho salmon and the river hosts runs of summer and winter steelhead.

The river frequently runs tinged with glacial till, especially during the warm months, but a few steelhead anglers eagerly anticipate the high-elevation freezes during autumn that lock up the glaciers and help the water clear. For a few weeks during the fall, steelhead fishing can be quite productive here for summer-run fish. The summer steelhead run usually continues from late May through autumn and the river puts out a fair number of fish in June.

Winter steelhead return to the Hood River in greater numbers and, along with salmon, are the subject of quite a lot of angling effort especially on the lower river. Powerdale Dam (river mile 4) was decommissioned and removal work began in 2010, with new temporary angling regulations in effect; be

Mount Hood looms above the Hood River.

sure to check the current ODFW angling synopsis for the latest details. Fall chinook salmon enter the river between August and November, along with a smaller run of coho salmon. Be sure to check current regulations for season dates and frameworks. Trout fishing is limited to catch-and-release with artificial lures and flies. Steelhead head well into the forks and a few anglers—both gear and fly fishers—target them from up as far as the forks. Access is difficult owing to lots of private land, so knock on doors for permission if you're not sure of access.

From the town of Hood River up to the old Powerdale Dam site, good trails follow along the river. The drive-in access is limited to the dam site itself and to the lower end of the river as it passes through town. This is almost exclusively a bank fishery, though boaters on the Columbia fish the mouth of the river up to the freeway bridge.

Hood River, East Fork (Hood River County)
no bait, catch-and-release

A fair fishery for small wild trout, the East Fork Hood River originates on the southeast slope of Mt. Hood and then parallels Hwy 35 north heading towards the town of Hood River. The East Fork joins the Middle Fork near Dee Flats and soon thereafter joins the main river. The lower half of the East Fork flows primarily through private property, but the decidedly scenic upper half lies within Mt. Hood National Forest. Easy access is available at three campgrounds and a county park along Hwy 35. The East Fork is closed to fishing for salmon and steelhead and opens for trout during late May to protect smolts.

Hood River, West Fork
closed waters

Hood River, Lake Branch
closed waters

Hood River Ponds (Columbia River/I-84)

A series of three small, elongated ponds located adjacent to the eastbound lanes of I-84 just east of Hood River, these warmwater fisheries offer bass, sunfish, crappie, yellow perch, and various non-game species. They are strung out between mileposts 66 and 67 and accessible only from the eastbound lanes. They are easy to fish from shore.

Horseshoe Lake (Olallie Lake area)

A popular drive-in lake located in the Olallie Scenic Area, 14-acre Horseshoe Lake offers stocked rainbows and brook trout. They range from 8 to 12 inches and only rarely does a big fish show up. Horseshoe is a pretty lake, so even if it holds little promise of large fish, it remains a pleasant family destination. See Olallie Lake herein for directions to the area.

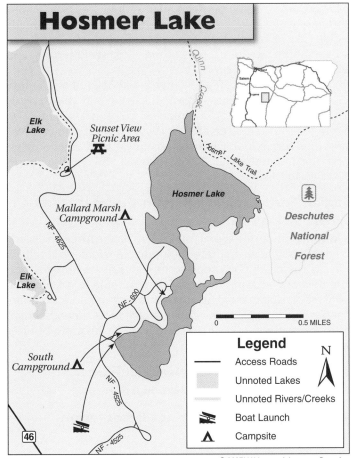

© 2007 Wilderness Adventures Press, Inc.

Hosmer Lake (Deschutes National Forest)
fly-fishing only, catch-and-release, boat recommended, float tube recommended, boat ramp, campground

A long-time perennial favorite fishery among Oregon's fly-angling community, Hosmer Lake is famed for its land-locked Atlantic salmon. The salmon, stocked here by ODFW, reach more than 20 inches in length and put up quite a fight, especially in pound-for-pound terms. The typical Hosmer salmon, during a good year, ranges from 14 to 18 inches and the lake also supports some of the state's largest brook trout. Big brookies here, which are notoriously difficult to land, range from 3 to 6 pounds.

Hosmer Lake spans about 160 acres, but reaches a maximum depth of only 12 feet. The shallow waters teem with life. Because energy from sunlight easily penetrates to the entire lake bottom, Hosmer is a veritable insect factory where Chironomids, *Callibaetis* mayflies, damselflies, caddis, and many other trout foods grow profusely. Obviously Hosmer's fish enjoy ample feed. Anglers enjoy plenty of dry fly opportunity: Mayflies, midges, damsels, and caddis hatch all summer long. When surface activity wanes, anglers rely on the more typical tactics of fishing wet flies or streamer patterns on sinking lines. The line of choice is one of the new-generation clear or camo intermediate or "still-water" lines. A wide array of flies does the job, ranging from Chironomid pupa and scud patterns to leech imitations and large marabou, bucktail, or rabbit-strip streamers.

Of these latter flies—the streamers—Hosmer's salmon seem prone to pounce on bright-colored Woolly Buggers, marabou leeches, and other such attractors. These flies are especially effective during the first two weeks after ice-out during May. Typically at this time snow blocks the access road, so dedicated Hosmer enthusiasts often hike or ski between 1 and 5 miles into the lake.

The *Callibaetis* hatch likewise begins before the road into Hosmer is free of snow. The mayflies hatch daily, between mid-morning and mid-afternoon, depending on the weather. The most intense hatches accompany those rare still, muggy, overcast days, but you can count on good mayfly activity most days, especially during June and July. The best dry fly opportunity occurs during still weather. Try fishing a Pheasant Tail Nymph or similar *Callibaetis* nymph imitation beginning about 9:00am. Then keep an eye peeled for fish to start splashing for duns and emergers.

Hosmer Lake also provides a rare chance to fish dry damsel adult patterns. The damsels hatch in enormous numbers during June and July. Watch for adults buzzing around the reed stands during mid-morning and keep an eye peeled for splashy rises near and amongst the reeds. Aim for the rise-forms and plop a blue or olive damsel adult pattern on the water. Wait for all the ripples to clear and then make a few twitches interspersed with long pauses. The takes are almost always violent.

The June and July fishing is very popular on Hosmer Lake and the campground usually fills up during summer weekends. Don't be surprised to see vehicles parked along the access road. August frequently brings a bit of a lull in the action along with an algae bloom. Fishing picks up again in the fall, which is a decidedly fine time to fish this scenic lake.

Fishing Hosmer Lake virtually requires watercraft of some kind because much of the lakeshore is lined with reeds and that which isn't is largely brushy and devoid of good backcast room. Anglers here effectively employ everything from float tubes and canoes to prams and drift boats. Only electric motors are allowed on the lake.

The lake is essentially divided into two parts. The boat ramp feeds into the south pool, which is connected by a narrow channel to the larger and shallower north pool. The channel is home to some of the lake's largest brook trout, whose numbers have seemingly decreased over the years. Hooking big fish in the channel is one thing; landing them there quite another. Once hooked, the big fish make a hi-speed dash into the reeds. However, hooking them there is a lot of fun.

The channel gets terribly busy with boat traffic at times, but if you can catch a day with minimal angling pressure and a bright sun, try this: Let the boat drift up against the reeds and then lower an anchor. Using a sinking line and a dragonfly nymph, scud, or mayfly nymph pattern, cast into the channel, but not beyond your sight line. Allow the fly and line to settle to the bottom. Then keep still and watch. When a big brookie or salmon cruises close to your fly, make three or four quick strips of line. If the fish is in a biting mood, it'll practically turn a somersault to get at the fly.

Though quite a few large trout are landed in the channel, it can get too crowded on busy days. At such times—all too common on Hosmer these days—fish either of the two main pools. The north pool seems to hold fewer fish, but often it holds fewer boats as well. The south pool is frequently most

Hosmer Lake

productive and most fly anglers here are respectful enough to give everybody ample space.

Hosmer offers two nice campgrounds. South Campground has 23 sites and nearby Mallard Marsh Campground offers another 15 sites. The main, paved boat ramp is adjacent to South Campground, but float tubes, pontoons, and canoes can also be launched at the informal ramp located at Mallard

Marsh Campground, between sites 14 and 15. If the campgrounds at Hosmer Lake are full, try the nearby campgrounds at Elk Lake or Lava Lake. Additional campgrounds are located to the south at Cultus Lake, Crane Prairie Reservoir, and various other destinations.

Hosmer Lake lies about 37 miles west of Bend on Century Drive. Follow the signs for Mt. Bachelor and the Cascade Lakes. Watch for signs announcing Elk and Hosmer Lake. From the south (Eugene), follow Hwy 58 over Willamette Pass and then turn left on CR 61 (Crescent Cut-off). After 3 miles, turn north onto Cascade Lakes Highway and continue north 36 miles to Hosmer.

Indian Ford Creek (Jefferson County)
no bait

Flowing from spring sources near Hwy 20 northwest of Sisters, Indian Ford Creek is a rather diminutive tributary of Squaw Creek. The creek flows mostly through private property and the meadow section north of Sisters is home to a few small, wild trout available only if you are willing to knock on doors for permission to fish. The upper stretch flows through Indian Ford Campground on the north side of the highway, but fish are few and far between here.

Irish Lake (Deschutes National Forest)
see Taylor Lake, Deschutes National Forest

Island Lake (Warm Springs Reservation)
see Trout Lake

Island Lake (Jefferson County)

Located in the southwest corner of Jefferson County not far from Santiam Pass, Island Lake is among the group of small lakes at Corbett State Park. Much larger Suttle Lake lies to the northeast. Eight-acre Island Lake is generally stocked periodically with brook trout and fishing ranges from slow to good. All-Terrain Vehicle (ATV) enthusiasts show up here on summer weekends, making the area rather dusty and noisy. The area was severely burned a few years ago by the Cache Mountain Fire. See Hand Lake herein for directions.

Jack Creek (Metolius River drainage)
closed waters

Jay Lake (Three Sisters Wilderness)
hike-in

A 13-acre brook trout lake near the southeastern edge of the Three Sisters Wilderness Area, Jay Lake is only lightly fished and usually produces catches in the 8- to 12-inch range. At 5,000 feet, Jay Lake is usually accessible by early June. An old trail route leads close to Jay Lake, but the maintained trail (Merle Lake/Cultus Trail) passes to the north. See Merle Lake herein for directions to the trailhead, located on FR 600, which accesses Irish and Taylor Lakes.

Nearby Raft and Strider Lakes are usually stocked with rainbows every few years and both are more than 20 feet deep. They have the propensity to grow rainbows to at least 15 inches and both are lightly fished owing to the lack of formal trails leading to them. A float tube is a nice luxury on these lakes 10 and 3 acres, respectively. Lots of smaller ponds dot the landscape here (all of which produce hordes of mosquito's), so study the contour map carefully.

Jean Lake (Mt. Hood National Forest)
hike-in

Beautiful Jean Lake is a fair to good producer of small stocked rainbow trout and is located in the Mt. Hood National Forest above larger and more popular Badger Lake. You can hike up the steep ridge west from Badger up to Jean Lake, but it's not easy going. The easier route is via a short trail from the west side of the lake, which begins near Camp Windy. From Hwy 35 across from the entrance to Mt. Hood Meadows Ski Area, follow FR 3550 southeast about 3 miles to a left-hand turn on the road to Camp Windy. At Camp Windy, stay to the left and head about a mile and a half to the Jean Lake Trailhead. From there it's an easy downhill hike about half a mile to this 6-acre lake, which sits in a timer-clad bowl guarded by steep ridges on three sides. The road and trail are usually free of snow by late June. Shore fishing is easy here, but the half-mile hike makes for an easy walk with a float tube. Some maps mislabel this lake as "June Lake."

Jefferson Creek (Metolius River drainage)
closed waters

Johnny Lake (Deschutes National Forest)
hike-in

A good brook trout lake a few miles east of Waldo Lake, 20-acre Johnny Lake is lightly fished yet easy to reach by a half-mile-long trail. The brookies here typically range from 6 to 12 inches, but a few beautiful 14-inchers inhabit the lake as well. At 5,400 feet, Johnny Lake is usually accessible by late May. The lake is ringed by trees with lots of downed timber in the lake; the shoreline is difficult to navigate around much of the lake, so a float tube offers a big advantage. From Eugene, follow Hwy 58 to the Waldo Lake turn-off and from there head for Charlton Lake. Follow FR 4290 east past the Charlton Trail for about 5 miles to a right-hand turn on FR 200, which leads a mile to the trailhead. From Bend, follow Century Drive from either direction towards Wickiup Reservoir. Just west of the Deschutes Arm, at the junction of South Century Drive and Century Drive (Routes 42 and 46), head due west onto FR 4290 about 4 miles to FR 200.

Kershaw Lake (Three Sisters Wilderness)
see Merle Lake

Kingsley Reservoir (Hood River County)
campground

A fair-to-good producer of stocked rainbow trout, Kingsley Reservoir lies in the forested hills southwest of Hood River. All methods produce here, and the reservoir offers ample bank-fishing space along with a launch area for small boats. The campground is strung all along the east shoreline, with attractive sites sitting nearly at water's edge. Bank fishing is usually good from this side of the lake and also from the earthen dam when the reservoir is at or near capacity. Kingsley is a good place for a family outing. Sometimes the campground fills up on summer weekends, but generally you'll have no problem getting a site.

The easiest way to get there is to take the westernmost of the three Hood River exits from I-84. Immediately after exiting the freeway and turning toward town, look for a right-hand turn on Country Club Road, which doubles back to parallel the freeway. Follow Country Club Road through several turns, heading south. Stay right at both stop signs and watch for the signs pointing towards Kingsley Reservoir. The road is paved all the way. If you don't mind rough, but easily passable mountain roads, you can drive past the back side of Kinglsey Reservoir for less than 2 miles to hook up with FR 2420, the road to Rainy Lake. Most maps show Kingsley as Green Point Reservoir or Upper Green Point Reservoir.

Kinnicinnic Lake (Three Sisters Wilderness)
see Merle Lake

Kolberg Lake (Columbia River/I-84)

Located adjacent to Kolberg Beach at Hood River, 5-acre Kolberg Lake offers fair prospects for a variety of warmwater species, including bass and crappie. A state recreation area with ample parking encompasses Kolberg Beach and the lake is across the highway.

Lady Lake (Three Sisters Wilderness)
see Brahma Lake

Lake Billy Chinook (Jefferson County)
boat ramp, boat recommended, campground, services

Lake Billy Chinook, sometimes called Round Butte Reservoir, is a huge three-pronged reservoir whose fingers fill the canyons once formed by the Metolius, Deschutes, and Crooked Rivers. Covering about 4,000 acres in total and reaching depths of more than 400 feet, Lake Billy Chinook offers a very productive fishery for kokanee along with good fishing for smallmouth bass and a unique opportunity to fish for trophy-size bull trout. The bull trout—a threatened species throughout most of its range in the West—is a piscivorous member of the char family, more closely related to Dolly Varden and brook trout than to the true trout.

Bull Trout in Lake Billy Chinook reach more than 20 pounds, with 2- to 8-pound fish being typical and double-digit specimens fairly common. The reservoir's population of bull trout is sizeable and stable enough that ODFW currently allows harvest opportunity for one fish 24 inches or longer. However, anglers should consider carefully releasing all bull trout as they can hardly compare to the abundant kokanee as

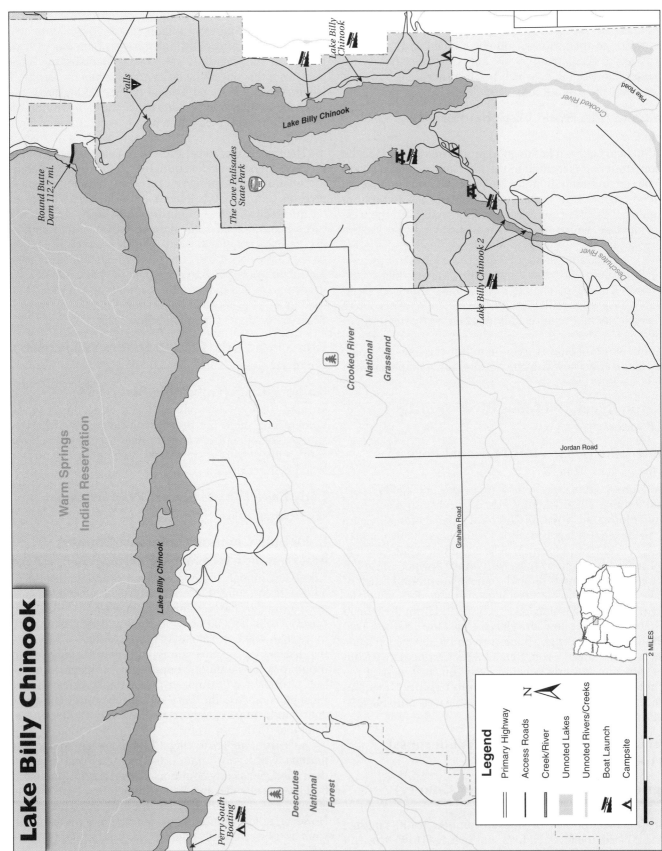

Lake Billy Chinook

Lake Billy Chinook

Lake Billy Chinook

Lake Billy Chinook 2

Lake Billy Chinook

Falls

Round Butte
Dam 112.7 mi.

The Cove Palisades
State Park

Warm Springs
Indian Reservation

Crooked River

Pike Road

Deschutes River

Crooked River
National
Grassland

Jordan Road

Graham Road

Perry South
Boating

Deschutes
National
Forest

Legend

	Primary Highway
	Access Roads
	Creek/River
	Unnoted Lakes
	Unnoted Rivers/Creeks
	Boat Launch
	Campsite

N

0   1   2 MILES

table fare and because a trophy-size bull trout has lived a long life. Most of the bull trout action occurs in the Metolius River Arm of the reservoir. You'll need large plugs, spoons, or jigs to target them in deep water and a fish finder is helpful. Angling for these large bull trout is much the same as fishing for Mackinaw—another type of char—in Crescent or Odell Lakes.

The Metolius Arm, which averages cooler temperatures than the remainder of Lake Billy Chinook, is also the prime region for targeting kokanee, although like the bull trout, these land-locked sockeye salmon occur throughout the reservoir. Kokanee here range from 10 to 20 inches, with the average size varying quite a bit from year to year. Trolling is the best method, using flashers and the usual array of kokanee lures or lure/bait combos. Finding the schools of fish is the key and when the reservoir is busy, you can find the fish just by watching the other boats. Kokanee fishing peaks from May through July and then again in the fall.

Smallmouth bass abound in Lake Billy Chinook. They can reach at least 5 pounds here, but most range from half a pound to 2 pounds. Once the water begins to warm during late spring, the bass hang out along the rocky banks, especially where talus or crumbled rock provides diverse cover. They can be taken on all methods, with jigs and small plugs being very effective. Even fly anglers fish for them using weighted Woolly Buggers and similar flies. The bass are most abundant in the Crooked and Deschutes Arms, although some of the largest fish are taken in the Metolius Arm.

In addition to its renown with anglers, Lake Billy Chinook is a popular playground for recreational boaters. In fact, it ranks among the state's top boating destinations with more than one million boating visitors per year. Shore fishing is somewhat limited, but available in each of the arms, especially in Cove Palisades State Park. The north bank of the Metolius Arm is on the Warm Springs Reservation and trespassing is not allowed.

The aforementioned Cove Palisades State Park is very popular and in total includes 5,200 acres, encompassing in its entirety the Deschutes and Crooked River Arms of the reservoir. The state park offers two huge campgrounds and four day-use sites. The campgrounds have lots of full-hookup RV sites among many other amenities, including Cove Palisades Marina. The marina offers rental boats, a store, deli, and other features. To reach the marina, call 541-546-3521. The main information number for the state park is 541-546-3412 and you can reserve campsites by calling Reservations Northwest at 1-800-452-5687.

The Metolius Arm offers two USFS campgrounds along with Three Rivers Marina, which has rental boats and supplies (541-546-2939). You must have a valid tribal fishing permit to fish the Metolius Arm and these are widely available at tackle shops and outdoor stores throughout the Willamette Valley and central Oregon. You can also get them at Cove Palisades Marina.

To reach Cove Palisades State Park, follow Hwy 97 north from Redmond or south from Madras and take the west turn-off to Culver. Then follow the signs to Cove Palisades. You can drive through the park and then head west to the Metolius Arm or you can reach the Metolius Arm from Hwy 20 west of Sisters. About 6 miles west of Sisters, take the north turn at Indian Ford Campground and follow this road (FR 11) for about 21 miles to a right-hand turn on FR 1170. After 5 miles, turn left on FR 64, a rugged primitive road, and head 2.5 miles up to Perry South Campground or 7 miles up to Monty Campground. Perry South has a boat launch.

With almost 75 miles of shoreline and three major rivers forming their own fingers, Lake Billy Chinook offers plenty of room to spread out. In addition to the fishing, this reservoir offers rather stunning geography highlighted by the sheer basalt cliffs rising out of the water in many places. The kokanee, bass, and bull trout action happens to be quite good, however, so don't allow the scenery to distract you from the business at hand. While you're at it, you might catch decent-sized rainbow and brown trout. Be sure to consult the ODFW synopsis for current regulations.

Lake Creek (Jefferson County)
no bait

Lake Creek is the outlet stream from Suttle Lake. It flows easterly to the Metolius River, splitting into three separate forks along the way. Private property prevents access to the lower end of the creek, including the forks. Otherwise, primary access is by hiking down from the highway near Suttle Lake or by hiking up or downstream from the crossing on the nearby Round Lake Road (FR 1270). A quarter mile below FR 1270, the creek splits into its branches and enters private property for about a mile. Each of the three branches then flows across a half section of public land 2 miles above the creek's confluence with the Metolius.

Lake Creek is rather lightly fished (except the popular stretch from Suttle Lake to Hwy 20) and offers wild rainbows, brown trout, and brook trout. Most of the fish range from 5 to 10 inches, but a few larger fish offer pleasant surprises from time to time. This is good dry fly water as well as perfect water for small spinners.

Forest Road 1270, the road to Round Lake, turns north off Hwy 20 about a mile east from the Suttle Lake access road. Follow this road for less than a mile to reach Lake Creek. To fish the lower public section, continue a short distance further north on the Round Lake Road and then turn east (right) on FR 1216, heading toward Camp Sherman. At the 3-mile mark, look for the Metolius-Windigo Trail. Follow the trail south about a mile to reach the North Fork and then the other two forks in succession (the Middle Fork carries most of the flow and most of the fish). Once you reach the creek, hike upstream to fish the public land. Alternately you can pick up the south end of the trail from the Metolius River Road (FR 14), half a mile north from the turn-off to Head-of-the-Metolius. There are several spur roads leading close to the creek in various places, but some of these may be gated—the best map of the area is the Sisters Ranger District Map, available from the R.D. Headquarters on the west edge of the town of Sisters.

Lake Simtustus (Warm Springs Reservation)
boat recommended, boat ramp, campground, services

You'll need both a tribal fishing permit and a boat to fish 7-mile-long Lake Simtustus, but the reward is good fishing for trout, kokanee, and smallmouth bass. Some large bull trout also inhabit the reservoir. This narrow lake is the first impoundment on the Deschutes River and is created by Pelton Dam, west of Madras and a few miles upriver from Warm Springs. Steep, rocky banks make shore fishing impossible except at the campgrounds.

Kokanee here tend to run large, with fish in the 14- to 20-inch range being typical and fish up to at least 22 inches taken from time to time. Likewise, the reservoir's trout can grow to trophy-class dimensions. The lake has thus far produced at least two rainbows weighing 24 pounds or better and 10-plus-pound fish are taken almost every year. The brown trout are no longer stocked, but some big old-timers still haunt the depths and they can weigh more than 15 pounds. If you're heading to Simtustus to target big fish, try large plugs, spoons, and jigs. A fish-finder is handy. Kokanee anglers generally troll or jig and the best kokanee and trout action occurs in The Narrows at the head of the reservoir, where sheer canyon walls squeeze the water into a spectacular gorge. The reservoir is regularly stocked with legal-size rainbows.

Smallmouth bass are quite common and the best fishing for them is found close to the banks, rocky points, and talus slides entering the water. To target the bass, you can't go wrong with ¼-ounce jigs and color seems of little matter. Steer the boat along the contour of the shoreline, casting in towards the bank and experimenting with depth until you locate fish. Most of the bass are less than 2 pounds, but the lake offers a few smallies in the 4-pound range.

Be sure to check the current regulations for Lake Simtustus, which is traditionally open from late April through October. The tribal fishing permit is available at many outdoor and fishing-tackle stores. The primary boat launch is located adjacent to Pelton Dam at Pelton Park, which also has a store and campground. The turn-off to the park is along Hwy 26 about 6 miles north of Madras. Simtustus is typically open during the statewide general trout season from late April through October. Check the current synopsis for specific dates.

Laurance Lake (Mt. Hood National Forest)
no bait, campground, boat ramp, float tube recommended, boat recommended

Popular with fly anglers, scenic 120-acre Laurance Lake is a good producer of stocked rainbow trout. The lake is actually an irrigation-storage reservoir on the Middle Fork Hood River drainage. To get there from Hood River, follow Hwy 35 heading south out of town and follow the signs to the community of Parkdale. After crossing the railroad tracks in Parkdale, turn south at the library and continue for about 2 miles to the signed right-hand turn leading to Laurance Lake.

Laurance opens in late April, but late-spring weather can put a damper on things here. Mid-May through July is prime time on Laurance, which offers a good summertime hatch of Callibaetis mayflies. The surface action can be quite good for stocked rainbows and a few wild cutthroat (catch-and-release only for all non-fin-clipped trout). For a short period during mid-July, the lake offers a hatch of giant *Hexagenia* mayflies ("giant yellow mayflies"). They hatch on the upper end of the reservoir, usually around dusk. Otherwise, stick to standard wet flies or fish small spoons and spinners. The Northwest end of the lake is usually a good bet. If the wind whips up, head for the small cove near the dam, where the lake's contour provides some protection. A float tube or small boat is very useful here. Laurance Lake and the surrounding drainage is a wild bull trout sanctuary, so if you catch a bull trout, be sure to carefully release the fish without removing it from the water. Sadly smallmouth bass have been illegally introduced to Laurance Lake, endangering the trout fishery and wild trout/char populations) and ODFW encourages anglers to keep and bass caught (no limit).

Lava Lake, Big (Deschutes National Forest)
boat recommended, boat ramp, campground, services

One of the more productive trout lakes located along Century Drive west of Bend, Big Lava Lake is well known for its propensity for growing fat rainbows in the 14- to 18-inch class, along with a few brook trout of similar size. At its best, Lava Lake produces trout to 4 pounds or more and is among the most consistently good fisheries in the area. Even at slow times during mid-summer, anglers can usually count on some action during morning and evening.

Most anglers fish Big Lava by boat because much of the shoreline is rather marshy. Effort is about equally divided between still fishing with bait and trolling, and both tactics pay dividends. The boat ramp is located on the southeast corner of the lake, as is the campground and Lava Lake Resort. The resort (541-382-9443) offers supplies, fuel, RV hook-ups, and rental boats. Typically Lava Lake is accessible by about mid-April (via the southern route in from South Century Drive) and fishable until mid-autumn. The resort closes around mid-October and this may well be the best time to fish this scenic lake.

The lake was formed by a natural lava dam created by an ancient flow from nearby Mt. Bachelor; and it has no permanent inlet or outlet stream. Instead, the lake is fed by springs found in the northeast corner under 20 to 30 feet of water. During summer, the area near the springs is prime trout country. Inquire at the resort for directions. The lake offers a fine view of snow-capped South Sister and nearby Broken Top and Bachelor.

During spring, follow Hwy 97 south from Bend to Sunriver and head west on Road 40 until you reach a right-hand turn on South Century Drive taking you up to Lava Lake. The northern approach from Century Drive, which heads west from downtown Bend, typically opens during early June and offers a shorter drive if you are coming from Bend.

Lava Lake, Little (Deschutes National Forest)
boat ramp, campground

The source of Oregon's famous Deschutes River, Little Lava Lake is a decent fishery for stocked trout, but illegally introduced tui chub seem to be putting a dent in the growth rate of the trout. The chub have also shown up in Big Lava Lake, continuing a problem of illegal introductions that has proven epidemic in the Cascade Lakes. The stocked rainbows don't often grow large here, but this lake is popular for its attractive forest setting. The lake spans about 110 acres and also offers brook trout and mountain whitefish.

Lemish Lake (Deschutes National Forest)
hike-in

Fairly productive and not too heavily used, scenic little Lemish Lake lies about 2 miles southwest of Little Cultus Lake. A good trail departs FR 600 and reaches 16-acre Lemish Lake in about half a mile. The trail itself sees lots of traffic, but anglers are actually uncommon. A float tube is advantageous here. Watch for the narrow pullout and Lemish Lake sign on the left-hand side of the road. See Little Cultus Lake for directions to the area. Brook trout here range from 6 to 12 inches.

Lily Lake (Deschutes National Forest)
hike-in

Fairly popular and usually quite productive early and late in the season, 13-acre Lily Lake lies just north of Charlton Butte, about 2 miles east of North Waldo Campground. The easiest route follows the Pacific Crest Trail from Charlton Lake for 1.3 miles and then a spur trail takes off to the right, leading to Lily Lake. You can also make an easy hike from North Waldo Campground or from the nearby horse camp on the Harrelson Trail. From the horse camp, this route follows the trail for 1 mile to the PCT and from there, you can cut a quarter mile cross-country to the lake. Lily is stocked periodically with rainbows and brook trout.

To reach Charlton Lake and the PCT or North Waldo Campground and Harrelson Trailhead, follow Hwy 58 east from Oakridge or west from Hwy 97 to the Waldo Lake turn-off (FR 5897). Follow the road north about 12 miles. The lake sits at 5,700 feet and is usually accessible by late June.

Lindick Lake (Three Sisters Wilderness)
hike-in

A beautiful alpine lake located on a narrow bench above the Pacific Crest Trail in the Three Sisters Wilderness, Lindick is periodically stocked with brook trout or rainbows. The fish are small, but the scenery is stunning and the lake is lightly fished. The shortest route covers more than 7 miles from the Skookum Creek Trailhead to the west and requires a short, steep scramble up to the lake. Lindick sits at 6,144 feet, spans 8 acres, reaching a depth of 25 feet. A quarter mile uphill to the southwest lies equally beautiful Dennis Lake, which offers similar trout prospects. Dennis spans 11 acres and reaches a maximum depth of 42 feet. These two lakes are ideally suited to the adventurous, backpacking angler. Consult the wilderness map for specific directions.

Lindsey Pond
(Columbia River/I-84)

This large, elongated pond forms next to the westbound lanes of I-84 at the mouth of Lindsey Creek, near milepost 54. If you're arriving from the west and headed east, exit the Interstate at Exit 56 and reverse course. Park at the wide lot at the west end of the weigh station. The pond offers smallmouth bass, crappie, sunfish, and non-game species and is conducive to float tubes or small rafts and the like. Try paddling up close to the railroad dyke and casting against the riprap for bass and crappie. The grassy edges are good for sunfish and

The Three Sisters Wilderness includes dozens upon dozens of trout-filled lakes.

largemouth bass. Except for the railroad tracks, the pond's shoreline lies entirely on public lands and, though this is one of the more productive of the I-84 ponds, its remains lightly fished.

Link Creek (Suttle Lake tributary)
closed waters

Link Lake (Jefferson County)
One of the small mountain lakes at Corbett Memorial Park near Santiam Pass, Link Lake is usually stocked with cutthroat trout. Fishing can be good, especially during June and October, but summer weekends increasingly attract ATV and dirt bike enthusiasts to the area, making it rather noisy and dusty sometimes. The 2003 B&B Complex Fire swept through the area, charring much of the timber, but the little pine trees seem to be growing rapidly around this lake. Consult ODFW for current stocking information

Lions Pond (Redmond)
This small pond in Redmond is reserved exclusively for kids and for disabled anglers. The wheelchair-accessible pond supports bluegill, largemouth bass, and legal-size rainbow trout and is located at the south end of town.

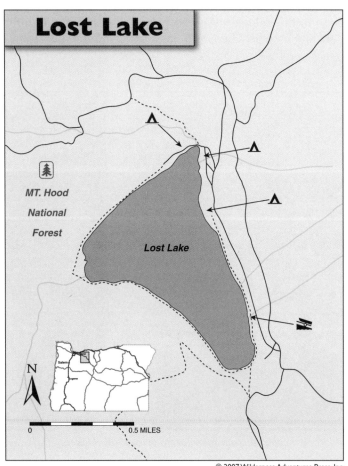

Little Three Creeks Lake
see Three Creeks Lake, Little

Lodgepole Lake (Three Sisters Wilderness)
see Merle Lake

Long Lake (Mt. Jefferson Wilderness)
hike-in

Located in the southeastern-most corner of the Mt. Jefferson Wilderness Area, 16-acre Long Lake is a fair producer of small trout and is comparatively lightly fished. Its immediate neighbors—Square Lake to the west and Round Lake to the east—are both far more popular. The entire area was burned over by the huge B&B Complex fire of 2003. The easiest trail route to Long Lake is from Round Lake and covers about a mile heading westerly. To get to the trailhead, follow Hwy 20 east past Suttle Lake and turn north on FR 12, after a mile, turn left on the signed route to Round Lake (FR 1210). If you're comfortable with cross-country travel, you can hike into Long Lake from the highway by parking at the Sno-Park 2 miles west from Suttle Lake. You can fish Long Lake from the banks, but I always used to carry a float tube in there as the lake is ideally suited to it.

Lost Lake (Mt. Hood National Forest)
campground, boat ramp, services, float tube recommended, boat recommended

The beautiful panorama of nearby Mt. Hood accentuates Lost Lake, a large, popular trout fishery situated at about 3,100 feet below the mountain's north slope. Lost Lake offers consistently good fishing for both rainbow and brown trout. The typical fish range from 9 to 14 inches and they reach about 20 inches maximum, though large fish are uncommon. This 230-acre lake also supports a few brook trout and a fishable but small population of wild kokanee.

Lost Lake is conducive to all methods of fishing and effort is about equally divided between still fishing with bait, trolling, or casting small lures and fly angling. During July, the lake hosts a good emergence of *Hexagenia* mayflies ("giant yellow mayflies") and at that time fly anglers show up in good numbers to fish over this unique hatch. These mayflies, which are indeed yellowish in color, average more than an inch in length, excluding the tails. Both the nymphs and duns make a robust mouthful for the lake's trout, which prey on them heavily during the hatch.

The best *Hexagenia* action occurs at dusk on the shallow shoal areas along the western corner of the lake. It's a long paddle via float tube from the roadside (east side) of the lake over to the shoals, so you are better off following the trail along the north shore and then launching closer to the action. The hatch begins with the big nymphs leaving their burrows on the bottom and swimming toward the surface. A large nymph pattern, fished with an active retrieve on an intermediate line can prove highly effective during the hour or so prior to the actual hatch. If you're lucky, the dry fly action begins an hour before sunset, but don't be too surprised to find that most of the surface action is compressed into the last 20 or 30 minutes of legal fishing hours around dusk.

A large USFS campground sits on the east side of the lake along with Lost Lake Resort (541-386-6636/www.lostlakeresort.org), which offers cabins, boat rentals, a store, and other amenities. The lake is encircled by a 3-mile-long trail, providing ready access to most of the shoreline. Typically Lost Lake is accessible by mid-May. From Hood River, follow Oak Street (the main east-west route through town) to a south turn onto 13th Street. Follow 13th leading south out of town and continue to the old mill site of Dee. At Dee, follow the road heading to your right, across the river and then stay left and follow the signs to the lake. From ZigZag on Hwy 26, turn left onto LoLo Pass Road and follow the signs to the lake.

Lucky Lake (Three Sisters Wilderness)
hike-in

A large, easy-to-reach brook trout lake on the edge of the Three Sisters Wilderness Area, Lucky Lake spans 30 acres and sits immediately southwest of Lava Lake near Century Drive. Lucky Lake's brook trout, which are usually quite abundant, range from 5 to 12 inches. A few 14-inchers show up in the catch. The lake is very deep and the best bet is to fish the fringes of the deep water. During summer, fly anglers enjoy a good hatch of *Callibaetis* mayflies here, with best surface action on still days. The trailhead is on the right-hand side of the road as you head south on Century Drive, just past Lava Lake. The hike covers just 1.3 miles, making this lake a prime candidate for a float tube or small raft.

Maiden Lake (Klamath Lake)

A 6-acre hike-in lake on the south slope of Maiden Peak, Maiden Lake offers fair-to-good fishing for small brook trout. Sprawling Davis Lake is due east and famous Odell Lake is a few miles to the south. Despite the crowds that gather on the much larger fisheries in the area, you will usually have Maiden Lake all to yourself, especially if you wait until autumn. The brookies here range from 5 to 13 inches, averaging about 8 inches. You can get there from the Rosary Lakes to the west (see listing herein), but the shorter trail, covering 2.7 miles, is from the east. From Hwy 58, turn northeast onto the Crescent Cut-off Road and then turn north onto the Davis Lake Road. Follow Route 46 about 3 miles to a left-hand turn on FR 4660. Follow FR 4660 about 3 miles to a Y-intersection, watching for the signs to the trailhead. FR 4660 veers north here, but continue on the spur going straight ahead and then take a right-hand turn on FR 4664. After a few hundred yards, turn left on Spur 100, which leads a mile up to the trailhead.

Marks Creek (Ochoco National Forest)

A slow producer of small redband trout, Marks Creek flows alongside Hwy 26 in the highlands east of Prineville. Public access begins when you cross onto the national forest about 8 miles east of Ochoco Reservoir.

Martin Lake (Mt. Jefferson Wilderness)
hike-in, cross-country

Martin Lake is a pleasant little lightly-fished, 4-acre hike-in lake stocked periodically with either rainbow or brook trout. The fish range from 5 to 14 inches, averaging about 9 inches. You can get there by several routes, so consult a map of the Mt. Jefferson Wilderness Area, on which you will see Martin Lake situated a few miles north of Santiam Pass and just east of the Pacific Crest Trail. Well-within the devastating B&B Complex Fire burn of 2003, Martin Lake nonetheless was somehow missed by the flames and remains a very scenic destination. The usual route begins just past Booth Lake and then follows the dry outlet stream up to Martin. If you prefer a more adventurous, demanding, and scenic route, make a short steep hike in and out of the lake from the PCT, before the trail begins its ascent of the south flank of Three-Fingered Jack. Each of the routes covers about 4 miles. At an elevation of 5,150 feet, Martin Lake is usually accessible by mid-June.

Matthieu Lakes (Three Sisters Wilderness)
hike-in

The oft-visited Matthieu Lakes sit nearly atop the McKenzie Summit; adjacent to the huge lava flows southeast of Belknap Crater. North Matthieu Lake spans 6 acres and reaches a maximum depth of about 14 feet. It offers modest-size rainbows. Tiny South Matthieu Lake is no longer stocked. From Sisters or from Hwy 126 on the west side of the mountains, head for the old McKenzie Highway, SR 242. At McKenzie Summit you will find Dee Wright Observatory and a half-mile to the east, turn onto the access road for Lava Camp Lake and the PCT Trailhead. Hike south about 3 miles to North Matthieu Lake. Despite being heavily visited, North Matthieu Lake is worth the hike just for the stunning view of the surrounding mountains. The shoreline is quite open and easy to negotiate.

McClure Lake (Columbia River/I-84)

McClure Lake is a large, productive pond positioned between I-84 and the Columbia River a few miles east of Mosier and west of The Dalles. McClure, which spans about 50 acres, offers sunfish, bass, yellow perch, bullhead, and crappie, along with non-game species. Bank fishing is good, but as with most of the ponds along I-84, a float tube or similar craft gives you an advantage, especially when fishing for bass. Access is by walking east from the rest area located at Memaloose State Park (westbound lanes).

Meadow Lake (Santiam Pass area)

Generally the best of the group of small lakes located southwest from Suttle Lake, Meadow Lake spans 16 acres and reaches a depth of about 30 feet. The lake is stocked periodically with cutthroat trout, which range from 6 to 12 inches, sometimes larger. This is a good lake for a float tube, raft, or small boat, but no motors are allowed.

The Meadow Lake area suffered through two fires during the summer of 2003. The first swept across the lake's basin, reversed itself, and swept back up Cache Mountain. A short time later the massive B&B Complex Fire reached into the area. Needless to say a lot of charred timber surrounds the lakes here, but lots of small pine trees now surround Meadow Lake. Perhaps the burned-over forest will temporarily dampen the enthusiasm of the ATV enthusiasts who, in recent years, have assembled in the lake basin here to camp, fish, and make a rather dusty mess of the many narrow access roads.

To reach Meadow Lake, head west from Sisters on Hwy 20 or east from Santiam Summit. Two miles west from Suttle Lake, watch for the turn-off to Corbett Memorial State Park on the south side of the highway. Forest Road 2076 heads south from the parking area here and leads down to Island, Link, and Meadow Lakes. For the latter, follow the road south for about 2.5 miles to a right-hand turn on a rugged access road (Spur Road 700).

Meek Lake (Deschutes National Forest)
hike-in

A consistent producer of brook trout and cutthroat, 11-acre Meek Lake is lightly fished despite the short, easy hike to this emerald beauty. The rugged access road probably discourages plenty of would-be visitors. Meek Lake sits at 5,580 feet between Summit Lake to the west and Crescent Lake to the east. Like its neighbors to the north—Snell and Farrell Lakes—Meek Lake has the ability to grow trout to decent size, considering the elevation. Most of the trout range from 6 to 12 inches, but a few fat 14- to 16-inch fish inhabit the lake. Shore fishing is easy here, especially for spin-casters, but the half-mile hike up to the lake offers easy passage for toting a float tube.

The rugged access road—a rocky, dirt track connecting Crescent and Summit Lakes—departs the west end of Crescent Lake (FR 6010), or you can descend from Emigrant Pass near Summit Lake to the west. This road is not maintained and is rather nasty, being best suited to high-clearance 4-wheel-drive vehicles. From Crescent Lake, it's 4 miles to the Snell/Meek Trailhead. The road is gated until the snow melts, so if you're heading up there during June or even early July, call ahead to the Crescent Ranger District to find out if the gate has been opened for the summer (541-433-3200). Beware the mosquitoes. Fishing holds up throughout the summer and can be especially good during the autumn. The lake has a couple of nice water-side camping spots with existing fire rings (check for potential fire bans in summer).

Merle Lake (Three Sisters Wilderness)
hike-in

Merle Lake is a fairly productive 9-acre brook trout lake located on the southern end of the Three Sisters Wilderness Area. Easiest access is from the trailhead to the south, a mile east of Irish and Taylor Lakes. To get there from the east, follow Century Drive to the turnoff for Cultus and Little Cultus Lake. Head toward Little Cultus and continue past the lake on the south shore. The road (FR 600) is rough and slow

Mount Jefferson rises above the Metolius River.

going, leading about 5 miles to the trailhead. From the south and west, turn north off Hwy 58 at Waldo Lake and follow the Waldo Lake Road 12 miles to North Waldo Campground. Then continue north on FR 514 and turn right at the intersection with FR 600. Head east about 2.5 miles, past Irish and Taylor Lakes.

The Merle Lake Trail (#15) makes a meandering loop through a basin dotted with other small lakes and ponds, some of which are stocked from time to time with brookies and rainbows. These lakes range from 1 to 10 acres and the deepest and largest of them are capable of producing the occasional 14- to 18-inch fish. Those that have been stocked in the past include: Lodgepole, Kinnikinnic, Phantom, Swede, Kershaw, Sundew, Harlequin, West Hanks, Middle Hanks, and East Hanks Lakes. The primitive campground at nearby Irish & Taylor Lakes serves as a nice base camp for exploring this interesting and scenic lake basin, but lock your valuables away from sight in your vehicle. A float tube comes in handy because many of the lakes have rather brushy, inaccessible shoreline margins.

Metolius River (Jefferson County)
no bait, catch-and-release, campground, services

One of the state's prettiest trout streams, the Metolius River springs to life from porous subterranean lava flows beneath the central Oregon ponderosa forest near Sisters. A tame, forested glide in its upper reaches, the Metolius soon gathers momentum from an increasing gradient. It rushes headlong through remote, steep sided canyons on its journey to Lake Billy Chinook.

Once a heavily stocked rainbow trout river, the Metolius has been managed strictly as a catch-and-release fishery for wild redband and bull trout since 1996. In the old days, the hatchery program largely defined the fishery on the Metolius as thousands of standard-issue hatchery rainbows were dumped into the river. The frequent stockings would be followed by a period of easy fishing even for the most casual of fly anglers.

These days, however, consistent success on the Metolius requires a bit more dedication as the river's wild redbands are less numerous and more selective than the hatchery clones. As of the late 1990s, biologists were uncertain as to how the river's wild trout populations would respond to the total absence of competition from hatchery fish. Estimated fish counts then suggested the population of native redband was less than 100 fish per mile of river, with the majority of these being juvenile trout. But in recent years the trout density seems to have increased slightly and the average size is edging up as well. Redbands typically range from 8 to 13 inches and they reach at least 20 inches. This challenging river offers quite a few 14- to 16-inch redbands and a handful of brown and brook trout also inhabit the river.

The Metolius offers rather sparse cover for trout when compared to lower-gradient streams. Its steep slope, which does not allow for meanders, coupled with its cold water (mid-40s) and relative lack of near-shore and overhead cover, effectively limit the population densities of the river's wild fish. The Metolius will never compare to the Deschutes or Crooked Rivers in terms of trout densities, but this unique river certainly compares favorably in the overall quality of experience and is as popular for its scenic splendor as for its fishery.

The key to fishing this river effectively lies in switching from the old-school method of pitching a hair-wing dry fly into the river, to fishing spring creek techniques: downstream, slack-line presentation, long leaders, spring-creek-style flies. Long, light leaders are the rule and spring-creek-style flies usually outperform attractor dry flies.

Among the better patterns are flies such as the X-Caddis and Sparkle Dun, both tied in the appropriate sizes to imitate specific insects. Important hatches on the Metolius include blue-winged olives (*Baetis*) mayflies, green drakes (*Drunella*) and several genera of caddis. Stoneflies abound as well, with the golden stonefly and Yellow Sally both being especially common. The abundant stoneflies, in fact, testify to the river's nature. The Metolius is indeed a spring creek, but because of the gradient, its nature is more that of a freestone river.

Despite its abundant hatches, Metolius River trout don't necessarily feed at the surface with great vigor. Numerous reasons might explain why the river's trout often ignore surface offerings, even in the midst of a good hatch. For starters, most angling effort has traditionally been concentrated around the campgrounds and roadside pools of the upper river waters, which have typically been dominated by hatchery trout. Anglers who explore the river's remote reaches, especially below Bridge 99, will find wild fish working the surface with a little more enthusiasm. Second, a lot of anglers simply don't recognize the best dry fly water and don't fish those places during the good hatches. The Metolius is dominated by swift riffles and runs—water that doesn't lend itself to dry-fly action during a dense hatch of mayflies or caddis. Third, the river's trout reside in a world of peril. They are assaulted from above by osprey, and from below by carnivorous bull trout. A trip to the surface makes for a venture wrought with peril.

Threatened elsewhere, bull trout thrive in the Metolius River.

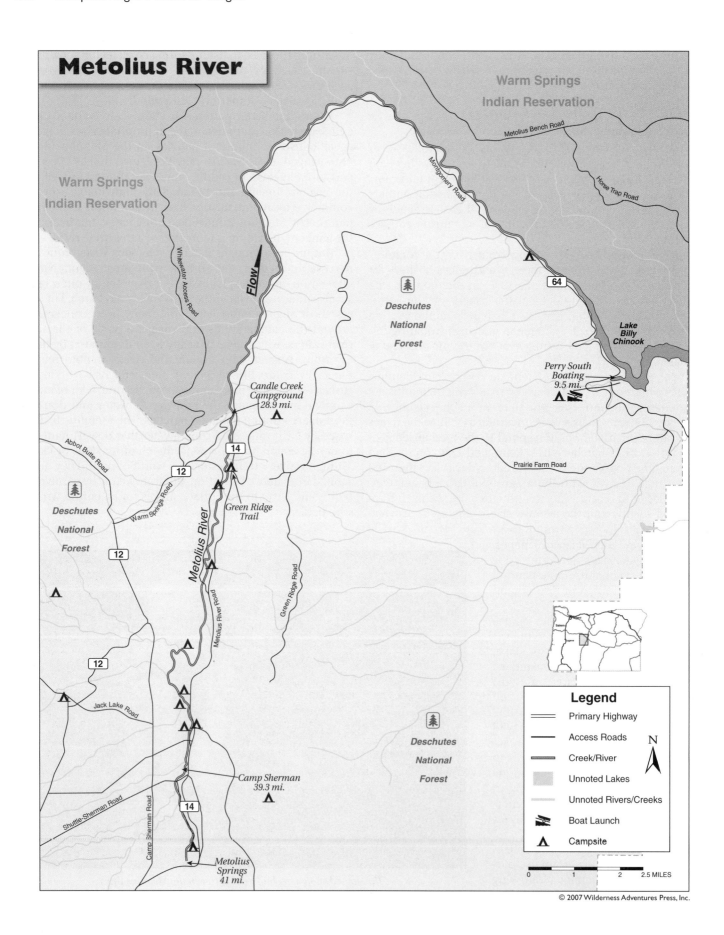

Metolius River

Warm Springs Indian Reservation

Metolius Bench Road

Horse Trap Road

Warm Springs Indian Reservation

Whitewater Access Road

Flow

Montgomery Road

Deschutes National Forest

64

Lake Billy Chinook

Perry South Boating 9.5 mi.

Candle Creek Campground 28.9 mi.

Abbot Butte Road

14

12

Warm Springs Road

Prairie Farm Road

Green Ridge Trail

Deschutes National Forest

12

Metolius River

Metolius River Road

Green Ridge Road

12

Jack Lake Road

Deschutes National Forest

Camp Sherman 39.3 mi.

Shuttle-Sherman Road

Camp Sherman Road

14

Metolius Springs 41 mi.

Legend

Primary Highway

Access Roads

Creek/River

Unnoted Lakes

Unnoted Rivers/Creeks

Boat Launch

Campsite

N

0   1   2   2.5 MILES

© 2007 Wilderness Adventures Press, Inc.

The river's bull trout (large, native char akin to Dolly Varden) offer another fishery for fly anglers who dredge the stream with big streamers. These beautiful char commonly reach 5 pounds, with 8- to 10-pound specimens caught and released by fly anglers each year. These predatory char feed heavily on kokanee, whitefish, sculpins, and native trout.

The migratory bull trout ascend the river during summer and fall to spawn in the upper Metolius and its tributaries. Many of these fish hang around for the winter or even take up permanent residence, so fly anglers have ample opportunity to fish for them. In fact, one of the Metolius River's best assets is its winter fishery. The river remains open to catch-and-release fishing through the winter (be sure to check current regulations for open area and season framework).

Winter brings a quiet time to the Metolius. Nymphs and wet flies account for most of the action, but hatches of *Baetis* mayflies and Chironomids bring trout to the surface from time to time. The Metolius offers many days of sunshine during the winter, and a dusting of snow makes for a surreal setting. Add some quality winter trout fishing and a complete absence of the weekend warrior, splash-and-giggle crowd and you may indeed be looking at the river's best season.

In years past, prior to the opening of the winter season, the Metolius River was more or less deserted from December through mid-spring. Now, however, the year-round economy in and around the little town of Camp Sherman seems to grow a bit each season. The Camp Sherman Store & Fly Shop (541-595-6711/www.campshermanstore.com) caters to all your needs, offering everything from fuel and food, to fine rods and rental cabins.

As winter eases its icy grip on central Oregon, the Metolius offers springtime hatches of blue-winged olive mayflies (*Baetis*), along with a few March brown mayflies and *Skwala* stoneflies. By late spring, caddisflies abound and anglers can count on daily hatches of the aforementioned green drakes and pale morning duns. Golden stoneflies emerge between May and September and the caddis hatches continue all summer and into autumn. Generally speaking, not a day passes between March and October that some kind of hatch doesn't occur, at least somewhere on the river.

Because the river and its major tributaries are spring-fed and flow across porous volcanic landscapes, the Metolius maintains stable flow, temperature, and clarity throughout the year. Only the most severe wet weather—such as heavy rain on top of melting snow—is likely to affect the flows. The river is always cold and only marginally wade-able owing to its rapid pace. Some pools and runs are easy to wade, but many others are simply too deep and fast for serious wade fishing. In fact, the Metolius offers a wide array of water types and the most successful anglers carry the tackle and the attitude to confront everything from shallow riffles where trout gorge on drifting nymphs to deep, glassy pools where the fish rise selectively and often sporadically.

The upper section of the river glides through open forest of stately ponderosa pines. From Camp Sherman down to Bridge 99, you can choose from any of eight attractive and popular campgrounds. The easiest water to fish—in general—extends from above Camp Sherman downstream a few miles to Gorge Campground. About a mile below the campground, the river enters "The Gorge," which is characterized by a steeper stream gradient and lots of water fishable only from the banks. From Wizard Falls Hatchery down to Bridge 99, the river takes on myriad personalities, which often change with each bend in the river. This stretch offers several large, fast, deep pools that hold lots of trout and better cover than is found in the pools further upstream.

Trails follow the river throughout its course, though two large parcels of private property force the trails to detour away from the river. From Camp Sherman to Canyon Creek Campground (on the west bank), the primary trail follows the east bank. Below Canyon Creek, primary trails follow both banks 7 miles down to Bridge 99. The road, meanwhile, follows along the east bank, usually at a respectful distance, and offers lots of park-and-walk access. At Bridge 99, the main road ends, yielding to a rugged dirt/rock primitive, tire-eating road that is gated several miles downstream. Few anglers drive this road, but quite a few hike or bike down to the remote and lightly fished stretch of river here.

On this section of the river—the lengthy reach downstream from Bridge 99—the Metolius gains even more momentum and becomes a rather fierce flow surging through a steep-sided, timbered canyon. Fishing can be just as good here as anywhere on the river, but it is best suited to adventurous souls who don't mind fighting through the brush, trees, and steep banks to shoot a few short casts into many likely pockets and runs.

About 10 miles below Bridge 99, the river swings easterly around the north extension of Green Ridge, appropriately called "Horn of the Metolius. All the land on the other side of the river—the west and then north bank—is closed to public access and belongs to the Warm Springs Indian Reservation. The reservation land extends on the west bank all the way south to Candle Creek Campground (on the west bank, about 2 miles below Bridge 99).

The so-called "Lower Metolius" is accessible from Lake Billy Chinook: From Hwy 20 west of Sisters, turn north at Indian Ford Campground and then follow FR 11 and then 1170 down to the Metolius Arm of the reservoir. From the campground there you can drive upstream to the river on Road 64. To reach the far better known "upper" stretch of the Metolius River, follow Hwy 20 west from Sisters or east from Santiam Pass and just west of Black Butte, watch for the signs announcing Camp Sherman/Metolius River.

Mill Creek (Wasco County)
no bait, catch-and-release

A lengthy trout stream open for catch-and-release angling, Mill Creek flows almost entirely through private lands on its journey from Shellrock Mountain northeast to the Columbia River at The Dalles. Fishing is largely by permission only and can be good in places, especially upstream from Mill Creek Falls. You'll need a good map and a full day to figure out access and property ownership, but the stream is only lightly fished.

Miller Pond (Columbia River/I-84)
see Deschutes Ponds

Monon Lake (Olallie Lake area)

A fairly popular brook and cutthroat trout lake located on the so-called McQuinn Strip atop the Cascade Range, Monon sits about a quarter mile due south of Olallie Lake. Monon offers mostly 6- to -8 inches fish, but with an occasional fish that reaches 16 inches. Best action occurs late in the season, especially during early October, but check the weather forecast before heading to these lakes during mid-autumn. Monon spans 91 acres with a maximum depth of 39 feet. The edges of the deep hole, on the north end of the lake, offer prime fishing prospects during the summer months. Camping is discouraged here because of past over-use and nearby Olallie Lake offers plenty of sites. For directions to the area, see Olallie Lake herein. A wildfire burned the area in 2001.

Moraine Lake (Three Sisters Wilderness)

A pretty little sub-alpine lake located immediately east of the main south-side hiking route up the South Sister, Moraine Lake tends to winterkill and is no longer stocked. It does provide a decent camping spot if you want to escape the crowds at over-used Green Lake to the northeast.

Mosier Creek (Wasco County)
no bait

A little stream flowing through a small, oak-clad ravine south from Mosier, Mosier Creek harbors a sparse population of trout. The entire creek flows through private property and even though the roads above are enticingly convenient, the prudent choice is to ask permission from landowners before walking to the creek. However, the property owners don't necessarily live close to the creek, so figuring out land ownership is a time-consuming proposition. For that reason, Mosier Creek is probably best left to the local kids.

Mosier Ponds (Columbia River/I-84)
float tube recommended

These two ponds offer fair-to-good prospects for bass, sunfish, yellow perch, brown bullhead, and other species. They sit on the south side of the Interstate and on both sides of the Mosier exit. The smaller of the two is West Mosier Pond and access to it is from the Rock Creek Access, which is used primarily by wind-surfers on the Columbia River: Exit the freeway at Mosier and then follow the sharp curve back to the west on Old Hwy 30. Immediately watch for the entrance to Rock Creek Access. Park here and walk over near the freeway embankment to reach the pond (some people follow the railroad right-of-way instead). There's another access point a bit further west on the old highway, but it would likely be imprudent to suggest that anglers park on the gravel pull-out, negotiate the steep incline to the tracks and then cross the tracks down to the pond.

The larger pond sits on the east side of the Mosier off-ramp and is also accessible by foot on its southwest corner. Both ponds offer only limited room on the bank unless you don't mind brush busting along the swampy shorelines. Whether you fish gear, bait, or flies, you'll likely be rewarded for the effort of carrying a float tube to these ponds.

Muskrat Lake (Three Sisters Wilderness)
hike-in

A fair brook trout lake on the Winopee Lake Trail north of Cultus Lake, Muskrat spans 8 acres and reaches a maximum depth of 17 feet. It's ideally suited to a float tube and offers a nice old trapper's cabin that is used as a shelter by skiers and hikers. Muskrat Lake is about 5 easy trail miles from the end of the road just past the campground at Cultus. See Teddy Lakes or Winopee Lake herein for directions.

Neptepah Lake (Warm Springs Reservation)
hike-in, float tube recommended

A small, deep lake in the Olallie Lake area, Neptepah Lake is stocked with brook trout that rarely exceed 12 inches. The lake lies immediately south of the southernmost tip of Olallie Lake. The trail begins at Peninsula Campground and heads southeast along the shore of Olallie Lake before branching due south the Neptepah, which sits on your left. A short distance further south, just before you reach Monon Lake, another 2-acre brook trout lake lies on your right. This is Mangriff Lake. These deep little potholes are perfect for a float tube and both will occasionally yield a 16-inch brookie.

Nena Creek (Deschutes River)

A well-known landmark on the west bank of the Deschutes above Maupin, Nena Creek is a seasonal flow and offers no trout fishing.

North Lake (Mt. Hood National Forest)
hike-in

The prettiest of all the lakes in or near the Hatfield Wilderness, 6-acre North Lake seems to glow a brilliant emerald green on sunny days as it catches the reflection of the dense alder and berry patches cloaking the talus slide above the west shoreline. Dense groves of elegant spire-shaped firs stand over the banks. North Lake offers brook trout, mostly from 5 to 11 inches, but also an occasional fish to 14 or 15 inches. The larger fish are usually quite plump.

Reaching the lake requires a short easy hike either from a

nearby trailhead or from Rainy Lake 1.3 miles to the south. See Rainy Lake herein for road directions and then watch for the trailhead about 2 miles before you reach the parking area for Rainy Lake. The trail, unmarked on the road at this time, is 9.8 miles up FR 2420, starting at the end of the pavement. Watch for a small pullout on the left and wilderness signs back in the trees on the right. By this trail (#411), the hike covers less than a mile. You can also drive over to FR 2420 from a rugged rock road leading past the end of Kingsley Reservoir.

Spin casters have an advantage bank fishing on North Lake because of the brushy shoreline. You can negotiate your way around most of the lake on foot, but the northwest corner is cloaked by an impenetrable tangle of alders. Fly anglers will be heartily rewarded for carrying a float tube in to this lake. North Lake is usually accessible by late May.

North Twin Lake (Deschutes County)
see Twin Lakes, North & South

Ochoco Creek (Crook County)

Ochoco Creek, east of Prineville, feeds Ochoco Reservoir and offers two more-or-less distinct fisheries for rainbow trout. The upper half of the creek flows through public lands in the Ochoco National Forest, providing easy access, first from the highway and then along Ochoco Creek Road on the way up to Walton Lake. Below the national forest boundary, the river flows mostly across private property down to the reservoir and also below the dam on Ochoco Reservoir. Be sure to ask permission before crossing private lands. Typical trout throughout the system range from 6 to 12 inches and all methods are allowed below the dam. Above Ochoco Reservoir the creek is open to fishing with flies and artificial lures (check current regulations). Three campgrounds are located in the upper drainage of the creek.

Al Shewey poses with an Odell Lake Mackinaw (lake trout).

Ochoco Reservoir (Crook County)
boat ramp, campground

Just a few miles east of Prineville, this large reservoir is a good bet for stocked rainbow trout, especially during spring. At full pool, the reservoir covers 1,100 acres, but it is progressively drawn down throughout the summer to feed regional irrigation needs. Most of the shoreline lies on private lands, limiting bank access to the dam and the area along the highway, including a nice state park but, all told, there is ample shoreline fishing available.

Fishing by boat is often better and recently, the boat ramp was extended so it can now be used even at low water levels. Boat anglers should try the mouths of Ochoco Creek and Mill Creek, which often attract lots of trout. Both creeks empty into the reservoir at the east end. Ochoco's rainbows, usually stocked as fingerlings, grow quite fat and typically range from 10 to 16 inches. A few 18 inchers show up in the catch, especially after two or more high-flow years. The upper end of the reservoir is a good bet for large trout. Black crappie have been illegally introduced, but they don't grow large here and currently there is no limit on them, so take as many as you want. The same holds true for brown bullhead.

The reservoir is open all year and is popular in every season. Late summer often brings a lull in the action, but the cooler weather of autumn revives the good fishing. All methods produce on Ochoco, with bank anglers mostly relying on bait and boat anglers divided between still fishing with bait and casting or trolling spoons and spinners.

To get there, first head for the town of Prineville. Head due east through Prineville on Hwy 26 and you'll see Ochoco Reservoir on your right 5 miles from town. Ochoco Reservoir State Park offers camping, drinking water, restrooms, picnic areas, and a boat ramp and is located about 2 miles east from the dam.

Odell Creek (Deschutes County)

Odell Creek is a gin-clear stream flowing north from Odell Lake into Davis Lake. The mouth of the creek is closed to fishing at Davis Lake, but a nice trail crosses the creek between East Davis and West Davis Campgrounds and provides a good opportunity to sneak up and view the huge rainbows that often ascend the creek from the lake below. The remainder of the creek offers marginal fishing at best.

Odell Lake
boat recommended, boat ramp, campgrounds, services

Odell Lake paints a scenic blue portrait across the forested crest of the Cascade Mountains about 80 miles east of Eugene. The lake is famous for its large Mackinaw, which reach more than 30 pounds. Fishing for them is good for those who know the lake and fair for anglers new to Odell (the limit is one lake trout with a minimum size of 30 inches). Odell also offers some nice rainbows along with lots of kokanee. Resident bull trout, though rare, are fully protected.

Odell's Mackinaw roam the depths between late spring and autumn, when the fishery attracts quite a bit of pressure. The fish can be as deep as 200 feet, but more commonly occupy the 80- to 160-foot depths. To enjoy a realistic chance at catching these beauties you'll need a boat equipped with fish-finding electronics and down-rigging gear. Some anglers prefer deep jigging instead of down-rigging. For the former method, you must first precisely locate a concentration of fish on the sonar. If you don't have your own boat, you can rent one at the two resorts on Odell—Odell Lake Resort (541-433-2540/www.odelllakeresort.com) and Shelter Cove Resort (800-647-2729/www.sheltercoverresort.com). Be sure to call ahead to reserve a boat—or for that matter a cabin or camp spot. In addition to the two nice lodges on Odell Lake, the Forest Service operates four campgrounds around the lake.

Spanning 3,562 acres, Odell Lake is 6 miles long and 1.5 miles across. The wind can whip up in a hurry here, so most Mackinaw anglers prefer to get out on the water early in the morning. The lake's Mackinaw were first stocked more than 100 years ago and their numbers were bolstered by additional stockings through the 1960s. Since then the fishery has prospered through natural reproduction. A state record fish weighing 40 pounds, 8 ounces and spanning 45.5 inches was taken here in 1984 by Kenneth Erickson. Kokanee are also taken by trolling. The fishery here ranks among Oregon's best, although the fish rarely exceed 15 inches. During the fall you can watch spawning kokanee in Trapper Creek at Shelter Cove Resort (on the west end of the lake).

Mackinaw often feed in pods of several to a dozen or more fish, pursuing schools of kokanee. Find concentrations of kokanee in deep water and you will often find Mackinaw nearby. Odell's lakebed is highly varied with several prominent shoals jutting into the lake and rising off the bottom. Jig anglers tend to focus on these areas and trollers, using down-rigging gear, work the edges. Flatfish and kwikfish reign supreme for most anglers. Check in at the lodges for current advice on tackle and locations.

You can target Odell's rainbows, which range from 10 to 20 inches, by trolling the shoreline margins, especially between July and October. Comparatively few anglers fish for the rainbows, even though fishing can be quite good. Fly anglers can even target them during late-morning through mid-day hatches of Callibaetis mayflies and again during the evening when the wind settles down.

The lake sits at 4,800 feet and traditionally opens during late April and closes October 31. At the beginning and end of the season, anglers sometimes find Mackinaw cruising near shore in just 15 to 30 feet of water. Like the kokanee on which they feed, however, the Macks prefer cold water and usually head deep before the opener and remain there throughout the open season.

Odell Lake, with its fine view of Diamond Peak, lies near Willamette Pass atop the Cascade Range. Highway 58 runs along the lake's north shore. Boat ramps are located at both resorts and at the campgrounds and all supplies, along with free advice, are available at the resorts. Additionally you can book guide service on Odell Lake through both lodges.

Olallie Lake (Mt. Hood National Forest)
campground, services

One of the state's more popular drive-to high mountain lakes, Olallie Lake sits at the foot of 7,215-foot Olallie Butte near the crest of the Cascade Mountains. The lake spans 238 acres and offers good fishing for stocked rainbow trout along with the occasional brook trout. In addition to the usual rainbows, ODFW stocks Olallie with several hundred brood trout each summer and these 4- to 15-pound lunkers have become a major draw for the lake. In 2003, the lake record was established with a fish weighing more than 17 pounds.

Anglers employ a wide range of tactics on Olallie Lake, from still fishing with myriad baits to trolling with gear or flies. In fact, slow trolling with wet flies and streamer flies is something of a tradition here. Because of the lake's no-motors rule, slow is the only speed really possible for trollers and it seems to work just fine. Many anglers drag woolly buggers, damsel nymphs, and other such flies, usually but not necessarily using fly tackle. You can launch any kind of small boat, but remember that all motors are banned, including electrics. The resort offers rental rowboats.

Bank angling is good at Olallie and a nice trail encircles the entire lake and roads reach all but the eastern and northeastern shorelines. There are three nice campgrounds on the lake along with the rental cabins, yurts, and campsites available through Olallie Lake Resort (541-504-1010/www.olallielakeresort.com). The resort also offers a store and tackle shop. The resort sponsors an annual summer fishing derby at the lake, with the winner usually receiving a free two-night stay in one of the cabins.

You can usually reach Olallie Lake by mid-June, but call the resort or the U.S. Forest Service to make sure the road is open. Fishing peaks from June through mid-July and then again from mid- to late September through late October. During late summer, the lake often gets too warm for trout stocking and fishing tends to slow down. At that time, however, you can still find very good action on some of the smaller, hike-in lakes in the Olallie Lake Scenic Area and on the adjacent Warm Springs Reservation.

From Portland, you can take one of two routes to Olallie Lake: Follow Hwy 26 toward Mt. Hood and then turn south on the Oregon Skyline Road (FR 4220), which leads 30 miles to the lake. Or you can head for Estacada and continue into the mountains on Hwy 224 and then follow the signs to Olallie. The last 7 miles are gravel and this route covers 65 miles after leaving Estacada. From Detroit on Hwy 22, follow FR 46 up the Breitenbush River drainage and then up to the Skyline Road.

Oldenberg Lake (Deschutes National Forest)
hike-in

A scenic and fairly productive 28-acre hike-in brook trout lake, Oldenberg occupies a shallow basin 4 miles due south of Crescent Lake and 3 miles northeast from Cowhorn Mountain. A 3-plus-mile hike gets you there from Crescent Lake's west shore to the northwest or from Windigo Pass to the south.

Take Hwy 58 to the turn-off for Crescent Lake and follow FR 60 for 7.5 miles to the trailhead. This route takes you past the Bingham Lakes—only Bingham, the largest of the Bingham Lakes, is still stocked with brook trout—and then up to Oldenberg on an easy and fairly popular trail that is open to both horses and mountain bikes, should you be so inclined. From the south, the Windigo Trail offers a scenic route past the Nip-and-Tuck Lakes (not stocked) and down to Oldenberg. However, by the time you drive to Windigo Pass (winding mountain roads from the west and a rugged dirt road from the east) you could have already walked into Oldenberg from the other trailhead.

One-Mile Pond (Columbia River/I-84)

So named because it spans a mile in length, One-Mile Pond lies between the east and westbound lanes of I-84 just east of The Dalles. It usually offers consistent action for bluegill, bass, yellow perch, and other warmwater species. Reasonably safe parking is limited to a gravel pullout that extends behind the guardrail in the eastbound lanes at the far western edge of the ponds. Use extreme caution when pulling off the freeway here. The safer bet is to have someone drop you off and then arrange for a pick-up later in the day.

Patsy Lake (Mt. Jefferson Wilderness)
hike-in

A tiny, but deep lake located a mile southeast from Cathedral Rocks in the Mt. Jefferson Wilderness Area, Patsy Lake used to be stocked with brook trout. As of my last visit there a number of years ago, the lake appeared to be fishless. Check it out if you happen to be in the area. The Junction Lake/Table Lake Trail takes you there.

Paulina Creek (Deschutes County)
no bait

A very pretty creek, and the outlet from equally scenic Paulina Lake southeast of Bend, Paulina Creek offers slow-to-fair fishing for small rainbow and brown trout. The upper few miles are best. Access is from the Paulina Falls Day Use Area, where a photogenic double waterfall plunges 60 feet. Hike downstream from there. The day-use area requires that you purchase the $10 pass for the Newberry National Volcanic Monument, available at the entry booth. Forest Road 21 to Paulina Falls (and Paulina Lake) heads east

from Hwy 97 about 24 miles south of Bend. From there, it's 12 miles up to Paulina Falls.

Paulina Lake (Deschutes National Forest)
campground, services, boat ramp

Famous for producing Oregon's state record brown trout several times over—and most of the state's truly large browns—Paulina Lake is a deep, natural beauty filling one of two craters left by a dormant volcano. The entire area, including nearby East Lake, is included in the Newberry Crater National Volcanic Monument. Paulina not only produces trophy-class brown trout, but also offers good fishing for large kokanee along with average-size stocked rainbows.

Paulina's brown trout typically range from 2 to 8 pounds, but not a year passes during which anglers there land fish pushing the 15- to 20-pound mark. The current state record, caught by Ron Lane in 2003, weighed 28 pounds, 5 ounces and stretched the tape to 37.5 inches. Lane, a trophy brown-trout expert from California, took this monster by trolling a 7-inch rainbow-pattern AC Plug—typical of the tackle and technique used to catch Paulina Lake's largest browns. Bank anglers, casting plugs and spoons, take a few large browns every year, but trolling produces most of these trophy-class fish.

Lane's record-setting trout came from the big point across from the resort and this shoal area is well known for being a consistent producer of big browns. Other popular trolling areas include the drop-offs between Red Slide on the north shore and Paulina Lake Resort on the west shoreline and, when the fish are shallow, from Red Slide east to Black Slide. One of the best techniques when the browns are shallow is flat lining: Trolling with at least 50 to 100 yards of line and a min-

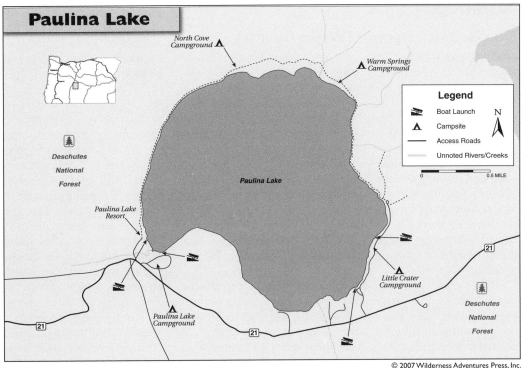

Paulina Lake

North Cove Campground

Warm Springs Campground

Legend
Boat Launch   N
Campsite
Access Roads
Unnoted Rivers/Creeks

0   0.5 MILE

Deschutes National Forest

Paulina Lake

Paulina Lake Resort

Little Crater Campground

Paulina Lake Campground

Deschutes National Forest

21   21   21

© 2007 Wilderness Adventures Press, Inc.

now-imitating plug. When the browns are deeper, use down-rigging gear.

Brown trout from 14 to 18 inches are fairly common and many of these are taken by bank anglers as well as boat anglers. Rich in prey, Paulina Lake is perfect habitat for growing double-digit browns. They feast on tui chub, kokanee, rainbow trout, and even crayfish. Bank anglers will find a good trail encircling the lake.

The kokanee in Paulina Lake reach several pounds and, in fact, the lake claimed the state record for this species until fairly recently. Kokanee from 14 to 17 inches are common and fishing for them can be very good at times. The key, of course, is to locate the depth and location of the schools. Trolling is the best method. Rainbow trout can reach several pounds, but typical fish are less than 16 inches. They provide lots of sport for both boat and bank anglers and can be taken using any method.

Paulina Lake opens in late April on the general statewide trout opener and closes for the season on October 31. The lake is generally accessible by opening day and by late October, snow flurries can occur any time. Despite the prospects for winter-like weather, October is one of the best—and least crowded—times to fish Paulina.

Because of its inclusion in the Newberry Volcanic National Monument, visitors to Paulina and East Lakes must pay an entry fee ($10 per 3-day pass at this time). Paulina features six campgrounds along with rustic Paulina Lake Lodge (541-536-2240/www.paulinalakelodge.com). The resort features rental cabins, boat rentals, restaurant, general store, fishing tackle, and other provisions.

Phantom Lake (Three Sisters Wilderness)
see Merle Lake

Pine Hollow Reservoir (Wasco County)
boat ramp, services

A good producer of both largemouth bass and rainbow trout, 240-acre Pine Hollow Reservoir is located in the foothills of the east slope of the Cascade's 5 miles west of Tygh Valley. Follow Hwy 197 south from The Dalles or north from the Hwy 216, west of Maupin. At Tygh Valley, turn west on Wamic Market Road and then turn right on Ross Road, leading to the reservoir.

Stocked rainbow trout here range from 9 to 16 inches, with a few fish reaching 20 or more inches. Largemouth bass reach at least 8 pounds, but typical specimens range from 10 inches to 4 pounds. When the water level is high, they thrive in the shoreline reed stands. At low water, look for them hanging along shoal areas. Bluegill and brown bullhead abound and, though they don't grow big here, they provide a great fishery, especially for kids.

Pine Hollow Reservoir is a popular summer playground with water skiers, jet skiers, and pleasure boaters, but a speed limit is enforced on the east side of the reservoir to provide better fishing conditions. Bank fishing access is limited by extensive private property, but can be quite good near both

boat ramps. One ramp is located at the campground on the southeast corner of the reservoir and the other is located at the north end of the dyke on the east shore.

The reservoir is open year-round and, when thoroughly frozen, can produce good ice fishing for trout. Most years, the stocked rainbows over-winter in good numbers. Be sure to check with the resort or with ODFW to check ice conditions. Peak ice fishing usually occurs during January and February. Pine Hollow Lakeside Resort (541-544-2271/www.pinehollow-lakeside.com) offers rental cabins, rental boats, store, RV park, and more.

Pinnacle Creek (Hood River drainage)
closed waters

Pocket Lake (Three Sisters Wilderness)
see Brahma Lake

Prineville Reservoir (Crook County)
campground, boat ramp, services

Smallmouth and largemouth bass, crappie, catfish, and trout command lots of attention on this popular and productive 3,000-acre impoundment on the Crooked River 15 miles south of Prineville. The stocked rainbow (and some cutthroat) trout typically range from 9 to 14 inches with quite a few fish to 16 inches. Smallmouth bass are plentiful and typically range from 8 inches to 2 pounds, but Prineville Reservoir held the state record smallie for years until it was broken in 1994 by a fish from Hagg Lake.

Largemouth bass are generally of modest size, but a few fish reach 5 pounds or more. They are not as abundant as the smallmouth bass, but are quite popular with a small assemblage of bass-fishing specialists. Crappie are quite plentiful and typically average 7 or 8 inches. Productive bass and crappie areas are scattered all over this large reservoir. The upper half of the lake is especially good. Popular bass areas include virtually all of the small bays and coves from Big Island past Jasper Point and Roberts Bay and all the way up the Crooked River Arm. Fishing for bass and crappie generally peaks from mid-May through September and by autumn the fish tend to disperse throughout the reservoir. Spring fishing (May) can be especially good for largemouth bass that spawn in the upper (Crooked River Arm) reservoir.

All three species are usually highly oriented to structure, ranging from stumps and docks to shoals and rocky points. The bass especially like the stump fields and, to create additional structure, ODFW has anchored dead junipers and Christmas trees in the reservoir. During the spring, look for wood structure in the backside of the bays and coves where shallow water warms more quickly than in the main reservoir. By summer, bass occupy the wood structures and also frequent rocky areas and gravel bars.

Trout fishing generally holds up reasonably well year-round owing to liberal stocking allotments for the reservoir. The rainbows are stocked as sub-legals and seem to over-win-

Prineville Reservoir is a busy but productive fishery for bass, panfish, and trout.

bullhead with bait. Trolling the shoreline margins also accounts for lots of trout. Prineville Reservoir attracts lots of casual anglers and also draws a dedicated assortment of serious bass anglers. These latter anglers rely on top-water plugs, spinner-baits, crank-baits, buzz-baits, and rubber worms along with a variety jigs. They always fish by boat, working the shorelines where appropriate cover holds bass. Bank fishing, however, is far more common here and still fishing with bait produces consistent action on a variety of species.

During summer, water skiers and pleasure boaters invade the reservoir; so many bass anglers do their best work during the morning hours before the traffic starts. Even when the reservoir is busy, you can escape the hustle and bustle by sticking to the upper end where a speed limit discourages pleasure boaters.

Prineville Reservoir offers two large, fully equipped campgrounds and a resort. The campground at Prineville Reservoir State Park often fills to capacity; so reserving a site is a good idea during the summer (call 1-800-452-5687). The state park campground features 22 full hook-up RV sites, 23 electric-only sites, 23 tent sites and five cabins. Jasper Point Campground offers 30 electric-only sites. Prineville Reservoir Resort (541-447-7468/www.prinevillereservoirresort. com) includes a seven-unit motel, large campground, a marina, rental boats, store, café, and tackle shop. The resort lodgings fill up frequently, so call well ahead for a reservation.

For a more secluded approach to fishing and camping at Prineville Reservoir, head for the Crooked River Arm east from the resort. Just before you reach the entrance to Jasper Point Campground, watch for the signed left-hand turn onto North Side Road. This is a rugged, steep, rutted, rocky primitive track not suitable for passenger cars or RVs, but it leads to a series of primitive campgrounds scattered along the north bank of the reservoir. North Side Road runs for 5.5 miles and connects to the Post-Paulina Highway east from Prineville and above the reservoir. Some campers take RVs down the North Side Road from the highway—the first 2 miles are far less treacherous than the remainder of the road.

To reach Prineville Reservoir, head for the town of Prineville and continue east through town to a right-hand turn onto Post-Paulina Highway heading southeast. Follow the road to a well-marked right-hand turn leading to the reservoir by way of a good paved road. To reach the upper end of the reservoir and the east terminus of North Side Road, continue easterly on the Post-Paulina Highway. When you reach the Crooked River, take the sharp right turn onto the dirt road.

To reach Bowman Dam from Prineville, turn south on SR

ter in good numbers most years, providing good ice-fishing opportunity during hard winters. During drought years—which have been quite prevalent in recent decades—all of the reservoir's fisheries take a heavy loss. The reservoir feeds water to regional agriculture and is drawn down steadily and substantially during the summer. Add a drought to the drawdown and the fishing can really suffer here.

During periods of good water supply, however, Prineville Reservoir ranks among the better still-water fisheries around for mixed-bag action. And even though the fish here rarely grow to trophy proportions, there are plenty of bass, crappie, trout, and bullhead to keep you busy; and big bass seem to be increasingly common.

They respond to all methods, but most anglers target bass and crappie with gear (jigs, spoons, and plugs) or trout and

27. The only reason to take this route is to reach the Powder House Cove boat ramp at the dam or the public bank access at Roberts Cove on the reservoir's south shore: Cross Bowman Dam and continue south to a left-hand turn on Salt Creek Road. During the spring, fishing for rainbow trout can be quite good near the dam and also in the Bear Creek Arm.

Raft Lake (Three Sisters Wilderness)
see Jay Lake

Rainy Lake (Mt. Hood National Forest)
hike-in

A fairly popular lake sitting on the east edge of the Hatfield Wilderness northwest of Hood River, Rainy offers brook trout in the 6- to 12-inch range. A tiny, primitive campground offers four spaces and sits by the road about a quarter mile from the lake. Rainy Lake spans about 10 acres and resides amidst stately conifers. The fish are fairly plentiful and a few reach 14- to 16 inches, though these are not common. From Hood River, follow Oak Street (the main east-west route through town) to a south turn onto 13th Street. Follow 13th leading south out of town and continue to the old mill site of Dee. At Dee, follow the road heading to your right, across the river and then stay right, doubling back to the north on Punchbowl Falls Road. Punchbowl Falls Road leads to a left-hand turn on FR 2420 (gravel), leading up into the mountains about 11 miles to Rainy Lake. Also see Black Lake and North Lake herein.

Red Slide Lake (Three Sisters Wilderness)
see Brahma Lake

Reynolds Pond (Deschutes County)

A nice little warmwater fishery located on public property east of Bend, Reynolds Pond once produced a red-ear sunfish that weighed about a pound. Most of the red-ears here, however, weigh just a few ounces and the largemouth bass rarely exceed a foot in length. The pond is fairly popular with youngsters and spans a shallow 20 acres or thereabouts. Flooded juniper snags provide cover for the fish and bank fishing is easy, though some anglers launch float tubes and other small watercraft. To get there, follow Hwy 20 east out of Bend to a left-hand turn on Dodds County Road leading to the tiny community of Alfalfa. At Alfalfa follow Johnson Market Road to the turnoff for the landfill and continue past the landfill to the pond.

Rim Lake (Three Sisters Wilderness)
hike-in, cross-country

A rather remote and highly scenic beauty with a fine view of the South Sister, Rim Lake lies in a shallow timber-clad depression north of Broken Top in the Three Sisters Wilderness. When I last visited, the lake offered good fishing for small brook trout without a soul in sight. This one is for the adventure-minded angler adept at cross-country navigation. Consult the map suggested below and fish this 4-acre lake between early July and late September. Might be a good idea to check the most recent stocking records by calling ODFW in Bend.

Rock Creek Reservoir (Wasco County)
boat ramp, campground

Located west of Tygh Valley, Rock Creek Reservoir is a fair-to-good producer of trout, bass, bluegill, and brown bullhead. ODFW stocks this 90-acre reservoir with a liberal allotment of legal-size rainbow trout along with a few hundred brood-stock fish when available. Bluegill and largemouth bass are fairly abundant, with the latter reaching at least 6 pounds, though 10- to 12-inch bass are more typical. Bluegill range from 4 to 8 inches. The lake's warmwater fish thrive in the willow stands at high water. At low water, look for them around any kind of wood structure and around the rocky areas.

Rock Creek Reservoir is an irrigation-storage facility and is steadi-

A float tuber samples Reynolds Pond east of Bend.

ly drawn down during the spring and summer. It can get quite low during dry years. Bank fishing is good here, especially for anglers still fishing with bait. Many anglers launch small boats and the boat ramp serves larger craft until the reservoir gets too low at mid-summer. The boat ramp is located at the campground on the south shoreline.

If you have a boat, try the inlet area on the northwest corner for the occasional carry-over trout that reaches 18 inches. The inlet arms are good bets most of the time and especially during April and May. When the reservoir gets low during late summer and autumn, try fishing the edges of the deep pool near the dam. Fly anglers will enjoy good surface action provided by early summer hatches of *Callibaetis* mayflies, along with occasional flights of flying ants. In the absence of surface action, try Woolly Buggers and small bead-head nymph patterns.

From Tygh Valley on Hwy 197, turn west on Wamic Market Road. At Wamic, head south and then veer right on Rock Creek Dam Road, which leads a few miles to the reservoir. If you're coming from the Portland area, follow Hwy 26 to a left turn on Hwy 35 and then a right-hand turn on FR 48, which is paved and leads directly to the reservoir.

Rock Rim Lake (Three Sisters Wilderness)
hike-in

A very pretty lake with small brook trout, Rock Rim Lake occupies a bench on the east slope of Irish Mountain, near the Pacific Crest Trail and due east from Cultus Lake. The shortest route is from the west via the Skookum Trailhead and the highly scenic Crossing Way Trail. You'll need sturdy boots, healthy lungs and a stout sense of adventure here, but the reward is solitude and scenery. Consult the wilderness maps for details and wait until late June when the snow clears out. Rock Rim Lake sits at 6,034 feet and its nearby neighbors also offer brook trout. These include Josephine Lake to the south and Stormy Lake to the north. Both about 4 acres in size, these lakes grow brookies to about 12 inches, but 8-inch fish are typical.

Rosary Lakes (Deschutes National Forest)
hike-in

Located along the Pacific Crest Trail a mile north of Odell Lake and over Maiden Peak from the ski runs at Willamette Pass, the three Rosary Lakes provide fair fishing between June and mid-autumn. All three are stocked with brook trout that commonly range from 6 to 10 inches. The largest of the three lakes, 42-acre Lower Rosary, also offers rainbows. Every once in a while a lucky angler will tangle with a 14- to 16-incher in Lower Rosary, but pan-sized trout predominate. The lakes are easy to reach via the Pacific Crest Trailhead atop Willamette Pass, across from the turnoff to Odell Lake's Trapper Creek Campground. Lower Rosary is 2 miles up the trail and Middle and North Rosary Lakes, both about 8 acres in size, are about 3.5 miles in.

Round Butte Reservoir (Jefferson County)
see Lake Billy Chinook

Round Lake (Jefferson County)
campground

Round Lake is a fairly popular, easy-access mountain lake located just east of the Santiam Summit and north of Suttle Lake. Unfortunately its shoreline and surrounding slopes were scorched by 2003 B&B Complex fire. Still, ODFW continues stocking the lake with rainbows and fishing remains productive. Round Lake spans 22 acres and reaches a maximum depth of about 17 feet. The campground is unimproved. At 4,900 feet, Round Lake is usually snowed in until at least mid-May, sometimes later. However, the ice comes off before the road is passable, making this a good bet for the adventurous types who might want to hike in during early May and have the place all to themselves. Consult with the Forest Service office in Sisters to check on road and ice conditions.

Salisbury Slough (Columbia River/I-84)
boat ramp, boat recommended

Salisbury Slough is a meandering slough on the Columbia River east from Mosier and west from The Dalles. The little town of Lyle, Washington lies directly across the Columbia. The slough offers good prospects for bass, crappie, yellow perch, and brown bullhead, along with an occasional sturgeon. Access is from Mayer State Park, which includes the west shoreline of the slough and offers a boat ramp and picnic area. There is a daily use fee at the park.

Shevlin Park Pond (Bend)

This small pond, open for kids only, is located next to the Aspen Shelter at Shevlin Park on the west side of Bend. It is stocked with catchable rainbows.

Simon Lake (Three Sisters Wilderness)
see Brahma Lake

Simtustus Lake (Warm Springs Reservation)
see Lake Simtustus

Sisters Mirror Lake (Three Sisters Wilderness)
hike-in

A very scenic and popular destination in the wilderness, Sisters Mirror Lake is prone to winterkill and is thus not stocked.

Snell Lake (Deschutes National Forest)
hike-in

Located amidst acres of small ponds between Summit Lake and Crescent Lake, Snell Lake is a rather lightly fished hike-in lake offering brook and cutthroat, with the relative abundance of each depending on the most recent stockings. Snell Lake spans 9 acres and reaches a depth of 17 feet. The trout tend toward the small side, but a few reach 14 to 16 inches and the lake is perfectly suited to a float tube.

Just a few hundred yards to the east, pretty little Farrell Lake offers the same scenario in a 4-acre package. Its brook trout average less than 10 inches, but the lake produces a few fish to 16 inches. Both lakes reside at 5,600 feet and are snowbound most years until mid-June. The same short trail that leads half a mile north to these lakes also extends south of the access road and reaches 11-acre Meek Lake after half a mile. Meek Lake is deep and, like Snell and Farrell Lakes, tends to provide good fishing all the way through the summer and well into autumn. All of these lakes are superb October fisheries, especially for spin fishers and fly anglers, but keep a sharp eye on the weather forecast.

The only downfall to these decidedly pleasant mountain lakes is the rugged access road—a rocky, dirt track connecting Crescent and Summit Lakes. It departs the west end of Crescent Lake (FR 6010) or you can descend from Emigrant Pass near Summit Lake to the west. From Crescent Lake, it's 4 miles up to the trailhead. This road is not maintained and is rather nasty, being best suited to high-clearance 4-wheel-drive vehicles. The road is gated until the snow melts in mid-June. The adventurous soul might head up to Crescent Lake in early June and hike or bike the road. If you do so, you'll find the lakes ice-free and completely deserted. Otherwise, if you're heading up there during June or even early July, call ahead to the Crescent Ranger District to find out if the gate has been opened for the summer (541-433-3200). Beware the mosquitoes.

Snow Creek (Deschutes National Forest)

A brushy little tributary to the Upper Deschutes, joining the river just upstream from Crane Prairie Reservoir, Snow Creek offers only fair fishing for small brook trout and a few rainbows. The South Century Drive cut-off road (FR 4270) crosses the creek a mile below its spring sources near Deschutes Bridge, and the road at Cow Creek Campground on Crane Prairie crosses the lower end of the creek. Currently catch-and-release rules apply to the rainbows here.

Snowshoe Lakes (Three Sisters Wilderness)
see Winopee Lakes

South Twin Lake (Deschutes County)
see Twin Lakes, North & South

Sparks Lake (Deschutes County)
boat ramp, boat recommended, fly fishing only

Sparks Lake is a broad, shallow lake sprawling across about 400 acres of wetlands and providing good fishing for small brook and cutthroat trout. Foot access is difficult owing to the lake's marshy shoreline, but Sparks is ideally suited to a small boat or canoe. It lies off Century Drive, a few miles past Mt. Bachelor.

The access road—FR 400—turns south from Century Drive and leads to the boat ramp and picnic area on Sparks. Often the water recedes beyond the boat ramp by late summer because the natural lava flow dam forming Sparks Lake is quite porous. The lava flow, on the south extension of the lake, is usually the best area for fishing. Sparks can provide consistent action all summer, but autumn is best. Rarely is it crowded because most anglers in these parts head for the nearby lakes that are both better known and inhabited by larger trout.

Sparks Lake is fertile enough to offer good hatches of *Callibaetis* mayflies and Chironomids throughout the season. Dry-fly action is best when the wind stays down. Damselflies appear by late June and can be prolific during July. A wide array of wet flies and small streamer patterns will entice the brookies here. Fine views of the surrounding mountains make this a camera-friendly destination. Currently anglers are not allowed to use a motor while actually fishing, but check the most current regulations.

The clear, skinny waters feeding Sparks Lake demand a stealthy approach.

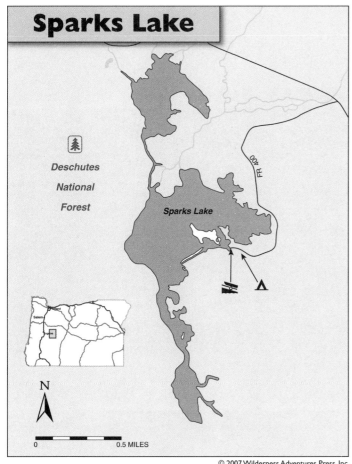

Sparks Lake

Deschutes National Forest

Sparks Lake

FR 400

N

0   0.5 MILES

© 2007 Wilderness Adventures Press, Inc.

Spoon Lake (Olallie Lake area)

A small, shallow lake south from Olallie Lake and north from Breitenbush Lake, Spoon Lake is no longer stocked owing to frequent winterkill.

Square Lake (Mt. Jefferson Wilderness)
hike-in

Located on the southern edge of the Mt. Jefferson Wilderness and immediately north of Hwy 20, Square Lake spans more than 50 acres and is generally stocked with brook or rainbow trout that reach 10 to 12 inches. The lake is easy to reach and popular. Watch for the signs announcing the Pacific Crest Trailhead on the north side of the highway across from Hoodoo Ski Area and then follow the PCT north a short distance to a right-hand turn leading about a mile to Square Lake.

Squaw Creek (Jefferson County)
catch-and-release, no bait

Squaw Creek flows through the town of Sisters, passing under the highway at the east edge of town. By mid-summer this section of the creek often runs dry due to irrigation draws.

The creek's lower few miles, however, are fed by springs and provide fair fishing for small wild redband trout. Nowhere abundant in the stream, these trout reach their highest densities in the creek's final mile before it dumps into the Middle Deschutes upstream from the Deschutes Arm of Lake Billy Chinook. Thanks to the springs, the lower section of Squaw Creek flows somewhat cooler than the Middle Deschutes immediately above the confluence.

Getting to the lower end of the creek requires that you first negotiate a series of fairly rugged back roads and then hike down to and across the creek, which flows through a deep canyon. You can get to the access roads from either side of the creek, but from the west side you must drive across the creek several miles above the prime trout water. You can avoid fording the creek by approaching from the southeast side, but the access point here is far less obvious. Rampant home building in the area has made access increasingly tenuous and, because Squaw Creek cannot take much angling pressure, I'll leave specific driving instructions up to the adventurous types willing to study the maps.

Stag Lake (Diamond Peak Wilderness)
hike-in

A good brook trout lake located in the wilderness between Crescent and Odell Lakes, 20-acre Stag Lake enjoys a commanding view of nearby 7,065-foot Lakeview Mountain. The hike to Stag Lake begins at either Crescent Lake Campground (Fawn Lake Trailhead) or at Odell Lake Resort (Crater Butte Trailhead). Both routes cover about the same distance, first to Fawn Lake (about 3 miles) and then west about 1 mile to a right-hand fork leading .7 of a mile north to Stag Lake. The lake is usually deserted, especially mid-week and offers several nice primitive camping spots. This deep lake sits at about 5,800 feet and is usually accessible by late June.

Strider Lake (Three Sisters Wilderness)
see Jay Lake

Summit Lake (Deschutes National Forest)
campground

Aptly named for its scenic perch atop the Cascade's summit south of Diamond Peak, 470-acre Summit Lake offers modest fisheries for rainbow and brook trout along with a few small Mackinaw. Sitting at 5,553 feet, Summit Lake is deep and sterile, so trout grow slowly. Typical brook and rainbow trout range from 8 to 10 inches, with a few larger fish taken. The Mackinaws here are rarely targeted and they range from 2 to 10 pounds. Most are less than 6 pounds.

You can approach Summit Lake from the east or west side of the Cascade Mountains, with either route capped off by several miles on rugged, barely maintained dirt/rock roads. The fastest route is from Crescent Lake to the east. Take Crescent Lake Road south from Hwy 58 about 7.5 miles to a right-hand turn onto FR 6010 (Summit Lake Road). This rough road, best suited to high-clearance, 4-wheel-drive vehicles, is usually gated until mid-June or later. From the gate, it's about 5 miles to Summit Lake.

From the west side of the Cascades, a long, winding mountain road—FR 21—departs Oakridge and follows the Middle Fork Willamette River to its headwaters. From the upper reaches of the Middle Fork you can choose from two different routes to Summit Lake—consult a map of the Willamette National Forest or the Crescent Ranger District Map, available from Deschutes National Forest. Summit Lake is a very pretty place even if the fishing is rather slow most of the time.

Sundew Lake (Three Sisters Wilderness)
see Merle Lake

Suttle Lake (Jefferson County)
boat ramp, boat recommended, campground, services

A popular early season lake located east of Santiam Pass and west of Sisters, Suttle Lake offers good-size brown trout, kokanee, and rainbow trout. This 250-acre lake often thaws by late April and brown trout enthusiasts appear immediately thereafter for a shot at fish ranging from 14 to 24 inches. Trolling plugs and spoons, working along the shoreline drop-offs early and late in the day, is generally the best method to target the brown trout.

Suttle Lake also offers good kokanee angling, which usually holds up throughout the summer except for a brief period during August when an algae bloom frequently erupts. Whether you target kokanee or trout, get out on the water early. By mid-day, the wind often rises and at the same time the lake becomes a playground for pleasure boaters and a few water skiers. After Labor Day the crowds disperse and the best brown trout action of the year occurs during October and sometimes into November.

The lake offers several campgrounds and boat ramps and The Lodge at Suttle Lake (541-595-2628/www.thelodgeatsuttlelake.com), on the east shore at the outlet, offers lodging, meals, supplies, rental boats, and other amenities. The turnoff to the lake is just west of a near-90-degree bend on Hwy 20. If you are arriving from the west, you will see the lake downhill to your right as the highway straightens after a number of curves on Santiam Pass.

Suzanne Lake (Deschutes National Forest)
hike-in, float tube recommended

Lightly fished and quite good, Suzanne Lake and its neighbor Darlene Lake offer excellent prospects for trout ranging from 8 to 13 inches with a rare fish reaching 16 or more inches. These lakes are easy to fish from shore, but a float tube is advantageous, especially for fly anglers. Suzanne is stocked with both rainbow and brook trout; Darlene usually with brook trout. Both lakes reside just below the 6,000-foot mark and are rarely accessible before June and sometimes not until mid-June.

To get there, follow Hwy 58 to the turn-off into Crescent Lake and then follow the access road to the west shoreline. Look for the Windy Lakes Trailhead just south of Tandy Bay Picnic Area. Both horses and mountain bikes are allowed

Suttle Lake, below the east side of Santiam Summit, provides boating opportunities for kokanee, rainbow trout, and a few large brown trout.

on this trail, which connects with the Pacific Trail above the Windy Lakes. After 4 miles and just before you reach the Windy Lakes, watch for a left-hand turn onto a second trail heading east. Suzanne Lake is a mile down this trail and Darlene Lake is just beyond.

Swede Lake (Three Sisters Wilderness)
see Merle Lake

Taylor Lake (Deschutes National Forest)
campground

A nice drive-to mountain lake, rather heavily visited, Taylor and its neighbor Irish Lake sit several miles due west from Little Cultus Lake in the old Taylor Burn area. A rugged dirt road leads west from Little Cultus and east from Waldo Lake to reach these two lakes, not to mention the trailheads for myriad smaller and often more productive lakes in the immediate vicinity. Taylor and Irish Lakes are both stocked with brook trout and sometimes with cutthroat. The trout rarely surpass 13 inches, but fishing can be quite good, especially if you have a float tube, pontoon, raft, or small pram. If you don't have such watercraft, hike along the meandering shore-lines of both lakes looking for shoal areas where trout feed.

Both fly angling and spin casting are effective here and both lakes offer good hatches of *Callibaetis* mayflies, caddis, and Chironomids, not to mention the occasional and sudden appearance of flying ants by the hundreds. In the absence of dry-fly action, try bead-head wet flies and small stream-er patterns, any of which can be effectively fished with a torpedo bobber and spinning gear. Small Rooster-tails and tiny Panther Martin spinners are also quite effective. You can usually locate fish by slow-trolling (no motors) with a flasher/fly combo or with a Woolly Bugger or similar streamer pattern on a sinking fly line.

Despite their general popularity, both Irish Lake (28 acres) and Taylor Lake (34 acres) are rarely if ever crowded as the fishing pressure is dispersed through the summer and fall. The rugged access road may be the main deterrent to large assem-blages of people here. Besides, both lakes are big enough that anglers can easily disperse and find solitude. The camping area between the two lakes is primitive and has just six tent sites, but lots of nice informal sites are scattered around the area. In reality, the informal sites are better because the estab-lished camp area seems to have a constant supply of broken glass, trash, and redundant fire rings.

To reach Taylor and Irish Lakes from Bend, follow the signs to Mt. Bachelor, taking the Cascade Lakes Highway (Century Drive) about 46 miles west and then south to a right-hand turn on FR 4635, leading toward Cultus Lake Resort. After about three quarters of a mile, turn left on FR 4630 heading toward Little Cultus Lake. From Little Cultus, take FR 4636 heading west (it becomes FR 600) for 6.4 miles to the lakes. The last 4 miles require high-clearance vehicles. This road is rocky and rugged and at nearly 5,600 feet, the lakes remain in-accessible until late June. If you're heading up this way during early summer, call the Bend Ranger District Office to check on road conditions. If you are coming from Eugene (Hwy 58), you can get to Irish and Taylor Lake from the northeast shore of Waldo Lake: From North Waldo Campground, head north on FR 514, which will intersect FR 600. Turn right and head a short distance east to the lakes.

Taylor Lake (Columbia River/I-84)

A productive and popular warmwater fishery, also stocked with rainbow trout, Taylor Lake is located adjacent to Inter-state-84 just west of The Dalles This is one of the best of the Columbia River/I-84 ponds and offers good fishing for large-mouth bass, red-ear sunfish, pumpkinseed, bluegill, brown bullhead, yellow perch, and a variety of other fish. Trout are stocked regularly; including some 2-pounders and the bass range from 1 to 6 pounds, with 10- to 14-inch fish fairly common. Red-ear sunfish and bluegill reach almost a pound, but the vast majority of sunfish are 4 to 7 inches in length. From time to time even a wayward sturgeon finds its way into the lake via the channel connecting to the adjacent Columbia River and bait anglers catch some large carp.

Taylor's varied topography and shoreline make it interest-ing to fish, especially if you have a float tube or small, carry-able boat. Most anglers fish from shore, primarily on the foot-bridge and adjacent south shoreline, which offers plenty of parking room. A boat or float tube, however, is the best way to explore the far margins of the pond and can give you a distinct advantage if you're looking for bass and large sunfish. You can launch small, lightweight boats from the beach, but don't back a trailer too far in without a 4-wheel-drive vehicle. Taylor Lake spans about 35 acres and reaches a maximum depth of 16 feet. All methods produce here and access is excellent.

Depart Interstate-84 at Exit 82. Head east, off toward the Columbia River, following the signs that point toward the port area. A short distance from the freeway take the signed left-hand turn on River Trail Way, following the signs pointing to Taylor Lake. The access road is very rugged, but people drive all sorts of vehicles right to the edge of the lake.

An angler lands a rainbow trout from Taylor Lake near The Dalles.

Teddy Lakes (Three Sisters Wilderness)
hike-in

A pair of productive hike-in trout lakes near Cultus Lake on the southern edge of the Three Sisters Wilderness Area, the Teddys are capable of producing a few of those highly coveted 2-pound brookies. Most of the fish range from 7 to 12 inches and rainbows are planted from time to time as well. The lakes have become increasingly popular with the population explosion in central Oregon, but don't be surprised to have them to yourself on any given day, especially mid-week and almost assuredly during late September and early October—a decidedly pleasant and productive time to visit these lakes, weather allowing.

South Teddy spans 17 acres and reaches a maximum depth of about 10 feet while North Teddy, half a mile farther along the trail, covers about 30 acres and reaches a depth of 28 feet. Both lakes are easy to fish from shore, but a float tube is a nice luxury, especially if you are fly angling.

The shortest route to the Teddy Lakes covers 3.5 miles and begins at the end of the road leading through the Cultus Lake Campground. The trail follows the north shore of Cultus, passes the junction with the Corral Lakes Trail and then reaches a right-hand turn onto the Winopee Lake Trail. Half a mile up the Winopee Trail you'll find the right-hand turn leading to the Teddy Lakes. You can cut more than 2 miles off the hike by boating over to the west side of Cultus. If you don't have a boat, ride your mountain bike along Cultus Lake until you reach the wilderness boundary (no bikes allowed in the wilderness) and then lock your bike to a tree out of sight from the trail.

Three Creeks Lake (Deschutes County)
campground, boat ramp

A very popular lake south of Sisters—and pleasant enough except on crowded weekends—Three Creeks Lake offers fair-to-good fishing for stocked rainbow and wild brook trout. Both species range from 6 to 16 inches, with 10- to 12-inchers being typical. Sometimes ODFW stocks the lake with some large brood-stock trout. All methods produce here, from still fishing with bait from the banks, to trolling spoons and flies, to casting and retrieving wet flies via float tube or pontoon boat. Even dry-fly action is a fairly regular occurrence.

Reaching a maximum depth of about 28 feet, Three Creeks Lake offers lots of shallow shoal areas that are prime fishing grounds, especially early and late in the season. During

Little Three Creeks Lake

August, try trolling or casting in the deeper water near the center of the lake and just out from the cliff on the south shore. During July and again in the autumn, bank anglers and boat anglers, mostly still fishing with bait and trolling, enjoy consistent action near the small dam on the lake's northeast corner. Trollers also frequent the shoreline in front of the campground and along the drop-off between the two creek inlets on the west side of the lake.

Many anglers fish Three Creeks Lake by boat, though motors are not allowed. The boat launch is located on the east shore adjacent to the small concession (541-345-7665) that offers rental boats. The lake is about 16 miles south of Sisters: From Hwy 20 in town, turn south on Elm Street, which climbs into the mountains, becoming FR 16 upon reaching the Deschutes National Forest. At 6,550 feet, Three Creeks Lake may not be accessible until late June or early July. Call the Sisters Ranger District to check road conditions if you are headed for the lake during early summer.

Three Creeks Lake, Little (Deschutes County)
hike-in

A scenic and fairly productive brook trout fishery south of Sisters, Little Three Creeks Lake lies at the foot of Tam McArthur Rim and just outside the wilderness boundary. Little Three Creeks spans about 15 acres and reaches about 12 feet in depth. The brookies here range from 6 to 12 inches and fishing usually peaks during June and again during the fall. Bank fishing is easy and interesting because the lake's shoreline winds through several attractive coves. During mid- to late summer, however, many of the trout retreat to the deeper area, whose shoals are not accessible from the shore. Carry a float tube in and you'll likely enjoy fine action along the edge of the deep water near the center of the lake and at the mouth of the channel leading into the lake from the southeast corner. All methods work, but small spinners and wet flies are especially productive and dry-fly enthusiasts can expect good hatches of *Callibaetis* mayflies. The trail covers about 1 mile and begins at the campground on the northwest corner of nearby Three Creeks Lake.

Three Sisters Wilderness Area

hike-in, cross-country

The Three Sisters Wilderness Area covers 242,400 acres in the Deschutes and Willamette National Forests north of Hwy 58 and south of Hwy 242 (the McKenzie Highway). The wilderness area offers numerous entry points on all sides and features dozens upon dozens of fishable lakes, most of them stocked periodically by ODFW. A few lakes offer naturally reproducing trout, these being wild populations that started from hatchery progeny at various times during the 20th Century. ODFW stocks rainbow, brook, and cutthroat trout in the wilderness lakes.

Most of the fishable lakes are listed in this guide, but there are always a few small, out-of-the-way gems, not listed in the books, that offer the potential for good fishing. If you cannot ascertain whether a particular lake has been stocked, consult the ODFW in Bend. Many wilderness lakes cannot support fish populations.

The Three Sisters Wilderness Area derives its name from the three snow-capped dormant volcanos known as the South, Middle, and North Sisters. South Sister is the highest of the three and also the state's third tallest peak at 10,358 feet. Good, established trail routes ascend both the South Sister and the Middle Sister (10,047 feet), which require no technical climbing. They are very steep, however, and should not be climbed by anyone not physically prepared for the challenge. The North Sister (10,085 feet) is a technical and dangerous climb for expert mountaineers.

With almost 300 trail miles in the wilderness, including a length of the Pacific Crest Trail, anglers can choose from myriad routes to the fishable lakes. The highest lakes in the wilderness are accessible by late July. Some out-of-the-way lakes require cross-country hiking, which should be left only to experienced hikers and backpackers. Cross-country hiking requires the most accurate and detailed maps. The best of these are the USGS topographical maps, available at various outdoor and book stores throughout the state. Another good map is the Geo-Graphics Three Sisters Wilderness Map.

Certain areas within the wilderness are considered high-use areas and in some of these places, visitors must use designated, established campsites. While fishing can be quite good in some of the heavy-use areas, anglers might want to consider visiting the dozens of lakes that are rarely visited and infrequently fished. Heavy-use areas include the Mink Lake Basin, the Obsidian Cliffs area, and the Green Lakes area. Virtually all of the wilderness entry points have a self-registration station at which all visitors must fill out a permit. Likewise, most of the trailhead parking areas require a Northwest Forest Pass.

Timber Lake (Olallie Lake area)

hike-in

A short, easy hike reaches 10-acre Timber Lake, a fairly popular brook trout and rainbow trout fishery just to the southwest of Olallie Lake. Take the Red Lake Trail heading south from the northwest end of Olallie and after half a mile turn left on the Timber Lake Trail, which heads about .75 of a mile up to the lake. Trout here range from 6 to 10 inches with an occasional fish to 12 or 14 inches. For directions to the area, see Olallie Lake herein. The area is usually accessible by late June.

Timmy Lake (Three Sisters Wilderness)

see Brahma Lake

Todd Lake (Deschutes National Forest)

hike-in

Todd Lake is a scenic and popular 45-acre brook trout lake located in a glacial cirque due north of Mt. Bachelor Ski Area. From Bend, head west on Century Drive and watch for the signed right-hand turn about 2 miles past the main entrance to Bachelor. Follow the road a short distance up to the parking area and hike a quarter mile up the well-worn trail to the lake. Because of its 6,151-foot elevation, Todd Lake is usually snowbound until early June, sometimes later.

The brookies here range from 4 to 14 inches, averaging about 8 or 9 inches. They are generally cooperative, especially during September and October. Bank access is good and trails encircle the lake, but a float tube or raft is a nice luxury for fishing the drop-offs along the shoals. During October you can walk to the backside of the lake on calm, sunny mornings and watch brook trout in the process of spawning. The campground is a walk-in primitive site.

Tooley Lake (Columbia River/I-84)

A fairly large warmwater fishery just west of The Dalles, Tooley Lake sits on the south side of I-84. The land between the freeway and the lake's north shoreline is all private, so the best access is from a small gravel pullout adjacent to the eastbound lanes at the west end of the reservoir or via a steep climb down from old Hwy 30, which hangs above the lake's south bank. If you are arriving from the west, head for the Dalles so you can drive past the lake to see the climb that awaits from Hwy 30. Then leave the freeway at the first Dalles exit and double back on the old highway. From the east, this is the last Dalles Exit (Exit 82).

Torso Lake (Santiam Pass area)

Un-named on many maps, 9-acre Torso Lake lies south of Hwy 20 on the east side of Santiam Summit, about 3 miles southwest of Suttle Lake. Torso, stocked from time to time with brookies or rainbows, lies just south of better-known

Meadow Lake south of the Corbett Memorial State Park. Forest Road 2076 heads south from the parking area for Corbett Park, which is off the eastbound lane of the highway about 2 miles west of Suttle Lake. The access road passes just to the north of Torso Lake and primitive roads reach the lake. During the summer of 2003 this area was burned first by the Link Fire and then by the massive B&B Complex Fire, so you'll find lots of charred timber here.

Tranquil Lake (Three Sisters Wilderness)
see Brahma Lake

Trout Lake (Warm Springs Reservation)
campground

Anglers need a tribal fishing permit to sample the brook trout action and to camp at 23-acre Trout Lake, which lies on the western edge of the Warm Springs Reservation a few miles east from Olallie Lake. Permits are available at Warm Springs Market and at fishing stores in central Oregon and the Willamette Valley. Or call the tribal office at 541-553-2000.

Other good lakes in the immediate vicinity include Island, Dark, and Long Lakes. They are interconnected by Mill Creek, which feeds into Trout Lake. Boulder Lake sits half a mile southeast from Trout Lake (see listing for Boulder Lake herein). The other lakes are accessible by trail from Trout Lake and all offer good fishing for brookies from 8 to 12 inches, sometimes larger. You can also reach them from the west by taking the Long Lake Trail east from the east shore of Olallie Lake (see Olallie Lake herein). To reach Trout Lake and the trail to Boulder Lake, Take Hwy 26 over Mt. Hood and easterly to the reservation, watching for Road P-600 leading 19 miles up to Trout Lake.

Tumalo Creek (Deschutes County)
no bait

A fair small-trout fishery near Bend, diminutive Tumalo Creek offers wild redband trout, along with some small brookies and brown trout. A big fish here measures 10 inches. Tumalo Creek attracts a fair amount of attention being conveniently located near the hub-city of central Oregon. Easiest access is at Shevlin Park on the northwest edge of Bend, where trails follow the creek and from Skyliners Road and Tumalo Falls Road west from Bend. Pretty little Tumalo Falls, about 10 miles west of Bend, offers a small campground. The entire Bend area has undergone rapid population growth in the past two decades; so many traditional access sites to the creek are no longer available due to housing tracts.

Tumalo Reservoir (Deschutes County)
closed waters

An irrigation storage reservoir near Bend, Tumalo Reservoir has trouble holding water and is not open to the public. It's a good spring bird-watching area, however.

Twin Lakes (Mt. Hood area)
hike-in

Popular and usually productive, these two deep hike-in lakes east of Mt. Hood offer brook trout from 8 to 14 inches. Follow Hwy 26 east from Sandy and past the ski areas. About 4 miles past the SR 35 turn-off (before you reach Blue Box Pass) watch for the trailhead signs near the Frog Lake SnoPark access. Follow the trail northeast about a mile to the first lake (12 acres) and another half mile to the upper lake (9 acres). The trail is usually snow free by mid-June.

Twin Lakes, North & South (Deschutes County)
campground, boat ramp, services

North Twin and South Twin Lakes are a pair of pretty and very popular stocked-trout fisheries located off Century Drive near the northwest corner of Wickiup Reservoir. Both are about the same size—120 acres for South Twin and 140 acres for North Twin—and both are about 60 feet deep. The lakes are liberally stocked with rainbow trout that range from 8 to 14 inches. South Twin puts out a fair number of 18- to 22-inch rainbows and North Twin, unfortunately, has been illegally stocked with brown bullhead. The bullhead will no doubt overpopulate and adversely affect the growth-rate of the trout.

South Twin is a popular boat fishery, with the action about equally divided between still fishing with bait and trolling with a flasher-and-bait combination. During the summer, fertile weed beds grow along the shoals, especially on the north shore, making it a popular and productive area. Fly anglers enjoy consistent success here, mostly on wet flies and streamers, but also with dry flies during the mayfly hatches. Flying ants are common and like patterns can produce plenty of action, especially on breezy days.

The campgrounds are spacious and attractive in their forested settings and the lakes are connected by trail. As is evident on any summer weekend, these lakes make for a fine family destination. You can camp here for more adventurous big-fish excursions to nearby Davis Lake and Crane Prairie or Wickiup Reservoirs. Many anglers head for South Twin when high winds blow across nearby Wickiup and Crane Prairie Reservoirs. Boats are handy on these lakes, but motors are prohibited. Shoreline access is excellent and anglers use all methods effectively. Twin Lakes Resort, at South Twin Lake, offers boat rentals, RV camping, store, tackle shop, and restaurant (541-382-6432/www.twinlakesresort.net).

To reach these lakes, head south from Bend on Hwy 97 and turn west at Sunriver, heading west on Century Drive until you see the signs announcing the Twin Lakes. From Eugene, follow Hwy 58 over Willamette Pass and turn left on the Crescent Cut-off Road a few miles past Crescent Lake. After a few miles, turn north toward Davis Lake. Continue north past Davis Lake and past Wickiup Reservoir to a right-hand turn on FR 42, leading a few miles to the turn-off into the Twin Lakes. The lakes are usually accessible by late April or early May.

Upper Lake (Olallie Lake area)
hike-in

Despite its proximity to the Pacific Crest Trail, 8-acre Upper Lake, located just southwest from Olallie Lake, usually offers good fishing for stocked brook trout. The fish typically range from 6 to 10 inches. To get there, take the Oregon Skyline Road to Olallie Lake and then follow the PCT south about 2 miles to Upper Lake. The easy route is certainly conducive to carrying a float tube. Make a day-hike of it by fishing Upper Lake along with nearby Timber and View Lakes (see separate listings herein). The area is usually accessible by late June.

Viento Lake (Columbia River/I-84)

A fairly productive warmwater fishery and easy to reach, Viento Pond lies adjacent to Viento State Park at Exit 56. The pond spans only 4 acres and you can fish from shore or launch a float tube or similar craft. Sunfish, brown bullhead, yellow perch, a few bass, and non-game species predominate.

View Lake (Olallie Lake area)
hike-in, cross-country

A 5-acre lake in the Olallie Lake Scenic Area near the crest of the Cascade Range, View Lake offers brook trout from 5 to 10 inches. This is a good lake to fish in conjunction with nearby Timber Lake and Upper Lake. All three are easily sampled during a day hike. Consult the map because only informal and faint trails head to View Lake. From Timber Lake hike half a mile south; from Upper Lake it's .75 of a mile east-by-southeast. From the Skyline Road, you can follow the dry outlet streambed from Monon Lake up to View Lake, which is so named because of the commanding view it offers. A wildfire burned the area in 2001.

Wahtum Lake (Hood River County)
hike-in

A large, deep lake on the edge of the Mark O. Hatfield Wilderness southwest of Hood River, Wahtum offers fair fishing for small brook trout. Scenic and fairly popular, Wahtum reaches a maximum depth of 184 feet and spans 62 acres. Motors are not allowed, but a float tube or carry-in boat is handy here. The hike covers an easy quarter mile and the adjacent campground, which is not within the wilderness area, has five sites and no water. To get there, head south from Hood River and follow the signs to the town of Dee. Just south of Dee, head southwest on Lost Lake Road (FR 13) about 9 miles to a right-hand turn on FR 1310, which leads 6 miles to the campground.

Two other nearby lakes—Ottertail and Scout—offer additional angling prospects. Scout is the better of the two. It spans 3 acres and generally provides fair-to-good fishing for small planted brook trout. Scout Lake lies near the end of FR 1310, half a mile south of Wahtum Lake. Ottertail Lake, half a mile east of Wahtum Lake, likewise offers small brook trout, though fishing is usually slow. You can hike there from Wahtum, climbing over the ridge dividing the two, but it's easier to drive to Ottertail from the town of Dee. Follow Punch Bowl Road toward Punchbowl Falls and turn left onto FR 2810, which leads 11 miles to the lake (located near the end of the road).

Walton Lake (Crook County)
campground

Located in a scenic forest setting east of Prineville, 18-acre Walton Lake would be a more enjoyable place if it weren't so popular. Despite the inevitable summer crowds, the lake offers fair-to-good fishing for stocked rainbows, the vast majority of which are the typical legal-size fish. During the spring, prior to the first stocking, you can catch a few carry-overs from the previous year and these fish range from 13 to 16 inches. Also, ODFW sometimes stocks the lake with 2-pound and larger hatchery rainbows. In 2009, Walton was chemically treated to remove illegally introduced brown bullhead and small-mouth bass, and then in 2010, the U.S. Forest Service closed the campground and access for renovation work; ODFW re-stocked the lake in 2011.

Actually an artificial impoundment, Walton Lake offers a campground, which attracts noisy generator-powered RVs along with car and tent campers. The lake is perfectly suited to float tubes, pontoons, and canoes and some folks launch car-toppers (electric motors only). All methods produce here and the best way to assure a little peace and quiet is to fish the lake late in the fall.

Warm Springs River (Warm Springs Reservation)

The Warm Springs River, a tributary to the Lower Deschutes, flows entirely within the Warm Springs Indian Reservation and originates high in the Cascades, just across the summit from the headwaters of the Clackamas River. Currently a short reach of the river at popular Kah-Nee-Ta Resort is open to fishing for trout with a river-specific fishing permit available at the resort or at the store in Warm Springs.

Warren Lake (Hood River County)
hike-in

A good 5-acre brook trout lake, Warren sits northwest of Mt. Defiance in the Mark O. Hatfield Wilderness not far from the town of Hood River. To reach the trailhead, take Oak Street in Hood River (the main east-west route through town) to a south turn on 13th Street. Follow 13th as it leads out of town and continue to the old mill site of Dee. At Dee, follow the road to the right, across the Hood River and then head right again on Punchbowl Road. From Punchbowl Road, head left on FR 2820 and then turn right FR 2821. The short trail begins at the end of the road. At 4,900 feet, Mt. Defiance is the tallest peak in the Columbia Gorge and is a fairly easy climb from this side.

Wasco Lake (Mt. Jefferson Wilderness)
hike-in

Offering good fishing for small cutthroat trout, 20-acre Wasco Lake lies northeast from Three-Fingered Jack in the Mt. Jefferson Wilderness Area. The Pacific Crest Trail passes by Wasco Lake just to the west, assuring a steady stream of visiting anglers, but the fishing tends to hold up through the season. Easiest access to Wasco Lake is from the trailhead at Jack Lake Campground 2 miles to the southeast. To get there, follow Hwy 20 west from Sisters or east from the Santiam Summit. One mile east of Suttle Lake, turn north on FR 12. After about 5 miles, swing left on FR 1230 and then after 2 miles take another left on FR 1234, which leads to Jack Lake Campground. This entire area was burned over by the huge B&B Complex Fire of 2003, lending an entirely different look to a lake once surrounded by dense stands of fir and hemlock. The lake is now surrounded by dense stands of burnt snags.

White River (Wasco County)
no bait, hike-in

A major Deschutes River tributary, the White River derives its name from the light-gray tinge of its water—a result of flowing directly off the Palmer Glacier on Mt. Hood. The warmer the weather, the whiter the river. Despite the color, the White River is a good trout stream, especially at and below White River Falls State Park. The falls provide a natural barrier to upstream fish movement, but below the falls the river is inhabited by Deschutes River "redsides," the indigenous redband trout of the basin. They range from 6 to 16 inches, with a few even larger.

Access is by hiking down the river canyon from the state park. From the falls—a 90-foot plunge off a basalt shelf—the river flows about 2.5 miles down to the Deschutes River just below Sherar's Falls. Fishing here can be good any time of year and even when running off-color, the river is often productive. To reach the White River Falls State Park, follow Hwy 197 to Tygh Valley and then head east on the Sherar's Bridge Road. The state park is a day-use facility with a nice picnic area. Above the falls, the White River is largely inaccessible owing to extensive private property and within Mt. Hood National Forest, the fishing is mostly for tiny natives.

Wickiup Reservoir (Deschutes County)
campground, boat ramp, boat recommended, services

Sprawling across 10,000 acres at full pool, massive Wickiup Reservoir is the largest and among the most productive of the fisheries on Century Drive. This huge reservoir offers consistently good fishing for brown trout, kokanee, rainbow trout, and even a few brook trout. The browns and kokanee share most of the spotlight here, even though fishing for rainbow trout can be very good at times.

Wickiup's brown trout reach trophy proportions, with 2- to 5-pound fish being typical. Double-digit-weight brown trout are caught every year at Wickiup and a few fish exceed 20 pounds. In 1998, an angler from Salem landed a fish that weighed 26 pounds. These trophy browns grow fat on a rich diet that includes everything from leeches and insects to kokanee, whitefish, and chub minnows. Given the size of these fish, it should come as no surprise that most brown-

trout anglers fish large plugs and spoons. Trolling is popular here and, whether you troll or cast, boat fishing is the best way to fish Wickiup.

Used for irrigation storage, Wickiup Reservoir is formed by a dam on the Upper Deschutes River. The dam is on the northeast side of the reservoir and releases during the summer result in a steadily diminishing water table. Owing to two deep channels running through the reservoir, however, Wickiup rarely gets low enough to severely affect the fishing. During autumn, in fact, Wickiup reaches its low point for the year at the same time that brown trout become highly aggressive and ravenous. The October fishing can be excellent here, with the size of the average trout superceding the fact that you rarely catch more than a few of them in a day's time.

Except for the deep channels, Wickiup Reservoir is relatively shallow throughout. The extensive shallows offer ample room for large browns and rainbows to prowl for abundant food. During summer, however, the channels in the lake create cool-water refuge for the fish; so most anglers focus their efforts in and near the channels, using sonar to locate the deep water. The Deschutes Arm begins on the north side of the reservoir, adjacent to South Twin Lake, and winds southward. Near the middle of the reservoir, the Deschutes Channel meets the Davis Channel. These deeper areas are always the best bet for kokanee, which range from 10 to 20 inches. The size, range, and abundance of these fish tends to be cyclic, so as the kokanee reach the 16- to 20-inch mark every four or five years, they are fewer in number.

Popular kokanee hotspots include not only the channels at mid-reservoir, but also just out from the face of the dam and southwest toward Goose Island. Trolling is the rule for kokanee fishing, but lots of anglers bank fish from the dam during June and July, using small bits of bait, such as corn or eggs, fished near the bottom. Late in the summer, Wickiup's kokanee go into spawning mode and begin to gather near the mouth of the Deschutes Channel. Upstream from West South Twin Campground, the Deschutes Arm is closed to fishing from September 1 until October 31. This closure protects spawning kokanee.

As with the kokanee fishing, brown trout action on Wickiup begins as soon as the reservoir opens in late April. Early on, the browns tend to be scattered but warm weather sends most of them toward the shelter of the channels. The most successful strategy, regardless of your chosen angling method, is to target the brown trout early and late in the day. The situation changes in late October, when the fish often remain active throughout the day. During autumn, try the face of the dam, the Deschutes Arm up to the closed area and the Davis Channel.

Most Wickiup anglers would agree that trolling fairly fast produces the best results here, perhaps because doing so triggers the chase-and-eat mentality of big browns foraging on fish. A wide array of plugs, spoons, and other lures are effective and fly anglers enjoy fairly consistent action with large streamer flies fished fast on sinking lines.

Rainbow trout in Wickiup range from 10 to 24 inches in length and are most abundant in the channels. During late April and May, try the Davis Arm for both rainbows and big whitefish (1 to 3 pounds). Brookies here can reach several pounds, but are fairly scarce and limited mostly to the Deschutes Arm. Largemouth bass also inhabit the reservoir, apparently having escaped from Crane Prairie Reservoir. Currently there is no limit on bass or other warmwater gamefish.

Wickiup Reservoir offers eight different campgrounds ranging from full-service camps to primitive sites. Retreating shorelines during the summer drawdown leave the dispersed camping areas rather far from the water. Most of the campgrounds have boat ramps, but large boats should use the ramps at Gull Point Campground or at West South Twin Campground. Rental boats are available through Twin Lakes Resort (541-382-6432).

To reach Wickiup Reservoir, follow Hwy 97 south from Bend and turn west off the highway at Sunriver. From Sunriver, South Century Drive (Route 42) heads southwest, reaching the Deschutes River between Crane Prairie and Wickiup Reservoirs. Watch for the signs to Wickiup and Twin Lakes on FR 4260, which heads to Gull Point and the Deschutes Arm and then continues south to the dam. Or continue west to a left-hand turn on Route 46, which heads south to the Davis Arm and then on to Davis Lake. If you're arriving from Eugene, follow Hwy 58 over Willamette Pass and past Crescent Lake Junction to a left-hand turn onto CR 61, the Crescent Cut-off. Follow this road east to a left-hand turn on Road 46 heading to Davis Lake and then on to Wickiup Reservoir.

Windy Lakes (Klamath County)
hike-in
A series of three lovely mountain lakes located near the crest of the Cascades south of Crescent Lake, the Windy Lakes offer fair fishing for small brook trout. A big fish goes 10 inches and they are generally skinny and few in number. But they live in a pretty place that is fairly easy to get to via a steep, maintained, 5-mile-long trail leading south from southwest shore of Crescent Lake (about a half mile south of Tandy Bay Picnic Area). Both horses and mountain bikes are allowed on this trail, which connects with the Pacific Trail above the Windy Lakes. The lakes range from 8 to 14 acres and sit above 6,000 feet. Autumn is best here and the lake is usually accessible by June.

Winopee Lake (Three Sisters Wilderness)
hike-in, float tube recommended
One of the better lakes in the southern portion of the Three Sisters Wilderness Area, Winopee spans 40 acres and offers both brook trout and rainbow ranging from 6 to 13 inches with a few fish to 18 inches. Winopee's shoreline, swampy in places, meanders south creating a long, narrow arm complete with two little islands. For fly anglers, Winopee offers a superb summertime hatch of *Callibaetis* mayflies, along with damsels, Chironomids, and a mid-summer evening hatch of large "traveling sedge," a type of caddis.

You can reach Winopee by trail from the north or from the south. The shortest route covers 7.5 miles and begins at the end of the road leading through the Cultus Lake Campground. The trail follows the north shore of Cultus, passes the junction with the Corral Swamp Trail and then reaches a right-hand turn onto the Winopee Lake Trail. You will pass the Teddy Lakes along the way (see listing herein). You can cut more than 2 miles off the hike by boating over to the west side of Cultus. If you don't have a boat, ride your mountain bike along Cultus Lake until you reach the wilderness boundary (no bikes allowed in the wilderness) and then lock your bike to a tree out of sight from the trail.

North of Winopee Lake, the Snowshoe Lakes, along with several other small lakes, offer fair-to-good prospects for brook trout. The area is lightly fished compared to the more popular Mink Lake Basin a little further north. At the north end of Winopee Lake, the Snowshoe Lakes Trail continues deeper into the wilderness, first passing 18-acre Snowshoe Lake, the best of the three, before reaching 3-acre Middle Snowshoe and then 30-acre Upper Snowshoe. Also try Big Finger Lake and Puppy Lake.

The South Sister looms ahead as hikers take to the trail in the Three Sisters Wilderness.

Yapoah Lake (Three Sisters Wilderness)

hike-in, cross-country

A lightly fished and very scenic rainbow trout lake with a commanding view of the North Sister, Yapoah Lake spans about 10 acres and produces fish in the 8- to 14-inch range. Take Hwy 242 east from the McKenzie Highway or west from Sisters to the top of McKenzie Pass. At Dee Wright Observatory, take the Pacific Crest Trail south 2 miles to Matthieu Lakes and then follow the Scott Trail east about 1 mile. From there you can follow a faint trail south about a quarter mile to the lake or just make your own course cross-country. If you follow the Scott Trail to its junction with the Green Lakes Trail, you have gone a bit too far, though you can use this junction as a starting point for an easy southwesterly course to the lake. Most of the shoreline is easy to follow, but a float tube is useful here. The route is usually free of snow by late June and there are two additional short routes arriving from the east (consult the map for these). The lake offers a couple nice camp spots for backpackers.

Yoran Lake (Diamond Peak Wilderness)

hike-in

A large, scenic lake near the eastern flank of the twin summits of Mt. Yoran, Yoran Lake is a popular stop for hikers on the Pacific Crest Trail and for hikers headed up the Yoran Trail from West Bay on Crescent Lake to the northeast. A fairly easy hike, the trail covers about 4.5 miles and gains about 1,100 feet. Yoran's northeast shoreline offers great views of Diamond Peak, and the adventurous types can take a side trail from the lake up to the Pacific Crest Trail and then make an ascent of Mt. Yoran. The trail is usually free of snow by late June. Wildflower enthusiasts will find plenty of scenery here as the trail passes through an extensive boggy meadow just a mile from the trailhead and then ends at sub-alpine elevations.

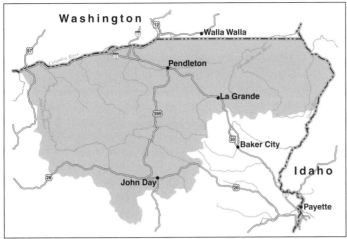

© 2007 Wilderness Adventures Press, Inc.

Northeast Zone

Northeastern Oregon is a region blessed by an angler-friendly combination of low human population density and myriad top-flight fishing opportunities. This zone encompasses the entirety of several major drainages, famous for their productive fisheries. Among them is the John Day River, one of the longest free-flowing streams in the country and home to a dense population of smallmouth bass and a good fishery for summer-run steelhead. Equally famous is the Grande Ronde River, also un-dammed, which supports strong runs of steelhead and lots of wild trout.

But the Northeast Zone also offers many lesser-known streams, including thoroughly wild rivers like the Minam, which flows almost entirely through roadless wilderness area and the forks of the Walla Walla, home to abundant native trout rarely seen by anyone other than local anglers. Oregon's least-known sizeable run of summer steelhead ascends the Imnaha River, tucked away in the northeastern-most corner of the state, while the unassuming Umatilla River, for many decades degraded by intense agriculture in the area, quietly offers revitalized runs of steelhead and salmon.

This region of Oregon also offers some of the state's most remote and seldom-fished lakes and streams. Only the hardiest and most adventurous anglers need apply for excursions into places like Joseph Creek or to the most isolated pack-in lakes of the Eagle Cap Wilderness. At the same time, however, the Northeast Zone offers countless productive, easy-access lakes and streams, the majority of which offer catch-and-keep opportunities.

Good maps are the key to unlocking the angling secrets of the Northeast Zone, especially if you venture off the beaten path and into the remote corners of Wallowa, Grant, Union, and Wheeler Counties. Topographical maps showing land ownership are invaluable and are available from both the U.S. Forest Service (ranger district maps) and the BLM. Both agencies sell maps by mail, although in many cases you must send a check ahead of time. As you study the maps, take note of the many unique geological and historical features of the area.

The Wallowa Mountains form one of Oregon's most picturesque backdrops and they break away to the east, where basalt crags plunge down to the Snake River forming Hells Canyon. Meanwhile the John Day River, well to the west and southwest of the Wallowa's, gathers its branches in the forested country of the expansive Blue Mountains and forms a substantial presence through the pastoral valley near the town of John Day. Soon, however, the John Day descends into one of the state's longest, most massive and most remote canyons. The increasingly popular float through the river's lower canyon covers some 70 river miles and takes upwards of a week.

As you travel northeastern Oregon, take time to introduce yourself to the region's many quaint and quiet little communities and to sample their unique offerings. You won't soon forget a meal at La Grande's Foley Station or Pendleton's Rafael's, and Terminal Gravity Brewery in Enterprise crafts ales well worthy of the day-long drive from western Oregon. And that's just a sampling.

Meanwhile bring your camera, for the rivers and lakes of northeastern Oregon are usually as scenic as they are productive.

Northeast Zone Contacts

Oregon Department of Fish & Wildlife
Northeast Regional Office
107 20th Street
LaGrande, OR 97850
541-963-2138

ODFW, John Day Watershed District Office
73471 Mytinger Lane
Pendleton, OR 97801
541-276-2344

ODFW, Baker City Field Office
2995 Hughes Lane
Baker City, OR 97814
541-523-5832

ODFW, Enterprise Field Office
65495 Alder Slope Road
Enterprise, OR 97828
541-426-3279

ODFW, Heppner Field Office
54173 Hwy 74, P.O. Box 363
Heppner, OR 97836
541-676-5230

ODFW, John Day Field Office
P.O. Box 9
John Day, OR 97845
541-575-1167

ODFW, Wenaha Wildlife Area
85060 Grande Ronde Road
Enterprise, OR 97828
541-828-7721

BLM, Baker Resource Area Headquarters
3165 10th Street
Baker City, OR 97918
541-523-1256

Umatilla National Forest Headquarters
2517 SW Hailey Avenue
Pendleton, OR 97801
541-278-3716

Heppner Ranger District Office
P.O. Box 7
Heppner, OR 97836
541-676-9187

North Fork John Day Ranger District Office
P.O. Box 158
Ukiah, OR 97880
541-427-3231

Walla Walla Ranger District Office
1415 West Rose
Walla Walla, WA 99362
509-522-6290

Wallowa-Whitman National Forest Headquarters
1515 Dewey Avenue
Baker City, OR 97814
541-523-6391

Wallowa Mountains Office
Eagle Cap Ranger District Office/
Wallowa Valley Ranger District
Hells Canyon National Recreation Area
201 East Second Street
Joseph, Oregon 97846
541-426-5546

Wallowa Mountains Visitor Center
115 Tejaka
Enterprise, OR 97828
541-426-4978

LaGrande Ranger District Office
3502 Hwy. 30
La Grande, Oregon 97850
541-963-7186

Pine Ranger District Office
General Delivery
Halfway, Oregon 97834
541-742-7511

Unity Ranger District Office
P.O. Box 29
Unity, OR 97884
541-446-3351

Aldrich Ponds (Grant County)

hike-in

Two walk-in ponds on the north side of Aldrich Mountain, on the ODFW's Phillip W. Schneider Wildlife Area, Aldrich Ponds are regularly stocked with rainbow trout fingerlings. The wildlife area was known as Murderer's Creek Wildlife Area until political correctness visited the ODFW. The headquarters are located near milepost 132 on Hwy 26, one-quarter mile east of Dayville and 30 miles west of John Day. To reach the ponds, which span 5 (Roosevelt Pond) and 8 (Stewart Pond) acres, respectively, head east from Dayville for 8 miles until you reach the Flat Creek Road Bridge spanning the John Day. From there it's a 5-mile drive over a rugged 4-wheel-drive road that is impassable when wet, followed by a hike of about 1 mile. The daily limit is two trout, and the ponds are open from late May through October (check current synopsis). Generally these ponds are managed to produce fast-growing trout; they are planted in fairly limited numbers as fingerlings (typically 750 annually for both ponds) and the fish grow rapidly in the fertile water. A few of the fish reach 20 inches. Two other very small hike-in ponds on the wildlife area are also stocked periodically (Wiley Gulch Pond and Aldrich Gulch Pond). Check with the ODFW office in John Day, (541) 575-1167, for directions and recent stocking updates.

Aneroid Lake (Eagle Cap Wilderness)

hike-in

Popular and rather heavily used, Aneroid Lake is a frequent destination for both day hikers and overnighters. By Eagle Cap Wilderness standards, this highly scenic 39-acre lake is easy to reach. From the trailhead south of Wallowa Lake, the East Fork Wallowa Trail (#1804) reaches Aneroid at the 6-mile mark. The first 2 miles are quite steep, switch-backing up more than 1,600 feet. After that the route is fairly easy going, through well-traveled but beautiful country. Aneroid, which has a number of nice campsites, offers brook trout and rainbows that occasionally reach 16 inches. They typically range from 7 to 10 inches.

Aneroid Lake's south shore is the site of the old Aneroid Lake Resort and the six rustic cabins there were built by then-owner Charles Seeber between 1896 and 1956. Originally the lodge featured nine cabins and a boathouse. The 60-acre site remains in private hands to this day and the cabins—also private property—are used both summer and winter. Like most of the Eagle Cap lakes, Aneroid is accessible by mid-July.

Anson Wright Pond (Morrow County)

campground

Morrow County's Anson Wright Memorial Park offers a small, handicapped-accessible pond regularly stocked with rainbow trout. The park is located along SR 207, 25 miles south of Heppner. A large camping area accommodates RVs and tent campers and Rock Creek flows through the park providing additional fishing opportunity.

Barth Pond (Umatilla County)

float tube recommended

Barth Pond is an old rock quarry pond supporting populations of crappie and largemouth bass. The pond spans about an acre in size and can get extremely low during drought years. Located near Interstate-84 east of Hermiston, Barth Pond fishes best from mid- to late spring and on summer evenings. Take Exit 193 from the Interstate (5 miles east of Stansfield) and then take the first right-hand turn on Whitmore Road. Follow Whitmore east for about 1.5 miles and then head north .3 of a mile on Nolan Market Road. Parking is on the wide pullout alongside the road.

Bear Creek (Wallowa County)

no bait

A small tributary to the Wallowa River, Bear Creek offers fair-to-good fishing for wild redband trout and wild brook trout. Most range from 5 to 10 inches, but an occasional redband from the lower end of the creek spans 12 to 14 inches. Brookies predominate in the upper end of Bear Creek. Entering the river at the town of Wallowa, Bear Creek is restricted to artificial lures and flies and is a nice dry fly stream during summer and autumn. Bear Creek Road follows the creek south from town, running right alongside for several miles, but mostly on private property. Be sure to ask permission to fish the lower end of the creek. A mile south of the national forest border, the road ends at Boundary Campground and from there the Bear Creek Trail follows the stream for almost 20 miles to its source at Bear Lake in the Eagle Cap Wilderness. In Wallowa, watch for the Bear Creek Road turn-off heading west from where the main highway takes a 90-degree turn midway through town.

Beaver Creek Reservoir (Union County)

no bait

During 2002, Beaver Creek Reservoir was opened to public access for the first time in 25 years. The lake is full of small brook trout, along with a few rainbows, and has since served as the sight for Free Fishing Day during June. From La Grande or Baker City, follow I-84 to the Ladd Canyon Exit and then follow Ladd Canyon Road to FR 4305. When you reach the gate at the end of the road, hike for about 1.5 miles to reach the reservoir. Check with ODFW in La Grande for Free Fishing Day dates. Beaver Creek Reservoir appears on many maps as La Grande Reservoir and it serves as a back-up water supply for the nearby city of La Grande.

Big Creek (Umatilla National Forest)

campground

A good small-stream fishery for brook trout in the 5- to 9-inch range, with an occasional 12-incher, Big Creek flows south into the North Fork John Day River southeast from Ukiah. Redband trout also inhabit the stream, mostly in its remote lowermost reach. Forest Road 52 crosses Big Creek 20 miles from Ukiah and a nice trail heads down the stream from Big

Creek Meadow Campground. The Tower Fire of 1996 burned over much of this area. Big Creek fishes best during early summer. Once the water drops, the fish get terribly skittish but mid-summer through fall, fly fishing can be quite good for those who hike down the creek.

Big Sheep Creek (Wallowa County)

A good fishery for wild rainbow trout, Big Sheep Creek flows northeasterly from the Salt Creek Summit area on the east side of the Wallowa Mountains. The creek is accessible through a series of primitive roads leading into the canyon and a trail that follows part of the stream. A rugged access road follows most of the lower creek from its confluence with Little Sheep Creek 3 miles south of the town of Imnaha. The road-accessible portion of Big Sheep Creek flows almost exclusively through private ranchlands, so be sure to seek permission to fish these waters. The creek is closed to fishing for salmon and steelhead.

Billy Jones Lake (Eagle Cap Wilderness)

hike-in

A small lake sitting at 8,300 feet along Hurricane Divide in the Eagle Cap Wilderness, Billy Jones Lake supports small, wild brook trout. Easiest access is to follow the trail to nearby Echo Lake and then climb over the ridge dividing the two lakes. The trail begins at Hurricane Trailhead south of Enterprise and west of Joseph. When you arrive in Enterprise from the west, follow the highway into town and around a 90-degree turn to the right. When the highway turns 90 degrees to the left, continue straight ahead, heading south on Hurricane Creek Road. The trail begins at the end of the road and leads 5 miles up to a right-hand turn on the 3-mile-long trail to Echo Lake.

Black Canyon Creek (Ochoco National Forest)

hike-in

Black Canyon Creek is the centerpiece of the 13,000-acre Black Canyon Wilderness Area and drains into the South Fork John Day after a tumultuous 12-mile tumble through one of the regions prettiest canyons. The creek's lower end snakes through a gorge lined by cliffs, and here the trail requires hikers to continuously ford the small creek. Black Canyon Creek offers fair-to-good fishing for small, wild trout. They are eager to pounce on dry flies. The best times are June and July, and then autumn; especially mid-September through October.

Access to the creek is strictly from the trail system because the canyon is too steep to negotiate cross country. The easiest and prettiest route is to start at the creek's mouth adjacent to the South Fork John Day and follow the trail through the gorge, heading upstream. From Dayville on Hwy 26, follow the South Fork John Day heading south on CR 42 for about 13 miles to the Black Canyon Trailhead. There's a small campground a few miles north of the trailhead.

Black Mountain Pond

see Walla Walla R.D. Ponds

Blue Lake (Eagle Cap Wilderness)

hike-in

Sitting at 7,703 feet and just south of Minam Lake, Blue Lake is a very pretty, lightly fished brook trout lake in the Eagle Cap Wilderness. The brookies range from 6 to 12 inches and are fairly abundant. The lake is 60 feet deep and covers about 30 acres. Just over the ridgeline to the west of Blue Lake, Wild Sheep Lake supports small, wild brook trout and is rarely visited. From the town of Lostine, head south on Lostine River Road. At the end of the road is Two Pan Trailhead and from there, the hike to Minam Lake covers 6 miles. From the south shore of Minam Lake, take the right-hand fork leading almost a mile up to Blue Lake.

Boardman Pond (Morrow County)

A good 1-acre bluegill pond located at the community of Boardman along I-84, Boardman Pond also supports white crappie and largemouth bass. It sits half a mile west from Boardman, south of the Interstate at Exit 164. The pond fishes best in the mornings and evenings during summer and is also a prime bird-watching area.

Boundary Pond

see Walla Walla R.D. Ponds

Brandon Pond (Grant County)

A 1-acre pond adjacent to the ODFW screen shop in John Day, Brandon Pond is stocked several times during the spring with legal-size rainbow trout. Most anglers enjoy fair success by still fishing with bait.

Bridge Creek (John Day drainage)

Bridge Creek is a lengthy tributary of the John Day River, reaching the river about halfway between Service Creek and Clarno. The creek flows through the famous Painted Hills, which are part of the John Day Fossil Beds National Monument, but the best trout fishing is found further upstream in the Ochoco National Forest, south from Mitchell. Wild redband trout here typically range from 5 to 10 inches, though the density of trout is relatively low. Fishing ranges from fair to good, depending on your exact location and on stream flows.

To get to Bridge Creek, follow Hwy 26 to Mitchell and then head south on CR 8, which becomes FR 22 upon reaching the Ochoco National Forest boundary. This road, however, swings away from the creek before reaching national forest lands, so access to the best reaches of Bridge Creek is rather precarious. The stream's upper stretch—diminutive but good for small, wild trout—is encompassed in the Bridge Creek Wilderness and like most of the creek from the wilderness boundary down to Mitchell access is by hiking.

This fishing is only for the bushwhacking adventurous type because there are no formal trails within this tiny wilderness area. Your best bet is to first head from Prineville to Walton Lake (see directions under Walton Lake in the Central Zone section). Then continue past Walton Lake on FR 22 and then FR 2630 up past Slide Mountain. At the junction with FR 450, turn right and drive 2 miles to Pisgah Springs, where there is a small campground. You will cross Bridge Creek just before you get there. From Pisgah Springs, hike northeasterly along the creek. Or follow FR 450 until it ends. You can then hike into the canyon from there. Be sure to consult a good topo map, as this is not easy country.

A 4-mile-long stretch of Bridge Creek flows alongside Hwy 26 west of Mitchell, requiring landowner access for fishing. North of the highway, Bridge Creek Road follows the stream through the Painted Hills. From the highway downstream to the Bear Creek confluence, fishing can be fair for wild redband trout, a few of which reach 12 or more inches. Again, respect private property.

Buck Creek (Umatilla National Forest)
see Umatilla River, North Fork

Bull Prairie Reservoir (Umatilla National Forest)
campground, boat ramp

Fairly popular and usually quite productive, 27-acre Bull Prairie Reservoir is located in the Umatilla National Forest about 15 miles north of Spray. From Spray (on the John Day River) or from Heppner to the north, follow SR 203 into the national forest. Just north of Fairview Campground or a few miles south of the Morrow County line, watch for the signed east turn to Bull Prairie Reservoir on FR 2039. The reservoir offers both rainbow and brook trout ranging from 8 to 18 inches. Most of the fish run from 9 to 13 inches in length. The reservoir has a campground, day-use picnic area and two boat launches, but motors are prohibited. Bull Prairie Reservoir generally fishes best from April through June and in the fall. During summer, when weed growth can be problematic, a small watercraft of some kind can be helpful.

Butte Creek (John Day drainage)
A small stream with limited trout-fishing opportunities, Butte Creek flows alongside the highway between Spray and Fossil offering fair access to the stream's upper reach. The lower end of the stream flows entirely through private property. Best fishing is usually during May and June.

Butter Creek (Morrow/Umatilla Counties)
A small stream with fair wild trout populations in its upper reaches, Butter Creek flows north from the Black Mountain area of the Blue Mountains. The old Heppner Highway (SR 74) crosses the creek at Vinson, about 10 miles west from Pilot Rock. From there, Gurdane Road follows the creek south and Butter Creek Road follows it north. The entire creek flows across private ranch and farmlands, so anglers must seek permission to fish here.

Cable Creek, South Fork (Umatilla National Forest)
A small wild trout stream in the Umatilla National Forest east of Ukiah, the South Fork of Cable Creek harbors redband trout ranging from 5 to 10 inches. Forest Road 52 crosses the creek about 16 miles east of town. The best fishing is in the Round Meadow section about half a mile north of FR 52. Deeper water here provides good summer habitat for the fish whereas the rest of the stream tends to get very low by mid-summer. Flyfishing is the best method. Follow Soap Hill Road south out of Ukiah (it becomes FR 52 when you reach the forest boundary).

Camas Creek (John Day drainage)
campground

Flowing through the town of Ukiah on its way to join the North Fork John Day River, Camas Creek offers fair fishing for wild redband trout. Best fishing is during early summer, but autumn fishing can be good on the lower end of the creek. Highway 395 follows Camas Creek south for 12 miles from Ukiah to the North Fork, providing ready access. Upstream from Ukiah, SR 244 parallels the creek through a mix of private and public land. Steelhead from the river ascend Camas Creek, but fishing for them is illegal.

Canyon Creek (Grant County)
campground

An easy-access, scenic little trout stream, Canyon Creek flows alongside Hwy 395 for more than half of the stream's 25-mile run to the John Day River at the town of John Day. The upper half of the creek is easy to access from FR 15. Canyon Creek is home to wild redband and cutthroat trout, along with a few brook trout. The fish typically range from 6 to 12 inches. The best fishing occurs in the stretch from Canyon Creek Meadows Reservoir down to Bear Gulch, near Hwy 395, but even the oft-fished waters along the highway can produce decent catches for those who put some time into the fishing. This is good water for both spin fishing and fly casting. Pick out a length of stream and work up or down the creek for a mile or more. Nice campgrounds are located at the reservoir and on the creek a few miles downstream, as well as near the Star Ridge Summit on Hwy 395 south of the turnoff on FR15.

Canyon Creek Meadows Reservoir (Grant County)
campground, boat ramp

At times a popular 25-acre reservoir from John Day in the Malheur National Forest, Canyon Meadows Reservoir has a leaky dam currently under study for either repair or removal. It does not hold water through summer. Wild cutthroat and brook trout in the impoundment range from six to 16 inches and most anglers still-fish with bait, although both spin- and fly-casting can be productive. To get there, follow Hwy. 395 south from John Day and head east on the Canyon Creek

Road (Forest Road 15), leading to a signed left-hand turn onto FR1520. From the south, follow the highway to Seneca and then head east on the Bear Creek Road (FR16). At Parish Cabin Campground, head west on FR 15 a few miles to the right-hand turn onto FR1520. Canyon Creek Meadows Reservoir—alternately referred to as Canyon Meadows Reservoir or Canyon Creek Reservoir—fishes best from April through June.

Catched-Two Lake (Eagle Cap Wilderness)

hike-in

A fair producer of small brook trout, Catched-Two Lake sits in a narrow, rocky bowl at nearly 8,000 feet in the Eagle Cap Wilderness Area. From the town of Lostine, follow Lostine River Road until it ends at Two Pan Campground/Trailhead. Head south on the West Lostine River Trail for about a mile to the side trail that leads steeply up to Catched-Two Lake.

Catherine Creek (Union County)

campground

A popular trout and steelhead stream among anglers from the surrounding area, Catherine Creek provides a scenic escape from the summer heat of the Grande Ronde and Powder River Valleys nearby. Between autumn and mid-spring, summer run steelhead ascend the creek via the Columbia, Snake, and Grande Ronde Rivers, respectively. Virtually all of these steelhead are of hatchery origin and only fin-clipped steelhead may be kept. Most of the fish show up during late winter and early spring, so they are usually fairly dark colored after overwintering in the rivers. The season is open until April 15 (be sure to check current regulations). Access to good steelhead water is restricted by private property, but bank anglers converge on Catherine Creek State Park, at a few places along the highway, and just below the town of Union. The popular state park is located 8 miles south of Union on SR 203.

Trout fishing on Catherine Creek ranges from poor to good, largely depending on the particular stretch of the creek. The best fishing is above the state park, extending into both main forks of the creek in the Wallowa-Whitman National Forest. Rarely does this portion of the creek produce large trout, but it abounds with small, wild fish ranging from 5 to 9 inches. The North Fork originates in the Eagle Cap Wilderness and its hike-in reaches are scenic and fairly productive for small trout. The South Fork is now essentially roadless in its middle reaches after the forest service gated several roads in the area.

To reach the forks, follow SR 203 south past Catherine Creek State Park and then turn east on Catherine Creek Lane (which becomes FR 7785). After about 3 miles, watch for a right-hand fork at Spur 700. This road is gated, but you can park here for the rather adventurous hike up the South Fork. FR 7785 continues along the North Fork to North Fork Catherine Creek Campground and from there a good trail follows the creek into the wilderness area.

Cavender Pond (Grant County)

A 5-acre reservoir stocked regularly during spring with rainbow trout, Cavender Pond sits half a mile north of the town of Monument and provides fair-to-good fishing during May and June. Fishing from the bank with bait is the most popular and productive method. Monument lies east of Kimberly on Hwy 19.

Chesnimnus Creek (Wallowa County)

campground

Hosting a small, protected run of wild summer steelhead, Chesnimnus Creek is a tributary of Joseph Creek, located north and east of the town of Enterprise. The creek offers only fair fishing for small, wild rainbows. Best access is in the vicinity of Vigne Campground. From Enterprise, head north on SR 3 for about 12 miles to a signed right-hand turn on FR 46. Follow FR 46 to a right-hand turn on FR 4625, leading to the campground.

Cheval Lake (Eagle Cap Wilderness)

hike-in, cross-country

A good producer of 6- to 10-inch brook trout, 10-acre Cheval Lake sits at 7,800 feet rather off the beaten path in the Eagle Cap Wilderness. From the town of Lostine, head south to the end of Lostine River Road. At Two Pan Campground/Trailhead, take the West Lostine River Trail heading south for 2.4 miles to a right-hand turn on the Elkhorn Creek Trail, continuing 5 miles to the junction with the Granite Trail. From there, pick up the trail heading southwest to Cheval or pick your way over the highest ridge, for a scenic approach down to the lake. Be sure to consult the map.

Chimney Lake (Eagle Cap Wilderness)

hike-in

A very scenic lake situated near Lookout Mountain in the Eagle Cap Wilderness, Chimney offers very good action for small brook trout. A 10-inch fish is a trophy here. Nearby Hobo Lake and Wood Lake also offer trout-fishing opportunities (see separate listings). Spanning 30 acres and sitting at an elevation of 7,604 feet, Chimney provides an idyllic view of the high ridgelines on both sides. The trail up to Chimney Lake gains nearly 2,600 feet in just 6 miles, most of it coming by way of an arduously endless series of switchbacks in the first 2 miles. The climb begins at the Bowman Trailhead on the Lostine River and passes Chimney Lake at the 5.3-mile mark. Follow SR 82 to the little town of Lostine and then head south on Lostine River Road, continuing past Williamson Campground and past Lostine Guard Station.

Cold Springs Reservoir (Umatilla County)

An irrigation-storage facility at Cold Springs Wildlife Refuge just east of Hermiston, this reservoir provides good fishing for crappie, along with smallmouth bass, bullhead, and yellow perch. The crappie can grow quite large here and during cycles of good water quality and supply, the fish range from 10 to 14 inches with a few fish reaching 15 to 16 inches. Bass range from half a pound to 4 pounds, with an occasional larger fish.

Bank access to the reservoir is limited both by regulation and by difficulty of getting there in places, so shore anglers usually fish from the dam. The boat ramp is usable unless and until the summer drawdown leaves it high and dry, but you can still launch by hand using small prams, canoes, or float tubes. A boat or float tube allows you to work the brushy edges during spring, where crappie congregate. Try ¼-ounce jigs in a variety of colors and experiment with depth until you find fish. Only electric motors are allowed on the reservoir. Be sure to check current seasonal closures as Cold Springs Reservoir is closed at certain times to minimize disturbance of migratory birds. For details, call 509-545-8588. The current standard regulations state: March 1 through September 30, according to State regulations. Bank fishing is permitted from October 1 through the end of February in a designated area near parking area B. Boating, only in non-motorized boats and boats with electric motors, is permitted from March 1 through September 30.

From Hermiston, follow SR 207 east for about 7 miles to a right-hand turn onto Wall's Road and then another right turn onto Tabor Road, leading to the dam. At full pool, Cold Springs Reservoir spans 1,600 acres and has 12 miles of shoreline.

Conforth Ponds (Umatilla Reservation)

Prior to being purchased from Conforth, these small ponds, located alongside SR 730 east of Umatilla, offered bass fishing. They are now part of the Wanaket Wildlife Area owned by the Umatilla Tribe and they provide wetland habitat to mitigate for similar habitat losses associated with the construction of McNary Dam. There are no fishing opportunities, though the tribe does offer regulated waterfowl and upland bird hunting.

Cottonwood Creek (Grant/Wheeler Counties)
hike-in

Reputedly offering fair fishing for wild rainbow trout during high-flow years, Cottonwood Creek reaches the John Day River near the top end of Picture Gorge. The creek's lower half flows through a mix of private and BLM land, while the upper half lies within the Ochoco National Forest. Trails, originating on FR 38 climb down into the canyon from the south. The Ochoco National Forest Map will get you pointed in the right direction.

Crawfish Lake (Elkhorn Range)
hike-in

A small, pretty lake on the west slope of the Elkhorn Range northwest of Baker City, Crawfish Lake is full of brook trout stunted by overpopulation. There is no limit on the size or number of brookies taken from the lake. Exit I-84 at North Powder and head west on the Elkhorn Drive Scenic Route, following the signs to Anthony Lakes and continuing about 4 miles past the ski area to the trailhead for Crawfish Lake, on the left-hand side of the road. The hike covers about 1 mile.

Crescent Lake (Eagle Cap Wilderness)
hike-in

Brook trout from 6 to 14 inches provide good action at 24-acre Crescent Lake, located in the popular Lake Basin area of the Eagle Cap Wilderness. To get there, head for Wallowa Lake south of Joseph. Then drive around Wallowa Lake and contin-ue south to the end of the road and the trailhead (about 1 mile south of Wallowa Lake). Follow the West Fork Wallowa Trail for about 5.5 miles to a right-hand turn up the Moccasin Trail, which leads into Lakes Basin. From the trail junction, the hike to Crescent Lake covers almost 5 more miles. You can camp at any of several pre-existing sites around Crescent Lake, but stay well back from the lakeshore. This area draws quite a lot of visitors during July and August, but fishing holds up all summer. The ideal time to visit Lakes Basin is later in September when the crowds disperse.

Cutsforth Park Ponds (Morrow County)
campground

Cutsforth Park is a pretty little county park located in the forested hills 22 miles southeast of Heppner on Willow Creek Road. The two interconnected ponds at the park are regularly stocked with rainbow trout and are handicap accessible. The park's campground offers 20 full hookup RV spaces, 16 camp spaces, and tent spaces.

Desolation Creek (John Day drainage)

A good fishery for redband, brook, and cutthroat trout, Desolation Creek is a scenic mountain stream flowing into the North Fork John Day River south from Ukiah. This is a good fly-fishing creek, with the best trout populations near and upstream from the Umatilla National Forest boundary. Access is good, but steep hillsides leading down to the creek help thin out the would-be crowds. From Ukiah, follow Hwy 395 south 14 miles to a left-hand turn on Texas Bar Road (FR 55). After 1 mile, turn right on FR 10, which follows Desolation Creek for most of the stream's length. Desolation Creek is closed to fishing for salmon and steelhead.

Diamond Lake (Eagle Cap Wilderness)
hike-in

Spanning about 11 acres and full of brook trout, Diamond Lake sits at 7,041 feet in the southwestern corner of the Eagle Cap Wilderness. Its outlet forms Elk Creek, which drains into the Minam River to the north. If you are traveling the Minam, you can make a 3.5-mile side trip up the Elk Creek Trail to sample Diamond Lake, whose brookies range from 6 to 13 inches. Otherwise, the shortest route to Diamond Lake is from the south, by way of either the Sand Pass Trail or the West Eagle Trail. The latter route allows you to more readily fish Tombstone Lake, which also offers brook trout. To reach the West Eagle Trailhead, follow SR 203 south from Unity or northeast from I-84. At Medical Springs, head east on FR 67 (CR 71 until you reach the national forest). Stay on FR 67 until you reach a left-hand turn on FR 77, leading north to the trailhead and campground. From here, the hike to Diamond Lake covers about 8 steep miles.

Divide Well Pond (Umatilla National Forest)
campground

A small, productive trout and bullhead pond west of Ukiah, Divide Well Pond is annually stocked with legal-size rainbows.

Nearby Potamus point, southwest of the pond, offers a spectacular vantage point overlooking Potamus Creek and the North Fork of the John Day River. From Ukiah, head west on FR 53 and then turn left on FR 5312, following it until it ends at a "T" intersection. Turn right onto FR 5320 and continue about 1.5 miles to the intersection of FR 5327 and FR 5320. The pond is located north of the 5320 and west of the 5327 road. An access road on the 5327 allows visitors to park at the edge of the pond. All methods of fishing work well in this pond, particularly in the early summer. Divide Well Campground is located about .75 of a mile from the pond along FR 5327.

Douglas Lake (Eagle Cap Wilderness)
hike-in

A pretty and popular lake in the heavily used Lakes Basin Area of the Eagle Cap Wilderness, Douglas offers good fishing for small brook trout. Sitting at 7,326 feet, Douglas Lake spans 44 acres and reaches a depth of about 80 feet. If you camp here, use only the existing campsites set well back from the lakeshore. Trails arrive at Lakes Basin from all directions, with the trailhead just south of Wallowa Lake being the most popular. However, the East Lostine River Trail from Two Pan Trailhead is slightly shorter, reaching Douglas Lake after 8.5 miles and begins 1,000 feet higher.

Downey Lake (Wallowa County)
private waters

Drift Fence Pond
see Ukiah Area Ponds

Eagle Creek (Union/Baker Counties)
see Southeast Zone

Eagle Lake (Eagle Cap Wilderness)
see Southeast Zone

Echo Lake (Eagle Cap Wilderness)
hike-in

A very pretty and fairly productive 7-acre lake supporting small, skinny brook trout, Echo Lake sits at 8,372 feet on Hurricane Divide in the Eagle Cap Wilderness. The trail begins at Hurricane Trailhead south of Enterprise and west of Joseph. When you arrive in Enterprise from the west, follow the highway into town and around a 90-degree turn to the right. When the highway turns 90 degrees to the left, continue straight ahead, heading south on Hurricane Creek Road. The trail begins at the end of the road and leads 5 miles up to a right-hand turn on the 3-mile-long trail to Echo Lake. The trail is generally free of snow by the first week in July.

Ellis Pond
see Ukiah Area Ponds

Frances Lake (Eagle Cap Wilderness)
hike-in

One of the better trout fisheries in the Eagle Cap Wilderness, Frances Lake supports wild brook trout to 12 or more inches and stocked rainbow trout averaging about 9 or 10 inches. Most of the fish range from 7 to 10 inches, but Frances supports quite a few 10- to 13-inchers. There are a couple different routes to 30-acre Frances Lake, but the formal route assures that you'll generally see few other anglers here: The trail covers almost 8 miles and gains 2,500 feet in an exhausting series of switchbacks. The trailhead is on the Lostine River south from the town of Lostine (Bowman/Francis Lake Trailhead). Experienced backpackers might want to haul in a float tube and camping gear.

Frazier Lake (Eagle Cap Wilderness)
see Glacier Lake

Glacier Lake (Eagle Cap Wilderness)
hike-in

A very pretty and popular destination in the Eagle Cap Wilderness, Glacier Lake sits at the foot of 9,572-foot Eagle Cap, one of the highest peaks in the Wallow's. This large, deep lake offers fair-to-good fishing for small brook trout, with an occasional fish reaching 12 or 13 inches. The lake is accessible by mid-July, sometimes earlier and is reached from the trailhead at Wallowa Lake. Follow the West Fork Wallowa Trail south about 10 miles to Frazier Lake and then continue climbing another 2 miles to reach the north shore of Glacier Lake.

Frazier Lake, much smaller and a thousand feet below Glacier Lake, is generally the better brook trout fishery of the two. Frazier's trout are similar in size, typically ranging from 5 to 9 inches, but the lake usually seems to support a few more 12-inchers. Both lakes are fairly popular with hikers, but anglers always seem to be in the minority and these lakes offer ample room to spread out. If you're traveling by horseback, bring a float tube. All methods work, with fly angling being especially productive for those with sinking lines and a selection of basic wet flies. *Callibaetis* mayflies hatch almost every day during the summer, and both caddisflies and black flying ants show up regularly. If the wind stays down, you can anticipate good dry-fly opportunities.

Grande Ronde Lake (Elkhorn Range)
campground

A very popular 10-acre lake in the Elkhorn Range northwest from Baker City, Grande Ronde Lake offers good fishing for small, stocked rainbow and brook trout. From North Powder or Baker City, just follow the signs to Anthony Lakes. The turn-off to Grande Ronde Lake is a mile west from the road to Anthony Lake. These lakes are generally accessible by late June and fishing holds up through September and often into October. Grande Ronde Lake is popular with fly anglers who use float tubes and pontoon boats.

Grande Ronde River (Wallowa County)
campground, boat ramp, services

Among the premier fisheries for upper Columbia Basin summer-run steelhead, the Grande Ronde River flows for nearly 220 miles through northeastern Oregon and southeastern Washington. The Grande Ronde meets the Snake River at Hellar Bar in Washington, about an hour's drive south from Clarkston. Many Oregon-based anglers buy a Washington license to fish the Washington portion of the river, especially during the prime season from October through early December.

The arrival of the bulk of the river's steelhead varies somewhat from year to year and is largely dependent on water temperatures cool enough to draw fish out of the Snake River. Typically the best action begins around the end of September and, most years, the October fishing is excellent, especially for those looking to rise steelhead to skated dry flies. The Grande

Grande Ronde River

Ronde is widely known as a superb fly-rod steelhead stream, but gear anglers are equally at home here. At the river's mouth—on the Washington side—is a 3-mile-long fly-only stretch that attracts lots of fly anglers during autumn. To get there, first head for Clarkston and then head north on Snake River Road until you reach the mouth of the Grande Ronde River at Hellar Bar. From there you can drive along the river for about 3 miles. Many anglers continue upstream on foot. A large BLM camping area usually fills up during the prime weeks of autumn.

The next easy drive-in access upstream is at Boggan's Oasis, located where Washington SR 129 crosses the river. South from Boggan's and up the steep grade, the road crosses into Oregon, becoming Oregon SR 3 and leading south to Enterprise. The reach—in Washington—from Boggan's down to the mouth (or rather to the end of the road 3 miles above the mouth) is a popular float, but should only be navigated by experienced boaters familiar with several severe hazards. One in particular, The Narrows Rapids, is a Class III or IV chute (depending on flows) that demands scouting. Float the river with someone who has run The Narrows before trying it yourself. The Narrows is located 4.5 river miles above the mouth and is followed by Class III Bridge Rapids, a short length of heavy water located just upstream from Concrete Bridge, which marks the end of the road access described above.

Upstream from Boggan's Oasis (which offers food, camping, and shuttle service), Asotin CR 100 (Grande Ronde Road) follows the river upstream to the Oregon border and the tiny town of Troy. The road provides excellent access to the Grande Ronde and steelhead fishing along the road is usually quite good from mid-autumn through spring. Troy marks the end of the drive-along access to the river and serves as a popular departure point for boaters making the 46-mile float down from the Minam River near Hwy 82. This float is popular with whitewater enthusiasts, who float this section during the high flows of spring. They are followed by the splash-and-giggle crowd during summer.

Serious anglers make up a minority of the river traffic, but trout fishing can be very good in this designated Wild & Scenic section, especially when the big stoneflies hatch during June and July and again during autumn when caddis hatches are quite prolific. The best trout fishing occurs when the spring runoff flows subside and, by comparison to spring, the autumn flows are quite meager, exposing lots more rock and making for a much slower journey down to Troy. The best trout fishing occurs at flows less than 2,000 cfs at Troy, but such flows also make for slow going in places. Be sure to scout all rapids.

Floaters on this section must adhere to a variety of strict regulations. You must have a self-issue river permit. These are available at the launch sites. In addition, all parties must use a fire pan if fires are used at camp and all parties must carry and use a portable toilet. No motorized equipment is allowed on the river between Sheep Creek (river mile 80) and Wildcat Creek (river mile 53.5). Call the BLM to obtain a river map to help you locate campsites, landmarks, and rapids (541-523-1256).

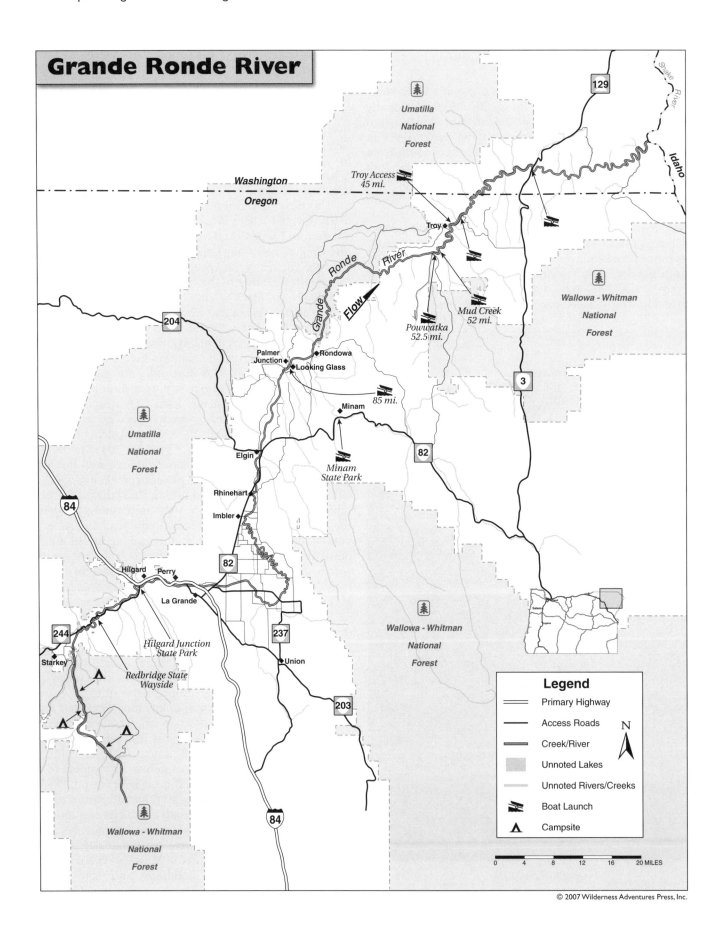

Grande Ronde River

The typical multi-day float on the Grande Ronde begins on the lower 10 miles of the Wallowa River. The Wallowa—and then the Grande Ronde—plunges through a deep, scenic canyon ripe with grassy ridges, forested draws, and massive basalt outcroppings. Wildlife abounds, including elk, deer, bear, and bighorn sheep. The popular launch at Minam is located adjacent to the highway bridge over the Wallowa River near its confluence with the Minam River. Or you can use the primitive launch 1.5 miles downstream at Minam State Park, which includes a campground. Additional access points include Palmer Junction at river mile 85 on the Grande Ronde itself, 4 miles upstream from the Wallowa River confluence. Launching at Palmer Junction cuts a few miles off the trip. Palmer Junction is located near Looking Glass, north of Elgin. You can get there from Elgin on CR 42 or by continuing easterly on SR 82. About a mile before you reach Minam Summit, watch for a left-hand turn on Yarrington Road (CR 49) and follow it north about 12 miles to Palmer Junction.

From any of the above launch points you are committed to floating the river through many miles of steep, roadless canyon. This float includes numerous rapids, including several Class III rapids. These include RedRock Rapids at river mile 7 on the Wallowa, Blind Falls at river mile 4.2 on the Wallowa, Sheep Creek Rapids at river mile 79.4 on the Grande Ronde, Martin's Misery Rapids at river mile 69.6, and Double Eddy, just upstream from Troy. Even experienced boaters should scout all rapids.

Drive-in access to Rondowa—where the Wallowa and Grande Ronde Rivers meet—is intermittent, but sometime available through a circuitous route traversing lands owned by Boise Solutions. The road is not marked and is frequently gated during logging operations and during the fire season. Your best bet is to check in with Boise Wood Products to find out if the road is open and accessible (541-962-2000).

You can take out at Troy—a tiny town offering basic services—or at the popular Mud Creek takeout at river-mile 52.7, just below Wildcat Creek Bridge (Powwatka) and 7.5 river miles upstream from Troy. You can drive to Mud Creek from Troy or from the town of Wallowa via Powwatka Road. Many anglers make the short drift from Mud Creek to Troy, where a primitive gravel launch area near the school allows easy access. Or continue another mile down to the sandy beach at Varney Park on the right-hand bank.

The Grande Ronde's steelhead are mostly of hatchery origin but, most years, a few thousand wild fish ascend the river. Only adipose fin-clipped steelhead may be kept. The fish typically range from 4 to 6 pounds, but the river has plenty of 7- to 12-pound fish also. Down at the mouth of the Grande Ronde, in Washington, a few 12- to 16-pound fish are taken each year. Many of these are steelhead from the Salmon River in Idaho.

During autumn, the weather on the Grande Ronde ranges from warm and pleasant to bitter cold. If warm weather persists into early November, anglers enjoy superb fishing on the river during seasons with high fish counts. Often, however, cold weather settles in by late October and as water tempera-

tures plummet, fly anglers usually switch to sinking or sinking-tip lines and/or weighted flies. Many of the late-arriving hatchery fish congregate near the acclimation pond at Cottonwood Creek, making the stretch of river here quite popular, especially with gear anglers who use spinners, spoons, and jig-and-float set-ups. Cottonwood is on the Washington side, about 3 miles upstream from Boggan's.

During winter, steelhead tend to hold in deeper pools and runs. Typically their migration more or less ceases until the spring thaw, at which time they again begin moving rapidly upriver. Their long stay in freshwater means that many of these fish darken considerably and the ice-cold water robs them of much of their fighting spirit. Nonetheless, spring steelhead fishing is very popular on the Grande Ronde and on the Wallowa River. The Wallowa River run, which arrives between February and April, is comprised almost entirely of hatchery fish bound for the facility upstream from Big Canyon. The bridge over the river at Big Canyon Road is a popular fishing spot during spring, but equally good prospects are found throughout the lower Wallowa River, much of which is easily accessible from Hwy 82 and from Minam State Park. The season closes in mid-April (check current synopsis).

Trout action on the Grande Ronde is primarily for wild redband/rainbow trout, along with some juvenile steelhead that fail to migrate out. The trout range from 8 to 18 inches, with quite a few perfectly proportioned fish in the 10- to 13-inch range. They are quite abundant in the Wild & Scenic stretch and the river is especially good for fly fishing. Look for summer hatches of stoneflies and caddisflies flies, the latter of which continue into autumn. Streamer patterns are also very effective, as are small spinners and spoons.

The Grande Ronde also supports a sizeable population of smallmouth bass and fishing for them can be very good in certain stretches of the river. The bass occur as far upriver as Troy, but the best numbers occupy the lower river, on the Washington side, with the best prospects downstream from Boggan's. They'll eat steelhead flies and lures or you can target them with dark-colored jigs or streamer flies. The bass here reach at least 16 inches, but smaller fish predominate.

Any float trip on the Wild & Scenic section of the Wallowa/ Grande Ronde begins with a call to the BLM to check water conditions or to obtain a list of the many licensed guides and outfitters serving the river (541-523-1256). Or call the river station at Minam (541-437-5580). Shuttle service can be arranged through the following: Shilo Troy Resort (509-256-3372/www.boggans.com), Minam Store (541-437-1111), Troy Oasis (541-828-7773/www.troyresort.com), Grande Ronde Outfitters (541-828-7902) and TRT Raft Sales in Elgin (541-437-9270).

Grande Ronde River, Upper (Union County)
campgrounds

Though its middle reaches are largely degraded and inaccessible owing to extensive private property between La Grande and Elgin, the Grande Ronde River's upper stretch offers fair-to-good trout fishing during summer and fall. Steelhead arrive in the upper river between late autumn and mid-spring. Only hatchery fish may be kept. The steelhead fishing deadline is at Meadow Creek, along SR 244, about 20 miles west of LaGrande.

The bulk of the steelhead reach La Grande and the upper river between February and early April. Many anglers fish the public access water at Riverside Park in La Grande. Local kids catch a few trout from the park waters during the trout season, but summer weekends bring a lot more swimmers than anglers. The trout fishing improves as you head upriver, first along I-84 west of La Grande and then along the road to Starkey (SR 244). Three parks offer fishing access along the highway, the first being Hilgard Junction State

The Grande Ronde River is one of the best streams for upper Columbia River summer-run steelhead. Prime season is October and November.

Park near the I-84/SR 244 interchange. Further southwest on SR 244 are Birdtrack Springs and Red Bridge State Wayside. All three parks have camping areas and facilities.

At Starkey, the river and the highway part company and FR 51 and 5125 follow the river up into the Blue Mountains towards its headwaters. The uppermost reach is accessible only by trail. Throughout its run from its sources in the Elkhorn Range to I-84, the river offers lots of good trout opportunity, but you'll want to carry a copy of the Wallowa-Whitman National Forest Map to figure out land ownership and access points. Best access to the diminutive upper roadless stretch is from the end of FR 5138, where an informal trail more or less follows the stream.

Green Lake (Eagle Cap Wilderness)
hike-in
A good brook trout lake, isolated and remote, Green Lake is a 15-acre wilderness lake occupying a narrow basin at 6,700 feet in Eagle Cap Wilderness. Reaching Green Lake requires a lengthy hike, with the shortest route beginning at Bowman Trailhead on the Lostine River. Follow Trail 1651 up and over Wilson Pass and all the way down to the North Minam River. Then head downstream to the left-hand turn on Trail 1666, leading 3.4 miles up to the lake. Total distance is about 13 miles. The lake is accessible by mid-July, but Wilson Pass may hold snow later than that.

Hat Rock Pond (Umatilla County)
campground
A nice 6-acre pond offering fair fishing for largemouth bass, smallmouth bass, and stocked rainbow trout, Hat Rock Pond is part of Hat Rock State Park, located on the shores of Lake

Wallula behind McNary Dam on the Columbia River. The park is about 9 miles east of Umatilla via SR 730. Hat Rock Pond offers plenty of shoreline access and is a good place to take the kids fishing. For a more concerted effort at the bass, launch a canoe or float tube. Fishing picks up during mid-spring and continues through the summer. During the long, hot summer in this part of Oregon, morning and evening fishing is best.

The state park offers numerous amenities and, at this time, there is no use fee except for the group picnic areas. Hat Rock was the first distinctive landmark passed by the Lewis and Clark Expedition on their journey down the Columbia, and is one of the few remaining sites not underwater. The park is a desert oasis surrounded by rolling sagebrush hills and outcroppings of basalt. Groves of cottonwood and black locust, ringed by acres of green grass, provide an oasis from the summer heat. A boat ramp provides access to Wallula Lake.

Hawk Lake (Eagle Cap Wilderness)
hike-in, cross-country
A small, seldom-fished lake on the Hurricane Creek drainage in the Eagle Cap Wilderness, Hawk Lake is periodically stocked with rainbows by ODFW. The lake is un-named on most maps, but lies at 8,000 feet almost due west of Matterhorn Peak and on the opposite (west) side of Hurricane Creek. No trails reach the lake so you must make the steep climb up the outlet creek (or the ridgeline just to the north) or follow the steep trail up to Echo and Billy Jones Lake and then follow the contour below the high ridgeline of Hurricane Divide, heading south to drop into Hawk Lake. The hike begins on the Hurricane Trailhead southwest of Joseph. You'll need a topo map showing the lake's location (even though it is not named on most maps) and you'll need a stout sense of adventure coupled with strong lungs.

Hideaway Creek (Umatilla National Forest)

A small brook trout stream, with some redband trout in the lower reaches, Hideaway Creek offers fair-to-good early summer fishing. The trout are small, but lightly pressured. To get there from Ukiah, head east on Hwy 244 about 14 miles to a right-hand turn heading south on FR 54. Follow FR 54 for 1 mile to a left-hand turn on FR 5440 and then follow 5440 to a right-hand turn onto the 075 spur, following it to the end of the road. From there, hike down the Chimney Rock ATV trail to the creek. From this point, the best fishing is downstream where there is more water. You can also fish the lower end of the creek by hiking upstream from the crossing on FR 54. The redband trout usually reside in this section.

High Lake (Strawberry Mountain Wilderness)
see Strawberry Lake

Hobo Lake (Eagle Cap Wilderness)
hike-in

A very high lake by Oregon standards, 8-acre Hobo Lake sits at 8,369 feet and offers fair fishing for stocked rainbows that don't attain much size. The trail up to Hobo Lake gains 3,300 feet in just 6 miles, most of it coming by way of an arduously endless series of switchbacks in the first 2 miles. The climb begins at the Bowman Trailhead on the Lostine River and passes Chimney Lake at the 5.3-mile mark. Follow SR 82 to the little town of Lostine and then head south on Lostine River Road, continuing past Williamson Campground and past Lostine Guard Station.

Honeymoon Pond
see Wallowa County Forest Ponds

Horse Camp Pond
see Walla Walla R.D. Ponds

Horseshoe Lake (Eagle Cap Wilderness)
hike-in

Horseshoe Lake is a very popular hiking destination in the Lakes Basin of the Eagle Cap Wilderness Area. Spanning 40 acres, Horseshoe Lake offers lots of small brook trout in a rather stunning alpine setting. The fish range from 5 to 12 inches and are usually quite abundant; and the shoreline offers lots of easy access. Both spin fishing and fly angling are productive throughout the late summer and fall.

From the West Fork Wallowa Trailhead 1 mile south of Wallowa Lake, hike south for 6 miles to the trail junction at Six-Mile Meadow. From there make the steep, 3-mile-long climb up the Lakes Basin Trail to Horseshoe Lake. Other, slightly longer routes arrive by way of the East Fork Lostine Trail and the Hurricane Trail. Lakes Basin is the most oft-visited area of the wilderness. Use only pre-existing campsites and check in ahead of time with the USFS in Enterprise as additional restrictions may be in effect.

Hurricane Creek (Wallowa County)
no bait, campground, hike-in

This pretty little wild trout stream originates in alpine meadows near the Lakes Basin in the Eagle Cap Wilderness. Hurricane Creek then plunges northward to meet the Wallowa River near Enterprise. Within the wilderness area, the creek is restricted to artificial flies and lures up to Slick Rock Creek. Hurricane Creek Trail follows the stream nearly to its source, providing almost 10 miles of fishing, although the best trout populations reside in the first few miles. Wild rainbows range from 5 to 10 inches, rarely larger. Downstream from the wilderness boundary, in the vicinity of Hurricane Creek Campground, access is from Hurricane Creek Road out of Enterprise (and Joseph). The lower third of the creek flows across private agricultural lands in the Wallowa Valley.

Ice Lake (Eagle Cap Wilderness)
hike-in

A stunning timberline gem, but heavily used during the summer, 45-acre Ice Lake is nestled in a granite cirque at the foot of the two highest peaks in the Eagle Cap Wilderness. Sacagawea Peak reaches 9,838 feet into the sky and her neighbor, The Matterhorn, stands nearly as tall at 9,826 feet. Both peaks are popular with experienced wilderness enthusiasts and both offer spectacular panoramic views. Ice Lake itself frequently serves as a base for those climbing the two peaks.

This deep lake supports small brook trout. A 10-inch brookie is a big fish here, but fishing for them is fairly easy from the accessible shoreline. Fly angling and spin casting are both effective. Heaviest use occurs during July and August, so if you want Ice Lake to yourself, wait until mid- to late September. Anglers always seem to make up only a small portion of the visitors at Ice Lake. Camping is very limited at this time because of ongoing riparian restorations efforts here—efforts aimed at restoring damage done by the all-too-frequent visitors.

To get there, take the West Fork Trail heading south from Wallowa Lake (the trailhead is at the end of the road about a mile south of Wallowa Lake). At the 2.8-mile mark, take the right-hand trail leading to Ice Lake (#1808). Expect plenty of steep country here, most of it somewhat tamed by switchbacks. The round-trip distance is 15.8 miles and well-conditioned hikers can easily handle it as a day trip.

Imnaha River (Wallowa County)
campground

A remote, scenic and productive river for steelhead and trout, the Imnaha reaches the Snake River near Hell's Canyon after a tumultuous 77-mile run that begins in the Eagle Cap Wilderness Area. Access to this river is difficult in many places owing largely to extensive private property and to the steep canyon through which the Imnaha flows. Nonetheless, the sections open to public use are well known and readily accessible. Moreover, recent acquisitions and landowner agreements worked out through the Nature Conservancy and ODFW have opened additional land to public access on the river.

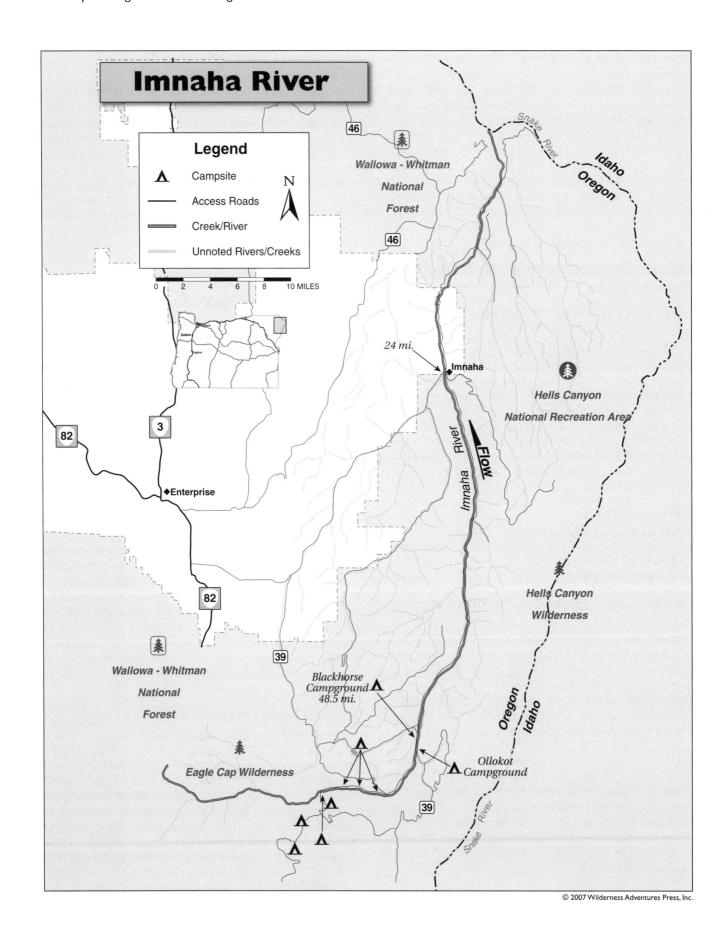

Imnaha River

Legend

▲ Campsite

N

— Access Roads

═ Creek/River

⋯ Unnoted Rivers/Creeks

0 2 4 6 8 10 MILES

46

🌲

Wallowa - Whitman

National

Forest

46

Snake River

Idaho
Oregon

24 mi.

◆ Imnaha

🌲

Hells Canyon

National Recreation Area

Imnaha River

Flow

3

82

◆ Enterprise

82

🌲

Hells Canyon

Wilderness

🌲

Oregon
Idaho

Wallowa - Whitman

National

Forest

39

Blackhorse ▲
Campground
48.5 mi.

▲▲

Ollokot
▲ Campground

🌲

Eagle Cap Wilderness

▲
▲

Snake River

39

▲

© 2007 Wilderness Adventures Press, Inc.

A wild rainbow trout from Inmaha River in the Eagle Cap Wilderness

mid-spring. During winter and spring, however, be very careful on the access road. Often the winter conditions are too severe for steelheading, so many Imnaha regulars wait for the longer days of late February through mid-April. If you can time your spring trip so that you are fishing prior to the season's first heavy snow melt, the river usually runs in fair shape.

Lower Imnaha Road and Upper Imnaha Road (upstream from Imnaha) both offer plenty of access to the river, but virtually all of the property along the road and the river is private. Anglers willing to take the time to seek landowner permission can enjoy plenty of access to good water. Above Imnaha, watch for signs that indicate the public access areas.

Despite the extensive private landholdings, steelhead angling can be very productive, especially around Imnaha and downstream.

By late September, summer-run steelhead gather near the mouth of the river and fishing here, and on the Snake, can be productive then. As water temperatures cool during October, the fish head up the Imnaha and, if mid-autumn brings a rainstorm or two, the fall fishing can be very good on the lower river between the mouth and the town of Imnaha. This section spans about 25 river miles, flowing mostly through a steep, scenic canyon. The lowermost 4 miles are accessible only by way of the Lower Imnaha Trail. The trailhead is at Cow Creek Bridge and reaches the Snake River at Eureka Bar.

To get to the trailhead, head easterly from Joseph on Little Sheep Creek Road, following the signs to the little hamlet of Imnaha (about 30 miles). At Imnaha, turn left on the paved road (CR 735) that, after about 6 miles, degrades into a steep, rugged dirt road. High-clearance 4-wheel-drive vehicles are best here, though you can negotiate the road by car under dry conditions. If the weather turns wet, use extreme caution. You will reach Cow Creek Bridge after about 14 miles. The trailhead and parking area is on the left.

From there, follow the trail down through the canyon. You'll find lots of good steelhead holding water amidst the steep, rugged flows here. In some places the river forms classic steelhead pools and runs, but also keep an eye peeled for small runs hidden amidst pocket-water stretches. The trailhead itself is located on private property so take care to leave the area in pristine condition to assure future public access. As you hike the canyon, watch for the resident bighorn sheep, along with lots of other wildlife.

This canyon section of the river offers good steelhead prospects throughout the season, from mid-autumn through

If the water rises and cools just a bit, the October and November fishing can be excellent during years of strong runs. The Imnaha attracts lots of fly anglers and lots of gear anglers and they employ the full spectrum of tactics here. The river is prime real estate for October surface action with skated dry flies.

The Imnaha also offers fair-to-good trout angling, primarily between the end of runoff in late June or early July and the end October. During years of heavy spring runoff, excessively high flows seem to flush a lot of the trout out of the system, but most years you'll find plenty of trout willing to take dry flies, nymphs, and small spinners. The Imnaha's wild rainbows typically range from 8 to 13 inches, with the average size decreasing as you head into the river's uppermost reaches. Bull trout, ranging from 12 to 25 inches, are fairly common in the Imnaha and law requires that they immediately be released unharmed.

Until you reach the national forest and the upper river, the Imnaha offers few lodging options. There are lots of primitive campsites on public lands around the area, but few alongside the river, except at several spots along the primitive road leading down to Cow Creek Bridge. One good option is the beautifully appointed Imnaha River Inn, a rustic but luxurious B&B that offers dinners and lunches. The owners can help you arrange guided fishing on the river (541-577-6002/www.imnahariverinn.com). The inn is located about 5 miles north (downstream) from Imnaha.

The other option is the Imnaha Store & Tavern, whose "Motel 3" offers exactly three rooms, which are coveted during the fishing and hunting seasons and especially during the annual Imnaha Canyon Day celebration held every September. The event has become regionally famous after it began as a bear and rattlesnake meat feed and now features plenty of food and drinks, along with a parade, tug-o-war, and other events. Canyon Day swells Imnaha's population from twelve to several hundred people. To reserve a room at the tiny motel, call the store at 541-577-3111.

Upper Imnaha Road follows the river all the way south into the Wallowa-Whitman National Forest. It's a slow, but scenic drive. If you are specifically headed for the headwaters however, take the Lick Creek Road/Wallowa Mountain Loop out of Joseph (FR 39). Twenty-two miles from Joseph, you'll reach Lick Creek Guard Station and Lick Creek Campground. From there, you can take the rugged and primitive FR 3925, which eventually leads to the Imnaha at Coverdale Campground. FR 39—the much better road and the usual route—continues down Gumboot Creek to the Imnaha and then doubles back to the west, following the river for 2 miles to a right-hand turn on FR 3960. Head west on FR 3960 to reach the four uppermost campgrounds and the Indian Crossing Trailhead, where the trail follows the Imnaha into the Eagle Cap Wilderness. These small campgrounds—Indian Crossing, Evergreen, Hidden, and Coverdale—rarely fill up except on a few popular summer weekends. They offer a combined 50 sites. Indian Crossing and Hidden have sites large enough to accommodate trailers.

Within the Eagle Cap Wilderness, the Imnaha offers fair-to-good summer fishing for small, wild rainbows and a few bull trout. Two miles up the trail you will find the beautiful, spring-fed pond, aptly named the Blue Hole. Four miles further is Imnaha Falls and a mile past the falls you'll reach the confluence of the Imnaha's North and South Forks. Trails follow both forks. The North Fork branches further at the Middle Fork. Although these trails are quite popular with both hikers and horse packers, anglers always seem to be in the minority. If you enjoy small stream fishing for small, wild trout, you'll be right at home on the wilderness branches of the Imnaha.

The trails are free of snow by mid- to late June, but fishing is substantially better after the snowmelt subsides in mid July. Fly anglers will find these waters most productive from late July through early October. Bull trout inhabit the upper river and its forks and they can reach 20 or more inches. Invariably they live in the deepest, most sheltered waters and can be enticed into chasing streamer patterns and lures. Be sure to release them unharmed and use only single-point, barbless hooks.

Jarboe Creek (Union County)
see Lookingglass Creek

John Day River
boat ramp

The second-longest un-dammed river in the United States, the John Day is a good steelhead stream and an excellent smallmouth bass river. The smallmouth fishery here has earned national repute, not only for the abundance of fish, but also for the spectacular and oft remote setting in which they thrive. The river draws its strength from myriad branches and forks through north-central Oregon, allowing the main river to form a substantial presence by the time it reaches the idyllic, narrow valley near Kimberley.

Unfortunately much of the river's flow is diverted to feed local and regional agricultural needs, thus explaining the elevated summer water temperatures that allow bass to thrive, but which have proven—among other things—a major detriment to native stocks of steelhead and salmon. The steelhead fishery still ranks among the better such opportunities in the state, but the timing of the run has changed and most of the fish are of hatchery origin. The bulk of the steelhead wait in the Columbia and the John Day Arm until cold weather and late-season precipitation create more favorable water conditions for their upstream migration. Thus the steelhead fishing usually doesn't begin until late autumn. The fishing picks up again during late winter and lasts until mid-April when the season closes.

Essentially the John Day offers two distinct fisheries for bass and steelhead. Most of the river is inaccessible except by boat, leaving a short section accessible by road. The best road access is from Hwy 19 and several side roads between Kimberly and Service Creek. Most of the land along this section is private so, when in doubt, you must seek permission from the landowners. Boaters can make day trips from Kimberly to Spray or Spray to Service Creek and there are a few other public access areas along the road. Maps of the John Day drainage show lots of backcountry road reaching the river or the rim above, but virtually all of these are private ranch roads and are closed to the public.

Service Creek also serves as the uppermost launch for multi-day trips through the inaccessible reaches of the John Day. From Service Creek to the river's mouth, there are but seven access points along 157 miles of river. Many floaters use the launch site downstream from Service Creek, at Twickenham Bridge on Rowe Creek Road (river mile 144). Or you can do a day-trip from Service Creek to Twickenham. The Twickenham Bridge access lies on private property and the landowner allows boaters to put-in, take-out and park. No camping, picnicking, fishing, hunting or any other activity is allowed here and continued public use depends on boaters obeying the rules.

Twickenham sits at river mile 144 and the next public access is below the famous Burnt Ranch Rapids at river mile 132. This is the Lower Burnt Ranch Access, which has a launch site (with a boater registration station) and restrooms. The next take-out/launch is at Clarno, at river mile 109. The drift from Burnt Ranch to Clarno takes two days at high water, but

John Day River

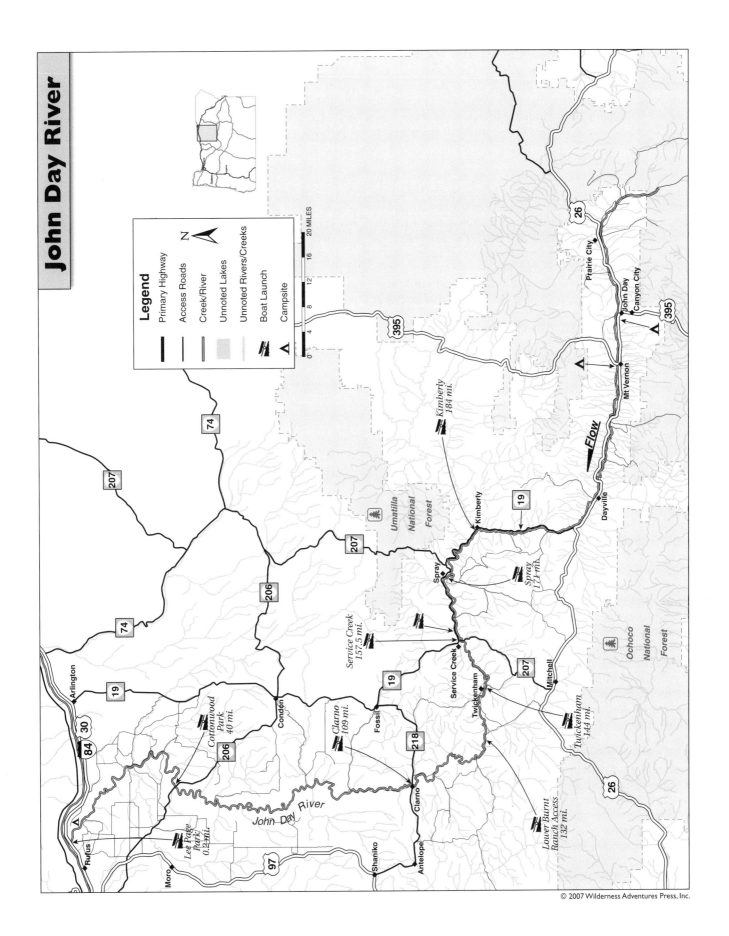

Legend

Primary Highway

Access Roads

Creek/River

Unnoted Lakes

Unnoted Rivers/Creeks

Boat Launch

Campsite

N

0 4 8 12 16 20 MILES

Prairie City

John Day

Canyon City

Mt Vernon

Dayville

Flow

Kimberly
184 mi.

Kimberly

Spray

Spray
171 mi.

Service Creek
157.5 mi.

Service Creek

Twickenham

Twickenham
144 mi.

Mitchell

Umatilla
National
Forest

Ochoco
National
Forest

Clarno
109 mi.

Clarno

Fossil

Lower Burnt
Ranch Access
132 mi.

Antelope

Shaniko

Condon

Cottonwood
Park
40 mi.

John Day River

Lee Page
Park
0.2 mi.

Moro

Rufus

Arlington

26

395

19

207

26

218

19

97

206

206

207

74

74

74

207

19

30

84

© 2007 Wilderness Adventures Press, Inc.

during low-flow periods—when fishing is best—you should plan three or even four days for this float and add a day if you launch at Twickenham and another day if you launch at Service Creek. A straight-through float from Service Creek to Clarno covers 48 miles and requires at least three days.

The Clarno access is at the State Route 218 Bridge west of Clarno. To get there, follow Hwy 97 north from Madras or south from I-84. From Madras, watch for the signs to Antelope and Clarno and head east. From the north follow Hwy 97 to Shaniko and from there, head south to Antelope and then east to Clarno. To reach the Burnt Ranch access, follow Highway 26 east from Prineville toward Mitchell. A few miles before you reach Mitchell, watch for the sign to the Painted Hills. The road here heads north along Bridge Creek and then follows the John Day's south bank to Burnt Ranch.

The Twickenham access is just about due north of Mitchell. From the south, follow State Route 207 about 9 miles north from Mitchell to a left-hand turn on the Girds Creek Road. From the north, follow SR 19 south from Fossil to Shelton State Wayside and turn south on Rowe Creek Road.

The bass fishing peaks at moderate to low flows, but boating can be tricky as the river drops and reveals lots of rock and plenty of slow-moving shallows. Splash-and-giggle enthusiasts prefer the high-water period of spring, but fishing is marginal then.

Clarno marks the beginning of the longest, most remote and most inaccessible drift on the John Day. The takeout is at Cottonwood Recreation Site. The drift covers 70 miles and takes nearly a week under low-water conditions. It's well worth repeating that moderate to low flows are best for fishing, but low water makes the drift laborious and slow. The take-out is at the bridge over the river on SR 206, which connects Wasco to the west and Condon to the east.

Both drift boats and river rafts are popular on the John Day, with rafts getting the nod at low water. Even kayakers use the river and these days, during the prime float season between April and June, the river is usually crowded, making for plenty of competition for campsites. The BLM's recommended minimum flows for various craft are as follows: drift boats, 800cfs; inflatable rafts, 500cfs; canoes, 300cfs; inflatable kayaks, 200cfs. If fishing for smallmouth is your goal, opt for the June through September

timeframe and watch for flows lower than 900cfs. When the river drops below 500cfs, fishing is excellent, even though you'll encounter plenty of difficulty in negotiating the rocky, shallow water in many places. Be sure to check with BLM (541-416-6718) before undertaking any such trip, especially at low flows.

Few boaters venture downstream from Cottonwood because of very difficult public access between Hwy 206 and Tumwater Falls. At Tumwater Falls, the entire river is forced through a narrow, black-basalt gorge, creating a treacherous chute that is essentially un-navigable at low water and very dangerous at any water level. Only a handful of experienced whitewater kayakers ever risk passage here.

However, boaters who drift below Cottonwood can depart at either of two different public-access easements. The first, at about river mile 22, is a BLM site called Rock Creek, on the east bank. You can get there from I-84 (Blalock Canyon Exit), from State Route 19 to the east or from SR 206 (via Ajax Road down to SR 19). Scout the take-out location before launching at Cottonwood so you will recognize it when you get there from the river. There is no formal ramp and the bank is steep here, but you can haul out an inflatable boat.

The second access, 1.5 miles below Rock Creek, is a public road easement at McDonald Crossing. At this ford, the road cuts across the riverbed, providing a 24-foot-wide public easement through otherwise private property. You can take out on the west bank and, with the road coming right into the river, this site is appropriate for trailer boats. Parking is problematic and currently the only legal parking area is at

The John Day River offers many faces and several major fisheries.

the Oregon Trail Monument parking area just up the road from the west bank. To get there, first consult your map and then head east from Morrow to Klondike and then east from Klondike to McDonald Ferry Lane, which leads to the river.

The reward for fishing the river during ideal smallmouth conditions is the very real possibility of catching bass by the dozens. A 50-fish day is pretty easy to accomplish. From July through most of September you'll get baked in the desert heat, but the warm water is what triggers smallmouth to feed aggressively. As temperatures moderate in late September and early October, you can enjoy the John Day at its best for bass fishing without suffering from the heat.

For steelhead fishing, conversely, a bit of fresh water often makes all the difference, so watch the October/November weather carefully and if rain sets in over the lower John Day River region, head for the river. The Cottonwood Site is a popular bank-fishing location and the steelhead season is the ideal time for the adventurous types to float the river from Cottonwood down to Rock Creek or the Oregon Trail site. Also, after October 1, motorized boats are allowed, so if flows permit, you can simply motor back up to Cottonwood.

Steelhead fishing continues through the winter, although the bite tends to taper off as water temperatures plummet. With the longer days of late February, however, fishing begins anew and anglers continue to pursue steelhead until the season closes during mid-April. These are summer-run steelhead, so by spring they tend to be dark, slender and not nearly so full of fight. Most are of hatchery origin, however, so anglers can keep them. Wild fish (non-fin-clipped) must be released.

Despite the popularity of the spring steelhead season, the John Day's steelhead are at their best during autumn when they are bright, fat and full of fight. These fish range from 4 to 15 pounds. Every autumn is different, however, and some years—especially dry years—few fish enter the system during October and November. Conversely, if the region gets sustained rainfall during October, the rising river (whose levels are further bolstered by the end of irrigation season upstream) draws lots of fish out of the John Day Arm and into the river.

The John Day has become quite popular with fly anglers. Steelhead fly fishers use a wide range of tactics, largely depending on water flows and temperatures. If the fishing picks up during October, the John Day offers good dry-line fishing with traditional unweighted wet flies. During November and December, most anglers switch to sinking-tip lines and/or weighted flies. Gear anglers enjoy consistent success—throughout the season—using everything from spoons and spinners to jig-and-float set-ups.

Smallmouth bass abound in the John Day River.

Bass-angling effort is about equally divided between fly anglers and gear anglers. Spin casters adept at fishing small jigs catch John Day smallies by the bucket load. Fly anglers use a wide array of sub-surface patterns, but a simple Woolly Bugger, dressed with a metal cone or metal eyes at the front, never fails. At low water, popping bugs and large dry flies are very effective. The John Day's smallmouth bass typically range from 8 to 14 inches in length, but the river offers quite a few fish in the 2- to 5-pound range.

Quite a few fishing guides now hold permits to work the John Day River and many of them offer multi-day float trips for both smallmouth bass and steelhead. The BLM can provide a list of these outfitters. Also, if you want to float the river on your own, the adventure begins by consulting the BLM. Ask for the BLM John Day River Boater's Packet and then review your plans with a BLM recreation specialist. They can also provide you a list of local shuttle-service operators. (BLM Central Oregon Field Office: 541-416-6700).

Fires are not allowed on the John Day River at any time between June 1 and October 1. Propane and white gas stoves are allowed. From October 2 through May 31, fires must be contained in a fire-pan and only charcoal or wood brought from home is allowed. Additionally, the BLM is now asking would-be floaters to voluntarily avoid launching on Fridays and Saturdays during the crowded season from Memorial Day weekend through July 4th Weekend.

John Day River, Middle Fork (Grant County)

A decent trout stream, also offering steelhead fishing during spring, the Middle Fork John Day River originates near Blue Mountain Pass, east from Prairie City and west from Unity. The river then travels about 75 miles to its confluence with the North Fork John Day. The lower end of the Middle Fork, difficult to get to, flows across private ranchlands while the rest of the stream journeys through a mix of private and public lands with fair-to-good access.

When in doubt about access, check with local landowners. To reach the headwaters from Prairie City or Unity, follow Hwy 20 toward Blue Mountain Summit and then take the north turn on SR 7 at Austin Junction. Just north of the junction, turn west (left) on Middle Fork Road, which follows the river all the way down to Hwy 395. It's slow going due to myriad curves and corners. Downstream (west) from Hwy 395, Long Creek-Ritter Road follows the river for another 10 miles. From John Day to the south or Ukiah to the north, simply follow Hwy 395 to the Middle Fork and head up or downstream from there.

Wild redband trout range from 6 to 18 inches and are not particularly abundant in any particular place. Find a productive stretch of river, however, and you can enjoy consistently good fishing. Most of the fish are in the 8- to 12-inch range and they respond to all methods. Best trout fishing is from June through October. The Middle Fork has a fair run of steelhead, which ascend the river between November and April, with best fishing prospects from February through the end of the season in mid-April. All non-fin-clipped steelhead must be released.

John Day River, North Fork (Grant/Umatilla Counties)

Flowing almost 120 miles from it source in the Elkhorn Range, the North Fork John Day offers good opportunities for summer-run steelhead between late fall and mid-April, along with only fair prospects for wild trout in a few reaches. Most of the autumn steelhead angling effort is concentrated on the lower section of the river, from Monument down to Spray, with best fishing during November and December. This stretch also sees quite a lot of pressure between February and the end of the season during mid-April, but the spring fishing tends to be more spread out as fish are scattered through the river all the way up to Hwy 395. Only hatchery steelhead may be harvested and these are most common on the lower end of the river.

Access is tricky on the lower portion of the river where the North Fork runs through mostly private lands. Seek permission before crossing private property. Otherwise stick to the road access points. You can float the lower end of the river, launching at Wall Creek on Wall Creek-River Road north of Monument or at the little town of Monument. The run from Wall Creek to Monument covers a fairly quick 5.5 miles or you can float from Monument to Kimberly, a stretch covering 16 miles.

State Route 402 follows the North Fork from Kimberly upstream to Monument and then River Road snakes along the river for several more miles before reaching the end of public access at Wall Creek. A private ranch road runs along the river all the way to Potamus Creek (about 17 miles). The road is posted "No Trespassing" on both ends, even though a lot of people use it to access the river on scattered BLM segments in that stretch. The prudent choice, however, is to stay off this

North Fork John Day River

road unless you have permission from the landowner, whose ranch lies upstream, off CR 15. Call the BLM office in Prineville to get his name.

Above Potamus Creek, public access begins again, extending upstream to Hwy 395. To reach this 20-mile-long stretch of the North Fork, take Hwy 395 south from Ukiah or north from Long Creek. The upper end of the North Fork is accessible by road upstream from Hwy 395 until you reach the North Fork John Day Wilderness Area. In its wilderness stretch, the North Fork is a small, rushing, canyon-bound stream inhabited more by juvenile steelhead than by resident trout.

Currently, regulations on the North Fork John Day require the release of all wild steelhead (non-fin-clipped). The season is open from September 1 through April 15, but check the most current regulations. Rarely will you find steelhead in the North Fork during September. Several of the North Fork's tributary streams offer fair trout prospects. Granite Creek is closed to protect wild steelhead. The entire system is closed to fishing for the few returning Chinook salmon.

John Day River, South Fork (Grant County)

Offering the best access of all the John Day's branches, the South Fork also offers fair-to-good fishing for wild redband/rainbow trout. The fish range from 7 to 14 inches and respond to all methods. The deeper pools found at bends in the small river and under cut banks are perfect places to work a small spinner, and the South Fork is ideally suited to fly angling. Owing to extensive public lands along the river, the South Fork John Day offers lots of elbowroom and is rarely if ever crowded. A good county road (South Fork Road) follows right alongside the river from Dayville south to the tiny wide spot called Izee—a stretch of about 50 miles. You can camp at any of numerous informal camping areas. Best fishing is from May through June and usually into early July. Autumn is as good if not better. During the hottest part of late summer, anglers should probably leave these fish alone due to elevated water temperatures.

John Henry Lake (Eagle Cap Wilderness)
hike-in

This shallow lake in the Eagle Cap Wilderness offers fair-to-good fishing for small brook trout. Access is via the Bowman Trailhead on the Lostine River, south from the town of Lostine. Watch for the trailhead about 4 miles south from Williamson Campground. The hike to John Henry covers almost 6 miles. After climbing Bowman Creek, you'll pass over a narrow summit and then begin a decent through several switchbacks into the basin occupied by John Henry Lake. When you reach Wilson Basin, watch for a side trail on your left, which takes you to the lake. John Henry Lake sits at 7,168 feet and is usually accessible by early July.

Joseph Creek (Wallowa County)
hike-in

Joseph Creek is a small, rugged stream meandering through a brutally steep and extremely remote rugged canyon north of Enterprise. Much of the stream flows through private property and even the public-land stretches are difficult to reach. However, Joseph Creek—largely owing to its remoteness—ranks among the best wild rainbow trout streams in the region. Trout here reach at least 18 inches and typically range from 8 to 14 inches. Flowing northward, the creek eventually crosses the state line into Washington, where it meets the Grand Ronde River. The lower reaches have smallmouth bass.

The only easy access to Joseph Creek is via the ranch operated by Ninebark Outfitters, which offers lodging packages that include access to a lengthy stretch of the creek. Ninebark Outfitters (541-426-4855) sits near the creek's headwaters, tucked away amid precipitous grassy slopes cloaked, in places, by extensive stands of conifers. The ranch offers rental cabins and also guided fishing packages (along with guided trail rides and guided or non-guided hunts). There is no other access to the upper portion of Joseph Creek, so anglers must have permission from Ninebark's owner or must be guests at the lodge.

The remaining access points to Joseph Creek are applicable only to those with the lung capacity and stamina of a mountain goat because after hiking in and out of the canyon you'll possess a better understanding of a mountain goat's lifestyle. The first of these access points is the Chico Trail, which heads on SR 3 about 18 miles north of Enterprise. Having mentioned it, I'll now suggest that you forget about this route, which requires a ridiculously long and arduous hike that dips down into and then back out of two brutal canyons before getting anywhere near the much larger Joseph Creek Canyon.

The better option is to use the primitive trail dropping into the canyon from the Joseph Canyon Viewpoint, 8 miles further north along SR 3. The trail here (Barton Trail) has not been maintained for years and is terribly degraded. Descending the trail is bad enough; climbing back out is brutal. From the overlook you'll get a good idea of what awaits you. If you persist in planning to fish Joseph Creek, schedule your trip for the prime times of mid-June or any time between mid-September and mid-October.

A third access trail into Joseph Creek follows the East Fork of Tamarack Creek down into the canyon from a place called Hunter's Camp Ridge, reaching Joseph Creek about 2.5 miles due south of the Washington border. To reach the trailhead, follow FR 46 (a right turn off SR 3 about 14 miles north of Enterprise) all the way to Coyote Campground. Then turn left on FR 4650 and then right on FR 4655. Follow FR 4655 (a rugged back-country road) until it ends at the trail. The hike covers about 3.5 miles.

Any angler adventurous enough to tackle Joseph Creek without the aid of Ninebark Outfitters might also want to explore the region's other extremely remote small-stream trout fisheries. These include Davis Creek, Swamp Creek, and Cottonwood Creek. The best map is the Wallowa Valley Ranger District Map available in Enterprise at the Wallowa-Whitman National Forest Office. You can get additional access tips and order maps by calling 541-426-4978.

Jubilee Lake (Umatilla National Forest)
campground, boat ramp

A good producer of pan-size rainbow trout, 90-acre Jubilee Lake is a popular man-made lake in the mountains northeast from Pendleton and north of Elgin. Tollgate Summit lies just to the south of Jubilee, which is a fine place to escape the summer heat that frequently overwhelms most of Umatilla County. From Pendleton, follow Hwy 11 northeast to Athena and Weston and then head east on the Tollgate Road (SR 204). When you reach Tollgate, turn left on FR 64, which leads up to Jubilee Lake. The fishing here usually holds up throughout the summer, although most regulars tout June and October as the top months. A boat is handy, but not necessary and this is a good place for a family fishing trip. Only electric motors are allowed.

Jumpoff Joe Lake (Umatilla National Forest)
hike-in, float tube recommended

A very scenic, though only marginally productive, high-elevation lake on the Desolation Creek watershed, Jumpoff Joe Lake offers small cutthroat trout in a photogenic setting. See Lost Lake herein for directions to the FR 10/FR 45 Junction. From that junction, follow FR 45 south 3.5 miles to the trailhead, which is located on a sharp switchback. The hike covers less than half a mile. Dense brush and downed timber make for difficulty in negotiating much of the shoreline, so a float tube comes in handy on this lightly fished lake.

Keyhole Pond
see Walla Walla R.D. Ponds

Kinney Lake (Wallowa County)
no boats

This privately owned lake near Joseph is open to public fishing by agreement with the owner, so anglers are asked to respect the property by removing all trash and restricting vehicle travel to existing roads. Camping and boating are both prohibited and the lake generally opens in late May. ODFW stocks the lake with legal-size rainbows and Kinney also offers good fishing for bullhead catfish. From Joseph, head east on the Imnaha/Hells Canyon Highway (SR 350). After about 5 miles, turn right on Tucker Down Road and then left on Kinney Lake Lane.

La Grande Reservoir
see Beaver Creek Reservoir

Ladd Marsh Pond
see Peach Road Pond

Lake Penland (Morrow County)
boat ramp

A popular and productive lake in the Blue Mountains south of Heppner, Lake Penland offers good fishing for rainbow trout from 8 to 18 inches, along with small bluegill. Most of the trout range from 10 to 13 inches. Camping is limited to a few primitive spaces and only electric motors are allowed on this fairly shallow, 65-acre lake. Shore fishing is good here, but fishing by small boat or canoe is the preferred method of many regulars. From Heppner, head south on Willow Creek Road (CR 678) for about 23 miles. Turn on to FR 21 and continue 3 miles to a left-hand turn on FR 2103, which leads 2 miles to Penland Lake. Penland is generally accessible by late spring, but FR 2103 can get very muddy. The nearest large campground capable of accommodating RV's is about 8 miles back to the north at Cutsforth Park.

Langdon Lake (Tollgate Summit)
private waters

Lee Lake (Eagle Cap Wilderness)
hike-in

A very pretty 9-acre lake in the Eagle Cap Wilderness, Lee Lake is a good bet for lots of 5- to 8-inch brook trout. It sits right in the heart of the popular and heavily visited Lakes Basin. You can reach the basin from the West Fork Wallowa River Trail heading just south of Wallowa Lake, the East Fork Lostine Trail or the Hurricane Creek Trail. See Horseshoe Lake herein for directions.

LeGore Lake (Eagle Cap Wilderness)
hike-in, cross-country

Sitting at 8,957 feet in the Eagle Cap Wilderness, 2-acre Legore Lake holds the distinction of being Oregon's highest fishable lake. The lake is stocked periodically with rainbow trout, though they are never abundant and the lake has been known to winterkill some years. Still, Legore is one of the most starkly scenic lakes in the wilderness, sitting entirely above timberline in a glacier-carved ravine just below the 9,673-foot summit of Twin Peaks. Permanent snowfields reach nearly to the edge of the lake, which is easy to fish from shore. You can reach Legore Lake by any of several routes, all of which demand competent alpine hiking skills. The shortest and steepest route follows the Fall Creek Trail from the Hurricane Creek Trailhead southwest of Joseph. The trail climbs precipitously up the creek for 2.4 miles. From there, you can continue by scrambling up the brutally steep scrim slopes, bearing west and then dropping back to the south to find the lake (or use any other scramble route that looks passable). Be sure to bring along a topo map, compass and all the gear you'll need for alpine travel and camping. The lake is usually free of ice by late July, but August or even September is a better time to visit Legore. Just beware the afternoon thunderstorms.

Little Sheep Creek (Wallowa County)

This small, lengthy stream originates on the northeast slopes of the Wallowa Mountains and flows north to meet the Imnaha River. The diminutive upper reaches offer slow action for small, wild trout, with fishing improving as you progress downstream. The creek flows alongside the Imnaha Highway for many miles, but access is limited due to extensive private lands here. Be sure to seek permission before fishing the creek. Rainbows range from 5 to 12 inches.

Little Strawberry Lake
see Strawberry Lake

Long Creek Pond (Grant County)

An old, flooded gravel pit located along Hwy 19, about 2 miles west from the town of Long Creek, this half-acre pond is stocked twice each spring during March and April. The fishing is fair to good through mid-May, sometimes later and most angler still fish with bait.

Long Lake (Eagle Cap Wilderness)
see Swamp Lake

Lookingglass Creek (Union/Wallowa Counties)

Restricted to artificial lures and flies (no hook gaps larger than ¼ inch), Lookingglass Creek is a fair producer of small, wild trout and is well known for its run of chinook salmon that return to the ODFW's Lookingglass Hatchery on the lower end of the creek. The salmon are dark and ready for spawning by the time they reach the hatchery, where they are used to propagate salmon for stocking elsewhere.

The creek's best trout action is found on a roadless section west of Tollgate Summit. On this 10-mile-long stretch, several old forest roads get you close to the canyon rim and trails that take you down into the creek. Easiest access is from the Luger Springs Trailhead located off a spur road from FR 63. Be sure to carry a Umatilla National Forest Map.

The wild trout here range from 6 to 12 inches, with some larger. Be sure to consult the synopsis for current regulations on Lookingglass Creek, which as of this writing is closed from 300 feet below Jarboe Creek to 200 feet upstream from the hatchery intake. Access to Lookingglass Creek is by way of FR 63 and 62 north of Elgin. Follow SR 82 to Elgin, turn left on Weston-Elgin Highway and then right on Palmer Junction Road. Continue into the national forest on FR 63. Also check out Mottet Creek along FR 63 and Jarboe Creek, which runs through a roadless canyon and is crossed only twice by forest roads.

Lost Lake (Umatilla National Forest)
hike-in

Lost Lake, situated near the more popular Olive Lake high in the Umatilla National Forest, offers good hike-in fishing for stocked rainbow trout. Some fish always seem to over-winter here; so a few 14- to 16-inch trout compliment the usual 9- to 12-inch rainbows. This is a good lake for fly angling, though all methods work. The lake is littered with tree snags, creating good cover for trout. Shoreline fishing is easy, but this is a fun place for a float tube.

From Ukiah, follow Hwy 395 south about 14 miles to a left-hand turn on FR 55 (Texas Bar Road). Follow FR 55 for 1 mile to a right-hand turn on FR10 and follow FR10 for 20 miles to a right turn on FR 45. After half a mile, turn left on spur road 020 and follow it about half a mile to the junction with spur road 030. Park at the gate and hike uphill about 2.5 miles to the lake, which is usually accessible by early June. Alternately you can reach Lost Lake from Sumpter to the east by following the Elkhorn Scenic Byway (CR 24) to Granite and then turning left on FR 10. From there follow FR 10 west to a left-hand turn on FR 45 and follow the direction above.

Lostine River (Wallowa Mountains)
no bait, campground

A productive, tumultuous little mountain river, the Lostine offers good fishing for small, wild redband trout and small brook trout. The river flows north, unfettered for more than 30 miles from its source at Minam Lake in the Eagle Cap Wilderness to the Wallowa River near the little community of Wallowa. For fishing purposes, the river can be divided into thirds: The uppermost stretch includes two branches, the Lostine proper and the East Fork Lostine. Both forks plunge rather rapidly down from their headwater sources at 7,300 feet and 7,500 feet elevation respectively. Combined they offer about 13 miles of small-stream, high-gradient, pocket water fishing. Within the wilderness, access is excellent via the trail system, but fishing the river can be a physically challenging affair. In places you must negotiate steep, boulder-clad banks and in other places it's easier just to walk right up the river channel. The reward for the effort includes the opportunity to cast dry flies into some truly beautiful little pools.

The East Fork joins the main river at the wilderness boundary and the Lostine Trail system follows right along both branches. These upper waters support trout in the 4- to 9-inch range, with most being 8 inches or less. Bull trout—fully protected by law—also inhabit these waters and can be found all the way down to the Wallowa River confluence. North from the wilderness boundary, the second section of the river is paralleled closely by Lostine River Road. The road allows easy access to more than 10 miles of water on national forest property. This area—including three campgrounds and five trailheads—is quite popular between July and early September. However, you can escape the crowds by fishing the river here during late September.

Downstream from the Wallowa-Whitman National Forest boundary, the Lostine River flattens and begins to meander through private ranch and farmlands for its final 14-mile run down to the Wallowa River. This lower section, which requires you to obtain landowner permission, offers the best bet for larger wild trout, a few of which reach 14 inches. In places, the lower section flows alongside the highway and alongside Lostine River Road, but the banks lay on private property. The prudent choice is to ask permission to fish, which is usually granted by most of the landowners. The lower reach of the river is good grasshopper water between July and September.

To get there, first follow I-84 to La Grande and then head east toward Elgin on SR 82. From Elgin, continue easterly on SR 82 heading toward Enterprise. Once you reach the Wallowa Valley, the first town you'll find is Wallowa. Two miles east of Wallowa, the Lostine River will be on your left (north) until you cross over it just before you enter the town of Lostine. At Lostine, pick up Lostine River Road heading south out of town from where the highway makes a 90-degree turn to the east.

Mac Pond (Union County)

A flooded rock quarry east of La Grande, this formerly popular little pond used to be stocked by ODFW. Recent ownership changes have eliminated public access and the pond is no longer stocked. Try Roulette Pond near Elgin or Ladd Pond (Peach Road Pond) at Ladd Marsh Wildlife Area.

Magone Lake (Malheur National Forest)
campground, boat ramp

Popular and fairly productive, Magone Lake is a 50-acre rainbow and brook trout fishery about 25 road miles north of John Day in the Malheur National Forest. Trout here typically range from 8 to 14 inches, with a few reaching 18 inches. The lake is usually accessible by late May and fishing tends to hold up throughout the summer unless the area suffers a prolonged heat wave. Autumn fishing can be especially good and the lake draws quite a few ice-fishing enthusiasts when conditions allow.

Magone Lake is quite fertile and conducive to all methods. Fly anglers should bring a float tube or pontoon boat. A nice hiking trail circles the lake, so shoreline access is very good; and many anglers still fish with bait.

To get to Magone Lake from the west or northwest, drive south on Hwy 395 past Long Creek and turn left on FR 36. The road leads east to the lake. The other road access, (26 miles north of John Day) is from Hwy 26 to CR 18, then turn onto Forest Service Road 36, which leads to the lake. A Malheur National Forest map shows the routes.

Marr Pond (Enterprise)

A small trout pond, stocked with rainbows by ODFW, Marr Pond is located in Enterprise and is the sight of a Free Kid's Fishing Day held annually during early summer. For details and dates, contact Wallowa Valley Ranger District in Enterprise at 541-426-5680. Fishing continues to be fair to good through early summer. Sometimes ODFW stocks the pond with a few trophy-size rainbows. Marr Pond is located in the southwest corner of Enterprise, near the railroad tracks.

Maxwell Lake

Maxwell Lake (Eagle Cap Wilderness)
hike-in

A very productive hike-in lake for 5- to 8-inch brookies, 16-acre Maxwell Lake is fairly popular during sunny weekends, but the steep 4-mile hike assures some solitude most of the time. The lake is situated at 7,729 feet high above the west bank of the Lostine River. The trail switches back time and again to gain the 2,200 feet from the trailhead, located near Shady Campground. Shaded in the evening by a high ridge to the east, nights tend to be very cold here. Use the pre-existing campsites on the north shore. From Elgin, follow SR 82 heading toward Enterprise. At the little town of Lostine, turn south onto Lostine River Road. The trailhead is about a mile from the end of the road.

McCormack Slough (Morrow County)
boat or float tube recommended

Covering about 500 acres, McCormack Slough is a backwater extending off the Columbia 5 miles east of Boardman. The slough offers a broad mix of warmwater fish species, including largemouth and smallmouth bass, crappie, brown bullhead, channel catfish, and yellow perch. Fishing can be very good at times, especially if you use a float tube or canoe. To access the slough from the inland side, follow I-84 to the Hwy 730/Irrigon Exit (#168) and head north to the Patterson Road Exit. Follow Patterson Road for 2 miles to a left-hand turn on a gravel access road, just past the information center/parking area for the Umatilla National Wildlife Refuge. The ponds and channels composing the southeastern part of the slough are fishable from the bank but some form of small watercraft also comes in handy here.

McGraw Pond
see Wallowa County Forest Ponds

McKay Reservoir (Umatilla County)
boat ramp

An irrigation storage reservoir 6 miles south of Pendleton, McKay (pronounced McEye) Creek Reservoir offers fair-to-good action for a variety of warmwater species, including crappie, yellow perch, largemouth bass, bluegill, brown bullhead, and a few channel catfish. Water levels at the reservoir fluctuate widely. At full pool, McKay spans 1,200 acres and at extreme low water can be drawn down to a mud puddle. During years of normal water flow, the reservoir starts out full and is steadily drawn down over the summer until it shrinks to several hundred acres.

At full pool or close to it, the reservoir offers flooded reed stands and shrubbery along with several channels and drop-offs that are good for crappie and bass. Be sure to check current regulations on bass fishing here. Most anglers fish from shore for bullhead, perch, and catfish, but quite a few anglers launch boats in search of crappie and bass. There is a boat ramp at each end of the reservoir, but the upper launch site (McKay South) is unusable at low water. The North McKay ramp is the better of the two.

McKay Reservoir is part of McKay Creek National Wildlife Refuge, which annually attracts thousands of migrating waterfowl and shorebirds in addition to the many hundreds of birds nesting there. Migrating shorebirds abound on the exposed mudflats left when the reservoir is drawn down. During autumn, fishing is not allowed, but the area is popular with pheasant hunters and waterfowl hunters (current fishing and hunting restrictions are posted at the refuge).

The McNary Ponds below McNary Dam on the Columbia offer good fishing for panfish and stocked rainbow trout.

To reach McKay Reservoir, follow I-84 to Exit 209 in Pendleton (Hwy 395). Turn south off the exit and follow Hwy 395 about 5 miles to the well-signed entrance to the refuge and reservoir.

McNary Channel Ponds (Umatilla County)

A good bet for bass, bluegill, crappie, catfish, and stocked rainbow trout, the McNary Channel Ponds are an assemblage of six small and medium-size ponds, some of which are interconnected by a ditch and all of which are connected by a convenient trail system. All of the ponds are easy to fish from various perches along the shorelines, but a float tube is an advantage on the two largest ponds. If you're still fishing with bait, get there early in the day to grab a good bank spot shaded by the small trees. The ponds are located just downstream from McNary Dam on the Columbia. Follow Hwy 730 east from Umatilla to Exit 184 and then turn north on Brownell Blvd, immediately west of I-84. Cross the tracks and then head east a few hundred yards to the McNary Wildlife Nature Area. Turn north to reach the ponds and the river. ODFW stocks the ponds with trout several times per year between April and July.

Meacham Creek (Umatilla County)
no bait, hike-in

Offering fair fishing for wild redband trout, Meacham Creek is a lengthy tributary to the Umatilla River east of Pendleton. Most of the trout range from 6 to 10 inches, but a few reach 14 or more inches, especially on the most inaccessible parts of the creek. An abandoned railway bed (Meacham Creek Trail) follows along the creek, making the stream ideal for those willing to walk. The best fishing is in the middle section where the creek wraps around Horseshoe Ridge.

Meadow Creek (Union County)
closed waters

Messner Pond (Morrow County)

A good fishery for white crappie, largemouth bass and—just for fun—big carp, Messner Pond covers 14 acres and is located just east of Boardman adjacent to the Columbia River. Take Exit 165 off I-84 and head north about half a mile. The bass and crappie fishing peaks from April through May and most years the carp seem to get increasingly numerous as summer wears on.

Milk Creek (Wenaha Drainage)
hike-in

Tributary to the South Fork Wenaha River, Milk Creek is a remote and productive little trout stream in the Wenaha-Tucannon Wilderness Area of northeastern Oregon. Access is by hiking. From Athena, Oregon, follow SR 204 to Tollgate Summit and then head north toward Jubilee Lake on FR 64. About a mile east of Jubilee Lake, turn left on FR 6415 and continue about 5 miles to the Timothy Springs Trailhead. The trail heads north, following the South Fork Wenaha for several miles before arriving at Milk Creek, where a branch trail heads upstream for almost 2 miles. Once this trail departs the creek, you can bushwhack further into the drainage.

Mill Creek (Walla Walla drainage)
no bait

Although most of the stream is located in Washington, diminutive Mill Creek crosses the border and runs through Oregon for a few miles, offering fair-to-good fishing for small, wild redband trout. Easiest access is by heading east from Walla Walla, Washington on Hwy 12 and then turning south toward Tracy and Kooskooskie. Just past Kooskooskie the road crosses into Oregon along Mill Creek and then follows the creek to the Umatilla National Forest boundary. The creek is limited to flies and artificial lures.

Minam Lake (Eagle Cap Wilderness)
hike in

This 33-acre lake in the Eagle Cap Wilderness is the source of the Lostine River and is inhabited by lots of small brook trout. Fishing is usually quite good for fish from 6 to 10 inches with a few larger fish available. The Lostine River Trail gains 1,700 feet on the 6-mile trek to Minam Lake. The lake sits at 7,373 feet and is usually accessible by early July. Prime time is mid-September through mid-October when the people disappear and the brook trout gain their bright fall colors. Just be mindful of the weather at that time of year. The trailhead near Two Pan Campground lies at the end of Lostine River Road, south from the little town of Lostine (located on SR 82 west from Enterprise).

Minam River (Wallowa/Union Counties)
hike-in

Largely a wilderness stream, the beautiful and wild Minam River originates high in the Wallowa Range and then carves out a deep, forested canyon on its journey to meet the Wallowa River northeast from Elgin. The Minam offers good fishing for wild rainbow, along with a few brook trout and a fairly sizeable population of piscivorous bull trout. All bull trout must be immediately released unharmed. These char can reach several pounds in the Minam and are usually found lurking under logjams, in deep pools, and under cut banks. The rainbows reach 15 inches, but 8- to 12-inch fish are more typical. If you look for the out-of-the-way pools and deep runs, you'll find quite a few 12- to 14-inch natives.

A 40-mile-long trail follows the Minam River though its wilderness run and is quite popular with horse packers. Numerous trails meet the Minam River Trail, so hikers and riders can choose a variety of entry points. Any trip to the Minam River should begin with a thorough study of the Eagle Cap Ranger District Map, available through any office of the Wallowa-Whitman National Forest. The lower river, from Meads Flats just north of the wilderness boundary, down to the confluence with the Wallowa River, is accessible by a network of rugged backcountry roads. The town of Minam is the starting point.

The Minam River is graced with the unique services of Minam Lodge, a privately-owned lodge situated within the designated wilderness. Operating on a special-use permit, the lodge offers guided fishing trips, horse treks and drop-camp service, along with rental cabins with meals included. They operate one of two airstrips within the wilderness boundary, so clients can fly in by charter flight or private plane. Charters originate from La Grande, Pendleton, Enterprise, Boise, and even from the Willamette Valley. For details about Minam Lodge, call 541-432-6545 or visit www.minamlodgeoutfitters.com.

The Minam usually runs high with snowmelt through June, making July through September the peak time to fish the river. October can be excellent when the weather cooperates. This swift, scenic stream is ideal for dry fly fishing and the trout are rarely fussy over specific patterns—just arm yourself with a selection of attractor-style dry flies.

Minam River bull trout

Mirror Lake (Eagle Cap Wilderness)
hike-in

One of the truly beautiful lakes of the all-too-popular Lakes Basin area in the Eagle Cap Wilderness, Mirror Lake spans 26 acres and offers good fishing for brook trout from 6 to 12 inches. Because the area is so rich in alpine splendor and reasonably easy to get to by Eagle Cap standards, Lakes Basin is overused during the summer and even the U.S. Forest Service encourages people to visit other parts of the wilderness. The basin even has its own management plan to deal with its popularity. Nonetheless, you can enjoy some very good action at Mirror Lake and the other nearby lakes, even though the brookies rarely exceed a foot in length. Best time to visit is after Labor Day when the crowds disperse.

The shortest route to Mirror Lake is from the East Lostine River Trail, which heads at Two Pan Campground on the Lostine River. Follow SR 82 from Elgin toward Enterprise and at the little community of Lostine, head south to the end of Lostine River Road. The hike to Mirror Lake covers 7.5 miles and gains almost 2,000 feet (Mirror sits at 7,595 feet). Well-conditioned hikers can make a day trip of it and avoid the overused camping spots at these delicate alpine lakes. Despite the heavy use, angling pressure is light on Mirror Lake and the intricate shoreline offers easy bank fishing and lots of room to spread out and explore. Take your camera along—9,572-foot Eagle Cap looms to the south.

Moccasin Lake (Eagle Cap Wilderness)
hike-in

A good bet for small brook trout and oft photographed for its reflection of nearby 9,572-foot Eagle Cap, Moccasin Lake sits in the heart of the Lakes Basin in the Eagle Cap Wilderness, south of Wallowa Lake. This area is heavily visited during the summer. The trail from the end of Lostine River Road travels about 8.3 miles and gains 1,800 feet. To reach the trailhead at Two Pan Campground, follow SR 82 from Elgin to the little town of Lostine and then watch for the signs for Lostine River Road. The trailhead and the small campground are at the end of the road. Alternately you can reach the lake from the West Fork Wallowa Trail at Wallowa Lake, but this route is both longer and substantially steeper.

Morgan Lake (Union County)
campground, boat ramp

Very popular with anglers from Union County, 60-acre Morgan Lake is a flooded pit pond sitting at 4,154 feet in the Blue Mountains southwest of La Grande. To get there from I-84, take Exit 265 and head northwest into town on Hwy 30/Adams Street. Turn left on Gekeler Lane, which becomes B Avenue, and then left again on Walnut Street. Walnut Street leads to Morgan Lake Road. Watch for the signs to the lake.

Morgan Lake offers rainbow trout, brook trout, and crappie. The crappie typically range from 6 to 9 inches, sometimes larger, and ODFW sometimes stocks the lake with a few hundred 1- to 2-pound trout along with the usual allotment of legal-size fish. Brook trout are included in the five-fish daily trout limit, but no size limit applies to them. No motors are allowed on the lake and the boat ramps are primitive. Bank angling is easy and most people fish bait here. The camping area is undeveloped, but popular. Morgan Lake fishes best during late spring and again during the fall.

Mottet Creek (Union County)
see Lookingglass Creek

Mud Creek (Wallowa County)

A small tributary to the Grande Ronde River, Mud Creek offers limited opportunity for small wild redband trout in steep canyon country north of Enterprise. Most of the creek flows through public property, but no roads follow along the creek, so you must hike in from above. Forest Road 3021 crosses the upper end of the creek just west of the Sled Springs Work Center, located along SR 3 north of Enterprise.

Olive Lake (Umatilla National Forest)
campground, boat ramp

Located high in the Blue Mountains southeast from Ukiah, Olive Lake is a scenic and fairly popular 160-acre fishery offering redband trout, brook trout, and kokanee, along with a few cutthroat trout. Sitting at 6,012, Olive Lake is rarely accessible until late spring and fishing is usually good right away for trout from 8 to 14 inches and kokanee of similar size. The fishing tends to hold up fairly well during the summer and can be very good during autumn.

From Ukiah, head south on Hwy 395 to a left-hand turn on FR 55 (Texas Bar Road). After 1 mile, turn right on FR 10 and continue easterly 26 miles to a right-hand turn on FR 480, leading to the lake. The developed campground at Olive Lake, on the northeast side, offers 23 sites and two boat ramps. Motors are allowed, but the lake is off-limits to waterskiers, which makes for a pleasant and typically quiet high lake fishing experience. A 2.5-mile-long trail encircles Olive Lake, allowing bank anglers easy access to secluded shorelines.

Angling success on Olive Lake is about equally divided between still fishing with bait and casting or trolling artificial lures. Fly anglers enjoy consistent success with sub-surface flies, either by casting and retrieving or by trolling slowly with a sinking line. Dry fly action occurs morning and evening and sometimes at mid-day when *Callibaetis* mayflies hatch along the lake's shallow fringes.

Peach Road Pond (Union County)

A good place to take the kids, this small pond on the Ladd Marsh Wildlife Management Area is annually stocked with legal-size rainbows and usually provides fair-to-good fishing from late April through May. As summer arrives, best fishing is morning and evening. As the name suggests, the pond lies alongside Peach Road. Follow I-84 to the Hwy 30/203 exit (Exit 265) and head easterly towards Hot Springs. Just past Hot Springs, turn north and follow Peach Road about 1 mile to the pond. (Also known as Ladd Marsh Pond).

Pearson Ridge Pond
see Ukiah Area Ponds

Penland Lake
see Lake Penland

Pocket Lake (Eagle Cap Wilderness)
hike-in, cross-country

If you rank solitude and good fishing on equal terms, little 9-acre Pocket Lake is one of the best destinations in the ever-popular Lakes Basin Management Area of the Eagle Cap Wilderness. A deep, blue gem surrounded by rocky crags, Pocket Lake sits just far enough off the trail that few people visit it and of those who do, only a handful are anglers. The brook trout typically range from 6 to 12 inches. Of the two cross-country routes to the lake, the easier way is to follow the Glacier Pass Trail (#1806) south from Moccasin Lake. Before you reach the top of the pass, the steepness of the terrain eases off a bit and the trail dips to the left to cross a streambed. You can simply follow the contour east about .8 of a mile to the lake, though you must negotiate one very steep side hill section. The other option is to follow the south bank of Lake Creek east from Moccasin Lake about a mile to the outlet creek from Pocket. Then follow the creek steeply uphill half a mile to the lake. Be sure to consult your topo map. For directions to the area, see Moccasin Lake herein.

Power City Ponds (Umatilla County)

Power City Ponds are part of the Power City Wildlife Area near Hermiston and offer fair-to-good fishing for brown bullhead and largemouth bass, along with a few bluegill and white crappie. The fish likely originate from Cold Springs Reservoir. The ponds are located east of Hwy 395, a few miles north of Hermiston.

Prairie Creek (Wallowa County)

A generally slow-to-fair producer of wild rainbows, Prairie Creek flows entirely through private ranch lands in the Wallowa Valley near Joseph. A few of the trout reach 16 to 19 inches, but the average fish is about 11 inches. Though not plentiful throughout the creek, the fish are fairly numerous in the scattered reaches of the stream with good habitat. Access to Prairie Creek is by permission only and landownership is usually easy to decipher. Knock on doors to gain access. Highway 82 crosses the creek once, 3 miles north of Joseph and the best fishing lies on the stretch upstream (east) from the highway crossing. The stream flows high and off-color through June, so best fishing is from July through early October.

Prospect Lake (Eagle Cap Wilderness)
hike-in, cross-country

Unique because it is more than 100 feet deep but only 14 acres in size, Prospect Lake is a fairly remote and very pretty rainbow trout lake in the Eagle Cap Wilderness south of Wallowa Lake. It lies just to the south of popular and much larger Glacier Lake. To get there, take the West Wallowa Trail from Wallowa Lake, and hike the 13 long miles to Glacier Lake. Consult your topo map and walk around to the southeast shore of Glacier Lake, then head up and over the ridgeline to reach Prospect Lake, which sits at 8,328 feet. The rainbows here, while not always abundant, range from 8 to 12 inches with a few fish to 14 inches or more. Be advised that Prospect Lake often remains ice covered until late July and sometime into early August.

Razz Lake (Eagle Cap Wilderness)
hike-in, cross-country

A very pretty and productive brook trout lake with fish ranging from 5 to 10 inches, Razz Lake is only lightly fished owing to its location. The surrounding area—Lake Basin—is very popular, but most people don't make the climb up to 14-acre Razz Lake, which sits at 8,103 feet. The informal route begins at the north side of Horseshoe Lake and follows Razz Lake's outlet stream for about a mile to reach the lake. It gets plenty steep in places. From the West Fork Wallows Trailhead 1 mile south of Wallowa Lake, hike south for 6 miles to the trail junction at 6-Mile Meadow. From there make the long climb up the Lakes Basin Trail to Horseshoe Lake. Follow the main trail north around the lake and watch for the creek.

Rhea Creek (Morrow County)

A small, fairly productive tributary of Willow Creek, Rhea Creek flows entirely through private ranch and farmlands south and west of Heppner. State Route 206/207 crosses the creek southwest of Heppner and east from Condon, and Rhea Creek Road follows it for most of its length. Even where the roads parallel the stream, Rhea Creek is entirely private so anglers must first seek landowner permission. Downstream from the highway bridge (SR 207), the creek dries up most summers, so the upper third of the creek supports the trout habitat. Redbands here can reach more than 18 inches, but most are much smaller. Ruggs Ranch, located upstream from the highway bridge, marks the downstream extent of the good water. The 70,000-acre ranch is a shooting preserve and offers guests the opportunity to fish a good section of the tiny creek (541-676-5390).

Road 53/Road 54 Ponds
see Ukiah Area Ponds

Rock Creek (Morrow County)

A small creek in the mountains south of Heppner, Rock Creek offers limited fishing opportunity for wild rainbows in the stretch at and near Anson Wright County Park on Hwy 207. This stream gets very low during summer, so try it during May or June. Most of the creek, rather degraded by agriculture, flows entirely through private lands, eventually meeting the John Day 22 miles above the river's mouth.

Roger Lake (Eagle Cap Wilderness)
hike-in

This shallow, spring-fed lake in the Eagle Cap Wilderness Area offers small brook trout. The lake sits about a quarter mile east of popular Aneroid Lake, on the east side of the trail. To get there, head for Wallowa Lake and follow the road around the lake until it ends at the trailheads for the Wallowa River and for Aneroid Lake. The hike covers about 5 miles.

Roulet Pond (Union County)

Roulet Pond is a tiny (half acre) pond located adjacent to SR 82 about 3 miles northeast from Elgin. The pond is stocked two or three times each April and May with legal-size rainbows. Often you can have the pond to yourself during midweek, but fishing tends to slow down appreciably by late June or early July.

Rowe Creek Reservoir (Wheeler County)

Sitting on private property, this popular 20-acre irrigation-storage reservoir on Rowe Creek due west of Service Creek and south of Fossil offers fair action for stocked trout. The landowner allows limited access through an agreement with ODFW that leaves the shoreline open to public fishing. Small boats are allowed, but there is no formal ramp and there is a 5-mph speed limit. The reservoir is ideally suited to float tubes and other such small craft. Most anglers still fish with bait from shore. Be sure to clean up all trash to help preserve good will with the property owners. To get there, first head for either Fossil or for Service Creek on the John Day River. On SR 19, halfway between Fossil and Service Creek, the state owns a strip of land along Service Creek called Shelton Wayside. Just west of Shelton Wayside, turn south on Rowe Creek Road and follow it about 8 miles to the reservoir. Fishing is best in the spring after the reservoir is stocked with legal-size rainbows.

Salt Creek Summit Pond (Wallowa County)
see Wallowa County Forest Ponds

Searcy Pond (Umatilla County)

Formerly open to public access and stocked by ODFW, this pond and the other ponds at the old Kinzua Mill site are currently closed due to a change in land ownership. However, ODFW is in the process of negotiating renewed access to these popular ponds east of Fossil. Check with ODFW for current details.

Seventh Street Pond (John Day)

This small pond in John Day is regularly stocked with legal-size rainbows by ODFW. Fishing pressure can be fairly intense in the days following stockings, so catch rates tend to fall off as the season wears on. Check with ODFW for current stocking schedules. As the name suggests, the pond is located off 7th Street, northeast from town.

Shimmiehorn Pond
see Walla Walla R.D. Ponds

Slide Lake (Strawberry Mountain Wilderness)
see Strawberry Lake

Slide Lake, Little (Strawberry Mountain Wilderness)
see Strawberry Lake

Steamboat Lake (Eagle Cap Wilderness)
see Swamp Lake

Strawberry Lake (Strawberry Mountain Wilderness)
hike-in

Scenic and productive Strawberry Lake spans 31 acres and offers good fishing for wild brook trout and rainbow trout. The fish range from 5 to 18 inches, with 6- to 12-inch trout being typical. The hike into Strawberry Lake covers an easy mile, making it conducive to carrying in a float tube or small raft. The lake offers excellent fly-angling prospects and surface action occurs most days with hatches of *Callibaetis* mayflies, caddisflies, and midges, along with flights of flying ants. Spin fishing is equally popular. Along with towering 9,038-foot Strawberry Mountain, Strawberry Lake is the centerpiece of a federally designated wilderness area encompassing 68,700 acres and featuring five fishable lakes.

Strawberry Lake is by far the largest and deepest of the lakes and usually the most productive. The other stocked lakes in the wilderness include 4-acre Little Strawberry Lake, 13-acre Slide Lake, 3-acre Little Slide Lake, and 5-acre High Lake. All of these lakes lie within easy hiking distance from Strawberry Lake and experienced wilderness hikers will have no difficulty fishing all of them over the course of a two- or three-day trip into the wilderness area.

The Strawberry Lake Trail begins at Strawberry Campground south of Prairie City on Hwy 26. Watch for the sign at Depot Park and then follow Strawberry Road (Route 60) 12 miles to the campground. This area is quite popular during the summer. Additional trailheads—far less busy—are found on the south side of the range, accessible via FR 16 leading east from Seneca to a left-hand turn on FR 1640. Be sure to carry a map of the area.

Strawberry Lake, Little (Strawberry Mountain Wilderness)
see Strawberry Lake

Sugarbowl Pond
see Ukiah Area Ponds

Swamp Lake (Eagle Cap Wilderness)
hike-in

Holding the distinction of being the last lake in Oregon where stocked golden trout persist, Swamp Lake was subsequently and regularly stocked with rainbow trout. However, an ODFW survey conducted in the early 1990s yielded a handful of 10- to 12-inch golden trout, so stocking of rainbow trout was halted. No reliable reports of golden trout supersede that time frame, but those small goldens proved that successful spawning has occurred in the lake's outlet. Originally Swamp Lake was stocked with golden trout in the 1960s and, in 1987, Swamp Lake produced a state-record 7-pound, 10-ounce golden trout. A golden trout of such size would likely have been at least ten years old and probably older. In any event, the lake remains a highly scenic gem offering at least a chance to find golden trout, even though they are rare in the lake.

The trail to Swamp Lake covers about 9 miles, gaining about 2,200 feet. The lake sits at 7,837 feet. To get there, take SR 82 to the town of Lostine and then follow Lostine River Road heading south along the Lostine River. The trailhead (Two Pan) is at the end of the road. Follow the Lostine River Trail (#1670) 2.6 miles to a right-hand swing onto the Copper Creek Trail (#1656), which leads 5 miles uphill to a right-hand turn onto the North Minam Trail (#1675). Swamp Lake is a mile down this trail. The trails are usually free of snow by mid-July. Swamp Lake's neighbors—Long Lake and Steamboat Lake—both provide good fishing for small brook trout, with typical fish ranging from 6 to 10 inches. Lost Lake is 1.5 miles by trail northwest of Swamp Lake and Steamboat Lake lies 1 mile to the north. You can easily sample all three lakes in a day's time and all three offer nice campsites.

Tatone Pond (Morrow County)

Located 2 miles west of Boardman, 1-acre Tatone Pond offers fair fishing for brown bullhead and stocked rainbow trout. The trout fishing is best during spring and tapers off as summer's heat arrives. The bullhead fishing peaks from April through July. Still fishing with bait is best for both species. Follow I-84 to the Tower Road exit (Exit 159) and turn north to the railroad tracks. Drive east next to the tracks for about a quarter of a mile to the small parking area and then follow the trail north a fifth of a mile to the pond.

Thirtymile Creek (Gilliam/Wheeler Counties)

A remote and lengthy tributary to the lower John Day River, Thirtymile Creek and its major fork (East Fork Thirtymile Creek) flow entirely through private ranchlands south of Condon. Where suitable habitat and stream flow exists, the two streams offer a few wild redband trout, although recent drought cycles have hit these waters hard. Access is entirely by permission of the landowners, so be prepared to spend time driving back roads and knocking on doors. With its best reaches in remote canyons and with land ownership difficult to decipher, Thirtymile Creek is best for local residents.

Tombstone Lake (Eagle Cap Wilderness)
see Diamond Lake

Trout Creek (Umatilla National Forest)

Located about 32 miles southeast of Ukiah, Trout Creek offers fair-to-good fishing for small brook trout and a few wild redband trout. The brookies, rather stunted from over-population, rarely exceed 10 inches. All methods produce here, with bait and spinners having the edge during the early season and dry flies being best during the low-water period of summer and fall. The public-access stretch of Trout Creek begins on the downstream side of FR 52. Hike downstream a little less than a mile to reach the meadow section. Camping is available at unimproved sites adjacent to the stream. From Ukiah head south on CR 531, which becomes FR 52 when you reach the national forest. Trout Creek is just past the Martin Creek Trailhead.

Trout Creek (Wallowa County)

A slow-to-fair producer of wild rainbow trout, with an occasional fish reaching 16 or more inches, Trout Creek flows almost entirely through private lands north of Enterprise in the Wallowa Valley. Access is by landowner permission and the productive reach is the creek's lowermost 2 miles. State Route 3, heading north from Enterprise, follows the creek and the last mile is accessible by local roads once you have secured permission to access the property.

Trout Farm Pond (Grant County)

A pleasant and relatively popular half-acre pond stocked with legal-size rainbow trout, this pond sits alongside the Logan Valley-John Day River Road about 15 miles southeast of Prairie City. There's a campground nearby and the pond usually fishes best from mid-May through June.

Twin Ponds (Umatilla National Forest)
campground

Stocked with both legal-size and trophy-size rainbow trout prior to the event, these ponds are the site of the annual Ukiah Kid's Fishing Derby held each June. The two ponds are located adjacent to Bridge Creek Wildlife Area, a major wintering area for elk and deer. In addition to stocked trout, the ponds harbor largemouth bass, which are most common in the south pond. All methods produce here and fishing generally peaks between May and late June. Summer evenings can be good for bass. The camping area is unimproved, but fairly popular and convenient. Drift Fence Campground is located 2 miles east of the ponds. From Ukiah, Twin Ponds are located about 6 miles southeast of town. Follow FR 52 toward Bridge Creek Wildlife Area and then turn down the 013 spur.

Ukiah Area Ponds (Umatilla National Forest)

The Umatilla National Forest and ODFW stock quite a variety of old rock quarry ponds located in the general vicinity of Ukiah. Most are located in forested settings and most are fairly lightly fished. They are stocked each spring with legal-size rainbow trout, usually before the general fishing season opens in May, and a few of the ponds offer warmwater species as well. Maps with the locations of these ponds and stocking information are available at the District office in Ukiah. Directions to the larger ponds are as follows (also see Twin Ponds herein):

Drift Fence Pond: Follow FR 52 southeast from Ukiah for 8 miles to the 440 spur road on your left. Drift Fence Pond has stocked trout and largemouth bass. Drift Fence Campground is nearby.

Pearson Ridge Pond: From Ukiah, take FR 52 heading southeast. The pond is located about 14 miles outside of town on the 270 spur, on the north side of FR 52. Stocked rainbows over-winter here so a few 14- to 16-inch fish are taken each spring. Primitive camping is available near the pond.

5318 Pond (5318 Rock Pit Pond): From Ukiah, follow Hwy 244 west to the junction with Hwy 395 and continue straight at the intersection towards Heppner on FR 53 (Blue Mountain Scenic Byway). Follow FR 53 about 12 miles to a left-hand turn on FR 5316 and continue 1 mile to FR 5318. Turn left and drive 1.5 miles, watching for the pond on the south side of the road, between the 020 and 030 spurs. A dirt road exits the 5318 at the pond. In addition to stocked trout, this pond offers black bullhead.

Ellis Pond: From the Hwy 244/Hwy 395 junction west of Ukiah, head west on FR 53 for 15 miles. The pond is on the left-hand side of the road, a little more than half a mile past the 140 spur road.

Sugarbowl 030 Pond: From the Hwy 244/Hwy 395 Junction west of Ukiah, head west on FR 53 for about 7 miles to a left-hand turn on FR 5309. Follow FR 5309 south to the 030 spur road on the right and head down the spur about a fifth of a mile, where the pond is on the north side of the road.

5411-020 Pond: From Ukiah, follow Hwy 244 east 14 miles to a left turn on FR 54. Head north to a left turn onto FR 5411 and continue half a mile to a left turn on the 015 Spur. The pond will be on the left about 200 yards miles from the 5411-015 Junction. A dirt road accesses the pond.

5415-050 Pond: Follow Hwy 244 east from Ukiah for 14 miles to a left turn onto FR 54 and head north to a left turn on FR 5412. Follow 5412 about 3.25 miles to the 050 Spur. The pond is located on the east side of the spur road.

Yellowjacket Pond: From Ukiah, follow Hwy 244 east 14 miles to a left turn heading north on FR 54. Follow FR 54 to a left-hand turn on FR 5412 and continue for 6.5 miles. The pond is located on the south side of the 5412 road, between the 150 and 160 spurs. This pond also has largemouth bass.

Umatilla Forest Ponds
see Ukiah Area Ponds and Walla Walla District Ponds

Umatilla River
The Umatilla River, though heavily degraded over the years owing to its proximity to major agricultural lands, offers an interesting mix of fisheries, ranging from small trout action in its upper reaches to salmon fishing in the city limits of Pendleton. Access to the river is the biggest challenge facing Umatilla anglers, but the fishing can be quite productive in certain places, especially for those with good timing.

Chinook salmon, mostly of hatchery origin, arrive in the Umatilla during the spring, with the open season currently extending from mid-April through June. Coho salmon, also of hatchery origin, arrive during late summer and fall. Current regulations allow for a September through November season. At the same time fall chinook salmon enter the Umatilla, but there is currently no open season on the adults, although anglers may fish for and keep fall chinook jacks. A small run of summer-run Columbia Basin steelhead makes its way up the Umatilla, with the first fish usually arriving during September. The bulk of the run arrives later in the fall when the river's temperature drops. Only fin-clipped steelhead may be kept during the season, which currently lasts from Sept. 1 through April 15. Be sure to check current regulations before pursuing anadromous fish on the Umatilla.

Many local anglers catch salmon and steelhead within the city limits of Pendleton, where access to the river is fairly good downstream from the Hwy 11 bridge on the east end of town. Upstream from the bridge, the Umatilla is on Umatilla Indian Reservation lands. You will need a permit to fish tribal lands upstream from the bridge (call 541-276-4109).

Umatilla River

Umatilla River, North Fork
(Umatilla National Forest)
hike-in, no bait, catch-and-release, campground

At just 20,144 acres in size, the North Fork Umatilla Wilderness is one of Oregon's smallest wilderness areas. The crown jewel of the wilderness is the North Fork itself, a gin-clear, clean mountain stream offering good catch-and-release fishing for small, native trout. The fish range from 6 to 12 inches, though you might find a larger bull trout in these waters and the river also supports a few spawning steelhead and salmon.

Except for a short length of river near the campground at Umatilla Forks, the entire North Fork is a hike-in fishery as it flows for about 10 miles through the wilderness, carving out a steep, scenic canyon. The trail is divided into two segments. The lower section follows the river upstream from Umatilla Forks for about 4.5 miles and is open to both foot and horse traffic. However, because horses are not allowed at the Umatilla Forks Day Use Area, horse riders must instead access the main trail by way of the Lick Creek Trailhead to the north. The upper section of the trail climbs steeply away from the river, ascending the ridge to the north before exiting the wilderness at the Coyote Ridge Trailhead south of Tollgate.

This upper trail offers a lengthy, but fairly expedient and scenic descent to the river for those who prefer to fish the uppermost reaches by more or less bushwhacking into the headwaters. Otherwise, stick to the lower trail, which provides ready access to the river. To reach Umatilla Forks and the main trailhead from Pendleton, follow Umatilla River Road east about 33 miles, continuing past Bingham Springs and past Corporation Guard Station. To reach Coyote Ridge Trailhead, take SR 204 toward Tollgate. About half a mile west of the shopping center at Tollgate, turn south on FR 3719 and then turn right on Spur Road 040.

The South Fork is perfectly suited to attractor-style dry flies, with specific pattern being inconsequential. Small spinners, fished barbless with a single hook, also work here. The fishing is best during June and July and again during autumn, when few people hike the trails. If you fish the river after the opening of deer and elk season, be sure to wear bright colors. Several other streams in the wilderness also offer good fishing for small natives. These include Buck Creek and Coyote Creek. The latter stream has no formal trail, but Buck Creek is followed by a good and lightly traveled trail that heads south from the next trailhead south of Umatilla Forks.

Umatilla River, South Fork
(Umatilla National Forest)
no bait, catch-and-release, campground

Partly accessible by road and partly by hiking, the South Fork Umatilla is a fair-to-good producer of small, wild rainbows and is open only for catch-and-release fishing with flies and artificial lures. The South and North Forks converge at Umatilla Forks about 33 miles east of Pendleton. From the confluence, FR 32 follows the South Fork upstream for about 3 miles, offer-ing easy access. After that however, access to the south fork is by trail only. The trailhead is located at the South Fork Bridge and from there the trail follows the river for about 2.2 miles, crossing it several times. An elk hunter's camp marks the end of the maintained trail, but you can bushwhack it from there and continue well south up the diminutive river. See Umatilla River, North Fork for driving directions to Umatilla Forks. Of the South Fork's major tributaries, Shimmiehorn Creek is the best and offers fair-to-good action for small native trout.

Unit Lake (Eagle Cap Wilderness)
hike-in

A good brook/rainbow trout lake spanning about 12 acres, Unit Lake is located on the east-facing slope not far from ever-popular Horseshoe Lake in the Eagle Cap Wilderness. From the West Fork Wallows Trailhead 1 mile south of Wallowa Lake, hike south for 6 miles to the trail junction at 6-Mile Meadow. From there make the long climb up the Lakes Basin Trail to Horseshoe Lake. As you reach Horseshoe Lake, watch for the trail to fork. Take the right-hand fork north to the right-hand turn onto the Unit Lake Trail, which leads about half a mile down to the lake. Unit Lake sits at 7,007 feet.

Victor Pond (Wallowa County)

Victor Pond, stocked two or three times each April and May, is a small irrigation-diversion pond situated next to SR 82, about 2 miles west from the little community of Wallowa. ODFW stocks legal-size rainbow trout here and the fishing remains fair through early June.

Walk-in Pond
see Walla Walla R.D. Ponds

Walla Walla R.D. Ponds
(Umatilla National Forest)

Beginning in 2003, ODFW and Umatilla National Forest began stocking several small rock-quarry ponds on the Walla Walla Ranger District of northeastern Oregon. These ponds are stocked spring and summer with legal-size rainbow trout and offer anglers a chance to escape the larger, better-known fisheries. The ponds are good family destinations with easy bank fishing access, but use care with small children because of the steep drop-offs into deep water. There are no developed campgrounds at the ponds, but plenty of opportunity for primitive camping. Be sure to check for fire restrictions. Umatilla National Forest Supervisor's Office in Pendleton offers a brochure with a map detailing the location of the ponds. Driving directions are as follows:

Black Mountain Pond: From SR 204 (Weston-Elgin Highway), follow FR 31 south to FR 3128. Then take FR 3135 to Spur Road 030. The pond is on the left, about a quarter mile down the spur road, but is not visible from the road.

Horse Camp Pond: From SR 204 (Weston-Elgin Highway), head south about 3 miles on FR 31 to Spur Road 287. The pond is just off FR 31 at spur 287.

Shimmiehorn Pond: From SR 204 (Weston-Elgin Highway) take FR 31 South to FR 3128, then FR 3130 to Spur Road 013. Shimmiehorn Pond is about one quarter mile down Spur 013 on the left. It is not visible from the road.

Keyhole Pond: From I-84 east from Meacham, take Exit 243 and head north on FR 31 about 12 miles to Spur Road 090. Follow Spur 090 to Spur Road 094. The pond is to the right of 094 and offers lost of flat ground for primitive camping.

Boundary Pond: From I-84 east from Meacham, take Exit 243 and head north on FR 31 about 3.5 miles to the 024 Spur Road. Watch closely for the spur road and do not go past FR 3104 (1.7 miles past Mt. Emily Sno-Park).

Walk-in Pond: Take FR 31 north from I-84, Exit 243 (Mt. Emily/Summit Road), then FR 3102 north and east about 1 mile to a locked gate. Park at the gate and walk about half a mile to pond, which is off FR 3102 near the 160 Spur. The pond sits about 100 yards to the right (south and east) of road and is not visible from the road

Walla Walla River (Umatilla County)

The mainstem of the Walla Walla River flows for less than 10 miles through Umatilla County before crossing the border into Washington. The stream receives a small run of summer steelhead, which begin arriving in the river by mid-autumn or thereabouts, but the season does not open until December 1. Only adipose fin-clipped (hatchery) steelhead may be taken and bait is not allowed. Most anglers fish the river for steelhead during December and then again during March and April. Because of their comparatively short migration, these Walla Walla steelhead tend to be in better shape come spring than their brethren well to the east in the Grande Ronde and its tributaries. Public access is problematic; so most fishing occurs in the city limits of Milton-Freewater and at a few other nearby spots. Mostly you'll need landowner permission to access the river. The steelhead season closes on April 15 (check current regulations).

Walla Walla River, North Fork (Umatilla National Forest)

hike-in, no bait

A fair-to-good bet for small, wild rainbow trout, the North Fork Walla Walla is accessible only by trail. The best bet is to follow the trail downstream from the Tiger Saddle Trailhead at the headwaters. Traveling through old-growth forest, this trail, and the river itself, provides a fine diversion from the summer heat that often settles into the surrounding lowlands. The trail is open to mountain bikes, horses, and motorcycles, so anglers may wish to avoid summer weekends. Also, quite a few hunters travel the trail by horseback during elk season. To get there, head from Pendleton to Walla Walla, Washington and then head east through town on Hwy 12 to a right-hand turn on Mill Creek Road. Follow this road back across the Oregon border to a right turn on FR 55. Continue past the junction with FR 6511 and then turn right on FR 6512, following it to the trailhead at the 020 Spur.

Walla Walla River, South Fork (Umatilla National Forest)

hike-in, campground, no bait

A consistently good producer of small, wild trout, the South Fork Walla Walla River, ranks among the better trout streams in northeastern Oregon. The river is especially good during autumn, when vibrant colors paint the leaves along the banks and the fork is largely devoid of anglers. Wild rainbows range from 5 to 14 inches, averaging perhaps 9 inches. They are eager to pounce on dry flies and will also take nymph patterns, streamer patterns, and small spinners.

You'll need a pair of hiking boots to enjoy the South Fork, as its upper half—the productive half—flows entirely through a fairly steep, scenic, forested canyon. This canyon is remarkably pristine and the riparian habitat surprisingly intact. The area managed to survive the era of rampant logging and mining largely unscathed, so the South Fork's trout now enjoy outstanding natural habitat. The river remains shaded by timber and steep slopes throughout the hot summers and several springs and feeder creeks contribute to the perpetually cold water.

The trail, which runs along the river for more than 12 miles, offers good access though in places you'll have to scramble down to the water. Often the best strategy is to get in the water at the downstream end of a promising stretch and simply fish your way up the river.

Most anglers begin their trek from Harris Park Campground: From Milton-Freewater, turn east, following the signs to Harris Park. The trail is open to horses, mountain bikes, and motorcycles so, if you want some solitude, fish mid-week and hike at least 3 miles upstream before making your first cast. Autumn fishing can be especially good—and quiet—but you'll still want to hike for about an hour before fishing. The fishing improves quite a bit when you reach the middle section of the canyon.

Wallowa County Forest Ponds (Wallowa-Whitman National Forest)

Several small ponds scattered around Wallowa County are stocked regularly with rainbow trout by ODFW. Each of the following is located in the Wallowa-Whitman National Forest and all fish best during the late spring and early summer.

Salt Creek Summit Pond: Salt Creek Summit Pond lies just east of the Salt Creek Summit Sno-Park on the Wallowa Mountains Loop Road southeast from Joseph and about 45 miles northeast from Halfway. Turn into the sno-park and then take the left-hand fork on FR 3915. About half a mile in, watch for the pond on the right. The pond is accessible between June and October.

McGraw Pond: Head east from Joseph on Little Sheep Creek Road for about 8 miles to FR 39. Head southeasterly on FR 39 about 25 miles to the McGraw Overlook Road (FR 3965). After about 3 miles you'll reach the McGraw Overlook and the pond is on the west side of the road.

Honeymoon Pond: Located in remote country north of Enterprise, Honeymoon Pond fishes best during May and June. Follow Hwy 3 north 14 miles to a right-hand turn on FR 46. Continue about 38 miles to FR 4680 (Cold Springs Road). The pond is located a quarter of a mile off a short spur road across FR 46 from the junction with FR 4680.

Teepee Pond: Follow SR 3 north from Enterprise about 14 miles to a right-hand turn on FR 46. Continue northeasterly about 32 miles to the Teepee Butte Road (FR 595) and head north on FR 595 about one quarter mile to the pond.

Wallowa Lake (Wallowa County)
campground, lodging, boat recommended, boat ramp

One of the state's best fisheries for kokanee salmon, Wallowa Lake enjoys the added bonus of being one of Oregon's prettiest drive-to lakes. Occupying a narrow, ancient glacier-scoured valley, 1,600-acre Wallowa Lake also offers good fishing for 9- to 18-inch stocked rainbow trout, slow-to-fair action for Mackinaw and even an occasional bull trout. The bull trout here are fully protected and must be released immediately. Currently the limit on all other species is five fish per day in any combination with no size restrictions.

A few of Wallowa Lake's kokanee reach 20 inches in length during a good year, but such trophies are rare even though the state record came from the lake in 2001, when angler Pamella Fahey landed a monster weighing almost 6 pounds, 12 ounces. Fahey's fish was the second state record kokanee to come from Wallowa Lake in just four years. Typical kokanee here range from 9 to 14 inches and most anglers troll during morning and evening, especially along the western shoreline in front of the numerous residences. Try this same area for Mackinaw using fish-finding equipment and down-rigging gear or deep-diving jigs. Mackinaw, though no longer stocked, still haunt the depths of Wallowa Lake and reach more than 30 pounds. Though hardly as good a Mackinaw producer as Odell or Crescent Lakes, Wallowa nonetheless attracts a handful of anglers who specialize in fishing for these deep-water char and at least one outfitter guides Mackinaw (and kokanee) anglers on Wallowa Lake (Tri-State Outfitters, 541-426-4468).

Mackinaw fishing is possible just about any time between ice-out and ice-up, but most anglers pursue these fish during May and June. Similarly, most of the kokanee fishing action occurs between May and July. Morning is prime time because afternoon winds frequently disrupt the lake and no matter what the wind does, you can count on the water skiers and jet skiers to arrive in hordes every weekend during the summer.

Trout fishing really seems to have no peak time on the lake and is consistently good from May through October. Even during the hottest part of August you can enjoy consistent action by fishing below the inlet on the south end of the lake. For this you'll want a boat, canoe, or float tube. The north end of the lake, incidentally, is the best bet for fly fishing. Bank fishing is best along the road, which follows the east shoreline. Each year, trout anglers catch plenty of rainbows from 14 to 22 inches long.

Rental boats are available at Wallowa Lake Marina (541-432-9115/www.wallowalakemarina.com) on the north shore (just west from the Wallowa River inlet). The marina includes a store. Mooring for private boats is available only through Wallowa Lake State Park, which also runs a huge campground with 121 full-hookup sites, 89 tent sites and a day-use area. Also adjacent to the lake's south end, the tiny community of Wallowa Lake lies dispersed through the forested flats, offering several restaurants and lodging options, including the rustic old Wallowa Lake Lodge (541-432-9821/www.wallowalakelodge.com) and quite a few rental houses and cabins. Nearby Joseph offers additional dining and lodging options just minutes from the lake's north shore.

Wallowa Lake is a popular and scenic getaway at the foot of the Wallowa Mountains in northeast Oregon. For anglers with boats (rentals available), the lake offers good fishing for kokanee salmon, rainbow trout, and Mackinaw.

Wallowa River (Wallowa County)

A good trout stream, also with a good spring fishery for steelhead, the Wallowa River offers several distinct personalities. Its headwater stretch tumbles through a scenic, forested glacier-carved canyon in the Eagle Cap Wilderness. Here the river offers fair-to-good action for small wild trout before dumping into Wallowa Lake just north of the town of Joseph. Upon departing the other end of Wallowa Lake, the river meanders through pastoral farmlands with the majestic Wallowa Mountains as a backdrop to the south. Finally the river enters a rugged, steep canyon and plunges more quickly down to its confluence with the Minam River. Emboldened further, the Wallowa then rushes northward through increasingly dramatic canyon lands until it finally joins the Grande Ronde River.

Through the Wallowa Valley, the river offers plenty of good trout fishing for wild fish ranging from 6 to 20 inches. Most of the rainbows here are in the 10- to 13-inch range, but 18-inch trout hardly raise eyebrows. For the most part, fishing this lengthy stretch of the Wallowa requires landowner permission because the entire stretch—from Wallowa Lake to the town of Wallowa—flows across private lands. Private property continues as the river enters the canyon downstream from Wallowa, but here the highway runs right alongside the stream. Access is good from the highway easement, but be sure to park only on the wide pullouts, at the Roadside Rest Stop, at the Big Canyon Road Bridge, or at the picnic area.

Regulations allow anglers to keep fin-clipped trout below Rock Creek, but these are hatchery-reared steelhead that never left the river. The wild fish, though not terribly abundant between Rock Creek and Minam, are beautifully marked rainbows. When the river clears during mid-summer, try for them with dry flies or small spoons and spinners.

Trout fishing on the Wallowa peaks between late June and October. Spin fishers enjoy consistent success, especially on the river's deeper pools, while fly fishing is especially good in the valley during hopper season and during autumn. Bait fishing is allowed downstream from Wallowa Lake; only flies and lures are permitted above the lake.

The Wallowa's spring steelhead fishery peaks between late February and the end of the season in mid-April. Only hatchery fish may be kept, but this is of little concern because very few wild fish (adipose fin intact) return to the Wallowa. These so-called "spring steelhead" are actually summer-run fish that enter the Columbia system as early as May the previous year. They over-winter in deep pools on the Snake and Grande Ronde Rivers before resuming their upriver journey in late winter. Most are quite skinny and dark by the time they reach the Wallowa, but they provide a great excuse to enjoy the spring sunshine on the river. Most anglers fish a relatively short section of river at and downstream from the hatchery facility at Big Canyon and also downstream from the Minam River confluence.

The Wallowa Valley and the Minam area offer lots of additional fishing opportunities, ranging from the lakes of the

The lower Wallowa River is popular for anglers seeking over-wintered steelhead during spring.

Eagle Cap Wilderness to the remote trout fishing found on the Grande Ronde. Campgrounds are scattered throughout the Wallowa-Whitman National Forest and the region's tiny towns—Wallowa, Lostine, Enterprise, and Joseph—offer all services and amenities.

Wallowa Wildlife Pond (Wallowa County)

A large pond covering about 3 acres, Wallowa Wildlife Pond lies adjacent to the Wallowa River about 2.5 miles northwest of the town of Wallowa. The pond is stocked regularly during the spring with legal-size rainbows and fishing tends to hold up through June. Local anglers often catch a few larger fish here during autumn. Still fishing with bait is best.

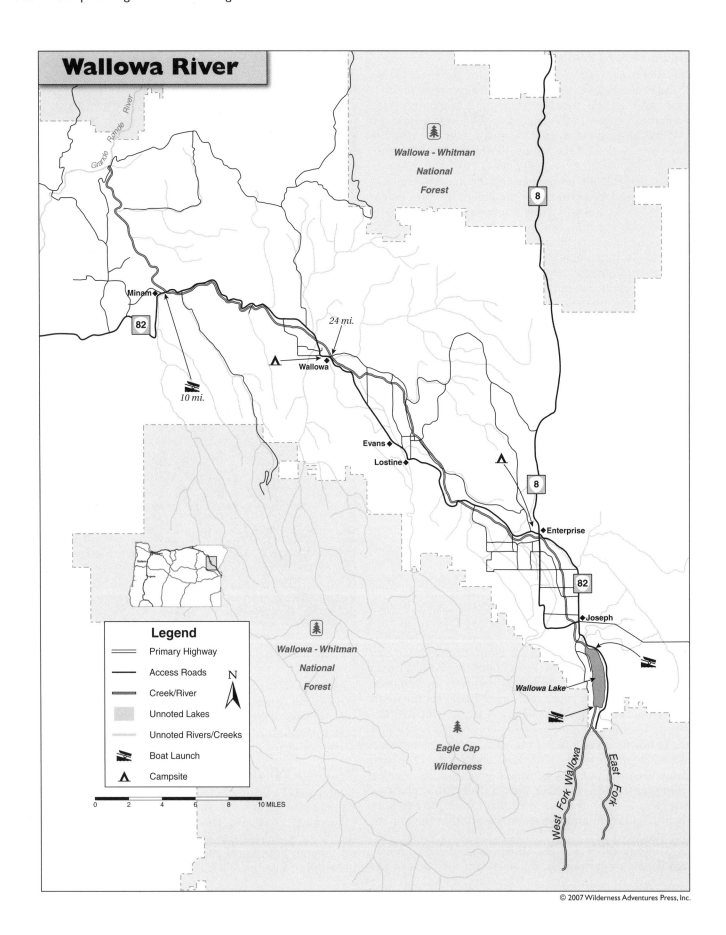

Wallowa River

Grande Ronde River

Wallowa - Whitman National Forest

8

Minam

82

24 mi.

Wallowa

10 mi.

Evans

Lostine

8

Enterprise

82

Joseph

Wallowa - Whitman National Forest

Wallowa Lake

Eagle Cap Wilderness

West Fork Wallowa

East Fork

Legend

⎯	Primary Highway
⎯	Access Roads
⎯	Creek/River
▨	Unnoted Lakes
⎯	Unnoted Rivers/Creeks
⛵	Boat Launch
⛺	Campsite

N

0   2   4   6   8   10 MILES

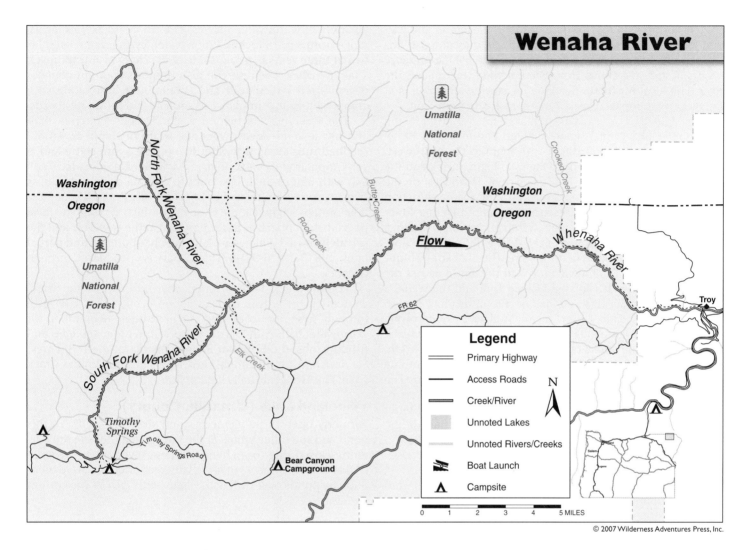

© 2007 Wilderness Adventures Press, Inc.

Wenaha River (Grande Ronde drainage)

hike-in

Truly a remarkable and wild river, the remote Wenaha flows entirely through roadless wilderness before meeting the Grande Ronde at the tiny town of Troy. Along its tumultuous journey, the canyon-bound Wenaha offers good fishing for wild rainbow trout ranging from 8 to 16 inches, with an occasional trout topping 18 inches. The trout are quite abundant throughout most of the stream and both they, and most of the river itself, are rarely seen by anglers. Solitude, fine scenery, and good fishing reward those who do make the trek into the Wenaha.

The Wenaha runs a northeasterly course after gathering the flows of several tributaries in the mountains north of Tollgate, east from Milton-Freewater and many miles due north of La Grande. Except for a few miles near its mouth, the entire river is included in the Wenaha-Tucannon Wilderness Area, which spans 177, 412 acres in total, 66,417 of which are in Oregon. Traditionally elk hunters have primarily used this area, but increasing numbers of anglers are sampling the

fine trout fishing on the river. Most anglers hike up from the town of Troy or use the comparatively short side trails dipping down to the river's south bank and intersecting the main trail that follows the Wenaha. To find total solitude, just hike up or downstream along the main trail to put some distance between yourself and the trail junctions. Or simply wait until autumn, when the fishing is exceptional and the pressure virtually non-existent.

The Wenaha River is also home to bull trout, a species of char listed on the federal list of threatened and endangered wildlife. All bull trout must be released immediately. These highly carnivorous fish reach several pounds and feed largely on other fish. They tend to inhabit the deep pools, especially where large boulders or logjams provide good cover. Large streamer flies, along with spoons and spinners can draw these fish out of their lairs, but fishing for them is strictly catch-and-release.

Steelhead, after running the Grande Ronde as far as Troy, ascend the Wenaha River in modest numbers. These are summer-run fish that arrive during the autumn. They are in peak condition from September through November, though many anglers continue to fish for them through the winter and well into spring. The season closes April 15 and only adipose-fin-clipped steelhead may be taken. Most of the fishing pressure occurs at and just above Troy, where a good trail follows the river. The legal upstream deadline for steelhead fishing is at the mouth of Crooked Creek, 7 miles upstream from Troy.

Forest Road 62 serves as the primary access route for hiking into the Wenaha River. A good road, and quite scenic, FR 62 connects Troy on the northeast with Elgin to the southwest. Follow SR 82 from La Grande to Elgin. In Elgin, turn left at the north edge of town when SR 82 veers right. Head west on the old Westin-Elgin Highway and turn right on Palmer Junction Road (CR 42), then follow the signs heading to Palmer Junction. Just before Palmer Junction, watch for the left-hand turn heading up to FR 63 (Jubilee Lake). At the FR63/62 junction, head right onto FR 62. When FR 62 reaches Lookout Mountain, watch for FR 6413, which turns to the left to access the uppermost trailheads (Jaussaud Creek Trail and the Wenaha Trail at Timothy Springs). Or stay on FR 62 heading east to reach the Elk Flat Trail, Cross Canyon Trail, and Hoodoo Trail, respectively. The Jaussaud Creek Trail covers 5.8 miles to reach the river, while the others range from 3.2 to 4.5 miles in length.

Along FR 62, you can find lots of good primitive camping spots, many of which are deer and elk hunter's camps. The only campgrounds in the area are above the headwaters of the Wenaha at Timothy Springs, Bone Springs, and Mottet Springs. All three of these campgrounds lie just outside the wilderness boundary, north and northeast of Jubilee Lake.

Weston Pond (Union County)

This half-acre pond is located adjacent to the gravel yard (Oregon Department of Transportation) on SR 204, 10 miles east of Weston. The pond is stocked twice each spring and fishing for legal-size rainbows is fair between late April and late May. Still fishing with bait is the most popular method.

Wildhorse Creek (Umatilla County)

Wildhorse Creek flows through private property from Athena down to the Umatilla River at Pendleton. The lower half of the creek offers a few rainbow trout, but fishing is slow. Be sure to get landowner permission before fishing the creek, which is closed to the taking of salmon and steelhead.

Wild Sheep Lake (Eagle Cap Wilderness)
see Blue Lake

Willow Creek

Willow, Rhea, and Butter Creeks, and McKay Creek above McKay Reservoir: Open April 26. Willow Creek will be stocked with catch-able trout in April and May through the cities of Heppner, Lexington and Ione.

Willow Creek Reservoir (Morrow County)
boat ramp, campground

Alternately called Willow Creek Lake, this 100-acre reservoir near Heppner offers good fishing for stocked trout and a variety of warmwater species. The trout, stocked as legals, range from 9 to 16 inches. When water levels remain solid for two or three years in a row, some of the carry-over trout reach a fat 18 inches. The reservoir also supports good numbers of decent-sized largemouth and smallmouth bass along with crappie, bluegill, pumpkinseed sunfish, and brown bullheads.

The reservoir sits behind a starkly solid concrete dam and fills a steep-sided ravine just south of Heppner. An old roadbed runs along the water line on the south shore and is very popular with bank anglers. Most bank anglers here still fish with bait, though jigs, both in crappie sizes and in bass sizes, can be very effective. Boats are also popular and the boat ramp is located at the west end of the reservoir. The local parks district operates a campground at the reservoir and the privately owned Willow Creek RV Park has both full and partial hook-ups (541-676-9618). The RV park is open March through October.

Willow Creek Lake is open year-round, but the frigid winters curb the fishing. Best action occurs from late April through June for trout and April through September for warmwater fish. With lots of support from other agencies and fishing clubs, the Heppner Ranger District of the U.S. Forest Service sponsors an annual kid's fishing derby at Willow Creek Lake. The event is usually held in June.

Wineland Lake (Umatilla County)

Formerly open to public access and stocked by ODFW, this pond and the other ponds at the old Kinzua Mill site are currently closed due to a change in land ownership. However, ODFW is in the process of negotiating renewed access to these popular ponds east of Fossil. Check with ODFW for current details.

Winom Creek (Umatilla National Forest)
campground

A small stream flowing alongside FR 52 (Blue Mountain Scenic Byway) 18 miles east of Ukiah, Winom Creek offers fair fishing for small, wild brook trout and redband trout. Bull trout reside in these waters and are fully protected, so anglers must make sure they can distinguish between bull trout and brook trout. Best brook trout action is downstream from FR 52.

Wood Lake (Eagle Cap Wilderness)
hike-in

A productive brook trout fishery in the Eagle Cap Wilderness Area, Wood Lake was among a very few lakes stocked with golden trout decades ago. The goldens are no longer present here, but brookies abound and reach at least 12 inches. The 7-mile hike gains about 2,900 feet and begins at Bowman Trailhead on Lostine River Road. From the little town of Lostine on SR 82, head south along the Lostine River. The trailhead is 3 miles south of Williamson Campground.

Yellowjacket Pond
see Ukiah Area Ponds

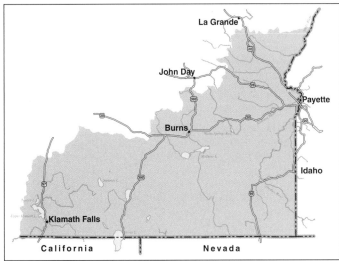

© 2007 Wilderness Adventures Press, Inc.

Southeast Zone

Southeastern Oregon is an arid but highly varied landscape replete with remarkable and stunning geography. Much of this region is encompassed by the much larger Great Basin—a 200,000-square-mile chunk of the intermountain west with no outside drainage. The Great Basin covers most of Nevada and parts of Utah, Idaho, California, and southeastern Oregon. This part of Oregon is characterized by massive fault-block mountain ranges interspersed with broad expanses of high desert. Some of the most awesome landscapes in the west rise up from the deserts of Malheur, Harney, and Lake Counties.

The must-see sights include the spectacular heights of Abert Rim, the colorful desert canyons of the Owyhee River, and the massive Steens Mountains, whose summit reaches 9,100 feet only to plunge precipitously off to the desert floor 5,000 feet below to the east. The southeast zone also includes the Malheur and Powder River drainages that originate in the rugged, forested Blue Mountains along with the superbly productive trout waters of the Klamath River/Klamath Lake drainage.

The southeast zone, encompassing most or all of the state's five largest counties (Malheur, Harney, Lake, Klamath, and Baker) is by far the most expansive geographical division made by Oregon Department of Fish & Wildlife. As you might expect, a region this large offers a wide array of interesting and productive fisheries, including some of the state's best big-trout waters and warmwater gamefish destinations. The Williamson River and nearby Upper Klamath Lake, for example, grow the state's largest wild trout. In the Klamath country, a 20-inch trout is hardly remarkable.

Further east, the arid expanses of southeastern Oregon are known for the many highly productive trout reservoirs where stocked rainbows grow fast and fat. The best of these include perennial favorites like Chickahominy, Malheur, and Thief Valley Reservoirs. In addition to the well-known reservoirs, the southeast zone offers a few tiny BLM reservoirs stocked with 500 to 1,000 trout annually by ODFW when conditions permit. ODFW feels, and I agree, that some of these little reservoirs are simply too small and fragile to stand up to statewide exposure. Thus several of them do not appear herein and anglers interested in an adventure must do a little homework through the ODFW offices out in southeastern Oregon.

This region also boasts the state's most remote wild trout waters in the form of tiny desert streams buried deep in the arid mountains of Lake, Malheur, and Harney Counties. Some of these streams remain the last strongholds for pure Lahontan cutthroat trout and others offer unique strains of redband trout. Both species are uniquely adapted to survive marginal conditions and climatic extremes of these desert waters.

All told, southeastern Oregon offers something for everyone, ranging from drive-up put-and-take fisheries to the waters accessible only to the most hardy and adventurous anglers. The one constant in this arid country is that the quality of the fishing usually depends on water supply. When drought cycles hit for two or three years in a row, many fisheries are devastated and when wet cycles occur, trout grow fast and furiously and countless southeast Oregon waters become amazingly productive big fish factories.

Contact List for Southeast Zone:

Oregon Department of Fish & Wildlife Headquarters
3406 Cherry Ave. NE
Salem, OR 97303
503-947-6200
www.dfw.state.or.us

ODFW--Klamath Watershed District Office
1850 Miller Island Road
Klamath Falls, OR 97603
541-883-5732

ODFW--Malheur Watershed District Office
237 S. Hines Blvd.
Hines, OR 97738
541-573-6582

ODFW--Lakeview Field Office
101 N. D Street
Lakeview, OR 97630
541-947-2950

ODFW--Ontario Field Office
3814 Clark Blvd.
Ontario, OR 97914
541-889-6975

ODFW--Baker City Field Office
2995 Hughes Lane
Baker City, OR 97814
541-523-5832

Fremont-Winema National Forest
1301 South G Street
Lakeview, OR 97630
541-947-2151

Fremont-Winema National Forest
2819 Dahlia Street
Klamath Falls, OR 97601
541-883-6714

Paisley Ranger District
Hwy. 31
Paisley, OR 97363
541-943-3114

Silver Lake Ranger District
Hwy. 31
Silver Lake, OR 97638
541-576-2107

Chiloquin Ranger District
38500 Hwy. 97 N.
Chiloquin, OR 97624
541-783-4001

Malheur National Forest
431 Patterson Bridge Road
John Day, OR 97845
541-575-3000

Emigrant Creek Ranger District
265 Hwy. 20 South
Hines, OR 97738
541-573-4300

Wallowa-Whitman National Forest
1550 Dewey
Baker City, OR 97814
541-523-6391

Baker Ranger District
3165 10th Street
Baker City, OR 97814
541-523-4476

Bureau of Land Management
Lakeview District Office
1301 S. G Street
Lakeview, OR 97630
541-947-2177

Bureau of Land Management
Burns District Office
28910 Hwy. 20 West
Hines, OR 97738
541-573-4400

Bureau of Land Management
Vale District Office
100 Oregon Street
Vale, OR 97918
541-473-3144

BLM Baker Resource Area
3285 11th Street
Baker City, OR 97914
541-523-1256

BLM Klamath Falls Resource Area
2795 Anderson Ave, #25
Klamath Falls, OR 97603
541-883-6916

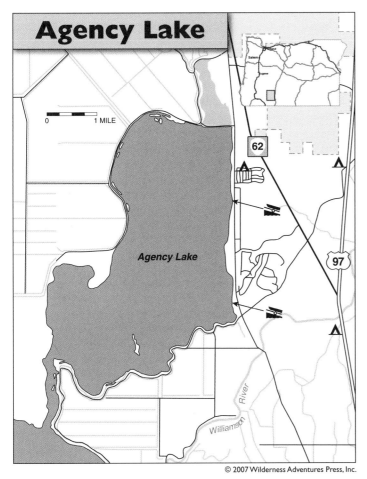

© 2007 Wilderness Adventures Press, Inc.

Agency Lake
boat recommended, boat ramp, campground

The northern neighbor of Klamath Lake, Agency offers a similar scenario of fishing fertile shallows for trophy-class redband trout, not to mention some big brown trout. Typical fish here range from 16 to 24 inches and a few exceed 30 inches, reaching double-digit weights. Fishing generally peaks during mid- to late spring and again during autumn, though the reservoir is open all year. All methods produce, with trolling hardware and fly angling both being popular. Fly anglers will need slow to medium-fast sinking lines and an assortment of leech, streamer, and attractor-style wet flies. During June, look for a chance to fish damsel nymphs and dry damsels against the reed stands, especially in the channel leading to Klamath Lake and at the mouth of the Wood River.

Agency Lake virtually requires a boat, which you can launch at public ramps on the southeast shore (Henzel Park) and the northeast shore (Petric Park). Use the launch at Henzel to fish the channel connecting Agency and Upper Klamath Lakes. This channel is a good place to fly fish throughout the spring. Many anglers fish the channel below the mouth of the

Wood River, a short run from Petric Park. Beware the wind here as it often blows hard across the lake during the afternoon.

Henzel Park offers a campground and additional campgrounds are located to the east along the Williamson River and north at Kimball Park on the Wood River. Anglers frequently use the Petric Park launch to run a ways up the Wood River, but remember that while Agency Lake is open year-round, the river is closed until late April and is limited to catch-and-release fishing. The lake currently has a one-fish limit. By ODFW definition, the Wood River extends "through the Wood River delta to emergent vegetation line in Agency Lake."

Alvord Creeks
closed waters

Stocked with Lahontan cutthroat during the 1970s, Big Alvord and Little Alvord Creeks are currently closed to fishing to help protect fragile remnant populations of these fish.

Ankle Creek (Steens Mountains)
hike-in, no bait

One of a handful of newly designated National Wild & Scenic Rivers in the Steens Mountains, diminutive Ankle Creek offers fair prospects for small wild redbands; and you'll have the place all to yourself, along with nearby Mud Creek and the adjacent Blitzen River. These waters are fishable from mid-summer through early October, with autumn being the best time. Until recently the Ankle Creek area was heavily grazed by cattle, but inclusion in a new wilderness area and accompanying land exchanges have removed the cattle, so recovery of the habitat should improve conditions for the native redband trout. For directions, see Mud Creek herein.

Ana Reservoir (Lake County)

Ana Reservoir, located in Lake County on the northern edge of the Summer Lake Basin, is best known for its thriving population of stocked striped bass/white bass hybrids, sometimes called "wipers." The fish reach double-digit weights and angling for them peaks during spring. ODFW plants about 2,000 fingerling "wipers" in the lake every other year along with annual stocks of legal-size rainbows. The reservoir is fairly fertile and some of the stocked trout carry over to reach 14 to 18 inches, although most of the catch is composed of the usual 10- to 12-inch variety. In recent years some largemouth bass have shown up here as well.

Spanning 58 acres, Ana maintains a consistent supply of water owing to the myriad springs in the basin. The springs also assure that Ana remains ice-free during winter. The hybrid bass fishery here attracts a handful of specialists who have learned the best techniques for targeting these superb gamefish. Most anglers fish for them from late winter through mid-spring, usually by boat and generally with deep-diving plugs and other hardware. The bass also take bait and some-

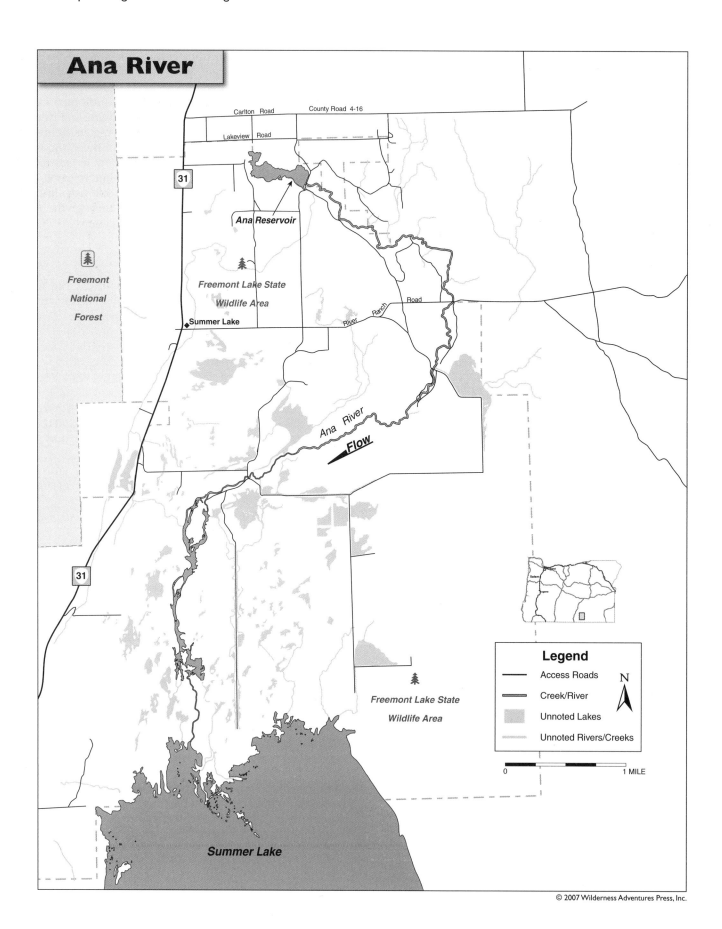

Ana River

Carlton Road

County Road 4-16

Lakeview Road

31

Ana Reservoir

Freemont
National
Forest

Freemont Lake State
Wildlife Area

Summer Lake

River   Ranch   Road

Ana   River

Flow

31

Freemont Lake State

Wildlife Area

Legend

—— Access Roads

—— Creek/River

Unnoted Lakes

Unnoted Rivers/Creeks

N

0   1 MILE

Summer Lake

Ana Reservoir near Summer Lake is Oregon's only fishery for striped bass/white bass hybrids, or "wipers."

times streamer flies tied in the 2- to 4-inch range. Fish flies on a sinking line. Sometimes the bass school up near the outlet at the south end of the dam, in which case you may be able to tempt them to chase a fly or lure. Often when they hold in the shallows, however, they are content not to feed. Be sure to consult current regulations on the bass fishery. As of this writing, the limit is one hybrid bass in any 24-hour period with a 16-inch minimum length.

The reservoir has no improved ramp, but you can launch car-toppers from the bank on the north shore. Likewise, you can easily launch a float tube. Most visitors here fish from the bank, either on the dam or from many locations around the shoreline, especially on the north side where access is easier. The trout, stocked as legals, provide most of the action. They take bait, lures, and flies about equally well. By autumn, some of these fish reach 14 to 18 inches, feeding on baitfish and a variety of other foods. Of note to fly anglers are the frequent evening rises to Chironomids.

Ana Reservoir lies just northeast from the tiny town of Summer Lake, a mile off the highway and about 75 miles from Lakeview. Three miles north of Summer Lake watch for the signed east turn onto CR 4-16, which is paved. If you're coming from the north (Silver Lake), head up and over Picture Rock Pass and when you finally reach the bottom of the grade, watch for the paved road leading east. Follow this road past the houses on your right and after about a mile-and-a-half make the right-hand turn on the dirt/gravel road heading a short distance down to the reservoir.

Ana River (Lake County)

A pretty little spring-fed stream flowing through the northern part of the Summer Lake Basin, Ana River offers fair-to-good fishing for planted rainbow trout ranging from 6 to 20 inches. ODFW stocks the trout as fingerlings—up to 20,000 of them per year—to provide a year-round fishery here. The river is popular with fly anglers, especially during spring when the trout rise for hatches of Chironomids and blue-winged olive mayflies. Summer heat can prove a major deterrent but, most years, the hopper fishing is worth the trouble. Autumn fishing is also quite good most of the time. Bait angling is allowed here and the current limit is five trout per day.

The river meanders through desert scrub characterized by greasewood and rabbit brush, with abundant spring wildflowers. In a few places, the canyon slopes are too steep to negotiate, but usually you can simply park on the spurs, walk along the rim and pick your water before descending to fish. Dry fly action predominates, but any deep pools (and the culvert holes) are prime candidates for a deep-fished streamer pattern.

Most anglers drive the sand roads that follow much of the river and simply hike the short distance down the steep slopes to get to the river. Occasionally you'll see a drift boat, raft, or float tube negotiate the stream, but considering Ana River's diminutive size, boating seems like overkill. If you float the river, be prepared for tight quarters and extensive shallows. After about 5 miles you can take out at the gravel road that crosses the river east of the town of Summer Lake.

The pretty little Ana River offers secluded small-stream fishing for trout in a desert setting.

From Bend, follow Hwy 97 south to the Silver Lake cut-off (SR 31) 2 miles south of Lapine. Follow HSR 31 past the town of Silver Lake and continue up and over Picture Rock Pass. When the highway levels out and straightens south of the pass, watch for a left-hand turn pointing toward Ana Reservoir. Follow the road past the houses to a right-hand turn leading to the dam on Ana Reservoir. Drive across the dam and turn east to follow the river. The river begins below the reservoir and a sand/dirt/gravel road follows along, sometimes at a distance. If you're arriving from the south, head north through the town of Summer Lake and watch for the right-hand turn to Ana Reservoir. From the east (Burns), follow Hwy 20 to Riley, turn south on US 395 and then, south of Wagontire, turn west on the Christmas Valley Road. At Christmas Valley, head south on Old Lake Road, which leads to Hwy 31 (east of Silver Lake). Turn left (south) and head over Picture Rock Pass.

Anderson Lake (Warner Valley)
Anderson Lake is one of the Warner Valley Lakes west of Hart Mountain and northeast from the tiny town of Plush. The lakes contain brown bullhead and largemouth bass but are primarily known as crappie fisheries. See Crump Lake for further information about this group of lakes.

Be sure to consult the maps and carry all necessary supplies in this remote country. Only the northern shoreline of Anderson Lake sits on public land, accessible from the road to Hart Mountain and from a side-road leading west along the north bank.

Annie Creek (Crater Lake National Park)
Annie Creek is the milky little creek that flows alongside Hwy 62 inside Crater Lake National Park. The creek has populations of small wild brown, rainbow, and brook trout. Best access is from pull-offs and day-use sites along the road. The fishing here peaks between late June and October.

Antelope Creek (Lake County)
no bait

Located a few miles southwest of the airport in Lakeview, Antelope Creek feeds into Goose Lake from the north. It is currently open for trout angling from late May through October (check regulations). This small stream offers fair fishing for wild redband trout, but flows entirely through private property. Mostly, it is fished by locals. You'll need permission from the landowners to join them. County roads cross the creek in several places. Check the map before seeking this one.

Antelope Creek (Malheur County)
closed waters

A remote and fragile desert stream tucked away in the southwest corner of Malheur County, Antelope Creek supports a protected population of Lahontan cutthroat trout. The stream is currently closed to fishing.

Antelope Reservoir (Malheur County)
A large, shallow and rather unproductive irrigation reservoir southwest of Jordan Valley, Antelope Reservoir offers stocked rainbow trout. The reservoir often suffers water supply issues and is also under a mercury contamination advisory. The trout here grow quickly and can reach 20 inches or more, but they are few in number. Bait anglers fishing from shore generally do best. To get there, head for either Burns Junction or Jordan Valley. Antelope Reservoir lies just south of Hwy 95 about 12 miles from Jordan Valley. You can camp at the lake; and Jordan Valley offers a couple motels.

Anthony Lake (Elkhorn Range)
campground, boat ramp

A popular and scenic 30-acre lake high in the Elkhorn Mountains west of Baker, Anthony offers good fishing for stocked rainbow trout and wild brook trout. The fish mostly range from 6 to 12 inches, with a few reaching 14 inches. In recent years, ODFW has added a few larger fish to the mix, stocking 14- to 16-inch rainbows. The catch rate here is high, especially early in the summer. Sitting at 7,100 feet, Anthony Lake is rarely accessible before July. A float tube is handy here and the local fly anglers who frequent the lake usually bring along the tube and have fast action with small wet flies and sometimes dry flies. Shore fishing is easy as well. Boats are limited to 5 mph. You can camp at the lake. Anthony Lake is easy to find from Interstate-84. Take the North Powder Exit and head west, following the signs to Anthony Lake.

Aspen Lake (Klamath County)

Aspen Lake is a huge swampy lake just west of Klamath Falls. According to ODFW it offers fishing for brown bullhead. It's a better bird-watching area and reputedly the rare yellow rail has nested here.

Augur Creek (Lake County)

no bait

A small tributary to Dairy Creek on the upper Chewaucan River watershed, Augur Creek harbors a sparse population of small native redband trout. Only the upper end of the creek flows through public land. Access is from FR 34 southwest of Paisley. See Dairy Creek herein for directions.

Baca Lake

closed waters

Closed to fishing, Baca Lake is a large irrigation-storage reservoir on the south end of the Malheur Wildlife Refuge near Frenchglen.

Badger Lake

see Sky Lakes Wilderness Area

Balm Creek Reservoir (Baker County)

Located in the foothills of the Wallowa Mountains northeast of Baker, Balm Creek reservoir offers fair-to-good fishing for mostly small planted rainbows along with illegally introduced crappie and smallmouth bass. The reservoir covers about 100 acres at full pool, which it achieves only during spring. The stocked trout can reach 18 inches, but most are pan-size. Bass average 8 to 12 inches. In 2009, ODFW conducted an anglers survey, the results of which indicated most anglers want Balm Creek managed as a trout fishery; consequently the agency is formulating a management plan for the reservoir that I suspect might include a plan to kill all the fish and start over with the trout stocking. Be sure to check with ODFW before heading here. Note the electric-only boat motor restriction for fishing. Shoreline fishing is plentiful and most anglers fish bait, although fly fishing can be good during late spring and fall. To reach Balm Creek Reservoir, turn east off I-84 at North Powder (north of Baker City) and head east on Telocaset Road. At Medical Springs, take the Eagle Creek Road southeast to FR 70, which heads 10 miles up to the reservoir. Snow can block access into May. You can rough camp at the reservoir or head another 10 miles east to Lily White Campground.

Bear Creek (Lake County)

no bait, campground

Bear Creek is a small, steep tributary of the Chewaucan River joining the river above Marsters Spring Campground some 8 miles southeast from Paisley on the Chewaucan Road (FR 33). The creek is home to small native redbands and a few wild brook trout (especially in the upper reaches). Most anglers simply walk up the creek, parking at the pullout where Bear Creek crosses under the Chewaucan Road. If there's already a vehicle parked there, you can access the upper reaches of the stream via a rather circuitous drive up FR 3315 (and its spurs), which heads northwest from the main road immediately west of Paisley. Highway 31 reaches Paisley south of Summer Lake and north of the US 395/SR 31 Junction at Valley Falls. Consult your map. Early spring (pre-snowmelt) fishing is possible on the creek's lower end if snow pack doesn't block the road, but the best action occurs from June through October. Near the mouth of the creek, Marsters Spring Campground on the Chewaucan is a decidedly pleasant and convenient camping spot.

Bear Creek (Grant County)

no bait, campground

A tributary to the upper Silvies River near Seneca, Bear Creek offers slow-to-fair fishing during summer for small, wild redband trout. The lower end flows through private ranchlands, but the creek's upper half is easily accessible along roads in the Malheur National Forest. Follow Hwy 395 from either Burns or John Day and when you reach Seneca, head east on FR 16, the route to Logan Valley. After 7 miles you'll enter national forest lands, picking up the creek, which then flows alongside the road for about 4 miles. To reach the upper half of the creek, watch for the signs to Parish Cabin Campground and head north on FR 15 a few hundred yards to a right turn on FR 1530. Forest Road 1530 follows the creek uphill for a mile, at which time you will turn left on Spur 065 (if it is open—otherwise walk it).

Bear Lake (Eagle Cap Wilderness)

hike-in

A small brook trout lake on the southern edge of the Eagle Cap Wilderness, Bear Lake is accessible from a well-marked side trail off the Main Eagle Trail heading at Boulder Park east of Medical Springs. See Eagle Lake for directions.

Becker's Pond (Ontario)

A fairly productive 12-acre lake at the city park (near Malheur County Fairgrounds) in Ontario, Becker's Pond offers largemouth bass, bluegill, and channel catfish. The bluegill run small but they are abundant and the bass range from juvenile-size up to 2 pounds with a few larger fish caught regularly. The catfish reach at least 20 inches. Shore access is excellent and the fishing generally holds up all summer long.

Bendire Creek (Malheur County)

no bait

Offering a few hatchery rainbows and an occasional wild redband trout, Bendire Creek flows between Murphy and Beulah Reservoirs north from Juntura. About 2 miles of the creek below Murphy Reservoir and 2 miles of stream above the reservoir flow through BLM land, but the only way to get there is by hiking down from the dam or up from the top end of the pool at Murphy. See Murphy Reservoir herein for directions. The creek is hardly productive enough on its own to justify the trip, but if you're checking out Murphy Reservoir, take time to explore the creek as well.

Bert Lake
see Sky Lakes Wilderness Area

Beulah Reservoir
boat or float tube recommended, boat ramp

During periods of average or better water supply, Beulah Reservoir ranks among the best trout producers in southeast Oregon. Unfortunately, in recent years the reservoir has experienced severe low water annually, so a call to the ODFW or a check of the agency's online fishing reports is warranted before making the long drive. Located about an hour and a half east of Burns and 30 minutes northwest from Juntura, Beulah Reservoir covers about 2,000 acres at full pool. The reservoir is quite fertile and stocked trout (along with a few

Beulah Reservoir

native redbands) grow rapidly. During a good year, the fish typically range from 13 to 16 inches and by autumn a few exceed 20 inches.

Many anglers still fish with bait and fly anglers are fairly common here. Shoreline access is good along the east edge of the reservoir and at the dam. Beulah Road follows the east bank for more than a mile and you can launch a float tube or pontoon boat just about anywhere to fish the shallow weed bed shoals along this edge of the reservoir. The boat ramp is located adjacent to the dam and some good catches are made from both ends of the dam and also from the tailrace below. If you have a boat, try running up to the Malheur River arm on the northwest corner.

Beulah's west bank is fairly steep, especially when the water is drawn down, but a rough dirt road follows above. Beware this road in wet weather. Except for the northeast corner, which is owned by Murphy Brothers Ranch, Beulah's entire shoreline sits on public land administered by the Bureau of Reclamation. The shallows adjacent to the Murphy Ranch can be very productive, but respect private property and fish only by boat or float tube.

Occasionally you'll catch a wild redband trout or bull trout, both of which should be released unharmed. Beulah's water level fluctuates widely and the reservoir is usually quite low by autumn. Generally turbid, Beulah is at its best as soon as it is accessible in the spring and again in October (during years of good water supply). Most years Beulah is ice-free by April, often earlier, but call ODFW in Hines to make sure.

To reach Beulah, follow US Hwy 20 east from Burns or west from Vale to the little town of Juntura. On the west end of town, take the signed right-hand turn leading 15 miles to the reservoir. Along the way you'll pass a nice campground (Chukar Park) on the North Fork Malheur a few miles out of Juntura. The town offers a restaurant and motel, but the gas station is closed, so arrive with a full tank (currently you can top off in Buchanan to the west). During high-water years, Beulah can be exceptional during October, but be forewarned that both Chukar Park and Oasis Motel in Juntura can fill up with chukar hunters most of the month.

Big Adobe Reservoir (Klamath County)
One of the impoundments below Gerber Reservoir in Klamath County, Big Adobe, a sometimes-producer of warm-water species, was completely dry as of 2010.

Big Creek
see Lake Creek (Grant County)

Big Indian Creek (Steens Mountains)
no bait

A redband trout stream in the Steens Mountains, Big Indian Creek cuts a deep, dramatic gorge into the mountains and flows through scenic stands of aspen on its journey to meet the Blitzen River. You can hike Big Indian Gorge by walking down from the top, off the Steens Loop Road, but this is steep, rugged country best negotiated by highly experienced and very fit hikers. Take a backpack and make a two-day trek of it, leaving ample time for fishing. The hike down to South Steens Campground covers about 8 miles. You can see what you're in for by looking down into the gorge from the loop road; so if the precipitous and rather perilous descent into the gorge doesn't appeal to you, hike the creek upstream instead. Just west from South Steens Campground, you can drive a rugged road down to Indian Creek (Newton Cabin Road).

To reach the rim overlooking the top of Big Indian Gorge, take the Steens Loop Road by following the signs from Frenchglen to Page Springs Campground and then up the mountain. This route is substantially smoother traveling than the South Loop Road, which turns east off Hwy 205 about 10 miles south of Frenchglen. However, South Steens Campground lies along the South Loop Road, 2 miles east from Blitzen Crossing and you can get there by driving the rugged road down from the top of the Steens or up from the highway.

Big Rock Reservoir (AKA Little Rock Reservoir) (Lake County)

A fertile and productive little reservoir in the Coyote Hills northwest of Plush, Big Rock offers consistent action for 12- to 18-inch trout in a remote setting—when it can maintain adequate water supply. The reservoir has gone dry several times in the few years up to 2010, so check with ODFW before heading out. The reservoir occupies a narrow gulch, which provides at least a little protection from the frequent winds. Most anglers fish bait from shore, though fly angling and spin fishing produce fair results. The reservoir tends to be muddy, but if water levels are high and winds low, it clears, revealing lush aquatic weed growth. There are no facilities of any kind. Naturally, Big Rock Reservoir peaks after two or more consecutive years of good water supply. From the tiny community of Plush, continue north of town and head north on the Hogback Road (CR 3-10) for 15 miles to the left-hand turn leading another 4-plus miles west and then south to the reservoir. The turnoff from the Hogback Road is well worn and easily identified. During wet weather, the access road—especially the last mile and a half of it—can get a little nasty. Big Rock fishes best during spring.

Big Springs Reservoir (Nevada)
float tube recommended

Big Springs Reservoir went completely dry in 2010, but the following synopsis is valid should the reservoir refill: Though actually in extreme northern Nevada, on the Sheldon Antelope Refuge, Big Springs Reservoir is little more than an hour east from Adel along Hwy 140 and is usually so productive for fat rainbow trout, that the trip is well worthwhile for anglers with a valid Nevada fishing license. Bait fishing and fly fishing by float tube or pram is especially productive during the spring (the reservoir traditionally opens in mid-May) and early summer, and again during autumn. Five consecutive dry years just after the turn of the century took a serious toll on Big Springs, but with adequate water supplies, this is one of northern Nevada's—and the region's—top producers. Camping is primitive and there are no services or amenities. For more information and to buy licenses online, go to www.ndow.org.

Big Swamp Lake (Lake County)

More properly called Big Swamp Reservoir, this 34-acre fishery supports a healthy population of brown bullhead. It is located just south of Heart Lake in the Fishhole Lake Recreation Area immediately south of Quartz Mountain Summit on Hwy 140 west of Lakeview. Forest Road 3715 turns south off the highway to reach the lakes.

Black Lake (Elkhorn Mountains)
hike-in, float tube recommended

A pretty, productive and heavily used little mountain lake located 1 mile by trail southeast from Anthony Lake in the Elkhorn Range west of Baker City. The lake offers fair-to-good fishing for small brook trout. The trail departs from behind the campground at Anthony Lake and gains about 400 feet in elevation. Along the trail you will pass aptly named Lilypad Lake, which blooms in a stunning display of yellow pond lilies each summer. Black Lake offers several nice campsites. Fly anglers should bring a float tube. For driving directions, see Anthony Lake herein.

Blitzen River (Steens Mountains)
no bait, campground

Formally known as the Donner und Blitzen River, this popular trout stream emanates from the springs and snowfields of the Steens Mountains. It gathers flows from several major tributaries before reaching the base of the mountains near the little town of Frenchglen. There the river enters the Malheur National Wildlife Refuge. From the refuge boundary upstream for nearly 20 miles the Blitzen flows rugged and free, providing good fishing for native redband trout ranging from 6 to 18 inches. Virtually the entire river flows across public lands on the newly formed Steens Mountain Wilderness.

Access to most of the river requires a sturdy pair of hiking boots. The Blitzen flows through a narrow canyon crossed by roads in only two places. Several rugged backcountry roads approach the canyon from BLM land above the west bank, but check with the BLM office in Hines before driving these roads because recent land exchanges and road closures in the area have altered access across a substantial portion of the Steens Mountains. The first road crossing is just east of Frenchglen at the entrance to Page Springs Campground (BLM). This popular and scenic campground is the starting point for most anglers, who simply hike up the river on fairly well-worn trails. A short hike upstream from the campground, a fish weir prevents non-native species from migrating upstream. The best fishing begins upstream (south) from the weir. A parking area at the back end of the campground allows immediate access to the trail.

About 18 river miles upstream, the next road crossing is on the South Loop Road. To get there, head south from Frenchglen on Hwy 205. After about 10 miles, watch for the big sign on the left announcing the Steens Mountains access. Head easterly for about 15 miles until you reach the river at Blitzen Crossing, where you'll find some great campsites. From Blitzen Crossing, hike up or downstream. From mid-July through September you can reach Blitzen Crossing from the top of the Steens Mountains Loop Road, but this side of the loop is rugged driving.

The jeeptrails that approach the river from the west begin with the Trough Road, which heads south from the west side of the river at Steens Mountain Resort (which offers rental cabins and a store). Gen-

The streams feeding off Steens Mountain support populations of native redband trout.

erally this rutted out track is so rough that you could walk it faster than you can drive it, but it does allow walk-in access to 5 miles of river. From the road you must hike upwards of a mile due east to climb down into the canyon. The other two backcountry roads—Burnt Car Road and Tombstone Canyon Road—approach the canyon from the South Loop Road.

Between Blitzen Crossing and Page Springs Campground, the river flows through a narrow canyon and in places you'll find easier going by just walking through the river instead of negotiating your way around steep rock walls. By July, the run-off subsides, leaving the river low and clear. Many anglers forgo the summer heat and opt to fish the Blitzen during autumn. This is fine dry fly water, where hopper patterns, caddis patterns, and various general use flies serve faithfully. The canyon is home to a wide array of wildlife, including plenty of rattlesnakes. Hiking the river also allows you to fish the lower reaches of Fish Creek (4 miles above Page Springs) and the Little Blitzen (3.5 miles downstream from Blitzen Crossing).

Below Page Springs, the Blitzen flows onto the Malheur Wildlife Refuge. On the refuge, the river is channelized in places, but harbors a few large redband trout. Generally, most anglers ignore these lower reaches, but the prospects of a 20-inch trout make a little exploration worthwhile. All access is by foot, however.

Blitzen River, Little (Steens Mountains)
no bait, catch-and-release
One of the main tributaries to the Blitzen (Donner und Blitzen) River, the Little Blitzen offers fair-to-good fishing for small native redband trout. The best fishing is on the stream's lower few miles beginning at the confluence with the Blitzen River. See Blitzen River above for directions to the area.

Blue Lake (Gearhart Wilderness)
hike-in
A fairly popular and scenic hike-in lake, Blue Lake is regularly and liberally stocked with rainbow trout. They range from 8 to 12 inches with a few fish to 14 or 15 inches. Blue Lake is the only lake in the Gearhart Wilderness. It spans about 20 acres. The shortest of several routes into the lake is from the trailhead near Lee Thomas Meadow on the north side of the wilderness area. From Hwy 140 to the south, FR 34 reaches the area. From Paisley, FR 33 approaches the wilderness and from Lakeview, you can reach the area by heading up Thomas Creek Road (CR 3-16 a few miles west of town off Hwy 140), which becomes FR 28. The latter two routes converge at Dairy Creek on the upper Chewaucan River. From there, head north up Dairy Creek on FR 3428. When you reach the intersection with FR 34, continue north on FR 3372. After about 8 miles, watch for the short spur leading to the trailhead. The hike covers a fairly easy 2 miles.

Blue Joint Lake (Lake County)
Blue Joint Lake is one of the Warner Valley lakes west of Hart Mountain and northeast from the tiny town of Plush. The lakes contain brown bullhead and largemouth bass but are primarily known as crappie fisheries. See Crump Lake for further information about this group of lakes. Be sure to consult the maps and carry all necessary supplies in this remote country.

Boyle Reservoir (Klamath County)
see Klamath River

Bridge Creek (Steens Mountains)
no bait

A redband trout stream flowing off the west slope of the Steens Mountains, Bridge Creek offers fair fishing in its lower reaches. It enters the Blitzen River on Malheur Wildlife Refuge a few miles north of Page Springs Campground near French-glen. The access road turns left after you cross the river on the way to Page Springs. If the road is gated, park at the campground and hike 3 miles down to the creek.

Bridge Creek (Lake County)
no bait

Like Buck Creek, its similar neighbor to the west, Bridge Creek flows northeasterly from its headwaters on Yamsay Mountain and reaches Paulina Marsh immediately west of the town of Silver Lake. The upper reaches of this small, forested creek offer small redband and brook trout. The top half of the creek is best and it flows through a narrow, steep-sided canyon. To get there, turn south at Silver Lake on CR 4-11, which becomes FR 27 when you enter the Fremont National Forest. Continue 3.5 miles from the national forest boundary to a right-hand turn heading west on FR 2804, which will cross the creek after about 4.5 miles. From there you can hike both directions or consult the map for directions to several spur roads that lead close to the stream. Best fishing is after runoff has subsided, so wait until late May or early June.

Buck Creek (Lake County)
no bait

Buck Creek flows northeasterly from the Yamsay Mountain area in northern Fremont National Forest. The stream reaches a delta near the highway at Paulina Marsh, just west of Silver Lake. The lower end of the creek flows mostly through private lands while the upper half flows across national forest lands. Fishing is for wild brook trout and redband trout, but they never seem abundant. I've often wondered what the lower reaches might hold as they meander through several miles of ranchlands, but you'd have to knock on doors to find out. Two small primitive campgrounds are located along the upper end of the creek. West from Silver Lake, turn west from Hwy 31 onto the Silver Lake-Klamath Marsh Road. After

about 5 miles you will cross the creek at a ranch. About 5 miles further west, watch for the left-hand turn on FR 2804 leading to the creek. From there several spur roads access the stream. Consult the national forest map.

Bully Creek Reservoir (Malheur County)
boat ramp, campground

A shallow, turbid reservoir near Vale, Bully Creek is fairly popular with area anglers who pursue crappie along with largemouth bass, yellow perch, and a hodgepodge of other warmwater species. The reservoir covers almost 1,000 acres at full pool, offering 7 miles of shoreline. During dry years Bully Creek is frequently drawn down to little more than a big mud puddle, but during wet years it recovers quickly and fishing can be quite good. Most of the crappie range from 6 to 9 inches, larger if several consecutive high-water years occur. There is a county-run campground adjacent to the reservoir. The road to Bully Creek (Graham Blvd.) leads north from Hwy 20 a few miles west of Vale.

Bumphead Reservoir (Klamath Reservoir)

A turbid reservoir on BLM land south of Gerber Reservoir, Bumphead offers good fishing for largemouth bass and crappie. It can get quite low by midway through the irrigation season, especially during dry years. With good water supply for several years running, Bumphead can grow crappie to 14 inches and bass to several pounds. The reservoir ranges from about 30 to 60 acres and lies just north of Willow Valley Reservoir. See driving directions for Willow Valley. The rugged road

The author fishes a remote section of Buck Creek.

to Bumphead begins with a left turn on the BLM's "CCC Road" off the Willow Valley Road a few miles before you reach Willow Valley Reservoir. If this road is gated (check ahead of time by calling BLM in Lakeview) you'll have to get there by driving south from Gerber Reservoir on the Round Valley Road: Just before you reach Gerber, turn southeast on the signed road to Round Valley Reservoir. Just past the reservoir, turn right on the CCC Road and continue south past Kilgore Reservoir. Two miles after the road turns westerly watch for a right-hand turn leading north up to Bumphead (Road #41-14.5-4).

Burns Pond (Harney County)

Located just south of Burns on Hwy 78, this small pond is a pleasant place to hang out and fish for stocked rainbows. It sits on the right side of the road as you head south from town. Check with the ODFW office in nearby Haines for stocking schedules (it is usually stocked heavily once in April and again in June). Most anglers fish bait here, but all methods produce with peak catches in the spring and early summer. though the pond always seems to have a few holdover trout during fall and winter before it freezes.

Burnt Creek (Lake County)
see Deep Creek

Burnt River (Baker County)
campground

Upstream from Unity Reservoir, the North and South Forks of the Burnt River offer fair fishing for small, wild trout and the South Fork is also stocked with catch-able rainbows in the stretch near the campgrounds. The West Fork also offers fair fishing, but is short and quite small. The South Fork flows for about 10 miles, but only the upper reaches of the stream offer good access on forest service lands. There are four campgrounds in the immediate area. Watch for the signs to the access road leading due west out of Unity.

The North Fork flows for more than 20 miles from its headwaters near Tipton Summit in the Blue Mountains. State Route 7 crosses the creek west of Whitney, but most of the stream along the highway lies on private property, leaving about 5 miles of fishable water on national forest lands. Watch for the turnoff at FR 1035 heading west about 3 miles north from Tipton Summit. This is high country and the fishing is best during summer. The lower reach of the North Fork offers slow-to-fair fishing for small rainbows. To get there from the north, turn south at Whitney. From the south head to Unity Lake State Park at Unity Reservoir and then head 2 miles east down the river to a left-hand turn heading north on Big Flat Road. You'll pick up the river when you reach the national forest boundary after 8 miles. There's a forest service campground along the river here.

Below Unity Reservoir, Burnt River offers a few rainbow trout, some smallmouth bass, and lots of non-game fish. The trout fishing is generally confined to the first 2 miles downstream from the dam on Unity Reservoir. Here the river flows through a scenic canyon, mostly on BLM lands, before meandering for the next 25 miles through a broad valley of ranch holdings. There is no public access, though I suppose you could try knocking on doors. At Bridgeport, the highway heads north and a gravel road continues east, picking up the river at the top of Burnt River Canyon (turn left when you reach the T-intersection). This rugged, rocky canyon has long been popular with miners and many active claims are still worked. Avoid trespassing. Here the river offers smallmouth bass and a few trout. It fishes best during late spring and autumn.

At Dixie, the river catches up to I-84 and flows south to join Brownlee Reservoir at Huntington. The river's lowermost reaches, mostly on private land, offer smallmouth bass, crappie, channel catfish, huge carp, and even a few largemouth bass.

Cached Lake
see Eagle Lake

Calderwood Reservoir (Lake County)

Calderwood Reservoir sits northwest from Mud Lake Reservoir (see listing herein) in the hills just east of Warner Valley. It has not been stocked in recent years and is both turbid and highly prone to drying up during drought conditions. After a few consecutive high-water years, anglers interested in remote waters might give a call to the ODFW biologist in Lakeview to inquire as to whether Calderwood has been stocked.

Camas Creek (Lake County)
no bait

Camas Creek is a pretty mountain stream that flows more or less alongside Hwy 140 on the east side of Warner Summit east from Lakeview. The section of Camas Creek flowing near the highway is rarely productive. The best section of the creek—though hardly productive compared to the middle reaches of Deep Creek several miles to the south—is the short canyon-bound stretch leading down to its confluence with Deep Creek. Give it a quick sampling if you're in the area, but don't expect many fish. This is hike-in water: Park along the highway shoulder where Deep Creek first reaches the highway west of Adel. Climb down to the creek and hike upstream into the canyon. Camas Creek enters from a dramatic gorge to the west and you can fish upstream from the mouth of the canyon. Redband trout here range from 6 to 10 inches. The water often runs off-color until autumn.

Camp Creek (Baker County)
no bait, campground

Camp Creek is a fair trout stream with two main branches flowing north out of the mountains near Unity and reaching the Burnt River to the north. The upper reaches of both branches offer good access on national forest land. Easiest access is from FR 16, which heads south from the highway just east of Murray Reservoir (east from Unity). The nearest campground is at Long Creek Reservoir near West Camp Creek or you can camp at Murray Reservoir.

Campbell Lake (Fremont National Forest)
campground, boat ramp

A pleasant and productive 21-acre mountain lake, Campbell is well stocked annually with rainbow and brook trout. Along with its neighbor Dead Horse Lake, Campbell Lake sits above the Chewaucan drainage in the Fremont National Forest southwest from the little community of Paisley. From the north, follow Hwy 31 to Paisley. Then head west up the Chewaucan River for 20 miles until you reach the junction with FR 28. Follow FR 28 about 11 miles to the signed left-hand turn leading to the lake. From Lakeview you can alternately head west out of town on Hwy 140, turn right on CR 2-16 and after 5 miles turn left on CR 2-16A (Thomas Creek Road) into the national forest, where it becomes FR 28. Follow FR 28 for about 28 miles to the signed left turn into Campbell and Dead Horse Lakes.

Sitting at an elevation of 7,195 feet, Campbell Lake is rarely accessible before late June. Check ahead by calling the Paisley Ranger District office in Paisley. Only electric motors are allowed on the lake with a 5-mph speed limit. You can camp at the lake or at nearby Dead Horse Lake.

Campbell Lake and Upper Campbell Lake (Warner Valley)

Upper Campbell Lake and Campbell Lake, sometimes called "Lower Campbell," are among the Warner Valley lakes west of Hart Mountain and northeast from the tiny town of Plush. The lakes contain brown bullhead and largemouth bass but are primarily known as crappie fisheries. During extended periods of high water the Warner Valley lakes produce large crappie, some up to 2 pounds. During drought cycles the lakes shrink to a fraction of their potential surface acreage and the crappie fishery all but collapses. The best fishing ever on the lakes occurred following the remarkably wet winters of 1982-84. By 1987 the crappie fishery had reached epic proportions only to be devastated by a three-year-long drought. The fisheries rebounded during the 1990s and then were devastated by another extended drought from 2000-2003. Most people fish these lakes from shore, although in a few places—especially some of the interconnecting channels at high water—a canoe comes in handy. Be wary of the frequent high winds. Plush is the jump-off point to reach these lakes and the main roads yield to numerous dirt roads and jeep trails. Be sure to consult the maps and carry all necessary supplies in this remote country.

Campbell Reservoir (Klamath County)

This shallow, but fertile irrigation reservoir sits just north of Hwy 140 near Bly and offers largemouth bass. At full pool it covers 200 acres, but this reservoir suffers severe water shortages during drought cycles. Access is from the BLM land on the east side of the reservoir. From Klamath Falls or Lakeview, follow Hwy 140 to Bly and then turn north on Campbell Road. After half a mile turn right (east) and head 4 miles up to the reservoir.

Chewaucan River (Lake County)
no bait, campground

A fine trout stream, the Chewaucan River is home to wild redband trout that can reach 18 inches. Most of the fish range from 8 to 12 inches, but since ODFW dispensed with stocking the river with hatchery trout in 1996, increasing numbers of large trout are showing up in the catch. The ODFW also began installing structure in the streambed to help stabilize the banks and create more deep-water refuge on this river, which for decades had been overrun by cattle.

Now the Chewaucan provides a true wild-trout experience and is especially popular with fly anglers. The river hosts regular hatches of stoneflies and caddisflies from late spring through early autumn, so anglers enjoy frequent dry fly action. When the trout aren't rising, they often respond to streamers and to nymph patterns drifted along the bottom. Most anglers fish the Chewaucan between June and September, but low snow winters provide op-

The Chewaucan River is one of southeast Oregon's best trout streams.

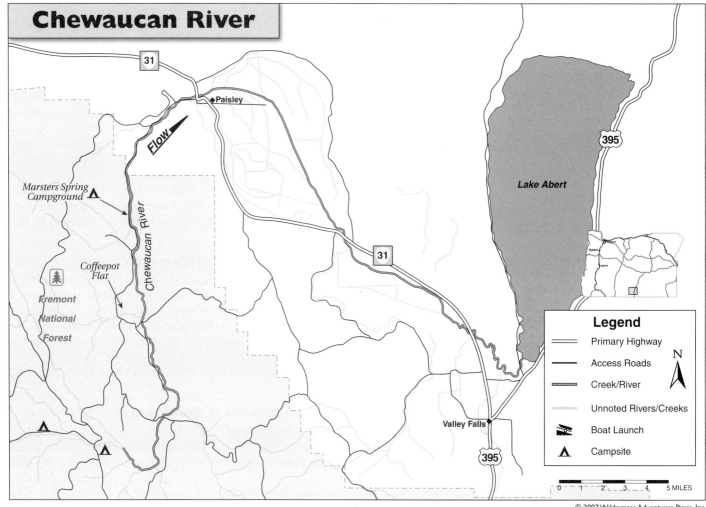

Chewaucan River

Flow

Paisley

Marsters Spring Campground

Coffeepot Flat

Fremont National Forest

Chewaucan River

Lake Abert

Valley Falls

Legend

	Primary Highway
	Access Roads
	Creek/River
	Unnoted Rivers/Creeks
	Boat Launch
	Campsite

N

0 1 2 3 4 5 MILES

© 2007 Wilderness Adventures Press, Inc.

portunity for good subsurface action between February and early April. When the snow melts in the high country to the west, the river runs high and muddy into June. The Chewaucan is also subject to sudden influxes of muddy water during summer, caused by thunderstorms in the mountains above.

The trout-bearing (upper) section of the river runs for more than 20 miles, but substantial stretches of the river's upper half flow across private ranchlands. Respect the fences and obey the signs where these properties are posted. Marsters Spring Campground sits right on the river 8 miles west of Paisley, and many fine primitive camping sites are available amidst the ponderosas both downstream and upstream from Marsters. From Paisley to a few miles past the campground, the Chewaucan flows alongside the road. At Coffeepot Flat, the road swings up and away from the river and walk-in access becomes the rule, although there are a couple jeep-track roads that lead to the river.

To find the Chewaucan, follow Hwy 31 south from Hwy 97 or north from Lakeview. The tiny community of Paisley lies on a bend in the highway about an hour north of Lakeview and about 30 minutes south of Summer Lake. Paisley has a good restaurant that serves up hearty meals, a friendly tavern, a mercantile, and a U.S. Forest Service ranger district office. At Paisley, turn west on Mill Street, which follows the river west into the mountains.

Chickahominy Reservoir (Harney County)
campground, boat ramp

One of the best and most popular trout fisheries in southeastern Oregon, Chickahominy Reservoir sprawls over a broad sagebrush basin nearly 100 miles east of Bend and about 30 miles west of Burns. At full pool, "Chick" covers almost 600 acres, but reaches a maximum depth of only about 25 feet deep. The deepest spot lies adjacent to the dam and the remainder of the reservoir rarely exceeds 10 feet in depth except in the main channel. Extremely fertile, Chickahominy provides ideal growing conditions for rainbows stocked as fingerlings. Three-year old trout here reach 20 inches and weigh 3 to 5 pounds. Most years the reservoir's typical trout spans a fat 13 to 16 inches.

An improved boat launch sits adjacent to the north end of the dam, near the camping and picnic areas. Many anglers

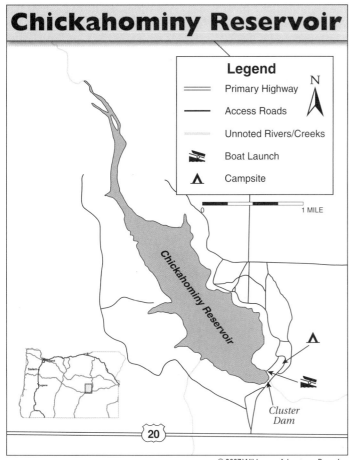

Chickahominy Reservoir

Legend

≡ Primary Highway

— Access Roads

⋯ Unnoted Rivers/Creeks

Boat Launch

⛺ Campsite

0   1 MILE

Cluster Dam

20

© 2007 Wilderness Adventures Press, Inc.

A massive rainbow comes to hand on Chickahominy Reservoir.

launch boats or float tubes, but the catch rate is just as good from shore because Chick's rainbows frequent the food-rich shallows. Two long, narrow bays reach out to the west from the reservoir's west-southwest corner and these so-called "fingers" are popular with fly anglers who simply walk along the shoreline and cast small nymph patterns to trout foraging for the reservoir's abundant supply of scuds, water beetles, Chironomids, and snails. Beware the rutted-out road leading to the west side of the reservoir—it has swallowed many a vehicle in deep mud during early spring. This road might prove frozen and easily passable during a March morning, but when it thaws out you'll find it an entirely different beast.

Bait anglers fish the entire south half of the lake, often setting up on shore and fishing Powerbait or various other offerings and doing quite well. Anglers with boats can run all the way up to the "Narrows" midway up the reservoir. Here Chickahominy is just a stone's throw wide and slightly deeper. If water levels permit, run north through the Narrows and fish the flats right where the reservoir starts to narrow and deepen. This is a good area for anchoring and still fishing with bait or casting and retrieving wet flies.

If I could select one must-have fly pattern for Chickahominy, I would never leave home without a fistful of Bead-head Prince Nymphs tied on size 10 through 14 hooks. However,

fly anglers enjoy consistent success on a wide range of offerings. Woolly Bugger and leech patterns are especially effective when trolled slowly behind a float tube, but can also be used to good effect from shore on a sink-tip or sinking line. One of my favorite tricks here and on all the trout reservoirs of eastern Oregon is to fish a small beadhead nymph (Prince, Zugbug or Pheasant Tail) about 2 feet behind a black or olive Woolly Bugger.

Any number of different general-use flies are equally effective and the reservoir offers several events of special note to fly anglers. Beginning in late February or early March, daily hatches of Chironomids get trout feeding during late morning. The best of these hatches is the March and April emergence of the large "bloodworm" midges, so called because the larvae have hemoglobin that gives them a reddish color. These Chironomids are big, requiring imitations in the size 12 through 16 range.

By late April, warm spring weather triggers water beetle flights wherein small water beetles fly in and out of the water, driving trout crazy. This uncommon event occurs late morning and evening on still days. By late May, Callibaetis mayflies and damselflies begin their annual emergence. If the weather remains fairly cool, fishing continues to be quite good during May. Throughout the spring, Chironomid hatches continue daily. By May, the midges are small and hatch most profusely during the evening.

Throughout the spring and again during autumn, keep your eyes peeled for trout cruising along the banks in less than a foot of water and rooting around for scuds and water beetles. When water supplies remain stable, autumn offers a brief window, usually during October, when fishing picks up after the doldrums created by hot desert summers. By October, Chick's remaining trout are in superb shape—absurdly fat and chrome bright. This is the time for the 5-pounders. Once winter sets in, Chickahominy offers ice-fishing opportunity, but call ODFW in Hines to check on ice thickness. Usually by mid- to late February, the ice melts and the spring fishing begins.

Chickahominy has its down sides. A ferocious wind frequently batters the lake on a daily basis, leaving only a brief window of pleasant fishing weather during the morning. When the wind picks up in the afternoon, boaters should head shoreward. Also, like all trout reservoirs in southeastern Oregon, Chick is highly susceptible to severe damage from drought conditions. Indeed, after memorable fishing years during the mid-1990s, the prolonged drought of the new century plunged the reservoir into total ruin. It completely dried up, but ODFW used the opportunity to make repairs on the dam and the drought had the added benefit of killing off a growing goldfish population. The goldfish had no doubt been introduced by some shortsighted angler who had been using them as live bait.

Chickahominy is easy to get to, being located adjacent to Hwy 20. Watch for the signed turn-off near mile marker 99. The gravel access road is good and leads first to a parking area on the south side of the dam before crossing over the dam to the camping and picnicking area. Most campers use RVs owing to the wind. The road to the "fingers" takes off to the left from the main access road before you reach the reservoir, but as I warned earlier, be careful during spring or any time during wet weather. You can walk to the fingers by parking at the lot on the south side of the dam. From there, just cross the fence and walk the shoreline heading west. Nearest supplies are available a few miles east at the store in Riley (541-493-2527).

Clover Lake (Mountain Lakes Wilderness)
hike-in
Clover Lake sits in a basin littered with small ponds about a mile southwest from far more popular Lake Harriette. Clover's brookies range from 4 to 14 inches, but big fish are rare. From Lake Harriette you can hike south and then west to climb up the ridge overlooking Harriette before following the trail south another mile to Clover. Take your float tube. From Harriette, the hike covers almost 3 miles. Or you can hike north from

the trailhead at Clover Creek. Five miles south of Lake of the Woods, turn east on the Clover Creek Road and then watch for a left turn on FR 3852.

Como Lake
see Lake Como

Cottonwood Creek (Lake County)
no bait
Cottonwood Creek feeds into Goose Lake from the north with most of the stream running across private property near Lakeview. The upper section, below Cottonwood Meadows Lake, flows through national forest property for a few miles, offering slow-to-fair trout angling, before again crossing private property just upstream from Cottonwood Reservoir. A trail follows the creek downstream from Cottonwood Meadows Lake and FR 3870 follows the south bank at a distance.

Cottonwood Creek (Bully Creek drainage)
no bait
Malheur County has Cottonwood Creeks scattered all over the county. This Cottonwood Creek and its branches, the South and West Forks, offer a few small native redband trout, mostly confined to the headwater areas. There is no easy way to reach them. You'll need the appropriate topographical maps and then you should stop in at the BLM office in Vale to get specific directions and information on road conditions. These backroads tend to be impassable during wet weather.

Cottonwood Creek (Trout Creek Mountains)
closed waters
At one time stocked with Lahontan cutthroat trout, Cottonwood Creek also supported or supports indigenous Lahontans. As of the mid-1990s, the creek still had a few fish, which are fully protected as the creek is currently closed to fishing.

Cottonwood Creek Reservoir (Harney County)
A turbid 100-acre reservoir located in the hills north of Drewsey and west of Beulah Reservoir, Cottonwood Creek Reservoir offers fair-to-good fishing during periods of good water supply. Bait anglers prevail here and the trout range from 9 to 16 inches. Best fishing is in late spring, but the road can get ugly during wet conditions. To get there, follow Hwy 20 east from Burns or west from Juntura. At the turn-off to the town of Drewsey, head north and after you pass through the tiny town, watch for the signed right turn on the Otis Valley Road. After about 4 miles, turn right again on the Altnow-Beulah Road, head east 2.5 miles and watch for the signed left turn leading north to the reservoir. You'll pass Altnow Reservoir (see listing herein).

Cottonwood Meadows Lake (Lake County)

boat or float tube recommended, boat ramp, campground

Cottonwood Meadows Lake is a 39-acre impoundment near Lakeview that offers good fishing for rainbow and brook trout. The rainbows range from 8 to 18 inches, averaging about 12 inches. Brook trout reach 18 inches, but average much smaller. The lake sits at 6,130 feet in an attractive forest setting dominated by large ponderosa pines and aspens. The lake is usually fishable by early May. Only electric motors are allowed, but a boat or float tube is handy here.

All methods produce here and the lake is fairly popular with fly anglers, especially in the fall when streamer flies, trolled slowly on a sinking line, account for some nice brookies. Additionally there is a good hatch of Callibaetis (speckled-wing dun) mayflies during the summer.

From Lakeview, take Hwy 140 west for 24 miles, then turn right on signed FR 3870. Follow FR 3870 for 8 miles and look for the campground and trailhead entrance signs. The small campground includes some fairly secluded tent sites scattered around the lake.

Cottonwood Reservoir (Lake County)

boat ramp

This 900-acre reservoir, located 12 miles northwest of Lakeview, is managed for redband trout, both wild and stocked. The fish average fairly small, but anglers catch a few 14- to 18-inch fish here. The reservoir sits on private land, but access is allowed. There is an improved boat ramp and a boat or float tube is useful. To get there, follow Hwy 140 west from Lakeview. About 7 miles out of town, watch for the signed north turn on CR 2-20, leading 5 miles to the reservoir.

Cow Lakes

see Upper Cow Lake

Cracker Creek (Baker County)

no-bait

Cracker Creek is a tributary to the upper reach of the Powder River north of Sumpter, flowing off the steeps of Elkhorn Ridge. The creek offers fair fishing for small rainbows and redband trout along a 3-mile section in Wallowa-Whitman National Forest. FR 55 follows the creek north from Sumpter.

Crater Lake (Crater Lake National Park)

no bait

One of Oregon's most splendid and recognizable natural wonders, Crater Lake occupies the extinct caldera of Mt. Mazama, whose eruption some 7,700 years ago scattered volcanic material halfway across the continent and left a discernable layer of ash throughout most of southeastern Oregon and beyond. The spectacularly beautiful lake covers 21 square miles and reaches a depth of 1,949 feet, making it the world's seventh deepest lake.

Between 1888 and 1941 Crater Lake was stocked with at least six different kinds of salmonids totaling some 1.8 million fish. Only kokanee salmon and rainbow trout remain today, both species spawning naturally in the lake's clear, clean waters. The kokanee are most abundant, numbering in the hundreds of thousands, but they are far less available to anglers than are the lake's rainbow trout. The trout thrive in the near-shore shallows while the kokanee generally stick to the open waters, feeding as deep as 450 feet.

Crater Lake's rainbows generally range from 9 to 14 inches and reach at least 6 pounds, though trophy-size fish are rare. The lake record is a 26-inch specimen that weighed 6.5 pounds. Anglers can fish from two places: Cleetwood Cove and Wizard Island. The trail to Cleetwood Cove drops 700 feet from the north rim and allows access to about a quarter mile of rocky shoreline. The popular, scenic ferry boat ride delivers you to Wizard Island, where you can fish through the day before the boat returns to retrieve you. Check with the Crater Lake National Park headquarters for schedules. No personal boats or float tubes are allowed on the lake.

Only flies and artificial lures are allowed at Crater Lake. No license is required to fish in the park and there is no limit on the size or number of fish you can keep from the lake. Rules forbid cleaning fish at the lake. The trout population is rather sparse here, so don't expect fast and furious action, but the experience itself is unique and the lake is postcard beautiful. Crater Lake National Park features two campgrounds along with rooms at Crater Lake Lodge at Rim Village and at the Mazama Village Motor Inn. To get information or make lodging reservations, call 541-594-3100.

Crater Lake

Crater Lake
(Eagle Cap Wilderness)
hike-in

Crater Lake is a 12-acre gem sitting at 7,500 feet in the southern portion of the Eagle Cap Wilderness Area. The lake offers brook trout that reach 12 inches or so. The shortest trail originates at the Kettle Creek Campground on the East Fork of Eagle Creek and gains elevation at a staggering pace over the 7-mile route to the lake. From Baker City or La Grande, head for Medical Springs on SR 203 and then head easterly on FR 67. At Tamarack Campground turn right onto FR 77 and after 5 miles take the left-hand turn heading north up the East Fork of Eagle Creek.

Crooked Creek (Klamath County)
catch-and-release, no bait

A tributary to the Wood River near Agency Lake, Crooked Creek is a good producer of large redband and brown trout. Best access to the creek is from its mouth by boat (See Wood River). Otherwise you'll need to ask permission from the landowners along Hwy 62. Fishing peaks from mid-summer through October.

Crooked Creek (Lake County)

Crooked Creek runs alongside Hwy 395 south of Valley Falls and north of Lakeview. It offers only a few small trout.

Crump Lake (Lake County)

Sprawling Crump Lake is one of the Warner Valley Lakes west of Hart Mountain and northeast from the tiny hamlet of Adel. Access is mostly from a mile-long section of BLM land along the road to Plush, a few miles north of Adel and from jeep trails running the length of the lake on the east shore. The Warner Valley lakes contain brown bullhead and largemouth bass but are primarily known as crappie fisheries. Crump Lake is usually the best of them.

During extended periods of high water the Warner Valley lakes produce large crappie, some up to 2 pounds. During drought cycles the lakes shrink to a fraction of their potential surface acreage and the crappie fishery all but collapses. The best fishing ever on the lakes occurred following the remarkably wet winters of 1982-84. By 1987 the crappie fishery had reached epic proportions only to be devastated by a three-year-long drought. The fisheries rebounded during the 1990s and then were devastated by another extended drought from 2000-2003. Most people fish these lakes from shore, although in a few places—especially some of the interconnecting channels at high water—a canoe comes in handy. Be wary of the frequent high winds. Plush is the jump-off point to reach these lakes and the main roads yield to numerous dirt roads and jeep trails. Be sure to consult the maps and carry all necessary supplies in this remote country.

Cucamonga Creek (Steens Mountains)

Cucamonga Creek, home to wild redband trout, flows virtually entirely across private ranch properties northeast from Frenchglen. Public access is unavailable.

Culver Lake (Eagle Cap Wilderness)
hike-in

A small, but deep brook trout lake in the southern part of the Eagle Cap Wilderness Area, Culver is highly scenic and lightly fished. It offers a few decent-sized brookies among the typical small fish. Culver spans 8 acres and sits at 7,600 feet. At these altitudes, the hiking season generally extends from early or mid-July to the end of September. Nearby are Bear Lake and Lookingglass Lake. See Eagle Lake herein for directions to the trailhead at Boulder Park.

Dairy Creek
no bait, campground

A small tributary to the upper Chewaucan River, Dairy Creek flows through scenic timber stands in the highlands just east of Gearhart Mountain. It provides fair fishing for native redband trout. The creek is usually accessible by late spring and holds up throughout the season despite low summer flows. Dairy Creek is about equidistant from Lakeview to the southeast and Paisley to the northeast. In Paisley, turn west at the restaurant and head up the Chewaucan River on FR 33. At the 20-mile mark you'll intersect FR 28. From there, turn left to reach the creek at Dairy Point Campground. From Lakeview, head west a few miles on Hwy 140 to a right (north) turn on Thomas Creek Road, which becomes FR 28 and leads all the way to Dairy Creek. While winter fishing on the Chewaucan can be quite good, the roads up to Dairy Creek are typically snowbound until April or even early May during high snow pack years.

Forest Road 3428 follows the south side of the creek for several miles, the first two of which are on private land. Respect the private property and drive to the upper reaches of the creek. Spur Road 047 heads up the north bank, crossing Augur Creek (see listing herein). There are two small campgrounds on the creek, one at Dairy Point where FR 28 meets the creek and the other upstream of the private ranch property.

Dead Horse Lake (Lake County)
campground, boat ramp

Dead Horse Lake is located in the Fremont National Forest southwest of the tiny community of Paisley. Like Campbell Lake, its neighbor to the east, Dead Horse Lake offers good fishing for pan-size rainbow and brook trout in a scenic forest setting. From the north, follow Hwy 31 to Paisley. Then head west up the Chewaucan River for 20 miles until you reach the junction with FR 28. Follow FR 28 about 11 miles to the signed left-hand turn leading to the lake. From Lakeview you can alternately head west out of town on Hwy 140, turn right on

Thomas Creek Road, which becomes FR 28 and leads 43 miles to the lake.

Sitting at an elevation of 7,372 feet, Dead Horse Lake is rarely accessible before late June and often not reachable until July. Check ahead by calling the Paisley Ranger District office in Paisley. Only electric motors are allowed on the lake with a 5-mph speed limit. You can camp at the lake or at nearby Campbell Lake.

Dean Creek (Baker County)
no bait

Dean Creek is a short tributary to Phillips Reservoir offering fair fishing for small rainbows. From the south side of Phillips Reservoir, half a mile east of Miller Lane Campground, follow the stream south on FR 1160.

Dee Lake
see Sky Lakes Wilderness Area

Deep Creek (Lake County)
no bait

Deep Creek is a remote, scenic and productive redband trout stream in southern Lake County, southwest from the tiny town of Adel and southeast from Lakeview. The creek draws its headwaters from the Warner Mountains, picking up several important tributaries before plunging into a rugged desert canyon just south of Hwy 140. The creek's upper reaches offer small trout in serene, forested settings and its canyon stretch, which has a few fish to 14 inches, tumbles through a boulder strewn cleft best accessed by those in good physical condition and with no fear of rattlesnakes.

The upper end of Deep Creek flows for several miles through Fremont National Forest before reaching extensive private ranch lands in Big Valley. A nice forested campground sits right alongside the creek: North of Lakeview, turn east on Hwy 140 and follow it over Warner Summit for 8 miles to a south turn on FR 3615. After half a mile, turn right on the old Hwy 140 and continue westerly for about 1.5 miles to a left turn on FR 3915. After 15 miles, turn right on FR 4015, which leads 1 mile to the campground.

In my opinion, the best way to access the canyon section of Deep Creek is to park along Hwy 140 about 6 miles west of Adel, where the creek reaches the road. Then hike upstream into the canyon from there. You have about 4 miles of the creek ahead of you, along with a short, productive stretch of Camas Creek. Most years, your best bet is to continue hiking for an hour before you begin fishing because trout densities increase substantially about 2 miles south of the highway. This canyon stretch frequently runs quite turbid—almost always so during spring and early summer. The fishing can be good from April through June when the water is off color, but naturally there's a big difference between off-color water and downright muddy water. The best fishing is during the fall, from mid- to late September through October.

Deep Creek offers remote, hike-in trout fishing in rugged canyonlands.

The section of the creek flowing along Hwy 140 produces a few nice redbands as well, though it is hardly as productive as the upper end of the canyon section. During dry years, you'll be lucky to find any trout along the highway. Throughout the lower reach, large flies, spoons, and spinners work during the spring when the water is murky. During autumn, Deep Creek is good fly water and hopper fishing usually lasts into early October.

Deep Creek's tributaries offer fair-to-good fishing also. These include Willow Creek, Dismal Creek, and Burnt Creek, all of which are small, attractive streams flowing through stands of stately ponderosa pines. A copy of the Fremont National Forest map will serve you well in this country. These tributary streams are accessible by late May or early June, but they fish better during summer and fall.

Deep Lake
see Sky Lakes Wilderness Area

Deer Creek (Baker County)

no bait

A nice little trout stream offering fair fishing for small, wild redband trout, Deer Creek is a tributary to Phillips Reservoir. The creek reaches the reservoir from the north near Mowich Picnic Area and a mile and a half to the west, Deer Creek Road heads north from the highway and follows the creek. The trout here range from 5 to 10 inches with a few larger trout available.

Deer Lake

see Sky Lakes Wilderness Area

Delintment Lake (Harney County)

boat ramp, campground

Nestled amidst ponderosa pines in the mountains northwest of Burns, manmade Delintment Lake is a popular and productive fishery for planted rainbow trout. The fish range from 6 to 16 inches, with an occasional 18-incher. Fat 10- to 12-inch trout are typical and usually abundant. Delintment spans 50 acres and is ideally suited to a small boat or float tube, though shore fishing is usually easy. The lake sits at 5,556 feet and is usually accessible by late spring. A decent damselfly hatch begins by early June, and fly anglers armed with damsel nymph patterns often enjoy fast action around mid-morning. Ice-fishing enthusiasts reach the lake by snowmobile, but check with ODFW in Hines about ice thickness before heading out. From Hines, turn north on the signed road (the old Hines Logging Road) across from the White Mountain Pine Industrial Park, head north 12 miles and then take the left-hand turn onto FR 41. After 26 miles turn left and follow the signs f5 miles to the lake.

Denio Creek

closed waters

Denio Creek is closed to protect remnant populations of Lahontan cutthroat trout.

Dismal Creek (Lake County)

see Deep Creek

Dog Hollow Reservoir (Klamath County)

Once a fair producer of bass (ODFW has never stocked it, so no one knows how they got there), Dog Hollow Reservoir dried up completely during the mid-1990s and the fishery has not been re-established as of this writing. As of 2010, Dog Hollow is very low. The reservoir is shallow and subject to being lost even during moderate drought cycles. It is located due south of Gerber Reservoir. Interestingly, the shoreline of Dog Hollow has the distinction of sheltering a substantial population of a rare wildflower, the Disappearing Monkeyflower (Mimulus evanescens).

Dog Lake (Lake County)

boat or float tube recommended, boat ramp, campground

Located southwest of Lakeview, Dog Lake is locally known for its trophy-size largemouth bass, though they tend to be few in number, and most visitors target other warmwater species. Currently the lake is closed to trout fishing (it is not stocked with trout and the closure is to protect native redband trout), and all bass less than 15 inches must be released. The lake, which covers almost 300 acres and sits at 5,100 feet, offers fairly abundant crappie, yellow perch, bluegill, pumpkinseed sunfish, and brown bullhead. Shoreline fishing is limited to the north bank and it's is a great place to take kids. To get there from Lakeview, take Hwy 140 west for 8 miles, turn left on Tunnel Hill Road and follow the signs 17 miles to the lake. The lake offers an improved boat ramp and a small campground. A good map of the area is the BLM Lakeview Resource Area Recreation Guide.

Donna Lake

see Sky Lakes Wilderness

Donner und Blitzen River

see Blitzen River

Doolittle Creek (Malheur County)

no bait, catch-and-release

This tiny, remote desert stream runs parallel to its neighbor, Fifteenmile Creek, beginning about 10 miles north of the Nevada border in the southwest corner of Malheur County. Supporting a fragile and very sparse population of native Lahontan cutthroat trout, Doolittle Creek is open at this time to fishing with flies and artificial lures, but check current regulations. A stream survey conducted in 1994 estimated that the entire creek supported only 300 trout—reason enough to leave them alone. The creek flows through about 7 miles of BLM land before joining Whitehorse Creek, but most of the stream goes dry during the summer and trout are found only below a small falls located on the lower end of the creek. The approaches to Doolittle Creek require lengthy drives over rugged backcountry roads, so carry two spare tires, extra fuel, shovel, and other emergency gear. Contact the BLM in Burns for specific directions; the BLM Sportsman Series Map, Trout Creek, details the area. Beware that the mountains in this corner of Oregon have recently become home to illegal marijuana grows reportedly guarded by armed men; consult the Malheur County Sheriff's Office in Vale (541-473-5125) for more information.

Drews Creek (Lake County)

campground, no bait

Drews Creek near Lakeview offers slow to fair fishing for wild redband trout. Highway 140 crosses the creek upstream from Drews Creek Reservoir and Dog Lake Road follows it for a few miles below the reservoir. The upper portion of the creek flows through about 5 miles of public land, while the lower reach below the reservoir, flows through public lands only in the vicinity of Drews Creek Campground. Check current regulations for open seasons on this creek.

Drews Reservoir
campground, boat ramp

A large irrigation-storage reservoir west of Lakeview, Drews Reservoir offers warmwater species, including crappie and catfish, along with a few large trout. The reservoir spans almost 2,000 acres at full pool, but is usually drawn way down. Fishing is usually slow, although the trout can reach 20 inches and catfish, which provide a popular local fishery, typically range from 2 to 6 pounds with some substantially larger. The reservoir also offers yellow perch, black crappie, white crappie, pumpkinseed, and brown bullhead. Shore fishing is popular and the reservoir has an improved boat ramp at the south end. Most of the shoreline lies on private lands, so seek permission before walking to a promising-looking spot on the bank. Drews Creek Campground is located 2 miles east from the dam. To reach the reservoir, follow Hwy 140 west out of Lakeview (or east from Klamath Falls). Ten miles out of town watch for a left-hand (south) turn on Andy Hill Road. Head south to a right turn on Dog Lake Road, which leads 4 miles to the reservoir.

Duck Lake (Wallowa Mountains)
campground

Duck Lake is a small trout lake on the east slope of the Wallowa Range 30 miles northeast from Halfway. From Baker City or La Grande head for Halfway and then continue east on SR 86 to a well marked left-hand turn on North Pine Creek Road (FR 39, the Hells Canyon Scenic Byway). Continue north about 14 miles to a left turn on FR 66 (Duck Creek Road). After about 6 miles watch for the right-hand spur leading down to Duck Lake. The lake, which spans 19 acres and reaches a depth of 50 feet, offers small brook trout and rainbow trout and has a pair of nice tent sites with tables.

Duncan Reservoir

A productive, oft-turbid trout reservoir located on a sage plateau a few miles southeast from the town of Silver Lake in Lake County. Duncan is stocked with rainbow trout annually and they tend to grow rapidly during periods of optimal water levels. Like most reservoirs in southeastern Oregon, Duncan peaks after two or three consecutive years of higher-than-average water levels. During drought periods, the reservoir is severely drawn down and becomes increasingly turbid. The reservoir is fairly popular during spring and is usually fishable by early April, though it's open year-round. During optimal conditions, give it a try during October when the water often clears somewhat and when the remaining fat trout can reach 20 inches.

Duncan Reservoir covers about 30 acres—the perfect size for a float tube or small boat. Shore fishing is easy, however, and many anglers still fish with bait from the dam and around the shoreline (bait fishing is usually the most productive method). Fly anglers armed with leech patterns can enjoy good sport here at times, especially in the fall when the water clears—but, again, remember that the reservoir is highly dependent on water supply. On late spring and early summer evenings, keep an eye peeled for fish rising for midges and chasing water beetles near the surface. You can camp at the reservoir. Though fishless because it is seasonal, Duncan Creek above the reservoir makes for a nice hike because it flows through a narrow box canyon.

From Bend, follow Hwy 97 south to Hwy 31, about 2 miles south of Lapine. Follow Hwy 31 approximately 5 miles past the town of Silver Lake and watch for a signed right-hand turn onto Emery Road (gravel) that leads to Duncan. From Burns, head for Riley and turn south on US 395 until you reach a right-hand turn on the Christmas Valley Road. Head through Christmas Valley until the road turns south. You'll come out on Hwy 31. Turn right and watch for the left-hand turn on Emery Road (near the power lines).

Eagle Creek (Wallowa Mountains)
campground

Eagle Creek is a scenic, productive trout stream flowing south out of the Eagle Cap Wilderness on the south side of the Wallowa Range. A popular summer destination, Eagle Creek is regularly stocked with legal-size rainbows. A few carryovers along with some wild trout reach 14 to 16 inches, but pan-size fish predominate. All methods are effective here, with fly angling being especially good during late summer and autumn.

Access is excellent, as FR 77 parallels the stream for many miles and the 5-mile-long Eagle Creek Trail follows the middle section of the stream through a roadless canyon just upstream from the Wallowa-Whitman National Forest boundary. The easiest way to get there is to follow SR 86 east from Baker City down the Powder River. Just before entering the town of Richland, head north on Eagle Creek Drive (CR 969), which becomes FR 7735 upon reaching the forest boundary. A mile past the national forest boundary you will reach Eagle Forks Campground, a good starting point for following the trail through the roadless reach of the creek.

At Eagle Forks, the road swings to the east and then returns to the creek upstream. Just stay on FR 7735 until you reach the left-hand turn onto FR 77. At the upstream end of the trail at Martin Bridge, FR 77 follows the creek all the way up to Boulder Park Campground near the Main Eagle Trailhead. Tamarack and Two-Color Campgrounds are situated creek side between Martin Bridge and Boulder Park. All told the campgrounds offer two dozen tent sites. If you're towing a trailer, head for Tamarack Campground. Additional camp-sites are located to the west at West Eagle Meadows—a very popular destination for campers, hikers, and anglers. West Eagle Creek offers only fair fishing for small trout and gets hit pretty hard during the summer.

Eagle Lake (Eagle Cap Wilderness)
hike-in

Source of Eagle Creek, this beautiful wilderness lake spans 37 acres and reaches a depth of more than 100 feet. The lake offers mostly small brook trout, but a few 12- to 16-inch fish are available. Eagle Lake sits at 7,400 feet and is only moderately busy compared to destinations on the north side of the Eagle Cap Wilderness Area. The hike from the trailhead at Boulder Park covers about 7 miles. From La Grande or Baker City, follow SR 203 to Medical Springs and then head easterly on FR 67. After about 15 miles turn left on FR 77, go 1 mile and turn right on FR 7755. Watch for the trailhead at Boulder Park after about 6 more miles.

Several other lakes in the area are worth a visit. Cached Lake sits 2 miles to the west, just south of the trail and offers small brook trout. Bear Lake and Culver Lake, also brook trout fisheries, are located off a side trail on the way up Eagle Creek 4.5 miles from the trailhead. All of these lakes are typically accessible by early July and fishing holds up well until the first snows fall.

Echo Lake (Eagle Cap Wilderness)
hike-in

A scenic 28-acre brook trout lake on the southern edge of the Eagle Cap Wilderness, Echo sits at 7,222 feet and usually offers good fishing throughout the short season between July and late September. The fish range from 6 to 10 inches, sometimes larger. The trail from West Eagle Meadows covers 5 miles and gains elevation rapidly. You'll cross the creek twice, which can be difficult during early summer. From Union, follow SR 203 south to Catherine Creek. Two miles past the park, turn left onto FR 77 (Eagle Creek Road) and follow it 15 miles up to West Eagle Meadows. From the south, you can follow FR 67 from Medical Springs up past Tamarack Campground to a left-hand turn onto FR 77.

Echo Lake (Mountain Lakes Wilderness)
hike-in

A fair-to-good brook trout and rainbow lake in the Mountain Lakes Wilderness Area northwest of Klamath Falls, Echo Lake sits about 200 yards north of much larger Lake Harriett. Use the Varney Creek Trail as described under the Lake Harriett listing herein.

Elder Creek (Lake County)
no bait, campground

A major, though diminutive tributary to the Chewaucan River, Elder Creek is a good bet for native redband trout ranging from 6 to 10 inches. The creek's best reaches flow through private ranchlands, for which you must seek permission; but the upper end of the creek flows for about 4 miles through the Fremont National Forest. The best section here is the last mile before the creek enters private property. To reach it you must hike downstream from FR 3315, which flows along the creek's headwaters. Drive west through Paisley and after you cross the Chewaucan River watch for a right-hand turn onto FR 3315. Eventually you'll reach FR 28. At that point the creek is immediately south of the road, flowing to the south. Park along 3315 and hike that direction. During drought years, this stream should be left undisturbed.

Elizabeth Lake
sees Sky Lakes Wilderness Area

Elk Creek (Baker County)
campground

A fair bet for small, wild rainbows, Elk Creek is a tributary to the upper end of the South Fork Burnt River, southwest of Unity. There are several nice campgrounds in the area and a handful of other trout-bearing streams. The South Fork itself is stocked with legal-size rainbows. For directions see Burnt River herein.

Emigrant Creek (Harney County)
no bait

A good choice for pursuing small, wild redband trout, Emigrant Creek is a fairly popular stream flowing through the Ochoco and Malheur National Forests north from the Burns area. The creek dumps into the Silvis River, but much of the lower half of the stream flows across private property. Access to the upper portion of Emigrant Creek is good. From Hines/Burns, take the signed north turn to Yellowjacket Lake (CR 127). At the Turner Ranch, turn west (left) on FR 43, which crosses onto public land after 3 miles and then parallels most of the creek's length.

Fifteen Cent Lake

During wet cycles, Fifteen Cent Lake has water, but does not support fish. It is one of the large, usually dry lakebeds on the west side of the Fields-Denio Road on the way into Mann Lake.

Fifteenmile Creek (Malheur County)
no bait, catch-and-release

This tiny, remote desert stream originates in the Oregon Canyon Mountains about 9 miles north of the Nevada border and flows through about 10 miles of BLM land before joining Whitehorse Creek. Most of it dries up during summer. Fifteenmile Creek, as of this writing, is open to catch-and-release fishing with flies and artificial lures, but anglers aren't likely to find any trout. The stream has in the past supported a fragile and very sparse population of indigenous Lahontan cutthroat trout, which clung to existence in the stream's short section of year-round flow. Surveys conducted in 1989 and again in 1994 suggested that the stream's trout population may have been extirpated. Beware that the mountains in this corner of Oregon have recently become home to illegal marijuana grows reportedly guarded by armed men; consult the Malheur County Sheriff's Office in Vale (541-473-5125) for more information.

Fish Creek (Steens Mountains)

no bait, hike-in

Fish Creek joins the Blitzen River 4 miles upstream from Page Springs Campground, a few miles southeast of the tiny town of Frenchglen. Like the Blitzen, Fish Creek offers fair-to-good fishing for wild redband trout, including a few that reach 16 inches. To get there, turn left off the highway at the south end of Frenchglen, following the signs to Page Springs. When you turn into the campground, head all the way to the back (south end) where a parking lot serves hikers. Follow the trail for about 4 miles to reach Fish Creek. You'll ford the river several times and find easier going in places by simply walking up the riverbed. Like the Blitzen, Fish Creek runs high with snowmelt well into summer. Wait until July to fish the river, or better yet, wait for the cooler weather of autumn. Fish Creek's redband trout are most abundant on the creek's lower few miles. Informal trails follow the creek, but in places you'll have easier going just walking in the stream.

Fish Lake (Wallowa Mountains)

campground

This is a pretty little high lake in the Wallowa Mountains about 30 miles north of Halfway. From either Halfway or Joseph (to the north) take the Hells Canyon Scenic Byway (FR 39) to the east side of the Wallowas and turn west on FR 66. After about 6 miles you will pass the road into Duck Lake and then ascend a steep ridgeline. From the top of the ridge it's about 6 miles to Fish Lake and along the way you will pass the Twin Lakes. Both Fish Lake and Twin Lakes have nice campsites and all three lakes offer fair-to-good fishing for small trout. During summer these lakes can get busy, especially on weekends, but by September you will often have them all to yourself. The best time is late September and early October when the larch trees turn a striking shade of yellow.

Fish Lake (Steens Mountains)

campground, boat recommended, float tube recommended, boat ramp

A popular summer destination low on the west slope of the Steens Mountains, Fish Lake offers good fishing for stocked rainbow trout and wild brook trout. The rainbows range from 8 to 13 inches. The brookies average smaller, but get bigger, with a few reaching 16 inches. Fish Lake covers 20 acres and sits at 7,400 feet. It is generally accessible by mid-June, but call the BLM office in Hines to find out if the road is passable if you intend to head there before July 4. You can camp at designated spots among the aspens at Fish Lake, but the area tends to fill up on summer weekends. Additional campsites are located 15 miles back toward Frenchglen at Page Springs and 2 miles further up the road from Fish Lake at Jackman Park. There are several informal deer hunter camps in the immediate area as well. The Steens are famous for many reasons, among them the mosquito's, so come prepared to do battle with them.

Fisher Lake (Lake County)

Sitting just southeast of Crump Lake, Fisher Lake is one of the Warner Valley Lakes west of Hart Mountain and northeast from the tiny town of Plush. These lakes contain brown bullhead and largemouth bass but are primarily known as crappie fisheries. Fisher Lake, however, has never been very productive and dries up during low-water cycles. Hart and Crump lakes are better.

Flagstaff Lake (Lake County)

Flagstaff Lake is one of the Warner Valley lakes west of Hart Mountain and northeast from the tiny town of Plush. The lakes contain brown bullhead and largemouth bass but are primarily known as crappie fisheries. During extended periods of high water the Warner Valley lakes produce large crappie, some up to 2 pounds. During drought cycles the lakes shrink to a fraction of their potential surface acreage and the crappie fishery all but collapses. The best fishing ever on the lakes occurred following the remarkably wet winters of 1982-84. By 1987 the crappie fishery had reached epic proportions only to be devastated by a three-year-long drought. The fisheries rebounded during the 1990s and then were devastated by another extended drought from 2000-2003. Most people fish these lakes from shore, although in a few places—especially some of the interconnecting channels at high water—a canoe comes in handy. Be wary of the frequent high winds. Plush is the jump-off point to reach these lakes and the main roads yield to numerous dirt roads and jeep trails. Be sure to consult the maps and carry all necessary supplies in this remote country.

Fish Lake on the west flank of Steens Mountain

Fort Creek (Klamath County)

no bait, catch-and-release

This pretty little spring creek is a tributary to the Wood River north of Agency Lake. The road alongside offers access to the upper end of the creek. Redband and brown trout inhabit the creek, but only a short stretch flows across public lands. The lower end of the creek is private, although you can fish the mouth by boat if you are floating the Wood River.

Fourmile Lake (Klamath County)

campground

A scenic lake sitting at 5,800 feet in the Cascade Range near the foot of 9,495-foot Mt. McLaughlin, Fourmile Lake offers a diverse fishery that features stocked rainbow trout, abundant small kokanee, wild brook trout, and lake trout (Mackinaw) recently introduced by ODFW. The stocked rainbows can reach good size here because they are able to over-winter successfully. Wild brook trout, though averaging pan-size, reach at least 15 inches. The kokanee tend to range from 8 to 12 inches and the lake offers a 25-fish limit on the kokanee in addition to the usual trout limits.

The Mackinaw were introduced by ODFW in hopes of producing a trophy fishery for them such as exists further north at Crescent and Odell Lakes. At 740 acres and 170 feet deep, and with kokanee for the lakers to feed on, Fourmile would seem an ideal setting for these fish. The first fish were raised at Klamath Hatchery from eggs obtained from a hatchery in Wyoming. To date little monitoring has occurred, but ODFW believes the first stocked Mackinaw could have spawned in the fall of 2003. That summer, anglers reported catching some lakers in the 20- to 24-inch range.

Naturally fishing for both kokanee and lake trout generally requires a boat, which is no problem during spring. There is no formal boat ramp, but anglers can back trailers into the lake on the sand beach at the campground. However, Fourmile Lake is managed as an irrigation reservoir for the Medford Irrigation District and it is substantially drawn down during the summer. By mid- to late summer, Fourmile is drawn down enough that launching boats becomes very difficult. The sand beaches slope gently enough that vehicles often flood out before the boat trailer is deep enough to float the boat.

Obviously this presents something of a problem during the fall, when fishing for Mackinaw peaks. So if you head for Fourmile Lake anytime after mid-summer, choose your watercraft and your vehicle appropriately and check with ODFW or Winema National Forest in Klamath Falls before heading up to the lake. Shoreline fishing is easy here because as the water is drawn down, a wide sandy beach appears around most of the lake making for easy access. If you launch any kind of watercraft, be aware of the stiff wind that usually whips up during the afternoon.

To reach Fourmile Lake, follow Hwy 140 west from Lakeview for about 35 miles to a north turn on FR 3661, which leads 6 miles to the lake. The road is generally free of snow by mid- to late June. Medford is about the same distance to the west. If you're coming from that direction watch for the turn-off after you pass the summit just east of Fish Lake.

Fourmile Quarry Ponds (Klamath County)

Located just west of Upper Klamath Lake off Cold Springs Road, these quarry ponds sit on Winema National Forest property and have in past years served as the site for Free Kid's Fishing Day, held during June. The ponds are then stocked with rainbow trout, including some big fish, and the forest service throws a fishing bash for the kids. For details, contact Winema National Forest in Klamath Falls at 541-883-6731. The ponds continue to produce a few trout in the weeks following the free fishing day, but they usually dry up during late summer. The U.S. Forest Service has proposed a project to deepen the ponds to produce a permanent fishery, but thus far the project has not been funded.

Francis Lake

see Sky Lakes Wilderness Area

Gerber Reservoir (Klamath County)

boat ramp, campground

Although it has gotten very low in recent years, sprawling Gerber Reservoir (3,830 acres at full pool) is well known for its productive warm-water fisheries. It sits about 50 miles west of Lakeview and about the same distance east from Klamath Falls. Gerber still holds the state record for white crappie, dating back to a 4-pound, 12-ounce specimen caught here in 1967. The crappie fishery remains the primary attraction at Gerber, but the reservoir also, at times, offers good fishing for decent-size yellow perch, largemouth bass, and brown bullhead. The bass here reach at least 5 pounds, but the big fish are uncommon. Gerber holds a sparse population of redband trout, along with rough fish of various kinds.

When full, Gerber's shoreline offers lots of good cover in the form of flooded trees and stumps along with rock piles, reefs, and shoals. Concentrate your efforts on these areas for both crappie and bass. A boat is handy to explore the far corners of Gerber Reservoir, but shore fishing and shoreline access is good. The reservoir offers two large BLM campgrounds, both with boat ramps, and a third ramp at the Barnes Valley Arm. The campgrounds usually open the weekend before Memorial Day weekend and close around the end of September. Some nice primitive campsites are scattered around the reservoir if you prefer to get away from the crowds.

Gerber lies south of Hwy 140 and about 19 miles from Bonanza. Head east about 20 miles from Klamath Falls and then take Hwy 70 to Bonanza. From Bonanza head south on Langell Valley Road to Lorella and follow the signed route up to the reservoir. From Lakeview you can head south from Bly on the Barnes Valley Road. Because of very low water in recent years, check with ODFW in Klamath Falls before heading out to Gerber as boat ramps may be high and dry and the fishery may be marginally productive.

Greaser Lake/Greaser Reservoir

A large, shallow natural lake, enlarged further by a dike/dam project, Greaser Lake (and Greaser Reservoir) sprawl across a wide basin several miles southeast of Adel. It is primarily inhabited by Warner Valley suckers.

Guano Creek (Lake County)
no bait

Guano Creek is the second largest stream emanating from Hart Mountain, site of the Hart Mountain National Antelope Refuge. The stream has recovered substantively since cattle grazing was discontinued on the refuge during the early 1990s. The creek was stocked with Lahontan cutthroat trout in 1957 and subsequently with other strains, and a few fish persist in the stream's perennial reaches on the mountain, occasionally dispersing downstream during high-water events (see Shirk Lake). Access is via a network of very rough desert jeep trails south from Hot Springs Campground, located near the Hart Mountain Refuge headquarters, but the creek contains so few fish that the effort is hardly worthwhile.

Haines Pond (Baker County)

Located along the road immediately north of Haines (north of Baker City), quarter-acre Haines Pond has largemouth bass and stocked legal-size rainbows. To get there, follow the old LaGrande-Baker Highway (US 30) north from Baker City or south from North Powder. The pond is on the east side of the highway a quarter mile out of town.

Harpold Reservoir (Klamath County)

A small BLM reservoir south of Bonanza, Harpold is lightly fished and offers largemouth bass, crappie, and brown bullhead. To get there, head east from Klamath Falls on Hwy 140 and then at Dairy turn south toward Bonanza head south on Harpold Road to a left turn on West Langell Valley Road. After about 2 miles watch for a left-hand turn onto BLM Road #39-11E-26, which takes you to the reservoir. Nearby Smith Reservoir sits on private land just to the east and requires that you get permission before fishing for its bass and crappie.

Harriette Lake
see Lake Harriette

Hart Lake (Lake County)

Massive Hart Lake, spanning 8,000 acres when full, is one of the Warner Valley lakes west of Hart Mountain and due east from the tiny town of Plush. These lakes contain large brown bullhead and a few largemouth bass but are primarily known as crappie fisheries. Hart Lake has always ranked amongst the most productive of the lakes here. During extended periods of high water the Warner Valley lakes produce large crappie, some up to 2 pounds. During drought cycles the lakes shrink to a fraction of their potential surface acreage and the crappie fishery all but collapses.

The best fishing ever on the lakes occurred following the remarkably wet winters of 1982-84. By 1987 the crappie fishery had reached epic proportions only to be devastated by a three-year-long drought. The fisheries rebounded during the 1990s and then were devastated by another extended drought from 2000-2003. Most people fish these lakes from shore, although in a few places—especially some of the interconnecting channels at high water—a canoe or car-topper comes in handy. Be wary of the frequent high winds.

Plush is the jump-off point to reach these lakes and the main roads yield to numerous dirt roads and jeep trails. Hart Lake is easy to fish because the Hart Mountain Road runs across its northern edge. A secondary road follows the entire east shoreline. Head north from Adel until you reach Plush and then continue north and then east on the Hart Mountain Road. The lake is 4 miles from town. Be sure to consult the maps and carry all necessary supplies in this remote country.

Heart Lake (Lake County)
boat ramp

Situated high in the Fremont National Forest south of Quartz Mountain Summit, 18-acre Heart Lake is a slow-to-fair producer of stocked rainbow trout and stocked kokanee. Like other lakes in the Fishhole Lake Recreation Area, Heart Lake has in the past suffered from tui chub infestation. Heart Lake is well suited to a float tube or small boat. You can camp at nearby Lofton Lake, or grab one of the two unimproved campsites at Heart.

From Bly, travel 13 miles east on Hwy 140, and turn right on FR 3715. Take FR 3715 (paved but narrow) for 7 miles, then turn right on FR 012. Continue on FR 012 for o1 mile and you should see the picnic area entrance. From Lakeview, follow Hwy 140 west 25 miles to the turn-off on FR 3715.

Heart Lake (Eagle Cap Wilderness)
hike-in

A rainbow trout fishery in the southern edge of the Eagle Cap Wilderness, 3-acre Heart Lake is accessible by way of a precipitously steep climb up Bench Canyon. The lake sits at 7,300 feet, more than 2,000 feet higher than the Main Eagle Trailhead on Eagle Creek. The lake is deep and easily over-winters trout, so a few of the 'bows reach 14 inches. From La Grande or Baker City, follow SR 203 to Medical Springs and then head easterly on FR 67. After about 15 miles turn left on FR 77, go 1 mile and turn right on FR 7755. Watch for the trailhead at Boulder Park after about 6 more miles. Alternately you can get there by heading north from Richland on Eagle Creek Drive.

Heavenly Twin Lakes
see Sky Lakes Wilderness Area

Hidden Lake (Eagle Cap Wilderness)
hike-in

As its name suggests, 16-acre Hidden Lake resides deep in the Eagle Cap Wilderness Area, about a mile north from Eagle Lake as the crow flies. You'll have to walk, however, and the route covers a long 8 miles, mostly along East Eagle Creek. Follow the main trail (#1910) north along East Eagle Creek 6 miles to the junction for the Hidden Lake trail and then climb about 2 miles up to the lake, which sits at 7,200 feet. Brook trout here are mostly small but plentiful, and fishing can be very good from mid-July through late September. On the way up the last segment of trail to Hidden Lake, you will pass by much smaller Moon Lake on your left. Don't mistake it for Hidden.

From La Grande or Baker City, follow SR 203 to Medical Springs and then head easterly on FR 67. After about 15 miles turn right on FR 77. Follow FR 77 down Eagle Creek to a left-hand turn on FR 7745, which leads up to the East Eagle Trailhead. Alternately head north on the Eagle Creek Road from the town of Richland, turning right on FR 7745.

Higgins Reservoir
no bait

Higgins Reservoir near Unity has in the past been a fair to good producer of fat rainbow trout and is restricted to flies and artificial lures. During years of good water supply, the stocked trout grew rapidly and averaged about 13 inches, with fish to 20 inches available. However, ODFW stocking of fingerling rainbows was discontinued in 2006 after the landowner decided to only allow walk-in access (the hike covers 0.75 mile), so check with ODFW in Prineville before venturing to Higgins. Rather lightly fished, Higgins is open to access by landowner agreement, which depends on anglers respecting the private lands. Haul out all trash. Only electric motors are allowed. Higgins covers about 100 acres at full pool and fishes best during late spring and again during autumn. To get there, follow Hwy 26 east from Unity about 1 mile to the gravel turn-off leading northeast to the reservoir.

High Lake
(Strawberry Mountain Wilderness Area)
hike-in

High Lake is a pretty little brook trout lake sitting at about 7,450 feet in the Strawberry Mountain Wilderness Area east from John Day. The lake is pretty enough, but I would not head up there just for the fishing as the self-sustaining brookies here average a skinny 6 inches. Fish it in conjunction with the other lakes in the wilderness area. (see Northeast Zone).

Highway 203 Pond (Baker County)

A large pond located adjacent to the I-84/Hwy 203 interchange 5 miles north of Baker City, this fishery is maintained by rainbow trout stockings from ODFW. The pond also has a few bass and panfish. The pond sits on the east side of the freeway and is accessed by the siding road off Hwy 203. Most anglers fish it from the bank by still fishing with bait.

Holbrook Reservoir
boat ramp

Traditionally a fair-to-good lake for fat, 12- to 18-inch rainbows, Holbrook Reservoir lies a few miles south of Hwy 140 near Quartz Mountain Summit west of Lakeview. The reservoir spans about 40 acres, much of it on private property where anglers are allowed access by the owner (no camping except at the designated campground). Bank fishing is fairly easy at Holbrook, but a float tube or small boat is handy. In recent years the lake has developed a tui chub problem which, coupled with back-to-back-to-back droughts from 2000-2003,

sent the trout fishery into depression. Holbrook still produces good catches however, and will improve with rising water tables. To get there, follow Hwy 140 east from Klamath Falls or west from Lakeview and watch for the south turn on FR 3715 at Quartz Mountain Summit. At the 5-mile mark on FR 3715 watch for the right-hand turn leading another mile to Holbrook.

Home Creek (Steens Mountains)
catch-and-release, no bait

Note that access to the public (BLM) lower stretch of Home Creek, as of 2010, is not possible owing to postings by Roaring Springs Ranch. Consult the BLM in Burns for further information. If the creek again becomes accessible, the following synopsis remains accurate.

Currently open to artificials-only catch-and-release fishing for its native redband trout, Home Creek flows westerly out of the Steens Mountains, reaching the Catlow Valley 8 miles south of Roaring Springs Ranch. The creek flows through a deep canyon and its lower 5 miles flow entirely through public property. Highway 205 crosses the creek, but the crossing lies on private property, which extends a few hundred yards upstream from the road. Just north of the creek, watch for a dirt road turning east off the highway. The road leads to the remnants of an old homestead, which is a popular (and shaded) camping spot. This is on public (BLM) land. From there you can hike up the canyon to fish for the creek's wild redbands, which reach at least 14 inches, but which usually range from 6 to 9 inches. This is good dry fly water for those adept at negotiating short-line casts through dense streamside foliage.

The entire upper watershed flows through private property beginning at the west edge of Township 35S, Range 32.5E, Section 16. Fishing is best during late spring and early summer and then again in the fall. Handle the trout carefully, release them immediately and double check the regulations to make sure the creek is still open. In recent years, Roaring Springs Ranch has posted signs indicating that you will need written permission to enter this area (only a tiny corner of public land touches the highway), so anglers should stop in at the ranch before fishing the creek and should have a backup plan in mind.

Honey Creek (Lake County)
no bait

A good redband trout stream, Honey Creek flows east from the Warner Mountains, emptying into Hart Lake near Plush. Most of the creek flows across private ranchlands with no public access and those stretches that run across BLM-owned sections are difficult to get to because of the maze of private lands surrounding the drainage. You can fish the headwater reach of Honey Creek in the Fremont National Forest north of Hwy 140, but the creek is quite small up here and the trout both tiny and scattered. Years ago I managed to figure out access to the lower canyon and the fishing was better, with redbands to 14 inches in a rugged setting. This one is for the adventurous angler willing to study the USGS topo maps alongside the BLM map. You will need a rugged 4-wheel-drive vehicle and make sure to pack extra tires, a jack, a shovel, and a sturdy pair of hiking boots. The access roads are terrible during wet conditions, so save this journey until a dry June or late September.

Hyde Lake (Klamath County)

Hyde Lake, covering 300 acres, is a private fee fishery located on the Yamsi Ranch east of Chiloquin. The lake produces large rainbow trout, some of which exceed 30 inches. Guests of Yamsi Ranch (see Williamson River, Upper) have access to the lake, and anglers can also book by the day (2010 rates were $125/day per angler). Take a float tube, pontoon, or small boat (electric motors only). To book, contact Yamsi Ranch (541-783-3008/www.yamsiflyfishing.com).

Isherwood Lake
see Sky Lakes Wilderness Area

Island Lake
see Sky Lakes Wilderness Area

Jackson Creek (Klamath County)
no bait, campground

Jackson Creek is a small, forested stream flowing north from spring sources on Yamsay Mountain east of Klamath Marsh. It offers fair fishing for small rainbows and a few brown trout. Take Hwy 97 to the Silver Lake Road that heads east across Klamath Marsh. The road traces a straight line across the open expanses of the marsh. When you reach the other side, continue northeast on Silver Lake Road about 12 miles to a right-hand turn on FR 49, which takes you directly to Jackson Creek. There's a nice little campground and upstream from there, the entire creek lies on public lands. Best of all, the creek is lightly fished once you get away from the campground because most of Jackson Creek remains hidden at a distance from the forest roads. Be sure to get a copy of the Chemult Ranger District Map, available from the Winema National Forest office in Klamath Falls.

Jenny Creek (Klamath County)
no bait

Home to a unique and long-isolated race of native redband trout, Jenny Creek flows south through the southeastern corner of Jackson County before crossing the state line and emptying into Iron Gate Reservoir on the Klamath River in California. The creek crosses under SR 66 about 18 miles east of Ashland. The redbands here typically range from 5 to 10 inches. Fishing is best on the creek's upper half. The lower end of Jenny Creek is traditionally drawn down rather dramatically and diverted for the Talent Irrigation District.

The upper reaches of Jenny Creek are contained within the new 52,000-acre Cascade-Siskiyou National Monument. Access is fairly easy as the creek winds through a patchwork of private timberland and BLM land north of the highway. Jenny

Creek Road follows the creek south from Howard Prairie Reservoir. Mostly on private land, the lower 2 miles of the creek support marginal populations of green and pumpkinseed sunfish, crappie, bullhead, and largemouth bass.

Juniper Lake (Harney County)

Completely dry in recent years, Juniper Lake is capable of growing fat trout during high water years. Juniper Lake is located along the Fields-Denio Road about 10 miles north of Mann Lake. When full of water, ODFW typically plants Juniper with rainbows and the lake is open to all methods. More turbid than nearby Mann Lake, Juniper Lake is better suited to bait and spinners, but streamer flies prove quite effective. The lake is easy to fish from the bank and unimproved campsites are available. To get there, follow Hwy 78 south from Burns, crossing over the north extent of the Steens Mountains and then turning south on the Fields-Denio Road (gravel). Follow the road past three lakebeds on the right (5-cent, 10-cent and 15-cent Lakes) and then past Juniper Lake Ranch, also on the right. Watch for the lake 2 miles past the ranch. Before venturing out to Juniper Lake, call ODFW in Burns to check current conditions.

Kiger Creek (Steens Mountains)
no bait

Kiger Creek flows through a deep, spectacular canyon cutting through the west slope of the Steens Mountains. The creek is accessible only by hiking into the gorge, which is generally possible after mid-July when the Steens Loop Road is open. Only experienced, well-conditioned hikers need apply, as this is treacherously steep, rugged terrain. He or she who climbs down into the gorge must also climb back out. Small, native redband trout inhabit the stream, whose lower reaches flow across private ranch lands.

Killamacue Lake (Baker County)
hike-in

Killamacue Lake is a 15-acre brook trout lake at 7,100 feet in the Elkhorn Range west from Baker City. The hike covers about 3 miles. From Baker City or North Powder head for Haines and then follow the Elkhorn Scenic Route west out of town for about a mile and a half and then turn left and follow the Rock Creek Road heading west. Watch for the trailhead about 2 miles after you enter the national forest.

Klamath Lake (Upper Klamath Lake)
boat recommended, boat ramp, campground

A massive natural lake with vast connected wetlands, Upper Klamath Lake ranks as one of the best trophy trout waters in the United States. Spanning more than 60,000 acres just north of the town of Klamath Falls, this huge, shallow fishery is home to indigenous redband trout that grow rapidly in the lake's fertile broth. Twenty-inch trout hardly deserve mention here as they are quite average and the lake boasts lots of fish reaching 24 inches. The maximum size is at least 18 pounds

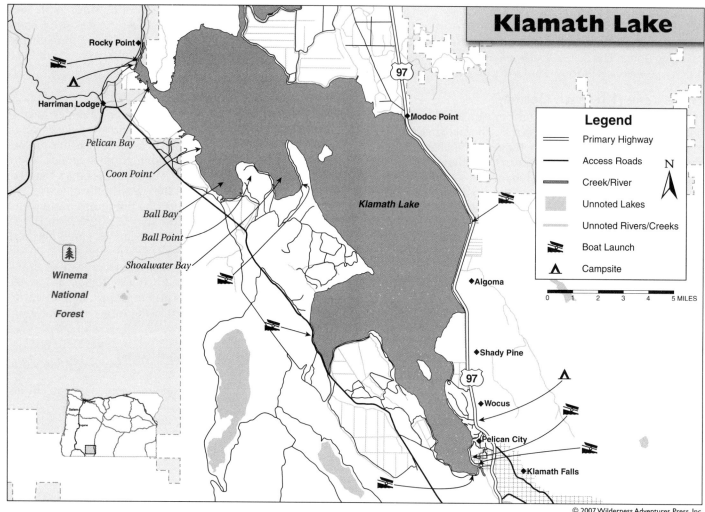

© 2007 Wilderness Adventures Press, Inc.

with typical trout ranging from 3 to 6 pounds.

All methods are used effectively on this lake. Many anglers troll with plugs and spoons or even with frozen minnows or parts thereof available at area tackle shops. Casting with plugs is also effective. The lake is home to a sizeable population of chub minnows and other non-game fish that provide forage for the fast-growing trout.

Klamath Lake enjoys substantial and well-deserved popularity with fly anglers, who enjoy consistent success from mid-spring through late autumn. The usual flies include myriad baitfish patterns, along with leech patterns and general-use nymph patterns. Most of the time, specific pattern takes a back seat to fishing the right place, especially when the trout start to congregate around creek mouths and springs in the lake. Hatch chasers can even enjoy the opportunity to fish a good damsel emergence during June, especially in the channel connecting Klamath and Agency Lakes. Callibaetis mayflies hatch during early summer as well, and from time to time they'll draw a few rises.

Most of the time, however, you can expect to fish streamer and leech patterns on sinking lines. The new generation slow-sinking "Stillwater Lines" are especially valuable here. A good basic selection of flies would include chub minnow patterns in both 3-inch and 5-inch lengths, leech patterns in shades of black, rust, and olive and a few basic wet flies. Of the latter, my favorites include Carey Specials in peacock and olive, bead-head Prince Nymph, olive damsel nymph patterns and patterns to mimic bloodworm Chironomid pupae.

Fishing for trout on Klamath Lake virtually requires a boat, although float tubers enjoy success near shore, especially in Pelican Bay. This huge lake is notorious for its high winds, so boaters fishing the main lake must keep an eye on the weather. Even canoes make effective fishing craft in Pelican Bay and along the lake's self-guided canoe trail that offers 9.5 miles of scenic and fishable water. Klamath Lake abounds with brown bullhead and yellow perch, both of which are easily taken by bank anglers.

Pelican Bay and its immediate surrounds, on the lake's northwest corner, is the lake's most popular fishing area, especially among fly anglers. The bay is spring-fed from several sources and its water remains clear during summer when the rest of the lake blooms with algae and grows extensive beds of aquatic plants. The summer broth causes water quality to suffer, so the trout tend to move to spring-fed areas, creek mouths and into tributaries. From mid-spring through the end of May or early June, you can find trout widely dispersed around the lake but, as summer sets in, head for the springs and tributaries. If one area doesn't produce, move to another spot. By October, angling pressure dissipates and fishing improves. The autumn fishing, from October into early November, can be very good.

The boat launch at Rocky Point Resort in Pelican Bay offers ready and easy access to the entire bay. The bay itself offers plenty of room for anglers to disburse and other popular areas include the "Fish Banks" just outside the bay to the north and the channel connecting Upper Klamath Lake to nearby Agency Lake. The mouth of the Williamson attracts lots of big trout, especially as water conditions in the lake deteriorate during the summer. The run from Rocky Point to the Williamson delta covers about 7 miles, so watch the weather and beware the wind.

Upper Klamath Lake

The aforementioned canoe trail has four segments: Recreation Creek, Crystal Creek, Wocus Cut, and Malone Springs. The segments connect to form a broad loop through the marsh at the lake's northwest corner. Often the best fishing is in the Crystal Creek/Malone Springs reach, whose springs attract schools of trout during summer and fall. However, you can usually find fish at Recreation Creek, immediately north of Rocky Point and at the mouth of Crystal Creek to the southeast. Recreation Creek feeds the top end of Pelican Bay while Crystal Creek reaches the main lake near the mouth of the bay. You can launch at the boat ramp at Rocky Point or shorten the trip to the springs by using the Malone Springs Launch adjacent to Crystalwood Lodge north of the lake.

Rocky Point Resort sits immediately north of the boat ramps at Pelican Bay and offers a wide range of services. The resort features rental cabins, lodge rooms, RV sites, tent sites, a restaurant, tackle store, rental boats and canoes, moorage, and more. They usually open on April 1. Be sure to call ahead to reserve lodging or rental boats (541-356-2287/www.rocky-pointoregon.com). Camping is available at several other places around the lake, including Eagle Ridge County Park, Odessa Creek Park, and Hagelstein Park. The former two parks are on the lake's west side, conveniently located for anglers heading for the popular fishing grounds around Pelican Bay, Ball Bay, and Shoalwater Bay. Other options include lodging in nearby Klamath Falls.

The town of Klamath Falls is the hub city for the adjacent lake. Highway 140 heads northwest from Klamath Falls and follows the lake's shoreline. Medford is 60 miles to the west. From either direction, follow Hwy 140 to the lake. Rocky Point Road (West Side Road) is well marked and turns north off the highway at the lake's northwest corner. Immediately south, the highway provides access to Odessa Creek, Eagle Ridge/Shoalwater Bay, and Ball Bay. Highway 97 follows the lake's east shore. To reach the Crystal Creek/Malone Springs, head north past Rocky Point Resort and watch for the signs.

Klamath River (Klamath County)
hike-in

In south-central Oregon, about three hours from Bend and just beyond the town of Klamath Falls at the little community of Keno, the Klamath River spills from Keno Dam, creating one of the state's best tailwater trout fisheries. Wild rainbows here typically range from 14 to 20 inches, but getting at them largely requires a substantial physical effort. Below Keno Dam, the river plunges rapidly through a rough and tumble boulder-strewn canyon and the water runs perpetually off color. The fishery here is closed during the summer when high water temperatures stress the trout. The river opens October 1 and closes in June.

The Keno Dam stretch can offer good fishing at any time during the river's open season, but if pressed for the best time I would choose the month of October. A close second would be anytime during spring when water releases at Keno Dam are minimal. At ideal flows the river is tinged a tea color, but

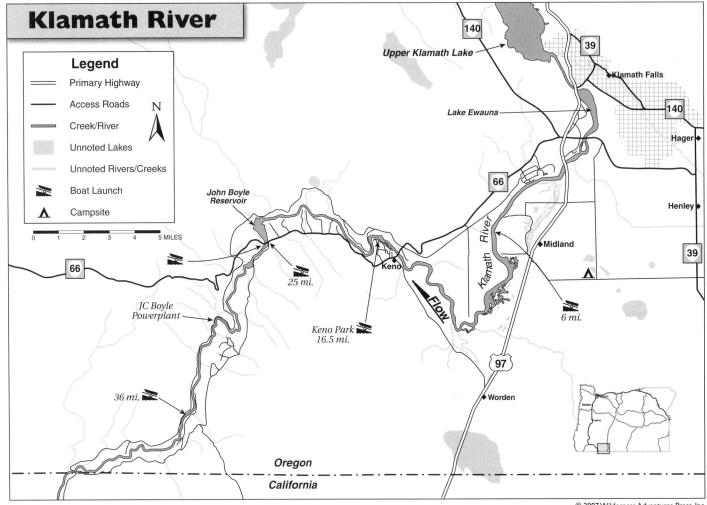

Klamath River

Legend

Primary Highway
Access Roads
Creek/River
Unnoted Lakes
Unnoted Rivers/Creeks
Boat Launch
Campsite

N

0 1 2 3 4 5 MILES

John Boyle Reservoir

JC Boyle Powerplant

25 mi.

Keno Park 16.5 mi.

36 mi.

140

Upper Klamath Lake

39

Klamath Falls

Lake Ewauna

140

Hager

66

Henley

Klamath River

Flow

Midland

Keno

6 mi.

97

39

Worden

Oregon

California

© 2007 Wilderness Adventures Press, Inc.

at high flows the water turns brown or greenish-brown and the fishing suffers accordingly. The best fishing occurs when flows from Keno Dam are well below 1,000cfs, with a few hundred cfs being ideal. You can call PP&L to check flows (800-547-1501).

Strewn with boulders and ledges that are terribly difficult to negotiate, the Klamath here makes for tough wading. Luckily many of the deeper runs, pools, and slots require little if any wading. Just negotiate the rocks to gain a position from which you can effectively fish these places.

Below Keno Dam the Klamath is one of Oregon's most fertile trout streams. It abounds with insects and baitfish, giving the wild trout plenty of food on which to grow fast and fat. Fly anglers usually fish heavily weighted nymphs and large streamer patterns. During spring and early summer, watch for awesome hatches of large stoneflies and caddisflies. Some trout respond to the hatches, but often the fish prefer to feed subsurface. Streamers are always good and top flies include heavily weighted woolly buggers, Clouser Minnows, and Zonkers. Gear anglers enjoy consistent success fishing with heavy spoons and spinners. Fish them on at least 8-pound test line.

Only two places offer easy access to the Keno-to-Boyle stretch of the Klamath River. One is the Pacific Power & Light public access site immediately west of Keno on Hwy 62 and the other is on the north bank just below the dam and across the river from the PP&L site. To get there from Keno, head west and cross the river near town. At the three-way intersection turn left (north) and drive a little more than a mile to a left-hand turn that follows the north bank of Keno Reservoir. The road wraps around that side of the reservoir and heads past the dam before ending at a turnaround. The entire road is rugged and the last few hundred yards are especially rough and can be almost impassable when wet. You can park just downstream from the dam and walk the final length of the road and then hike downstream from there.

Other than these two easy-access areas near Keno Dam, getting to the Klamath River here requires a steep, treacherous climb down into the canyon from Hwy 66. Several informal trails drop off the roadside and plunge down to the river. Naturally you'll have to climb back up at day's end. The trails are easy to find: Drive west out of Keno on Hwy 66 and after the road climbs up out of the valley, watch for the pull-offs on your right. Park at the pull-outs and carefully negotiate the trails into the canyon. The faint of heart and physically unfit need not apply.

About 6 miles below Keno Dam the Klamath River is backed up at J.C. Boyle Reservoir. This 450-acre impoundment is mostly a warm-water fishery, though some big trout live at the top end. Crappie, perch, brown bullhead, and large-mouth bass inhabit the reservoir, which fluctuates between 1 and 4 feet daily as water is drawn for power generation. The large-mouth bass reach several pounds but most are a lot smaller and they never seem abundant. Generally the better fishery is for crappie. You can fish the reservoir from shore or by boat.

The Klamath River in Oregon offers several different stretches inhabited by wild redband trout.

Hwy 66 crosses the narrow reservoir on a low dike-like bridge that offers no underpassage for boats. Topsy Campground, on the southeast shore, offers a boat ramp and barrier-free fishing dock. Watch for the signs as you approach the reservoir from the east or as you cross the reservoir from the west. You can drop a small boat in on the north side of the bridge. Most of the bass come from the shoals near Topsy, but by late summer you can find them in the shallows north of the highway. Crappie are far more abundant and easier to find.

Downstream from Boyle Dam, the river flows through a shallow but steep-sided canyon accessible by dirt roads below the spillway area. The turnoff to Boyle Dam is 1.7 miles west of Boyle Reservoir and heads south. After half a mile take the third left off this access road and head down the hill to the river. At the bridge, turn right on the gravel road that follows the cement flume along the river. Here you have access to about 2 miles of river. This access road catches up to the main road at the lower spillway and from there you can fish another 2 miles of river down to the Boyle Substation. This entire stretch is characterized by rugged fishing for mostly small, wild redband trout. Typical fish here range from 6 to 12 inches, but they are eager dry fly biters and also respond well to small spinners and spoons. The water is tea-colored and strewn with boulders and ledges, so be very careful wading and use a wading staff.

Below the huge flumes of the substation, the Klamath runs another 11 miles down to the California border. This lower reach, fairly popular with highly skilled whitewater experts, offers some good fishing for wild rainbows in the 10- to 20-inch class. However, discharges from the turbines at Boyle Dam triple the size of the river here and leave only narrow windows of opportunity between discharges. Your best bet during the summer is to be on the water at sun-up and enjoy a brief respite before the outflows begin. Often the flows decrease again in the evening. Be careful in this stretch for several reasons, especially because of treacherous wading made all the more brutal by sudden and dramatic increases in flows.

Most anglers fish this stretch from the Topsy Road, which follows the east bank south from Hwy 66 at J.C. Boyle Reservoir. The river down here runs mostly through BLM land and many anglers fish the creek mouths, especially when the river is at high levels. The Topsy Road, always dusty and rough during dry weather, gets terribly sloppy during wet weather and is best suited to 4-wheel-drive vehicles. You can call J.C. Boyle Power Plant to get information on water releases to the lower stretch of the river (800-547-1501).

Krumbo Creek
see Krumbo Reservoir

Krumbo Reservoir (Harney County)
boat recommended; boat ramp, float tube recommended

Under ideal conditions, 150-acre Krumbo Reservoir ranks among the best big-trout waters in southeastern Oregon. During the high water years of the mid-1980s, Krumbo put out good numbers of 20- to 25-inch rainbows and lots of 14-to 18-inch fish. Subsequent drought and conditions took a toll, but the reservoir tends to spring back to its full potential any time Mother Nature offers two or three consecutive high-water years. Krumbo is ideally suited to all methods of fishing and float-tubing fly anglers are a common sight at the reservoir, which also harbors a solid population of fair-sized largemouth bass.

Krumbo is located an hour south of Burns, at the foot of the Steens Mountains, on the Malheur National Wildlife Refuge. The nearest town is Frenchglen, 15 miles to the south on Hwy 205. Krumbo lies to the east of the highway—watch for the signs about 2 miles south of the spot where the highway rounds a sharp curve cut right into the bedrock. Many anglers fish Krumbo from shore, but a small boat or float tube is a decided advantage, though no motors are allowed. Camping is not allowed at the reservoir, so your options include the Frenchglen Hotel, for which you'll need advance reservations (541-493-2825), Page Springs Campground on the Blitzen River a few miles southeast from Frenchglen, or several decent primitive campsites located on BLM land a few miles northwest of the reservoir. To find these, head back north on the highway and as you wrap around a tight right-hand curve, watch for a broad gravel pullout on your left with a dirt road leading north. Turn up the road and pick a spot in the junipers to your right.

Krumbo Creek feeds the reservoir and during high-water years the creek is worth fishing, as you'll often find some of the reservoir's fat trout residing there. Below the reservoir, Krumbo Creek is closed to fishing. The reservoir opens in late April and closes at the end of October (check current synopsis).

Lake Creek (Grant County)

no bait, campground

Lake Creek is a small tributary to the Malheur River at Logan Valley east of Seneca. The stream offers small wild redband trout and brook trout. Nearby Big Creek is similar, offering small wild trout with the best fishing from June through September. Trails follow both Lake Creek and Big Creek up into the Strawberry Mountain Wilderness Area. Turn east at Seneca on FR 16 and when you reach Logan Valley watch for the signed left-hand turn on FR 924.

Lake Como (Mountain Lakes Wilderness)

hike-in

Lake Como sits a mile northwest of Lake Harriette in the Mountain Lakes Wilderness Area near Klamath Falls. Como offers brook trout and rainbows reaching about 12 inches, sometimes a little larger. The shortest route to Lake Como is via the Varney Creek Trail coming in from the north. Follow Hwy 140 northwest from Klamath Falls. At about the 16-mile mark, watch for the signed left-hand turn on FR 3637. After about 1.5 miles, turn left again on FR 3664. Shortly thereafter take the right-hand fork up to the trailhead. From Medford, you can get there by taking FR 361 from Lake of the Woods, but you'll make better time following Hwy 140 up and around, past Pelican Bay, to the turnoff on FR 3637. The trek to Lake Como covers 4 miles.

Lake Harriette (Mountain Lakes Wilderness)

hike-in

The largest and most popular of the lakes in the 21,000-acre Mountain Lakes Wilderness Area, Harriette generally holds up well to the fishing pressure and offers fair-to-good action on brookies and rainbows ranging from 6 to 14 inches. Harriette spans 70 acres and offers plenty of shoreline fishing, although a float tube is always useful. Be sure to camp in pre-existing spots well back from the lakeshore. The easiest way to reach Harriette is from the north on the Varney Creek Trail: Follow Hwy 140 northwest from Klamath Falls. At about the 16-mile mark, watch for the signed left-hand turn on FR 3637. After

about 1.5 miles left again on FR 3664. Shortly thereafter take the right-hand fork up to the trailhead. From Medford, you can get there by taking FR 361 from Lake of the Woods, but you'll make better time following Hwy 140 up and around, past Pelican Bay, to the turn-off on FR 3637. The hike to Harriette covers about 5 miles.

Lake of the Woods (Lake County)

boat ramp, campground

Lake of the Woods is a popular, attractive mountain lake well known for its booming kokanee fishery and also offering brown and rainbow trout, bullhead, yellow perch, and some largemouth bass. It is likewise popular with water sports enthusiasts, and many of the lakeside residents water ski on the lake during summer. Fishing holds up well from late spring through mid-autumn and a few hardy souls ice fish here during winter.

The lake's kokanee reach 14 inches, while stocked rainbows range from 10 to 16 inches. Brown trout here reach at least 8 pounds and most range from 14 to 20 inches. Brown bullhead abound and yellow perch also seem to be thriving in the lake's shallow shoreline areas. Bass are rare, but they can grow big here. The limit on kokanee is currently 25 fish and there is no limit on brown bullhead. Moreover, Lake of the Woods is open to angling 24 hours per day, so anglers specifically seeking large brown trout enjoy a unique opportunity to pursue these oft-nocturnal predators after dark using plugs, spoons, and streamer flies.

Lake of the Woods lies nestled amidst evergreen forests just east from the summit of the Cascade Range west from Klamath Falls and immediately south of Hwy 140. Medford is 50 miles to the west. There's an information center just off the highway and forest roads circle the lake. Two nice, spacious campgrounds occupy the east shore.

Little Malheur River

see Malheur River, Little

Little McCoy Creek

closed waters

Flowing off the east face of the Steens, Little McCoy Creek is closed to angling to protect a possible remnant population of Lahontan cutthroat trout.

Little Rock Reservoir

see Big Rock Reservoir

Lofton Reservoir (Lake County)

A scenic and consistently productive rainbow trout fishery, Lofton Reservoir covers 41 acres in the highlands west of Lakeview. Perched at 6,100 feet in the Fishhole Lake Recreation Area, Lofton is usually accessible by May. It tends to hold up throughout the summer and angling improves during autumn. Lofton's stocked rainbows range from 8 to 18 inches. Shoreline fishing is easy, but the reservoir is ideally suited to a float tube or small boat. Only electric motors are permitted. A nice wheelchair-accessible fishing dock overlooks one side of the lake. The campground has 25 spaces.

From Lakeview, travel 25 miles west on Hwy 140 and turn left on FR 3715. Take FR 3715 for 7 miles, and then turn left on FR 013. Continue on FR 013 for 1 mile and you should see the campground entrance sign.

Long Creek Reservoir (Baker County)
campground

A tiny reservoir near Unity with a fine view of Monument Peak, Long Creek Reservoir is stocked with legal-size rainbows and fishing can be fair to good depending a lot on water supply. The reservoir covers only 2 acres but reaches a depth of 25 feet. To get there, head for Unity and then turn south just east of town onto FR 1680. Follow FR 1680 to a left turn on FR 1692, leading down to the reservoir.

Long Lake
see Sky Lakes Wilderness Area

Long Prairie Creek (Klamath County)

Home to a residual population of redband trout, Long Prairie Creek is a tributary to the Klamath River, reaching the river south of the state line. The creek has suffered plenty of habitat damage from decades of logging, grazing, and other activities and fishing is quite marginal.

Lookingglass Lake (Eagle Cap Wilderness)
hike-in

A scenic 31-acre hike-in lake near Eagle Creek, Lookingglass Lake offers good fishing for brook trout. Most of the fish range from 8 to 12 inches with some bigger fish available. The trail begins at the Main Eagle Trailhead at Boulder Park and covers about 6.5 miles, going up the canyon along Eagle Creek before climbing up into a glacial cirque, where the lake lies nestled up against Hummingbird Mountain. This is a beautiful camping spot that draws quite a few people, but don't be surprised to have the lake all to yourself. From La Grande or Baker City, follow SR 203 to Medical Springs and then head easterly on FR 67. After about 15 miles turn left on FR 77, go 1 mile and turn right on FR 7755. Watch for the trailhead at Boulder Park after about 6 more miles.

Lost Lake (Elkhorn Range)
see Summit Lake

Lost River (Klamath County)

The Lost River makes a broad 90-mile loop through southern Klamath County before returning to California at Tule Lake. Its headwaters are Clear Lake in California, just 25 miles east from Tule Lake. The river is a low-gradient stream that provides good habitat and good fishing for warmwater species, including largemouth bass, crappie, pumpkinseed sunfish, yellow perch, Sacramento perch, brown bullhead, and even some large goldfish. Largemouth bass here reach at least 6 pounds and 2- to 4-pound bass are not unusual. Much of the river is quite small and shallow, but a series of springs, dams, diversions, dikes, and meanders make for a highly varied watercourse that even puts out an occasional large redband trout.

Most of the river flows through private property so bank access is limited to just a few places, including Crystal Springs County Park southeast of Klamath Falls near Henley. Follow Hwy 140 or SR 39 southeast through Klamath Falls. Just before you get to Henley on SR 39, turn east on Short Road and then south on Reeder Road to another east (left) turn on Crystal Springs Road. The boat ramp here allows you to launch and then fish both directions on Wilson Reservoir—about 3 miles in length. Boat fishing here represents the best access of any reach on the river.

About 10 miles to the east, you can find bank access at Harpold Dam, where the river is backed up into a shallow pool that provides good fishing, mostly for brown bullhead and largemouth bass. Harpold Dam is located 4 miles west of Bonanza and is downstream from Big Springs, which is a major component to the Lost River water supply. The other popular bank-access area is at Malone Dam, located just north of the state line about 20 miles south of Bonanza. To get there, head south from Bonanza through Langell Valley. West Langell Valley and East Langell Valley Roads meet at the dam, which forms Malone Reservoir. Malone Reservoir is a 20-acre impoundment and is a good producer of warmwater species, including some good-sized largemouth bass and crappie. It also offers brown bullhead and Sacramento Perch. Bank access is at the dam.

Lower Campbell Lake
see Campbell Lake

Lucky Reservoir (Lake County)

A turbid but fertile reservoir located south of the tiny hamlet of Adel east from Lakeview, Lucky Reservoir spans only 6 acres but can produce fair catches of fat rainbow trout. Because of the muddy water, most anglers fish bait, but lures and flies work well, especially during autumn when the water sometimes clears slightly. The trout here range from 10 to 20 inches with 12- to 14-inch fish being typical. Catch rates range from slow during turbid, low water periods to fair during ideal conditions. The south end of the reservoir is very shallow and when the wind blows, which is usually every day, the mud spreads to the deeper north end. The road into the reservoir can be impassable during spring. To get there, follow Hwy 140 to Adel and turn south. At the junction of Lake County Roads 314 and 314A, take 314A to BLM Road 7132 swinging back to the north. Follow the road to the power lines and then to the reservoir. Leave all gates as you find them (open or closed).

Malheur Lake
see The Narrows

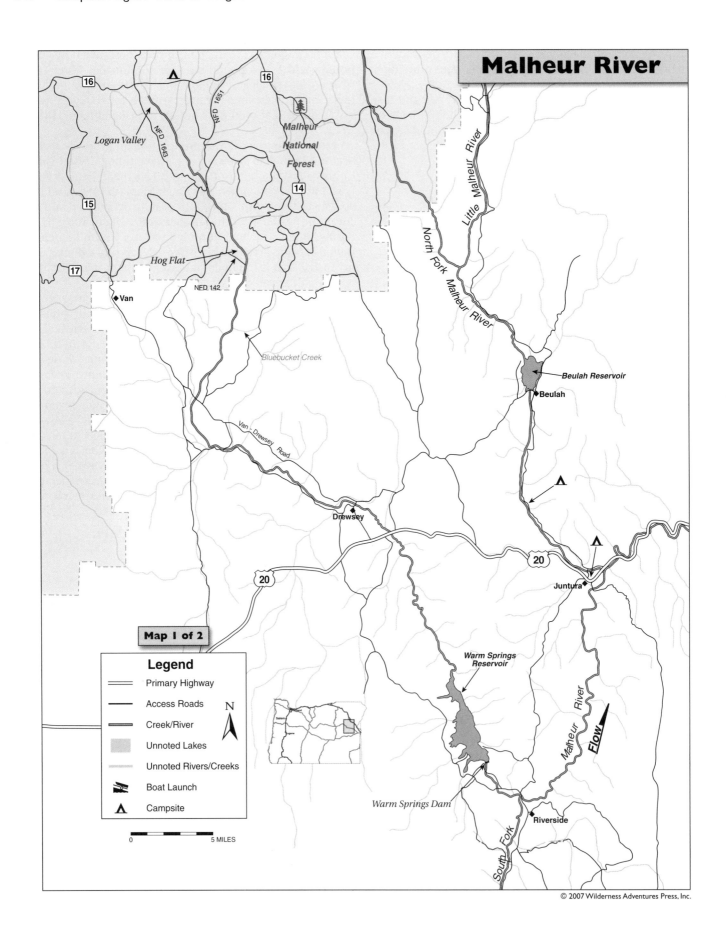

Malheur River

16

16

NFD 1651

Logan Valley

NFD 1643

Malheur National Forest

14

15

17

Hog Flat

NFD 142

Van

Bluebucket Creek

Little Malheur River

North Fork Malheur River

Beulah Reservoir

Beulah

Van - Drewsey Road

Drewsey

20

20

Juntura

Warm Springs Reservoir

Malheur River

Flow

Map 1 of 2

Legend

Primary Highway

Access Roads

N

Creek/River

Unnoted Lakes

Unnoted Rivers/Creeks

Boat Launch

Campsite

0   5 MILES

Warm Springs Dam

South Fork

Riverside

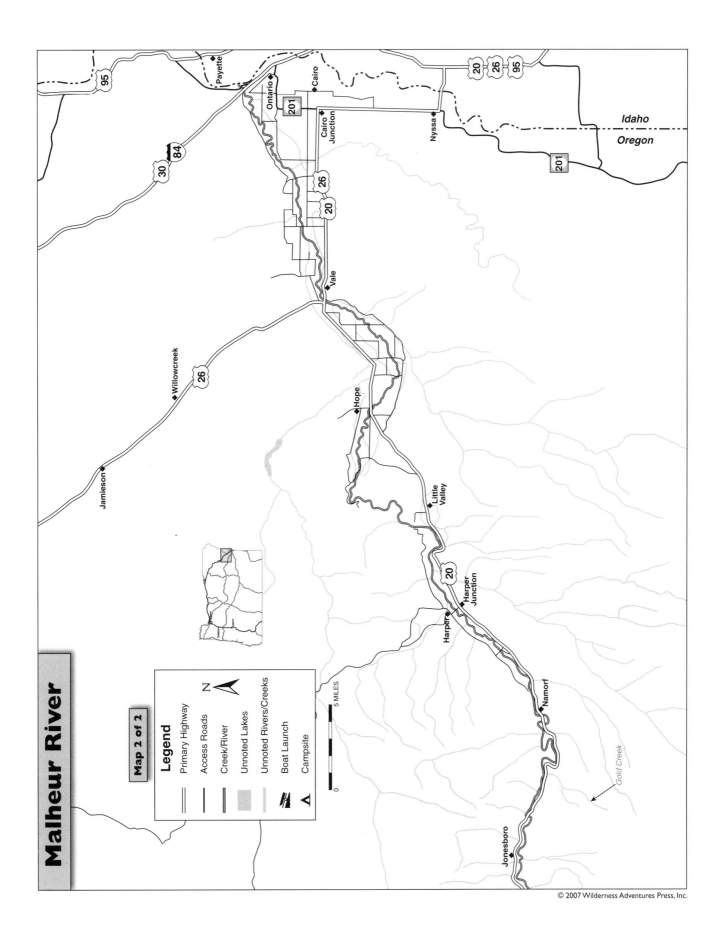

Malheur River

Map 2 of 2

Legend

Primary Highway
Access Roads
Creek/River
Unnoted Lakes
Unnoted Rivers/Creeks
Boat Launch
Campsite

5 MILES

© 2007 Wilderness Adventures Press, Inc.

Malheur Reservoir (Malheur County)

One of the most fertile and productive reservoirs in eastern Oregon, Malheur offers fast-growing rainbow trout that typically range from 12- to 18 inches and reach at least 22 inches. The fishery peaks after three or more consecutive years of average or better water conditions and has been known to dry up under prolonged drought conditions (it went completely dry in 2003). At full pool, Malheur spans 1,400 acres, but averages less than 20 feet in depth.

This fertile reservoir is rich in trout foods and the stocked rainbows grow fat on scuds, snails, Chironomids, leeches, damsels, and *Callibaetis* mayflies. The fishing peaks from mid- to late spring and can be especially good during fall if water levels allow. The reservoir abounds in perfect float tube water, offering lots of near-shore shoals and shallows where trout feed morning and evening. During the day they feed in slightly deeper water, where extensive weed beds harbor abundant insects, scuds, and other foods. An improved boat ramp is located adjacent to the dam and unimproved campsites lie scattered about near the dam and access roads. Bank anglers usually fish bait and generally do quite well.

Relatively remote, Malheur Reservoir lies north of Hwy 26, northwest from Brogan and northeast from Ironside. Willow Creek Road reaches the reservoir from either side, departing Brogan on the east and Ironside on the west (watch for the signs). If you are coming from I-84 to the east, exit the freeway at the Rye Valley Road (Dixie) at Exit 340. Head west to a left turn on the Mormon Basin Cut-off Road and then a right turn on Willow Creek Road. The reservoir sits at 3,400 feet; so if you head out in the spring, call ahead for road and water conditions (call the ODFW office in Baker or Vale).

Malheur River, Logan Valley to Drewsey
campground

The Malheur River begins at the confluence of several creeks in Logan Valley east of Seneca. A diminutive forest stream in its uppermost reaches, the Malheur heads south, flowing almost 20 miles across public lands before reaching the narrow valley west of Drewsey. The upper stretch of the river is characterized by decent access and by fair fishing for wild redband trout. Easiest access is in the Dollar Basin area, where several forest service roads reach and approach the river. The spider-like network of roads here is easier to decipher by map than by description, so consult a copy of the Malheur National Forest Map.

To reach the Malheur at Dollar Basin, head for the little town of Seneca, located on US 395 north of Burns and south of John Day. At Seneca, head east up Bear Creek on FR 16 and follow it all the way to the west edge of Logan Valley. Just past milepost 16, turn south on FR 1643 and follow it south all the way to Dollar Basin. Watch for a left turn on FR 1651 leading down to a little recreation site called Malheur Ford. From there you can follow the Malheur Trail downstream for miles, fishing lots of small pocket and meadow water that doesn't see much pressure. The other end of the trail is at Hog Flat about 6 miles downstream. To get there, head back to FR 1643 and turn south. About 7 miles later watch for a left-hand turn on FR 142. The trailhead is at the end of this road. This is small water, ideal for dry flies.

Below Hog Flat, the Malheur flows off the national forest and through a patchwork of private and BLM land. Adventurous types can hike into the river canyon from the east to fish 2 contiguous miles of public property near the mouth of Bluebucket Creek, north of the Van-Drewsey Road. A spur road down Bluebucket Creek reaches a short distance toward the river and from there it's a hike-in affair down into a very steep-sided canyon. To get to Bluebucket Creek, follow Hwy 20 east from Burns and past Buchanon to a north turn on Pine Creek Road. Head north on Pine Creek Road until you meet the Van-Drewsey Road. Turn right and after about 2 miles turn left on CR 14. Bluebucket Creek is about 7 miles north and the river is off to your left (west). Once you cross Bluebucket Creek on the main road (just past milepost 19) watch for a spur leading off to your left (west).

Downstream from Bluebucket Creek, the Malheur begins a lengthy meander through Drewsey Valley, all of it on private property. There is some good fishing available upstream from Drewsey, but you must get permission from the landowners. The Drewsey-Van Road follows the north side of the river at a distance and Market Lane follows the south side of the valley from Drewsey to Pine Creek. Currently this portion of the Malheur carries a five-fish daily bag limit and bait is allowed only downstream from Bluebucket Creek.

During years of adequate water supply, Malheur River rainbows grow fast.

Malheur River, Drewsey to Warm Springs Reservoir

Downstream from Drewsey the Malheur River flows entirely across private ranch lands until finally entering state-owned property 1 mile south of Hwy 20. From that point, the river flows entirely on public lands all the way to Warm Springs Reservoir, a reach of about 10 river miles and a remote section of river capable of producing fine catches of smallmouth bass for the adventurous angler. Like most waters in this country, this reach of the Malheur peaks when Mother Nature offers up several consecutive years of above-normal water supply.

To reach this section of the river, turn south off the highway at the signs for Warm Springs Reservoir, about 2 miles west from the Drewsey turnoff. From the road into the reservoir, several rugged spurs head easterly to reach or approach the river. You'll need a good map and don't drive this country without 4-wheel-drive, extra tires, a shovel, and all other such supplies. You'll also need a sturdy pair of hiking boots. The river fishes best during late spring and early summer and again during the autumn.

Malheur River, Warm Springs Dam to Juntura

campground

Warm Springs Dam—quite monolithic for a dam out in this desert—creates a fertile, fish-food-rich tailwater on the Malheur River just downstream. During years when water levels permit, ODFW adds the other piece of the puzzle in the form of liberal stocks of hatchery rainbows. The fish grow rapidly in this river and many range from 14 to 18 inches. After two or three good seasons, the Malheur here offers fat 20-inch specimens as well. Over the past few years, low flows resulting from low-snowpack winters have severely curtailed the trout fishery, but the river bounce back quickly during times of good water supply.

Access is the tricky part on the 20-odd-mile stretch from the dam down to Juntura, where Hwy 20 catches up with the river. Public access extends from the dam downstream to the Warm Springs Reservoir Access road. Downstream from the road, the river flows through private property for about a mile and a half down to the BLM's Riverside Recreation Site. Here the gravel road to Juntura crosses the river. From Riverside, you can fish downstream for several miles, more if you're up for the hike. However, the abandoned railroad grade that follows the river through the canyon is privately owned and is not open to public use. As of this writing the landowner is negotiating with the state to possibly trade a length of the south end of the railroad bed into public hands. Check with ODFW in Hines for the latest word.

You can float this section of the river in a sturdy raft at high flows between late April and September. Take out at the diversion dam above Juntura, which you should scout first. The folks at Oasis Restaurant in Juntura can point you in the right direction and they serve up a hearty meal for breakfast, lunch, or dinner. Don't float this river at low flows.

Riverside offers little in the way of amenities, but it is a popular camping spot during the early part of the chukar hunting season in October. Turn left off the road just south of the bridge over the river and stake out a campsite amidst the dust and sagebrush. The aforementioned Oasis Restaurant in Juntura also has a small hotel.

Malheur River, Juntura to Vale

Downstream from Juntura, the Malheur picks up the North Fork Malheur and then enters a deep, arid canyon. Highway 20 follows along the river, winding through the canyon and providing ready access. Throughout the canyon run, the river flows through a mix of public and private property. Be sure to seek permission before fishing on private lands. The trout fishing deteriorates progressively as you get farther and farther east of Juntura. Halfway through the canyon, rough fish become more numerous than trout. Trout fishing here is always highly dependent on river flows and water condition. During high-water years, water releases from Warm Springs Reservoir feed agricultural needs downstream and keep the river running high and dirty from mid-spring through the summer.

Fishing streamer flies on the Malheur River

Beautiful little wild redband trout inhabit the North Fork of the Malheur above Beulah Reservoir.

The best fishing is thus restricted to early spring and autumn when flows from the reservoir are reduced, shrinking the Malheur River to a much more fishable entity. March and October are generally the two best months, especially for fly anglers. Bait and spin-fishers can do reasonably well even at high water provided the water is running more greenish than brownish. ODFW stocks the river liberally with rainbows and they grow quickly in this river. No trout are stocked below Gold Creek, about 20 miles downstream from Juntura.

Below Gold Creek, the river is inhabited by a variety of non-game species along with a few smallmouth bass and a few trout. The river is slowed by Namorf Dam, below which non-game fish predominate. The river's last few miles, from Vale down to the Snake River, are likewise populated by lots of non-game fish but bass, bullhead, and some large catfish also live here, though you wouldn't want to eat them owing to the intense agricultural run-off.

Malheur River, North Fork
(below Beulah Reservori)

The tailwater fishery immediately below the dam on Beulah Reservoir produces some nice rainbows to bait, gear, and fly anglers. Downstream from this short reach, the river flows entirely through private property except for the 1-mile section of BLM land at Chukar Park, 5 miles from Juntura. Downstream from Juntura, Hwy 20 crosses the North Fork immediately above its confluence with the Mainstem Malheur.

Malheur River, North Fork
(above Beulah Reservoir)

Upstream from Beulah Reservoir, the North Fork Malheur offers fair-to-good fishing for wild redband trout in a remote mountain setting in the Malheur National Forest. Access is by a series of forest roads and trails on the eastern edge of the Malheur National Forest southeast from Prairie City.

The Malheur National Forest map will guide you here. Redband trout predominate and these waters are also home to fully protected bull trout. If you catch one, release it carefully.

Malheur River, Little
hike-in, no-bait

The Little Malheur is a fair fishery for small redband trout and flows through some remote country south of Unity, but only the uppermost headwater section lies on public land in the Malheur National Forest. The Little Malheur begins as a small stream emanating from the Monument Rock Wilderness Area, leaving less than 5 miles of road-accessible water north of FR 16. From just east of Unity, turn south on West Camp Creek Road, which intersects FR 16 or follow the highway east to Eldorado Pass and turn south on FR 16. From Burns, you can follow US 395 north to Seneca and then turn east on FR 16 for a very long, but scenic back way into the river, which also takes you to the upper reaches of the Malheur River and the North Fork Malheur River.

Malheur River, South Fork

The diminutive and oft water-starved South Fork of the Malheur joins the Middle Fork a few miles downstream from Warm Springs Reservoir. It has a sparse population of native redband trout, which are probably best left undisturbed by anglers, and smallmouth bass in the lower reaches. If you care to give it a try, you'll have to knock on ranch doors. A good gravel road more or less follows the river from Riverside south to Senator and from there the Norman Ranch Road follows the rest of the way. Only 2 miles of the South Fork flow across BLM land, north from Senator (consult the map: *BLM Sportsman Series, Senator*).

Malone Reservoir (Klamath County)
see Lost River

Mann Lake (Harney County)
no bait

Desolate, dry and dusty; howling winds, total lack of shade and drinking water, too cold or too hot; 50 miles from anything. Doesn't sound like much fun until you throw in a fertile lake teeming with 20-inch Lahontan cutthroat. That's the deal at southeastern Oregon's Mann Lake, or at least it used to be before the illegal introduction of goldfish, which proliferated in the lake. In September, 2010, ODFW treated the lake to remove the goldfish and will start over with stocking trout in the spring of 2011. Once the trout fishery is restored, the following synopsis will again be accurate and the good times will return to this eastern-Oregon fly angler's favorite, where most anglers are only too happy to tolerate the inhospitable remoteness in return for the trophy cutthroat fishing.

The massive Steens Mountains trap virtually all the moisture arriving from the west, leaving the narrow basin to the east in an expansive rain shadow. Some 5,000 feet below the rugged Steens Mountain summit, Mann Lake receives a precious few inches of precipitation each year. Even when wet winters dump massive snow pack on the Steens, Mann Lake can experience a net loss in water volume. Evaporation is the enemy in the scrub deserts of the Great Basin West. Alkalinity is one result of this incessant evaporation, and it is the alkaline water of Mann Lake that makes its cutthroat such unique trout, able to withstand water conditions that most salmonids would not survive.

Historically, this race of cutthroat hailed from the Lahontan Lake Basin east of Reno, Nevada. Their greatest stronghold today is Nevada's massive Pyramid Lake, where cutts to 10 pounds are reasonably common. Other western states have long traded in Lahontan stocks and several states now maintain Lahontan cutthroat hatchery programs. Traditionally, Mann Lake has provided the brood stock for Oregon's Lahontan cutthroat program, but recent problems with the rearing of these fish have led biologists to look for new stock from Washington's Lake Lenore (the region's other well known Lahontan fishery). In Mann Lake, these trout survive for five to six years, reaching a maximum size of about 25 inches. Typical fish range from 14 to 20 inches.

Mann Lake's season begins as early as February, before snowmelt begins in the Steens Mountains. Don't venture out there in February without first calling the ODFW office in Hines/Burns to check on whether the ice has thawed. The best spring fishing occurs between late March and early June.

The rich broth that comprises Mann Lake is home to huge quantities of virtually every significant stillwater trout food, from Chironomids to 2-inch-long giant diving water beetles. Spring offers exceptional hatches of Chironomids (midges), with the bloodworm hatch of mid-spring being especially prolific. During cold weather, the midges hatch mid-morning before the wind arrives. By late May, evening hatches are common. Wading anglers line up in the near-shore shallows, in fish pupae patterns subsurface, or in the surface film. Cold weather, which forces the adult midges to dry their wings before taking flight, creates the opportunity to fish dry flies.

Both morning and evening, especially dusk and dawn, trout cruise the shoreline shallows, rooting out scuds, water beetles, and water boatmen, all of which abound in the lake. These shallow-water cruisers are the lake's most challenging trout, requiring that you stalk quietly along the beach making delicate casts well ahead of visible targets. Use a 12- to 15-foot leader and a 4X or 5X tippet. Cast a small scud or water beetle pattern (sizes 12 to 18) that will penetrate the surface instantly and sink quickly to the bottom in 6 inches to 2 feet of water. My personal favorites include a size 14 or 16 Zugbug, slightly weighted with lead, or a tiny bead, and a size 14 or 16 olive-tan scud, tied on a 1XL wet fly hook, and weighted with a single strand of .020 lead wire tied along the shank. At dusk and dawn, leech patterns can draw savage strikes in mere inches of water, but they don't land very quietly, forcing you to cast well ahead of an oncoming trout. Even with small flies, lead these shallow-water cruisers by about 10 feet so the line splash and fly splash won't spook them. When the target fish closes to within 2 or 3 feet of the fly, start stripping. A series of quick 2- to 5-inch pulls, followed by a pause, should do the trick.

Once the wind starts blowing, between mid-morning and early afternoon, the stalking is over. You either can't see below the rippled surface or the mud gets stirred up and clouds the water (this is especially true when lots of people are wading the shoreline). The wind usually subsides during the evening (at least during calm weather), at which time the sight fishing begins anew. Look for areas protected from the wind's full force, and thus from the clouding mud.

Callibaetis (speckled-wing dun) mayflies emerge during May and June, rarely in dense numbers, but often heavy enough to bring trout to the surface. The damsel hatch begins about the same time, and as spring weather warms and days lengthen, evening Chironomid hatches occur, and water beetle activity increases. Throughout the spring, Mann Lake's trout feed on all these foods, along with snails, leeches, and dragonfly nymphs. During lulls in the shoreline action, try tubing the center of the lake, fishing leech and scud patterns slow and deep. Use a medium-rate sinking line, or a 10-foot, sink-tip line. Otherwise, intermediate and floating lines are ideally suited to Mann Lake.

Summer brings an end to the fishing as water temperatures soar and algae blooms erupt. Each year differs, but you can expect the fishing to come to an end sometime between mid-May and late June. Cool weather and shorter days in September kill off the bloom. Fishing improves and remains good through fall, assuming you can tolerate the bitter cold nights common in the desert basins of eastern Oregon.

Mann Lake is uniformly shallow, reaching a maximum

Mann Lake Lahontan cutthroat trout

depth of about 14 feet during high-water periods. Its surface covers about 300 acres on average, but the lake's size fluctuates wildly. During the flood years of the mid-1980s, Mann Lake tripled in acreage, but 20 years later the lake had shrunk to about 200 acres.

To reach Mann Lake, head first for Burns, Oregon. Then take Hwy 78 south out of Burns and past the tiny communities of Lawen, Crane, and New Princeton. Continue southeasterly, climbing up and over the Steens foothills at the Malheur/Harney County Line. As you wind down the other side, you will see a sprawling sage basin on the right, with a wide gravel road cutting across its center. Turn right onto this road, whose signs point towards the town of Fields. This is the Folly Farm Road, more commonly called the Fields-Denio Road and it leads some 25 miles to Mann Lake, which lies on the right (west) side of the road. Along the way you

Steens Mountain provides a fine backdrop to Mann Lake.

will pass Juniper Ranch and Juniper Lake on the right, then sprawling Tudor Lake on the left (Tudor will have little or no water most years). After driving past Tudor, and over a slight rise, you will descend to Mann Lake. The only turnoff heads straight to the lake's northeast shore, and then wraps around the north end to reach the west shore.

The entire north end of the lake provides excellent fishing, while the south shore, which is the private property of the Mann Lake Ranch, is usually posted. You can reach the south end by tube or boat, but foot traffic is limited to the un-posted areas. Shoreline fishing, including stalking sighted fish, is available virtually all around the north and west edges of the lake.

A few years ago, the BLM installed outhouses and improved the gravel parking areas. These are the only improvements: There is no drinking water and you won't find a single tree anywhere in the area. Take your own shade, and if you pitch a tent or a tarp, make sure it can withstand the constant battering from winds that commonly reach 30 to 40 miles per hour. Gravel boat ramps are located on both sides of the lake. Burns is almost 100 miles behind you, and the tiny village of Fields (store, fuel, cafe) is located nearly 40 miles to the south. The "gravel highway," once notorious for eating tires, has largely been supplanted by pavement during the past five years (in this country, always bring one or two extras, along with a full gas tank and perhaps some extra fuel, and plenty of water). You can also reach or depart Mann Lake via Fields and Frenchglen; this latter hamlet being located more than an hour away on the west side of the Steens Mountains. Both tiny towns are well worth a visit: Fields for a milkshake and burger or a hearty breakfast (also four motel rooms, fuel, and a store) and Frenchglen for a stay at Frenchglen Hotel and a visit to the Malheur National Wildlife Refuge or the Steens Mountain Loop Road.

Margurette Lake
see Sky Lakes Wilderness Area

MC Reservoir (Lake County)

A large, intermittent reservoir located just north of Hwy 140 about 20 miles east from Adel, MC has been stocked in years past with rainbow trout that tend to grow quickly. Usually the lake is too intermittent to support fish, so it has not been stocked in many years. Check with ODFW in Lakeview to get up-to-date information.

Meadow Creek (Klamath County)
no bait

A nice little forested stream with small, native redband trout, Meadow Creek flows north through the Winema National Forest east of Klamath Marsh and a few miles west from the Upper Williamson River. It is accessible from FR 49 and its spurs. For directions to the area, see Williamson River, Upper, herein. You will want to carry a map here.

Midway Reservoir
See Upper Midway Reservoir

Miller Creek (Klamath County)

The outlet from Miller Lake, this small, forested stream offers fair-to-good fishing for small brown and rainbow trout. Below Miller Lake, for about 4 miles, the creek runs through a shallow ravine south of the road. You can pull off along the road and walk down into the creek or hike down from Miller Lake. This is good dry fly water with trout that reach about 10 inches.

Miller Lake (Klamath County)
boat ramp, campground

A large, natural lake in the forested highlands west of Hwy 97, Miller Lake offers a good fishery for large brown trout along with modest-sized planted rainbows. The lake also offers a fairly dense kokanee population, but the fish are mostly stunted, making them ideal prey for carnivorous browns. The brown trout here typically range from 12 to 24 inches, with lots of fish in the 14- to 20-inch range, although they are not always easy to catch. Every year the lake produces a few trophies to 8 pounds, usually to anglers fishing spoons and plugs.

Fly anglers can enjoy good sport here also, especially with a pontoon boat or float tube, from which you can troll large streamer patterns on fast-sinking lines. Concentrate on the near-shore drop offs. At low light—early in the morning and around sunset—large browns often cruise very close to shore in less than 10 feet of water. Uniquely Miller Lake is open to fishing 24 hours per day, allowing anglers the opportunity to target big brown trout when the fish feed most actively. During daylight hours they tend to be deeper, so match your tackle to the water depth. The lake spans nearly 600 acres, so you'll generally find ample room. The lake is usually accessible by May, but call ODFW in Klamath Falls to check before you drive down there. Fishing generally holds up well during the summer, but the best action occurs from late September through October.

Miller Lake offers a boat ramp and a nice campground. To get there, follow Hwy 97 south from LaPine or north from Klamath Falls. The signed turnoff to Miller Lake is just north of the town of Chemult near milepost 202. From there a good gravel road leads 12 miles to the lake. A small boat comes in handy here.

Moon Reservoir (Harney County)

Highly turbid most of the time, Moon Reservoir nonetheless can be a good producer of bass, panfish and a few trout. It occupies a narrow canyon on Silver Creek, south of Hwy 20 between Burns and Riley. Watch for the signed south turn on the 00 Ranch Road leading to a right-hand turn onto a dirt/gravel road that reaches the reservoir. Water supply problems doom the fishery here each time a drought cycle occurs and the reservoir usually needs about three consecutive high-water years to grow largemouth bass and crappie to good size; at which time fishing can be quite good, mostly with jigs for crappie and plugs or rubber-worm jigs for the bass. You can launch small boats at the upper end when the water is up. The fishing here usually peaks during May and June.

Mosquito Creek
closed waters

Mosquito Creek was once stocked with Lahontan cut-throat and if any of the fish remain, they are protected as the creek is closed to angling. It flows off the east escarpment of the Steens south of Mann Lake.

Mountain Lakes Wilderness (Klamath County)
hike-in

The Mountain Lakes Wilderness Area is a 36-square-mile block of mountainous terrain surrounding several prominent peaks southwest from Upper Klamath Lake. The dominant peaks, all in the neighborhood of 8,000 feet tall, include Mt. Harriman, Mt. Carmine, Aspen Butte, and Whiteface Peak. Hidden among the pine and fir forests here are a number of fishable lakes, most of them stocked every other year with brook trout and/or rainbow trout. Lake Harriette is the largest and most popular. Other stocked lakes include: Clover, Como, Echo, Mystic, Paragon, South Pass, and Weston. You can easily fish from shore, but a float tube is handy.

The hiking season here generally begins in late June. Mountain Lakes Wilderness is easy to reach. The hub of the maintained trail system is the Mountain Lakes Loop Trail in the core of the Wilderness. It traces an 8.2-mile path around the caldera rim. You can reach it from the north by way of the Varney Creek Trail (4.4 miles); from the west on the Mountain Lakes Trail (6.3 miles); or from the south by way of the Clover Creek Trail (3.3 miles). See separate listings for the lakes.

Mud Creek (Steens Mountains)
hike-in, no bait

Mud Creek is a fairly productive little walk-in redband trout stream that joins the upper reach of the Blitzen River upstream from Blitzen Crossing. One rugged backcountry road gets you within about 2 miles of the mouth of the creek, but check with the BLM in Hines to make sure the road is still open for travel. To get there, head for Blitzen Crossing by following Hwy 205 south from Frenchglen about 10 miles to the left-hand turn at the well-marked entrance to the Steens South Loop Road. Follow this gravel road until you reach Blitzen Crossing. Now backtrack from the crossing for about a mile until you see the dirt road leading south. Stay on this road until it ends at the rim of the Blitzen River's canyon. Hike the top of the canyon or drop down to the river and head downstream. You'll pass Ankle Creek and then Mud Creek, both of which reach the Blitzen from the east. Best fishing here is in September and early October.

Mud Creek (Steens Mountains)
hike-in, no bait

The Steens Mountains boasts three different Mud Creeks. This one feeds the Blitzen River downstream from Page Springs Campground, on the Malheur Refuge. A pretty canyon-bound stream, Mud Creek supports a small population of redband trout, with the lower reach of the creek offering an occasional large fish. You can hike down to the mouth on the refuge service roads on the east side of the Blitzen River or hike into the canyon from the Steens Loop Road a few miles uphill and east from Page Springs Campground. Consult the map—*BLM Sportsman Series, Baca Lake*—first. The area was severely burned by a wildfire in 2006.

Mud Lake Reservoir ("Mud Lake") (Lake County)

This aptly named 100-plus-acre reservoir sits amidst heavily grazed sage/juniper hills east of Adel and north of Hwy 140 in southern Lake County. It has not been stocked in recent years, so call ODFW before venturing here. It nearly dried up during the prolonged drought of 2000-2003 but, when full, can produce slow-to-fair fishing for fast-growing rainbows. Mostly it's a bait-fishing show because the turbid water never clears. Best fishing is from the earthen dam on the south end, below which is a decent camping spot. There is an unimproved boat launch site, but I'd recommend against hauling in any kind of trailer/boat. To get there head east from Adel across Warner Valley. At the east edge of the valley, follow the highway as it turns south. Four miles past the highway's south turn, watch for a sharp-angled left turn heading north from the pavement. This road leads past two large playas, the first of which has water during wet years before reaching the reservoir. It's about 10 miles from the highway to the reservoir and the road can get rugged (and sloppy during wet weather).

Murray Reservoir (Baker County)

A good little trout fishery 10 miles southeast of Unity, Murray Reservoir offers stocked rainbows that range from 9 to 18 inches. Most are pan-size but, if water levels remain high, some nice, fat trout are available during autumn. The reservoir sits right alongside Hwy 26 on private property, but the landowner allows access for anglers. Boats and float tubes are not allowed on the reservoir.

Myrtle Creek
see Silvies River

Mystic Lake (Mountain Lakes Wilderness)
hike-in

Mystic Lake is a scenic little gem offering 8- to 12-inch brook and rainbow trout, with a few fish growing a bit larger. The lake covers just a few acres and lies just south of the trail to South Pass Lake, about a mile south from Lake Harriette and almost at the foot of 8,208-foot Aspen Butte. Be sure to consult your topo map to find this one as it lies off the formal trail. Any of the three trails into the lake basin will get you to the general vicinity. Mystic is a nice place to camp if you want to escape the other visitors to the area.

North Pine Creek (Baker County)
campground

A fair trout stream, mostly for stocked rainbow trout, North Pine Creek flows south right alongside the Wallowa Mountain Scenic Loop Drive, which heads northeast from Halfway in eastern Baker County. Access is very good along the road and a nice campground sits off a short spur road about halfway up the creek. The water generally runs a little off color during summer, clearing substantially during autumn. Stocked rainbows range from 9 to 12 inches and a few wild fish reach at least 12 inches.

North Powder Ponds (Baker County)

Stocked with legal-size rainbow trout, the two North Powder Ponds provide fairly consistent fishing, especially during late spring when ODFW plants them regularly. North Powder Pond #1 is a mile south of town on the west side of the freeway off Hwy 30. From North Powder, follow the highway south going toward Haines and watch for the short access road leading west. North Powder Pond #2 is a few miles to the west, off Elkhorn Drive. Four miles west of North Powder, after the road makes a sharp turn to the south (left), watch for the pond on your left, on the east side of the road.

Obenchain Reservoir (Klamath County)

A medium-size impoundment located on private land off FR 335 northeast of Bly, Obenchain offers largemouth bass, brown bullhead and bluegill, with the bass being most prevalent. From Klamath Falls or Lakeview, follow Hwy 140 to Bly and then turn north onto Campbell Road. A half mile up the road turn east towards Campbell Reservoir and then take the left-hand turn heading north past Campbell on FR 335.

Oregon Canyon Creek (Malheur County)
no bait

A tiny remote desert stream with a very sparse population of rainbow-cutthroat hybrids in its upper reaches, Oregon Canyon Creek is an adventure only for the hardiest desert explorers. At one time stocked with rainbows, the creek is originally home to rare indigenous Lahontan cutthroat trout. The hybrids are the result, though the creek has not been stocked for many years. Rugged desert roads approach the canyon-bound headwaters, but you must hike into the creek. You can get there from back roads leading west from Hwy 395 or from the west via the Whitehorse Ranch Road. Study the maps and beware these roads during wet weather. Beware that the mountains in this corner of Oregon have recently become home to illegal marijuana grows reportedly guarded by armed men; consult the Malheur County Sheriff's Office in Vale, (541-473-5125), for more information.

Overton Reservoir (Lake County)

Overton Lake (Reservoir) is a pretty little stocked trout pond high on the forested south end of Abert Rim. It sits amidst tall pines and white fir and is a decidedly pleasant place to hook a few trout on a summer day. At 6,600 feet elevation, Overton is rarely accessible before mid- to late May. From Hwy 395 just north of Lakeview, head east on Hwy 140 about 8 miles to a left-hand turn on FR 3615. Follow this road for 12.5 miles and then turn left on FR 3624 and continue 2 miles to a right turn on Spur Road 011. The pond is a short distance up the spur road.

Owyhee Reservoir (Malheur County)
boat ramp, boat recommended, campground

Backing up the Owyhee River south of Vale, Owyhee River stretches south through a deep flooded canyon for more than 50 miles. It provides good fishing for a variety of warmwater

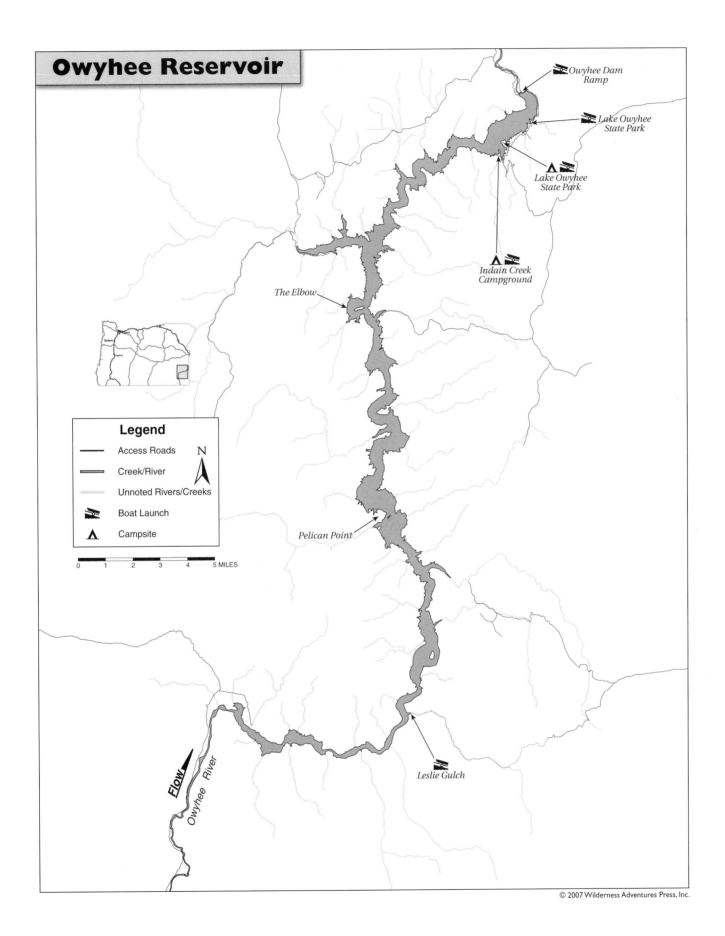

Owyhee Reservoir

Owyhee Dam
Ramp

Lake Owyhee
State Park

Lake Owyhee
State Park

Indain Creek
Campground

The Elbow

Legend

— Access Roads

▬ Creek/River

┄ Unnoted Rivers/Creeks

Boat Launch

⛺ Campsite

N

0 1 2 3 4 5 MILES

Pelican Point

Leslie Gulch

Flow

Owyhee River

© 2007 Wilderness Adventures Press, Inc.

gamefish and is especially well known for its crappie fishery. Black crappie here reach at least 14 inches and typically range from 8 to 10 inches in length. Owyhee Reservoir also offers very good fishing for largemouth and smallmouth bass and good action for brown bullhead, yellow perch, and channel catfish.

Smallmouth bass become increasingly common as you head south up the reservoir and are the dominant gamefish on the upper (south) end of the reservoir. They typically range from 8 to 14 inches, but the reservoir produces a few smallies in the 4- to 5-pound class. Largemouth bass are more common on the north half of the reservoir, where you can target them in the shallow near-shore margins of the coves and inlets. Crappie inhabit the same areas. Largemouth bass range from 1 to 4 pounds. All the reservoir's fisheries suffer during extended drought conditions.

During high-water cycles, however, fishing here is very good. High water tends to flood some of the shoreline brush, making superb shallow water habitat for crappie and bass. Under such conditions crappie are easy to catch from the shoreline through the state park and some nice largemouth bass roam these areas as well. If you're serious about bass fishing however, bring your boat and run south, up the reservoir, and explore the myriad coves, inlets, and shoals. For smallmouth fishing the boat is a virtual necessity because the smallies inhabit the remote south (upper) half of the 13,000-acre reservoir. If you make the long run to the upper end, pack your camping gear and make an adventure of it.

Although a boat is certainly a nice luxury here, shore-fishing access is plentiful, beginning with Lake Owyhee State Park, which offers two large campgrounds and several boat ramps. The state park is located 3 miles south of the dam on the east bank and you can fish along the road just about anywhere along the way. Even small craft such as canoes, float tubes, kayaks, and pontoon boats give you an advantage at times, but beware of strong afternoon winds that sometimes blow through the canyon. All methods produce on the reservoir and anglers well versed in jig fishing can have banner days on crappie. Be advised that the lake carries a mercury warning; so eat the fish at your own risk.

Heavily used, but with ample room for anglers to spread out, the two campgrounds here offer 31 sites with electrical hookups, eight tent sites and about 50 primitive sites. These are available on a first-come, first-served basis, but you can reserve the park's two teepees by calling 800-551-6949. Fuel, ice, and other supplies are available at Indian Creek Campground (formerly Lake Owyhee Resort).

Another drive-in access area is at the Dry Creek Arm on the west bank about 10 miles south of the dam. The roads in get quite rough but, when the reservoir is at or near full, this is a good place for crappie and largemouth bass. You can reach Dry Creek Arm by two different approaches. Consult the BLM map for specifics. Likewise you can drive the long road in from Succor Creek to the east and reach the reservoir's east shore at Road Canyon. Always consult the BLM office in Vale before venturing out on these rugged back roads.

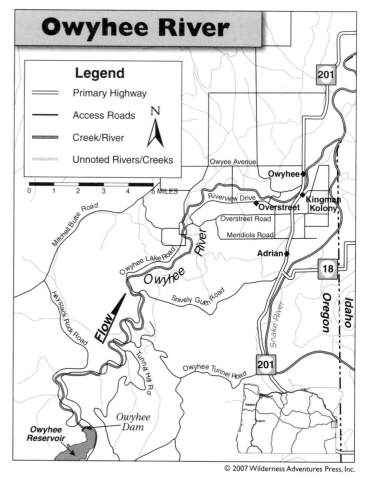

© 2007 Wilderness Adventures Press, Inc.

The main access to the reservoir takes you to the dam via the lower Owyhee River south of Nyssa. From Nyssa, follow the highway 12 miles south to a right turn on Owyhee River Road, which leads 12 miles to the dam. Continue past the dam 3 miles to Owyhee Lake State Park.

Owyhee River, Lower (Malheur County)

The pet fishery for many Boise fly anglers, the Owyhee River below Owyhee Dam offers about 10 miles of prime water for large brown and rainbow trout stocked by ODFW. Idaho license plates almost always outnumber Oregon plates on the vehicles parked along the river during the prime season from mid-autumn through mid- to late spring. Access to the lower Owyhee's prime pools has become so competitive that fly anglers, mostly from Boise, park along their favorite pools during the pre-dawn hours to make sure they have first choice of water. Naturally weekends are the most crowded, especially between February and April.

Below Owyhee Reservoir the river is characterized by slack-water pools interspersed with shallow riffles. During autumn, when irrigation season winds down, the dam is corked and the river shrinks down to a mere fraction of its summer flows. The river then remains very low until the following spring when flows are again increased dramatically to feed irrigation needs in the basin downstream. So summertime fishing is difficult, although a few hardcore anglers make a science out of probing the river's edges during summer for big brown and rainbow trout. Most anglers fish the river during low flows when the Owyhee's water allowance ranges from 10 or 12 cubic feet per second to about 30cfs, depending on water supply in the reservoir.

Often the slack-water pools freeze over during winter, usually in January. During severe winters the entire lower river locks up in ice. Otherwise the river remains fishable all winter. Highest angler use is from February through April. October and November—a time of year that used to attract only chukar hunters to the lower Owyhee—now see lots of anglers fishing the river. During winter, expect bitter cold weather. By March, however, this part of Oregon enjoys quite a few warm, sunny days and hatches of Chironomids, blue-winged olive mayflies and little winter stoneflies often bring a few trout to the surface at mid-afternoon. More often anglers rely on small nymph patterns and streamer patterns. The brown trout here typically range from 13 to 20 inches, but the older fish reach at least 10 pounds. Rainbows average smaller, but get nearly as large.

During the low-flow periods of winter and spring, fishing the Owyhee resembles stillwater fishing as anglers use sinking or sink-tip lines (or floating lines and heavily weighted flies) to strip streamer and nymph patterns through the slack-water pools where the brown trout often reside. As the water rises with releases from the dam, concentrate on the slow-water edges and current seams in the same pools that are virtually current-free during winter. Though the river has a population of large stoneflies, small nymph patterns tend to be more productive than larger flies. If you go this route, arm yourself with a selection of basic beadhead nymph patterns in sizes 12 through 18.

Because the river can get severely de-watered during dry winters, many fly anglers are beginning to impose on themselves a voluntary cease-fishing rule when the water drops to precariously low levels during winter. Fishing for brown trout is strictly catch-and-release here. A five-fish limit is in effect for rainbow trout, so bait-fishing is allowed.

To get there, head for the town of Nyssa and then follow the highway south 12 miles to a right-hand turn on Owyhee River Road, which follows the river up to the dam.

Owyhee River, Upper

boat ramp, boat recommended, no bait, campground

Upstream from Owyhee Reservoir, the Owyhee River is one of Oregon's great natural treasures. It flows for many miles through starkly scenic arid canyon lands and is far more popular with rafters than with anglers. Nonetheless, the upper Owyhee offers good fishing for smallmouth bass, channel catfish, and a few redband trout. The river is only floatable at high spring flows and even during wet years the rafting season is usually over by late May. Unfortunately the river fishes best at lower flows, so the ideal way to fish the river is to drift it

towards the end of the whitewater season, as the river's spring flows begin to drop. Wait too late and you'll be dragging the raft through all sorts of shallow rock gardens and then paddling through miles of slack water to reach the take-out at the head of Owyhee Reservoir.

Floating the Owyhee at normal spring flows requires experience at the oars and is a trip best done with an outfitter the first time, so you can learn the river's peculiarities. The typical Owyhee float requires four or five days, especially if you want to leave ample time for fishing and sightseeing. The BLM office in Vale can provide you with a list of outfitters permitted for float trips on the Owyhee. The river has two main drifts and four major access points. The upper reach covers 40 miles from Three Forks (where the river's branches converge) to the Rome Launch. The lower float goes from Rome, 40 miles down to Birch Creek Ranch or 50 miles down to Leslie Gulch. If the road to Birch Creek Ranch is passable, you'll save a lot of time on the oars because reaching Leslie Gulch requires that you traverse the upper end of Owyhee Reservoir.

The Owyhee's smallmouth bass typically range from 8 to 14 inches and they tend to be aggressive biters. In some reaches they abound in surprising numbers and a few fish reach 3 or 4 pounds. You would be hard pressed to find a lure they won't take, but most gear anglers rely on jigs or small spoons while fly anglers use streamer flies, such as the ever-effective cone head woolly bugger and similar patterns. The catfish, most abundant on the lower drift, reach at least 8 pounds and typically range from 14 to 20 inches. They are highly aggressive and will actively chase spoons, spinners, and streamer flies, even in relatively fast-moving water.

If you decide to float the Owyhee on your own, your first step is to contact the BLM in Vale (541-473-3144). They can provide all required information and fill you in on conditions and specific rules governing the river. The launch sites on the river offer primitive campsites and are generally open from March through September. By mid-summer the ramps are often high and dry, but you can still use these areas to gain foot access to fish the river. A sturdy pair of hiking boots and a sense of adventure can lead to some very good bass fishing in these areas. All of these river launch sites are accessed via backcountry roads that can get nasty during wet spring weather. Check road conditions by calling the BLM in Vale.

To reach Three Forks, follow Hwy 95 west from Jordan Valley for about 15 miles to a south turn on Three Forks Road and continue 35 miles. To get to the Rome Launch, follow Hwy 95 west from Jordan Valley for 32 miles and the turn south at the signed access to the Rome Launch. The Leslie Gulch/Slocum Creek access is near the top end of Owyhee Reservoir: Follow Hwy 95 north from Jordan Valley to Leslie Gulch Road or, from the north, follow the Succor Creek Road south from Hwy 201. A fourth river access is at the old Birch Creek Historical Ranch. The road to the ranch is a 4-wheel-drive track that is not passable during wet weather. From Hwy 95, 8 miles north of Jordan Valley, turn west on Cow Creek Road (at the Jordan Craters sign) and follow the BLM Owyhee River Access signs 28 miles to the river.

Paiute Reservoir (Lake County)

If it ever again manages to refill and stay filled, Paiute Reservoir is a sleeper for big rainbows. It occupies a shallow canyon immediately south of Hwy 140 just above the west edge of Guano Valley off the Antelope Flat Road (it is visible from the highway). Generally the access road is not marked, but after descending the last hill on your way from the west (from Lakeview and Adel) and dropping down into the west edge of Guano Basin, watch for a right-hand (south) turn onto a rutted dirt/gravel road that has a stop sign where it meets the highway. After the road crosses the outflow stream in a shallow draw, continue up the hill and watch for a several two-track dirt roads leading to your right to the bluff above the reservoir (if the gate across the main road is closed, be sure to likewise close it behind you). This reservoir suffered severely during the prolonged drought of 2000-2003, then again during the latter years of that decade. In 2005 and 2006, renewed water supply revitalized the rainbow trout fishery (it carried water throughout the year in 2006 and provided some ice fishing that winter), but then dried completely in 2010. Also, after the ODFW had battled a leak in the dam for several years, the dam somehow fixed itself, so the reservoir no longer drains, so when and if it does refill and can be restocked, it will again provide good fishing during all but the hottest months. The reservoir sits at about 5,200 feet, so spring arrives fairly late here; fishing picks up around the end of March and remains productive into June. During years of good water supply October fishing is a good bet, but this has been a rare privilege in the past couple decades. Check with ODFW to find out about current water levels and stocking schedules. Shallow, fertile and fairly turbid, Paiute Reservoir offers no facilities and the wind can flat out howl through this high range country. Shore fishing with bait is the most popular and productive method, but you can easily drop a float tube or small boat in the reservoir. During fall, fly fishing can be good using large, black woolly buggers and other attractor patterns. Ice fishing is possible during January some years, but this is remote country so only experienced ice anglers—those who recognize unstable ice conditions—need apply. Solid ice one day can and often does yield to unstable ice the next day. Be extremely careful.

Paragon Lake
(Mountain Lakes Wilderness Area)
hike-in

Paragon Lake is a small pond located along the trail west of South Pass Lake in the Mountain Lakes Wilderness northwest of Klamath Falls. Paragon is stocked with brook trout, which usually range from 6 to 10 inches. From Harriette Lake, head south around the west flank of Mt. Carmine and then at the next trail junction, turn east towards South Pass Lake. After about .75 of a mile you will find Paragon Lake on the left-hand side of the trail. See Lake Harriette and Clover Lake herein for trailhead directions.

Pelican Lake (Lake County)

Pelican Lake is one of the Warner Valley lakes, which during times of good water supply are widely known for producing large crappie. Pelican, however, is a better place for water birds and sits on private ranchlands near Adel.

Pence Spring Reservoir (Malheur County)

Pence Spring Reservoir is a small BLM impoundment located in rugged, remote country on the Cottonwood Creek drainage north-by-northwest from Harper. As a crow flies, it's about 15 miles due east from Beulah Reservoir. During high-water years, ODFW has been known to stock a few rainbows here and they can grow quickly. Don't bother trying to find this one before finding out from ODFW if the reservoir has been stocked and then prepare for a long, rugged journey over miles of rough back roads.

Phillips Reservoir (Baker County)
boat ramp

Located on the Powder River west of Baker City, Phillips Reservoir is a solid producer of 6 to 12-inch yellow perch and a slow-to-fair producer of fat 12- to 16-inch trout with a few fish to 4 pounds. White crappie and smallmouth bass also inhabit the reservoir. At full pool it covers about 2,350 acres, but is drawn down during the irrigation season. Local anglers sometimes ice fish the reservoir, but most folks fish here during spring, early summer, and autumn. A boat is handy here, although shoreline access is excellent as the reservoir sits on National Forest land. State Route 7 follows the north shore for 6 miles, along which are four formal access sites, including Union Creek Campground. At the west end of the reservoir, a road cuts south to reach the south shoreline and three additional campsites. A trail follows the east half of the south shore. The boat ramps are at Union Creek Campground, Southwest Shore Campground, and near the dam. To reach Phillips Reservoir from Baker City, follow SR 7 south and then west for about 15 miles

Pike Creek
closed waters

Pike Creek flows off the east face of the Steens Mountains and is closed to fishing to protect a possible remnant population of Lahontan cutthroat trout.

Pilcher Creek Reservoir (Union County)

Pilcher Creek is a popular and generally productive crappie and rainbow trout fishery located north of Baker City and west of the little community of North Powder. Exit I-84 at North Powder and head west on North Powder River Road to a right turn on Tucker Flat Road. At full pool the reservoir spans more than 100 acres and a boat or float tube is handy here but certainly not necessary. Most anglers fish bait, but fly anglers enjoy consistent action via float tube, especially spring and fall. The reservoir is generally drawn down rather heavily during summer, so drought years tend to take a heavy toll. The rainbows reach 18 inches, but most range from 9 to 13 inches. You can camp at the lake. Wolff Creek Reservoir lies just to the east and you can easily fish them both in a day's time.

Pine Creek (Baker County)

Pine Creek is a pretty little mountain trout stream, originating high on the south slope of the Wallowa Range before meandering across the scenic Pine Valley near Halfway in northeastern Baker County. The creek's only downfall is that it flows mostly through private ranchlands, but property owners in the valley seem willing to grant permission to anglers who take the time to knock on doors. If you're not willing to do so, you'll never enjoy Pine Creek at its best, even though you can access the creek along the road from Halfway up to Cornucopia and in places along the road leading toward the Snake River. Quite a few diminutive smallmouth bass occupy the creek's lowermost mile or so.

Upstream from Halfway the creek is stocked with legal-size bows. Wild redband trout inhabit the entire drainage and some small brook trout live in the upper reaches of the creek and its tributaries. The best stretch for fair-sized wild trout is in the valley near Halfway and down past the stream's confluence with East Pine Creek and Clear Creek. Trout here are not abundant, but you'll find a few 12- to 16-inch fish and few other anglers willing to do the legwork to get permission to fish the creek. All methods produce here and bait fishing is legal. No matter what method you use—flies, bait, or spinning gear—keep moving and cover a lot of water. A network of local roads approach and cross the creek through the valley while CR 413 follows Pine Creek up to Cornucopia.

Pine Lakes (Eagle Cap Wilderness)
hike-in

A pair of scenic lakes near Cornucopia in the southern part of the Eagle Cap Wilderness, the two Pine Lakes offer good prospects for brook trout from 6 to 14 inches. The Pine Creek Trail is lengthy and steep, beginning at the north outskirts of the old mining camp of Cornucopia, at the end of CR 413. The trail from Summit Point Lookout is easier and more scenic: About half way between the towns of Richland and Halfway, turn north on FR 77 and follow it all the way up to McBride Campground. From there take FR 7715 north to the parking lot for Summit Lookout Trailhead. From here head north on the trail, which traverses open sub-alpine meadows dotted with small stands of fir and pine. At the 4.2-mile mark, take the left-hand fork heading down to the lakes.

Poison Creek (Harney County)
no bait

A small stream flowing south along Hwy 395 north of Burns, Poison Creek is not very productive but offers a few small redband trout. You can access it from the highway and from several spur roads leading west. It tends to run turbid during spring and then get quite low by mid-summer.

Pole Creek Reservoir (Baker County)
float tube recommended

Despite its preponderance for water-supply issues Pole Creek Reservoir, 25 miles northwest of Vale, can at times rank among the better stillwater trout fisheries in the southeast zone. Given two or three straight years of heavy snow pack in the nearby mountains, Pole Creek produces fat, 14- to 18-inch rainbows. Bait anglers usually set up from shore while the occasional float-tubing fly angler puts in an appearance. This reservoir has all but dried up several times in the past few decades, so call ODFW before venturing here. The reservoir is easy to reach from Hwy 26. Head northeast from Vale, past the tiny of Hamlet of Brogan and watch for the signed left-hand turn about 2 miles to the east. From John Day, follow Hwy 26 all the way past Ironside, then up and over the Brogan Hill Summit. The turnoff is about 5 miles east of the summit. Malheur Reservoir is about 20 minutes to the northwest and if Pole Creek is producing big fish, likely Malheur will be in good form as well.

Powder River (Baker County)

Draining a fairly large area of eastern Oregon, the Powder River offers several different faces to anglers. The Powder begins at the old mining town of Sumpter, at the convergence of McCully Fork and Cracker Creek. The river immediately dumps onto private ranchlands until it reaches Phillips Reservoir, 7 miles to the east. Though it meanders attractively through open meadows, the upper Powder River offers only a few trout and requires that you get permission from the landowners, whose cattle generally graze right to water's edge.

Far more appealing is the tailwater section below Mason Dam on Phillips Reservoir. This short reach (about 3 river miles) offers good fishing for planted rainbows that can reach 20 inches. Most of the fish range from 9 to 13 inches, but they tend to be fat and healthy. If you don't mind knocking on doors to get permission to fish, the next few miles below the public access reach offer equally good action. The Mason Dam tailwater is open during the general season for catch-and-keep angling with bait allowed and remains open throughout the balance of the year for catch-and-release angling with flies and artificial lures (check current regulations). Fly anglers have become increasingly enamored with the off-season fishery here, when nymphing tends to prove quite effective. The river enjoys a fair hatch of *Skwala* stoneflies during mid-spring, not to mention solid evening caddis hatches during summer and some great hopper action from July through September most years. There is ample camping space available at the three campgrounds just up the road at Phillips Reservoir.

Just below the Mason Dam tailwater fishery, the Powder enters a lengthy run through private ranch and farmlands in the vicinity of Baker City. This entire reach is very difficult to access and most of the river is highly denuded anyway. After meandering its way northward and then eastward, the Powder finally dumps into Thief Valley Reservoir (see entry herein). Thief Valley Dam creates another tailwater fishery capable of producing 18-inch trout, though most range from 12 to 14 inches. The tailwater here is private property, but the rancher allows anglers to walk down and fish the river. When you reach Thief Valley Reservoir, watch for the road on your left that wraps around the big cove south of the parking area and then winds a mile down to the dam. During spring, a bad mud hole often forms where this dirt road fords Cusick Creek, in which case you are better off walking down to the dam.

The tailwater fishery extends only half a mile or so downstream, but the river again enters BLM land 3 miles below Thief Valley Reservoir. This section of the Powder allows you to escape the inevitable crowds that gather below the dams and it flows almost 10 miles through hard-to-reach BLM canyon lands. Often you'll need 4-wheel-drive and high clearance to negotiate the access road: From Baker City, follow I-84 for 4 miles north to Exit 298 and then head east on SR 203, the Medical Springs Highway, which crosses the river after about 10 miles. Half a mile after you cross the river, watch for the left-hand turn heading north. This is the road to Big Creek, which enters BLM lands half a mile north of the highway. From there it parallels the Powder River, which lies hidden in its canyon half a mile to the west. Just before you reach the Big Creek canyon, a left-hand spur cuts westerly toward the river. Consult you map, lace up your hiking boots, and have at it.

Downstream from the Medical Springs Highway (SR 203), the river again enters private ranch and farmlands in the Lower Powder Valley. Access without permission is virtually non-existent until the river enters the canyon on its final run down to Brownlee Reservoir. Access is good on the BLM lands in the canyon and SR 86 follows right alongside the river. Here the Powder offers an interesting mix of rainbow trout, smallmouth bass, and some large squawfish (northern pike-minnow). The trout inhabit the well-oxygenated riffles, while the bass and squawfish live in the pools. The river here is highly structured, being studded with boulders. When the river runs clear, you can sight fish for the bass—and squawfish, which I mention only because they reach at least 14 inches and sometimes rise for dry flies. The bass here are small but feisty and the rainbows average about 10 inches, with some larger.

As you approach Richland, the river again enters private properties and finally dumps into the Powder River Arm of Brownlee Reservoir. Forming an 8-mile-long arm of Brownlee, this stillwater fishery is an excellent producer of smallmouth bass, crappie, and catfish. All three species can reach impressive sizes. Best fishing and best access is by boat. You can launch (and bank fish) at the popular Hewitt Park Boat Launch, 2 miles east from Richland on the north bank.

Priday Reservoir (Lake County)

A trout and crappie reservoir located north of the town of Adel and about 5 miles south of Plush, Priday can produce some large fish when water levels are stable for two or more years. The trout can reach 20 inches and typically range from 12 to 14 inches. White crappie range from 8 to 14 inches. The reservoir sits adjacent to the main road connecting the two towns and fishes best from mid- to late spring. You can fish from shore, but a float tube or small boat is handy and there is an unimproved launch site. Most of the bank lies on private land. The water is always muddy, so most anglers fish bait, although crappie specialists often rely on jigs.

Pronghorn Lake Ranch (Klamath County)

Situated in a truly scenic setting in the Langell Valley, about 45 minutes southwest from Klamath Falls, Pronghorn Lake Ranch is a private fee fishery offering a two very large lakes, one boasting hard-fighting, fast-growing Kamloops rainbow trout (as well other strains), the other offering robust largemouth bass. The property includes two small, cozy cabins (bring sleeping bags/pillows), as well as RV hookups, and a boat. The 2010 rate was $150/day (special rates available for groups). For details, visit www.pronghornlakeranch.com, or call 541-882-2180.

Puck Lakes
see Sky Lakes Wilderness Area

Red Mountain Lake (Elkhorn Range)
see Summit Lake

Renner Lake (Lake County)
closed waters

Renner Lake is a 500-acre lake situated on a private ranch near the California border. There is no public access.

Rock Creek (Hart Mt. Refuge)
no bait

Rock Creek is a tiny high-desert stream flowing easterly off Hart Mountain and providing refuge for a remnant population of redband trout that are geographically isolated from others of their kind that inhabit the streams flowing off the west slope of the Steens Mountains. During high-water periods the trout distribute themselves throughout a fairly lengthy reach of the creek, but usually they reside only in the upper reaches, primarily in the canyon in the general vicinity of the Hart Mountain Refuge headquarters, from the Hot Springs Campground area downstream past Rattlesnake Draw. Catch-and-release is a good idea on these beautiful little natives, though I recommend not fishing for them at all unless high water persists for three or more years in a row, which hardly seems likely these days. The best reaches of the creek are accessible only by hiking, so refer to a good topo map before setting out. Best fishing occurs during late spring and again during autumn, but during low-flow years anglers should consider leaving the trout alone, at least during the fall. Check current regulations.

Rock Creek Lake (Baker County)
hike-in

A scenic, high mountain lake on the south end of the Elkhorn Range, Rock Creek Lake offers good fishing for brook trout and rainbows along with some small Mackinaw, or lake trout.

Sitting at 7,600 feet, the lake covers 35 acres and reaches a depth of 104 feet. From Baker City or North Powder head for Haines and then follow the Elkhorn Scenic Route west out of town for about a mile and a half and then turn left and follow the Rock Creek Road heading west. The road deteriorates when you cross onto the Wallowa-Whitman National Forest and the trailhead is at the end of the road.

Rock Creek Reservoir (aka Taft-Miller Reservoir) (Lake County)

A remote, widely fluctuating irrigation-storage reservoir located about 20 miles northeast of the Hart Mountain headquarters, Rock Creek Reservoir offers fair fishing for white crappie. Until fairly recently, it was known as Taft-Miller Reservoir. The feeder stream, Rock Creek, is home to a remnant population of indigenous redband trout, some of which migrate downstream into the reservoir. In order to protect these stocks, the reservoir is no longer stocked with fish. The crappie persist on their own and a few largemouth bass reside here also. At full pool, the reservoir spans more than 200 acres, but it is usually drawn down well below that level. The area is windswept and heavily grazed, but during high-water periods the crappie fishing can be good, making the trip worthwhile. From the west (Lakeview) follow Hwy 140 to the Plush cutoff and at Plush head northeast on the Hart Mountain Road. Continue up and over Hart Mountain and follow the road another 20 miles to the reservoir. From the east (Burns), head south on Hwy 205 to Frenchglen. South of Frenchglen, watch for the turnoff to Hart Mountain (Rock Creek Road) and head west to the reservoir (Rock Creek Road heads west from Hwy 205 just after you reach the south end of the high rimrocks on your right).

Rogger Pond (Lake County)

Rogger Pond is a small, flooded borrow pit in the Warner Mountains east of Lakeview. It's a fairly good producer of stocked legal-size rainbows during the spring. Follow Hwy 140 over Warner Summit and then turn south on the Twin Springs Road to reach the pond (about 3 miles east of the summit).

Round Valley Reservoir (Klamath County)

A good bass fishery located in rugged country south of Gerber Reservoir, Round Valley offers bass that reach several pounds. Just before you reach Gerber Reservoir from the west on Gerber Road, turn south at the signed route leading 6 miles down to Round Valley Reservoir. Water levels fluctuate dramatically here depending on irrigation draws and on climate, but the bass fishery seems to hold up well. There's no formal boat ramp, but you can drop a car-topper in with no problem unless the reservoir is severely drawn down. Like most of the reservoirs in the immediate vicinity, Round Valley dried up during the drought of 1994 and fisheries have been slow to recover, especially after another severe drought from 2000-2003. So call ODFW in Klamath Falls before making the journey out here.

Sagehen Creek (Lake County)

Prominent on maps because of its length, Sagehen Creek is actually a dry creekbed. Seasonally it feeds runoff to Spaulding Reservoir.

Sawmill Creek (Harney County)
campground

A lengthy tributary of Silver Creek northwest from Riley, Sawmill Creek offers fair fishing for small, wild trout. Access is good from FR 4540, which follows the creek most of the way to the headwaters. The road turns west from FR 45 and leads up to Buck Springs Campground. For directions to the area, see Silver Creek.

Sevenmile Creek (Klamath County)
no bait

A productive tributary to Agency Lake, Sevenmile Creek offers redband trout, brown trout, and brook trout. The brook trout predominate in the creek's upper reaches, while brown and redband trout inhabit the meandering section in the Wood River Valley. The lower end of the creek is channelized above Agency Lake. Sevenmile Creek is fine dry-fly water, especially during the summer when hoppers appear in the valley. The best fishing is from July through early October.

Much of this stream flows through private ranchlands, so make sure to ask permission to fish the meanders downstream from Nicholson Road on the west side of the valley. Upstream from Nicholson Road the creek flows entirely through national forest lands and is easily accessible from FR 3334. From Klamath Falls or Medford follow Hwy 140 to West Side Road just west of the Upper Klamath Lake. Follow the road past Rocky Point and continue north until you reach the turnoff at FR 3334. From the north, follow Hwy 97 south to the Chiloquin cutoff and head west to a right-hand turn on Hwy 62. Follow the highway north to Fort Klamath and head west on Nicholson Road.

Sherlock Gulch Reservoir (Lake County)

During years of adequate water supply, Sherlock Gulch Reservoir is capable of growing fat rainbows to at least 18 inches. Typical trout range from 10 to 14 inches. The reservoir is shallow and turbid, not to mention remote, being located east of Hwy 395 and east of Abert Rim's precipitous drop-off. There's no easy way to get there, so call ODFW in Lakeview to check current conditions before heading out. Then follow Hwy 140 east from Hwy 395 and turn right on the cutoff road to the tiny town of Plush. From Plush, head north and then take the Hogback Road (CR 3-10) north 10 miles to a right-hand turn on the Flagstaff Road (CR 3-11). After half a mile, turn left and then head north almost 7 miles to another left turn leading to the Sunstone Area. Continue 9 more miles to the reservoir. It's a long drive over gravel/dirt surfaces, so take all needed supplies along with a good map.

Shirk Lake (Lake County)

Shirk Lake is a large, shallow wetlands managed for waterfowl and water birds by the BLM. It sits on the old Shirk Ranch site on the northwest corner of Guano basin, an hour east from Lakeview on Hwy 140. The turnoff (signed for Guano Lake) is on the west end of the long, flat stretch of highway that crosses Guano basin leading to the precipitous climb up Dougherty Grade. I offer such detail only because anglers might want to file away in their memories the fact that during the record high-water years of the early 1980s, trout (apparently from Guano Creek) entered the swollen Shirk Lake and grew huge, creating a short-lived, closely held secret fishery.

Sid's Reservoir (Sid Luce Reservoir) (Lake County)

A remote and productive high-desert reservoir sitting above the tiny town of Plush, Sid's Reservoir usually offers fair-to-good fishing for fat rainbow trout. Most range from 12 to 16 inches, but Sid's yields a few 20-inchers almost every year. A few years ago, someone illegally introduced largemouth bass to the reservoir and the bass seem to be thriving, so now this fertile fishery is home to both fast-growing rainbows and a few fairly decent bass. From Plush head north to the end of the pavement and then take the Schneider Creek Road up the plateau to the power lines. Cross Schneider Creek and head up to the top of the plateau and watch for the left-hand turn leading to the reservoir. The notoriously bad road requires a high-clearance four-wheel-drive vehicle, though as of 2010, rumor suggests Bonneville Power Administration has plans to improve the road, which is used to access the power lines for maintenance.

Silver Creek (Baker County)

no bait

Silver Creek joins Cracker Creek just north of the old mining town of Sumpter, west from Baker City. The creek offers fair fishing for small rainbows and is followed by a rough spur road. From Sumpter head north on FR 55 and then turn left on FR 5540.

Silver Creek (Harney County)

no bait

Silver Creek flows for miles through private ranchlands west of Burns, but originates in the national forest north of Riley, near popular Delintment Lake. Its upper reaches offer fair fishing for small trout in an attractive pine forest setting. Most of the creek is accessible by a short walk from myriad spurs heading east off FR 45. From the spur roads you must hike down into a shallow but steep canyon to reach the creek. A mile and a half west of Riley, turn north off Hwy 20 on Silver Creek Road, which will become FR 45 when you cross onto the national forest.

Silver Creek (Lake County)

no bait, campground

Lake County's Silver Creek flows under Hwy 31 immediately west from the town of Silver Lake. It offers slow-to-fair fishing for redband trout and stocked rainbows with prospects improving considerably when several consecutive high-water winters occur. Forest Road 27 reaches the upper stretch of the stream's west fork at Silver Creek Marsh Campground, while FR 28 leads to a right turn on FR 2917, which crosses the creek at Bunyard Crossing.

Most years, the main branch offers marginal prospects because it gets dewatered frequently; the diminutive West Fork is better, but both can be fair after several high-water seasons. During wet climate cycles, the main fork is fishable in the canyon stretch between Thompson Valley Reservoir and Bunyard Crossing. You can hike the canyon or walk in from the end of several spur roads leading towards the creek from both sides, off FR 28 and FR 2917. Downstream from Bunyard Crossing, you can approach the canyon from the east on a BLM road, but most people just hike down from the crossing or from the end of Spur 413, just to the east. A Silver Lake Ranger District map (Fremont National Forest) comes in handy here.

Silver Creek Diversion Reservoir is located just a few miles south of town and backs up the creek into a two-pronged, narrow impoundment, the upper branches of which are on BLM lands. Dirt roads lead to the upper ends of the diversion reservoir, which you can easily fish from shore. Given three or more consecutive years of high flows, this turbid reservoir can produce trout to at least 18 inches, though they tend to be few in number. To reach the reservoir, head south near the ranger district office on County Road 4-12 (FR 28) and watch for a dirt track leading west about 4 miles down the road.

Silver Creek Diversion Reservoir

see Silver Creek, Lake County

Silvies River (Harney County)

The Silvies River flows south out of the Blue Mountains, eventually meandering out onto Harney Basin where the river dissipates with no outlet from the basin. Its lower reaches are drawn upon for local irrigation needs and private lands lock up its upper reaches that flow through the scenic high prairies near Seneca. A few miles of the uppermost section of the river flow across public lands in Malheur National Forest offering only fair fishing for small redband trout. Downstream (south) from Seneca, the river again reaches national forest property. This middle reach of the Silvies is home to a few redband trout, but is dominated by smallmouth bass and other warmwater species. Access begins at the crossing on FR 31, which turns west from Hwy 395 about 20 miles north of Burns. Best fishing is downstream from the road, where the river flows through a wide, deep canyon. A few spur roads reach the canyon rim, but from there it's a hike-in affair. The canyon stretch offers about 9 miles of public river corridor, ending near the confluence of Myrtle Creek.

Myrtle Creek is a lengthy tributary flowing north to south through an even steeper, more dramatic canyon. A forest service trail follows the creek all the way through the canyon, but the stream is only moderately productive with small redband trout becoming increasingly common as you head upstream to higher elevations.

In 2003 the state received news of a $1.7 million federal grant aimed at supporting conservation for imperiled species on private lands and part of the grant was earmarked for a restoration of the West Fork Silvies River in Harney Basin southeast of Burns. The project should help in restoring redband trout populations on the lower Silvies River. Presumably in historic times redband trout from the Silvies could have included fluvial populations that reared in Malheur Lake.

Skull Creek

closed water

Skull Creek originates high in the Steens Mountains and eventually meets SR 205, the Catlow Valley Road, south of Roaring Springs Ranch. Skull Creek is closed to fishing and flows entirely through private property. Catlow Valley redband trout, once indigenous here, are likely extirpated from the creek.

Skull Creek Reservoir

closed water

Though prominent on maps of the Steens Mountains area, Skull Creek Reservoir lies completely on private ranch lands and is closed to any public access.

Sky Lakes Wilderness Area (Klamath County)

hike-in

The Sky Lakes Wilderness Area occupies 116,300 acres in the high Cascades south of Crater Lake National Park. The wilderness offers a wide array of attractions, including some two-dozen fishable lakes offering planted rainbow, brook, and cutthroat trout. Many visitors come here to climb 9,495-foot-high Mt. McLoughlin, whose volcanic bulk dominates the skyline. The mountain encompasses the south end of the wilderness while the fishable hike-in lakes are found further to the north, largely in three main lake basins. Approaches to the wilderness are from the east side in the Winema National Forest and the west side in the Rogue River National Forest. The wilderness has more than 140 miles of trail. Be sure to obtain the map before planning your trip. Most of the lakes are accessible by late June and fishing holds up all summer and into October.

Trout in these high lakes typically range from 8 to 12 inches, but many of the lakes produce both brook trout and rainbows up to 16 inches. Fly anglers often enjoy fast action using basic wet flies and small streamer patterns. Dry fly action coincides with afternoon hatches of Callibaetis mayflies, which occur throughout the summer and into early autumn. Flying ants end up on the water quite frequently and a like imitation often draws explosive rises. Also look for Chironomid hatches during the evening. Spin fishermen account for plenty of trout too, especially with small rooster-tails and small spoons. Most of the lakes are easy to fish from shore, but a float tube comes in handy and allows you to have the middle of the lakes all to yourself.

The Seven Lakes Basin is the northernmost of the lake basins and offers four fishable lakes, all of them stocked with brook trout, usually every other year. Some natural reproduction occurs here as well. Alta, Grass, and Middle Lakes all span about 30 acres. Nearby Cliff Lake is about 9 acres. These lakes sit in a scenic basin whose rivulets and streams join to form the headwaters of the Middle Fork Rogue River. Direct access from the east side of the wilderness is on the Sevenmile Trail heading at the end of FR 3334. The trail reaches Grass Lake after 4.5 miles. You can camp at the trailhead. From the west side of the mountains, the easiest route to Seven Lakes Basin is via the Seven Lakes Trail, beginning near the end of FR 3780.

About 5 miles south from Seven Lakes Basin is the popular Sky Lakes Basin, which offers quite a few productive lakes. Big Heavenly and Isherwood Lakes are sometimes stocked with cutthroat trout. Otherwise all these lakes offer the usual brookies and/or rainbows, planted every other year. The fishable lakes here include Deep, Deer, Donna, Margurette, Trapper, Wizzard, Sonja, and Elizabeth. The most direct trail to this basin is from the east side of the wilderness on the Cherry Creek Trail at the end of FR 3450. The trail reaches Trapper Lake after about 5 miles. Experienced backpackers might prefer a much shorter cross-country route heading due west to Wizard Lake from the end of FR 3419. Don't try it unless you're well versed in cross-country travel by map and compass. The southernmost of the group—ever-popular Heavenly Twin Lakes, Isherwood Lake, and Elizabeth Lake—are easy to get to from the Cold Spring Trailhead (see below).

The southernmost basin in the Sky Lakes Wilderness is the Blue Canyon Basin, featuring brook trout action at Bert, Blue, Blue Canyon, Camp, Dee, Island, Pear, and Horseshoe Lakes. Rainbow trout are stocked in a few of these waters as well. The basin is fairly popular, but rarely as busy as Sky Lakes Basin to the north. Bert, Dee, and Island Lakes lie on the east side of the wilderness and are easy to reach via the Bert Lake Trail: From Hwy 140, about halfway between Rocky Point Road to the east and Lake of the Woods to the west, turn north on FR 3651. Follow this road north toward Cold Springs Camp/Trailhead, but 2 miles before you reach Cold Springs, head west on FR 3659. Watch for the trailhead for Bert Lake, a little over a mile up the road.

Bert Lake lies just off the trail to the north, about a mile from the trailhead, but the trail continues on to Island Lake and also intersects both the Pacific Crest Trail and the Blue Canyon Trail, the latter of which reaches the other cluster of lakes in about 2 miles. From the west side of the wilderness, use the Blue Canyon Trail heading at the end of FR 3770.

A handful of more isolated lakes offer equally good fishing. Long Lake is a fair fishery and is located south of Island Lake. It sees a fair amount of traffic on the trail from Fourmile Lake. Just north of Fourmile Lake (located just outside the southeast corner of the wilderness), Woodpecker Lake has been stocked in years past. Better than either of these are the Puck Lakes, located northeast of the Sky Lakes group and southeast from Seven Lakes Basin. You can get to the Puck Lakes from either lake basin or by a short hike up the Nannie Creek Trail leading in from the east side of the wilderness at the end of FR 3484.

Except for the Cold Springs Trailhead and Bert Lake Trail, the trailheads on the east side of the wilderness are all reached by taking Hwy 140 to Rocky Point Road and then driving north past Upper Klamath Lake to the forest roads leading uphill to the west. If you're arriving from Bend, you can save a lot of driving by cutting over north of Agency Lake. From Hwy 97 north of Chiloquin (south from Collier Park), turn west on the Chiloquin cutoff road, which takes you to a right-hand turn on the Crater Lake Highway (SR 62). Head north up the Wood River Valley and then turn left on Weed Road. Stay on Weed, which continues as Sevenmile Road, until you reach a left-hand turn on West Side Road—the north extent of Rocky Point Road.

Slide Lake (Lake County)
hike-in

Slide Lake is a small walk-in lake situated below the awesome steeps of Slide Mountain. The lake offers pan-size brook trout and rainbows. From Paisley, on Hwy 31, head west on Mill Street towards the Chewaucan River. Just west of town, turn right onto FR 3315 and go 6 miles to another right turn on FR 3360. After about 9 miles watch for the trailhead sign on the west side of the road. From there it's about half a mile to the lake on an old closed spur road. Forest Road 3360 can get a little rugged and is usually passable by June 1. Check ahead by calling the Paisley Range District office. You can camp at the trailhead or at the lake.

Sonja Lake
see Sky Lakes Wilderness Area

South Pass Lake (Mountain Lakes Wilderness)
hike-in

A popular and productive 10-acre lake on the southwest edge of the Mountain Lakes Wilderness, South Pass Lake offers pan-size brookies and rainbows. To get there, follow the 2-mile trail south and then east from Lake Harriette or hike in from the Clover Creek Trail to Clover Lake (see listing herein for Lake Harriette and Clover Lake).

Spaulding Reservoir (Lake County)

Spaulding Reservoir ranks among the state's most remote trout reservoirs, requiring a 19-mile drive over rough gravel and dirt roads. Covering about 20 acres at full pool, Spaulding is located north of Guano Rim on the southeastern edge of Lake County, about 90 miles east of Lakeview. To get there, follow SR 140 east from US 395 north of Lakeview. Route 140 leads up and over the Warner Mountain Summit, passing through the hamlet of Adel and then heading toward the Nevada border. Twenty miles east of Adel, the highway makes a sharp turn to the south after crossing the Guano Valley, to head up the steep grade of Guano Rim (Dougherty Grade). Just before the highway turns south, watch for a left-hand turn on a gravel road (with a sign for Spaulding Reservoir). This is the Beatty's Butte Road. After about 13 miles heading north you'll see a signed right-hand turn that leads up to the reservoir. The Beatty's Butte Road is fairly easy going, but if you travel here in the spring, beware the sinkhole that forms during wet weather after you make the turn onto the Spaulding Reservoir road.

Spaulding fares okay during dry years, but always check ahead by calling the ODFW office in Hines or Lakeview. In 2010, the reservoir dried up completely, testifying to the importance of getting an up-to-date status report before you make the long drive. Stack two or more wet years together and Spaulding becomes a great place to pursue fat 12- to 18-inch rainbows. The water gets turbid after spring runoff and during windy conditions, especially during low-water periods, so bait is a popular choice here. Still, fly anglers enjoy consistent action fishing woolly buggers and leech patterns along with Zugbugs and other small nymphs. Shore fishing abounds, though a float tube or car-topper comes in handy (beware the submerged barbed wire—look for the fence posts on the north and south shores). During winter—when the road is either dry or frozen—a few locals ice fish at Spaulding, but only experts who know stable ice conditions need apply. Camping is limited to primitive sites and you'll likely have the place to yourself save for the howling coyotes.

Spencer Creek (Klamath County)
no bait

A fairly productive tributary to the Klamath River, Spencer Creek offers wild brook and redband trout, a few of which reach 14 or more inches. Most range from 6 to 10 inches. The creek feeds the Klamath River at J.C. Boyle reservoir after a 16-mile run from the mountains to the northwest. Unfortunately most of Spencer Creek flows through private lands, but you can get access from some of the road right-of-ways. Carry a BLM map to decipher the network of roads and if you have any questions over access, seek permission. From Hwy 66 on the west side of Boyle Reservoir, turn north on the Keno Access Road or follow the Clover Creek Road north from the east side of the river at Keno. Those two roads get you close to the creek and then a web of secondary roads follow the creek.

Sprague River (Klamath County)

A lengthy tributary to the Lower Williamson River, the Sprague River ranks among the more varied and interesting streams in the region. At its mouth, the Sprague forms the famous "Blue Hole" on the Williamson, renowned for its ability to produce trophy-class migratory redband trout from Klamath Lake and a few huge brown trout that are residents here and in the lower Sprague. The Blue Hole and mouth of the Sprague are boat fisheries: Launch at Chiloquin and drift down or from the public access point just east of Hwy\ 97 on the road leading to Chiloquin (you'll need a motor to run upriver to the mouth of the Sprague).

The lower mile of the Sprague River, below Chiloquin Dam, flows across private property, but you can access the north bank from behind the high school in Chiloquin. Otherwise, public access begins on the Winema National Forest. From

Chiloquin head east on Sprague River Road. A mile from town, a left turn (FR 5810) leads across the river and heads south, crossing onto public land at about the 2-mile mark. From there, secondary roads allow access to a mile of river. Back on Sprague River Road, public property begins half a mile east from the FR5810 turnoff. Here the road parallels the river for a mile and a half, enters half a mile of private land, and then emerges on public land for another half mile. This lower end of the river produces some heavy redband and brown trout and is open to all methods. Access is excellent from the road.

The next bridge upstream lies just east of Potter's RV Park, upstream from the mill site (Braymill). From Potters upstream, most of the Sprague flows through private property. The river meanders for many miles through Sprague River Valley. Here the river is home to trout, largemouth bass, and brown bullhead. Access is difficult and except for a couple launch points in the valley getting to the river requires that you seek permission from the landowners. Even seeking permission can be a daunting proposition because of the numerous large ranches and the many parcels of land with non-resident owners.

The river here generally runs rather turbid, except at a few spring-fed pools, where ODFW snorkel surveys reveal the presence of trophy-size redband trout that run up the river to spawn during the winter. These fish come from Upper Klamath Lake and run all the way up into the Sprague and even the Sycan River to spawn. One radio-tagged fish from the Sycan was later tracked all the way down to Agency Lake. More abundant are the resident redband trout, which commonly range from 14 to 16 inches.

Fishing for largemouth bass peaks during the summer and early autumn, though don't expect world-class action. Like the trout here, the bass are difficult to target owing to extensive private property. The river is floatable, but I'm not sure I'd recommend it unless you carry a stout sense of adventure. Launch sites are primitive and spaced far enough apart to make for a very long day in the boat on a river where you cannot get out on the banks due to private property.

The uppermost launch is adjacent to Hwy 140 about 2 miles east from the town of Beatty. Watch for the power lines just after you round a sharp bend on the highway. The launch here is suitable for a drift boat. From here you must cover 20 miles of meandering river to reach the takeout, so be prepared for a long day. Given the distance and the slow-moving current, an electric motor might be a good idea. In any event, the take-out is near the town of Sprague River on Malheur Road: On the north side of the river, follow Drews Road and watch for the south turn on Malheur Road.

You can use the county access at Malheur Road to launch for a trip downstream or, if you don't mind using a long rope or cable to get the boat into the river, you can launch a little farther downriver at the Sprague River Road Bridge. From either of those two launches you can float down to the Saddle Mountain Pit Road and take out at the bridge there. Be sure to scout the take-out, which is located about 8 miles west from Sprague River and about 15 miles east from Chiloquin. Watch for the south turn at milepost 15. The take-out works for a trailered boat, but expect some difficulty during low flows when the river here gets quite shallow. This drift covers about 15 river miles.

To float the lower river, you can launch at Saddle Mountain Pit Road and do a short drift down to the next primitive launch site, located at the picnic area on forest service property 2.5 miles downstream. Or from there you can make the 15-mile meandering journey through private lands down to the take-out east of Braymill, near Williamson River Road. Again, this requires a long day on the water. Below this launch, the river gets shallow and rocky, making for risky travel with a drift boat. This lower reach of the Sprague is better suited to skilled canoeists. You can take out at the next bridge crossing, at Chiloquin Dam, or down on the Williamson (portaging the dam).

Remember that the Sprague is generally a slow, meandering river so floating it can consume an entire summer day. Be sure to scout the put-in and take-out locations. Also beware that some of the locals along the river don't think much of people floating the Sprague. Stay off the banks on private lands.

The Sprague's middle reaches, from Godowa Springs Road at Beatty down to Saddle Mountain Pit Road, is open to fishing with bait, primarily to allow anglers to take advantage of a good population of brown bullhead. Bullhead are quite abun-

Sprague River

dant and reach good size here. Godowa Springs Road Bridge is only a crossing and offers no public access.

You can follow the Sprague River from Chiloquin on Sprague River Road or you can get to the Sprague Valley by following Hwy 140 east from Klamath Falls or west from Lakeview. At Beatty, head north to cross the river. Drews Road follows the north side of the river for about 11 miles between Beatty and the town of Sprague River.

The upper Sprague flows through pretty country high in the Fremont National Forest, though some of the best water lies on private ranch property. A good 2-mile section flows through a canyon and offers mostly rainbows, including a few of good size. Consult the map on this one. To get there, take Hwy 140 to the tiny town of Bly and half a mile east of town, turn north on Campbell Road. Go 5 miles to FR 3411. When 3411 crosses the river, you are on public land and you can fish upstream for about 2 miles. Higher up, the North Fork Sprague offers good fishing for mostly small rainbows and brookies on about 8 miles of river. There are two nice, small campgrounds in the area, Sandhill Crossing and Lee Thomas Meadow. Continue north on FR 3411 to reach them. Though most of the fish are small, this is a decidedly beautiful and pleasant part of the forest and well worth a summer visit.

Spring Creek (Klamath County)
campground

A major tributary to the Lower Williamson River, Spring Creek is a beautiful but rather infertile spring-fed stream that offers good action on stocked legal-size rainbows. ODFW stocks the stream weekly during summer. A few of the migratory redbands from Klamath Lake make it up this far to spawn during late winter and others arrive during the heat of summer, but don't expect to see many of them here. Mostly the creek serves as a put-and-take fishery in a truly beautiful setting easily accessed from Hwy 97 a few miles north from the Chiloquin exit. The stream flows for about 2 miles and the middle of it crosses private lands. Access to the headwaters is at Spring Creek Campground and extensive Collier Park encompasses the stream's lower .75 of a mile. You can fish either end by foot or you can drop a canoe in at the picnic area near the top and take out at Collier Park on the east side of the highway.

Squaw Lake (Lake County)

Squaw Lake is a natural pond hidden behind Squaw Butte near Picture Rock Pass just a few miles north of Summer Lake in Lake County. During high-water years the lake spans about 10 acres, but it shrinks considerably during low-water cycles. Still, Squaw Lake retained year-round water even during the severe drought years that accompanied the turn of the century. During years of sufficient water, ODFW has been known to drop a few rainbows in Squaw Lake. They can grow quite large but are few in number (the last time the lake was stocked was in the 1980s).

Fishing Squaw Lake is hardly worth the rugged drive over primitive roads to get there. Those interested in the history of indigenous peoples, however, may very well want to visit the lake for a chance to see Boulder Village, one of the state's largest concentrations of stone "rings" that remain from the pit houses built by the natives over the past two thousand years or so.

You can get to Squaw Lake and Boulder Village from the north or from the south. Both routes are rugged and rocky, the south route being slightly shorter but much rougher. I prefer the north route: Head east on Hwy 31 past the town of Silver Lake. After the highway finally turns south, approaching a high rim (Egli Rim) on your left and the bed of dry Silver Lake on your right, watch for the turnoff to Christmas Valley (Old Lake Road). This is the second road you will pass leading to Christmas Valley (the first, still on the straightaway past Silver Lake, points to Silver Lake and Fort Rock). Turn left (east) and drive about a mile and a half, watching for a rough, unmarked gravel road on your right. Follow this road about 5 miles until you reach the top of a small valley. After the road levels off, watch for the first right-hand turn, which dips down to Squaw Lake. Never drive this road during wet weather—even a 4-wheel-drive vehicle is no match for the desert mud. Boulder Village is located in the tree line along the base of Squaw Butte, to the south of the lake. This is an archaeological site, so look and wonder, but don't disturb or take anything.

Stinking Water Creek (Harney County)

Sharing their name with the creek, the Stinking Water Mountains form a prominent landmark in southeastern Oregon. The creek, however, is too intermittent to support trout.

Stone Corrall Lake (Lake County)

Stone Corrall Lake is one of the Warner Valley Lakes west of Hart Mountain and northeast from the tiny town of Plush. These large, natural lakes contain large brown bullhead and a few largemouth bass but are primarily known as crappie fisheries. During extended periods of high water the Warner Valley lakes produce large crappie, some up to 2 pounds. During drought cycles the lakes shrink to a fraction of their potential surface acreage and the crappie fishery all but collapses. The best fishing ever on the lakes occurred following the remarkably wet winters of 1982-84. By 1987 the crappie fishery had reached epic proportions only to be devastated by a three-year-long drought. The fisheries rebounded during the early mid-1990s and then were devastated by another extended drought from 2000-2003, and then again at the end of that decade. Most people fish these lakes from shore, although in a few places—especially some of the interconnecting channels at high water—a canoe comes in handy. Be wary of the frequent high winds. Plush is the jump-off point to reach these lakes and the main roads yield to numerous dirt roads and jeep trails. Be sure to consult the maps and carry all necessary supplies in this remote country.

Summit Lake (Elkhorn Range)

hike-in

Perhaps the most starkly scenic of the high lakes in the Elkhorns, Summit Lake is surrounded on three sides by sheer rock escarpments. Summit Lake covers 22 acres and reaches a depth of 43 feet. It offers good fishing for mostly small brook trout. The shortest trail to the lake covers just over a mile and is very steep. Access to the trailhead is over a rugged 4-wheel-drive road leading up the North Fork of the North Powder River (FR 7301).

From Baker take Hwy 30 to Haines and then head west on the Elkhorn Scenic Route or, if you're arriving from the north, exit the freeway at North Powder and follow the Elkhorn Scenic Route west about 8 miles to a left turn on Foothill Road (CR 1144). From that direction, just continue south on Foothill to a right-hand turn on Bulger Flat Lane. If you're coming from Haines, head north to a left-hand turn on Muddy Creek Road or a mile further north on CR 630. Both roads connect to Foothill Road. Turn north and watch for the left-hand turn leading west on Bulger Flat Lane. This road will deteriorate and lead to the North Powder River, heading south up the river to the national forest boundary. Here it becomes FR 7301, a rugged affair leading 5 miles to the Summit Lake Trailhead. Another trail here leads up the other side of the canyon to reach Meadow Lake and Lost Lake and a mile back down the road you'll find the trail to Red Mountain Lake.

Lost Lake sits at 7,700 feet and supports stunted wild brook trout that rarely exceed 8 inches. They live in a pretty place, however, accessible only by foot or horseback. You can also get there by a longer and highly scenic route from Anthony Lake: 5 miles south on the Elkhorn Crest Trail and then 3.5 miles to Lost Lake. Red Mountain Lake, at 7,100 feet, is a productive and scenic little brook trout lake accessible by way of a steep, mile-long trail.

Swamp Lake (Lake County)

Swamp Lake is one of the Warner Valley lakes west of Hart Mountain and northeast from the tiny town of Plush. The lakes contain large brown bullhead and a few largemouth bass but are primarily known as crappie fisheries. See Stone Corrall Lake for a further description.

Sycan River (Klamath/Lake Counties)

campground

The beautiful little Sycan River ranks among the region's best wild trout fisheries and is especially suited to fly angling. Its upper reaches flow entirely through public lands on the Fremont National Forest and offer fairly abundant small brook and redband trout during times when the river is not severely dewatered. The fish here typically range from 5 to 10 inches, but a few 14- to 18-inchers inhabit these waters, especially on the upper river's final mile or two above Sycan Marsh. The further away from the roads you hike, the better the fishing gets. However, sufficient water supply is always an issue, so be sure to consult ODFW before venturing up to the river.

To reach the upper river from the north, head for the little town of Silver Lake and just east of the Forest Service offices, turn south on CR 4-12, which becomes FR 28 and heads for Thompson Valley Reservoir. About 10 miles past the reservoir, you'll reach the junction of FR 28 and FR 3239. Forest Road 28 continues southeast about 10 more miles to a right-hand turn on FR 30, which takes you down to Pikes Crossing on the Sycan. Forest Road 3239 heads southwesterly about 5 miles to the river. Here the land to the east of the road is public property and the ranchlands to the west of the road are private with no public access. For the next few miles heading south, you can pull off and hike east to reach the river. Be sure to carry a forest map in this country.

From the South, you can get to the upper Sycan by taking either Hwy 140 or Sprague River Road up to the town of Beatty. From Beatty continue east on Hwy 140 to a north turn on FR 30 (Ivory Pine Road). Follow this road all the way to Pike's Crossing or to a left turn on FR 3239.

At Forest Road 3239, the river flows onto extensive private ranchlands and into sprawling Sycan Marsh. When the river

Sycan River

re-emerges from the marsh, it flows southwesterly towards the Sprague River. Immediately below the marsh, the Sycan is often dewatered during summer by irrigation draws, but a series of springs recreate the river a short distance downstream. From there the "lower" Sycan flows almost 20 miles through the Winema National Forest. This lower section is home to redband trout typically ranging from 9 to 14 inches with quite a few 15- to 18-inch trout. Brown trout of similar size also occupy this stretch.

Forest Route 27 crosses the Sycan about a mile below the marsh and you can hike down from there. However, I've seen this section completely dry more often than not; so don't be surprised to find that the FR 27 bridge spans nothing more than a brush-choked riverbed.

Generally the better fishing is farther downstream, below a series of springs that re-create the river. A network of forest roads approaches the Sycan here. Throughout this lower section, the Sycan flows mostly through a shallow, forested canyon where stately old ponderosa pines stand guard over the river. Spur roads reach the river in several places, but the best fishing is found where you must hike down into the canyon. You will need a map to decipher the network of roads and, because many spur roads have been closed to vehicle access, you should obtain the ranger district map that shows current closures.

The upper Sycan originates high on the west approach to Winter Rim, which rises precipitously above sprawling Summer Lake. The upper river is rarely accessible until late May or early June and it fishes best after snowmelt has subsided in July. Prime time is September. The lower section of the river is a good late spring and early summer fishery, but can be quite productive during autumn, especially during high-flow years. There's a nice camping area at Pike's Crossing on the upper river and from the lower river, you can easily drive the 15-odd miles west to Head of the River Campground near the Williamson River.

Taft Miller Reservoir
see Rock Creek Reservoir

Ten Cent Lake
During wet cycles, Ten Cent Lake has water, but does not support fish. It is one of the large, usually dry lakebeds on the west side of the Fields-Denio Road on the way into Mann Lake.

The Narrows (Harney County)
The Narrows, along with adjacent Mud Lake, connects Harney and Malheur Lakes. Combined, the two huge shallow lakes create the largest lake in the state, at least during times of high water. The last time these two lakes enjoyed high water was after the record-setting winters of the early 80s. Shortly thereafter, the Narrows became a productive spot to catch catfish. Keep an eye on it for similar situations in the future. During the 80s, most anglers fished from the shoulder of the road where Hwy 205 spans the narrow channel, about 30 minutes south of Burns.

Thief Valley Reservoir (Baker County)
boat recommended, float tube recommended, boat ramp
Located on the Powder River north of Baker City and a few miles east of I-84, sprawling Thief Valley Reservoir offers good action for 12- to 18-inch planted rainbows, with a few larger fish available. Its proximity to Baker City and LaGrande assures moderate to heavy fishing pressure, but this reservoir never really seems crowded because boat anglers disperse to the far corners. Ice-off usually occurs by early April and during years of good water supply the action lasts into early July. Following three or more years of high water, the reservoir is especially productive in late September and October.

All methods produce here and anglers employ a wide array of tactics, from still fishing with bait from the bank, to trolling hardware, to fly angling with searching patterns on sinking lines. Unless you have a boat, shoreline access is essentially limited to the southeast edge of the reservoir. At high water, a broad cove just south of the access road is a good bet morning and evening. If you have a motorized boat, make the mile-long run up to the inlet arm, which can be very productive during spring.

A mid-day wind frequently turns Thief Valley into a white-capped froth. If you can tolerate the wind, switch to trolling tactics. Don't be surprised to catch a few bass,

Thief Valley Reservoir

bullhead, catfish, or crappie, as they tend to migrate down from the river above. Also, the tailwater reach below the dam is a popular and productive fishery for fat rainbows.

To reach Thief Valley Reservoir, take Exit 285 off I-84 (the North Powder Exit). Turn east off the freeway and follow the main road through the little town of North Powder. About 5 miles from the freeway, turn right on Government Gulch Lane, then drive about 2 miles to a right turn across the railroad tracks. Cross the tracks and continue another 3 miles to the top of a high summit from which the reservoir is visible to the west. Follow the road down to the county park on Thief Valley's east bank, where you will find ample float tube launches, lots of camping space, and precious little shade.

Thomas Creek (Lake County)
no bait
Thomas Creek, just west and northwest from Lakeview is mostly a ditch in its lower portions, but the upper section offers a few wild trout. Follow the highway west from town and turn north on Thomas Creek Road. Once you cross onto the Fremont National Forest, the creek follows the road (FR 28) for several miles. It fishes best between June and October.

Thompson Valley Reservoir (Lake County)
boat ramp, boat recommended, campground
At times a fine fishery for fast-growing rainbow trout, Thompson Valley Reservoir suffered the indignity of being illegally stocked with largemouth bass, which seem to be thriving here. Several years of drought around the turn of the century further degraded the trout fishery, but Thompson Valley is always a fair bet for 13- to 18-inch rainbows with a few fish exceeding 20 inches. The trout fishery peaks after two or three consecutive years of average to above-average water supply, at which time the rainbows grown fat and fast. They respond to all methods.

The reservoir lies in the pine forests south of the little town of Silver Lake in Lake County. From Silver Lake, turn south on CR 4-12, which becomes FR 28 upon crossing into Fremont National Forest. Continue south for 13 miles then turn right on FR 014 to Eastbay Campground. Or you can drive to the west shore by heading south from Silver Lake on CR 4-11, just west from the Ranger District office. After about 13 miles, this road takes you to Thompson Reservoir Campground. Continue south from either campground to circle around the reservoir on FR 3142.

Between them, the two campgrounds offer 36 tent sites and both have boat ramps. A boat is a valuable asset here and fly anglers often use float tubes. If you are specifically angling for largemouth bass, seek out the myriad submerged stumps, logs, channels, and shoals. ODFW has also stocked the reservoir with white bass/striped bass hybrids, which have yet to make much of an appearance. Thompson Valley sits at almost 5,000 feet and is usually accessible by late April, although low snow-pack years allow ready access for ice fishing during winter.

Threemile Creek (Harney County)
closed waters
Threemile Creek flows west from the Steens Mountains, crossing the Catlow Valley Road south of Roaring Springs Ranch. The creek is closed to fishing to protect a supposed remnant population of Catlow Valley Redband Trout.

Trapper Lake
see Sky Lakes Wilderness Area

Traverse Lake (Eagle Cap Wilderness)
hike-in
A hike-in brook trout lake near the southern edge of the Eagle Cap Wilderness, 19-acre Traverse offers brook trout from 6 to 12 inches, with an occasional larger fish. The West Eagle Trailhead reaches Traverse Lake after about 6.5 miles and along the way you'll enjoy spectacular scenery, abundant wildflowers, and a rather stunning view of Echo Lake (see listing herein). From Union, follow SR 203 south to Catherine Creek. Two miles past the park turn left onto FR 77 and follow it 15 mile up to West Eagle Meadows. From the south, you can follow FR 67 from Medical Springs up past Tamarack Campground to a left-hand turn onto FR 77.

Trout Creek (Harney County)
no bait, hike-in
One of Oregon's most remote trout streams, Trout Creek offers fair fishing for small wild cutthroat/rainbow hybrids in a tiny desert creek. The fish range from 5 to 12 inches and are mostly confined to the upper reaches of the creek. This is rugged desert country a long way from everything in the southeast corner of Harney County. Be sure to carry two extra tires, extra fuel, a shovel, water, and all other necessary supplies for traveling backcountry 4-wheel-drive roads. The roads are passable by late spring and fishing peaks during early summer and again during late September and October.

The trout here are unique in that they may represent a fairly pure strain of Alvord cutthroat trout. The famed trout biologist Robert Behnke considers the Alvord cutthroat to be extinct, while ODFW says these fish persist in Trout Creek, but with possible introgression with hatchery-born rainbows suspected to have been planted by Nevada during the 1940s. According to Behnke the Alvord cutthroat became separated from the Lahontan cutthroat due to a landslide that redirected Mahogany Creek from Lahontan Basin to the Alvord Basin about 20,000 years ago.

Most of Trout Creek runs across private ranchlands with only about 40 percent of the drainage on BLM property. The upper end of the creek, which supports the best trout fishery, flows through BLM land that historically been decimated by intensive livestock grazing. More modern grazing practices are slowly yielding a recovered riparian zone on the creek, which is critical to the survival of these trout.

To reach Trout Creek, head for Fields on the Fields-Denio Road. The easiest route to Fields is to follow Hwy 205 from

Burns to Frenchglen, then south past the Catlow Valley and finally up and over Long Hollow to the tiny village of Fields. Stop at Fields for a milkshake, burger, fuel, and local directions. Then continue south toward Denio about 9 miles to a left-hand turn on CR 203 to Whitehorse Ranch. Before you reach the ranch, head south on the Trout Creek Mountain Road, which follows the ridge above Little Trout Creek before turning west to meet Trout Creek after about 15 miles. Be sure to check road conditions and closures at the BLM office in Hines. Beware that the mountains in this corner of Oregon have recently become home to illegal marijuana grows reportedly guarded by armed men; consult the Malheur County Sheriff's Office in Vale (541-473-5125) for more information.

Tudor Lake (Harney County)

Tudor Lake is a large, dry lakebed about 7 miles north from and on the opposite side of the road from Mann Lake. During the flood years of the early 1980s, Tudor lake filled with water and was subsequently stocked with rainbows. The fish grew rapidly in the super-fertile broth and by 1984 and 1985, Tudor Lake was quietly producing rainbows to 26 inches to the few anglers who knew about the fishery. By the late 80s the lake had become a mud puddle and by the early 90s it was again a

Unity Reservoir

dry, dusty flat. I mention this here because I was lucky enough to enjoy Tudor during those precious few years when it ranked among the state's best big-trout producers. Should flood years ever again occur in southeastern Oregon, keep an eye on Tudor Lake.

Twentymile Creek (Lake County)
no bait

Located in the remote foothills of the Warner Mountains south of Adel, Twentymile Creek offers fair fishing for small, wild redband trout. The problem here is access, as most of the stream flows through private ranchlands along the road south of Adel. A few miles of the upper creek flow through BLM lands. Consult the BLM map for access. The fishing here peaks in early summer and again in the fall.

Twin Lakes (Elkhorn Mountains)
hike-in

A pair of small brook and rainbow trout lakes just west of Elkhorn Peak, Twin Lakes offer good fishing in a very scenic setting. You can get there by several different routes. The usual route follows the 4-mile-long trail up from the end of FR 030 north of Phillips Lake on the Powder River. Head for the west end of the reservoir and then turn north on Deer Creek Road. Follow the road up to Deer Creek Campground and then continue north on FR 030. This route requires a steep uphill hike that gains 2,065 feet.

You can also get to Twin Lakes from the trailhead at Marble Pass. This route saves a lot of steep hiking, but getting to the trailhead is plenty rugged on your vehicle. Follow Pocahontas Road west from Baker City and turn left at Marble Creek Road, which will deteriorate steadily as you climb up the drainage. From the trailhead at the top of Marble Pass, hike west about 4 miles and then turn left at the trail junction to reach the lakes. This last section of the trail is a series of switchbacks heading down a steep talus slope. Keep an eye peeled for mountain goats on the ridge to the west of the lakes.

Twin Lakes (Wallowa Mountains)
see Fish Lake

Unity Reservoir (Baker County)
boat ramp, campground

Impounding the Burnt River just north of the town of Unity, this large reservoir offers fair-to-good fishing for stocked rainbow trout ranging from 9 to 14 inches with a few larger carry-over fish available. It also supports some small bass and crappie. Many anglers tow boats to Unity, though shoreline fishing is easy and productive. Most anglers fish bait or troll with spoons and blades. A few fly anglers show up with float tubes during spring and fall. The reservoir is used for irrigation and is drawn down steadily during the summer. Most years it maintains ample water supply for productive fishing all the way through October. Ice fishing during winter can be good as well, but check on ice thickness by calling the ODFW office in Baker City. To get there, follow Hwy 26 to Unity and watch for the signs marking the north turn 2 miles north of town. You can camp at the state park near the dam.

Upper Campbell Lake
see Campbell Lake

Upper Cow Lake (Malheur County)
boat ramp

A large, shallow and highly turbid lake in the desert near Jordan Valley, Upper Cow Lake attracts moderate angling pressure for its white crappie, brown bullhead, and largemouth bass. Like so many waters in this parched part of Oregon, the lake fishes best after two or three consecutive years of above-average water supply. At such times, Upper Cow Lake grows crappie to at least a foot long. Structure here comes in the form of steep banks, underwater shoals, and other such submerged terrain features—figure them out and you'll find the fish. A boat is handy to reach the different coves and points, but you'll find ample shore fishing. Beware the wind if you're fishing by boat. Try for bass on the westernmost finger of the lake, where the water reaches the lava flow, west from the boat launch. From Jordan Valley, follow Hwy 95 west 5 miles to a right-hand turn on Danner Loop Road and then follow the signs 14 miles to the Cow Lakes. The lower lake is usually fishless and the upper covers about 1,000 acres when full. The BLM campground has ten sites, but bring your own drinking water and everything else.

Upper Klamath Lake
see Klamath Lake

Upper Midway Reservoir (Klamath County)
campground

A 40-acre BLM reservoir south of Gerber Reservoir, about 22 miles southwest of Bly, Upper Midway was a good producer of decent-sized largemouth bass before somebody illegally introduced yellow perch into the reservoir, which soon became over-populated with masses of very small perch. In 2005, the reservoir was drained, and then, in 2006 and in 2007 after it refilled, it was re-stocked with largemouth bass, which held their own and grew to modest sizes. Then Upper Midway did not fill in the spring of 2010, and the fish appeared to have succumbed to winterkill. As of 2010, ODFW plans to restock bass as soon as water levels allow, which could be as early as spring of 2011, but they will need a year or two to grow. The campground here is a primitive site provided by the BLM, and while there is no ramp, small boats can be easily launched from shore.

Van Patten Lake (Elkhorn Mountains)
hike-in

A productive and scenic lake in the Elkhorn Range west of Baker City, Van Patten offers brook and rainbow trout from 6 to 14 inches with most rarely reaching 10 inches. This is good float-tube country and fly fishing is especially productive during the July-through-September hiking season at this elevation (7,396 feet). From the lower trailhead, the hike to Van Patten covers a steep mile and a half. From Baker City, follow Hwy 30 north to Haines and then head west on Elkhorn Drive toward Anthony Lake. Watch for the Van Patten Lake Trailhead signs a few miles before you reach Anthony Lake. Turn up FR 130 to reach the trailhead. Parking spaces are available near the maintenance shed at the base of the hill. Four-wheel drive vehicles may continue on Forest Road 131 for a mile to the upper trailhead (Trail 1634), for additional parking spaces. This road is steep, rocky, and has a short turning radius on the switchbacks. It is also severely out-sloped in places. The trail to Van Patten offers fine views of the valley off to the east and the Wallowa Mountains beyond. Some nice campsites are located along the lake's west shore.

Vee Lake (Lake County)
boat recommended, boat ramp, float tube recommended

Vee Lake, sometimes called "V Lake," is located on the northern edge of the Warner Mountains northeast from Lakeview. It is surrounded by sparse stands of ponderosa pines and aspen, on the edge of the high desert where the Warner Mountains to the south transition to the high-elevation sage steppe of Abert Rim on the north. Sometimes one or more bald eagles perch atop the snags along the reservoir. During periods of good water supply, Vee Lake is an excellent fly-angling impoundment. It is uniformly shallow and weedy with drowned timber and holds an abundance of trout foods. *Callibaetis* mayflies, damsels, water beetles, and Chironomids provide surface action from late spring through mid-summer and again during the fall. Bank fishing is good, but this 12-acre lake is ideally suited to float tubes and small boats (electric motors only/5 mph speed limit).

During persistent drought conditions, Vee Lake suffers and becomes a shallow, turbid puddle that provides only poor-to-fair fishing. Luckily it is high enough to survive single-season droughts and normally its stocked rainbows grow rapidly to reach lengths of 12 to 18 inches. Vee Lake is generally accessible by May, but before venturing out there, check with the Forest Service office in Lakeview.

From Hwy 395 north of Lakeview, turn right on Hwy 140. Head east up into the Warner Mountains for 8 miles, then turn left on FR 3615. Follow FR 3615 for 13.5 miles and then turn right onto FR 3616. Follow FR 3616 for 5 miles to the lake.

Walls Lake Reservoir
Walls Lake Reservoir is a small, fishless desert reservoir near Frenchglen.

Warm Springs Reservoir (Harney County)
boat ramp, campground

One of Oregon's more productive warmwater and trout fisheries, this sprawling reservoir occupies a broad basin on the Middle Fork of the Malheur about an hour east of Burns and south of Hwy 20. In recent years, extended severe drought has decimated the fishery, but recovery occurs fairly rapidly here when water levels return to normal. Given some normal winters, look for Warm Springs to return to glory.

The reservoir spans more than 4,000 acres at full pool, which it achieves early in the spring during years of normal water supply. The reservoir supplies a stable flow of water for downstream agricultural interests and is steadily drawn down until autumn. Often the boat ramp is left high and dry by summer and during severe drought conditions the reservoir is drawn down to minimum pool, when fish tend to be lost through the dam.

Warm Springs offers good fishing for smallmouth bass that range from 8 to 20 inches. They congregate around the reservoir's abundant rock structure. Catfish, largemouth bass, and yellow perch are fairly common as well; and the reservoir is also known for its fast-growing rainbow trout. The fat trout typically range from 13 to 18 inches and during years of optimal conditions, many trout from 18 to 20-plus inches inhabit the reservoir. During spring, still fish with bait or troll with lures or flies. If the fishery holds up through the fall, fly anglers can enjoy some fair action on a few very large trout. Mid-October is prime but again, only after several years of optimal flows. Otherwise, fish the reservoir between March and June.

The reservoir is surrounded entirely by public land (Bureau of Reclamation and BLM), so access is good via a network of rugged dirt and gravel roads. The main access road follows more or less along the west shoreline. The boat ramp is located on a broad peninsula jutting out into the reservoir's southwest corner. There are countless campsites all around the reservoir, but no formal facilities. Three miles below the dam there is a BLM campground at Riverside, where the road crosses over the Malheur River.

Several different roads lead across the desert to Warm Springs Reservoir, but only two of them are worth driving. During spring (or any time the roads are wet), the best route is the road connecting Riverside with the town of Juntura. At the west edge of town, watch for the signs to Riverside and head south. At Riverside, turn right before you cross the river and drive another few miles up to Warm Springs. The total distance is about 20 miles. During dry conditions, the oft-rugged Warm Springs Reservoir Road is slow but shorter by distance, covering about 12 miles after turning south off Hwy 20 east of the Stinking Water Summit and 2 miles west of the turn-off to Drewsey.

Warner Pond (Lake County)

ODFW stocks rainbow trout in this small pond on the Hart Mountain Antelope Refuge. Fishing is best from mid- to late spring with most of the catch ranging from 9 to 13 inches.

West Sunstone Reservoir (Lake County)

This turbid little desert reservoir offers fair fishing only during high-water years, especially if two or three such years occur consecutively. It spans about 10 acres at full pool. Only occasionally stocked, rainbows grow quickly during favorable conditions and reach 18 inches. The reservoir dried up completely during the drought of 2007-2010. West Sunstone sits a mile and a half east of Sherlock Gulch Reservoir and northwest from the Sunstone Collecting Area, which is north from the little town of Plush. See Sherlock Gulch Reservoir for directions—the turnoff to West Sunstone heads north from the main road about 2 miles before you get to Sherlock Gulch, but don't bother with the long drive unless ODFW gives it the thumbs up (check with the office in Lakeview or Klamath Falls).

Weston Lake (Mountain Lakes Wilderness)
hike-in

Diminutive Weston Lake spans just a few acres, but often produces good catches of brookies and rainbows ranging from 8 to 13 inches. It lies on the west edge of the Mountain Lakes Wilderness, 3 miles due east from Lake of the Woods, and is lightly fished compared to the other lakes in the wilderness area. Access is from the Mountain Lakes Trail heading on FR 3660, which turns east off Hwy 140 a mile north of Lake of the Woods. Weston Lake sits off the formal trail, so be sure to consult your map for this one.

Warm Springs Reservoir

Legend
Access Roads
Creek/River
Unnoted Creeks
Boat Launch

N

Malheur River

Warm Springs Road

Warm Springs Landing

Warm Springs Reservoir

Warm Springs Creek

Warm Springs Dam

Warm Springs Rd

0   1   2   2.5 MILES

© 2007 Wilderness Adventures Press, Inc.

Whitehorse Creek (Malheur County)
no bait, catch-and-release

One of Oregon's most remote desert trout streams, Whitehorse Creek is also one of the last strongholds in the state for indigenous, genetically pure Lahontan cutthroat trout. The fish are most numerous in the upper watershed and also inhabit Willow Creek and Little Whitehorse Creek, along with short reaches of Doolittle and Fifteenmile Creeks. These Lahontans once occupied drainages on both sides of the mountains here, but in some waters they were doomed by introduced brown and brook trout and in a few streams they hybridized with stocked rainbows. None of these waters are stocked now, nor have they been for decades. Still, the pure Lahontan cutthroats exist only in the Willow-Whitehorse Basin, though there may be a few in Line Canyon Creek and Sage Creek on the Quinn River drainage.

The most recent population surveys for the basin estimated the total population of trout in these waters at about 4,000 fish, mostly in Willow, Whitehorse, and Little Whitehorse Creeks. At that time, Doolittle Creek had an estimated 300 fish and none were found in Fifteenmile Creek. Since that time, this part of the Great Basin has been subjected to some severe drought conditions, especially around the turn of the century, so populations now may well be substantially lower than these numbers.

To sample these waters, you'll need a stout sense of adventure, a high-clearance 4-wheel-drive vehicle, a sturdy pair of hiking boots, and good maps. Access begins at the Whitehorse Ranch Road, which heads east from the Fields-Denio Road about 10 miles south of Fields. From there, the Willow Hot Springs Loop Road (along with several other rugged 4-wheel-drive roads) gets you close to the upper watersheds on Willow and Little Whitehorse Creeks and the lower canyon reach of Whitehorse Creek. After that you must hike the canyons. You can make a long circuitous and rugged drive south from the loop road on Trout Creek Road to an east turn on the Fifteenmile Reservoir Road to approach the upper section of Whitehorse Creek.

All of this country is characterized by small streams that run through brushy canyon bottoms. As you gain elevation in the Trout Creek Mountains you will find pretty little aspen groves. Don't even try to negotiate these roads until late in the spring, when they have dried out for the year. The best time to visit is during September when the aspen leaves begin to turn yellow. Be sure to carry two extra tires, a shovel, water, fuel, and all other gear required for traveling well off the beaten path in southeast Oregon. You can get local information at Fields Store & Café, which also serves up a mean burger and milkshake. In addition, Fields has a small motel, as does Denio down on the Nevada side of the border.

Beware that the mountains in this corner of Oregon have recently become home to illegal marijuana grows reportedly guarded by armed men; consult the Malheur County Sheriff's Office in Vale (541-473-5125) for more information.

Wild Billy Lake (Klamath County)
fee fishery

Wild Billy Lake is a private 200-acre lake in the Sprague River Valley and is operated as a fee-fishing location known for its large rainbows. The lake is fly-fishing only and has a cabin available for rent. For rates and reservations call 541-747-5595 or visit the website at www.wildbillylake.com.

Wildhorse Creek (Steens Mountains)
hike-in

The outflow from Wildhorse Lake, this scenic stream flows rapidly down the east side of the Steens Mountains, eventually reaching the Fields-Denio Road north of Fields. The Lahontan cutthroat trout in the creek reproduce naturally, but they rarely reach more than 10 inches in length, and most range from just 3 to 7 inches. The lower half of the creek flows entirely through private ranch lands, leaving 6 miles of fishable water flowing through BLM land. You can hike down from Wildhorse Lake or you can drive and then hike in from the Indian Creek Road, across from Alvord Hot Springs on the Fields-Denio Road ("East Steens Road"), but because the upper end of the creek is best, hiking down from the lake makes the most sense. Don't bother with this creek unless you're in good physical condition.

Wildhorse Lake (Steens Mountains)
hike-in

No doubt one of Oregon's prettiest places, Wildhorse Lake occupies a deep glacial cirque near the summit of the Steens Mountains. Its introduced Lahontan cutthroat trout reproduce naturally and give this lake the distinction of a two-way tie for the highest lake in Oregon that supports spawning trout (the other is Billy Jones Lake in the Eagle Cap Wilderness).

Wildhorse Lake spans about 20 acres and its Lahontan cutthroat reach at least 16 inches but most range from 4 to 10

Wildhorse Lake on Steens Mountain is not for the timid.

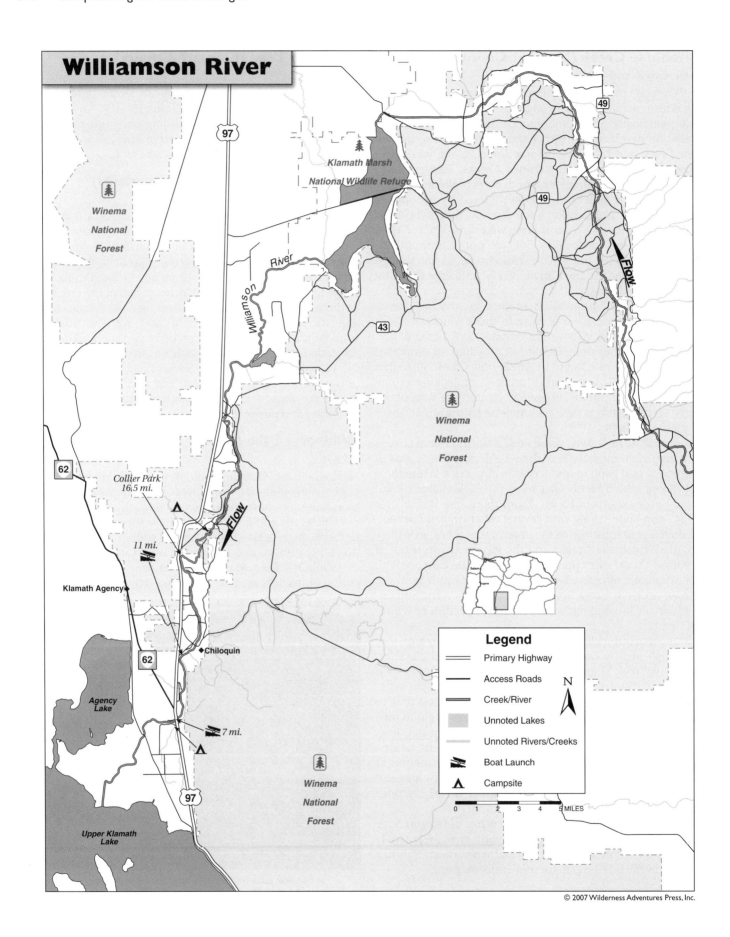

Williamson River

Klamath Marsh
National Wildlife Refuge

[97]

[49]

[49]

Williamson   River

Flow

[43]

Winema
National
Forest

Winema
National
Forest

[62]

Collier Park
16.5 mi.

Flow

11 mi.

Klamath Agency

[62]

Chiloquin

Agency
Lake

7 mi.

Winema
National
Forest

[97]

Upper Klamath
Lake

Legend

⎯	Primary Highway
⎯	Access Roads
⎯	Creek/River
▢	Unnoted Lakes
⎯	Unnoted Rivers/Creeks
⚓	Boat Launch
⛺	Campsite

N

0   1   2   3   4   5 MILES

inches (I've caught two 16-inch specimens myself and have heard rumors of 18-inchers). Many of the fish are quite skinny due to their relatively sparse food supply, but a few fat 12-inchers show up in the catch. They respond to all methods, but small spinners and flies tend to do best.

During the morning and evening rise, try a Griffith's Gnat or similar small midge pattern. At mid-day keep your eyes peeled for the *Callibaetis* mayflies, especially on the occasional days when the wind doesn't blow. Sometimes you can take up residence near the shore and cast ant patterns to sighted fish within a few feet of the bank. In the absence of surface activity my favorite tactic is to fish two flies: a No. 6 black bead-head Woolly Bugger or similar pattern about 2 feet ahead of a No. 14 Pheasant Tail Nymph or Zugbug. Usually the fish take the smaller fly, but the big fly gets their attention. You'll want a sinking or sink-tip line along with a floating line.

Plenty of shoreline fishing waits, as there are no trees in the way. Half the lake is dominated by gentle meadow-clad banks and the other half by talus slides reaching the lake shore. The rockslides are easily negotiated so you can fish from any point along the banks. Nonetheless, Wildhorse Lake is tailor-made for a float tube, so if you're tough enough to carry in the tube, waders, warm clothes, and fins, you won't be disappointed.

To tackle the hike into—and out of—Wildhorse Lake you should be in good physical shape. The trail is steep and rocky and begins at nearly 9,500 feet before losing 1,000 feet in elevation over the course of about 1 mile. Naturally you must regain that altitude on the way out and at such elevations, the out-of-shape need not apply.

The trail is often passable by July 4, though you may need to negotiate your way around a broad snow bank clinging to a very steep, treacherous slope (if the snowbank is too large or the upper end of the trail too daunting, walk the access road up to the repeater tower above the parking lot and hike down the back side to the lake). The fishing is better later in the summer anyway, so you are best served to wait until late July. Anytime between late summer and early autumn is ideal. To get to the trailhead, take a left turn out of the south end of the town of Frenchglen, following the signs toward the Steens Loop Road. Climb the Steens Road until you reach the summit, where three roads converge and follow the middle fork whose sign points towards Wildhorse Lake. Park at the trailhead and walk down to the overlook atop the cliff. You'll see the trail winding its way steeply down the mountain.

Williamson River, Lower (Klamath County)
boat recommended, campground, catch-and-release

In terms of sheer numbers of big trout, Oregon's Klamath country fisheries are virtually beyond compare, the famed Williamson River being the flagship water in this southern Oregon valley. The spring-fed Williamson feeds massive Upper Klamath Lake, whose shallow super fertile waters teem with fast-growing wild trout.

Outside of Alaska, you won't find a region whose waters are so densely populated with native, trophy-class rainbows. Five-pound specimens won't raise any eyebrows among those who regularly ply the waters of the Williamson or Wood Rivers, or of Upper Klamath or Agency Lakes. Moreover, any angler with average casting ability can catch the fish of a lifetime several times over on any given day on these waters.

The Williamson is a split-personality river. Its lower half, below Klamath Marsh, runs through pastoral farmlands and secluded housing tracts down to its confluence with Upper Klamath Lake. Without Klamath Lake and its huge wild rainbows, this "lower" Williamson River would hardly be worth your time. But the behemoth rainbows of the lake wander up the river like steelhead. By mid-summer, the river is full of 2- to 12-pound "redbands" from Klamath Lake.

During late spring, the big redbands begin to trickle into the Williamson, where they occupy many different pools and runs. Often they form substantial pods or schools in the larger pools. The fishing begins by late May, picks up speed during and June, and peaks between July and September. The water, always slightly tea-colored on the lower reach below the town of Chiloquin, often runs off-color during late spring. Even the upper reach (above Chiloquin), which draws most of its volume from the clear waters of Spring Creek, can run a little cloudy early in the season.

Indeed, the Lower Williamson may be further divided into its upper section below Collier Park and its lower section from the town of Chiloquin down to the mouth. The upper reach, below Collier Park and the Spring Creek confluence, is virtu-

Its fishery created by migrant trout from Upper Klamath Lake, the Williamson River is perhaps the best wild trophy-trout stream in the lower 48 states.

ally inaccessible to bank anglers except for a short segment at and immediately below Collier Park. While plenty of fine fish are landed each season near Collier Park, the best reaches of the upper stretch are fishable only by boat or by access to private property along the banks. Most anglers fish the upper stretch by hiring one of the several fly-angling guides who enjoy access to this section. This upper stretch is improved after mid-summer; so most anglers concentrate on the 7 miles of river from Chiloquin down to Williamson River Resort.

This lower half of the Lower Williamson offers better public access than the reach from Collier Park down to Chiloquin. But because bank access is still quite limited on the lower section most anglers float the river in drift boats, anchoring to fish favorite pools and runs. The Williamson offers no technical water, but low late-summer flows can expose ledge rock in a few places. The most popular drift goes from Chiloquin down to the takeout at the Rapids Motel near Hwy 97, a reach of 5 miles. In some places, you can fish from a float tube or pontoon boat. Two good spots for small craft are the public access area just below Chiloquin, behind the airfield and on the west side of Hwy 97 at the so-called Williamson River Resort, which charges a modest launch fee.

In any event, the trout of the lower Williamson are migratory fish that behave oddly most of the time and inexplicably some of the time. Despite voluminous hatches of major insects, sometimes the river's trout eat and sometimes they don't. That's the bottom line. They are quirky fish that, once in the river, often act more like steelhead than trout. On the lower Williamson, a perfectly good mayfly hatch can go completely unmolested by hundreds of huge trout. Then the next day the same hatch arrives flush with rising trout. Float the river and you see pods of trophy trout. Catch them in an eating mood and you enjoy uncomplicated fishing for some of the biggest trout of your life. Otherwise you just see lots of big trout and maybe find a few willing to eat a wet fly quartered down and strip retrieved.

The Lower Williamson is a fairly large river and its trout literally average about 4 pounds. They demand stout tackle, so most anglers opt for a 6- or 7-weight fly rod. Bring two reels or spools, one rigged with a floating line and one spooled with a sinking line. In recent years, the clear, monofilament-core sinking lines have gained a substantial following on the river. On the sinking line, attach a short leader of at least 6-pound test (2X and 3X tippets are the norm). Rig the floating line with a 9-foot, 4X leader and keep a spool of 5X handy just in case you encounter fish feeding on tiny blue-winged olive (*Baetis*) mayflies. Other common mayflies include pale morning duns and Tricos.

The Williamson River is home to huge, wild redband trout that migrate up from Upper Klamath Lake between late spring and autumn.

Two strategies prevail on the Lower Williamson, but you must first find the fish by looking for good holding water characterized by depth and some form of cover along with a break from strong currents. Most often you will fish sinking lines with wet flies ranging from small nymphs to medium-size streamer-type flies. Cast across and slightly down, allowing the line time to sink. As the fly starts to drag and swing across the flow, retrieve line in slow, short strips. Cover the good water thoroughly in this manner, working downstream through the pools. Every Williamson River regular has a favorite wet fly, but most would agree on the general effectiveness of a sparsely dressed leech-style pattern in olive or brown and tied on a No. 6 hook.

The second tactic is classic dry-fly fishing and the opportunity to do so can appear at any time anywhere on the river. At times it seems every trout in the river is feeding at the surface. More often, isolated pods of fish or individual fish begin feeding on a specific hatch. During May and June, the predominant mayfly is the aforementioned blue-winged olive. During June, to varying degrees, the river enjoys hatches of giant yellow mayflies (*Hexagenia*), green drakes, and pale morning duns. When you visit the Williamson, come prepared for dry-fly action and be ready to match specific hatches.

Sometimes the Williamson's monster trout are easy to fool when they rise consistently during a hatch, but often they prove as spooky and selective as more typical spring-creek trout found on places like Idaho's Silver Creek. So make a habit of careful approach and delicate presentation. Meanwhile, don't stray too far from that sinking line/wet fly setup because a perfectly grand mayfly hatch can and often does go utterly ignored by the quirky lunkers of the Williamson.

You can float the Lower Williamson on your own, but

unless you have lots of time to dedicate to the task, you are better off hiring a guide the first time. And the bank access is so limited, that boat-less anglers are certainly well served to fish with a guide. Some pools hold pods of fish and some don't. As the season progresses, the fish often move to different locations and the pattern can change from year to year. You could spend half a season just figuring out where best to cast the fly. So unless you have a boat and lots of time on your hands, hire a guide.

Certainly you can explore the Williamson on your own, but you'll need a few days to figure things out. And you'll need a boat. In any event, the Williamson River offers one of the country's most impressive big-fish factories in a region blessed with remarkable scenery. Anglers willing to ferret out the river's secrets and understand the whimsical nature of her fish may hook the trout of a lifetime several times over.

You can arrange guide service through southern Oregon fly shops or through some of the lodges in the area, including highly reputed Crystalwood Lodge (866-381-2322/www.crystalwoodlodge.com) and Lonesome Duck (800-367-2540). Or call the ODFW office in Klamath Falls for suggestions on guides working the waters in the area.

Williamson River, Upper (Klamath County)
no bait

Upstream from Klamath Marsh, the Williamson River is an entirely different fishery than the more famous "Lower" Williamson located along Hwy 97 to the west. The Upper Williamson flows almost entirely through private ranch lands. One of these ranches—John Hyde's Yamsi Ranch—caters to fly anglers and offers complete lodging/fishing packages during the summer. The Yamsi Ranch property begins just downstream from Williamson Springs, the river's birthplace in the Winema National Forest. Spanning 5,000 acres, the Yamsi Ranch is well known for large rainbow and brook trout and for terrific mayfly hatches, including the famous "Black Drake" emergence of mid-summer. Yamsi Ranch can be reached at 541-783-2403/www.yamsiflyfishing.com.

The Yamsi Ranch property extends for several miles downstream and then the river alternates between tracts of private and public property. Access to the public reaches is essentially impossible from the east bank, but available via several forest roads on the west side of the river. To get there, follow Hwy 97 to the Klamath Marsh cutoff road leading east towards Silver Lake (Route 76). Follow the road east across Klamath Marsh. At the east edge of the marsh, the highway turns southeast for a mile-and-a-half. Watch for the right-hand turn onto Forest Primary Route 49 (immediately east of the adjacent turn-off on FR 45). All of the accessible public water is reached by FR 49 and its spurs, so study the Winema National Forest map. A few old spur roads approach the river while other stretches of the Williamson require a short hike. Including the meanders, you have access to about 5 river miles here. The fishing peaks from late June through September.

Willow Creek (Lake County)
see Deep Creek

Willow Creek (Malheur County)
no bait

Willow Creek flows alongside the road leading to Malheur Reservoir from the little town of Ironside on Hwy 26. Although the road provides easy access to the diminutive creek, which harbors a sparse population of redband trout, Willow Creek flows almost entirely through private property. Downstream (east) from Malheur Reservoir, Willow Creek flows mostly through private property with about 3 miles of non-contiguous BLM land along the way. Willow Creek Road follows the public sections, but this part of the creek carries little of interest to anglers even though it harbors some large rainbows during high-water periods. Be sure to seek permission before fishing private stretches of the creek.

Willow Creek (Trout Creek Mountains)
no bait, catch-and-release

A remote stream in the Trout Creek Mountains southeast from Fields, Willow Creek supports a sparse population of wild Lahontan cutthroat trout. The stream is currently open to catch-and-release fishing, but check the most recent regulations as Willow Creek has been closed to angling in years past. See Trout Creek for directions to the area. Beware that the mountains in this corner of Oregon have recently become home to illegal marijuana grows reportedly guarded by armed men; consult the Malheur County Sheriff's Office in Vale (541-473-5125) for more information.

Willow Creek (Steens Mountains)
closed waters

Flowing off the east side of the Steens Mountains, Willow Creek is closed to protect a possible remnant population of Lahontan cutthroat trout, though they are likely extirpated.

Willow Valley Reservoir (Klamath County)
boat ramp

A remote but easy-to-reach reservoir located on BLM land near the California border, Willow Valley offers fair-to-good fishing for largemouth bass and crappie, along with yellow perch and bluegill, and stocked Lahontan cutthroat trout that can reach at least 18 inches after several consecutive years of good water supply. Largemouth bass here reach several pounds. From Klamath Falls, head east on Hwy 140 and when you reach the little town of Dairy, turn southeast toward Bonanza on SR 70. At Bonanza take the East Langell Valley Road heading for Lorella. About 9 miles south of Lorella, watch for the signed left-hand turnoff to Willow Valley Reservoir. Bass fishing peaks during late spring, and the reservoir has a primitive BLM campground and a boat ramp. Typically the reservoir gets very low by late summer and fall, and the boat ramp can then be unusable, but bank fishing is generally good.

Wilson Reservoir (Klamath County)
see Lost River

Wind Lake
see Sky Lakes Wilderness Area

Withers Lake (Lake County)
hike-in

Actually a small but scenic irrigation reservoir, Withers Lake is a nice little walk-in brook trout and brown trout fishery atop Winter Rim off the Government Harvey Road south of Summer Lake. From Paisley head west toward the Chewaucan River and just outside of town turn north onto FR 3315 and after 6 miles turn right on FR 3360. Follow FR 3360 to a left-hand turn on Spur Road 359. Drive to the end and walk a short distance to the lake. Withers is easy to fish from shore, especially with bait or spinning gear, but a float tube is useful. The small brook trout reproduce naturally here and the lake has been planted with brown trout in recent years. Heavy weed growth can be troublesome by late summer, but fall can provide excellent fishing with few people.

Wizard Lake
see Sky Lakes Wilderness Area

Wolf Creek Reservoir (Union County)
boat recommended, float tube recommended

Locally popular and productive, this 200-acre reservoir offers fair-to-good fishing for planted rainbow trout that reach 18 inches, and decent fishing for crappie. Most of the fish range from 10 to 13 inches and they are usually fat and healthy.

This is a good float tube reservoir for fly anglers, though bait anglers predominate. At times (when the water level is high) you must tolerate water skiers and jet skiers. To get there, take I-84 to the little town of North Powder (north of Baker City), but exit the freeway 2 miles to the north at the Wolff Creek Lane Exit (#283). Head west 5 miles to the reservoir. The reservoir fishes best from April through June and again during the fall, during years of good water supply.

Wood River (Klamath County)
no bait, catch-and-release, boat recommended

The major tributary to Agency Lake, the Wood River is a scenic, meandering flat-water spring creek renowned for its large redband and brown trout. Both species commonly range from 14 to 20 inches. Many of the fish—especially the big redband trout—ascend the Wood River from Agency Lake. Some of these fish reach 30 inches in length. The river is a catch-and-release fishery and is popular with fly anglers.

The river flows almost entirely through private ranchlands, so access by foot is limited. Most anglers fish the Wood by boat, usually by floating down from the bridge on Weed Road. The put in at Weed Road is an informal launch. Some anglers slide drift boats into the water here, but most use canoes and pontoon boats. From the bridge, you can spend the day fishing your way downstream to the river's mouth at Agency Lake. Then turn left and row over to the BLM launch site. If you have a boat with a motor, head a little farther west to the ramp at Petric County Park.

Some anglers motor from Petric Park over to the mouth of the Wood, run up the river and then drift back down to fish. If you choose this course, beware the shallow bar at the mouth of the river. Since the BLM purchased the Wood River Ranch, far more anglers are using pontoon boats and canoes to drift the river, so conflicts with boaters motoring upstream are perhaps inevitable. On the river's glassy flows, feeding trout are easily disturbed by boaters motoring upriver, so I'd suggest you opt instead to float down from the bridge.

Occupying the river's west bank, the BLM's Wood River Ranch property begins about 2 river miles upstream from the mouth of Crooked Creek, which enters the Wood from the east and about 2 miles as the crow flies downstream from Weed Road. Until you get there, the banks are private property. Once you reach the BLM land however, you can walk the dike road on the west bank and fish from shore.

You can access the upper half of the river and launch canoes and small boats at Kimball Park near the headwaters, at the day-use park near Fort Klamath and

The productive Wood River meanders quietly through a bucolic valley.

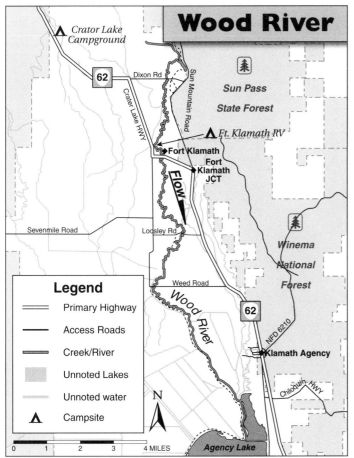

trout from Agency Lake ascend the river and many of these fish range from 4 to 6 pounds and sometimes larger. You won't catch lots of fish on the Wood, but most of them are large.

To find the Wood River, follow Hwy 97 to the Hwy 62 Junction at the Williamson River. Head northwest on Hwy 62 into the valley and past Agency Lake. The river is off to your left at this point until you cross it near the little town of Fort Klamath. Kimball Park sits on the east bank north of Fort Klamath—watch for the signs.

Woodpecker Lake
see Sky Lakes Wilderness Area

Yamsi Ranch
see Williamson River, Upper

Yellowjacket Lake (Harney County)
campground, boat recommended, float tube recommended

Located in the Malheur National Forest about 35 miles northwest of Burns, 30-acre Yellowjacket Lake is a local favorite in the Burns area of southeast Oregon. It grows fat rainbow trout. When water levels remain high for two or more consecutive years, a few fish reach 18 inches. Most of the time, the fishery offers 8- to 14-inch rainbows that are planted as fingerlings; often Oregon Department of Fish and Wildlife (ODFW) plants legal-size trout as well. A fingerling planted in May reaches about 8 inches by fall.

The reservoir is fertile, growing dense weedbeds during summer, and is a great place for float tubes and fly rods; a gravel launch allows access for prams and other small boats. Shoreline fishing access is also easy and extensive, and at times during spring and fall, wader-clad anglers can enjoy plenty of action without ever setting foot in a boat or float tube (note the posted private property on the upstream end of the reservoir). Before the weeds grow, you can even set a chair at water's edge and still-fish with bait. When the aquatic weeds grow thick, anchor in open water and also fish the dropoff along the east side of the small reservoir. The weedbeds support ample trout food: scuds, chironomids, damselfly nymphs, callibaetis mayflies, snails, leeches, and more.

Yellowjacket is popular with local anglers and can be a little busy on weekends during late May and June. During October, especially during times when several high-water years occur consecutively, the fishing can be especially good for piggish trout. The weeds die off during fall, and large Woolly Buggers and leech patterns account for plenty of savage fish. In the spring and summer, try those same patterns, along with smaller Zugbugs and Prince Nymphs, damselfly nymphs and dragonfly nymphs, and chironomid patterns fished on sinking-tip or sinking lines.

To get to Yellowjacket Lake, which sits at about 4,800 feet elevation, watch for the signed turnoff on Hines Logging Road (Harney County Road 127) in Hines (the satellite community contiguous with Burns). Continue 12 miles to a signed right-

at the road right-of-way on the Loosley Road bridge. If you launch at any of these upriver access points and are bound for Weed Road Bridge, be aware of the irrigation-diversion dam upstream from Weed Road. The banks above the dam are on private property, but the owners allow anglers to portage on the east bank. Make sure you do nothing more than portage around the dam on this property, returning immediately to the water. The landowners have tolerated problems with trespassers in the past, so be respectful.

You can camp at Kimball Park, at Henzel Park on Agency Lake, or at campgrounds nearby on the Williamson River. Two lodges in the Wood River Valley cater to fly anglers and both offer guided fishing: Horseshoe Ranch (541-381-2297) and Crystalwood Lodge (541-381-2322/www.crystalwoodlodge.com).

The Wood River fishes best from late June through early October and offers regular hatches of pale morning duns and Callibaetis mayflies. The best dry-fly action, however, occurs during late summer when hoppers abound along the river's grassy, undercut banks. If hopper patterns don't draw the big fish out from under the cut banks, try large streamer patterns fished on high-density sink-tip lines. The river's resident fish typically range from 10 to 16 inches, but plenty of double-digit brown trout lurk under the banks. During summer, redband hand turn on Forest Road (FR) 47 and continue 7 miles to another signed right-hand turn on FR 37, then 2.5 miles to a third right-hand turn leading to the reservoir. If arriving from the west, turn north (left) on Spring Creek Road just west of the tiny town of Riley, following the well-marked routes. You can gas up and pick up basic supplies at the Riley Store. To check fishing/water conditions, call the ODFW in Hines, 541-573-6582.

This small impoundment has a nice campground with bathroom facilities and water pumps. Deer, elk, and porcupines frequent the area, and also interesting is the ongoing natural recovery from a huge forest fire that swept through the area a few years ago.

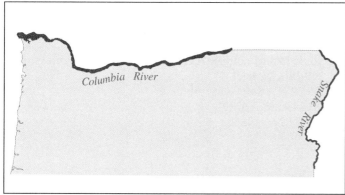

Columbia & Snake River Zones

The mighty Columbia River, once a superhighway for the world's most robust runs of salmon and steelhead is a waterway much changed by man. Today's Columbia River only superficially resembles that known by the indigenous peoples as far back as the Clovis culture that thrived at the end of the last ice age, at least 13,000 years ago. Indeed, one of the continent's most famous discoveries of Clovis-associated stone blades was discovered on the Columbia Plateau in Washington State (the Wenatchee Clovis Site).

Filled with fish virtually throughout the year, the Columbia no doubt sustained countless generations of native peoples. Still, it is much changed as a result of the arrival of immigrants of European descent hailing from the then far away and fledgling United States of America. Modern salmon and steelhead runs cannot compare to the bounty of centuries long past, yet the Columbia still manages to produce some of the state's best opportunities for salmon and sturgeon fishing and, despite arduous passage at the river's myriad dams, steelhead and salmon still manage to find their way to natal streams as far upriver as central Idaho.

The Columbia River dams have influenced the river's habitat so profoundly that they have created ideal conditions for non-native fish to thrive. These include smallmouth bass and walleye, whose populations are burgeoning. Shad, another import, run the lower Columbia by the millions. Along with the Columbia's sturgeon and salmon (chinook and coho), these non-native species have created valuable and highly productive fisheries on the river.

Forming part of the border between Idaho and Oregon, the Snake River offers a similar scenario. That section of the Snake flowing alongside Oregon's rugged eastern border offers some of the best smallmouth bass, crappie, and catfish angling in the entire Pacific Northwest. Here the mighty Snake River is tamed by several dams, including Brownlee Dam and Hells Canyon Dam. The reservoirs formed behind these dams create perfect habitat for these warmwater species and, their tremendously productive fisheries, perhaps to some degree, provide a minor mitigation for the fact that Hells Canyon Dam was built with no fish-passage facilities and thus cuts off hundreds of river and stream miles that were once home to salmon and steelhead.

In total, Oregon's share of the Columbia and Snake Rivers offers a bewildering array of super-productive fisheries. Anglers arrive here from all quarters to pursue everything from salmon at the mouth of the Columbia, to walleye and sturgeon upriver, to warmwater fish along the border country.

Columbia Zone Contacts

**North Willamette Watershed District Office
(Regional Office)**
17330 SE Evelyn Street
Clackamas, OR 97015
(503) 673-6000

Fish Division Programs in Astoria
Marine: (503) 325-2462
Inter Jurisdictional (Columbia River sturgeon and
salmon): (503) 325-3418

**Sauvie Island Wildlife Area/North Willamette Watershed
Wildlife District**
18330 NW Sauvie Island Road
Portland, OR 97231
(503) 621-3488

Snake River Zone Contacts

**Northeast Region
Grande Ronde Watershed District Office
(Regional Office)**
107 20th Street
LaGrande, OR 97850
(541) 963-2138

Baker City Field Office
2995 Hughes Lane
Baker City, OR 97814
(541) 523-5832

Columbia River, Mouth

The most renowned and productive salmon fishing grounds on the Columbia River, the fishery at the mouth is popularly called "Buoy 10" and annually yields thousands of salmon to boat anglers fishing mostly out of Warrenton and Astoria. Technically speaking, the Buoy 10 fishery extends from the Buoy 10 line upstream to a line projected from Rocky Point on the Washington bank through red Buoy 44 to the navigation light at Tongue Point on the Oregon Bank.

Anglers begin probing the Buoy 10 fishery immediately upon the opening of the salmon season on August 1. In most years, plenty of fish ply these waters at the opener, a mix of both chinook and coho salmon, wild and hatchery origin. Only the fin-clipped hatchery coho may be kept and all wild fish must be immediately released unharmed. Currently, anglers may keep both wild and fin-clipped chinook salmon. The Buoy 10 salmon season closes on December 31, and is then open for hatchery fish only from January 1 through the end of March. However, salmon seasons are subject to constant changes, so be sure to check the current angling synopsis provided by ODFW.

Also beware that beyond the Buoy 10 line, the mouth of the Columbia is subject to ever-changing ocean salmon fishing regulations, which are set each April by the Pacific Fishery Management Council (PFMC). The annual regulations are published each May and are available from license agents and from ODFW. These regulations frequently change during the actual season, so anglers must be aware of such changes.

The Buoy 10 fishery is primarily the haunt of sled boats and other large motor-propelled craft because the Columbia estuary here is subject to severe tidal currents and, on the western edge of the fishing zone, heavy swells and chop. Also beware the shipping channels and remember that the ships have the legal right-of-way. The most popular launch points in Oregon are at Hammond, Warrenton, and Astoria; on the Washington side, boaters use the ramps at Fort Canby State Park and Chinook Harbor.

Among the Buoy 10 salmon-fishing crowds, the method of choice is to drift or troll with herring. Typically anglers rig herring on 5- to 7-foot-long mooching leaders with two single hooks snelled tandem. Rig a swivel chain above the mooching leader to avoid twisting. According to widely respected Oregon angler Buzz Ramsey, "You can enhance the effectiveness of your herring by fishing it in combination with a 101 Herring Rig [Luhr-Jensen], which is a snelled mooching leader combined with beads, tubing spacer and spinner blade attached to a plastic clevis. The 101 Herring Rig is available with different blade colors and in whole or cut plug rigging versions."

Trollers at Buoy 10 generally prefer diving rigs over lead-weighted setups, but all sorts of trolling setups are used for this fishery and anglers should be prepared to troll at a variety of depths. In general, coho salmon are caught closer to the surface than chinook salmon.

The Buoy 10 fishery can get very crowded, so much so that boat operators must exercise extreme caution in order to maintain a safe and congenial atmosphere. If possible, fish mid-week and be on the water as early as possible. Lots of guides work this fishery (and the sturgeon fishery at the mouth), and a guided expedition is a great way to enjoy it for anglers without the appropriate watercraft and for boat owners wishing to learn their way around.

Sturgeon comprise the second-most favorite fishery on the Columbia River estuary and this portion of the river is even more productive for legal-size fish than the famous sturgeon grounds below Bonneville Dam and in the Bonneville Pool. The Columbia estuary annually yields several tens of thousands of white sturgeon and quite a few of the scarcer green sturgeon. The best baits are anchovy, herring, sand shrimp, and a few other local favorites.

The top sturgeon areas on the estuary are within easy reach by boat of the ramps at Warrenton, Hammond, and Astoria, mostly just downstream from the Hwy 101 bridge and throughout and adjacent to the Desdemona Sands shoals off the mouth of Youngs Bay.

In addition to its well-known sturgeon and salmon fisheries, the mouth of the Columbia River also offers excellent prospects for shellfish ranging from Dungeness crabs to various clams, and for a variety of marine fishes, including redtail surfperch, striped seaperch, black rockfish, blue rockfish, cabezon, greenling, lingcod, and starry flounder. Crabbing is best along Clatsop Spit on the Oregon side and in and near Baker Bay on the Washington side. Both sides provide very good jetty fishing (you will need a Washington license to fish from the north jetty). In addition to perch and bottomfish, jetty anglers often catch salmon but, be sure to consult regulations before targeting or retaining salmon from the jetties.

Bottomfish and perch, of course, are even more available to boat anglers, but beware the strong tidal currents and rough conditions prevalent between the jetties. Striped perch, greenling, and flounder are especially apt to take bait. Rockfish, lingcod, and redtail surfperch eagerly take bait, and can also be great fun on jigs of various kinds. Big is better for lingcod, which can reach double-digit weights on the Columbia jetties. Black rockfish are the most common of the *Sebastes* genus, but large blue rockfish sometimes come from the outer reaches of the jetties. Shore-bound anglers must always exercise extreme caution when fishing from the jetties.

Columbia River, Astoria to Bonneville Dam

From Astoria, past Portland to massive Bonneville Dam, the mighty Columbia River is at its mightiest, gathering the flows of large tributaries, including the Sandy and Willamette Rivers. This section of river offers good prospects for sturgeon and salmon, along with a superb fishery for shad, and good action for walleye and steelhead. Smallmouth bass, yellow perch, and crappie become increasingly common as you move upstream, and the numerous sloughs and backwaters harbor all manner of warmwater species.

The lower Columbia offers numerous productive and

popular salmon and sturgeon fishing areas and these are literally scattered throughout the entire stretch of river. The mouth of the Multnomah Channel near St. Helens attracts salmon anglers in hog-line numbers and produces lots of fish; likewise the mouths of the Cowlitz and Kalama Rivers on the Washington side. Various islands (among them Tenasillahie, Wallace, Crims, Lord, Shell, respectively moving upstream) provide ideal places to seek salmon as the fish congregate in channels formed by the currents wrapping around these islands.

Boat anglers certainly enjoy the advantage of mobility on the lower Columbia River, but bank anglers enjoy fairly consistent success at a number of very popular beaches along the river. These include oft-crowded Dibblee Beach (near Rainier), Rainier Beach (in Rainier), and Prescott Beach (at the town of Prescott north of St. Helens). Boat ramps and moorage facilities are located all along the river, from Portland to Astoria. The most popular launch points on the Oregon side of the river are as follows, starting at Astoria: Astoria East Mooring Basin, John Day Ramp (John Day River), Aldrich Point Ramp, Westport Ramp, Rainier City Marina, Scipios Goble Landing (private, 503-556-6510), St. Helens Marina, Scappoose Bay Marina. Several marinas and ramps are available on Sauvie Island and along Multnomah Channel.

Just downstream from Portland, Sauvie Island serves as a tiny community, major waterfowl migration area, and fishing destination. Its various sloughs and ponds are home to warmwater species, while the channels and adjacent river offer fair-to-good prospects for salmon and a steelhead, along with sturgeon and, increasingly it seems, fair-sized walleye. Sauvie Island is a popular salmon-fishing destination for boat and bank anglers.

Upstream, east from Portland via I-84, Bonneville Dam is the lowermost of the huge Columbia River dams. From the fishing deadline below the dam, downstream for several miles, this section is popular and productive for sturgeon and shad along with walleye, bass, and some fair action for salmon and steelhead. The shad, which arrive by the hundreds of thousands during May and June, comprise a very popular fishery for bank and boat anglers. Access for bank anglers is good from the hatchery below the dam. Boat anglers can launch in Portland at Hayden Island, adjacent to I-5 (Doubletree Columbia River Ramp and Jantzen Beach Ramp), or from any of several ramps along Marine Drive between I-5 and I-205. The public ramp, operated by Metro, is the M. James Gleason Ramp at 4300 NE Marine Drive (river mile 109.5). Nine miles upstream is another public launch at Chinook Landing.

Two good ramps are located alongside I-84 between Troutdale and Bonneville Dam; the first at Rooster Rock State Park (river mile 128) and the other at Dalton Point, about 6 miles farther east. Rooster Rock State Park is a superb facility (fee) with a double-width ramp leading into a narrow cove, which in turn leads out to the Columbia. The large park here has a decidedly pleasant picnic area, along with some bank access to the Columbia. Likewise, Dalton Point also includes some

bank access.

The lower Columbia walleye fishery has become increasingly productive in the Portland area. Most anglers look for pilings, rock piles, submerged reefs, and other structures. Among these walleye-attracting structures are the bridge pilings at the I-5 and I-205 bridges spanning the river. Only experienced power boaters should approach and fish the bridge pilings, which continue to put out some nice-size walleyes. Also, throughout the Columbia's lower run from Bonneville Dam to Astoria, a wide array of side channels and sloughs offer very productive fishing for warmwaters species, including smallmouth and largemouth bass, catfish, bullhead, bluegill, crappie, and yellow perch.

For kayaking anglers out for a day of fishing or ready for the adventure of a multi-day paddle, the Lower Columbia River Water Trail (www.columbiawatertrail.org), managed by the Lower Columbia River Estuary Partnership, is a 146-mile paddle trail on the Lower Columbia, stretching from Bonneville Dam to the Pacific. The trail website features full details on access points, campsites, points of interest, and more.

Columbia River, Bonneville Dam to John Day Dam

This middle stretch of the Columbia River spans about 70 miles and includes the river's first three massive dams and two huge impoundments. The stretch of river backed up by Bonneville Dam is called Bonneville Pool; The Dalles Dam creates "Celilo Lake," better known as The Dalles Pool. Bonneville Pool stretches more than 40 miles, but the lower half of it comprises the slack-water section. The entire reach is productive for sturgeon, smallmouth bass and walleye, along with salmon and steelhead. For steelhead and chinook salmon, the mouths of the White Salmon and Klickitat Rivers are especially productive and popular. Launch at Hood River Marina or Bingen Marina (on the Washington side) to fish off the river mouths.

Upstream, at the quaint little community of Lyle, Washington, the mouth of the Klickitat River is a productive destination for steelhead during autumn. The easiest launch site is at Meyer State Park, almost across the river from Lyle, adjacent to I-84. This stretch of the Columbia also features some highly productive sturgeon and walleye areas. In The Dalles, the river swings close to the freeway and bank anglers often congregate along the city walking trail, adjacent to the interstate, to fish for sturgeon. Walleye fishing can be good through town.

Just upstream from The Dalles Dam, the Columbia runs alongside several rocky reefs that provide excellent prospects for smallmouth bass. Parking is difficult, however, so even though bank fishing is good here, you rarely see many anglers. Boaters enjoy the advantage, but smallmouth fishing is secondary to the productive fisheries for sturgeon, steelhead, and walleye, so few boaters probe the rocky shorelines here. Ramps on both sides of the river provide ready access to the lower end of The Dalles Pool—Avery Park in Washington and Celilo Park in Oregon. The most popular steelhead fishery on the Oregon side of the river occurs at the mouth of the Deschutes, upstream from Celilo Park. The easiest run is from Heritage Landing on the west bank of the mouth of the Deschutes River. From there you can run a sled boat down into the Columbia. You can also launch at Celilo and run up the Columbia, a better option for large boats, but it is a longer run covering several miles and not much fun if a heavy wind arrives.

Farther upriver, walleye, sturgeon, and smallmouth bass provide good fishing. Look for bass around structure, including the gravel piles near Biggs, the bridge pilings near Biggs and Rufus, and the numerous rock reefs upstream from Rufus. This stretch of the river produces some big bass and walleye, yet it is comparatively lightly fished. The gravel piles along the Oregon side provide bank-fishing opportunities on this stretch of the Columbia—for all three of the above-mentioned species, along with a variety of other warmwater and non-game fishes. In addition to the ramps at Heritage Park on the Deschutes and at Celilo Park, a conveniently located ramp on the Washington side across from Biggs, provides easy access to the upper end of the pool. Cross the river on Hwy 97 and watch for the turnoff into Maryhill State Park.

Columbia River, John Day Dam to McNary Dam

The John Day Pool ("Lake Umatilla") stretches for 76 lonely miles and along the way provides the Northwest's premier trophy walleye fishery, along with a wide array of other prospects. There is some very good and little-known action for large smallmouth bass, including fish up to 6 pounds. Much of the John Day Pool is remote by angling standards because I-84 (Oregon) and Washington SR 14 provide only minimal bank access, and because the well-spaced boat ramps leave plenty of broad river open to exploration between the mouth of the John Day River and Boardman well to the east. Only a few tiny communities sit beside the river on this arid stretch of freeway—Arlington, Boardman, Irrigon, and Roosevelt (Washington).

From the mouth of the John Day River up to Boardman, during the peak seasons for walleye, sturgeon, and smallmouth bass—mid-spring through mid-autumn—boaters can have huge tracts of the river here all to themselves. Ramps are located at Arlington and across the river at Washington's Roosevelt Park, at Quesnel Park about halfway between Arlington and Boardman, and at Boardman. Anglers fishing for big walleye below McNary Dam often use the popular ramp at Umatilla.

The Columbia River may well yield the next world record walleye, as the fish seem to be getting bigger and more abundant. Certainly they enjoy a food-rich environment that allows for rapid growth and the available habitat encompasses virtually the entirety of Oregon's stretch of the Columbia. The best fishing, especially for big "marble-eyes," traditionally occurs in the John Day Pool as far upriver as Umatilla (an especially popular reach extends from McNary Dam down to Boardman).

In the John Day Pool, walleye typically range from 5 to 14 pounds and quite a few larger fish are taken each year. The current state record is just a shade less than 20 pounds. In some places on the Columbia, walleye seem to occur just about everywhere, but most walleye specialists learn to identify the most likely places to hold fish at different times of year. The largest fish, especially, seem to consistently come from the same areas of the river. Walleye tend to be rather structure oriented and in particular like rocky or gravel slopes coming off the mouths of tributary streams, back-water eddies and slicks, side channels, and just about anyplace where the bottom offers ridges, deep-water shoals, islands edges, and other such attractions. Also, slightly off-colored water is better suited to walleye fishing than clear flows, so wind chop—generally a fact of life on the Columbia—often aids in the fishing.

Walleye prey heavily on other fish, and the Columbia offers them a smorgasbord that includes pike minnow, sculpins, sucker minnows, and other bottom dwellers in addition to salmon and steelhead fry. Any area that concentrates bait is sure to attract walleyes, explaining the popularity of the dam outflows themselves as prime fishing areas. The spillways and turbines provide a conveyor belt of dead, injured and healthy prey fish, so walleye congregate to feed on them. Popular spots include the legal fishing areas immediately downstream

from McNary, John Day, The Dalles, and even Bonneville Dam.

Spring fishing, from March through June or thereabouts, often occurs at depths of 20 to 50 or more feet as the walleye begin staging to spawn. Sonar equipment can prove very helpful in marking fish holding along submerged reefs, bars, and other structures. The actual spawning generally occurs over gravel bottoms at shallow to moderate depths, out of the main river current. Once the spawn is over, the best fishing of the year begins and the most successful Columbia River walleye anglers are able to effectively fish a wide range of depths, locations, and water conditions.

In the prime water from McNary Dam down to Boardman, walleye hotspots include the slicks and eddies downstream from the dam, and the various seams and slow channels created by islands and submerged reefs and shoals. A depth finder helps mark the edges where these underwater structures drop off into deeper water—typical hangouts for walleye of all sizes. A good topographical chart for the Columbia River can also aid in your search for ideal walleye habitat.

Walleye anglers use a broad range of techniques, with the most popular being deep-water jigging and trolling or casting plugs and spinner/bait combos. During the early season, jigs—often tipped with bait—are popular because the fish don't seem to move around much and because they occupy deep water. In the main river, you need jigs weighing at least half an ounce, if not more, to keep the lure on or near the bottom. Later in the year, as the water warms, plugs and other lures become increasingly effective. During the heat of summer, some anglers continue fishing well into the night.

In addition to the superb walleye prospects of the John Day Pool, the mouth of the John Day River itself provides very good prospects for steelhead (mostly trolling) and smallmouth bass, including some big bass. Catfish, crappie, yellow perch, and bullhead also abound, along with some huge carp and other non-game fish. Access to the mouth—which stretches for about 8 miles to the south—is primarily by boat, with a convenient launch site located off I-84 (Exit 114) at LePage Park. Upstream is the popular boat-in-only Philippi Park, which attracts both anglers and water skiers. Steelhead fishing peaks from about August through November. Bass fishing picks up during mid-spring and even a few nice walleye come from the lower end of the John Day Arm.

Bank angling prospects, though limited, are certainly worth exploring on the John Day Pool. The interstate often runs at a bit of a distance from the river, but a few key pullouts offer walk-in access from the westbound lanes. Also, bank access at Arlington offers a shot at good smallmouth bass fishing and these same waters put out a variety of other species, from the occasional sturgeon to crappie and catfish. Heading east, the next easy bank access is at Quesnel Park, near the Willow Creek Wildlife Management Area at Exit 151. The river here offers some good bank fishing for a variety of species, along with about 20 primitive campsites and a boat ramp.

At Boardman, the really serious fishing for trophy-class walleyes begins, with the prime fishery extending up to McNary Dam at Umatilla. Boat ramps are located at Umatilla, just downstream from the freeway bridge over the Columbia, at Irrigon, at Patterson Junction, and at Boardman.

Columbia River, McNary Pool

Upstream from McNary Dam, the McNary Pool extends across the state line and into Washington, leaving the lower 15 miles of the pool within Oregon. This stretch is called Lake Wallula and offers good fishing for smallmouth bass, walleye, catfish, yellow perch, and fair prospects for steelhead and some upriver bright chinook salmon. Most anglers fish salmon and steelhead near the boating deadline upstream from McNary Dam, though some bank fishing is available on both the Oregon and Washington sides of the river. Easiest bank access on the Oregon side is from Hat Rock State Park, located east of Umatilla on SR 730. Upstream from Hat Rock State Park, the highway offers several pullouts that allow anglers to get to the water.

This stretch of the Columbia puts out quite a few 1- to 4-pound smallmouth bass, and a few trophy-class smallies up to 6 pounds. The fishing peaks from April through June, but can be good any time during the summer and fall. Steelhead fishing peaks from late October through early December. Boat anglers usually launch at Hat Rock State Park or at either of the two McNary Dam ramps. A boat is advantageous here because the river offers lots of structure unreachable to bank anglers; submerged reefs and rock piles usually hold bass and walleye.

Snake River, state line to Hells Canyon Dam

Hells Canyon Dam is the upstream limit for anadromous fish—steelhead and salmon—on the Snake River because the dam includes no fish-passage facilities. The rugged, remote and awe-inspiring canyon here provides a remarkable backdrop for anglers seeking the river's abundant smallmouth bass, catfish, sturgeon, and steelhead. Most anglers fish by jet boat because access from the banks is very limited. The steelhead fishery—primarily for hatchery fish—peaks from November through February and has become very popular in recent years. The most popular areas for steelhead include long stretches of river near the mouths of Oregon's Imnaha River and Idaho's Salmon River. This entire stretch of the Snake River is highly regarded for its productive sturgeon fishery. Smallmouth bass abound in certain places and, where the water tends to be too swift for bass, anglers find lots of rainbow trout, including a few that reach 16 to 18 inches.

Boaters can launch at the ramp on the Oregon side of Hells Canyon Dam, or downstream above the mouth of the Imnaha River, at the Dug Bar launch. To reach the popular Dug Bar launch, head first for Enterprise, Oregon and then follow the highway up to Joseph. At Joseph, head east following the signs to Imnaha and from there, head north along the Imnaha River until you descend to Dug Bar. For the uppermost launch at Hells Canyon Dam, follow SR 86 east from Baker City, through

Richmond and Pine, and down to Oxbow Dam. Cross to the Idaho side and follow the winding paved road downstream to the crossing at Hells Canyon Dam. A few lengthy trails reach down to the river in places, but are rarely used by anglers. Hikers and anglers should consult the Hells Canyon National Recreation Area map, available from the Wallowa-Whitman National Forest offices in Enterprise, (541) 426-4978.

Many outfitters and guides work the Snake River downstream from Hells Canyon Dam, mostly specializing in steelhead and sturgeon fishing. Because this lengthy section of river is remote, rugged, and increasingly dangerous as you progress upstream toward and into Hells Canyon, first-time anglers should consider hiring a jet-boat guide to learn the river. Wallowa-Whitman National Forest maintains a list of guides who work the river: http://www.fs.fed.us/r6/w-w/recreation/outfitters.html.

Snake River, Hells Canyon Dam to Brownlee Dam

By Snake River standards, the stretch of rugged canyon reaching from Hells Canyon Dam up to Brownlee Dam is relatively short. It includes Oxbow Dam, which forms 11-mile-long Oxbow Reservoir, and Hells Canyon Reservoir, which spans about 20 miles from Oxbow Dam downstream to Hells Canyon Dam. All told, this 30-plus-mile stretch of impoundment water offers excellent prospects for bass, crappie, rainbow trout and catfish, along with a few other species, including yellow perch, white sturgeon and some truly large carp.

Hells Canyon Reservoir is the lowermost reservoir on the Snake River and the most remote. It offers good prospects for 12- to 22-inch rainbow trout, taken primarily by trolling, and bass—both largemouth and smallmouth. Hells Canyon Reservoir often boasts the clearest water of the three impoundments (Brownlee and Oxbow being the other two), so bass anglers often must fish deeper, at least during the high-sun hours. The banks offer lots of "stair-step" rock drop offs, which provide good cover for bass and crappie, though the crappie fishery here seems to fluctuate rather wildly between fair and poor. In recent years, hatchery steelhead have been stocked annually into Hells Canyon Reservoir, usually during late fall or winter. Once in the reservoir, they are counted as trout and the current trout limits apply.

On the Idaho side, a good paved road snakes along the entire length of the reservoir, providing access to lots of bank fishing (Idaho license required) and taking anglers to the launch site at Idaho Power's Hells Canyon Park, which has about two dozen RV sites and tent sites. On the Oregon side, Homestead Road leads down the reservoir about 8 miles from Oxbow Dam and provides lots of good bank fishing and quite a few dispersed primitive campsites. To get to the river, take SR 86 from Baker City, and head through Richmond and Pine, down to Copperfield. Homestead Road leads north, or cross the river to access the Idaho side. Bank fishing from the Idaho side requires an Idaho license.

Idaho Power's Copperfield Park is a popular facility offering 62 RV sites with water, electricity, fire pits, and picnic tables. There are 10 tent sites with picnic tables, barbecue stands, and some mature trees. It also offers a convenient RV dump station, extra vehicle parking spaces, handicapped accessible restrooms with showers, and a large, grassy picnic area adjacent to the Snake River. The Copperfield Boat Launch is about 1 mile downstream from Copperfield Park, on the Oregon side of Hells Canyon Reservoir. Facilities include a double-lane concrete boat ramp, boat docks, parking, garbage receptacles, and seasonal toilets.

Oxbow Reservoir, the middle of the three border impoundments on the Snake River, offers excellent fishing for smallmouth bass, including plenty of large fish. Largemouth bass are available, but not nearly as common as in Hells Canyon Reservoir. Oxbow Reservoir also offers fair-to-good prospects for crappie and catfish—both channel cats and flathead cats—along with a mixture of other species, including a few decent-size rainbow trout.

Bank access is very good on the Oregon side, as Oxbow Road follows the reservoir between Oxbow and Brownlee Dams. To get there, take S 86 east from Baker City, past Richland and Pine, and down to the river

Brownlee Reservoir smallmouth bass

Brownlee Reservoir, forming the Oregon/Idaho border, is one of the Northwest's most prolific fisheries for smallmouth bass, crappie, and catfish.

at Copperfield. Turn south to follow the reservoir. Several primitive launches serve boaters on the Oregon side, the most popular of which is The Oxbow Boat Launch, a day-use-only site located about 10 miles downstream of Brownlee Dam and 2 miles upstream from Copperfield Park. Facilities include a gravel boat ramp, docks, composting toilet, garbage pickup, and parking. An improved ramp is located on the Idaho side at Idaho Power's McCormick Park Campground, located about 1 mile below Brownlee Dam. The campground has 34 RV sites with electricity and water, along with quite a few tent sites.

Bear in mind that water fluctuations occur daily on the Snake River impoundments. The average outflow from Brownlee Dam can fill Oxbow Reservoir to capacity in about six hours, thus nighttime water releases are the norm at Oxbow. For current water level information, call Idaho Power's recreation line at (800) 422-3143.

Snake River, Brownlee Reservoir

Brownlee Reservoir may well be the single best combination crappie/smallmouth bass fishery in the Northwest. Anglers have taken state-record smallmouth and crappie from Brownlee Reservoir, which ranks annually among Oregon's most oft-visited fisheries. Moreover, Brownlee also offers a very productive fishery for channel catfish, which commonly range from 2 to 8 pounds.

In fact, Brownlee teems with big fish; 12- to 18-inch bass are common. Better yet, if you spend a little time on Brownlee, you stand a fair chance of hooking a 20-inch smallmouth. The fish are big by Northwest standards—bigger on average than the bass in the John Day or Umpqua—and there are lots of them. Likewise, black and white crappie abound and often

provide non-stop action. These aren't the usual 7-inch crappie familiar to anglers west of the Cascades. These are the big boys: They typically span 9 to 12 inches and 14-inchers show up regularly. The reservoir also holds a few surprises: large bluegill, fat yellow perch, huge carp, and even a few big rainbow trout.

Located upstream, or south, of Hell's Canyon, Brownlee Reservoir forms a 57-mile-long portion of the Idaho/Oregon border. Towering canyon slopes clad in sage, rabbitbrush, and cheatgrass, rise precipitously from the rocky shorelines. Brownlee lies far from just about everywhere save the border town of Ontario and a few tiny hamlets strung through the region. Interstate-84 leaves Portland and travels some 340 miles before reaching Exit 345, which leads through the small community of Huntington and then down to the southern reaches of Brownlee's massive pool. Between Huntington on the south and Richland on the north, Snake River Road (gravel) follows the reservoir for almost 30 miles through the canyon.

Brownlee's northern reaches (along with Oxbow Reservoir) are best accessed from the towns of Richland and Halfway. Interstate-84 delivers you to Baker City, where Exit 302 leads to SR 86. This road heads east, picking up the Powder River, itself a fine smallmouth stream in its lower reaches. At Richland, where the Powder River Arm of Brownlee Reservoir offers fine prospects for crappie and bass, SR 86 swings northeasterly and climbs over the hill to Halfway and then turns east again, leading a dozen or so miles down to Oxbow Dam. After the long descent to the river, the road swings abruptly south and follows Oxbow Reservoir to Brownlee Dam before crossing over to the Idaho side as Hwy 71.

No roads access the lower third of Brownlee reservoir, but anglers wishing to ply the waters of Oxbow and Brownlee would be well served to head for the town of Richland. From Richland you can follow SR 86 to Oxbow or turn south on Snake River Road, climb over the rim, and wind your way down to Brownlee. While the road offers excellent bank access downstream from Huntington, boaters have the advantage of covering far more water. The boat ramps are scattered along the reservoir for convenient use. A good boat ramp is found just north of Huntington. Otherwise, you can launch car-top boats and pontoons at various informal sites along the road. Or launch at Richland on the Powder River Arm, itself a highly productive bass and crappie fishery. As long as you remain on the water, you can fish anywhere on the reservoir with an Oregon or an Idaho license. Bank anglers must possess a license for the state from whose bank they are fishing.

Fishing picks up during late spring when crappie, smallmouth bass, catfish, and bluegill congregate in channels, off steep points, and in deep coves. When warm weather arrives during late May or June, spawning crappies invade the shallows and bass follow along feeding on crappie fry. You needn't worry too much about disturbing spawning crappies because their spawning season extends for several weeks with some fish spawning early and others later. During the spawning period, look for gently sloping shorelines dominated by shale beds and slack water. Crappies abound in these areas. Among them are active spawners, but these are always in the minority. Bass occupy these same places, feeding heavily on juvenile crappies, crayfish, and on just about anything else that moves.

Indeed, early summer offers the best mixed-bag fishing with both crappies and bass abundant in the shallows. A 1995 sampling by Oregon Department of Fish & Wildlife (ODFW)

determined an average Brownlee Reservoir white crappie to span more than 10 inches in length. These big white crappie, while numerous, are less abundant than the black crappie, which average slightly smaller. In my experience, the big white crappie typically inhabit the shale beds while black crappie predominate in channels, along rock faces, and over steep-sloping banks. That's not a hard and fast rule and you often catch both species in the same places. In any event, don't linger too long in one location when searching for Brownlee's crappie. Instead, fish each spot thoroughly, making sure to fish all depths. Move on if you don't hit crappie within a reasonable number of casts.

During July, crappies seek deeper water during much of the day, but often feed in the shallows around dusk. Throughout the summer, steep rocky drop-offs and creek channels remain prime areas to find both crappie and bass. Also look for wood structure in the form of rotting trees anchored in place by ODFW, dead snags lying in shallow water, stick-ups in the creek channels and coves, and flotsam drifted into floating piles. These structures attract schools of crappies, especially during the post-spawn period lasting from late June through September. Water levels fluctuate rather wildly on these Snake River impoundments, so you may luck into a chance to study the reservoirs at low drawdown levels. If so, record the locations of structures that will hold fish at higher water levels.

Brownlee Reservoir offers a few nice camping areas located along the access road. Otherwise, you can find motel space in Ontario to the south, Richland to the west or the larger community of Baker City located along I-5 to the west. Most maps show the boat launch at Farewell Bend State Park, located alongside Brownlee Reservoir south of Huntington, but for the most part, you can forget about using this launch because it often sits well above the slack-water portion of the reservoir, thus requiring you to run down to the reservoir and then back up the river. The launch downstream from Huntington (Spring Park) is the best site for boaters on the upper (south) half the reservoir, while Woodhead Park, off Idaho SR 71 near the dam, serves better if you want to fish the lower (north) end. Woodhead Park, an Idaho Power facility, is very popular because of its 124 full-hookup RV sites.

Seven-year-old Alex Shewey, the author's nephew, hooked this huge flathead catfish in Brownlee Reservoir.

Appendix I
Warmwater Fisheries In Oregon (By County)

Courtesy Oregon Department of Fish & Wildlife

Baker County

Snake River Reservoirs: Brownlee Reservoir—14,000 acres; Hells Canyon Reservoir—2,300 acres; Oxbow Reservoir—1,400 acres; Largemouth bass, smallmouth bass, black crappie, white crappie, yellow perch, brown bullhead, channel catfish, bluegill, pumpkinseed, flathead catfish.

Haines Pond #1: 1 acre; .25 of a mile north of Haines. Largemouth bass.

Highway 203 Pond: 10 acres; 4 miles north of Baker City at junction of I-84N and Hwy 203. Largemouth bass.

Phillips Reservoir: 2,350 acres; 12 miles southwest of Baker City on Hwy 7. Smallmouth bass, largemouth bass, black crappie.

Thief Valley Reservoir: 700 acres; east of North Powder. Brown bullhead, black crappie, white crappie, largemouth bass, smallmouth bass.

Unity Reservoir: 926 acres; 4 miles north of Unity on Hwy 245. Black crappie, smallmouth bass.

Benton County

Adair Pond: 6 acres; Hwy 99W south of Adair Village at ODFW Regional Office. Largemouth bass, redear sunfish, channel catfish.

Bonner Lake: 3 acres; from Hwy 233 go west to Hoskins. From Hoskins take Summit Road west 1.3 miles. Largemouth bass, brown bullhead.

Willamette River Sloughs: From mouth of Santiam River to Harrisburg. White crappie, bluegill, largemouth bass, brown bullhead, black crappie.

Clackamas County

Roslyn Lake: 135 acres; north of Sandy approximately 3 miles via Ten Eyck Road. Largemouth bass.

Willamette River Sloughs: From Milwaukie to mouth of Pudding River. White crappie, bluegill, largemouth bass, smallmouth bass, brown bullhead, black crappie.

Wilsonville Pond: 6 acres; west of I-5 one mile south of the Wilsonville Rest Area. From Butteville Road take Boones Ferry Road north 0.5 miles. Largemouth bass, bluegill, brown bullhead.

Clatsop County

Blind Slough: 194 acres; north of Knappa Junction or Brownsmead Junction off Hwy 30. Yellow perch, white crappie, largemouth bass, black crappie, yellow bullhead.

Brownsmead Slough: southeast of Brownsmead, 20 miles east of Astoria. Access via Brownsmead Junction off Hwy 30.

Burkes Lake: 6.3 acres; 1 mile west of Warrenton off Ridge Road. Largemouth bass.

Cemetary Lake: 10.3 acres; south of Warrenton at the Astoria Cemetery. Black crappie, bluegill, largemouth bass, warmouth, yellow perch.

Clear Lake: 8 acres; 1 mile northwest of Warrenton. Largemouth bass.

Coffenbury Lake: 50 acres within Fort Stevens State Park, 2 miles west of Warrenton. Yellow perch, brown bullhead.

Crabapple Lake: 22 acres within Fort Stevens State Park, 2 miles west of Warrenton. Largemouth bass, yellow perch.

Creep and Crawl Lake: 5 acres within Fort Stevens State Park, 2 miles west of Warrenton. Bluegill.

Cullaby Lake: 200 acres; 4 miles north of Gearhart and east of Hwy 101. White crappie, black crappie, yellow perch, largemouth bass, brown bullhead.

Gravel Pit: 4 acres; 0.5 miles east of Gearhart. Bluegill.

Grizzley Slough: off Blind Slough north of Knappa. Bluegill, largemouth bass, yellow perch.

Rilea Slough: Camp Rilea (National Guard), 3.5 miles southwest of Warrenton and west of Hwy 101. Yellow perch, white crappie, largemouth bass, bluegill.

Seaside Log Ponds: 7 acres; east of Hwy 101 near Seaside city limits. Yellow perch, black crappie, largemouth bass, brown bullhead.

Slusher Lake: 20 acres at Camp Rilea (National Guard). 3.5 miles southwest of Warrenton and west of Hwy 101. Brown bullhead, yellow perch, largemouth bass.

Smith Lake: 41 acres; 2 miles south of Warrenton and west of Hwy 101. Largemouth bass, yellow perch, bluegill, white crappie, black crappie.

Sunset Lake: 107 acres; 4 miles north of Gearhart and west of Hwy 101. Access via Sunset Beach Road. Yellow perch, brown bullhead, largemouth bass, black crappie.

West Lake: 32 acres; 3 miles north of Gearhart and west of Hwy 101. Brown bullhead, largemouth bass, yellow perch.

Westport Slough: 233 acres; north of Hwy 30, near Westport, 10 miles west of Clatskanie. White crappie, largemouth bass, yellow perch, bluegill.

Wildace Lake: 1 mile southwest of Warrenton off Ridge Road. Largemouth bass, black crappie, bluegill, warmouth bass.

Columbia County

Beaver Slough Complex: northeast of Clatskanie. White crappie, yellow perch, black crappie, largemouth bass.

Clatskanie Slough: north of Clatskanie off Hwy 30. White crappie, yellow bullhead, yellow perch, bluegill, largemouth bass, black crappie.

Columbia River: Mainstem. Walleye, largemouth bass, yellow perch.

Crim's Island Slough: 6 miles northeast of Clatskanie. White crappie, black crappie.

Deer Island Slough: 68 acres; northwest of Columbia City off Hwy 30 at Reichold Chemical. (Access only at south end). White crappie, brown bullhead, yellow bullhead, largemouth bass, bluegill, yellow perch.

Dibblee's Slough: 18 acres; Dibblee Point northwest of Rainer. White crappie, black crappie, brown bullhead, yellow bullhead, largemouth bass.

Dike Slough: access by boat from Wallace Slough on the Columbia River north of Clatskanie. Largemouth bass, black crappie, white crappie.

Goat Island Slough: 55 acres; northwest of Columbia City off Hwy 30 at Reichold Chemical. (Access at south end only). White crappie, brown bullhead, yellow bullhead, largemouth bass, bluegill, yellow perch.

Magruder Slough: off Westport Slough. Located north of Hwy 30, 3 miles east of Westport. Yellow bullhead, bluegill, black crappie.

Mayger Slough: 3 miles northwest of Downing, east of Crim's Island. White crappie, black crappie.

Prescott Slough: 9 acres, along Hwy 30 at Prescott Junction. West of Trojan Nuclear Power Plant. White crappie, largemouth bass, brown bullhead, yellow perch, bluegill, black crappie, warmouth, yellow bullhead.

Recreation Lake: 27 acres; along Hwy 30 at Trojan Nuclear Power Plant. White crappie, bluegill, brown bullhead, yellow perch.

Reichold Chemical Discharge Canal: 1 acre; (Access and species same as Deer Island Slough).

Rinearson Slough: north of Hwy 30, northwest of Rainer. White crappie, largemouth bass, yellow bullhead, bluegill.

Sandy Island Slough: north of Goble. Black crappie.

Santosh Slough: off Multnomah Channel north of Scappoose, approximately 2.7 miles beyond Columbia County Airport via Dike Road off Hwy 30. Black crappie, white crappie, yellow perch, largemouth bass, brown bullhead.

Sauvie Island lakes and sloughs: 2,500 acres; northwest of Portland and east of Hwy 30. White crappie, black crappie, largemouth bass, bluegill, brown bullhead, yellow perch.

Scappoose Bay: 600 acres; south end of the city of St. Helens, off Multnomah Channel. Brown bullhead, white crappie, black crappie, yellow perch, largemouth bass.

Vernonia Lake: 45 acres; southeast part of Vernonia off Hwy 47. Bluegill, yellow perch, largemouth bass.

Westport Slough: 233 acres; north of Hwy 30 near Westport, 10 miles west of Clatskanie. White crappie, largemouth bass, yellow perch, bluegill.

Coos County

Beale Lake: 12 acres; south of Lakeside and west of Hwy 101. Bluegill, yellow perch, largemouth bass, warmouth.

Bluebill Lake: 35 acres; within National Dunes Recreation Area north of North Bend. Largemouth bass. However, the population has likely declined because the lake dried up several times in the 1990s.

Bradley Lake: 14 acres; 3 miles south of Bandon. Brown bullhead.

Coquille River: the tidal portion from Riverton upstream to Myrtle Point. Brown bullhead, largemouth bass, striped bass.

Eel Lake: 350 acres; 13 miles north of Coos Bay on Hwy 101, 1 mile north of Lakeside. Largemouth bass, black crappie.

Empire Lakes (Upper & Lower): 45 acres; within Empire District of Coos Bay. Largemouth bass, yellow perch, brown bullhead, bluegill, black crappie.

Horsfall Lake: 250 acres; within National Dunes Recreation Area, north of North Bend. Yellow perch, largemouth bass, brown bullhead.

Johnson Mill Pond: 2 miles south of Coquille. Largemouth bass.

Jordan Lake: 10 acres; within National Dunes Recreation Area north of North Bend. Yellow perch, Largemouth bass, brown bullhead.

Powers Pond: 30 acres; at Powers. Brown bullhead, largemouth bass, crappie.

Rock Creek Pond: 5 acres; 3 miles east of Remote on Hwy 42. Brown bullhead, largemouth bass, bluegill.

Saunders Lake: 57 acres; 8 miles north of North Bend. Bluegill, largemouth bass, yellow perch, warmouth.

Snag Lake: 30 acres; west of Hauser. Largemouth bass, yellow perch, brown bullhead.

Tenmile Lakes (North & South): 1,700 acres; at Lakeside, 12 miles north of Coos Bay. Bluegill, brown bullhead, largemouth bass, striped bass/white bass hybrids, black crappie, yellow perch.

Crook County

Ochoco Ponds: 3 acres; 5 miles east of Prineville on Hwy 26. Just below Ochoco Dam. Largemouth bass, bluegill.

Prineville Reservoir: 3,000 acres; 17 miles south of Prineville on Hwy 27 to Bowman Dam or Juniper Canyon Road to the State Park. Largemouth bass, smallmouth bass, brown bullhead.

Curry County

Floras Lake: 260 acres; near Langlois, west of Hwy 101. Largemouth bass.

Garrison Lake: 160 acres; in Port Orford, west of Hwy 101. Largemouth bass, yellow perch.

Libby Pond: 10 acres; 7 miles up the Rogue River from Hwy 101. Brown bullhead.

Deschutes County

Crane Prairie Reservoir: 4,960 acres; southwest of Bend 46 miles via Century Drive (Hwy 46). Largemouth bass.

Fireman's Pond: 1 acre; .25 of a mile east of Hwy 97, south end of Redmond city limits. Restricted by city of Redmond to kids and handicapped. Largemouth bass, bluegill, brown bullhead.

Reynolds Pond: 5 acres; 1.25 miles southeast of Alfalfa off Dodd's Road. Largemouth bass, redear sunfish.

Douglas County

Ben Irving Reservoir (Berry Creek Reservoir): south from Roseburg on I-5 to Hwy 42, to Tenmile CR 141—5 miles to reservoir. Largemouth bass, black crappie.

Canyonville Pond: 10 acres; 1 mile east of Canyonville. Black crappie, largemouth bass, brown bullhead.

Cooper Creek Reservoir: 160 acres; 2 miles east of Sutherlin. Black crappie, largemouth bass, bluegill.

Elbow Lake: 12 acres; north of Reedsport, west of Hwy 101. Largemouth bass, bluegill, yellow perch.

Fords Mill Pond: 100 acres; on Hwy 138, 1 mile west of its junction with Hwy 99. Bullhead catfish, bluegill, yellow perch, black crappie, largemouth bass.

Galesville Reservoir: 630 acres; 10 miles east of I-5 at Azalea exit. Largemouth bass, bluegill, smallmouth bass, black crappie, brown bullhead, pumpkinseed.

Loon Lake: 269 acres; east of Reedsport, south of Hwy 38, up Mill Creek. Largemouth bass, brown bullhead, white crappie.

Marie Lake: 18 acres; 3 miles south of Reedsport on Hwy 101. Yellow perch, largemouth bass.

Plat I Reservoir: 140 acres; east of Sutherlin on Plat I Road. Largemouth bass, bluegill, black crappie, bullhead catfish.

Stewart Park Pond: 2 acres; within Stewart Park, Roseburg. Black crappie, largemouth bass.

Tahkenitch Lake: 1,800 acres; north of Reedsport, east of Hwy 101. Largemouth bass, bluegill, yellow perch, black crappie, brown bullhead, warmouth.

Threemile Lake: 67 acres; north of Reedsport, 3 miles west of Hwy 101. Yellow perch.

Gilliam County

John Day Pool: (See Sherman County)

John Day River: from Kimberly to mouth via Hwy 19, Hwy 206 and I-84. Smallmouth bass, channel catfish. From Tumwater to mouth: Smallmouth bass, white crappie, brown bullhead, channel catfish.

Willow Creek Arm (John Day Pool): 9 miles east of Arlington. Smallmouth bass, white crappie, bluegill, bullhead catfish, yellow perch, pumpkinseed.

Grant County

Carpenter Pond: 1 acre; 1 mile west of John Day via Hwy 26. Largemouth bass, bluegill.

Harney County

Cottonwood Creek Reservoir: 90 acres; 40 miles east of Burns and 10 miles north of Hwy 20. Largemouth bass, white crappie.

Diamond Crater Lake: 2 acres; Malheur Refuge, northeast of Diamond. Largemouth bass. (Winterkills periodically).

Krumbo Reservoir: 200 acres; 50 miles south of Burns on Malheur Refuge. Largemouth bass, white crappie.

Malheur River: 30 miles of river above Warm Springs Reservoir; 40 miles east of Burns near Hwy 20. Smallmouth bass.

Moon Reservoir: 619 acres; 5 miles southeast of Riley, or 25 miles southwest of Burns. Largemouth bass, white crappie, yellow perch.

Warm Springs Reservoir: 4,420 acres; south of Drewsey. Largemouth bass, smallmouth bass, bluegill, brown bullhead, yellow perch, channel catfish.

Hood River County

Bonneville Pool: 20,400 acres; on Columbia River behind Bonneville Dam (Hood River and Wasco Counties). Smallmouth bass, largemouth bass, black crappie, white crappie, bluegill, brown bullhead, yellow perch, pumpkinseed, sturgeon, walleye.

Button Pond, Government Cove, Hood River Pond No. 1, Hood River Pond No. 2, Iris Lake, Kolberg Lake, Lindsey Pond, Line Pond, Viento Lake, Wyeth Lake: total 174 acres; adjacent to Hwy 30 (84N). Largemouth bass, black crappie, bluegill, brown bullhead, white crappie, yellow perch, pumpkinseed.

Jackson County

Agate Reservoir: 239 acres; east of White City off Hwy 140. Largemouth bass, brown bullhead, black crappie, bluegill.

Applegate Reservoir: 988 acres; south of Ruch off Applegate River Road. Largemouth bass, smallmouth bass, black crappie, brown bullhead.

Emigrant Reservoir: 878 acres; southeast of Ashland off Hwy 66. Largemouth bass, smallmouth bass, brown bullhead, bluegill, black crappie.

Gold Ray Forebay: 80 acres; northwest of Central Point off Hwy 99. Largemouth bass, brown bullhead, white crappie, black crappie, bluegill.

Hoover Ponds: 20 acres; east of White City off Hwy 140. Largemouth bass, black crappie, bluegill, brown bullhead.

Howard Prairie Reservoir: 2,070 acres; east of Ashland off Dead Indian Road. Brown bullhead, (Primarily a trout fishery).

Hyatt Lake: 957 acres; east of Ashland off Hwy 66. Largemouth bass.

Jackson County Expo. Ponds: 20 acres; near Central Point off I-5. Largemouth bass, bluegill, black crappie, brown bullhead.

Keene Creek Reservoir: 10 acres; east of Ashland off Hwy 66. Pumpkinseed, brown bullhead.

Kenneth Denman Wildlife Management Area Ponds: 152 acres; near White City off Agate Road. Largemouth bass, black crappie, brown bullhead, bluegill.

Little Hyatt Lake: 13 acres; east of Ashland off Hwy 66. Brown bullhead, black crappie.

Lost Creek Reservoir: 3,428 acres; northeast of Shady Cove off Hwy 62. Largemouth bass, smallmouth bass, brown bullhead, black crappie.

Medco Pond: 25 acres; south of Prospect off the Prospect - Butte Falls Highway. Largemouth bass, black crappie.

Squaw Lakes: 60 acres; south of Ruch off Applegate River Road. Brown bullhead, black crappie, bluegill, largemouth bass.

Willow Lake: 345 acres; southeast of Butte Falls off FR 30. Largemouth bass, black crappie.

Jefferson County

Haystack Reservoir: 240 acres; 8 miles south of Madras and 2 miles east of Hwy 97. Black crappie, largemouth bass, smallmouth bass, bluegill, brown bullhead.

Lake Billy Chinook (Round Butte Reservoir): 4,000 acres; 9 miles southwest of Madras on the Deschutes River. Largemouth bass, smallmouth bass. (Primarily a kokanee and trout fishery).

Lake Simtustus (Pelton Reservoir): 540 acres; 7 miles west of Madras on the Deschutes River. Largemouth bass. (Primarily a trout fishery).

Josephine County

Flanagan Slough: 14 acres; west of Grants Pass off Riverbanks Road. Brown bullhead, largemouth bass.

Josephine County Sportsman's Park Pond: 5 acres; north of Merlin off Hwy 99. Largemouth bass, black crappie, bluegill, brown bullhead.

Lake Selmac: 148 acres; east of Selma off Deer Creek Road.

Largemouth bass, bluegill, brown bullhead, black crappie.

Klamath County

Aspen Lake: 500 acres; west of Klamath Falls. Brown bullhead.

Bumphead Reservoir: 50 acres; southeast of Lorella (T40S, R14E, S31) on rough dirt road. White crappie, largemouth bass.

Campbell Reservoir: 200 acres; 7 miles northeast of Bly off Road 34. Largemouth bass. (Public access on east end of reservoir).

Devil Lake: 85 acres; 10 miles southeast of Bly on Fishhole Creek Road. Yellow perch, brown bullhead, largemouth bass.

Gerber Reservoir: 3,830 acres; 50 miles east of Klamath Falls, 12 miles northeast of Lorella off Gerber Road. White crappie, black crappie, yellow perch, largemouth bass, brown bullhead, pumpkinseed.

J.C. Boyle Reservoir: 450 acres; 15 miles west of Klamath Falls on Hwy 66. White crappie, brown bullhead, largemouth bass, Sacramento perch, pumpkinseed.

Klamath Lake: 80,000 acres; Klamath Falls. Yellow perch, brown bullhead. Fishery mainly in Rocky Point area, north of Hwy 140.

Lake of the Woods: 1,113 acres; 32 miles northwest of Klamath Falls off Hwy 140. Largemouth bass, brown bullhead.

Malone Reservoir: 20 acres; on Lost river at south end of Langell Valley near the state line, 20 miles southeast of Bonanza. White crappie, Sacramento perch, brown bullhead, largemouth bass.

Obenchain Reservoir: 40 acres; 10 miles northeast of Bly off Road 335. Largemouth bass, brown bullhead.

Round Valley Reservoir: 150 acres; 23 miles south of Bly on Round Valley Road. Pumpkinseed, yellow perch, largemouth bass, brown bullhead.

Upper Midway Reservoir: 40 acres; 22 miles south of Bly, 3 miles east of CCC Road. Largemouth bass.

Willow Valley Reservoir: 200 acres; 15 miles southeast of Lorella, via East Langell Valley Road and Willow Valley Road. White crappie, largemouth bass, black crappie, bluegill.

Wilson Reservoir: 200 acres; on Lost River 8 miles southeast of Klamath Falls on Crystal Springs Road. Yellow perch, Sacramento perch, black crappie, white crappie, largemouth bass, brown bullhead, pumkinseed sunfish.

Lake County

Ana Reservoir: 58 acres; 75 miles northwest of Lakeview near Summer Lake. White-striped hybrid bass.

Big Swamp Lake: 34 acres; west of Lakeview via Hwy 140 and south of Quartz Mountain. Brown bullhead.

Cottonwood Reservoir: 900 acres; 12 miles northwest of Lakeview, north of Hwy 140. Smallmouth bass.

Crump Lake: 3,200 acres; 35 miles east of Lakeview via Hwy 140 near Adel. Brown bullhead, white crappie, largemouth bass, black crappie.

Dog Lake: 300 acres; 20 miles southwest of Lakeview, south of Hwy 140. Largemouth bass, yellow perch, white crappie, black crappie, bluegill, pumpkinseed, brown bullhead.

Drews Reservoir: 1,978 acres; 15 miles west of Lakeview, south of Hwy 140. Yellow perch, white crappie, black crappie, pumpkinseed, channel catfish, brown bullhead.

Hart Lake: 8,000 acres; 35 miles east of Lakeview, via Hwy 140 near Plush. Brown bullhead, white crappie, black crappie, largemouth bass.

Priday Reservoir: 130 acres; 30 miles east of Lakeview, via Hwy 140 near Adel. White crappie.

Taft Miller Reservoir: 115 acres; 20 miles northeast of Hart Mountain Antelope Refuge Headquarters. White crappie, largemouth bass.

Lane County – Coastal

Carter Lake: 28 acres; south of Florence, west of Hwy 101. Largemouth bass, yellow perch.

Clear Lake: 149 acres; north of Florence, east of Hwy 101. Largemouth bass, yellow perch.

Cleawox Lake: 82 acres; south of Florence, west of Hwy 101 at Honeyman State Park. Largemouth bass, yellow perch, black crappie, brown bullhead, bluegill.

Collard Lake: 31 acres; north of Florence, east of Hwy 101. Largemouth bass, yellow perch, bluegill, brown bullhead.

Mercer Lake: 341 acres; north of Florence, east of Hwy 101. Yellow Perch, largemouth bass, black crappie, brown bullhead.

Munsel Lake: 93 acres; north of Florence, east of Hwy 101. Yellow perch, largemouth bass, bluegill, brown bullhead.

Siltcoos Lake: 3,500 acres; south of Florence, east of Hwy 101. Black crappie, brown bullhead, yellow perch, bluegill, largemouth bass.

Sutton Lake: 101 acres; north of Florence, east of Hwy 101. Yellow perch, largemouth bass, brown bullhead, bluegill.

Woahink Lake: 787 acres; south of Florence, east of Hwy 101 at Honeyman State Park. Yellow perch, largemouth bass, brown bullhead, bluegill.

Lane County – Inland

Ayers Pond: 33 acres; Junction of Ayers Road and North Delta Highway in Eugene. White crappie, bluegill, largemouth bass.

Cottage Grove Ponds (6): 15 acres; east of Cottage Grove on Row River Road near truck scales. Largemouth bass, bluegill, brown bullhead.

Cottage Grove Reservoir: 1,150 acres; 6 miles south of Cottage Grove on London Road. Largemouth bass, brown bullhead.

Creswell Ponds (4): 20 acres; east side of I-5 freeway at Creswell. Largemouth bass, bluegill, brown bullhead.

Delta Ponds: 200 acres; along Delta Highway in Eugene near Valley River Center. Bluegill, largemouth bass, white crappie, brown bullhead.

Dexter Reservoir: 1,000 acres; at Lowell, east of Eugene on Hwy 58. Largemouth bass, brown bullhead, white crappie.

Dorena Reservoir: 1,840 acres; 7 miles east of Cottage Grove on Row River Road. Largemouth bass, brown bullhead.

Eugene Rest Area and Junction City Ponds (7): 13 acres; between Junction City and Eugene, west side of Hwy 99W. Largemouth bass, bluegill, brown bullhead.

Fern Ridge Ponds: 5 acres; just below Fern Ridge Dam west of Eugene. White crappie, largemouth bass, brown bullhead.

Fern Ridge Reservoir: 9,000 acres; adjacent to Hwy 126, 10 miles west of Eugene. White crappie, brown bullhead, largemouth bass, bluegill.

Hills Creek Reservoir: 2,735 acres; 5 miles southeast of Oakridge on Middle Fork Willamette River. Brown bullhead, white crappie, largemouth bass.

Long Tom River: from Fern Ridge Dam 25 miles to Willamette River. White crappie, largemouth bass, brown bullhead.

Lookout Point Reservoir: 4,200 acres; north side of Hwy 58 about 20 miles southeast of Eugene. Largemouth bass, white crappie, brown bullhead.

Triangle Lake: 293 acres; 40 miles east of Florence on Hwy 36. Largemouth bass, bluegill, yellow perch, brown bullhead, pumpkinseed.

Willamette River sloughs: between Eugene and Corvallis (Lane, Linn, and Benton Counties). Largemouth bass, white crappie, brown bullhead, black crappie, bluegill, warmouth, channel catfish.

Lincoln County

Big Creek Reservoir No.1: 20 acres; on Big Creek Road northeast of Newport. Brown bullhead.

Big Creek Reservoir No.2: 17 acres; on Big Creek Road northeast of Newport. Brown bullhead, largemouth bass.

Devils Lake: 680 acres; at Lincoln City on Hwy 101. Largemouth bass, brown bullhead, yellow perch, channel catfish, black crappie, white crappie, bluegill.

Eckman Lake: 45 acres; 3 miles east of Waldport on Hwy 34. Brown bullhead, largemouth bass.

Olalla Reservoir: 100 acres; 4 miles north of Toledo. Brown bullhead, largemouth bass, bluegill.

Linn County

Bond Butte Pond: 35 acres; east of I-5 Freeway at Bond

Butte overpass, 15 miles south of Albany. Channel catfish, white crappie, largemouth bass.

Foster Reservoir: 1,200 acres; near Foster. Largemouth bass, smallmouth bass, bluegill.

Freeway Lakes: 10 acres; 3 miles south of Albany. White crappie, bluegill, largemouth bass, brown bullhead.

Green Peter Reservoir: 10 miles east of Sweet Home. Largemouth bass.

Jefferson Junction Borrow Pit: 5 acres; north of Albany, west of Hwy 99. Largemouth bass, brown bullhead, bluegill.

Timber-Linn: 11 acres; east edge of Albany. White crappie, bluegill, brown bullhead, largemouth bass.

Waverly Lake: 5 acres; in Albany (juveniles only). White crappie, bluegill, largemouth bass, brown bullhead.

Willamette River Sloughs: from mouth of Long Tom River to mouth of the Santiam River. White Crappie, bluegill, largemouth bass, brown bullhead, black crappie.

Malheur County

Beckers Pond: 12 acres; Ontario City Park. Bluegill, largemouth bass, channel catfish.

Bully Creek Reservoir: 1,000 acres; 9 miles northwest of Vale. White crappie, largemouth bass, smallmouth bass, channel catfish, yellow perch, brown bullhead.

Cow Lakes: 1,000 acres; 20 miles northwest of Jordan Valley. White Crappie, largemouth bass, brown bullhead.

Dunaway Pond: 1 acre; south of Nyssa. Bluegill, largemouth bass, black bullhead.

Granite Creek Reservoir: 15 acres; southeast of Riverside. Largemouth bass, bluegill. (Private - permission required).

Malheur River: lower 10 miles; near Ontario. Channel catfish.

Malheur River South Fork: lower 10 miles; near Riverside. Smallmouth bass.

Owyhee Reservoir: 12,740 acres; 20 miles southwest of Adrian. Largemouth bass, smallmouth bass, black crappie, channel catfish, yellow perch, brown bullhead.

Owyhee River: lower 15 miles; 10 miles south of Nyssa. Channel catfish.

Owyhee River: 116 miles; from Owyhee Reservoir upstream to the Idaho State Line. Smallmouth bass, channel catfish.

Snake River: 76 miles; from Idaho State Line downstream to Brownlee Reservoir. Smallmouth bass, channel catfish, flathead catfish.

Marion County

Bluegill Lake: 7 acres; Cascade Gateway Park in Salem off Hwy 22. Largemouth bass, bluegill, crappie.

Brown-Minto Island Complex: south of Salem on the Willamette River. (Borrow pits and sloughs). Largemouth bass, white crappie, bluegill, brown bullhead.

Goose Lake: 9 acres; 7 miles north of Salem. White crappie, largemouth bass.

Horseshoe Lake: 45 acres; west of St. Paul (fee charged). Largemouth bass, bluegill, white crappie, brown bullhead, channel catfish.

Mission Lake: 40 acres; Willamette Mission Street Park, 2 miles east of Wheatland ferry landing. White crappie, bluegill, largemouth bass, black crappie.

Santiam River: from confluence with Willamette River upstream to Jefferson. Largemouth bass, smallmouth bass.

St. Louis Ponds (7): 54 acres; 2 miles west of Gervais on west side of freeway (no boats - special regulations). Black crappie, white crappie, bluegill, channel catfish, largemouth bass, redear sunfish, green sunfish.

Skookum Lake: 20 acres; 3 miles south of Newberg (fee charged). Bluegill, largemouth bass, white crappie, brown bullhead.

Walling Pond: 8 acres; 16th and McGilchrist Streets in Salem. Largemouth bass.

Walter Wirth Lake: 20 acres; Cascade Gateway Park in Salem. Largemouth bass, bluegill, brown bullhead, white crappie.

Willamette River Sloughs: from Wilsonville to mouth of Santiam River. White crappie, bluegill, largemouth bass, brown bullhead, black crappie.

Woodburn Pond: 14 acres; east of I-5 from Woodburn north on Boones Ferry Road to Crosby Road then north on Edwin Road to pond. Largemouth bass, bluegill, black crappie, white crappie, channel catfish.

Morrow County

Boardman Pond: 1 acre; .5 of a mile west of Boardman, south of I-84N (exit 164). Largemouth bass, white crappie, bluegill.

John Day Pool (Lake Umatilla) includes John Day Arm and Willow Creek Arm: 52,000 acres; on Columbia River behind John Day Dam. Smallmouth bass, channel catfish, largemouth bass, white crappie, black crappie, brown bullhead, walleye, bluegill, pumpkinseed, sturgeon, yellow perch.

McCormack Slough: 500 acres; 5 miles northeast of Boardman. Highway 730 to milepost 171.9. Turn north on Patterson Ferry Road, go 1.9 miles. Turn west on gravel road (0.1 of a mile past Umatilla National Wildlife Refuge Information Center and parking area). Largemouth bass, brown bullhead, smallmouth bass, channel catfish.

Messner Pond: 14 acres; I-84N exit 165, north 0.5 of a mile (1 mile east of Boardman). Largemouth bass, white crappie.

Tatone Pond: 1 acre; 2 miles west of Boardman between I-84N and Columbia River. I-84N exit 159 (Tower Road Exit). Turn north to railroad tracks. Drive east along tracks to parking lot. Walk 0.2 of a mile north to Tatone Pond. Brown bullhead.

Willow Creek Reservoir: 88 acres; 1 mile southeast of Heppner on Western Route Road. Largemouth bass, black crappie, white crappie, smallmouth bass, bluegill, pumpkinseed.

Multnomah County

Benson Lake: 40 acres; Multnomah Falls. White crappie, largemouth bass, brown bullhead.

Blue Lake: 64 acres; 3 miles northwest of Troutdale. Largemouth bass, brown bullhead, black crappie, bluegill.

Bybee Lake: 275 acres; North Portland Road, Portland. White crappie, brown bullhead, largemouth bass, bluegill, black crappie, yellow perch.

Columbia River: mainstem. Largemouth bass, walleye, yellow perch.

Columbia Slough: in north Portland between Marine Drive on north and Hwy 30 on south, numerous road crossings. Black crappie, white crappie, brown bullhead, largemouth bass, yellow perch.

Delta Park Ponds: 100 acres; North Portland in West Delta Park. Brown bullhead, bluegill, largemouth bass.

Gary Island Slough: access by boat from Columbia River just east of mouth of Sandy River. Largemouth bass, yellow perch.

Government Island Slough: access by boat from Columbia River, north of Portland International Airport. Yellow perch, white crappie, black crappie, brown bullhead, yellow bullhead, bluegill.

Mirror Pond: 64 acres; Rooster Rock State Park south of Hwy 30. White crappie, brown bullhead, largemouth bass, bluegill.

Oregon Slough: (North Portland Harbor) south of Hayden Island. Largemouth bass, yellow perch.

Rooster Rock Slough: 5 acres; north of I-84N at Rooster Rock State Park. Brown bullhead, white crappie, black crappie, largemouth bass, yellow perch.

Smith Lake: 60 acres; North Portland Road, Portland. Brown bullhead, white crappie, black crappie, bluegill, largemouth bass.

Willamette River Sloughs: from Milwaukie to mouth of Willamette River. White crappie, bluegill, largemouth bass, brown bullhead, black crappie, channel catfish.

Polk County

Grossman Pond: 2 acres; Independence. From Monmouth Street take Talmadge Road south 0.6 of a mile. Largemouth bass, bluegill.

Mercer Reservoir: 60 acres; 10 miles west of Dallas via Ellendale Road and Boise Cascade logging road. Largemouth bass. (City of Dallas regulated).

Willamette River Sloughs: from Wheatland Ferry to mouth of Santiam River. White crappie, bluegill, largemouth bass, brown bullhead, black crappie.

Willamina Pond: 5 acres; in Huddleston Park, Willamina. Black crappie, brown bullhead, largemouth bass, yellow perch.

Sherman County

Bibby Reservoir: 16 acres; 5 miles west of Kent on Buckhollow Creek. Largemouth bass.

John Day Pool: 54,000 acres; on Columbia River behind John Day Dam (Sherman, Gilliam, Morrow, Umatilla Counties). Smallmouth bass, largemouth bass, white crappie, black crappie, bluegill, channel catfish, brown bullhead, sturgeon, walleye.

John Day River: river mile 95 to mouth. Smallmouth bass, channel catfish.

Rufus Slough and East Deschutes River Pond: 27.5 acres total; immediately east of mouth of Deschutes River adjacent to Interstate 84N. Largemouth bass, black crappie, bluegill, brown bullhead, white crappie, yellow perch, pumpkinseed, walleye, channel catfish.

The Dalles Pool: 10,500 acres; on Columbia River behind the Dalles Dam (Sherman and Wasco Counties). Smallmouth bass, largemouth bass, black crappie, white crappie, walleye, sturgeon, brown bullhead, channel catfish, yellow perch, pumpkinseed.

Tillamook County

Cape Meares Lake: 65 acres; 7 miles west and north of Tillamook along Bay Ocean Road. Largemouth bass.

Crescent Lake: 7 acres; east of Manhatten Beach, 1 mile north of Rockaway. Largemouth bass.

Hebo Lake: 2.2 acres; 5 miles east of Hebo. Brown bullhead.

Lake Lytle: 70 acres; north of Rockaway. Largemouth bass, black crappie.

Marie Lake: 0.6 acres; Twin Rocks east of Hwy 101. (Public access limited). Largemouth bass.

Smith Lake: 40 acres; north of Garabaldi, west of Hwy 101. Largemouth bass. (Access limited to portion adjacent to Hwy 101).

Spring Lake: 11 acres; north of Garabaldi, east of Hwy 101. (Access limited to portion adjacent to Hwy 101). Largemouth bass, brown bullhead, black crappie, bluegill, pumpkinseed.

Town Lake: 9 acres; 2 miles north of Woods. Largemouth bass, black crappie.

Umatilla County

Barth Quarry Pond: 1 acre; I-84N exit 193. Go north 50 yards. Turn east on Whitmore Road and go 1.6 miles, then north 0.3 of a mile on Nolin Market Road. Largemouth bass, white crappie.

Cold Springs Reservoir: 1,550 acres (200 acres at low pool) 6 miles east of Hermiston. Hwy 207 to milepost 3.5. Turn east on E. Punkin Center Rd. Go 3 miles to Cold Springs National Wildlife Refuge. (No gas powered motorboats). Largemouth bass, brown bullhead, bluegill, white crappie.

Hat Rock Pond: 5.9 acres; 9 miles east of Umatilla. Hwy 730 to milepost 192.1. Turn north into park, follow the signs. Largemouth bass, smallmouth bass.

McKay Reservoir: 1,200 acres; (less than 40 acres at low pool), 6 miles south of Pendleton on Hwy 395. Open March 1 to September 30. Largemouth bass, black crappie, yellow perch, brown bullhead, bluegill, channel catfish.

McNary Channel Ponds: 25 acres; 1 mile west of McNary Dam on Columbia River. Hwy 730 to milepost 184.1. Turn north on Brownell Blvd (100 yards west of I-82). Cross tracks, go east 0.1 of a mile to McNary Wildlife Nature Area. Turn north to ponds and river. Largemouth bass, smallmouth bass, white crappie, bluegill, channel catfish.

McNary Pool (Lake Wallula): 11,640 acres; on Columbia River above McNary Dam. Smallmouth bass, largemouth bass, white crappie, black crappie, bluegill, brown bullhead, yellow perch, channel catfish, sturgeon, walleye.

Union County

Catherine Creek Slough: 10 acres; east of LaGrande to Elgin. Brown bullhead, largemouth bass, white crappie, yellow perch, channel catfish, warmouth, bluegill, smallmouth bass.

Grande Ronde River: near Elgin. Largemouth bass, brown bullhead, smallmouth bass, white crappie, bluegill, yellow perch.

Grays Slough: 10 acres; lower Cove Road, 3 miles east of Conley. Black crappie, white crappie, largemouth bass, brown bullhead.

Morgan Lake: 65 acres; 3 miles southwest of LaGrande. Black crappie, brown bullhead.

Roulet Pond: 1 acre; east of Elgin. Brown bullhead.

Wallowa County

Kinney Reservoir: 20 acres; southeast of Joseph. Brown bullhead.

Wasco County

Bikini Pond, Cliff Lake, Deschutes Pond No. 1, Deschutes Pond No. 2, Lone Pine Pond, Long Pond, McClures Lake, Miller Pond, Mosier Pond, One-mile Lake, Salisbury Slough, Sand Lake, Sand Dune Lake, Tooley Lake, Tunnel Lake, West Deschutes River Pond, Wilson Lake: total 234 acres; adjacent to I-84N. Largemouth bass,

black crappie, bluegill, brown bullhead, white crappie, yellow perch, pumpkinseed, walleye.

Cody Ponds No's. 1, 2, 3, 4: 2 to 6 acres; near Rock Creek Reservoir, 6 miles west of Wamic. Largemouth bass, bluegill.

Taylor Lake: 35 acres; 2.5 miles northwest of The Dalles between I-84N and the Columbia River. Largemouth bass, black crappie, channel catfish.

Washington County

Dormans Pond: 8 acres; junction of Gales Creek Road and Hwy 6. Black crappie, brown bullhead, bluegill, warmouth, largemouth bass.

Henry Hagg Lake: 1,110 acres; west of Hwy 47 about 5 miles south of Forest Grove. Smallmouth bass, yellow perch, largemouth bass, brown bullhead, yellow bullhead.

Tualatin River: from Scholls to mouth. Largemouth bass, bluegill, white crappie, channel catfish, brown bullhead.

Wheeler County

John Day River: from Kimberly to river mile 97 off Hwy 19. Smallmouth bass, channel catfish.

Searcy Pond: 10 acres; 1 mile south of Kinzua via FR 21. Yellow perch, brown bullhead.

Wineland Lake: 17 acres; 18 miles southeast of Fossil via FR 21. Largemouth bass, bluegill, black crappie.

Yamhill County

South Yamhill River: boat ramps: Kiwanis Park, McMinnville, and Monroe Landing west of Whiteson. Largemouth bass, white crappie, bluegill, brown bullhead.

Willamette River Sloughs: from Newberg to Wheatland Ferry. White crappie, bluegill, largemouth bass, brown bullhead, black crappie, channel catfish.

Withy Lake: 10 acres; 3 miles west of Amity on Amity Bellevue Road. Largemouth bass, bluegill, bullhead.

Yamhill River: from Lafayette Locks to mouth. Boat ramp at Dayton. White crappie, bluegill, largemouth bass, brown bullhead

Appendix II

Northwest Forest Pass

List of vendors at:
http://www.fs.fed.us/r6/feedemo/vendors.shtml
Available at any U.S. Forest Service Office
Order by phone at: 1-800-270-7504
Order online at: www.naturenw.org

Columbia River Gorge

Northwest Forest Pass Required Sites
Trailheads
Bonneville
Bridge of the Gods
Dog Mountain
Eagle Creek
Herman Creek
Larch Mountain
Sams Walker
Wahclella Falls
Wyeth

Picnic Areas
Eagle Creek
Larch Mountain
St. Cloud

Deschutes National Forest

Northwest Forest Pass Required Sites
Trailheads
Aspen
Big Eddy
Black Butte
Booth Lake
Broken Top
Cabot Lake
Crane Prairie
Devils Lake
Dillon Falls
Elk Lake
Green Lakes/Soda Creek
Head of Jack Creek
Jack Lake
Lava Camp
Lava Island
Little Three Creek Lake
Lucky Lake

Meadow/Meadow Climbing
Osprey Point
Pole Creek
Sisters-Mirror Lake
Six Lakes
Skyliner
Slough
Sparks Lake
Tam McArthur Rim
Todd Creek (Horse Camp Trailhead)
Todd Lake
Tumalo Falls
Wickiup Plains
Winopee Lake

Picnic Areas
Beach
Besson
Crane Prairie
Cultus Lake
Dillon Falls
Meadow/Meadow Climbin
Mile Camp Day Use
North Wickiup
Osprey Point
Quinn River
Rock Creek
Scout Lake
Slough
South Twin Lake
Sunset View
Suttle Lake Water Ski
Tumalo Falls
Interpretive Sites
Brown's Mountain Crossing
Osprey Point
Tumalo Falls
Boat Launches
Aspen
Besson
Big Eddy
Blue Bay
Brown's Mountain
Crane Prairie
Cultus Lake
Dillon Falls
Hosmer Lake
Lava Island

Link Creek
North Wickiup
Quinn River
Rock Creek
Slough
South Shore
South Twin Lake
Sparks Lake
Suttle Lake Water Ski

Mt. Hood National Forest

Northwest Forest Pass Required Sites
Trailheads
Badger Creek
Bagby Hot Springs
Barlow Pass PCT
Billy Bob Snow Park
Bottle Prairie
Burnt Lake North
Burnt Lake South/West ZZ
Cast Creek/Horseshoe/Sandy River at Riley
Cloud Cap
Crosstown/Glacier View
Dog River
Douglas Lower
Douglas Upper
East Fork at Robinhood
Elk Meadows/Clark Creek
Fish Creek
Frenches Dome
Frog Lake PCT
Hidden Lake
High Prairie
Indian Henry
Knebal Springs
Little Zigzag Falls
Lolo PCT
Lower Dry Fir
Mazama
McCubbins
McCubbins Overflow
McGee Creek
Mirror Lake
Old Salmon River - All Sites
Old 1916/Headwaters/PCT on Rd 42
Paradise Park
Pinnacle Ridge
Pioneer Bridle at Tollgate
Pollali
Ramona Falls-Sandy River
Salmon Butte
Salmon River West
Shell Rock Lake
Surveyors Ridge North

Surveyors Ridge South
Tamanawas
Tilly Jane
Top Spur
Umbrella Falls
Underhill Site
Vista Ridge
Whatum Lake
Zigzag Mtn/Rd 19
Picnic Areas
Eight Mile
Frog Lake
McCubbins Gulch
Rock Creek
Trillium Lake

Rogue River National Forest

Northwest Forest Pass Required Sites
Trailheads
Big Pine Interpretive
Chetco Divide/Vulcan Pk
Francis Shrader Old Growth
French Gulch
High Lakes*
Limpy Botanical
Myrtle Tree
Oregon Redwoods
Redwood Nature
Snow Camp
Tincup
Upper Chetco
Vulcan Lake/Johnson Butte
Whiskey Spring Interpretive*
*Concessionaire-operated site. The Northwest Forest Pass
 is honored, but not required.
Picnic Areas
Big Pine
Fish Lake*
Sam Brown
Seattle Bar
*Concessionaire-operated site. The Northwest Forest Pass
is honored, but not required

Siuslaw National Forest

Northwest Forest Pass Required Sites
Trailheads
Baker Beach
Bluebill
Cape Cove-Cape
Cape Perpetua Overlook
Captain Cook-Cape
Carter Dunes
Conners Camp-Marys Peak

Cummins Creek-Cape
Devils Churn
Discovery Loop-Cape
Drift Creek Falls
Giant Spruce-Cape
Goosepasture Staging
Hauser-N Parking Lot
Hebo Lake DU
Horsefall DU
Horsefall Beach DU
Lagoon
Meadow Edge-Marys Peak
N Ridge/Summit Lak/Mary's Peak
Oregon Coast Trail-Cape
Oregon Dunes Overlook
S Jetty Parking Lot #1
S Jetty Parking Lot #2
S Jetty Parking Lot #3
S Jetty Parking Lot #4
S Jetty Parking Lot #5
S Jetty Parking Lot #6
S Jetty Staging
Siltcoos Beach
Siltcoos Lake
Siuslaw Vista
Spinreel DU
St Perpetua-Cape
Stagecoach
Sutton Trails
Tahkenitch Creek
Tahkenitch/Threemile
Taylor Dunes
Umpqua Beach Parking #2
Umpqua Beach Parking #3
Umpqua Dunes
Waxmyrtle
Wild Mare DU

Picnic Areas
Carter Lake DU
Dune Lake
Hall Lake
Hebo Lake DU
Holman Vista/Sutton Beach
Lodgepole
Ocean Beach
Sandtrack
South Jetty Crab Dock
Sutton Group
Boat Launches
Blackberry
Carter Lake Boat Ramp
Spinreel
Sutton
Tahkenitch
Tahkenitch Landing

Visitor Center
Cape Perpetua VC

Umatilla National Forest

Northwest Forest Pass Required Sites
Trailheads
Burnt Cabin
Coyote Ridge
Crane Creek
Deduct
Elk Flats
Meadow Creek
N Fork John Day
N Fork Umatilla
Panjab
Rattlesnake
Rough Fork
Teepee
Timothy Springs
Touchet Corral
Twin Buttes
Godman
Tucannon
Three Forks

Umpqua National Forest

Northwest Forest Pass Required Sites
Trailheads
Howlock Mountain
Mt. Thielsen
North Crater
Toketee Lake
Umpqua Hot Springs
Picnic Areas
Soda Springs
Boat Launches
N Ramp Diamond Lak
Poole Creek Ramp/Lemolo Lake
S Shore Ramp/Diamond Lak

Wallowa-Whitman National Forest

Northwest Forest Pass Required Sites
Trailheads
Baldy Creek
Bear Creek
Bowman-Francis Lake
Buck Creek
Buck Creek NRA
Deadman
Dutch Flat
Eagle East
Elkhorn Crest
Freezeout

Hat Point
Hurricane
Indian Crossing
Main Eagle
Maxwell Lake
McCully
Moss Springs
N Fork Catherine Creek
Oregon Trail Interpretive Park
PO Saddle
Summit Point
Two Pan
Warnock Corral
West Eagle Meadows

Picnic Areas
Oregon Trail Interpretive
West Eagle Meadows

Willamette National Forest

Northwest Forest Pass Required Sites
Trailheads
Benson Lake
Betty Lake
Bobby Lake
Crag Mountain (Jeff Wld.)
Crescent Mountain
Crossing Way (3-Sis Wld.)
Daly Lake
Duffy (Mt. Jeff Wld.)
Erma Bell
Foley Ridge (3-Sis Wld)
French Pete (3-Sis Wld)
Fuji
Gordon Lakes - East
Gordon Lakes - West
Hackleman Old Growth Grove
Hardesty/Goodman
Harralson
Iron Mountain - Civil Road
Iron Mountain - Road 15
Larison Creek
Linton Lake (3-Sis Wld.)
Lower East Fork (3-Sis Wld)
Maiden Peak
Marion (Mt. Jeff Wld.)
Maxwell (Mt. Jeff Wld.)
Mt Ray (Waldo Wld.)
Obsidian (3-Sis Wld.)
Opal Ck Gate
Pamelia (Mt. Jeff Wld)
Pat Saddle (3-Sis Wld)
PCT - Santiam Pass
Proxy Falls (3-Sis Wld.)
Pyramids

Rebel (3-Sis Wld.)
Robinson Lake (Mt. Wash Wld.)
Rooster Rock (Menag Wld.)
S Breitenbush (Mt Jeff Wld.)
S Pyramid Creek - West
Santiam - Lwr
Santiam - Upr
Scott (3-Sis Wld.)
Separation Ck (3-Sis Wld)
SWR - Mountain House
SWR - Sevenmile Camp
Taylor Burn
Timpanogas/Indigo
Tombstone Pass (Srv Cone Pk)
Trout Creek (Menagerie Wld.)
Twins Peak
UpperGold Lake
Waldo Lake (all trailheads)
Whitewater (Mt Jeff Wld.)
Woodpecker (Mt Jeff Wld.)

Boat Launches
Bingham
CT Beach
Echo
Islet
Larison Cove
Lookout
North Waldo
Shadow Bay
Slide Creek
Interpretive Sites
Salt Creek Falls Observ. Area
Picnic Areas
Ct Beach
Echo
Larison Cove

Appendix III

Oregon Game Fish Records

Oregon Cold Water Game Fish Records

Species	Weight (pound/ounces)		Year	Where	Angler
Salmon, Atlantic	no data		-	-	-
Salmon, Chinook	83	0	1910	Umpqua River	Ernie St Claire
Salmon, Chum	23	0	1990	Kilchis River	Roger Nelson
Salmon, Coho	25	5.25	1966	Siltcoos Lake	Ed Martin
Salmon, Kokanee	6	12	2001	Wallowa Lake	Pamella Fahey
Shad	6	6	2004	Willamette River	Larry Arendt
Sturgeon*(see below)	-		-	-	-
Trout, Brook	9	6	1980	Deschutes River	Burt Westbrook
Trout, Brown	28	5	2002	Paulina Lake	Ronald Lane
Trout, Bull	23	2	1989	Lake Billy Chinook	Don Yow
Trout, Cutthroat	9	8	1986	Malheur River	Phillip Grove
Trout, Golden	7	10	1987	Eagle Cap Wilderness	Douglas White
Trout, Macinaw or Lake	40	8	1984	Odell Lake	H V Hannon
Trout, Rainbow	28	0	1982	Rogue River	Mike McGonagle
Trout, Steelhead	35	8	1970	Columbia River	Berdell Todd
Whitefish	4	0	1974	McKenzie River	Todd Fisher

*There is no state record information for sturgeon in Oregon because the maximum size limit is 60 inches. It is unlawful to remove an oversized sturgeon from the water.

Updated August 18, 2004

Oregon Warm Water Game Fish Records

Species	Weight (pound ounces)		Year	Where	Angler
Bass, Hybrid White	18	8	2002	Ana Reservoir	Justin C. Marks
Bass, Largemouth	12	1.6	2002	Ballenger Pond, Springfield	B. Adam Hastings
Bass, Smallmouth	7	14	2000	Henry Hagg Lake	Kevin Silver
Bass, Striped	68	0	1973	Umpqua River	Beryl Bliss
Bluegill	2	5.5	1981	Farm Pond	Wayne Elmore
Catfish, Bullhead	3	7	2001	Henry Hagg Lake	Bob Junkins
Catfish, Channel	36	8	1980	McKay Reservoir	Boone Haddock
Catfish, Flathead	42	0	1994	Snake River	Joshua Kralicek
Catfish, White	15	0	1989	Tualatin River	Wayne Welch
Crappie, Black	4	6.1	1995	Pond, Corvallis	John Doss
Crappie, White	4	12	1967	Gerber Reservoir	Jim Duckett
Perch, Yellow	2	2	1971	Brownsmead	Ernie Affolter III
Perch, Sacramento	0	11.2	1998	Lost River	Jonathan Cogley
Sunfish, Green	0	11	1991	Umpqua River	John Baker
Sunfish, Pumpkinseed	0	7.68	1996	Lake Oswego	Linda Mar
Sunfish, Redear	1	15.5	1992	Reynolds Pond	Terence Bice
Walleye	19	15.3	1990	Columbia River	Arnold Berg
Warmouth	1	14.2	1975	Columbia Slough	Jess Newell

Updated August 18, 2004

Index

Y

Z